SUCCESS IN

POLITICS

A COMPARATIVE STUDY FOR ADVANCED LEVEL

D1465215

Success Studybooks

Advertising and Promotion

Book-keeping and Accounts

Business Calculations

Chemistry

Commerce

Commerce: West African Edition

Communication

Economic Geography

Economics: West African Edition

Electronics

Elements of Banking

European History 1815–1941

Information Processing

Insurance

Investment

Law

Managing People

Marketing

Office Practice

Politics

Principles of Accounting

Principles of Accounting: Answer Book

Principles of Catering

Statistics

Twentieth Century World Affairs

World History since 1945

SUCCESS IN

POLITICS

A COMPARATIVE STUDY FOR ADVANCED LEVEL

NEIL MCNAUGHTON

JOHN MURRAY

© Neil McNaughton 1996

First published 1996
by John Murray (Publishers) Ltd
50 Albemarle Street
London WIX 4BD

Typeset by Colset Private Ltd., Singapore
Printed in Great Britain at the Bath Press, Avon

A CIP catalogue record for this book is available from the British Library

ISBN 0-7195-7200-2

Contents

Synoptic

Syrople

CROSS

Foreword

I congratulate Neil McNaughton on recognising that at a time when all the examining boards are launching new A level syllabuses in Government and Politics which must conform to the core prescribed by the Schools Curriculum and Assessment Authority, there is a clear need for a book which embraces all the principal areas of the subject on which examiners are liable to set questions.

Of course, in contrast to many subjects, A level Government and Politics is not something to be studied in classrooms alone. It happens all around us all the time. Year after year, Chief Examiners urge students to read newspapers, visit Parliament or local councils, take a continuing interest in pressure groups, political parties and elections as well as paying attention to political analysis in the media and to contemporary issues and controversies in general. I am pleased to say that more and more candidates now score high marks because the matters they are discussing are clearly within their own experience.

Nevertheless, acquiring a good awareness of current affairs is only part of the preparation a serious student of government and politics needs to undertake. Those who will score the highest marks are the students who know that facts, examples and evidence are useful only when they contribute to a relevant answer which must also contain concepts, theories, analysis and interpretation. So a book such as this text is important because it will undoubtedly help students to set in context and organise systematically the information necessary to gain a good grade.

On a personal level, I have to thank Neil McNaughton. I believe this book will help more students to achieve good grades – and if that means that my fellow A level examiners and I will in future be seeing stronger scripts than sometimes in the past, then we shall all be pleased. I have yet to meet an examiner who likes failing anyone; we like to give good scores – but can obviously do so only when they are justified.

This is a relevant, carefully prepared text which can only strengthen the performance of students taking A level Government and Politics and similar examinations. By its direct, no-nonsense style, this book will also help the general reader to cut through the evasions and competing claims of some politicians and – as a result – I believe it will contribute to the wider understanding of politics, which is essential in a democracy such as Britain.

Anthony Batchelor, OBEC,
Chief Examiner for A level Government and Politics
for the Associated Examining Board

Acknowledgements

While every effort has been made to trace copyright holders the publishers apologise for any inadvertent omissions. The publishers would like to thank the following sources for permission to reproduce material.

Photographs
Cover illustration, Robert Harding Picture library; Popperfoto, pp. 128, 136, 140; 'PA News', p. 145; Press Association/Topham, p. 147; 'PA News'/Sean Dempsey, p. 148; Popperfoto, p. 167; Rex Features, pp. 176, 179; Rex Features/Nils Jorgensen, p. 189; 'PA News', Adam Butler, p. 191; Popperfoto/Reuter, pp. 183, 195; The Associated Press Ltd, p. 202; Popperfoto, pp. 207, 210, 214; Rex Features, p. 220; The Associated Press Ltd, p. 227; Popperfoto/Reuter, p. 243; Press Association/Topham, p. 260; Wandsworth Council, p. 266; Associated Press/Topham, pp. 295, 300; Brown Brothers, Sterling, PA 18463, p. 358; Topham, p. 362; Range/Bettmann, p. 371; Popperfoto/Reuter, pp. 387, 389; Range/IME, p. 392; Associated Press/Topham, p. 393; Popperfoto/Reuter, p. 398; Popperfoto/AFP, p. 417; Popperfoto, p. 419, top and bottom, p. 241; Popperfoto/J. David Ake/AFP, p. 426; Popperfoto, pp. 428, 430, 433, 435; Range/IME, p. 148; Associated Press/Topham, p. 452; Popperfoto, p. 462; Rex Features, p. 477.

Written Material
Macmillan General Books, pp. 47, 112, 136, 144, 147, 148, 149, 150, 168, 217, 224, 226, 237, 265, 487; Longman Group, p. 76; The *Independent*, pp. 234, 285, 287, 488, 493–94; Cartermill Publishing, p. 297; The *Guardian*, p. 489; McGraw-Hill, p. 498.

The following examination boards have given permission for the exam questions on pages 487–98 to be reproduced:
The Associated Examining Board; Northern Examinations and Assessment Board; University of Cambridge Local Examinations Syndicate; University of London Examinations and Assessment Council; University of Oxford Delegacy of Local Examinations.

Introduction

A comprehensive and comparative approach to politics

This book is designed to reflect both the substance and the philosophy of the A level core subject core, and it covers most of the compulsory aspects of syllabuses produced by the various examination boards. As well as dealing in some detail with the institutions, processes and culture of British politics, it answers the requirement for a more comparative approach to institutions and concepts as well as knowledge of the nature of the European Union and its impact on politics in the UK. In addition, most of the principal optional fields of study which have been offered are covered.

The most important aspect of the book's comparative approach is the emphasis given to American government and politics, which is the focus of the second part of the book. This is a natural choice since the USA offers us both insights into, and contrasts with, the British political system. It is similar enough to help our understanding of basic principles – the separation of powers, checks and balances and common-law rights immediately come to mind – but also different enough to introduce key contrasts. In the latter respect, federalism, constitutionalism and presidential government are important examples.

The study of political concepts, as dealt with in Unit 1, was originally incorporated into the London University syllabus under the auspices of Professor Bernard Crick, whose work on political education has been possibly more influential than any other's. More recently the importance of such concepts has slowly been absorbed more widely, so much so that the subject core now fully reflects their value. All students of Advanced level politics must now understand these concepts.

Also given a clear focus in this book are ideologies other than those which have characterised modern British political life. Though this is a common option in syllabuses, it is not universally offered at this level. Nevertheless, any genuinely interested student of the subject may develop a deeper understanding of many modern issues in politics by gaining some specialised knowledge of ideologies. Naturally, ecological or gender questions will be better appreciated with a good knowledge of environmentalism and feminism which underpin the arguments. Similarly, anarchism or communism provide us with radical alternative philosophies whose contrast with modern capitalist, liberal democracy throw into sharper relief the true nature of 'orthodox' modern Western politics. A knowledge of the nature and practice of various totalitarian forms of government is clearly essential for all students of modern politics.

The institutions and influence of the European Union are constantly developing. This is reflected in the unit on the government and politics of the EU. It is now impossible to be genuinely knowledgeable about British politics without understanding how the impact of Europe has affected the system and is likely to do so in the future. It is particularly recommended that, when studying such institutions as legislatures, executives and law courts, students should understand their characteristics and operation in Europe as well as in Britain and the USA.

Much can be learned by thinking about the reasons why important differences exist, what political realities lie behind those differences and what recommendations for reform may be developed as a result of such knowledge. The same may be said about such political concepts as the nature of rights, constitutions, sovereignty and law. Indeed, questions concerning all these ideas have been called into question in Britain at the end of the twentieth century as a result of widespread disillusionment with the political system. As constitutional issues come increasingly to the fore, vital lessons can be learned from both the American and the European experience.

In several sections of this book, the reader is supplied with summaries of the main points of comparison which can be identified between differing political systems and philosophies. The contrasts and similarities between the British and American systems are possibly most evident, but there are also passages and summaries concerning contrasting outlooks on both concepts and ideologies. An empathetic approach, showing understanding of such contrasting outlooks, is both useful and, indeed, requested by many examiners.

No political or constitutional issues are simple and all are viewed differently by groups who hold different philosophies. The good student of politics must understand this reality and be able to express the way in which such groups will consider the issues from their own different standpoints. This empathetic approach is especially important when considering interpretations of political concepts such as equality, representation, rights or justice. It is also useful when considering issues and attitudes.

Although this book is designed to deal comprehensively with the new common core and to provide a thorough introduction to all the main options at advanced level study, it would be impossible to cover every aspect of every optional politics syllabus in one volume. Naturally, a good deal of extension reading is recommended for these options. The recommended reading list at the end of the book acts as a guide to such further study. In addition to the many excellent specialist books which are available, there are a number of journals which are now produced especially for students at this level. The Politics Association's own *Talking Politics* (four editions per annum) and Leicester University's *Politics Review* (five editions per annum) are both extremely useful. Finally, a good deal of interesting material is produced by the Politics Association Resource Centre (PARC) in Manchester. Many of PARC's publications have the dual merit of being brief and of enabling students to update themselves on the most recent developments in politics.

How to use this book

The student who is new to politics faces two particular difficulties. One is that few political issues are clear cut. There are usually two or more sides to take on any idea or question. Used to being presented with relatively certain information at more elementary levels of education, the advanced student is confronted with a whole series of doubts about where truth and accuracy lie. The second problem involves understanding how to use examples and illustrations to underpin arguments. Examiners are all anxious that the better candidates in their examinations are able to demonstrate a good knowledge of relevant, contemporary political events and developments. The question is, what examples should be used? Which authorities should be quoted? In both cases this book attempts to provide help.

At the end of each section a summary is provided, usually in a convenient tabular form. As well as providing an aid to detailed revision of the material, the summaries also indicate the important elements of disagreement which can be identified among different political parties and philosophies. Students are encouraged to learn and understand all these key points. They are vital to good examination organisation and technique.

From time to time brief narratives or quotations are included. These are designed both to help with an understanding of the text, and to provide suggestions for the illustrations and evidence which is needed to bring relevance and authority to any answer in politics examinations. Of course, the good student will add his or her own examples, but the illustrations shown can act as a guide to how such material can be effectively used.

Key terms and concepts

The nature of politics

One useful definition of politics is to describe it, as Professor Bernard Crick has done, as the peaceful resolution of conflict. This implies that the alternative is some form of violent means of settling differences, such as revolution, civil war or simply armed struggle, while in politics the clash of ideas and interests is resolved through legal, organised methods which have been agreed by consenting citizens. Under this definition, autocratic or totalitarian rule must also be ruled out as forms of politics. Instead they are merely means by which a state is governed.

Crick's definition of politics can be applied on any scale. Disputes within a family, for example, where there is a struggle for supremacy and possibly heated discussion about holidays, home alterations, education or pet keeping, could be described as the peaceful resolution of conflict. So, too, could manoeuvring for advantageous positions and promotion in a work situation. Above all, it can refer, of course, to the way in which whole states are run.

A more conservative and limited view has been described by the modern philosopher, Michael Oakeshott. He was attracted by the original Greek roots of the word *politiki*, meaning the affairs of the state. For him politics is, and should be, merely the organisation of the running of the state. This implies doing whatever may be necessary to preserve the security and promote the well-being of the people. This shares common ground with Crick's definition, but also allows for other forms of rule.

So, politics can relate to the power struggles on the high peaks of government, to the internal disputations of parties, the campaigns of local groups of activists, elections to a school sixth-form committee or even contests for influence among groups of friends. All these circumstances may conform to one or the other of our two alternative descriptions.

To sum up a definition of politics, three ideas can be identified:

- Politics concerns the resolution of conflicts by non-violent means.
- It necessarily involves a struggle for power and influence.
- In its fullest sense, it refers to the manner in which a state is organised and run.

Here we will confine ourselves to treating politics as the manner in which the affairs of government are handled and the conflicts which are involved in the running of those affairs. For our 'scale' we will be dealing with government at local, regional, national and supra-national level. The 'micro-politics' of the home, the classroom and the workplace need not concern us here.

A glossary of common political terms is to be found on pp. 503–9.

The nature of state and government

These two terms cause considerable confusion to new students of politics. This is with good cause. They can, indeed, be difficult to define and distinguish from each other. As with the term 'politics', a number of different descriptions could be adopted without harm to our general understanding. In this book the following usages of the terms are generally applied.

The state   The term 'state' refers to the permanent institutions which exercise sovereign power within a defined territory. 'Sovereign power' may be defined as the monopoly of the right to enforce laws. These institutions are permanent in the sense that they do not change when a new government is elected or when new political leaders replace existing ones. State institutions in Britain include the following:

- Those bodies which administer laws – the courts, police and other enforcement agencies, the tax and welfare authorities.
- Those public bodies, often known as 'quangos' (quasi-autonomous national government organisations), which carry out many of the functions of government, such as the allocation of public funds, the regulation of large private organisations and the development of policies.
- Local and regional levels of government which either make decisions themselves or administer services whose nature has been determined by central government institutions.
- Parliament itself, which may be considered to be part of the state. Although its personnel may change after each general election, it is permanent as an institution.
- The civil service, including the executive agencies which have now replaced parts of the old bureaucracy, is very much at the heart of the state, establishing a stability which does not exist in ever-changing government structure.
- The armed forces, including the security or intelligence services, which play a vital role in the protection of the state.

The Head of State is the monarch (a term referring to the individual who holds the position) or Crown (referring to the office itself). This implies that there is one personality who has the authority to speak on behalf of, and represent the whole nation. Though this may theoretically be the case, a problem arises in that the monarch is not elected and cannot be held accountable to the people for what she does. In those systems – the majority in the world of politics – where the Head of State is elected and is normally known as 'President', this difficulty does not arise. Thus, although the Queen may have the technical authority to speak for all her subjects, it is not expected in a modern democracy that she should attempt to do so without guidance.

The British non-political monarch, therefore, cannot represent the state. In her place the Head of Government must do so. This is the Prime Minister. The confusion between the role of Head of State and Head of Government presents problems, as we shall see below.

The Government   Although the word 'government' can refer to the 'act of governing' and often does so, 'the Government' itself is a more specific term. It applies to those elected ministers who claim the authority to run the state which is described above.

We have seen that the institutions of the state are permanent; the Government, on the other hand, is transient. It represents a temporary majority thrown up in Parliament by the results of the previous general election. By their votes the people give it a temporary mandate (authority) to control the institutions of the state, pass laws and administer services in accordance with the manifesto which it put before them at the election.

The idea that the Government controls and runs the institutions of the state is not quite sufficient for the fullest understanding of the relationship between the two. We must also take into account certain other realities:

- For its period of office the British government effectively *is* the state. It is almost impossible to distinguish between the two. All key national decisions – when to hold elections, whom to appoint as ministers, what foreign treaties to sign, what military actions to take – are taken by the Government.
- The Head of State (the monarch) does have reserve powers which may be used in exceptional circumstances. Thus, the Queen could theoretically dismiss a minister or the whole Government, could refuse to give royal assent to legislation and could command her troops not to take action ordered by the Government. Whether this would be tolerated by those troops or by the people remains an open question.
- Parliament also enjoys the power to veto Government legislation. Though rarely used, this is a real power. When used we can say that Parliament is working on behalf of the state in the sense that it is acting in the national, long-term interest against a temporary, partisan Government.
- The situation is now further complicated by the European Union. In some areas of jurisdiction, such as trade and environmental protection, the Council of European Ministers is the government of the UK. Short of leaving the Union, there is nothing the British Government or Parliament can do about the Council's decisions where there is no national veto available. Similarly, the permanent institutions of the Union – the Commission, the European Parliament and the Court of Justice – are now part of the state. Unlike specifically British state institutions, however, the Government cannot speak on their behalf.

1 Political concepts

Introduction Politics has its own vocabulary, much of which is familiar to us in every-day speech. However, if we are to be serious students of the science of politics, it is essential that we understand that common terms may have different meanings and usages. The expression 'usage' refers to the fact that many political concepts are treated in a particular way by people who hold differing philosophical outlooks. In other words, the 'use' of political terms may vary greatly. For example, the word 'freedom' may mean one thing to a liberal, but another to a traditional Conservative. In the former case it may suggest the idea of an absence of restrictions, as in 'free speech' or 'free movement'. In the latter case, to a Conservative, freedom may be used to express the idea of maximum opportunity. Thus the concept 'freedom' must be used carefully and explained fully according to its context.

Similarly, there are a number of political terms which are used in one way in everyday language, but can mean something different or more precise to the student of politics. Take, for example, the word 'responsible'. Normally it can imply behaviour which is sensible, perhaps caring for the feelings of others. This is too vague for the political scientist. Responsible **political** action specifically means action for which an individual may be held to account, just as ministers must be **responsible** to Parliament. We also tend to treat the words 'power' and 'authority' as interchangeable, meaning roughly the same thing. In politics, how-ever, the distinction is crucial, as we shall see below.

Professor Bernard Crick's work on political literacy in the 1970s sug-gested that concepts fall into three broad categories which provide us with a useful scheme. These were:

- concepts concerning the process and status of government
- concepts concerning the status and interests of individuals in society
- concepts concerning relationships between government and the people.

We will consider below the following concepts within these three categories:

Government	Individuals	Relationships
Order	Freedom	Representation
Power	Individualism	Responsibility
Authority	Rights	Law and legal justice
Legitimacy	Welfare	Social justice
Consent	Equality	
Sovereignty		

Concepts concerned with government

Order At first sight the concept of social order may appear to be simple and uncontroversial. However, there are a number of different political perspectives which can be applied to the subject. Not least is the question of how fundamental order is to the human condition. For some, such as the seventeenth-century English philosopher **Thomas Hobbes** (1588–1679), or the early conservative commentator **Edmund Burke** (1729–97), the need and desire for order is man's most basic instinct once he has provided for himself in a material sense. Others, such as the eighteenth-century liberal **John Stuart Mill** (1806–73), have argued that individual freedom comes first.

'Good Order is the foundation of all Good things.'
Edmund Burke, 1790

To simplify the issues surrounding order, we can identify four political traditions which have their own view of what the term implies.

Authoritarian conservatism or totalitarian dictatorship

Here order is considered to be so vital that the means by which it is achieved are less important than the result of those methods. All that matters is that sufficient **force** can be exerted upon society and in extreme cases even **terror**. Thus order is maintained by propaganda and fear of punishment and not just by law alone.

Mere conservatives would tend to stress the use of law more than the totalitarians, but both would agree that there may be times when pure force is justified in order to preserve the security of the state and the individuals who live in it. Typical of this view was that of the Italian Renaissance writer **Niccolo Machiavelli** (1469–1527). He argued that wise and successful rulers should use a shrewd combination of legal and military methods to maintain their own power, as well as the internal and external security of the state. But we should not think that this is a purely historical idea. Twentieth-century dictators such as Mussolini and Stalin adopted much the same view.

Traditional conservatism

The maintenance of order and security is just as important to these conservatives as it is to those described above. However, they approach the problem from a very different perspective. For them there is a '**natural order**' in any society, that is, a social structure which has developed over a long period of time. It becomes part of the traditions of the people and they feel comfortable and secure within it.

Possibly the most striking example was the feudal system which flourished in Europe throughout the Middle Ages. There, every individual knew his position within the structure, understood his rights and his duties and rarely questioned the system. The result was long periods of peace and order. There were, of course, periodic breakdowns in order, when thrones and territory were disputed, or where poor harvests or disease created unrest, but for the most part feudalism was a guarantee of good order. A more extreme form of this kind of stratified society is the Indian **caste** system. Each person is born into a caste or level of society, connected to specific occupations and roles in that society. It is forbidden, under strict Hindu religious teaching, to leave one's caste or marry out of it. The reward for caste loyalty is spiritual salvation and the result has been a remarkably well-ordered society.

It can be seen that, as long as such natural forms of order are maintained, society is likely to enjoy peace and security. Conservatives have, therefore, observed that the best way for governments to maintain order is to respect traditions. The greater individual liberty or social equality which liberals and socialists have sought has, they believe, caused upheaval and disorder.

> *'What is the fundamental principle of the feudal system, gentlemen? It is that the tenure of property shall be the performance of its duties. Why, when William the Conqueror carved out parts of the land, and introduced the feudal system, he said to the recipient, "You shall have the estate, but you shall do something for it; you shall feed the poor; you shall endow the Church; you shall defend the land in case of war; and shall execute justice and maintain truth to the poor for nothing."'*
>
> Benjamin Disraeli, 1882

Feudal order has all but disappeared in the modern world, but traditionalists still believe that an ordered society can be promoted if time-honoured institutions are preserved and respected. The conventional family, established religion, moral principles and traditional political bodies are examples of how security can be carried forward from one generation to the next.

Liberalism and democracy

Liberals and democrats attempt to reconcile the principles of freedom and self-determination of peoples with the need to maintain order. The conservative notion – that it is sufficient for the people to respect traditional forces of order – is rejected by liberals. There must, instead, be a specific and explicit agreement by the people as to how they are to be governed. The system of government and its laws must enjoy, broadly, the consent of the people. Thus, even if there are political disagreements and different parties may compete for power, order is maintained because people respect the **principle** of democratic government.

This is not to say that force is never required to maintain good order. It is understood that there will always be those of a criminal frame of mind, and others who disagree fervently with the actions of government and are therefore prepared to break the law in pursuit of their beliefs. Nevertheless, the principle holds good that order will only be preserved if there is popular consent to government.

> *'The basis of order in any society is agreement upon how we are governed.'*
>
> John Hume, Northern Ireland MP, 1994

The practical implications of this liberal–democratic view of what constitutes order can be identified as follows:

- The vast majority of the people support the system of government.
- The rule of law prevails – governments are subject to legal constraints.
- Only a small minority are prepared to break the law for political reasons.
- There is an organised and effective law enforcement system.
- Power is transferred peacefully from one government to the next.

Anarchism and communism
All the views on order described above depend upon the existence of a political state which has powers to maintain security. Both anarchists and Marxist-inspired communists, however, oppose the existence of a state. While they accept that the state maintains some form of order, it is seen as an artificial creation which is an unwarranted interference in man's true freedom.

Anarchists, for example, believe that good order is possible without a state, provided conditions exist within which man can exercise his own judgements, free from the many corruptions of modern society such as private property, the use of force and the existence of class distinction. The communist view is remarkably similar. For communists it is a just **economic** order which must be imposed in order to remove the need for the powerful state. In the latter case, it is the equal distribution of income and wealth, together with the absence of private ownership, which constitutes such an order.

> 'We know that, if our descendants are to reach their high destiny . . . they will owe it to their coming together more and more intimately, to the incessant collaboration, to this mutual aid from which brotherhood grows little by little.'
>
> E. Reclus, nineteenth-century anarchist

Power

Power is the ability that an individual or a body has to make others do something. We may qualify this by adding that we assume that the subject of power is doing something **that they would otherwise not do**. We can also differentiate between different **degrees** of power.

Degrees of power
Power may be **absolute** in the sense that we can say the subject will obey **virtually without fail**. Of course, no power can be totally absolute in this sense as, if a person is willing to die, there can be no way of forcing him to act in a certain way. The political or religious martyr who will sacrifice himself for his belief cannot be controlled and power ceases to have any meaning. Power may also be relatively weak. Here we are suggesting that power merely means affecting people's behaviour without fully controlling it. In this sense, power is better described as influence. In between these two extremes are an infinite number of levels of power.

To illustrate, we can say that military leaders of totalitarian states have absolute power. They control all the forces of law and order and may put to death, or at least imprison, any opponent. There may be a few brave individuals willing to risk death to defy a dictator's power, but he has virtually absolute power. At the other end of the spectrum, we often speak of the 'power' of trade unions or of big business. Clearly, such bodies cannot physically force anybody to act in a certain way, but they do possess influence. By threatening sanctions, such as strikes or lack of co-operation, they may influence governments or other bodies and individuals to behave in a particular way which suits them. In between the two, we can point to democratic governments which exercise power through legitimate institutions. Ultimately, they are in the hands of the people who have elected them and may, in the future, remove them from office. Between elections, however, they are able to get their way on the whole.

How power is exercised

How and why is power exercised? To answer this question we must examine the basis of power.

Coercion is perhaps the clearest source of power. It concerns the use of **force** to secure compliance. Force implies threat of torture or execution in extreme circumstances, but more commonly uses the threat of imprisonment if its subjects will not obey.

It should be emphasised at this point that **all** states reserve the use of coercive power, no matter how peaceful or democratic the government may be. This is because states are not voluntary organisations, so that it is almost inevitable that there will be people who will not agree with some of its laws and customs. Such people must, therefore, be forced to conform in the interests of the security of others. If they will not conform, they must be removed from society by imprisonment or even execution.

By contrast, if we freely join a club, society, business/company or college, for example, we have voluntarily joined and, by so volunteering, have agreed to abide by its rules. Should we find the rules unacceptable, we may leave or be expelled. By and large, states do not have these options. Instead they must reserve the right to force people into compliance.

Of course states do not need to exercise such coercive power most of the time. Most people will conform either through natural consent, or through fear of punishment. Thus, coercive power is usually reserved or latent, that is, it exists and people know it exists, even when it is not in use. In peaceful ordered states, notably Western democracies, coercive power remains on the whole latent. On the other hand, in less stable situations, such as Northern Ireland from the 1970s to the 1990s, when sections of the population did not consent to the regime which governs them, force is openly needed. Thus, there were soldiers in the streets and suspension of many individual rights. The same has been true in military dictatorships such as Chile or Cuba.

'Political power grows out of the barrel of a gun.'
Mao Tse-tung, 1938

Political power is that which is exercised without force (despite Mao's extremist view shown above), but which is nevertheless highly effective. Thus, governments and law-making bodies possess such power because they enjoy the force of law behind them. They can use laws, but also persuasion, offers of rewards and threats of sanctions to get their way. How, for example, does the British Cabinet exert political power over Parliament? The answer is that it can reward those MPs who are loyal to the Cabinet (e.g. advancement in their careers) and threaten sanctions against those who defy them (for example, reduced career prospects or even expulsion from the party in extreme circumstances). Of course, in this particular example, Parliament as a whole can defy such **political** power by exerting the **coercive** power which they possess as the supreme law-making body. In other words, the forces of law and order – the police and courts – must enforce Parliament's wishes above those of the Cabinet if there were to be a conflict.

Finally, **influence**, as we have seen above, refers to the ability to affect decisions in the political arena, but is not real power in the sense of being able to ensure that certain actions are undertaken. Thus, pressure groups often **influence** government, but none of them can actually make decisions and carry them through to implementation. We can now rank forms of power in descending order of effectiveness thus:

1. Coercion
2. Political power
3. Influence

So far we have not discussed the question of whether these types of power are being **rightfully** exercised. The sources and levels of power tell us nothing about this issue. In other words, power can be judged by its **results** but this does not tell us anything about its justification. To examine this issue we must introduce the concept of **authority**.

Authority

As we have suggested above, the terms 'power' and 'authority' are often treated as interchangeable terms, but this would be inaccurate. While 'power' refers to the ability to achieve certain ends, 'authority' refers to the right to exercise that power.

Hereditary authority

Until the sixteenth century questions about authority were largely redundant in Europe. A combination of the doctrine of the 'Divine Right of Kings' and the strength of the tradition of the hereditary principle prevented any questioning of the sources of royal power. Divine Right referred to the belief, widely held, that monarchs owed their right to govern to the sanction of God. They were, in other words, God's servant on earth, doing his will. The hereditary principle was a matter of both tradition and expediency. It was the accepted way of determining who should govern, but also provided a peaceful means of transferring power on the death of a ruler. (Of course, it did not always work perfectly and disputes over succession to the throne were not uncommon.)

Hobbes's interpretation of authority

Thomas Hobbes (1588–1679), writing at the time of the English Civil War and the execution of King Charles I, asked who was the real 'author' of the King's power. His answer was that 'authority' can only be granted by the people. The notion that God or tradition could sanction the use of power must, he argued, be rejected just as Parliament had abolished (though only temporarily) the monarchy. But Hobbes was not a democrat. He asserted that popular authority could not be granted to each individual ruler, and could not be removed by the people. Rather, authority was given to an absolute, all-powerful ruler on the grounds that this was necessary to ensure peace and security. Thus, Hobbes's kind of ruler was little different to any existing seventeenth-century monarch. However, he had found a basis for his authority, a better justification for the use of power. In short, he had developed the concept of political authority.

Weber's alternative sources of authority

With the growth of democratic ideals in the nineteenth century, Hobbes's limited notion of authority became increasingly unsatisfactory. The German sociologist Max Weber (1864–1920) understood that political authority could have more than one single source, any of which could be considered as legitimate. Three such sources were identified:

Traditional This is the idea that if the exercise of power by an institution has been accepted by the people over a long period of time, certainly several generations, it has gained real authority. In other words, it has stood the test of time. Prominent examples would include hereditary monarchy, as we have seen above, but the British House of Lords could also be included. The ruling families in a variety of Arab states in the Middle East certainly base their authority on tradition and there is relatively little challenge to the principle.

Charismatic The term 'charisma' refers to the ability to inspire others and to attract a following. Originally applied to actors or religious leaders, it has come to have political significance. Here authority is granted purely on the basis that a leader is so persuasive and respected that he is allowed to exercise power over his followers. Such examples as Mahatma Gandhi or Benito Mussolini may be said to have been granted such authority by large numbers of people.

Legal–rational This refers to any organised system for establishing proper authority. In the modern world this is likely to consist of free elections. It may, therefore, be described today as 'elective' authority. In democracies it has become the only fully acceptable basis for authority, though it is often combined with traditional or charismatic forms. Thus, a Prime Minister such as Margaret Thatcher could claim special authority on the grounds of charismatic appeal in addition to her elected position. Similarly, some democracies such as Britain's still accept the authority of traditional institutions alongside elected bodies.

Before leaving the subject of authority it is worth noting how different political movements tend to deal with it:

Conservatives have been much more willing to accept traditional forms of authority, especially in the nineteenth century. Of course, during the twentieth century elective authority has become increasingly important, but there remains an acceptance of some traditional sources of authority relating to the House of Lords, the Church and the monarchy. In addition, Conservatives have placed great store by leadership so that charismatic authority is accepted more readily by them as a legitimate basis for power than, for example, by liberals. Individuals such as Churchill and Thatcher illustrate such beliefs.

Liberals are very much more concerned with popular authority and so accept only fair and free elections as a basis for authority. Furthermore, it is essential that government be fully responsible to the people in order to retain that authority.

Socialists too insist on elective authority and completely reject the claims of traditional regimes. Nevertheless, there are occasions when the implementation of socialist objectives may clash with the will of the people, precipitating a crisis of authority. This is particularly the case when socialist governments are especially dogmatic in their ideological outlook.

Power and authority

We can see from the above that power and authority are closely related concepts, but do not mean the same thing. It should also be noted that there can be circumstances where power is being exercised without recognised authority, as in unpopular military dictatorships. It may also be that an individual or body is exceeding the authority which it has been granted. Thus, a hereditary monarch might have some traditional authority, but nevertheless be acting in a dictatorial manner by not consulting others in the exercise of power.

In some unusual cases it could also occur that authority has been granted to an individual, but he is unable to exercise power because he does not have control of sufficient force. For example, the Pope is unable fully to enforce his rulings on the personal conduct of Catholics today, even though they may pay lip service to his authority.

Ultimately, it is likely to be the case that, where an institution or an individual enjoys the broad **consent** of those who are being governed, and if sufficient **coercive power** is also available to deal with those who do not consent, then power and authority may coincide in the most effective way. Stable liberal democracies, on the whole, conform to this pattern.

Legitimacy

The concepts explored above – of order, power and authority – are all descriptions of circumstances we may observe in the real world. They are theoretically measurable and there are few disputes as to their meaning or significance. The term 'legitimacy', however, presents us with considerable problems.

When we ask the question, 'Is power being rightfully exercised?' there is no indisputable reply. It depends very much on what we consider to be legitimate authority, what we believe is the justified use of power. Democrats, for example, only accept elections as a means of bestowing authority, while many Conservatives argue that tradition is an acceptable basis for the exercise of power. Who is right? The answer is that there is no single answer. Legitimacy is a matter of opinion. It depends entirely upon the individual's political outlook. There is a considerable selection of versions of what constitutes legitimate rule. The principal examples are as follows.

Tradition

As we have already seen, a regime which has held power without serious popular challenge for a long period of time, could claim legitimacy.

Control

Some would say that any ruler who can control the state, provide internal security and protect it from external attack has a right to govern. This theory, sometimes called 'might is right', is often accepted as the basis for the international recognition of a regime. It can be argued that, once a government has proved that it controls a territory, it deserves to be recognised by other states, even if they disapprove of the way it has achieved power.

Religion

Some Islamic regimes today, for example, such as Iran or Libya, argue that the basis of their authority lies with religious belief. As long as the rulers are following the teachings of Mohammed the Prophet, this is sufficient reason for the people to obey it. Such so-called 'theocracies' have flourished from time to time in the name of other religions too.

Legality It could be suggested that, if there is a recognisable system of laws in a state, and if the government operates within those laws, it is a legitimate regime. There is, of course, a major problem with this proposition since we must also ask how the laws came about, but it can also be said that such a regime does at least accept limitations on its own actions.

Morality Here judgements about the conduct of a regime must be made in order to assess a claim to legitimacy. Questions such as, 'Are human rights respected?', 'Does the government respect large minorities?' and 'Is true democracy allowed to flourish?' may be asked. Naturally such criteria must be subjective so that legitimacy based on moral grounds may be hotly disputed.

Consent Possibly the most widely accepted basis for legitimacy is that a regime enjoys the consent of its people to govern them. This is examined in more detail below.

Consent

It is a fundamental principle of modern democratic societies that they should feature government by consent. Without this the whole basis of government can be called into question.

Nevertheless, the concept of political consent causes great difficulty among scholars. Superficially, it may often seem clear when a regime enjoys the consent of its people to govern; yet it is often a problem to determine whether a people are so much in fear of their government that there appears to be no significant opposition. It was not clear, for example, whether the rulers of the former Soviet Union did, as they claimed, enjoy the support of their subjects or whether the sanctions against opposition were so great that little of it was seen. Only when Mikhail Gorbachev opened the country to free expression and Boris Yeltsin inspired the people to embrace political reforms was it apparent that real consent had been absent.

Though faced with such problems, some attempt has to be made to identify positive signs of consent if we are to make a valid judgement as to whether regimes are legitimate. The following may be used as criteria:

- There is widespread participation in free elections. Where turnouts at the polls are very low, it could be deduced that there is little confidence in the regime. In countries such as Britain or France, where 60–80 per cent of the electorate vote without the need to make voting compulsory, as is the case in Australia, it is clear that broad consent does exist. It should be stressed here that there may be periods when the actual government in power is unpopular, but this does not mean that the system itself is opposed.
- In the absence of truly free elections it may be tempting to say there can be no proof of popular consent. This would not be valid, however. There may, for example, be clear and regular demonstrations of support for the regimes in ways other than voting. Distasteful though we may find it, there is little doubt that Hitler's Third Reich enjoyed a long period of strong support even when democracy had been suspended. Less controversially, the Sheikhdoms of the Middle East certainly appear to be well loved even though they are far from free societies in Western terms.

- While open manifestations of support give us strong clues as to a regime's popularity, it is less clear when we observe a state in which the people are enthusiastic in neither support nor opposition to their government. The sullen populations of East European socialist regimes up to the 1990s, the silent masses of China and the apparently peaceful societies of South-East Asia could be the result of either of two phenomena. As we have said above, it may be that the people simply live in abject fear of their rulers. On the other hand, the silence of the people could signify unenthusiastic yet genuine consent. However, it can certainly be argued that lack of any significant opposition over a long period of time suggests a people are content to be governed as they are.
- Finally, there are political systems which have survived for such a long period of time and are so absorbed in the traditions of a society that consent can be assumed. Few questioned the right of hereditary monarchies to rule for many centuries largely on the grounds that many generations before had accepted them as a reality. Today the traditional regimes of the Middle East and North Africa fall into this category.

Sovereignty

In general terms the expression 'sovereignty' simply means 'supreme power', but an investigation into most political systems reveals that a more sophisticated approach is needed. It is useful to divide sovereignty into two main types, that is, legal and political sovereignty.

Legal sovereignty

This describes the point where the ultimate ability to make laws, which will be enforced, resides. Thus, in Britain this point is indisputably Parliament. The police, the courts and other law enforcement agencies will only administer laws which have been properly passed in Parliament and given the Royal Assent by the Queen. It may sometimes appear that other bodies are making law, such as ministers or local authorities, but in reality they are acting only on the authority of Parliament. They may be overruled or have their powers cancelled by Parliament at any time. In some other 'democracies' legal sovereignty may be divided, often between a legislative assembly and an elected presidency.

Regimes which are not democratic in nature usually grant legal sovereignty to a ruler or ruling body which governs 'by decree', but the principle holds good that, if such decrees are enforced, the ruler is indeed sovereign. This illustrates that the concept of sovereignty has nothing to do with questions of legitimacy or genuine authority.

Sovereignty and the European Union

Membership of the EU means that each member state agrees to accept and enforce decisions made by the Council of Ministers rather than by their own government or Parliament. Although such jurisdiction lies over a limited range of functions such as trade, agriculture and consumer protection, it is often said to mean a **transfer of legal sovereignty** from member states to the EU. Is this so? The answer lies with voting arrangements in the Council of Ministers. On some key issues a unanimous vote is required. In other words, each member has a **veto**. In these cases sovereignty is **not** lost. However, where only a **majority** vote is needed, there is a loss of sovereignty since each member state can be outvoted.

We should not forget, however, that any member may withdraw from the Union, so the loss of sovereignty is not irrevocable. It should also be stressed that any loss of legal sovereignty is accompanied by a gain in the influence which each member has over the affairs of all the others. In other words, there is a trade-off between national sovereignty and international influence.

Political sovereignty Here we are concerned with effective, rather than merely legal power. The difficulty arises when we ask the question, 'Where does ultimate political power reside?' Most states have written constitutions which describe who is legally sovereign and, even where there is no such constitution, as in Britain, it is usually clear who has such sovereignty. Power, on the other hand, is a more elusive idea.

Britain provides us with an ideal example of the problem. As we have said, Parliament alone is legally sovereign, a reality which is explored further in Unit 7. But real power seems to lie elsewhere. The Cabinet, in particular, is considered the centre of power. Yet it must not be forgotten that Parliament can, and sometimes does, overrule the Government. Then there are the people. At the polls it is they who decide who shall form the government. Thus, the people could be considered to be 'politically sovereign', at least at election time.

In other political systems the political sovereignty of a President may be considerably more important than the legal sovereignty of a legislative body. In the Russia of the 1990s, for example, the power of Parliament is relatively weak in comparison to the power of the Head of State.

The two types of sovereignty described above refer to the internal workings of a political system. However, the term does have a further connotation. This concerns the status of political rulers in relation to other states.

Northern Ireland sovereignty

Since the partition of Ireland between North and South in 1921, the sovereignty of Northern Ireland has been hotly contested. The dispute also concerns an issue of consent. The claim of the Republic of Ireland and of the Republicans in the North is that the people of the **whole** of Ireland did not consent to partition. Furthermore, they argue, since Ireland is traditionally a single community it should not be split. Thus, sovereignty is claimed rightfully to lie in Dublin. The British claim to sovereignty, supported by the Loyalist community in Ulster, is that the majority of the people of Northern Ireland **alone** wish to remain part of the United Kingdom. Thus, both communities argue that their claim is the more legitimate.

International or external sovereignty

This refers to the criteria by which we judge who is actually in control of a certain territory. In practice, this opens the question of which government should be officially recognised by other governments. There are two principal ways of viewing this problem.

First, we can ask who is effectively in control of a territory, that is, which institution or institutions possess coercive power. This says nothing about the morality, legitimacy or desirability of the regime in power. It is simply a pragmatic question. If we accept the reality of the situation and we wish to have dealings with a regime – economic or diplomatic – we might put aside our opinions and simply recognise the rulers in power. Secondly, we might care more about the legitimacy of the regime. If it does not come up to certain standards of behaviour, we may choose not to grant recognition of its sovereignty. Its record on human rights or the effectiveness of its democratic institutions may be the criteria we use.

China and the United States

The strange case of American reluctance to recognise the People's Republic of China illustrates the problem of external sovereignty. In 1949, led by Mao Tse-tung, the communists took control of China following a civil war. The deposed rulers, under Chiang Kai-chek, fled to the offshore island of Taiwan and set up a rival government, still claiming to be the rightful government of all China. The USA continued to recognise the government-in-exile until 1977, arguing that they had been wrongfully deposed and were the only elected government of China. Most of the world, however, took a more realistic view and accepted the regime in Peking on the grounds that they controlled the country and there was no real prospect of a return to the former government.

Concepts concerned with the individual

Freedom

Introduction

At first sight, the concept 'freedom' or, as it is often termed, 'liberty', may seem reasonably straightforward. On the whole, we think of it as meaning an 'absence of restraint'. Prisoners, for example, are said to be given their freedom at the end of their sentence; the bars which imprisoned them have been removed. When whole peoples – colonies, conquered territories and the like – are released from subjugation by a foreign power, we say they are now 'free'. But this is a limited interpretation of freedom. Political thinkers and politicians alike have used freedom to describe a number of different phenomena. In some cases, as we shall see below, complete political doctrines are based on a specific usage of the concept. It is, therefore, crucial that its various meanings are understood.

Licence

If there were to be absolutely no restraints upon man's actions, a state of complete 'licence' would exist. Some philosophers, notably **Thomas Hobbes**, the seventeenth-century English writer, imagined mankind in a total 'state of nature'. This refers to pre-history when there was no state, no laws and no form of social organisation. This would indeed have been a state of complete licence. However, Hobbes pointed out that this would certainly not constitute true freedom simply because there would be no artificial controls. Rather, mankind would be enslaved by a constant state of fear. The individual's property and even his life would be threatened by all the other free individuals in the world. Thus, licence leads to the utter loss of real liberty.

Hobbes's close contemporary, **John Locke**, developed a similar analysis of pre-society, but suggested that man is subject to natural laws which are rules of conduct instinctively understood. These include social feelings and an understanding that each individual should respect the lives and property of others. At first sight this may appear to suggest that no artificial restraints are needed, that there is no such condition as complete licence since we would control our own behaviour. Locke realised that not all men would follow these laws of nature so that there would indeed be a need for man-made laws.

Freedom as 'private judgement'

The philosophy of anarchism, which developed during the nineteenth century, suggested an optimistic view of mankind living in such a state of nature. In the view of anarchists, mankind is naturally sociable, uncompetitive and co-operative. He does not need to be guided towards 'good actions' and does not naturally wish to harm his fellow man. It follows from this belief that it is possible to achieve real freedom without recourse to artificial laws. In short, the state becomes unnecessary (the term 'anarchism' literally means 'absence of government', not chaos as many believe).

The early English anarchist William Godwin (1756–1836) referred to man's potential to use complete freedom positively and for good ends as the exercise of private judgement. This is not the same as 'licence' because man actually **restrains himself**. He is certainly not free to do absolutely anything. Indeed, the Russian anarchist Mikhail Bakunin (1814–76) insisted that man was actually subject to social necessities so that, even in the total absence of laws and government, there can be no such thing as complete freedom.

> *'It is earnestly to be desired that each man should be wise enough to govern himself, without the intervention of any compulsory restraint.'*
>
> William Godwin

Negative liberty

The terms 'negative' and 'positive' liberty were coined by a modern English philosopher, Isaiah Berlin, in 1958. However, the meanings of these two concepts were of particular relevance to the development of liberal principles in the seventeenth, eighteenth and nineteenth centuries. It is therefore convenient to employ the two expressions in this context even though they had not been developed at the time.

John Locke (1632–1704) and **Jean-Jacques Rousseau** (1712–78) both understood that man can only be truly free when he places the protective cloak of laws around himself and his fellow men. Locke referred to this as 'freedom within the laws', while Rousseau suggested an even more striking 'paradox'. He suggested that mankind is naturally reluctant to be bound by laws but finds himself in a dilemma. Man not being perfect, as anarchists were later to accept could be the case, realises that the absence of laws creates more limitations than the laws themselves. As Hobbes had said, a state of licence leads men to fear each other. Therefore, argues Rousseau, man must be 'forced to be free'. In other words, he must be compelled, however reluctantly, to accept laws which he dislikes, in order to be truly free.

The idea of the freedom of action we possess within laws can be described as **negative liberty**. It was **John Stuart Mill** – England's most celebrated nineteenth-century liberal – who developed the idea of negative liberty to its fullest extent. In his view, we have a right to be free to undertake any action which does no harm to others. He called these **self-regarding actions**. In practice, this referred to most personal conduct and it certainly implied thoughts and beliefs. These areas constituted the realm of negative liberty. **Other-regarding actions**, on the other hand, do affect others and must be subject to legal controls. Here negative liberty only exists within the laws, as Locke had insisted.

The importance of safeguarding the maximum amount of such negative liberty became the central value of nineteenth-century Classical Liberalism. Its most important arena was the economic sphere where it was felt that capitalism could only achieve its full potential if the maximum degree of economic freedom could be guaranteed. This theme was later to be resurrected by the 'New Right' which was successfully led by Margaret Thatcher in the 1980s. In practice, the maximisation of negative liberty requires that the power of the state be reduced as far as possible, while laws or regulations should be kept to a minimum.

'The only purpose for which power can be rightfully exercised over any member of a civilised community, against his own will, is to prevent harm to others.'
John Stuart Mill, 'On Liberty', 1859

Positive liberty   For liberals, as their name suggests, liberty is a fundamental value. It therefore became a major problem for them when the accepted notion of negative liberty was seriously called into question later in the nineteenth century. At that time excessive liberty was creating a society in which large sections of the population were experiencing extremes of social and economic deprivation. The freedom of the more able and fortunate to benefit from capitalism was balanced by the freedom of others to fail to do so, often through no fault of their own.

But if the state or any other organisation were to step in to alleviate such suffering there would be a loss of negative liberty for all. Taxation to fund such social welfare, for example, would seriously curtail the individual's freedom to spend his income as he wishes. It therefore became necessary for liberals to attempt to redefine freedom.

Without abandoning negative liberty as a desirable end, liberals began to see that, by maximising the opportunities open to people to realise their full potential and to lead the kind of life they prefer, a new form of freedom could be created. This was a 'positive' kind of freedom resulting from better social conditions and welfare such as education, training, health care, good housing, employment opportunities and pension provision. 'Positive liberty', as Berlin was later to describe such an idea, became the new central belief of the liberal movement as well as that of modern socialism and social democracy. Indeed, by the 1940s it was a concept around which moderate politicians from all political traditions could rally.

Collective freedom   A considerably more difficult conception of freedom has been offered by such philosophers as **Friedrich Hegel** (1770–1831) and T.H. Green (1836–82). For them, personal freedom, meaning the pursuit of our own self-interest, does in fact enslave us. We are not really free under such circumstances because we are forced to battle against a world which we see as separate from us. We are, in other words, alienated by the rest of the world and society. Even if that society places few restrictions upon our actions, it still confronts us threateningly. In practical terms, for example, we may be forced to compete against our fellow man in our economic lives, to struggle against economic forces which seem to be beyond our control. Yet it is the very freedom in modern liberal societies which has unleashed those forces against us.

In a contemporary setting we may consider that those consumers who have adequate means are free to purchase whatever goods they wish. In reality, however, the producers of those goods have already decided what is available and so the apparently free choice of the consumer is actually in the hands of those producers.

True freedom, Hegel and Green suggest, can only flourish if each individual is totally at one with the rest of society. This implies, in perhaps a sinister way, that each individual should lose his own personal identity into that of society as a whole. In this way there is no contradiction between the goals of society and the goals of any individual within it. Everyone is now 'free' because there is no contradiction between the actions of individuals and the actions of all. Thus, it need not be such a dangerous concept if we consider such a state as one of perfect harmony between the actions of the individual and the needs of society as a whole.

For Green, a liberal, this suggested nothing more radical than a welfare state in which all freely contribute to the protection of others. However, it is also an idea which has been taken up by **fascists** to justify the totalitarian state, and by some **Marxists** to justify the imposition of communist ideology at the expense of individual liberty. In other words, this difficult conception of freedom is extremely flexible in its implications.

Forms of freedom

1. **Licence** The complete absence of artificial restrictions.
2. **Private judgement** The anarchist conception wherein each individual is guided by his own conscience.
3. **Negative liberty** The freedom which exists within the laws. For early liberals the only practical form of freedom.
4. **Positive liberty** Associated with modern liberals and socialists, it refers to circumstances where opportunities for people are maximised.
5. **Collective freedom** The belief that we are only truly free if there is no distinction between the goals of individuals and those of society as a whole.

Individualism

Closely allied to ideas of freedom is individualism, a concept which has been adopted by conservatives, liberals and socialists alike.

It encompasses a number of goals which individuals may wish to attain including maximising personal opportunities, realising one's potential, the fulfilment of aspirations, enjoyment of wealth, property and privacy as well as the security which results from a well-ordered and peaceful society. These are all qualities which may allow us to enjoy and express our own individuality.

The idea has coincided with freedom as a desirable end for the simple reason that, for many, it is personal liberty which is the best guarantee of one's ability to express such individuality. For example, only if we are free to enjoy our own private property without threats from others or interference by the state can we pursue a truly individual lifestyle. However, various political philosophies have stressed different aspects of individualism and propose radically different ways of achieving it.

Conservatives

For conservatives, the key lies in the creation of a well-ordered and secure society. Individualism certainly cannot flourish, they argue, if we are constantly in fear of encroachments on our property or attacks on our person. Similarly, there must be a regulated economic, social and political environment in which individuals feel secure enough to be able to engage in freely chosen activities in the knowledge that the future will be much like the past, that there will be no violent social upheavals which may create uncertainty.

The liberal–conservative economist, **John Maynard Keynes** (1883–1946), used such an argument to promote his proposals for extensive state intervention in the national economy. The free working of the capitalist system was all very well, he observed, but it resulted in too many uncertainties for individual economic enterprise to flourish. The Great Depression of the 1930s, for example, created a climate in which there was insufficient optimism for individuals to undertake new economic enterprises. Intervention by the state could have prevented the slump and protected individuals, workers and entrepreneurs from its worst effects.

Conservatives have always insisted that there should be a strict dividing line between matters which should be in the public domain and thus be the concern of the state – such as maintenance of law and order or measures to alleviate the conditions of the poor – and those which should remain in an individual's control, that is, in the private sphere – such as the enjoyment of property and the nature of family life. It is this observance of a protecting barrier around private concerns which distinguishes conservatism from forms of totalitarianism. The latter recognises no such divisions; everything becomes the legitimate business of the state. The scope for individualism is, thus, eliminated.

Liberalism

For the original eighteenth- and nineteenth-century liberals, the so-called classical liberals, individualism was best served by reducing external interference with individual action to a minimum. Freedom of thought, belief, expression and action were manifestations of individualism and should therefore be jealously guarded.

More modern liberals, however, have modified this view, arguing that such freedom is not the only guarantee of individualism. There must also be equality of opportunity through such devices as accessible education, career chances and the elimination of artificial privilege. At the same time, they have accepted that social evils such as poverty, ill-health, unemployment and poor housing reduce the scope for individualism. Thus, the state can be justified in stepping in to reduce such disadvantages.

Socialism It is often argued that socialism is the enemy of individualism. Its emphasis on **collective** solutions to economic and social problems appears, at first sight, to preclude any scope for significant individual action. However, this would be a false assumption. Socialists have suggested that the creation of greater equality in the economic world, together with greater control by workers over their own labour activities, does increase the scope for individuals. While they have accepted that education, welfare, housing and industrial relations may be better managed by collective action (through the state or trade unions), freedom from the uncontrolled forces of capitalism does release the individual from economic struggle.

The moderate social democratic element of the socialist movement shares the liberal view, however, stressing equality of opportunity and welfare capitalism as the main guarantees of individualism.

Rights

Feudal rights Until the seventeenth century the notion of 'rights' was a relatively limited one. They were only considered to exist in relation to strict hierarchy which existed in society. Thus, slaves or medieval serfs had very few rights, being limited in their movements, work and personal lives. The nobles, on the other hand, possessed extensive rights, including entitlement to own and manage property and to exercise control over large expanses of land.

Not only were rights limited, but they were also sometimes only granted in return for specific duties. The more rights one possessed, the more duties one was expected to perform. The role of maintaining the peace was, for example, carried out by those who were also entitled to ownership of great estates. In practice, therefore, rights were both traditional and an integral part of the social hierarchy. The Magna Carta of 1215 was an expression of this hierarchy of rights and an attempt (largely in vain) to remind the King of their existence.

Natural rights In the seventeenth century came the first conceptions of natural rights, opening the door to a whole new world of political ideas. Two English philosophers of the period, Hobbes and Locke, both asserted that men are actually born with rights. These rights come into existence as soon as an individual enters the world. For Hobbes they consisted of the right to life, to liberty and to the pursuit of happiness. Locke added the enjoyment of property to Hobbes's list.

It followed from this new belief that any attempt to curtail these rights was against nature. Man alone could give up his rights, they could not be limited by others unless it were with his consent. This firmly put paid to the controlled forms of feudal rights described above and set strict limits on the ability of rulers to exercise their powers over men.

Ironically, though the concept of natural rights was developed largely in England, their practical application was at first confined to France and America. The American Declaration of Independence, part of which is shown below, was written by **Thomas Jefferson** in 1776 as a direct challenge to the absolute colonial monarchy of George III.

> *'We hold these truths to be self-evident, that all men are created equal, that they are endowed by their Creator with certain inalienable rights, that among these are Life, Liberty and the Pursuit of Happiness. That to secure these Rights, Governments are instituted among men, deriving their just powers from the consent of the governed. That whenever any form of Government becomes destructive of these ends, it is the right of the people to alter or abolish it.'*
>
> American Declaration of Independence, 1776

Similar declarations were made by the French revolutionaries, inspired by another Englishman, Tom Paine, in 1789. We can see from the Declaration that the notion of natural rights opened the door to a number of political principles including:

- limited government
- government by consent
- responsible government
- individual liberty
- equal rights.

The absolute belief in natural rights went into something of a decline during the nineteenth century, replaced largely by concerns with the idea of freedom, but it has returned to favour in the second half of the twentieth century as will be indicated below.

Equal rights As we have seen above, a natural result of the idea that all men are born with equal rights is the belief that we must all enjoy equal rights. After all, why should nature (or indeed God) endow us with unequal rights? So it was that the early revolutionary liberal movements were based on equality of rights. They sought to sweep away the hierarchical system of rights which remained from the feudal age.

It has since become a basic principle of all societies which profess to be just and democratic that every citizen shall enjoy equal rights under the law and in their dealings with government. During the twentieth century equal rights were steadily extended to women who had been left behind by all but the most radical of liberal thinkers.

Citizenship Before the development of ideas about natural and equal rights, all people, other than monarchs, were known as subjects. This meant that all were 'subject' to the power of the Crown and to the strict legal structure at whose head the monarch stood. Citizens did not exist and had not done so since the classical civilisations of Greece and Rome.

The term 'citizen' implied the holding of certain rights which could not be removed or curtailed except by proper process of law. Thus, the prominent members of ancient Greek and Roman society were given privileges under the law, for example, to travel or to take part in political decision making – rights which others did not possess. In the Middle Ages no such concept existed since all were subject to the absolute authority of the monarch.

When the notion of equal rights became established the concept of citizenship returned. This time, however, citizenship was not limited to a privileged few, but to everybody by virtue of equal entitlement to rights. Indeed, in the days following the French Revolution it was customary for people to address each other as 'Citizen' in celebration and recognition of their new-found equal status.

Thus, in modern democracies we are all both citizens and subjects. We are subject to the laws but we also have rights with regard to those laws and the governments which enforce them. In order to qualify as citizens, however, we must also accept our **obligations** under the law. It is expected that we obey the law, that we pay our taxes and that we respect properly constituted authority. In some states, though not Britain, there is even a legal obligation to vote in elections. Sometimes, too, in the interests of defence, citizens may be obliged to serve in the armed forces. This was the case in the United Kingdom during both World Wars and into the 1950s. Thus, citizenship implies a balance between our civil rights and obligations.

Human rights After World War Two and the defeat of a number of totalitarian dictator-ships, academics and world statesmen began to search for a new universal conception of rights. These were rights which all people in all parts of the world could hope to enjoy. In 1948 the United Nations' Declaration of Human Rights was formulated and signed by all members of the UN. This represented a new and fuller description of basic rights and was the modern version of the original concept of natural rights.

It contains a vast array of rights, both traditional and modern. As well as legal and political rights, such as free speech, movement and associa-tion, there are also economic and social rights included. All are con-sidered entitled to education, health care, employment opportunities and welfare.

Of course it would be intensely optimistic to expect all such rights to be respected everywhere and there is certainly no way of enforcing them. It is also true that some of the poorest countries simply cannot afford to guarantee many of them. Nevertheless, such conceptions of human rights do provide a standard by which political systems can be tested.

Apart from the UN Declaration, many states have their own Bill of Rights within which governments and lawmakers are forced to operate. The European Convention of Human Rights, administered by its own court in Strasbourg, is one to which many European states are now subject. Even Britain, with its traditional reluctance to accept strict formulations of human rights, invariably accepts its rulings even though it is not legally bound to do so.

Legal or civil rights Since many modern states have codified constitutions setting out the rights which citizens enjoy both collectively and individually, it is often the case that rights are legally **guaranteed**. These can be described as **civil rights**. The term has almost become synonymous with the struggle waged by black Americans for full legal and political rights in the 1950s and 1960s. Up to that time they did not enjoy the same legally guaranteed, or 'civil', rights as whites so that the movement came to be known as the 'Civil Rights Movement'.

Rights and ideologies Although there are now a number of institutions which lay down basic human rights, attitudes towards rights still differ among various political philosophies. British **Conservatives**, for example, have traditionally been suspicious of most abstract concepts. The idea of natural or universal human rights, has, therefore, never been fully embraced by them. They prefer instead to think of rights as **traditional**. That is, rights only have a valid existence within the context of a particular society. This implies that rights evolve and develop with society. They are not an unchanging concept and so will vary at different times and between different communities. Thus, for example, rights which may suit Americans do not necessarily belong in Britain or other societies. For instance, it is a closely guarded principle of American life that there is a right to carry weapons for self-defence. The British are, on the whole, fearful of such a practice; even the police are not normally armed.

For liberals rights remain paramount. There is very little justification for individual rights to be limited. Wars and other emergencies may be an acceptable reason for their suspension, and there must be some balance between the needs of the whole community and the rights of individuals. Nevertheless, liberals have always been antagonistic to threats to basic rights which they perceive as highly valued and in need of clear protection. Unlike conservatives, liberals do see some rights – such as freedom of thought and of expression – as universally applicable.

Socialists are often accused of being careless of individual rights. Their beliefs in collectivism and the power of the state are seen as threats to the individual. Certainly the track record of many socialist states in eastern Europe was very poor in terms of respect for human rights. However, modern democratic socialists and social democrats have accepted the value of rights and now insist they must be safeguarded. Indeed it has normally been socialists who have most effectively championed the cause of equal rights for such groups as women and ethnic minorities. In addition, certain economic and social rights have entered the socialist creed. Ideas such as the **right to work**, to a decent **education**, to a decent wage and to **welfare** provision have largely been the result of socialist thought. Many consider such rights to be a basic necessity to ensure a minimum standard of life.

Welfare

Welfare can be defined as the achievement of goals and the satisfaction of demands of individuals through the **collective** provision of goods and services. It follows from the idea of collective provision that there must be **general** agreement as to what shall be provided.

The philosophical ideas behind welfare provision are explored in some detail in Unit 3, notably in the sections on democratic socialism and liberalism. However, there have also been a number of more practical considerations which have resulted in the state provision of welfare in Britain. Essentially, there are two non-ideological reasons (described on the next page) for providing welfare services.

- There are some aspects of the quality of life which may be considered vital in a civilised society. Personal medical care, relief from the effects of involuntary unemployment, low-cost housing and education are among these. It follows that some provision must be made by the state for those who are unable to provide them for themselves.
- Most members of a community would agree that there are some minimum obligations of care which everybody has for those who are less fortunate than themselves. State welfare thus becomes the vehicle for the performance of these obligations.

Clearly socialists and many liberals would add that welfare should be used to create greater social equality between the classes, and it can ensure that some services are paid for by those who can best afford it. Thus, welfare provision can be seen by those on the centre-left of British politics as an essential aspect of social justice.

A more extreme view is associated with a broad conception of rights. It can be argued that a decent standard of living, education, good housing, etc, are actually **human rights**, so that all societies should provide them, in the form of welfare, to all their people.

It was the link between the concept of rights and that of welfare which also inspired liberal social reformers such as **William Beveridge** and **John Maynard Keynes** in the 1930s and 1940s. They viewed such qualities of life as a good standard of living, regular and secure employment, decent housing as basic human rights even more important than civil rights upon which liberals had traditionally concentrated. Indeed, they represent the central theme in the transformation of liberalism from a purely political movement to one which embraced **social reformism** – a key element in mid twentieth-century British politics.

Equality

The breakdown of the rigid types of social hierarchy in the eighteenth and nineteenth centuries cleared the way for various new liberal- and socialist-inspired concepts of social equality. The notion of natural rights, which had been developed in the seventeenth century, provided the foundation for ideas of equal rights, but this could not take hold until the traditional social order had declined. Once established, however, the concept of equality quickly grew and expanded into a number of different applications:

Equal rights

The development of ideas about equal rights has been described in the section 'Rights', on page 23 above. It is notable for its influence upon the revolutionary movements in Europe and America which flourished in the late eighteenth and early nineteenth centuries. Since then, the principle of equal rights under the law has become established as an essential feature of any political system which claims to be democratic.

While most political philosophies accept that humans possess unequal powers and abilities, there is almost universal acceptance today that all are born with **equal worth**. It is equality of worth upon which the idea of equal rights is based.

Women's equality
Apart from a brief period in the 1640s when the English 'New Levellers' suggested that women should have equal political and property rights alongside men, the issue of women's equality has been relatively late in appearing within political thought as a viable proposition.

One of the earliest English campaigners for women's equality was **Mary Wollstonecraft** (1759–97), wife of the most celebrated English anarchist, William Godwin. Wollstonecraft firmly believed that women have the same potential abilities as men and are therefore entitled to equal treatment. It was not just equal political and legal rights which she wanted to see for women, but also equality of opportunity. Education and career possibilities must be equally open to women, she argued.

Despite much interest in women's equality after the French Revolution, little progress was made for women until the second half of the nineteenth century. John Stuart Mill and his wife, Harriet (née Taylor) Mill, led the way in Britain. John Stuart Mill's principal target was the notorious 'Married Women's Property Act' which denied to married women the right to own property and so condemned them to arranged marriages and denied them opportunities to divorce. Meanwhile, Harriet was more concerned with voting rights. Many other social reformers were also campaigning for equal pay and employment rights for women, including the Chartist movement of the 1840s.

Nevertheless, lack of success in the economic and social fields achieved by the early campaigners for women's equality led to a belief that true progress would only be made if women were granted equal voting rights with men. Thus, movements for women's suffrage grew up all over America and Europe in the late nineteenth century. During the first quarter of the twentieth century most Western democracies granted votes to women.

Even then, equality for women was far from assured. Only when the feminist movement gathered strength in the 1960s were the final steps towards full equality made. Such objectives as equal pay, employment rights, equal opportunities in education and careers have largely been achieved. In the United States the battle to enshrine women's equality through the **Equal Rights Amendment** has not yet been won, but most legal statements of rights now include some guarantees of women's equality.

There are still a number of important exceptions to this steady movement towards women's equality in the world community. One is Muslim countries, where there is most resistance to change. This has a religious basis since the Koran appears to grant women a different, perhaps inferior, status to that of men. The religious–cultural barrier to women's equality in such countries seems unlikely to change in the foreseeable future. For similar cultural reasons, many poor countries, especially in Africa, also deny equal rights to women.

Equality of opportunity
It is now widely accepted that considerable natural inequalities exist among people. Only a few extreme thinkers of the anarchist or communist varieties base their political ideas on the belief that we can be equal in our powers and abilities. However, this is not to say that all people should not be given equal chances in life on the grounds that we have equal rights and are of equal worth as human beings.

So it is that societies which claim to be both democratic and just have sought to create greater equality of opportunity. The key element in this regard is the provision of good quality education which is accessible to all. In addition, supporters of such equality have advocated the opening up of careers to all with the relevant skills and an end to artificial privileges being granted to a fortunate few.

After World War Two, many of these objectives had been achieved, but sociologists continued to point out that those who had been brought up in relatively 'deprived' backgrounds continued to 'fail' in both education and employment. Even with free education and improved opportunities in many of the professions, equality of opportunity did not seem to be working. Why was this so? The answer, the same sociologists (led in Britain by **Peter Townsend**) suggested was that inequality results from causes more complex than simple lack of educational and employment opportunities. The effects of poverty, poor housing, unsettled family background and racial prejudice were also key factors. In other words, whatever the state did to try to promote equality of opportunity, social background would continue to inhibit real equality.

This problem gave rise to suggestions for the introduction of positive discrimination. This device not only attempts to eliminate disadvantages, but also substitutes deprivation with positive advantages. Thus, inner city schools were to be granted extra resources. Measures were to be taken to promote employment opportunities for members of ethnic minorities and the disabled. Better housing and support for deprived families were seen as vital ingredients in promoting opportunities for children. More recently attempts have also been made, notably within the Labour Party organisation, to discriminate positively in favour of both women and black or Asian members. Thus, equality of **political** opportunity can also be a goal of egalitarians.

So we see that equality of opportunity is a social issue as well as a legal one. It can never realistically be fully achieved, perhaps, but liberals and socialists especially continue to struggle to reduce the unnatural inequalities which still abound.

Racial equality Aspirations for racial equality have only become an issue in modern times with the advent of multi-racial societies. Throughout history it has been acknowledged that there are important differences between races and national conflicts have often been exacerbated by racial rivalry. However, it has been modern theories of racial superiority and inferiority which have given rise to much controversy over the significance of racial differences.

J.A. Gobineau (1816–92), the French social theorist, and Houston Chamberlain (1855–1929), an Englishman who was an early adviser of Adolf Hitler, popularised theories of racial inequality. Such theories had considerable influence on right-wing philosophies, especially fascism. Similarly, the post-war white regime in South Africa adopted a policy of 'apartheid' which systematically discriminated against non-whites, based on a fundamental belief in the racial superiority of the white races.

But it has not only been pseudo-scientific theories which have created the problem of racial inequality. Racism and racial prejudice, often fuelled by economic deprivation, have taken hold in many societies, not in terms of theory but simply in people's minds and emotions. This has led to considerable discrimination against racial minorities, resulting in a loss of equality in education, employment and other legal and social rights.

As a result, the search for racial equality has become a key issue in the late twentieth century. To some extent solutions have been legal and constitutional in nature. Thus, race relations laws in Britain, civil rights legislation in the USA and a variety of international declarations of human rights have sought to establish racial equality. However, it is also widely recognised that prejudice is one of the main causes of unequal treatment for racial minorities. Solutions to this aspect of the problem are more difficult to find. They centre on education and public campaigning and, as such, remain long-term goals.

Equality of outcome
Also referred to as **economic equality**, this concept is usually associated with socialism and communism. It is an idea based on ethics or morality, arguing that all are of equal worth, even though they may make a different contribution to society. What is considered important is that all who make the best contribution they can, should be entitled to equal rewards.

In its most extreme form, this suggests that all who work will receive exactly the same income. Certainly after the Russian Revolution in 1917, Lenin intended this to be the case. Very soon, however, he learned that this took away the incentives which could persuade individuals either to work diligently or to undertake long periods of education and training in order to carry out more socially valuable jobs. Thus, he introduced limited inequality in wages. Nevertheless, it was still claimed to be a 'just' system since each was paid on a rational basis, according to the social value of his contribution. Capitalism, communists claim, grants rewards according to market forces, which results in random and unjustifiable inequalities, nothing to do with the true value of one's contribution.

> '[Society can inscribe on its banners] "From each according to his ability, to each according to his needs".'
> Karl Marx, 'Critique of the Gotha Programme'

Milder forms of socialism do not go so far. Rather, the idea of equality of outcome implies that gross inequalities should be reduced and that rewards should be more fairly distributed than the free market capitalist system usually achieves. It remains a moral question for socialists. Equality is seen as the natural state of mankind, rather than inequality as liberals and conservatives believe.

Concepts concerned with relationships between citizens and the state

Representation

Introduction

When ideas concerning popular government emerged in the seventeenth and eighteenth centuries, when the notion that the authority to govern must be granted by the people and that mere tradition or divine right were no longer acceptable, immediate problems presented themselves.

Three principal difficulties can be identified:

- Most people at that time were either illiterate or only semi-educated. They would have had difficulty reading about, let alone understanding, political issues. Even the most tolerant, liberal of thinkers such as John Stuart Mill recognised this difficulty.
- The demands and beliefs of the mass of the people would most likely be incoherent, driven by emotion rather than reason, and subject to undue influence by dictatorial leaders. The great American democrat, **James Madison**, understood this when contributing to the shape of the United States' Constitution in 1787.
- Such ideas of pure democracy would result in the people making decisions derived from pure self-interest. The good of the community as a whole could be overlooked. Even the French eighteenth-century philosopher of the Enlightenment, **Jean-Jacques Rousseau**, rejected popular democracy altogether on these grounds.

Thus, representative systems were developed to deal with such problems. Although there are a number of forms, which are described below, in all cases the same principle applies. That is that the people do not govern themselves, but have representatives who govern on their behalf.

Burke's model   The great eighteenth-century English politician **Edmund Burke** became concerned that new ideas emerging from Europe and America would lead to Parliament becoming merely a forum for the promotion of sectional interests and demands. For him the role of a representative should be to promote the **national** interest, not the interests of a minority or even the majority. True, MPs might hold particular views and be influenced by their own philosophy, but in the end they should seek to further their own view of the interests of the whole community.

So, Burke's model of the ideal representative suggests an independent individual who takes into account the mood and sentiments of his constituents, but then uses his own judgement in making decisions. Ultimately, if his judgement is flawed or becomes unacceptable to the voters, he can be removed at the next election.

The balance between political philosophy and national interest is nicely expressed in Burke's definition of a political party:

> '*A body of men united for promoting by their joint endeavours the national interest upon some particular principle in which they are all agreed.*'
> Edmund Burke, 'Reflections on the Revolution in France',
> 1790

Social representation   A related idea to that of Burke is the creation of a body which is a **microcosm** or miniature version of the community which it is representing. For example, such a group would be likely to be half women, half men, would reflect the social class structure and would include a fair representation of ethnic minorities as well as a good age range. In this way, it might be expected to make the same kind of collective decisions which the whole community would make if it were to meet together. Here again, representatives would be using their own judgement as well as taking account of the way other like-minded people might act.

The jury system operates on this principle in the legal rather than the political field, but illustrates its value in ensuring just decision-making. In addition, to some extent, any elected body may be considered to be more democratic if it can be socially representative in such a manner. Thus, there are calls to increase female membership of the British House of Commons and for more members of ethnic minorities to be represented. In 1994 there were only 60 women out of 651 members in the Commons (though there was a woman speaker, Betty Boothroyd, and a recent woman Prime Minister for eleven years!), and only two members of Afro-Caribbean origin. A similar principle can be applied to the civil service, in view of its influence over policy making. The higher levels of the civil service have been notorious for their bias towards Oxford and Cambridge graduates, who have invariably come from middle-class backgrounds (a tendency which is, more recently, less marked). There are also very few women in the higher echelons of Whitehall.

However, the representatives of the people, it can be argued, ought to be superior to the majority of the community. We should, perhaps, expect representatives to be better educated and more experienced than most of us. It therefore becomes inevitable that there will be a majority of the well-educated, older and successful individuals in our governmental institutions.

It is sometimes suggested that, in order to encourage the election of more women and members of ethnic minorities, positive discrimination should be applied whereby a quota, or minimum number, drawn from such groups, are guaranteed places. The Labour Party operates such a system on behalf of women within certain sections of its internal organisation. There is, indeed, a feminist pressure group, known as the Three Hundred Group, which aims to increase the number of women MPs to the number suggested in its title. Opponents of positive discrimination, however, point out that such quotas may result in some inferior individuals gaining seats simply to fulfil the requirements of the system.

Delegation

This is the clearest form of representation. A delegate is one who is elected or appointed to mirror accurately the views of those whom they represent. In the most extreme of circumstances a delegate may have no flexibility whatsoever, having instead to follow a specific mandate or strict instructions. Parties in the USA, for example, hold **Primary Elections** to choose delegates who will support a particular candidate for office. These delegates **must** follow the instructions of their party voters, at least until their chosen candidate may be knocked out of the race in an early ballot.

The example described above is the strictest form of delegation. In practice, a delegate is one who is expected almost invariably to follow the wishes of his electorate, but may stray from these in certain circumstances. Again, the USA provides a useful example here. Members of the House of Representatives must seek re-election every two years. They must, therefore, pay special heed to the wishes of their constituencies. Too much independent action, as Burke recommended, is likely to result in loss of the seat.

Totalitarian representation

As we have seen above, Rousseau suggested in the eighteenth century that representative democracy was likely to be flawed by the dominance of sectional interests. He was concerned that the collective good of the whole community, what he called the '**general will**', should be served. Since the people or their representatives could not be trusted to establish the general will, it must be left to a single superior individual to establish that will. This person – called the 'legislator' – would govern as a **representative** of the community **as a whole**, as a single **collective** body. This highly controversial position has often been used to justify totalitarian government and certainly the dominant Jacobin Party, led by the notorious **Robespierre** during the French Revolution, claimed to represent the mass of the people in such a way.

Summary of representative forms

1. **Burke's view** Representatives should use their judgement and not slavishly follow the beliefs of their constituents.
2. **Social representation** A representative body should be a microcosm of the community which it represents.
3. **Delegation** A representative who follows closely or exactly the instructions of those who appointed or elected him.
4. **Totalitarianism** The idea that an individual or small elite party can represent the collective interests of a society.

More recently such communist leaders as Lenin and Mao Tse-tung have adopted a similar position. They both led elite parties which claimed to represent the best interests of the masses. Since communist ideology was, in their view, clearly in the best interests of the people, its ruthless imposition could be justified in terms of representative government.

The case of the British MP

In some ways the position of British MPs summarises the variety of representative forms which can flourish. We should bear in mind that he is a member of a highly disciplined party, largely united in purpose and with a clear election manifesto expressing its policy intentions. He is also elected to represent a constituency, is expected to consider the national interest and may be sponsored by an interest or pressure group to provide publicity and influence for their cause. Yet voters rarely elect him for his personal qualities and beliefs. Instead, they generally elect him because he is a member of the party which they wish to support. Thus, he may experience a number of conflicting influences in his representative role. We can summarise these as follows:

- The party whips expect him to 'toe the party line'. His constituents may do the same.
- Sometimes the interests of his constituency may conflict with government policy.
- He may support a particular cause which leads him into conflict with party policy.
- If he believes his party's policy is not in the national interest he faces a dilemma.
- His own personal principles may cut across some considerations shown above.

Having established these potentially difficult conflicts, the student may consider how an MP should react in the following circumstances:

- He is anti-European when his party policy is for closer European integration.
- His own party proposes an unpopular new motorway in his constituency.
- He is sponsored by the National Union of Students and his party proposes cuts in student grants.
- His party supports return of the death penalty, to which he is morally opposed.
- His constituency party wants him to vote one way on a key issue against party policy. His party whip insists he takes the opposite, official party line. His constituency threatens to 'de-select' him so that he will not be their official candidate at the next general election. This will guarantee defeat for him at that election.

Responsibility

Responsible government

It is a general principle of any representative system that government should be responsible to those who have elected it. This can imply two principles.

First, that electors have opportunities to find out what government is doing, to be able to subject its actions to scrutiny and, in extreme circumstances, to remove it if it is proving unsatisfactory. The performance of our representatives must be judged before we can know whether to renew their mandate. This idea is often known as 'accountability'.

Secondly, it can mean that government acts in a way which is in the genuine national interest and is not merely concerned with satisfying the demands of a section of the population, or is not only concerned to ensure its own re-election in the future. Such governments need to be relatively free from constant control by the electorate. They need the opportunity to ignore short-term popularity concerns in order to benefit the long-term interests of the community.

In either case responsibility is a vital partner to representation. It is also crucial to the effective operation of democracy. Power without responsibility is indeed a recipe for absolute, autocratic government. All rulers need the discipline of responsibility if they are to keep in touch with the people.

Responsibility in practice

There are a number of ways in which government can be made responsible in practice. The British system of parliamentary accountability is perhaps the most ancient. Just as absolute monarchs were required to report their actions to Parliament on a regular basis, modern ministers are also called to account on a regular basis.

Such responsibility applies both individually and collectively:

- The doctrine of **individual ministerial responsibility** insists that every government minister must attend Parliament regularly to answer questions, to justify decisions, explain the thinking behind policy and to be subject to cross-examination by MPs. In effect the minister is being held accountable to the people, but MPs are performing the function on behalf of the community.

It is also argued that a minister whose department makes a serious error should actually resign. In recent years this principle has fallen into disrepute, so reluctant are ministers to relinquish their posts despite strong parliamentary pressure to do so.

The question may be asked, 'Why must ministers answer for their department when most of the work and most of the decisions are taken by civil servants?' The answer lies in the principle that all civil servants must remain politically anonymous in order to protect their neutrality. Thus, their political boss, the minister, must be prepared to answer for them.

The minister who resigned and the minister who didn't ...

In 1982, when Britain was caught unprepared for the Argentine invasion of the Falkland Islands, it was clear that someone in government was to blame and would have to accept responsibility. In the event, it was Lord Carrington, the Foreign Secretary, who 'did the honourable thing' and resigned.

In 1983 a number of dangerous Republican (IRA) prisoners escaped from the Maze prison in Northern Ireland. It was revealed that security at the prison had been very poor. The responsible minister was Northern Ireland Secretary, James Prior. He refused to accept responsibility and the prison governor had to resign instead.

- **Collective responsibility** refers to the fact that the Government is collectively responsible for its actions and the quality of its performance. Of course, it is at general elections that a Government is principally called to account, but continuous scrutiny is exercised by Parliament. The ultimate sanction is the passage of a 'vote of no confidence' in the House of Commons which must result in the removal of a Government, but this is rare as the Government usually commands a loyal majority. The Labour Government of 1979 is the only modern example of such an occurrence. In practice, it is merely in the course of debates that Government accountability is exercised.

  The doctrine is so important in British politics that individual ministers are required to defend the Government position even if they disagree privately. By insisting on such loyalty, the Government stands or falls together. A minister who is not willing to accept responsibility for a Government decision must resign his post. **Michael Heseltine's** resignation after the Westland affair in 1986 was the most significant example in recent times.

Law

Introduction

Here we can define law as a body of rules which is binding within the whole of a community. Many other types of rules may exist, of course, such as military law, church law, regulations within clubs, societies, schools and sports, but these only apply in particular circumstances and among certain sections of the community. Law itself is binding on all and, as such, must effectively be enforced by the state. Three main reasons exist for the creation and enforcement of laws:

- State laws are not the only rules by which people abide. Many are guided in their conduct by their own sense of morality or by religious principles. Indeed, in an ideal world, the laws would conform to a common sense of moral behaviour. However, views on morality vary from individual to individual so that the state must set standards for all to follow.

- In addition to such rules of conduct, laws are needed to ensure that government policy is properly implemented. Thus, for example, businesses must abide by laws which govern the employment of their staff and the quality of the goods they sell, individuals must pay various taxes and schools must implement educational objectives.
- The modern world can prove extremely competitive and circumstances frequently arise where individuals may come into conflict with one another. To avoid the disordered and sometimes violent settlement of such conflicts, laws act as a guide for the resolution of disputes.

Purposes of law

1. Setting common standards of behaviour
2. Ensuring that government policy will be implemented
3. Dealing with disputes which may arise between citizens

Types of law
- **Statute law** refers to those laws which have been passed by Parliament. These are known as statutes or Acts. If there is any conflict between a statute and any other kind of law, the statute is considered superior.
- **Secondary legislation** is produced by bodies which are sanctioned to do so by Parliament. In the main these are government ministers, local authorities and public corporations. Such secondary authorities act within powers granted to them by primary or **enabling legislation** and the orders and by-laws which they make are as binding as any other laws. Thus, the Secretary of State for Trade and Industry may be granted powers to establish a wide range of industrial or commercial regulations. Similarly, local authorities have statutory powers to regulate vehicular traffic and to set building regulations.
- **Common law** is uncodified (that is not written in an organised form). It is a body of rules which has evolved over a long period of time. Although such law has not been passed by Parliament, it is considered binding by the courts. Much common law has now been replaced by statutes which are more precise. It is still often applicable in commerce and family law, but it is in the process of being phased out.

  Lawyers are charged with the task of studying past legal judgments in order to discover what the common law says about a particular case with which they are involved. In practice it is judges who declare how common law applies and these judgments must be followed in any similar case.
- **Case law** is developed where judges must decide how a law, whether common or statute, should apply in a particular case. Having established such principles, any future similar case must be treated in the same way. For example, the equal opportunities laws seek to establish equal rights for women. However, there may be many instances where it is not clear whether these rights are being abused. So a body of case law builds up over the years until a new statute can be passed which tidies up such practical applications. This kind of law is often referred to as **judge-made law** because the interpretation is made by the judge in each case and becomes binding on all other courts.

Constitutional law Such law is normally superior to other kinds of law. That is, all actions by government or laws passed by a legislature must conform to constitutional principles. In Britain this is not the case, however, since constitutional statutes are no different to ordinary laws. The doctrine of the sovereignty of Parliament means that the legislature cannot be limited by any superior law. This is not to say that there are no constitutional statutes in Britain – the laws governing local government, ministerial powers and citizens' rights fall into this category. What it does mean is that they are not binding on Parliament.

In either the British case or that of other liberal democracies the functions of constitutional law are the same, as described below:

Functions of constitutional laws

1. Determining the distribution of power between the various institutions of government
2. Setting the limits to those powers
3. Establishing the rights of citizens, both in relation to each other and to the state
4. Defining the territory controlled by the state and the nature of citizenship
5. Setting out procedures for amending the Constitution itself

Further details and issues concerning the British Constitution are included in Unit 12.

The rule of law It is clear that all organised societies need laws which can be enforced by the state. It is only liberal democracies, however, which lay claim to the principle of the 'rule of law'. In a very general sense this principle simply refers to systems where government always operates within the laws rather than in an arbitrary fashion which was the custom of medieval absolute monarchs. In 1885 Professor A.V. Dicey set out a full and precise definition by which all democracies can be judged. His definition has four parts:

- All are equal before the law. No one, including government, is above the law and no one should be at a special disadvantage when being dealt with in law.
- Citizens may only be punished through the proper application of law. In other words, the law enforcement agencies must abide by legal procedures.
- Only laws passed by Parliament or under authority granted by Parliament (in other states this would be applied to whatever constituted the sovereign body) can be enforced.
- Laws should be just and respect the rights of citizens.

Few would argue that the first three principles hold largely true in Britain and in most democratic countries, but the fourth, concerning rights and justice, is open to considerable question. In states with a codified constitution and . or a guaranteed Bill of Rights, rights may well be protected, but Britain's lack of such features creates a major problem. Rights are at the mercy of the sovereign Parliament. The rule of law is, therefore, always vulnerable.

Law and justice   There is often confusion between these two terms. If we define justice in a general way, as 'fairness', it may certainly conflict with law. We all have our own conception of what is 'fair' in any particular circumstance. The laws cannot hope to reflect all these different views of justice. If each judge were to attempt to take into account various ideas, the outcome of the law would be too uncertain. Those who come to be involved in legal cases can only hope to be treated according to the law as it stands, whether it is 'fair' in our eyes or not. As Dicey argued, as long as we are all treated equally under laws which are consistently enforced, we can at least be sure that we have been treated with 'justice'. If we do not like the laws as they are applied, the best we can do is to seek to influence the political system so as to have those laws changed.

The consistent and equal application of the law, including fair trials and impartial judges or juries, can be described as **legal justice**. This should not be confused with **social justice** which is the final concept to be described here.

Social justice

Social justice can be defined as different conceptions and beliefs about how 'goods' should be distributed within a community. Here the term 'goods' refers not only to material goods and services or money income, but also desirable conditions such as rights, power, status, freedom or welfare. In other words, everything that most would describe as desirable.

The use of the word 'beliefs' above gives a clue to the nature of social justice. It is an evaluative term, that is, its meaning depends upon the ideological or philosophical standpoint of the person using it. For example, a socialist does not mean the same as a conservative or a liberal when describing social justice. This is because his beliefs and values are different. By contrast, 'legal justice', as described by Dicey, is a positive or universal term which can be generally applied.

The table below indicates a number of commonly held principles which can be described as conceptions of social justice. In each case the particular philosophies which incorporate the beliefs are identified:

Principles of social justice	Philosophies supporting the principle
Equality of outcome where all are given approximately equal economic rewards	Communism Anarchism Extreme socialism
Equality of opportunity where inequalities are accepted but artifiical advantages and disadvantages are reduced	Socialism Modern liberalism Social democracy
Equal legal and political rights	Socialism Social democracy Modern and classical liberalism
Economic rewards awarded strictly according to merit	Classical liberalism Conservatism New Right neo-liberalism
The use of taxation and welfare to reduce income inequalities	Socialism Social democracy
The provision of welfare only to ensure all have a minimum standard of living	Conservatism New Right neo-liberalism
Economic rewards determined only by markets.	Classical liberalism New Right neo-liberalism

The beliefs shown above can be studied in more detail in Units 3 and 14.

There are a few extreme thinkers who deny the validity of social justice at all. Such **libertarians**, as they are known, envisage a society where no such principles exist. Each becomes responsible totally for their own welfare and no one has any obligation to ensure justice for others. However, as a concept, it is social justice which is the most important characteristic of all political beliefs.

2 The United Kingdom – social and political context

The United Kingdom

The UK has existed in its present political form since 1922. At that time, Eire (now the Republic of Ireland) was granted its independence, leaving Northern Ireland within the Kingdom as part of an entity known as 'Great Britain and Northern Ireland'. This title broadly describes what is also known as the United Kingdom. Territories which are part of the UK must fulfil the following criteria.

- They are subject to the authority of the **Queen** as their Head of State.
- Their laws are, ultimately, subject to the sovereignty of **Parliament** in London.
- There are a few 'dependent territories of the UK' such as the Isle of Man, the Channel Islands and the Falkland Islands, but these are not strictly part of the UK itself and not all their citizens have the right of permanent abode in Great Britain.

There are some **Commonwealth countries** of which the Queen is still the ceremonial Head of State, such as Canada, Australia and New Zealand, but they are **not** subject to the sovereignty of the London Parliament and so are not in the UK.

Some **colonial** territories still exist, notably Hong Kong (until 1997 when it returns to the jurisdiction of China) and Gibraltar, which are subject to full UK rule, but constitutionally they are **colonies of the UK**, not part of the UK itself.

The main political parts of the UK are as follows:

England

England is the largest part, of course. In terms of government, there is little difference between England and Wales, but just enough to give it a separate identity. Foreigners, and indeed many Britons, can be confused by such anomalies as the existence of a distinct 'England football team', a cricket team which plays as 'England' but may include Welshmen, Scots and Ulstermen, and an Olympic team which competes as the 'United Kingdom'. The student of politics, fortunately, can safely ignore such distinctions; they arise from the strange nature of various sporting bodies which do not recognise strict political boundaries.

Wales

Wales has not been a separate kingdom since the early Middle Ages. We understand where its borders lie, it has its own language – spoken intermittently by less than a quarter of its population and it considers itself distinctive in a number of ways. Nevertheless, it is more a cultural reality than a political one.

Laws passed in Parliament at Westminster all apply to England and Wales equally. At the same time, all important policies which are developed in the Cabinet will apply to Wales as well as England. It would be wrong to say, however, that there is no Welsh government.

The **Welsh Office** came into existence in 1964, with a Cabinet minister at its head and a full civil service department. This administers such services as education, transport, the health service, industrial support and local government, using a large grant given by central government in London. However, this is more 'devolved administration' than actual government; what is more, there is no separate law-making body in Wales. There are also a number of 'quangos' in Wales. They are committees of various kinds which distribute public funds and determine local policy with relative freedom from central government interference. The most important example is the **Welsh Development Agency**, giving grants to encourage industrial investment in the principality. Again, however, these quangos do not constitute full government. (They will be described fully in Unit 8.)

An attempt to establish devolved (semi-independent) government in Wales was made in 1978–9, but this failed following decisive rejection by the Welsh people in a referendum. These events, and prospects for future independence, are discussed further in Unit 10. To all intents and purposes, therefore, Wales need not be treated separately, in a political sense, from England.

Scotland The Scottish and English Crowns were united in 1603 when James VI of Scotland became James I of England and Scotland. It was at this time that the 'United Kingdom' first came into existence. There was still, however, a separate Scottish Parliament which made law in that country. Legislative unity was not established until the 'Act of Union' of 1707. This joined the governments of England and Scotland to follow the merging of the two Crowns a century before.

Scotland has, therefore, enjoyed a longer and stronger history of 'separateness' from England than has Wales. Furthermore, the Church of Scotland is very distinct from its English Protestant counterpart and there is a separate education system, including the universities. In addition, the arrangement of courts is quite different from that of England and Wales. Above all, however, Scotland is different in that it has its own laws.

Scottish law is made at Parliament in London, but it is not the same as English law. There are separate laws, made on separate occasions. Before the student jumps to the understandable conclusion that English and Welsh MPs may be making Scottish law, and that this would be politically absurd, it must be pointed out that Parliament does have special arrangements to avoid this. Though it is the Cabinet which proposes any changes, the **Scottish Grand Committee** of all MPs representing seats in Scotland passes the law in their own country. Any controversial matters are still resolved in Cabinet, but effectively English and Welsh MPs have no authority in Scotland. The casual observer or visitor to Scotland would notice little difference, but there are significant distinctions in laws concerning property, contracts and the conduct of criminal trials.

As in Wales, there is a Scottish Office which administers most local services, as well as the usual variety of quangos and official committees which relate only to Scotland. Again, however, this is not separate government. Prospects for devolved government or even full independence appear considerably more realistic in Scotland than in Wales. The main issues are described in Unit 8.

Northern Ireland　Sadly for its people, the political system of Northern Ireland has been in a state of turmoil since 1968. Resolution of the problems remains the subject of great controversy. The history of the province since its establishment in 1921 bears witness to the difficulties of creating a permanent arrangement.

When Eire became independent in 1921, the province of Northern Ireland remained within the UK. It should be pointed out at this stage that Northern Ireland and 'Ulster' are not quite the same. Ulster is one of the four ancient provinces of Ireland. It comprises nine counties in all. When Northern Ireland came into being, only six of Ulster's counties were included in it. Thus, although reference is often made to the 'Ulster problem', we should be aware that it is really Northern Ireland, the main part of Ulster, to which reference is being made.

Having a Protestant majority which feared Catholic-inspired rule from Ireland (including the acceptance by Catholics of the Pope's authority in family and moral concerns), the six counties of Northern Ireland wished to remain under the jurisdiction of the Crown and Parliament. The Protestant community does not consider itself to be English, but does feel its culture has more in common with Britain than with Ireland. It was, therefore, an understandable, though fateful, decision by Lloyd George's Liberal Government to partition Ireland. The alternatives may have included civil war or at least mass disorders.

Until 1972 Northern Ireland had its own Parliament and from its majority was drawn a Government and Prime Minister, very much along the lines of the main British government. So although under the Crown Northern Ireland was virtually a separate, independent political entity, with its own laws, social and economic policies, police and courts, the London government still controlled defence, foreign affairs and currency as well as collecting taxes from the people.

The Catholic minority (about 40 per cent) had always been uneasy about its position, but systematic discrimination in such fields as politics, housing, education and employment by the Protestant majority eventually brought matters to a head. Unrest, which became apparent in 1968, quickly grew into violence, ultimately resulting in the abolition of devolved government in Northern Ireland in 1972. **Direct Rule** from London was established. This was still in place in 1995.

Direct Rule means that Northern Ireland laws are made at Westminster, the Cabinet makes key decisions and the Northern Ireland Office, headed by a Secretary of State, runs the day-to-day affairs of the province. A number of attempts to solve the political deadlock in Northern Ireland by political rather than military means have all failed to date. A Protestant, largely loyalist majority, represented by Ulster Unionist politicians, continue jealously to guard their position in the UK. The nationalists, mostly Catholic, are represented by both moderate politicians and militants in the IRA and Sinn Fein. They wish either to be reunited with the Republic of Ireland, or at least to be given some degree of independence from majority Protestant rule. The situation remains unresolved.

The cultures of Britain

As we have seen above, there are a number of different national cultures which have flourished in Britain for centuries. However, these are not only long established, they are also mostly confined to fairly well-defined territories – Wales, Scotland and Northern Ireland. More recently, Britain has become very much more of a multi-cultural society with the influx of a variety of immigrant groups.

Statistics showing the numbers of 'immigrant groups' in the UK are notoriously unreliable. It must also be emphasised that, as such groups become established, they eventually cease to be 'ethnic minorities' and become instead fully British. Some figures are, nevertheless, illuminating.

'Heads of Families' born overseas 1991			
West Indies	**India, Pakistan, Bangladesh**	**Others**	**Total**
433,641	1,295,810	905,960	2,635,411

Source: National Census, 1991

With the 1991 population being 57,998 million, we can see that the 'first generation' ethnic minority population amounted to 4.5 per cent of the total population. If we included the dependants of these individuals, who are second generation and beyond, we find a much larger group who are not immigrants, but who may be considered so by the rest of the population and thus suffer discrimination. The proportion of the population which comes originally from other cultures is also reflected in growing religious diversity, which is considered below.

The political implications of the multi-cultural nature of modern British society are various. The most important include:

- The need for policies and legislation which will reduce and, if possible, eliminate discrimination against the 'ethnic minority' community. This includes measures to combat racially motivated crimes against property and persons.
- Though the total number of people from ethnic minorities is small overall, there are some areas, especially in the inner cities, where they form a significantly large proportion of the population. This now affects voting patterns substantially and the parties have become aware of the importance of such ethnic groups in the selection of candidates for Parliament and for local council elections. Marked effects in the make-up of councils has already been felt. There are still relatively few members of ethnic minority groups in the House of Commons (four in 1992), but there are indications that this number will grow in the near future.
- The multi-cultural and religious nature of society needs to be reflected in educational practice, both in the main curriculum and in acts of collective worship.

Religion

Two important developments in the religious character of the UK have political implications. One is the general decline in religious observance among traditional Christian communities. The other is the increasing numbers of adherents to religions other than Christianity.

Religious observance

The decline in commitment to the Christian religions is difficult to measure, since statistics of church attendance are unreliable and, in any case, do not indicate accurately how important religion is in people's lives.

Some indication can be gleaned from Church of England figures relating to membership of church parishes – that is, those who are registered as 'members' of the church. The number has fallen from 140 per thousand in 1921 to only 44 per thousand in 1990 (figures for York and Canterbury). This is a crude but informative indication of how the Church of England plays a declining role in society.

Politically, the effect falls largely upon the nature of legislation covering family, social and moral issues. There has been a general liberalisation of laws on divorce, homosexuality, abortion and pornography since the 1960s. Part of this has certainly been the result of a reduction in adherence to religious principles. Church leaders have not ceased to speak out on the great moral and social issues of the day, but politicians are increasingly aware that they reflect a declining set of values in British society.

'Minority' religions

While Christian religions have been experiencing diminishing popularity, there has been a growth in the significance of other religions, due largely to overseas immigration in the past forty years.

The statistics since 1970 tell their own story:

The growth of non-Christian religions in Britain				
Year	Hindus	Muslims	Sikhs	Buddhists
1970	50,000	204,000	75,000	6,000
1980	120,000	306,000	150,000	17,000
1990	140,000	505,000	250,000	28,000

Source: Registrar General Estimates

Not only are these numbers growing, but members of these religions tend to show a much higher level of regular worship and a greater commitment to their values than Christians. They may therefore have a significance much greater than that implied by the simple numbers shown in the statistics.

The implications of this for politicians are now quite considerable. If we include the estimated 326,000 Jews in the UK, there may be as many as 1.5 million regular adherents to non-Christian religions. When we consider that regular attendance at Church of England services is probably well below four million, it is clear that the dominant place of Protestantism in British society is coming to an end. As we have seen above, these trends inevitably affect social and moral attitudes (witness the antagonism of the Muslim community in the 1990s to the author Salman Rushdie following publication of *The Satanic Verses*, a book critical of the Islamic religion). Schools must also take account of the plurality of beliefs when establishing their curriculum.

The 'established' Church

As far as England and Wales are concerned, the Church of England is politically 'established'. This is largely the result of historical realities. When the Church did play a significant part in British life, it was clear that its leaders should be allowed to play an important role in politics. Furthermore, there were various devices which were designed to ensure that the values of the Church of England should remain entrenched in the culture. These are still in place and include the following:

- The monarch must be a member of the Church and be married to a spouse who is also a member.
- The monarch may not be married to a divorced person.
- The Archbishops of York and Canterbury, together with other senior Bishops of the Church of England, sit in the House of Lords. (Note that senior Catholic clergy do not enjoy this right.)
- Anglicanism (i.e. the teachings of the Church of England) is the established religion of schools in England and Wales. There must be regular acts of worship (though these are not compulsory for members of other religions).
- Archbishops and Bishops of the Church are appointed by the Prime Minister on the advice of the Archbishop of Canterbury.

The declining importance of Anglicanism in Britain has led to some calls to 'dis-establish' the Church from political life. The effects of such a development would have little political significance, but would be of immense symbolic importance. It would officially recognise the decline in religious observance and so clear the way for more open political debate on a number of issues affecting marriage and divorce, morality and even the role of the monarchy.

Social class

The significance of class

Until the 1960s it was the accepted political wisdom that the class divisions in British society determined the nature of politics and the issues over which elections were fought. Most of the population considered themselves to be members of one of the two great social classes – working or middle – and saw their interests in terms of their position in that simple class structure. Of course not everybody fitted into this simple scheme. There was a substantial section of the working class which supported the Conservative Party on the grounds of 'deference', a feeling that they would prefer to be governed by their superiors. There were also members of the middle class, largely professionals and those occupied in 'caring' careers such as teaching, nursing, charities and social work, who supported the Labour Party or the Liberals on intellectual and emotional grounds. Yet, on the whole, politics revolved around allegiance to the two larger classes and the attitudes which were associated with those classes.

Elections were fought over the 'middle ground', over those issues which might attract the support of people who were unsure of their class position or who were willing to vote according to issues rather than traditional class allegiance. The shift of a few hundred thousand votes could make a vital difference in the nature of the government which resulted.

Thus, the Labour Party was seen as the party of the Welfare State, of powerful trade unions, of high taxation but also high spending on public services, of a commitment to equality of opportunity in education and employment, and of support for the aims of nationalised industries. The Conservatives were not radically opposed to any of these ideas, but tended to try to keep taxes down, to be more concerned with economic stability than the rights and conditions of workers, and were more concerned with property rights and business than with those dependent on welfare. Otherwise there was a broad consensus to political values with which both middle and working classes could agree.

Since the 1960s, however, the traditional class structure has broken down. There are several reasons for this development:

- The decline of traditional industries such as coal, steel, shipbuilding and heavy engineering has reduced the size of the traditional manual working class.
- There has been a corresponding growth in service industries such as computing, financial services, entertainment, retailing and sales whose employees have no specific class identification.
- The difference in the wages of skilled manual workers and those in the service industries described above has narrowed or disappeared.
- The general rise in prosperity has rendered income and lifestyle differences less significant. Most families (about 70 per cent) now own their own homes. A similar proportion possess cars, travel abroad and enjoy a wide range of entertainments.

As a result of these changes, voting has become more volatile and support for the political parties is considerably fragmented. It is no longer true that Labour is purely a working-class party, while the Conservatives now enjoy support across the whole social spectrum. The Liberal Democrats have also benefited from class fragmentation. Their support is drawn from a wide range of social and economic groups.

The modern class structure

The extremely varied nature of Britain's occupational structure can be illustrated by reference to the proportions of household heads in different types of occupation. These are shown below:

Occupational group of head of household in 1991	
Type of employment	**% of Total**
Professional	5
Employers and managers	13
Intermediate and junior non-manual	13
Skilled manual	19
Semi-skilled manual	8
Unskilled manual	2
Retired	27
Unoccupied	12
Other	1

Source: *Social Trends 1994*, General Statistical Office

We can see that no occupational group is dominant and especially that manual workers, from unskilled to skilled, comprise only 29 per cent of the total. This is what might have formerly been described as the working class, before 1960 the dominant class in British society. It is now quite small and declining in size.

The statistics do reveal, however, a large group of unemployed (12 per cent) and also hide the fact that there are a significant number of workers who are either severely under-employed or very low paid. It is this group, heavily dependent on welfare and charity, which have been described as a new 'underclass' which is causing political concern. Apart from their dependence on welfare, members of this 'class' are prone to homelessness, display social and health problems, are susceptible to criminal behaviour and drug abuse, and their children frequently experience educational difficulties. The principal danger in the development of an underclass is that it may transform itself from merely an **economic** category – the very poor and deprived – into a kind of **sub-culture** which becomes permanently alienated from the rest of society and, thus, a threat to its security. Extreme left- and right-wing movements are also likely to flourish in such a sub-culture.

Still, class is considerably less significant than it used to be on the British political scene, but this is not to say that poverty and deprivation are not still with us. Most disturbing is the suggestion that political parties, in their search for the 'centre ground of support', will ignore this new underclass in their programmes of action.

The media

Broadcasting

Britain's radio and television companies are remarkable in the degree of freedom they enjoy from interference by the state. Although the BBC is a public corporation (i.e. publicly owned), it is guaranteed its independence by the Charter which established it and which is renewed regularly by Parliament. Thus, the freedom of the BBC remains in the hands of Parliament, apparently safe from the ambitions of any government to control it. Attempts to stifle political debate and controversy have always met with staunch opposition from all elements in society, and sometimes, when necessary, by the courts.

The commercial broadcasting stations are also guaranteed independence by a series of Acts of Parliament. Here there is no link at all with the state. Only the Independent Broadcasting Authority (independent indeed, as its title suggests) can regulate private companies and even then it is more to ensure good public taste and political impartiality than to attempt any undue influence.

As a result, there is a vigorous tradition of extensive and free political debate on TV and radio. Programmes concerning current affairs and other social or economic issues are popular and remain serious and of high quality.

The Press

As in broadcasting, Britain enjoys an extremely active and forthright press. However, it cannot be said with the same confidence that the newspapers are free from political influence. Indeed, it has often been argued by politicians on the left of centre that the British Press has an inbuilt bias towards the Conservative Party. This, they claim, was never more apparent than when Margaret Thatcher was Prime Minister. The

Sun's 1992 headline **'IT WAS THE SUN WOT WON IT'**, referring to that newspaper's unrelenting campaign against the Labour Party and the unexpected election victory by the Conservatives, reinforced this view.

Since then, however, the *Sun* has changed its allegiance and, while not being an enthusiastic supporter of Labour, has abandoned its apparently slavish attachment to the Conservatives. Indeed, during the mid 1990s, virtually the whole of what is known as the 'Tory Press', including the *Daily Mail* and the *Daily Telegraph*, lost faith with the leadership of John Major and ran campaigns to remove him. This has restored some political balance to the British Press establishment, especially taken together with the tendency of the *Guardian, Independent, Observer, Sunday Times* and *Independent on Sunday* to take a left-of-centre line on many issues.

The Press is not as subject to guarantees of political neutrality as are the broadcasting media. The BBC Charter and the rules of the Independent Broadcasting Authority (IBA) contain strict regulations concerning the treatment of current affairs. The Press Complaints Authority, on the other hand, is largely confined to issues of good taste and the preservation of privacy rather than political balance.

The following figures taken from the 1983 election, when political partisanship was at its height within the Press, are illuminating:

Circulation of newspapers supporting the Conservatives	11.26 million (78%)
Circulation of newspapers supporting Labour	3.27 million (22%)
Circulation of newspapers supporting the Liberals	0.42 million* (3%)
* figure exceeds 100% owing to some dual allegiance.	

Source: *British Political Facts, 1900–94*, Butler and Butler, Macmillan

By the mid 1990s, however, the position had changed markedly. The information relating to the modern British Press, shown below, indicates the greater degree of balance which now exists:

Newspaper	Circulation (approx.)	Normal political stance
Daily Express	1.4 m.	Right wing
Sun	3.8 m.	Independent
Daily Mirror	2.5 m.	Left wing
Daily Star	0.8 m.	Right of centre
Daily Mail	1.8 m.	Right wing
Daily Telegraph	1.0 m.	Right wing
Guardian	0.4 m.	Left of centre
Independent	0.3 m.	Independent
Today	0.5 m.	Independent

Before the 1980s it was accepted political wisdom that the Press had little influence over voting behaviour. Since then, however, it is believed that there is some marginal influence, especially from the popular tabloid newspapers. The kind of statistics shown above, therefore, are now of more than passing interest to a student of politics.

The Welfare State

Since its creation in the 1940s, the Welfare State has been woven into the fabric of British society and politics. Indeed, until 1980 no politician dared challenge its basic principles without risk of being branded an extremist. The arrival of a Conservative Government with radical views on the economy and welfare threatened such certainties and even began to challenge the whole basis of the Welfare State.

The British welfare system was founded upon a number of principles the main ones being:

- All employed members of the population must contribute to welfare provision, partly on the basis of an equal payment, partly on the basis of ability to pay (i.e. level of income).
- A wide variety of services and benefits are available, free on demand and without regard to income. These include education, health care (including mental health), child benefits, family support services, unemployment benefit and old age pensions.
- A further range of benefits is available for those in special need, such as those in extreme poverty, or those suffering from disablement or bad housing conditions, although these awards are based on an assessment of needs (i.e. a 'means test').

To some extent there has been a mild erosion of the Welfare State provisions since 1960, with charges being levied, for those who can afford them, on dental care, eye testing and the provision of glasses, medical prescriptions and a range of other marginal medical services. More stringent tests to determine who is in most need have also been introduced. Nevertheless, no serious challenge was mounted to the basic philosophy of the Welfare State until a section of the Conservative Party took a turn to the political right wing in the 1980s. There is now on the agenda some suggestions that a number of these services and benefits will no longer be automatically supplied, such as old age pensions and free education. Furthermore, there are tentative proposals to allow some people to opt out of the Welfare State altogether. It can no longer be assumed that the Welfare State will be with us indefinitely.

Foreign relations

Britain is possibly unique among the world community of nations in enjoying close alliances with four international bodies simultaneously. These are:

- Links with her Commonwealth countries, such as Canada, Australia, New Zealand, South Africa and India.
- The traditional alliance with the USA – the so-called 'special relationship'.
- The relatively newly formed association with the European Union.
- Membership of the North Atlantic Treaty Organisation (NATO).

In addition to these unusual circumstances, Britain possesses a number of other features which give it a special position in international relations. They are:

- The possession of an independent nuclear deterrent (largely Trident, submarine-based missiles).
- A place on the United Nations Security Council (the UN's inner circle of members) which gives her an effective veto over United Nations action.
- A disproportionately influential role in international relations, based on its past military strength and the persistence of a number of alliances described above. Margaret Thatcher's prestige abroad also helped to sustain this position through the 1980s.
- Military strength and access to foreign bases such as Cyprus, the Falkland Islands and the Caribbean, well beyond its apparent economic strength. The size and sophistication of the Royal Navy is especially important in this regard. Britain is, therefore, able to deploy tactical forces round the world at short notice better than many larger, richer states.
- Many states, notably in the Middle East and in Africa still accept a degree of moral authority from Britain. This is the result of its long attachment to democracy and history of struggle against tyrannical regimes.

Of course the complexity of Britain's network of alliances also brings problems and extra responsibility with it. There have been occasions when it has found itself in conflict with one traditional ally while seeking to support another. Thus, the joint British, French and Israeli action against Colonel Nasser's closure of the Suez Canal in 1956 resulted in decisive opposition from the USA. More recently, there have been difficulties over British involvement in the Bosnian civil war, and in 1995 a fishing dispute between Spain and Canada found Britain caught between its conflicting loyalties to a Commonwealth ally and a European partner.

As the century draws to a close, however, the traditional links with the USA and the Commonwealth appear to be weakening. It may be that future British foreign policy will have to be increasingly integrated with that of the European Union.

Britain's principal social and economic problems

Crime

There has been a general tendency for the incidence of recorded crime to rise during the course of the twentieth century. Since about 1970, however, the rise has accelerated markedly. This is illustrated in the table on page 50.

These dramatic figures bring a number of political implications with them. First, there is clearly an increasing need for provision of policing, law courts, crime prevention, prison facilities and other forms of punishment or rehabilitation. Secondly, there is a clear message that social conditions must be responsible for the large increase in criminal behaviour. These may include unemployment, poverty, poor housing and lack of leisure facilities, especially for the young. Politicians must make decisions regarding the basic causes of crime, often choosing between preventative measures and mere enforcement of the law.

Incidence of recorded crime						
Year	Murder	Wounding	Robbery	Burglary	Rape	Theft
1900	312	1,212	256	3,812	231	63,604
1930	300	1,443	217	11,169	89	110,159
1950	315	5,177	1,021	29,834	314	334,222
1970	393	38,735	6,273	190,597	884	1,463,469
1990	664	177,200	36,200	529,300	3,400	2,374,400

Source: Home Office Official Crime Statistics

Thirdly, there is a constant need to update the powers which the police and courts have in dealing with crime. Policy on sentencing is particularly critical in view of the rising prison population which has gone hand in hand with the 'crime boom'.

Declining industries　There has been a significant decline in Britain's traditional manufacturing industries in the last quarter of the twentieth century. Statistics on production in three industries illustrate this trend:

Industry	1970	1992
Cars	1.641 million	1.292 million
Steel	27.868 million tons	16.212 million tons
Coal	145 thousand tons	84 thousand tons

Source: *Annual Abstract of Statistics*

In itself the decline may not be politically important, provided there is a corresponding rise in output and employment in other industries, such as services. To some extent this has been the case. However, this kind of well-established industry is usually highly concentrated in a few localities. Their decline has, therefore, resulted in high local levels of unemployment and falling living standards. Save for measures to reverse the decline, it has become necessary for governments to consider intervention in these localities to try to provide new employment opportunities and to prevent the whole region from falling into long-term deprivation. As we have seen above, high levels of unemployment and poverty may also give rise to an increasing incidence of crime.

Whatever the social consequences, British political parties and governments have had to adjust to the fact that Britain is no longer a leading world industrial power. Some have even described the recent history of British government as 'the management of economic decline'. This may be exaggerated, but does reflect the fact that our economic horizons have had to be lowered in recent times.

Poverty and the income gap

Although the importance of class differentials has declined, there is much evidence to suggest that the gap between those who enjoy a decent standard of living and those who are significantly deprived is growing.

In 1963, for example, approximately 10 per cent of households received an income of below half the average income for the whole country. By 1990 this percentage had risen to just over 20 per cent. Further evidence of growing poverty is indicated by the number of households needing to claim housing benefit (i.e. help from the state with rents or mortgages). This number rose from 1.8 million in 1981 to 4.3 million in 1992. Many other statistics support the same story.

Increasing burdens on the taxpayer, social problems and growing crime rates are examples of problems which result from this phenomenon, apart from the human misery it causes. In the longer term, increasing social conflict may result. The inner city riots of 1981 were indicative of a growing problem. Tension, racial and economic, continues to be a danger in Britain's cities.

Inflation and unemployment

Britain has been bedevilled by chronic economic problems since Prime Minister **Harold Macmillan** was able to declare during the 1959 election campaign that 'Britain has never had it so good'. Governments of both major parties have struggled and often failed to deal with the twin evils of inflation and unemployment, which have held back Britain's economic growth. Both have grown in economic and political significance since Macmillan's 1959 claim.

Although there have been fluctuations in the levels of inflation and unemployment, the problems of these have persisted. Whenever governments appear to have them under control, a new bout of difficulties arises. The relevant statistics indicate how endemic the problem has become:

Inflation rates	
1963	2.0%
1968	5.2%
1973	8.8%
1976	16.4%
1981	11.9%
1986	4.4%
1993	3.2%

Source: *Annual Abstract of Statistics*

The unemployment story is a similar one:

Number of unemployed	
1960	0.461 million
1970	0.628 million
1975	1.152 million
1980	2.244 million
1985	3.346 million
1990	1.850 million
1993	3.062 million

Source: *Annual Abstract of Statistics*

Thus, government economic policy since 1960 has been dominated by the need to control these two economic evils. Neither party has succeeded in the interim in conquering either with any permanence.

Britain's political culture

The term 'political culture' refers to the dominant values and attitudes concerning politics which exist within a community. This culture is different in every country and has important effects upon the way parties, politicians and pressure groups behave. It also determines the nature of the political institutions through which they work. Some of the prominent aspects of Britain's political culture include the following:

- A respect for democratic institutions, notably Parliament and the party system.
- An acceptance of the continued authority, albeit limited, of the monarchy and, to a much lesser extent, other traditional institutions such as the House of Lords and the civil service.
- A generally liberal and pluralist approach to politics. There is a tolerance of competing political views, provided they do not threaten the state and its democratic institutions.
- Political moderation. Extreme political philosophies of both left and right attract little support.
- A conservative (small 'c') attitude to political change. The British prefer gradual evolution to revolutionary change in politics.
- A strong sense of patriotism, often verging on notions of national superiority and sometimes xenophobia. This also includes intense pride in Britain's history and heritage.
- Broad support for the concept of a Welfare State where all are willing to contribute to support those who may be in need through no fault of their own.
- A deep attachment to the importance of private property.

The 'Thatcher Revolution'

The political culture described above came under considerable pressure for change during the period of Margaret Thatcher's premiership and immediately after it. In many ways significant changes were to be observed, though whether these will become permanent remains to be seen.

Some of the developments were:

- A suspicion of the economic power of the state and a desire to restore greater freedom of enterprise.
- A greater sense of individualism and feeling that each person is largely responsible for their own welfare.
- Suspicion of, and opposition to, the power of trade unions in society.
- Increased challenges to the traditional authority of such institutions as the Church of England, the civil service, the monarchy and the House of Lords.
- A less liberal approach to matters concerning the family and morality.
- An established desire to maintain a low level of personal taxation.
- A deep suspicion of traditional socialism as expressed by the left wing of the Labour Party.

> *'If power has shifted away from politicians to markets and bureaucrats, so that things that are central to our lives – the cost of money, the availability of work, the regulations that govern our leisure and countryside – are decided without political discussion, plenty of people will be unworried by that. It could be called the final victory of paternalism and liberalism over politics.'*
> Andrew Marr, *Ruling Britannia* (Michael Joseph, 1995)

Thus, Britain seems to be more conservative and **less** liberal in matters concerning **morality** and **political** controversy. At the same time, however, the country is **more** liberal in its **economic** outlook, preferring greater individual freedom of action and considerably less state regulation.

These developments have brought about several fundamental changes in the character of the British political culture. In particular, a number of features of society, which had appeared to be well established, have now declined markedly. Among them are the following:

- Britain has always been considered to enjoy a highly **homogeneous** society, that is, one where social differences were generally not great enough to breed fundamental disgreements about the direction of political action. The established class system created stability and order in a way which was often absent in many of the more fragmented social systems in some western European states such as Italy and France. The disintegration of the traditional class system which occurred in the 1980s has led to a more individualistic, more diverse society.
- As the settled, ordered nature of society disappeared, there was also a noticeable decline in the postwar **consensus** which had characterised party politics for over thirty years. This consensus – a general agreement on the nature of the Welfare State, the mixed economy (state-owned industry alongside private enterprise), the role of trade unions and the interventionist control of the economy – relied on the homogeneous nature of society. Consensus was replaced by so-called 'conviction politics' where there are deep political disagreements about policy. The great issues concerning welfare provision, ownership of industry, taxation, local government, Europe and trade unionism are the subject of bitter controversy instead of broad acceptance of agreed goals.

*Thatcherism has been more about restoring state authority
and the political fortunes of the Conservative Party than it has
been about constructing a free economy.*
Andrew Gamble, 'The Politics of Thatcherism' in
Parliamentary Affairs (July 1989)

● The attacks which successive Thatcher administrations made upon the
social, economic and political Establishment of Britain have
substantially changed public attitudes towards leadership. The British
characteristic of **deference** – a respect for those enjoying positions of
authority, whether traditional or elected – has been significantly
reduced. Margaret Thatcher had little respect for the established
leaders of the judiciary, civil service, Church of England, financial
institutions, aristocracy and the professions. These **elites**, as political
scientists term them, were seen as obstacles to her reforming zeal.
Their privileged position was attacked with varying degrees of success.
Thus, Britain became less subject to control by these elites, while, at
the same time, the public eventually lost their traditional deference
towards them.

*The simple top-down world in which politicians took turns at
flicking the levers of power, offering the rest of us more jobs
and predictably rising prosperity, has gone, and our political
imaginations have hardly begun to cope with the change. This
toppling of the old order faces every developed and open
country.*
Andrew Marr, *Ruling Britannia* (Michael Joseph, 1995)

For exam questions relevant to this unit, see page 487.

Introduction Outside Northern Ireland Britain has an essentially two-party system, with some challenge from third parties – Liberal Democrats in various regions and nationalists in Scotland and Wales – yet its ideological background is considerably more complex and fragmented. It is therefore inevitable that these ideological traditions do not coincide precisely with the party structure.

Thus, we can divide political traditions into as many as seven main philosophical movements, all of which are still flourishing at the end of the twentieth century. These may be described as:

- Traditional Conservatism
- Authoritarian–nationalistic Conservatism
- 'New Right' Conservatism
- Liberalism
- Democratic socialism
- Social democracy
- Liberal nationalism.

At first sight this may appear confusing when set against the simpler party system. The reason is that each party is really a coalition of groups who belong to these ideological movements to a greater or lesser extent. If we place each movement into the party structure we obtain a scheme as follows:

Conservative Party	Labour Party	Liberal Democrat Party	Scots & Welsh Nationalists
Traditional Conservatism	Democratic socialism	Liberalism	Liberal nationalism
Authoritarian–nationalists	Social democracy	Social democracy	Liberalism
'New Right' neo-liberals	Liberalism	Liberal nationalism	Social democracy

We can now see that three identifiable forms of conservatism flourish within the same Conservative Party and that liberalism and social democracy can be discovered in four different parties. It is even the case, not shown above, that some members of the Conservative Party on its moderate wing hold views in common with pure liberals or even social democrats.

So we must be careful to distinguish between the political parties with their various internal factions and their ideological traditions, which we will now examine.

Traditional Conservatism

The most effective and convenient way to trace the development of traditional conservatism is by reference to a number of individuals who have either proposed or practised political principles which can be grouped into this category of belief. Having reviewed the ideas of these conservatives, we can summarise the position as it stands today.

Opinions vary considerably as to when British Conservatism came into existence. Some go back as far as the English Civil War in the 1640s, citing the supporters of the Stuart monarchy as the original Conservatives, reacting as they did against the new ideas of the Parliamentary faction. Others suggest it began with the opponents of the Whig Party who established Parliamentary sovereignty and a limited, constitutional monarchy following the Glorious Revolution of 1688. Indeed it was at this time that the term 'Tory' was first introduced to describe such a conservative faction. For convenience, the actual formation of a 'Conservative Party' by **Sir Robert Peel** in the 1840s could be used as a starting point. However, the period which can, perhaps, best be selected as seeing the birth of the tradition is the years immediately following the French Revolution, that is the 1790s. The key figure was, ironically, a Whig MP rather than a Tory, but his philosophy was unmistakably conservative. He was **Edmund Burke.**

Edmund Burke (1729–97)

After the French Revolution in 1789, and more particularly the 'reign of terror' of 1792–3 when many aristocrats and opponents of the ruling party lost their lives or their liberty, fear gripped much of the British political establishment that the radical ideas of the revolutionaries would be exported across the Channel, sweeping away the authority of traditional institutions such as the monarchy, landed aristocracy and the Church of England. These ideas included such 'extreme' (in terms of late eighteenth-century belief) principles as equal political rights, democratically elected institutions and religious freedom. Burke was among these reactionaries or 'conservatives' who opposed the radical new ideas. His major work, entitled *Reflections on the Revolution in France*, expressed these fears, but went further still, developing into a full account of early conservative principles.

His ideas follow a logical series of steps:

- Man is not a rational creature, but is driven by basic instincts and emotions. The new ideas of the seventeenth century, often referred to as the 'Age of Reason' or the 'Enlightenment', assumed that men were capable of rational thought and action, so that society and politics could be moulded in such rational ways. Burke would have none of this. Not only did mankind follow emotions rather than reason, but responded to such base instincts as selfishness and greed. It would therefore be futile to conduct politics in a rational manner. The imperfections of man had to be recognised.

- Since man is imperfect and, furthermore, is not capable of being made perfect through education or moral example, he must have disciplines imposed on him, just as children must be disciplined. Such control can only be imposed from above, by some form of superior force. Democracy and equality, he argued, involved man being able to control his own actions rationally. He was not capable of this, Burke insisted.

- The most basic need of man is for order and security. Such qualities in a society are far more desirable than characteristics such as individual freedom and tolerance. Thus, the purpose of political power is to create and to maintain good order.

- Order and security are best achieved through continuity and respect for traditional institutions. By preserving strong links between the past, present and future, security is maintained. It was the preservation of traditional institutions such as landed interests, the family and the Church, which could provide such continuity.
- Violent and rapid change is, thus, to be avoided. There may be times when gentle reforms are required, but these should only be undertaken when absolutely necessary and with regard to traditional practices.
- Property ownership brings with it a sense of responsibility. Not all are capable of this, so that property ownership cannot be shared by all. However, those who are privileged enough to own property do have a duty to protect the security of the whole of society, including the propertyless.

Sir Robert Peel (Prime Minister 1834–5, 1841–6)

After Burke the Conservative movement fell into danger of becoming a purely reactionary movement, opposed to any form of social reform or progress. Thus, Conservatives were opposed to reform of the political system (which was a key issue in the early 1830s), to the introduction of free trade rather than protectionism (also an issue) during the same period and to equal political rights for Catholics. Peel recognised that such a reactionary movement would be politically doomed.

In his so-called 'Tamworth Manifesto' issued in 1834, he urged Conservatives to accept reforms if they were clearly desirable and inevitable. Thus, he linked the movement to progress and reform. His maxim was that it was sometimes necessary to 'reform in order to preserve'. However, he insisted that such change be moderated and, to achieve this, traditional forms of authority would need to be combined with the new democratic institutions which were promoting reform. Thus, the conservative movement added the principle of a 'mixed' political system to Burke's earlier ideas. More popular democracy could be accepted provided some power was retained by traditional institutions.

Peel's support for an ordered society was demonstrated by perhaps his best known achievement, the creation of an organised police force when he was Home Secretary in 1822.

Benjamin Disraeli (Earl of Beaconsfield, Prime Minister 1868, 1874–80)

Disraeli had formed his political beliefs under Peel, and the two men had a great deal in common. Disraeli took the idea of the mixed political system and developed it further into the concept of 'Tory democracy'. He urged Conservatives to accept the right of all people to a share in democracy. In effect, they should be granted voting rights. Recognising the dangers of democracy, however, he proposed a political system designed to reduce the threat to society. For him, the dangers were:

- The huge voting power of the working classes might create revolutionary change, sweeping away order and authority, replacing it with anarchy or even socialism.
- Alternatively, the wealth of the newly enriched capitalist middle classes could be converted into political power. If they were to exercise power in their own interests – and he believed they would – the working class would be disadvantaged, creating the seedbed for discontent and

revolution (1848 had seen a series of revolutionary upheavals in various parts of Europe). Capitalist power, he predicted, was creating 'two nations', one of the rich and powerful, the other of the poor and powerless.

- The traditional power of the aristocracy, monarchy, landed gentry and Church had always been a moderating and unifying influence. If their power were to be undermined by democracy, moderation would disappear. The landed classes were the natural ruling class since they alone could govern in the interests of the whole nation rather than purely in their own interests.

Thus he warned against a divided nation, torn by class conflict and destroyed by the uncontrolled pursuit of self-interest by the two great social classes. The answer was to ensure that Britain remained 'one nation', living with order and security, so as to preserve the power of traditional institutions and to combine it with new democratic institutions. This was Disraeli's vision of Tory democracy. He also believed that a strong sense of nationalism and pride in the Empire (which was at its height then) could unite the nation.

On a more philosophical level, Disraeli believed that society was a single organism, one great united whole which could exist in a state of harmony if the 'natural order' were preserved. He firmly believed that men are not equal, but that some are naturally superior to others. Any social and political system, therefore, had to reflect that social order and not destroy it, as nineteenth-century liberals and socialists were proposing. Each level in society has its part to play in preserving order and creating prosperity and so the levels depended on each other. But this did not mean that rank and privilege should be abolished. On the contrary, they should be maintained. At the top there should be a permanent ruling class made up of the traditionally superior class – the aristocracy and landed gentry.

In summary, Disraeli's contributions to the conservative tradition can be described as follows:

- Popular democracy is necessary, but carries such dangers of disorder that democratic institutions must share power with traditional centres of power which have proved themselves to be superior and more responsible in the past.
- It is vital for peace and prosperity to unite the nation (his views are often described as 'one nation Toryism'). Unity can only be preserved if no section of society is able to profit unduly at the expense of others.
- Nationalism is to be encouraged as a further means of unifying society.
- There is a natural order in society which should be preserved. This order serves to unify and not divide the nation. At the top is a natural ruling class who should govern fairly and responsibly. Ideas of social equality are, therefore, artificial and false.

Michael Oakeshott (1901–90)

For nearly a century after Disraeli the Conservative movement, and much of the Conservative Party itself, adopted his principles. As with Peel, they learned to accept reforms where they were necessary and to argue that Conservatives were the best suited to manage such changes for the good of the whole nation and not just sections of it. However, by the mid-twentieth century this was not enough. The steady march of liberal and socialist ideas represented a threat to traditional Conservative beliefs. A restatement of philosophy was needed and was provided by the modern conservative philosopher, Michael Oakeshott.

Faced with increasingly high levels of involvement by the state in society, Oakeshott questioned the basis upon which any political action should be undertaken. His answer was to oppose all forms of action which were based on abstract principles or artificial ideologies. Thus, for example, 'equality' was an abstract principle, not natural to mankind. If political measures were simply designed to promote greater equality **for its own sake** – a socialist objective – it would be seen as unnatural and would lead to disruption in society. Ideologies too are to be treated with great suspicion, he suggested.

Like all Conservatives, Oakeshott opposed the imposition of rigid ideologies on the grounds that this could easily lead to tyranny – political leaders who were driven by the desire to impose the ideology would tend to accept no opposition, often ruthlessly putting down any resistance to it. This had clearly occurred after the French Revolution of 1789 when the Jacobins hunted down all opponents, whether real or imagined. Similarly, in the twentieth century, communism adopted tyrannical methods in order to impose itself upon society. Oakeshott, however, added a further objection: ideology and abstract principles do not take account of the traditions and sentiments of the people. **All** political action, Oakeshott said, must take account of such natural features of a society. If not, the people will not readily accept it, disorder is likely to result. He suggested that politics should be 'a conversation not an argument.'

The implication of Oakeshott's beliefs is that there should be no sense of **progress** in politics. Politicians should **not** see their task as moving society in a particular direction, towards a goal or a series of goals. Rather, they should allow the people to set their own direction naturally and should simply ensure that the state is maintained in a safe and secure condition. For him, the art of politics was something similar to steering a ship. The course is set by the passengers and the politician should merely ensure it keeps safely to that course. It is this particular aspect of Oakeshott's philosophy which perhaps defines the term 'Conservatism' most aptly today. It includes the idea of conserving what is good and what is in accordance with the wishes of the people. The alternative is to lead the people towards goals which they may not desire, with unpredictable consequences which may threaten the preservation of the better features of society.

'If the main strength of Conservatism is adaptability, its main enemy is ideology.'
Francis Pym (Conservative Cabinet Minister 1979–83),
The Politics of Consent, (Hamish Hamilton, 1984)

Harold Macmillan (Prime Minister 1957–63)

From World War One onwards there was a steady expansion in the activities and scope of the state. For Conservatives, traditionally suspicious of state power, this represented a major challenge. Macmillan adopted the approach of Peel and Disraeli to such developments while updating their beliefs to suit the second half of the twentieth century. Thus he 'modernised' the Conservative tradition without distorting it.

He recognised that the new powerful state should play a similar role to that of the ruling class in the nineteenth century. It should prevent class conflict and act as a neutral arbiter between the competing claims of different sections of society. By creating a stable society the state would maximise the opportunities for individualism to flourish. Thus the powerful state would not threaten individual action, but would enhance it. In practice, this implied such policies as firm economic management, control and support for industrial development, protection of the rights of both employers and trade unions and maintenance of an effective Welfare State for the benefit of all. Since the Labour Party could support such objectives, the period surrounding Macmillan's premiership is often referred to as that of 'consensus politics'.

Macmillan also understood that, if the state were to remain benevolent and popular, it was necessary to involve the representatives of important sections of society in the governing process. Thus trade union leaders, employers, financiers, agricultural and military interests were incorporated into the state. So far did the process go, in fact, that Macmillan's vision was often described as the 'corporate state'.

His objectives were still those of Disraeli. He believed that those of a conservative disposition should govern. He saw social unity and harmony as vital. He understood that all should feel they have a stake in the activities of the state and that no single class should be allowed to dominate.

Traditional Conservatism today

Margaret Thatcher transformed the nature of the Conservative Party during the 1980s. Many of the traditional values described above were abandoned. Those Conservatives who adhered to them were steadily removed from power and declined in numbers. They referred to themselves as 'one-nation' Tories; 'Disraelian Conservatives' or sometimes merely as 'traditional' Tories. Thatcher's supporters disparagingly dubbed them 'wets' on the basis that they had insufficient nerve to support the radical reforms which were being proposed. Such proponents of the tradition as **Francis Pym**, **John Biffen** and **Ian Gilmour** were driven from office and fought a losing rearguard action against radical Thatcherism.

> 'The aim [of Conservatism] has always been to conserve what is good and to improve what is bad.'
> Francis Pym (Conservative Cabinet Minister 1979–83),
> *The Politics of Consent* (Hamish Hamilton, 1984)

A few heirs to the tradition of Burke, Peel and Disraeli retain powerful positions. These include **Michael Heseltine** and **Kenneth Clarke**. It remains to be seen whether the traditional form of Conservatism can reassert itself as the century draws to an end.

Summary of traditional conservative beliefs

1. Man is imperfect, irrational and imperfectible so that no political action should be based on rational ideas or be designed to grant excessive amounts of personal freedom.
2. The desire for order is the most important instinct of mankind so that any political system should be aimed at preserving order.
3. Rapid and radical social change should be avoided. Reform, if necessary, should be gradual and carried out in accordance with traditions. Whatever changes are allowed, what is good in society should be conserved.
4. Traditional institutions and an established ruling class are crucial in maintaining continuity between the past and the present.
5. There is a natural order in society which should be preserved.
6. Society should be a unified, harmonious whole and political action should be designed to preserve such a situation.
7. Abstract political principles and ideologies are to be treated with great suspicion and generally opposed.
8. The state should take into account the interests of all sections of society in creating order and general prosperity. In so doing it should promote individualism and maximum opportunities for the people.
9. Ownership of property is a privilege and brings with it the responsibility to preserve and maintain an ordered society.

Authoritarian–nationalistic Conservatism

On the extreme edge of the Conservative movement a group has survived often described as its traditional right wing. It has invariably been in a minority, but has, nevertheless, survived. Its two main characteristics are authoritarianism and entrenched nationalism. Of its modern adherents perhaps **Enoch Powell**, a minister in the 1960s and long-time prominent MP, has been the most important example.

Its stance on social and political issues includes:

- A particularly strong position on law and order issues including support for widespread use of the death penalty, severe sentences for crime in general, increased powers for the police and courts and support for corporal punishment in schools.
- Opposition to 'progressive' theories of education, the family, sexuality and crime prevention.
- Support for the preservation and extension of traditional institutions such as the Church, the monarchy and the House of Lords.
- Strong defence of the rights of property owners.
- Strong support for the preservation of private education and health.
- Emphasis on the concept of a ruling class with support for the preservation of the aristocracy, the 'traditional' public schools and universities. Also, particularly strong support for the continued authority of the monarchy.

The group's stress on nationalism also includes the following points:

- Preservation of the 'Union' of the UK. This implies total opposition to further degrees of independence for Scotland and Wales.

- They are confirmed 'Unionists' in the context of Northern Ireland. Any movements towards reducing the authority of the British Crown in the province, or of granting any influence to the Republic of Ireland, is totally opposed.
- Further immigration to the UK is opposed. Existing immigrant communities should be encouraged to return to their countries of origin. Measures towards enforcing racial equality are opposed.
- They were initially opposed to Britain's entry into the European Community. Some favour Britain's leaving the Community while others accept membership but wish to see a looser attachment to Europe.
- Britain's declining influence in world affairs is regretted. They support continuing involvement in those areas of the world where Britain continues to have vital interests. They tend to support the British alliance with the USA rather than European states.
- Continuing high expenditure of the armed forces is supported in order to facilitate a stronger world role.

Although some aspects of this movement may appear to be close to fascist ideology, there is a crucial distinction. Such Conservatives do support the principle of parliamentary democracy and the rule of law. Fascists would oppose democratic institutions and support instead dictatorial forms of government. Thus, they are very much a part of a Conservative rather than a fascist tradition.

'New Right' Conservatism

Although various elements of New Right Conservatism have flourished separately over the past two centuries, it was only in the 1980s that they were brought together into a single ideology. It came to dominate the political agenda in western Europe and the USA and was led by its best known proponent **Margaret Thatcher** (Prime Minister 1979–90). It was she and her close political allies such as **Sir Keith Joseph** who fused a number of political traditions into a single philosophy.

In broad terms, the New Right is a synthesis of what have been called 'neo-Liberalism' and 'neo-Conservatism' – in other words, modern versions of two traditional nineteenth-century movements. However, we can divide it further into as many as four historical tendencies. These can be identified as follows:

Classical liberalism

With the growth of the Industrial Revolution in Britain and the capitalist system which was a natural companion to it, there developed the study of economics as a science. The early economists such as **Adam Smith** and **David Ricardo** in the late seventeenth and early eighteenth centuries believed that the reason for the extraordinary growth in production and wealth resulting from capitalism was the degree of individual freedom in the economic sphere which the system allowed. This freedom released the forces of enterprise and innovation which facilitated such progress. At the same time, the preservation of such freedom required that governments should resist the temptation to interfere with economic affairs. Any such interference would inevitably reduce the wealth-creating capacity of capitalism. These economists further believed that all would benefit from the free operation of capitalism – workers, consumers and employers alike – as it guaranteed that production could be carried out at the most efficient level possible.

As the eighteenth century progressed and the political movement known as liberalism advanced, these **economic** theories came to be linked with the new **political** interest in personal liberty. Thus, the original – now known as 'classical' – liberals, such as **John Stuart Mill, Richard Cobden** and **Herbert Spencer**, advocated free trade and competition, the absence of state interference in the operation of product and labour markets and control of monopoly power resulting from large companies squeezing out smaller firms.

NOTE: More detail on classical liberalism can be found in the section on liberalism on pages 66–68.

Classical liberal ideas were falling out of favour by the end of the nineteenth century, to be replaced by political doctrines which involved more state interference in social and economic affairs. However, in the 1970s economic progress in the developed world seemed to be faltering. Interest was revived in the classical liberal ideas of a hundred years before. The Swiss philosopher **Friedrich Hayek** and American economist **Milton Friedman** suggested that excessive interference by the state in economic affairs, together with the growth in the influence of trade unions, were robbing capitalism of its ability to promote real growth in prosperity. Not only that, but unduly high taxes, over-regulation of industry and high levels of public expenditure were reducing economic and political liberty unjustifiably.

Margaret Thatcher and her close adviser, Sir Keith Joseph, were heavily influenced by these neo-classical liberals and set about converting fellow Conservatives to their beliefs. Their goal was to 'roll back the frontiers of the state', as they put it. This involved reducing public expenditure and taxation, removing state control over industry and restoring the operation of free markets wherever possible. At the same time, what was seen as the undesirable influence of trade unions was to be destroyed. It is these beliefs which are now referred to as 'neo-liberalism'.

American populism

The term 'populism' refers to any political movement which appeals to the mass of the people. The American populist party which flourished in the 1890s, however, was considerably more. It championed opposition to any form of vested interest which threatened the independence of the individual. The targets were big business, big government and especially excessive taxation. In a modern context a number of institutions have come under attack. These have included the civil service (including the bureaucracy involved in the European Union), over-powerful local government, trade unions, monopolies, the established Church and the Welfare State.

Populism has also appealed to feelings of extreme individualism, self-responsibility and independence which are so widespread in the USA. Whatever threatens these emotions is, therefore, to be mistrusted. Welfare, for example, is believed to rob people of the necessity to provide for themselves. If there is over-reliance on the state families will lose the will to fend for themselves. Big business and over-regulation reduce the effectiveness of small business. Thus, populism appeals to the 'small man', the rugged individualist. It follows that those who are unwilling to support themselves should not be rescued by the state.

Whiggism

In the nineteenth century the Whigs were essentially liberals who adapted their belief in individual liberty to defend the interests of the capitalist and property owning classes. The New Right is also a neo-liberal movement and, in common with the Whigs, wishes to defend the importance of property ownership. Thatcher added a modern aspect to the movement by encouraging widespread ownership of shares in private industry. Thus, the opportunity to accumulate wealth and property is seen as fundamental and the role of the state should be to sponsor and defend such rights.

Conservative authoritarianism

Although the New Right opposes the over-powerful state and defends the rights of individuals against it, there remains an acceptance that individuals do need to be protected in their lives and property against attacks from others. Small though the state may be, therefore, it should be a powerful, centralised institution. In common with traditional Conservatives the New Right takes a strong position on law and order issues. Its attitude to crime is to concentrate on punishment rather than social cures, while on social issues in general a conservative line is taken.

Although there was some element of moralism in the British New Right, greater stress was placed on it in the USA. It was certainly recognised that the increases in personal freedom which were resulting from New Right policies created the danger that society would disintegrate, with individuals in permanent conflict with each other and lacking any sense of moral responsibility. The answer lay in a stress on traditional values of family and religious morality. Such apparent immoralities as crime, homosexuality, single parenthood, pornography and sexual permissiveness were opposed. They threatened the integrity and security of society in a way which is unacceptable to any brand of Conservatism. As an additional unifying force in a potentially fragmented society, patriotism has been promoted, forming a bond with the nationalist form of Conservatism described above.

It is this modern application of traditional Conservative values which is often described as 'neo-Conservatism'.

We can now summarise this 'New Right' form of Conservatism:

New Right & neo-liberalism

1. Great stress on economic freedom
2. Disengagement of the state from economic control
3. Restoration of free markets wherever possible
4. Dependence on the Welfare State discouraged, self-responsibility in its place
5. Opposition to vested interests such as trade unions, big business, bureaucracy
6. Support for small independent businesses
7. Encouragement for widespread property and share ownership
8. Stress on morality and traditional values
9. Maintenance of a limited but disciplinarian state

A NOTE ON THE TERM 'RIGHT WING'
With the fragmentation of the Conservative movement in the 1980s, the term 'right wing' has become somewhat confusing. Unfortunately, it is apparent that there are now **two** accepted meanings of the word. It refers both to the 'Thatcherite' New Right form of Conservatism, as well as the authoritarian–nationalistic form of Conservatism.

Liberalism

Origins During the eighteenth century two major developments were occurring in Europe. First, the traditional forms of authority and the existing social order – both political and religious – were coming under challenge. Secondly, the Enlightenment ushered in new forms of rational, scientific thought.

The challenge to traditional authority and order

The religious Reformation which had earlier gripped much of northern Europe was not only of spiritual significance. The traditional authority of the papacy and the religious intolerance which had characterised Roman Catholicism were also called into question. The rigid doctrines of Rome, including its insistence on the authority of the Church, had been defeated by free-thinking, radical members of the Protestant movement. At the same time as papal authority was being weakened, the institution of hereditary, absolute monarchy was also coming under attack. The execution of Charles I in England represented a warning shot. It was soon followed by the Glorious Revolution of 1688 which ushered in a limited, constitutional form of monarchy. A century later both the French and the Americans rid themselves of hereditary monarchy (the French temporarily) and replaced it with more rational forms of government, based on a limited degree of democracy.

Along with these challenges to traditional authority there arrived a new outlook on human society. The notion of a 'natural order' in society was soundly rejected in favour of the view that each person is an individual with unlimited potential. The traditional order stratified mankind into social layers. This order was rigid and denied man his individuality. As the nineteenth century dawned, bringing with it the onset of capitalism and industrialisation, this insistence on individuality became an essential ingredient in economic development.

The Enlightenment The Enlightenment, which underpinned the historical developments described above, challenged existing religious and irrational modes of thinking. The movement encompassed the worlds of science, politics, religion, the arts and literature. Enlightenment philosophers were offering rational explanations of the world and suggested new ways of ordering society along such rational lines. They stressed man's particular ability to apply his reason to problems instead of merely responding in an emotional, instinctive manner.

Rational thinking gave rise to such possibilities as equal rights, individual liberty, government by popular consent and even full-scale democracy. The old order had denied the possibility of any of these new ideas.

The original ideas of liberalism

1. Tolerance of new beliefs and ideas
2. Rejection of traditional forms of religious and political authority
3. Replacement of the philosophy of a 'natural order' by a stress on man's individuality
4. Rational analyses of society and proposed social reforms
5. Belief in the importance of 'government by popular consent'
6. The possibility that equal rights could be introduced

Classical liberalism

The term 'classical' refers to the early form of liberalism which flourished for much of the nineteenth century. However, before it came to maturity, liberalism was preceded by two parallel movements, **natural rights** and **utilitarianism**.

Natural rights The doctrine of 'natural rights' had emerged in seventeenth-century England, developed by **Thomas Hobbes** and **John Locke**. They argued that each individual is born with certain rights which are natural and cannot, therefore, be denied to him by other men. These suggested rights included the right to life and liberty, to pursue happiness, avoid pain and enjoy one's own property. It followed that these rights could only be limited if man himself consented to accept controls. Thus, government had to be founded on consent and, at least in Locke's case, was subject to some degree of popular control.

This philosophy also viewed man very much as an individual, entitled to be free yet understanding that, in order to enjoy his freedom successfully, he would have to set up government over himself.

By the end of the eighteenth century, natural right philosophy had been taken further by the French romantic thinker **Jean-Jacques Rousseau** and the British revolutionary **Tom Paine**. They suggested that all men have not only **natural** rights but also **equal** rights and equal potential. By contrast, the inequality of rights which had existed within traditional society was artificial and could not be justified.

Utilitarianism Like Locke and Paine, **Jeremy Bentham** (1748–1832), the founder of the **Utilitarian** movement, saw men essentially as individuals. However, he rejected the notion of natural rights, calling it 'nonsense on stilts'. In its place he developed the principle of utility. This was based on the belief that man is motivated by the desire to achieve happiness and to avoid pain. Happiness, for utilitarians, meant the consumption and enjoyment of goods and property. The provision of such happiness was described as **utility**. Pain meant the deprivation of such pleasures and was referred to as **disutility**.

The kind of society which was envisaged was one of free individuals, pursuing their own interests as workers, producers and consumers. The role of government was to ensure that these individuals enjoyed a society where their **utility** would be maximised. On the whole, this would imply little action by government, save to ensure the free operation of the economy. However, where state action could be seen to increase the **total sum of utility** in a society it could be justified. Thus, the goal of any political system was to achieve the 'greatest good for the greatest number'. All government action could be judged on rational grounds. To ensure that the state pursued such goals the utilitarians insisted on a large degree of democracy and that government be answerable to the people. Indeed, popular control of government was essential since each individual knows what is best for himself. It is not for governments to decide what is best for their people. These beliefs suggested a number of principles:

- Each individual should be free to pursue his own goals.
- No person has a right to determine what is best for another individual.
- Each has an equal right to opportunities to achieve his own happiness.
- The role of government should be limited to maximising utility.

The most important disciple of Bentham was the son of James Mill, one of Bentham's close associates. This was **John Stuart Mill** (1806–73). J.S. Mill (it is important to distinguish him from his less liberal father) synthesised many of the earlier principles of liberalism with utilitarianism and so became the founder of classical liberalism in the nineteenth century. His views have been at the centre of British political philosophy ever since.

John Stuart Mill   Though he rejected the concept of natural rights, J.S. Mill was close to Locke in his view that each individual has a basic right to be free. He also accepted Bentham's belief that social utility should be maximised if possible. But he differed from the Utilitarians on two important points:

- He believed that man may have higher personal goals than merely the consumption of goods and the accumulation of property. Governments which acted on this limited view of man's motivations were arrogant and mistaken. Man's individuality in thought, belief and action should be recognised. He argued that 'it is better to be a human being dissatisfied than a pig satisfied; better to be Socrates dissatisfied than a fool satisfied'.
- If governments concentrate only on achieving maximum social utility, there is a danger that this will interfere with the basic freedom of action and thought of the individual. In order to determine how much freedom individuals should be allowed, he suggests a basic rule – that if an action does no harm to others it should suffer no outside interference.

> *'The only purpose for which power can be rightfully exercised over any member of a civilised community, against his own will, is to prevent harm to others. His own good, either physical or moral, is not a sufficient warrant.'*
>
> John Stuart Mill, *Utilitarianism*, 1841

Other classical liberals J.S. Mill was not the only nineteenth-century liberal who advocated high levels of individual liberty and a minimum role for the state. The so-called **Manchester School** of liberalism, led by **Richard Cobden** and **John Bright**, concentrated on freedom in the economic life of the country. They advocated free trade and the retention of 'market forces'. Following the theories of the economist **David Ricardo**, they argued that only free trade and free markets could ensure maximum wealth creation. J.S. Mill himself had agreed that freedom in economic life would release the innovative and enterprising spirit in the individual.

On the extreme wing of the classical movement lay **Herbert Spencer** (1820–1903). Spencer was a follower of the evolutionary theories of Charles Darwin. He applied them to human society by arguing that it is the individual who adapts best to his environment – principally the economic environment – who will progress. Those who fail to do so will fall behind. Similarly, he believed that men are naturally unequal, just as animals are, so that some will inevitably do better than others. Governments were beginning, in the second half of the nineteenth century, to interfere with the natural state of society by providing education, welfare and a variety of local services. Spencer believed this was tampering with the processes of nature and so was to be opposed.

Samuel Smiles, a contemporary of Spencer, campaigned against welfare provision on the grounds that it is up to each individual to make the best of his own life according to his abilities. If he comes to rely upon others he does himself no good. Thus, Smiles and Spencer were both fervent opponents of state interference in society.

Summary of classical liberal ideas

1. The most basic value which must be preserved in society is individual liberty.
2. The free working of the economic system is vital in maximising prosperity.
3. The state should play a minimal role in society.
4. Inequality is natural. Creating greater equality is an interference with nature.
5. On the whole individuals are responsible for themselves and their own welfare.

New liberalism

The problems of classical liberalism As the nineteenth century progressed, the apparent divide between rich and poor widened, concern grew that the exceptional spread of industrialisation and capitalism was resulting in excessive levels of deprivation. It was becoming clear that, while there were many beneficiaries of the new prosperity, there were even more losers. Two main concerns taxed liberal minds in the second half of the century:

- How to deal with the clear evidence that free market capitalism combined with an inactive state was actually **causing** poverty and social ills among the masses.

- The realisation that, while individual freedom might be desirable, and while it might seem just that each person should be responsible for his own successes or failures, there was also fundamental **injustice** in the system. This was that individuals may be disadvantaged simply by circumstances of birth and social environment. In other words, not everyone begins life from the same starting point.

Thus, solutions were required to these two problems: first, how to alleviate the condition of the poor without interfering too much in society and so reducing individual freedom; secondly, how to provide **equality of opportunity**, again without jeopardising freedom.

Three liberal philosophers and three politicians were the principal architects of a new form of liberalism aimed at providing such answers.

T.H. Green (1836–82)

Green was a moral philosopher who re-examined the nature of freedom. The earlier liberals saw freedom only in terms of freedom from the restrictions of laws and over-powerful governments. Green argued that we are not **truly** free if we do not have a sense of caring, or obligation, towards our fellow man. As Rousseau had argued a century before, we may be **enslaved** by the pursuit of our own self-interest. Such a pursuit was very much what liberals had been advocating. According to Green, we must balance our own personal liberty with our obligations to others. In so doing we achieve harmony with the society within which we live. With this harmony comes a higher form of freedom.

William Ewart Gladstone (Prime Minister 1868–74, 1880–85, 1886, 1892–94)

Gladstone, who effectively founded the modern Liberal Party, shared Green's sense of social morality as well as recognising the growing injustices in late Victorian society. He was mostly concerned to increase opportunities by providing some degree of education for all and to encourage local government to be more active in the care of the poor. At the same time, he attempted to open up access to British institutions to a broader section of the population, in particular the civil service, higher education and the military. For Gladstone injustice was itself a barrier to freedom, so that stronger government measures to restore justice could not be considered illiberal.

Leonard Hobhouse (1864–1929)

At the 'socialist' end of the new liberal movement, Hobhouse argued that the poor and the low-paid workers had no control over the operation of capitalism. They were, therefore, not free, but subject to economic forces beyond their control. It was therefore up to the state to free them from such forces by ensuring a decent standard of living and the right to work. His contribution to the debate was essentially to justify considerable extensions in the activities of the state.

Joseph Chamberlain (1836–1914, Mayor of Birmingham and Cabinet minister)

In common with Hobhouse, Chamberlain argued that the state should step in to improve the conditions of the poor and underprivileged. He believed that it was local government which should achieve this and so he urged municipal provision of hospitals, housing, schools, parks, libraries and the like. Like Hobhouse, he was very much a socialist-style liberal. Indeed, his brand of politics was known as 'municipal socialism'. Although Chamberlain left the Liberal Party at the end of his career, he did not join the new Labour Party, which appeared to be his natural political home. Nevertheless, he represents the beginning of a style of liberalism which was closer to socialism than classical liberalism.

J.A. Hobson
(1858–1940)

Unlike Chamberlain, Hobson did transfer to the Labour Party later in life. As a liberal he had developed a test against which to judge any extension of the activities of the state. For him, if an action extends the social freedom and opportunities for individuals, if it maximises the possibility for each to reach his desired potential, it can be justified. Thus, for example, compulsory education might seem a threat to liberty, but its effects – to enhance opportunities for all – justify its provision.

David Lloyd George
(Prime Minister 1916–22)

The culmination of the transition from classical to new liberalism was largely realised in the achievements of Lloyd George, both as his predecessor Asquith's Chancellor of the Exchequer and later as Prime Minister himself. It was he who extended the provision of education and public housing, introduced pensions and a system of state-organised welfare to cushion individuals against poverty and unemployment. Fear of state intervention as a threat to individual liberty was finally placed in the background of Liberal thinking. Since then the Liberal Party has championed the cause of the poor and underprivileged and has accepted that the state must play a vital role in creating greater social justice.

Ironically, Lloyd George was perhaps the most effective, but also the last, Liberal Prime Minister of the century. The rise of the Labour Party squeezed the Liberal Party out, especially as many of its ideas were adopted by Labour. There was simply too little difference between the two parties for voters to differentiate between them. Nevertheless, prominent Liberal politicians have continued to be influential in British politics.

Summary of new liberal ideas

1. Liberty does not only consist of freedom from restriction. There is a higher form of freedom which results from a collective sense of harmony and cooperation.
2. The state is justified in intervening to reduce clear social injustices.
3. Equality of opportunity is essential to maximise each individual's potential.
4. The state has an obligation to care for those who are unable to support themselves.

Modern liberalism

The Welfare State –
William Beveridge
(1879–1963)

Just as the Liberal Party was entering a catastrophic decline in its electoral fortunes, a report published in 1942 by a committee led by a leading civil servant and Liberal, William Beveridge, set out a blueprint for post-war British society. It was based on the idea that liberty was less threatened by laws and governments than by social evils such as poverty, unemployment, ill health and generally poor living conditions. It followed from this that state action to reduce such evils would provide greater freedom. For Liberals this was the end of Samuel Smiles' old idea, that individuals must fend for themselves. Beveridge now proposed that the state has a responsibility to care for all, 'From the cradle to the grave'.

The practical results of Beveridge's thoughts were the introduction of a compulsory Welfare State, free provision of secondary and higher education, the National Health Service and large increases in the social activities of local government. Once again, however, it was for others, not the Liberal Party, to implement such plans.

> *To my mind there are three things above all that every citizen of this country needs as a condition of a happy and useful life after the war. He needs freedom from Want and fear of Want; freedom from Idleness and fear of Idleness enforced by unemployment; freedom from War and fear of War.*
> Sir William Beveridge, 'Why I am a Liberal' (1945)

State Economic Management – John Maynard Keynes (1883–1946)

Keynes was the leading economist of his day. Like Beveridge he found further cause for the state to intervene in order to enhance personal liberty. For him, a stable economy was vital to provide the environment in which each individual – worker, consumer or employer – could fulfil his potential. Free market capitalism was characterised by periods of boom and slump, the worst example of the latter having occurred in the Great Depression of the 1930s. Thus, if governments could reduce these natural economic cycles, replacing them with steady growth and stability, all individuals would be freer to pursue their own goals.

Constitutional reform

The Liberal Party enjoyed something of a political revival during the 1970s, but it was still searching for a distinctive identity. The only area where it has been decisively successful in this regard has concerned proposals for constitutional reform. Two successive party leaders, **David Steel** and **Paddy Ashdown**, have been instrumental in supporting these reform proposals.

Their view is that British parliamentary democracy is flawed, largely as a result of the two-party system which has resulted in government which is too powerful, too centralised, too uncontrolled and too secretive. As a result, individuals have become politically powerless, lacking influence and sufficient opportunities to participate.

The solutions to these problems lie in proposals for extensive reform of the political system. The introduction of proportional representation in voting is a central feature, reducing, as it would, the stranglehold of the two main parties. Of almost equal importance is their support for a 'Bill of Rights' to guarantee the rights of individuals and important minority groups. Other measures include reform of the House of Lords, introducing fixed-term Parliaments, forcing government to be more open and restoring powers to local and regional government.

Just as Liberal Party fortunes were reviving in the 1970s, Scottish and Welsh nationalism experienced growth in popular support. Such nationalist sentiments were seen as manifestations of people's desires to take control of their own lives and to have greater influence over the activities of government. It was not, therefore, surprising that Liberals have taken up the nationalist cause.

Environmentalism As interest in environmental issues grew during the 1970s and 1980s, Liberals came to be aware that individuals were feeling that the quality of their lives was under threat from excessive industrialisation, intensive agriculture and urbanisation. It was seen as an appropriate concern for them on the grounds that freedom was threatened by reductions in the quality of life.

Equality Although Liberals have always believed that inequalities among people are natural, they have also insisted that all individuals, no matter what their qualities and abilities, should have equal rights. The battles for equal legal and political rights have largely been won. However, equal rights for women, for various groups of the underprivileged and for ethnic minorities have not yet been fully secured. This objective remains, therefore, a central element in modern liberalism.

A summary of modern liberalism

1. Individual freedom is still its main goal.
2. Equality of opportunity should be promoted.
3. Social justice should be created, if necessary by the state.
4. The political system should promote opportunities for individuals to influence and participate in government.
5. Government should be as locally based as possible.
6. Equal rights should be protected.
7. State action is justified if it enhances individual opportunity and freedom.
8. It is the role of the state to protect the physical environment in order to enhance the quality of life.

Where is liberalism today? The ideas of both 'classical' and 'New' liberalism have largely been incorporated into other political movements. As we have seen above, much of the liberalism of Lloyd George and Joseph Chamberlain, Green and Hobhouse, Beveridge and Keynes, was soon absorbed by the new successful Labour Party. Indeed, once so-called 'consensus' politics had set in after World War Two, much of the Conservative Party was happy to accept the same principles. At the same time, there has been a resurrection of neo-classical liberal ideas by such thinkers as Friedman and Hayek and their implementation by 'New Right' Conservatives, led by Margaret Thatcher.

In both cases the Liberal Party itself (now the Liberal Democrats) has found itself without its own distinctive policies. It must be stressed, however, that liberalism itself has been a highly successful movement, challenging both conservatism and socialism with great effect. It is only the Liberal **Party** which has declined. In short, most of the liberal clothes have been stolen by others and are still being worn by them.

Democratic socialism

Introduction Like conservatism and liberalism, the term 'socialism' does not have a single meaning. But unlike Britain's other two principal ideological traditions, democratic socialism has taken on a quality which is noticeably distinct from its counterparts in Europe. How could there be, for example, any relationship between the kind of philosophy adopted by the Labour Party and the ideology of the former socialist republics of Eastern Europe? Even the socialist parties of France and Spain have emerged from a very different tradition.

We should be alerted to the distinctive nature of British 'socialism' by the very fact that the party which has been its home for the whole of the twentieth century did not choose to title itself a 'Socialist' party at all, preferring the somewhat ambiguous name 'Labour' to inscribe on its banners. Indeed, those socialists who expressed admiration for such regimes as the Soviet Union or the People's Republic of China have always been marginalised in the Labour Party, and often expelled, on the grounds that their views were revolutionary and anti-democratic.

Some terms defined

The name 'socialism' in the context of Western democracy is, therefore, an imprecise one, so much so that it is more helpful to consider it as essentially three separate movements.

In its most moderate form it has come to be known as 'social democracy', which should not be confused with an earlier revolutionary movement flourishing particularly in Germany, Russia and much of central Europe in the late nineteenth and early twentieth centuries. Modern social democracy, by contrast, is neither revolutionary nor truly socialist in nature. It is described in some detail later in this unit.

More extreme forms of the movement have been described as 'state' or 'revolutionary' socialism. Its followers reject the notion of parliamentary and pluralist democracy in which parties with differing philosophies may compete freely for power. Rather, the state is to be taken over as the main instrument for the transition to a socialist society. In such circumstances, only limited opposition is envisaged. Democratic institutions would also be severely restricted in their role. This extreme form of socialism is described in Unit 14.

The form of socialism which represents the central origin of the British Labour Party and many other left-wing parties in Europe has come to be known as 'democratic socialism'. As its name suggests, it proposes to retain a democratic system of government, but is, at the same time, more committed to a radical socialist programme than are social democrats. It is this branch of the movement which we are considering here.

In the context of the British Labour Party we can certainly assert that the radical, revolutionary form of state socialism now has relatively little influence in the party. The efforts of **Neil Kinnock** in the mid-1980s to rid Labour of its extreme left wing proved largely successful. The schism between the moderate centre of the party – i.e. the 'democratic socialists' – and the moderate 'social democrats' (who have always refused to accept such a description of their beliefs) has continued since the 1950s when leader **Hugh Gaitskell** attempted to shift the party to the centre ground, with a certain amount of success. By the 1990s, under the reforming leaderships of **John Smith** and **Tony Blair**, the term 'social democrat' became both widespread and acceptable within the party. However, it is that form of democratic socialism, which has been the principal philosophy of Labour for much of its life, which is considered in this section.

The perhaps unique form of socialism which has flourished in Britain has been the result of a wide variety of influences. It is that variety which has given it its unusual character. We shall examine these origins first.

Origins

Trade unionism

The British trade union movement grew steadily through the nineteenth century. Unlike its contemporary counterparts in Europe, however, it rarely assumed a radical political character and kept some distance between itself and the main political arena until the turn of the century.

Instead the trade unions tended to concentrate upon economic, social and industrial issues such as decent wages, improved factory conditions, safety and bargaining rights. There were few attacks on the capitalist system in general, but rather on those individual businesses and entrepreneurs who were guilty of using their economic power against the interests of workers. Of course the trade union movement has had its fair share of revolutionary socialists and Marxists in its ranks, including in recent times the miners' leader **Arthur Scargill**, but these have been exceptions and not the norm.

As far back as 1848, when much of Europe erupted in a series of revolutionary upheavals in which workers and trade unionists played a leading part in attempts to bring down the established order, Britain remained largely calm. The **Chartist** movement of the 1830s had made some radical demands – for example, for trade union recognition, votes for the working classes and negotiating rights with employers – but it did not threaten the existing political and economic order. Since then the picture has remained much the same. Despite widespread union membership and periodic outbreaks of militant action such as the general strike of 1926 and the campaign against extensive reform of industrial relations in 1971, British trade unionism has remained moderate and limited in its aims.

This form of non-radical trade unionism is sometimes described as 'labourism', a working-class struggle which does not assume the full characteristics of class warfare. The movement accepts capitalism as a necessary vehicle for wealth creation, but wishes to ameliorate its worst effects through state-led controls and an extensive and powerful trade union movement.

Despite the relatively limited horizons of the trade union movement, it has been a major influence upon the nature of British socialism. The central position which unions have enjoyed within the Labour Party itself is testimony to its importance.

Christianity

Many British socialists derived their belief in social justice and equality from firmly held Christian faith. For them there was no essential difference between the basic teachings of Christ and the socialist creed. The virtues of shared wealth, caring for the poor, equal rights and pacifism were, for them, the essence of basic Christian values.

The historian **R.H. Tawney** (1880–1962), for example, rejected scientific analyses of capitalism, such as Marx's, to justify its overthrow. Instead he concentrated on the idea that the 'injustices' of capitalism, such as wide disparities in wealth and opportunities, were matters of conscience and morality rather than class conflict. Indeed, such figures as Tawney and the contemporary socialist, **Tony Benn**, are notable for their rejection of class warfare as the basis for socialism. For them the clear **justice** which they feel is inherent in socialism should be enough to persuade people to vote for such a future.

Nonconformism In the traditional industrial regions of Britain, such as the North, South Wales and the Scottish Clyde Valley, a particular brand of Protestant Christianity took hold during the eighteenth and nineteenth centuries. Such varieties as Methodism, Presbyterianism and Congregationalism were all manifestations of the movement which was collectively known as Nonconformism. In such cases the motivation which lay behind their formation was a reaction to the conservatism and paternalism of the Church of England.

The established Church was seen as a representative of the landed gentry and the middle classes. The working classes could not identify with its traditionalism, its strict hierarchy and its association with the ruling class. The nonconformist churches, while each having their own characteristics, had in common a sense of internal democracy, equality among their membership and a strong sense of brotherhood and social solidarity.

The specific influence which Nonconformism had upon British socialism is widely acknowledged, yet difficult to define. Certainly there was a strong sense of social equality present, derived from a certainty that all men were created equal by God. It could also be argued that a strong commitment to democracy arose out of these egalitarian churches, as well as a distrust of all powerful vested interests. Above all, however, a well-developed sense of local community was associated with Nonconformist churches and chapels which helped to form close bonds between Church, trade union and local Labour Party branch. Certainly British socialism has been especially deeply rooted in such small communities.

Fabianism In 1884, when a modest British interest in Marx's radical and revolutionary brand of socialism was first awakening, a group, composed mainly of middle-class intellectuals, formed the **Fabian Society**. Named after the Roman general Fabius, who fought wars by a process of long-term attrition rather than by attempting a decisive military blow, it was a movement committed to a gradual transition to a socialist society.

Its founders, who included the playwright **George Bernard Shaw** and the celebrated socialist couple, **Sidney and Beatrice Webb** (the former of whom founded the London School of Economics), believed that capitalism was a doomed system. There was no need for revolution since socialism would naturally evolve out of capitalism. Thus, what was required was for intellectuals and workers to prepare themselves for the inevitable onset of socialism. This was to be largely achieved through education and planning the the form of the future socialist state. This movement which was extremely influential around the turn of the nineteenth century, went some way to ensuring that British socialism remained evolutionary rather than revolutionary in nature.

Fabianism was unusual in another more important regard, however. Its leaders were committed to the idea of a form of socialism to be run by a centralised state. This state would take over the principal industries and commercial activities, running them in the interest of the whole community, with fair wages and guaranteed employment. However, this was not to be a workers' state. The Fabian leaders did not believe that the working class was able to govern itself. Instead they were elitist paternalists, believing that intellectuals would understand how best to realise a socialist future. These ideas contrasted sharply with many of those of the European socialist movement. There, especially in France, it was envisaged that workers themselves would take over the means of production, distribution and finance. The state was seen as the potential enemy of the working class. Thus it was expected to remain limited in size and weak in nature. The Fabians were committed to a strong, wide-ranging state.

'Labour works by the inevitability of gradualness. Building democratic socialism is an existential process, done slowly by perseverance, patience and education.'
Austin Mitchell, *The Case for Labour* (Longman, 1983)

Liberalism and parliamentary democracy

As we have seen above, when the liberal movement of the nineteenth century was transformed from its so-called 'classical' to its 'new' variety, it took on many characteristics now described as socialist. Such liberals as **Hobhouse** and **Hobson** preached the virtues of **equality of opportunity** and the notion of **state-sponsored welfare**. At the same time, Liberals had always promoted equal rights and protection for the especially weak in society. All these ideas appealed greatly to the moderate form of socialism which the British seemed to prefer.

British socialism is also notable for its strong attachment to parliamentary democracy. In much of Europe, socialists have been traditionally less concerned with individual liberty or with democratic institutions. On the whole they have been more interested in a powerful centralised state and other collective institutions which tend to operate in opposition to individualism. In Britain, however, there has always been a strong bond between liberal democracy and mainstream socialism.

In practice this has created a commitment to such principles as equal political rights, pluralist party politics and guarantees of individual liberty through democratic institutions. Apart from the Social Democratic Federation, led by the neo-Marxist **H.M. Hyndman** (1842–1921) who was suspicious of parliamentary politics, preferring instead a more direct transition to a socialist system, British socialists have mostly been committed to liberal democracy. Even the **Independent Labour Party** – the more radical of the two main working-class parties which emerged around the turn of the nineteenth century – chose the parliamentary route to power. It was finally squeezed out by its more moderate and powerful counterpart, the orthodox Labour Party, in the 1930s. As we have seen above, such liberal figures as Lloyd George, William Beveridge and J.M. Keynes have had more influence on the British socialist movement than the great European socialists such as Marx, Bernstein or Blanqui, all of whom favoured direct action to achieve working-class goals.

'Of political parties claiming socialism to be their aim, the Labour Party has always been one of the most dogmatic – not about socialism, but about the parliamentary system.'
Ralph Miliband, *Parliamentary Socialism* (Merlin, 1972)

Miscellaneous influences   There is a remarkable richness in British socialism which is largely the result of the wide variety of influences which have moulded it. The principal examples are described below:

Robert Owen (1771–1858), a philanthropic industrialist, believed that capitalists themselves had a moral obligation to ensure the welfare of their workers. His experimental **New Lanark Mill** provided the employees with education, health care, housing and subsidised goods in the hope that it would provide a model for all employers to follow. In the event the experiment failed, but his ideas were largely instrumental in moulding the character of British trade unions. Unions might have become politically radical and revolutionary in character, as they had done in parts of Europe. Instead they tended to concentrate on achieving the kind of benefits which Owen had provided for his own workers. Thus, ironically, Owen, one of the most radical socialists of his day, went some way to moving unions into a moderate position on workers' conditions.

The **Co-operative movement**, which was founded in 1844, differed from its European counterparts in that its objectives were to protect the interests of **consumers** from capitalist 'profiteering'. By contrast, the producer co-ops, which particularly flourished in France and Spain, were designed to free **workers** and **small producers** from exploitation by big business. Ever since the development of the co-operative movement, British socialism has included a commitment to protect the interests of consumers from the monopoly power of capitalism.

William Morris (1834–96) is still celebrated today for his contribution to interior design, but it was his **romantic** and **anarchistic** brand of socialist principles which have endeared him to many trade unionists during the twentieth century. Morris was suspicious of the centralised state and abhorred the effects of large-scale industrialisation on the lives of workers. He favoured the small-scale worker's co-operative as the ideal form of economic organisation. He practised his own beliefs in the company which he set up and ran in consultation with the workforce. As we have seen above, the workers' co-operative movement has had little success in Britain, despite many attempts to popularise it. Nevertheless, Morris has remained a model for the many small craft unions which flourished through much of the twentieth century. Such unions have had some success in protecting the interests of their members and ensuring organised training facilities and expanded educational opportunities.

Guild socialism, the inspiration of the socialist historian **G.D.H. Cole** (1889–1959), was a similarly romantic ideal to that of Morris. Cole also advocated a system of small, powerful trade unions, akin to the ancient craft **guilds** which had protected free, skilled workers within the feudal order. These unions would be granted democratic rights within each business. They would not be producing organisations, however. Instead they would ensure a degree of worker influence over capitalist organisations, guaranteeing both the welfare of employees and some say in the running of enterprises. As with Morris, there was little practical application of these ideas, but there was considerable influence. Such measures as employment protection, minimum wages and better working conditions were achieved through a system of **trades councils** which became a model of small-scale, decentralised socialism at work. Their influence over industrial relations continued until the 1980s.

Summary of British democratic socialist origins

1. **Trade unionism** A particularly moderate form with largely economic rather than political goals. The influence of a non-radical working class has resulted in a moderate form of socialism.
2. **Nonconformism** Re-inforced the social solidarity of socialism and rooted it firmly in local communities.
3. **Fabianism** Imbued British socialism with a sense of gradualism and paternalism. Socialist goals were to be achieved by evolution, not revolution.
4. **Liberalism** Most modern liberal aims have been absorbed within the socialist movement, especially the pursuit of equal rights and a commitment to popular, parliamentary democracy.
5. **Christianity** A strong moral atmosphere was added, arising out of an interpretation of Christian teaching which proposed social justice and equality.
6. **Other influences** Including consumerism, industrial democracy and a strong attachment to welfarism.

Characteristics of British democratic socialism

Collectivism

It is the basis of **all** socialist thought that there are a large number of human goals which are better achieved by **collective** rather than by **individual** action. This is based on assumptions that this is both the most **efficient** and the **fairest** way of providing a wide variety of services. Some examples will serve to illustrate this idea.

Health care could be arranged so that each individual should pay for care as they receive it, perhaps through voluntary private health schemes. This is very much how health care is organised in the USA. Thus, it would be up to each individual **how much** care they receive, **how often** and **of what type**. The collective road to health care is likely to involve either a **national health care** system, where everybody who is able **must** contribute but everybody receives free health care on demand, **or** a state-run **health insurance** system, where all would contribute to an insurance scheme and claim back any expenditure on health provision which may be needed. In either case, a collective health system requires compulsory contribution, while an individualistic solution does not.

The pay and conditions of workers of any kind could simply be left to free market forces and individuals negotiating the terms of their own employment. Socialists support strong trade unions which negotiate **collectively** on behalf of their members. However, for unionism to be effective it is almost essential that all or most workers are prepared to support the union and take industrial action where required. If not, employers would be able to divide their employees and weaken their collective bargaining power.

Finally, **welfare** is a typical example of collective action. Here it is expected that **all** should contribute through various forms of tax, so that **all**, however rich or poor, may be relieved from such problems as poverty, homelessness, unemployment and the need for an old age pension.

Collectivism can also be applied to such provisions as education, housing, industrial training, child care and employment creation, all of which have, from time to time, been the responsibility of central or local government in Britain. The key philosophy behind collectivism is that contributions should be calculated according to **ability to pay**, but care, welfare and services should be given equally on the basis of **need**. Virtually the whole of the socialist movement has been based in this fundamental belief.

> *'Socialism is the creation of a society in which it is easier to secure self-fulfilment through serving society than through the exclusive pursuit of self alone.'*
>
> Stuart Holland, *The Socialist Challenge* (Quartet, 1975)

Distributive justice The effect of free market capitalism is to distribute rewards, in the form of incomes, corporate profits and wealth, unevenly. It is inevitable that some workers, investors or entrepreneurs will do better than others financially. For socialists this is both random and unjust. For them, rewards should be distributed according to worth and merit. The capitalist system takes no account of this, operating merely on the basis of an individual's position in the market.

It would be an error to assume that socialists advocate that financial rewards should be distributed **equally**. Such a belief belongs in communist philosophy rather than among less radical socialists. Instead, socialists wish to see the distribution of rewards made on a rational basis, most commonly according to how much an individual's work is perceived to be worth to society. How is such 'distributive justice' to be achieved?

The simplest solution lies with the **tax** system. By implementing a progressive tax system – where those with higher incomes pay a larger proportion in taxation – the inequalities in income can be reduced. At the same time, accumulations of **wealth** in too few hands can be broken up by taxes on inheritance or even through wealth taxes based on the value of total assets owned rather than on income. Company profits can be redistributed more evenly through **corporate taxation**.

The **welfare system** can also be used in the redistributive process. Those on particularly low incomes can receive financial subsidies from the proceeds of taxation. This can be in such forms as family benefits, housing subsidies, unemployment benefit and a host of other forms of extra benefits.

The state can have a more direct effect on income distribution through its own employment policies. Government employees may be offered wages higher than those which would normally prevail in markets operated by private companies. There may also be a tendency to employ more workers than private companies would normally use. In this way some workers, who would otherwise be unemployed and on very low incomes, receive decent incomes.

The most radical measure which can be adopted to achieve such economic 'justice', short of complete control of commerce and industry by the state, is to introduce strict controls over incomes, forbidding excessively high wages and adopting minimum wage legislation. In practice the former is virtually impossible to implement, but a national minimum wage has long been a socialist dream.

Welfarism We have seen above that welfare can be used as a means of redistributing income to the less well off. However, it can also be seen as a desirable end in itself. Socialists accept that there are some who are unable to provide adequately for themselves, such as the old, the very poor, the disabled, the unemployed and the long-term sick. Society, therefore, has an obligation to contribute to their welfare so that all can enjoy at least an acceptable standard of living.

The principal means of achieving this is the **Welfare State** itself, a system where all who are able make compulsory contributions to a state-run organisation which then distributes welfare benefits on the basis of need.

Social ownership of the means of production

Possibly the most controversial issue among British socialists surrounded the commitment which the Labour Party appeared to make in Clause IV of its constitution formulated in 1918. The wording of the main part of this clause is shown below:

> *'[we aim] to secure for the workers . . . the full fruits of their industry and the most equitable distribution thereof that may be possible upon the basis of the common ownership of the means of production.'*
> Clause IV, The Labour Party Constitution, 1918

The questions which have been asked since are: 'How is this to be achieved?' and 'Does it really imply the complete takeover of production and distribution?' and, in the 1990s, 'Is this an outdated concept following the privatisation of most state-run industries in the 1980s?'

The first issue was largely resolved in Britain when **Herbert Morrison**, a leading member of the post-war Labour Government, produced a blueprint for the creation of publicly owned and state-run industries. While 'syndicalists', mostly on the continent of Europe, were arguing for the takeover of major industries by trade unions, Morrison was convinced that ownership by the central state was the most effective form of social ownership. This would ensure that major industries would be run for the benefit of the **whole community** and not just for the workers in them.

The extent of collective ownership was also hotly disputed. Candidates for **nationalisation** – the Morrisonian method for bringing economic enterprises under public control – were:

- **natural monopolies** such as railways and gas supply
- **public utilities** which the whole community consumes, such as electricity and telecommunications
- **infrastructure** industries upon which all other enterprises rely, such as iron, steel and coal
- **very large companies** on the grounds that their economic power may operate against the interests of workers and consumers.

In the event, nationalisation was confined to the first three categories, although more radical members of the movement advocate public ownership of all large enterprises.

The purposes of nationalisation were several. In general, any profits can be distributed throughout the community rather than to a small group of shareholders. More specifically, prices can be controlled, workers pay and conditions protected, and output geared to the needs of the economy in general rather than purely to the making of profit. Finally, nationalised industries can protect the less fortunate in society by ensuring that they receive goods and services which might not be supplied to them by private enterprise. Thus, for example, transport and other utilities can be subsidised to serve isolated communities or special low prices may be charged to old-age pensioners.

The issue of Clause IV and its implications was transformed when **Tony Blair** became Labour leader in 1994. He was determined to modernise the party in general and Clause IV in particular. After a short struggle against radical elements in the party and some of the larger trade unions, he succeeded in changing the clause fundamentally. The commitment to public ownership was dropped and replaced by the goal of achieving full employment opportunities and the control of large-scale industry for the public good, rather than public ownership itself.

Equality of opportunity

In common with liberals, socialists argue that the state should create conditions which will give maximum opportunity to all sections of society. Education, from the nursery through to higher institutions of learning, should, thus, be open to all and should not discriminate on the grounds of wealth or privilege. A strong, comprehensive system of secondary schooling, colleges and universities which are accessible to everyone, and the provision of student grants have all been supported to enhance equality of educational opportunity.

Socialists oppose entrenched privilege. Measures to open up career opportunities are an essential feature of the socialist goal of creating a society based purely on merit. Discrimination against women, ethnic minorities, the disabled or any other minority group has been firmly opposed. More radical proposals for **positive discrimination** in favour of disadvantaged groups have been suggested, underpinned by specific legislation to outlaw discrimination.

Trade unionism

Although the main agent of socialist collective action has, in Britain, been the state, through both central and local government, unions are seen as playing a key role in protecting workers' rights. Without the **collective** power of unions, individual workers are powerless in the face of market forces and control exercised by large employers.

Socialists therefore insist on the preservation of union privileges, including the guaranteed right to undertake collective bargaining, to take industrial action without undue fear of legal restrictions and to be recognised by employers if sufficient workers wish to be represented.

In addition to their right to defend the interest of workers at the place of their employment, unions are expected to play a key role in the state planning of industrial development and economic management. It is not sufficient, argue socialists, for workers to be able to express their aspirations through the ballot box every few years. They must also have a continuous role in public policy-making if their interests are to be properly protected. Thus the state is expected to be a 'corporate state', where employees as well as employers are fully represented on official policy-making bodies.

The 'dirigiste' state

It can be seen from many of the features described above that British democratic socialism has been very much the friend of the powerful state. The collective goals which they wish to pursue are seen as the business of the state rather than of voluntary secondary groups. In addition to welfare provision and the redistribution of income, socialists have supported a 'dirigiste' state, meaning one which seeks to direct and control key aspects of the economy.

Centralised planning has long been a socialist dream. Indeed, in 1964 a Labour Government was elected with a commitment to implementing a **National Plan** detailing future raw material, production and employment requirements. The state was to establish targets for all aspects of industrial and commercial activity. The achievement of these targets was to be facilitated by the state, both through the enterprises under its direct control and through private companies. The incentive for these companies was a guarantee of a healthy, growing economy.

In the event, the National Plan failed after less than two years of life simply because the state could not deliver its promises of economic growth and so failed to secure the co-operation of those who were to implement the plan. It was not only economic circumstances which destroyed this unique experiment with state planning in a liberal democracy. For many, both in and out of the Labour Party, it was simply too radical an idea, threatening as it did opportunities for individual initiative.

In addition to full-scale planning, socialists have also promoted state interference in industrial relations, the supply of finance and investment for industry, the provision of grants and incentives for businesses to set up in areas of high unemployment, and even nationalisation of land.

Municipalism

Somewhat ironically, it was a Liberal – **Joseph Chamberlain** – who inspired the Labour Party to adopt local government as a suitable vehicle for a number of socialist endeavours. It is at this level that such provisions as subsidised housing, public health protection, social services to protect families in need and support for the elderly were introduced by early labour administrations. It is in this regard that the community-based, nonconformist roots of socialism in Britain have been particularly influential. There is a residual fear among socialists that the centralised state could become excessively powerful. The best protection against this, many have argued, is a strong, independent system of local government. In the modern era, **Ken Livingstone**, the last leader of the abolished Greater London Council, has remained a champion of this kind of municipal socialism.

The end of democratic socialism?

Between 1979 and 1992 the Labour Party suffered four successive election defeats. During this period the onslaught of Thatcherite, New Right policies shifted the centre of British political opinion markedly to the right. The 'frontiers' of the state had been rolled back; trade unions had been stripped of most of their influence, and individualism and private enterprise were widely preferred over the collectivist ideals of traditional socialism.

In eastern Europe all the so-called 'socialist' regimes fell to democratic movements which adopted free market capitalism to replace state-run socialist economic systems.

Thus, democratic socialism had become discredited and unpopular. Many of its cherished monuments had been destroyed or were suffering threatening attacks. Privatisations removed huge sections of British industry from state control. Reforms had demolished many of the trade unions' rights and privileges, local government functions were reduced and its independence severely curtailed. Direct taxes on incomes and profits were reduced dramatically, having the effect of increasing the gap between rich and poor. The National Health Service was reformed by introducing an internal market. Even the Welfare State, possibly the greatest jewel in the socialist crown, was being threatened in the 1990s.

The reaction of socialists was not to fight back, but to respond by adopting a more moderate position. A few stalwarts of the movement continued to struggle against the tide as the twentieth century came to a close, but most socialists drifted towards social democracy.

British democratic socialist achievements

1. Nationalisation of natural monopolies, including:

- Water
- Electricity generating and supply
- Gas
- Telecommunications
- Railways
- Municipal public transport.

2. Nationalisation of other key industries:

- Iron and steel
- Airports
- National airline
- Seaports
- Oil exploration
- British Leyland (Motors)
- British Aerospace.

3. Steeply progressive personal taxation with a top rate of 83 per cent, rising by another 15 per cent for investment income.
4. Municipal socialism, including:

- Child and ante-natal care
- Subsidised council housing
- Grants to students in higher education
- Care of the elderly
- Subsidised public transport
- Colleges of higher education
- Adult education.

5. Protection for private tenants against landlords.
6. Equal pay for women.
7. Employment protection and compulsory redundancy pay.
8. Free state education for all from 5 to 18 years of age.
9. The Welfare State.
10. The National Health Service.

Social democracy

Socialists are frequently accused of a slavish attachment to **institutions** which have become either meaningless or which have placed too little importance on the individual. The role of trade unions is a prime example. It is a fundamental aspect of the socialist creed that strong, active unions are essential in the protection of workers' rights and conditions. This does not present a problem until the suspicion takes hold that over-powerful unions and their leaders may hold back the aspirations of some workers while appearing to protect their interests. At the same time, the 'conservatism' of unions in terms of work practices and new technology may hold back economic progress. Social democrats, therefore, recognise the need for worker protection, decent pay and fair conditions, but also understand that each individual worker is entitled to choose whether to participate in union activity, and should certainly have the opportunity of influencing the way in which unions operate on their behalf. Thus it becomes more important to create a better **climate** of industrial relations, to establish **agreed values** about how workers should be treated, than merely to allow powerful unions to struggle against stubborn employers.

The nationalised industries were a further example of how important cherished institutions became to the socialist movement. They were designed to act in the interests of their workers and of the whole community. Yet many of them, such as gas, electricity and the railways, were simply state monopolies which had replaced private monopolies. Not only did they not always operate efficiently or sensitively enough, but they also stifled much economic initiative in the community, owing to their enormous market power. Again, social democrats are more concerned with how industry can best benefit the community rather than merely on the **form** it takes. Large or small scale, state-run or private, protected or subject to full competition, free or controlled, enterprises should be judged by how well they serve consumers and employees, rather than by whom they are run. **Prosperity with social justice** is what social democrats wish to see achieved by industry, rather than mere state control.

We can perhaps say, therefore, that social democracy represents original socialist values, such as equal rights, equality of opportunity and social justice, but is not inevitably linked to any specific socialist institutions.

Traditional socialism has always been associated with an analysis of society which suggests that **class differences** are crucial, in particular that the middle classes, composed of professionals, managers and business owners, have gained at the expense of the working classes under capital-ism. In short, the interests of the two great classes are seen to be in conflict. Social democrats now accept that society is more complex than this simple class analysis would suggest. They see, instead, a community of individuals and many different interest groups. Class interest thus becomes outdated in such a **pluralist** society.

A further criticism of socialism has been that it is too rigid and intolerant in its outlook. We have seen above that it has been firmly attached to certain institutions and has been reluctant to accept that there may be a number of alternative ways of achieving the same goals. In addition, it has made assumptions that all people will ultimately benefit from such socialist objectives as social equality, public ownership of major industries and the imposition of comprehensive education. Social democrats are willing to accept that it is for each individual to **choose** what type of services he wishes to consume and whether he wishes to make his own arrangements for education, health care, pensions and the like.

It follows from this that a vital goal of social democracy is to enhance and facilitate choices for individuals and therefore to oppose socialist measures which may limit such choices. For example, a well-resourced and organised state education system may be vital for the creation of equality of opportunity, but this should not preclude the existence of private education alongside the state provision. Both should flourish together to provide maximum choice and opportunity. Similar arguments can be brought to bear in the field of a large number of welfare and social benefits which may be provided in a variety of different ways.

> 'Pluralism offers the prospect of a more interesting, relevant and stimulating democracy, where difficult problems will evoke different solutions and where decisions more fully reflect the wishes of particular communities.'
> David Owen, *Face the Future* (OUP, 1981)

Individualism   While socialism has been an essentially **collectivist** doctrine, insisting that many goals are better achieved by collective action rather than individual endeavour, social democracy places greater emphasis on the individual. Indeed, for the latter, the only acceptable purpose for collectivism is to improve opportunities and choices for those individuals. In other words, collectivism is a desirable **end in itself** for socialists, but it is only a **means to an end** for social democrats.

> 'The essential principle of the left of centre – whether democratic socialists or social democrats – is the belief that society must work together for the individual to succeed.'
> Tony Blair, 1994 Speech

Freedom   The American philosopher, **John Rawls,** in his theory of **distributive justice,** has asserted that, while there should be a fair distribution of income in society, this should not be achieved at the expense of personal liberty. Social democrats, many of whom follow and admire Rawls' work, accept the importance of such freedom. Socialism has often been accused of curtailing freedoms through its insistence on compulsion in such areas as taxation, contributions to welfare and industrial regulation. Collective values, in other words, have often pushed individual liberty into the background.

Social democrats, by contrast, believe both that liberty should be better protected than it has been in the past by socialists, and also that the creation of wider opportunity and choice is, in itself, an enhancement of freedom. The state should not, therefore, concentrate on prohibiting activities on the grounds that they may not promote greater equality, but should try to improve the range of opportunities open to citizens. Housing provision is a good example of the distinction. Socialists have tended, in the past, to argue that local council-owned housing is the fairest way of providing homes for the less well-off. The private rented sector and opportunities for home ownership have, meanwhile, either been opposed or discouraged. Social democrats accept the need for some public provision of low-cost housing, subsidised out of taxes, but also wish to encourage **all** types of housing provision to increase **choice** and to encourage a **free** housing market.

Equality of opportunity

Equality of outcome has been a central objective of traditional socialism. This ignores the possibility that individuals are unequal in their abilities and the contribution they make to society, replacing it with the idea that all are of equal **worth**. The implication is that all are deserving of equal rewards.

Social democrats prefer to accept natural inequality which implies that individuals enjoy different levels of merit and potential. Artificial advantages or disadvantages, based on inherited privilege, gender, ethnic origin or a deprived childhood should be removed, but thereafter we are not of equal worth so that rewards must reflect this in a just society. Like liberals, therefore, it is equality of opportunity, not of outcome, which social democrats prefer.

Distributive justice

What degree of inequality should be allowed in a just society? This is a question which taxes social democrats. Democratic socialists have less problem with the same question. For them the answer is simply, 'relatively little'. The former, however, have more difficulty, as inequality is both inevitable and necessary in any economic system which seeks to maintain incentives for enterprise and endeavour.

An answer has been supplied by **Rawls** again. He argues that inequalities can be justified if they do not interfere with the liberty of others, and if the least well-off in society are not made worse off as a result of those inequalities. For example, it can be justified for a capitalist entrepreneur to make very large profits, provided he is not benefiting directly from losses suffered by the lowest-income groups. Indeed, the incentive of high profits may result in more enterprise, resulting in greater income and employment for others.

Key distinctions between social democracy and democratic socialism

1. Social democrats are more concerned with values, while democratic socialists wish to preserve socialist institutions.
2. Democratic socialists analyse society in simple class terms, while social democrats have a more pluralist approach to both social organisation and political ideas.
3. While socialism has always been a collectivist doctrine, social democrats lay greater stress on individualism.
4. Social democrats criticise traditional socialism's apparent disregard for individual freedom.
5. Social democrats stress the need for equality of opportunity, while democratic socialists are more concerned with equality of outcome.
6. Social democrats are prepared to accept greater economic inequalities than democratic socialists provided this can be shown to benefit society.

Social democratic values

It will quickly become apparent here that the principal values of social democracy bear a resemblance to those of both democratic socialism and modern liberalism. It is certainly true that the movement is something of a synthesis of liberal and socialist ideals, though this is often denied by its supporters. It is for the uncommitted observer to decide from the following descriptions.

Equality of opportunity

The very same goal is pursued by liberals and socialists. However, like liberals, social democrats would not feel it necessary to destroy such so-called 'artificial' advantages as inherited wealth and private education as purer socialists might.

The mixed, pluralist economy

It was the leading moderate Labour Party ideologue of the 1950s and 1960s, **Tony Crosland**, who suggested that the idea of the state controlling the **commanding heights** of the economy – the great industries, financial institutions and communication facilities – was no longer desirable. He asserted instead that there should be a pluralist approach to ownership of the means of production, distribution and finance. Some enterprises were ideal for private ownership, some for local government control, some for producer co-operatives and only some for the central state to run. In other words, there should be a **mixed economy**, with the type of ownership depending on circumstances. His views are now fully accepted by social democrats.

The Welfare State

The main development here is that the welfare system should not stifle individual enterprise, but rather enable people to widen their own opportunities. For example, single parents should not be subsidised to stay at home and merely receive benefit, but should be given the facilities to be able to return to work and support themselves, possibly through child care and retraining. The same applies to the unemployed and young school-leavers as well as for the homeless.

> 'With a few inevitable exceptions, welfare should be an investment in productive and capable people, not a last resort for the incompetent.'
> Ralph Miliband, *Reinventing the Left* (Polity Press, 1994)

Pragmatic economic management

Both New Right Conservatives and traditional socialists have tended to link themselves firmly to one particular style of economic management, the former to **monetarism** and **laissez-faire**, the latter to **Keynesian** policies. Social democrats reject such a dogmatic stance. They accept the need for a pragmatic and pluralistic approach to economic policy.

Constitutional reform

There is a recognition by social democrats that the centralised state is too powerful. They accuse both Conservatives and democratic socialists of carrying the process of centralisation too far, to the detriment of popular democracy. Thus, like liberals, they propose decentralisation, open government, reform of the second chamber and enhanced powers for Parliament. Some, but not all, advocate reform of the electoral system.

Social justice Although this principle is much vaunted among all members of what is called the 'centre left' of British politics, it is extremely difficult to define. Indeed, it can mean anything its advocates want it to mean. It must, therefore, be left somewhat flexible as a concept. In practice, it concerns such policies as **fair taxes**, involving a certain amount of redistribution of income, the use of **welfare** to protect the vulnerable in society, the establishment of **equal rights** for all sections of the community and the use of **public expenditure** to aid parts of the country which suffer economic disadvantages.

Employment Without being dogmatic about methods, social democrats would claim to place greater emphasis on the creation of employment than other political creeds. Whether it be through economic management, public expenditure or job creation schemes, social democrats place a high priority on keeping unemployment at low levels.

Liberal nationalism

Introduction The Liberal form of nationalism which flourishes in Britain should not be confused with so-called 'British nationalism'. The latter is an extreme right-wing movement, often described as 'neo-nazi' or 'neo-fascist', which is concerned with maintaining British unity, discouraging immigration and laying stress on patriotism, isolationism and the restoration of Britain's pre-eminence in world affairs, and establishing a strong, authoritarian state.

By contrast, Scottish and Welsh nationalism are essentially liberal movements with completely different roots and aspirations. (Nationalism in the context of Northern Ireland is dealt with elsewhere.)

Welsh nationalism

The principle vehicles for Welsh nationalism are **Plaid Cymru** (the Welsh National Party), the **Welsh Language Society** (a political and cultural campaign group), and **Sons of Glendower** (a militant separatist group).

The last named is committed to an independent Wales, with its own sovereignty and, therefore, political institutions. It operates outside democratic politics, preferring direct, sometimes violent, action to further its aims. It is a small, relatively insignificant movement.

The Welsh Language Society, despite its apparently innocuous title, has proved an effective force in Welsh politics. As its name suggests, it is concerned with the preservation and extension of the use of the Welsh language. However, it goes further than that. It is also committed to safeguarding and promoting Welsh culture in general, including literature and the arts. It has become political in the sense that English culture is seen as the main threat to its objectives. Thus, greater independence for Wales in the political and social spheres is also likely to preserve the culture. It is, naturally, closely allied to Plaid Cymru.

Few Welsh nationalists wish to see full political independence for Wales. However, they do campaign for a greater degree of self-determination for the Welsh people and for the preservation of a separate Welsh identity.

Some of their principal objectives are:

- An elected Welsh assembly to oversee government
- Local control over education, social services, higher education, health and transport
- Greater Welsh control over funds for local industry and commerce
- Equal status with English for the Welsh language
- Local control over funding for the arts and broadcasting.

It should be noted that there is no indication above of the separation of Wales from the UK. Defence, foreign affairs and broad economic policy would remain in the hands of Westminster.

Scottish nationalism

Unlike Wales, Scotland has long enjoyed a good deal of administrative independence from England. Since the last century there has been a Scottish Office, with its own funds for the administration of education, health, transport and a wide range of other services. In addition, Scotland has its own legal system, very different from that of England and Wales, and its own laws, although these have to passed by Parliament in London. There is a separate education system, from primary through to universities, and the Church of Scotland has long been distinct from its Anglican counterpart.

Thus Scotland has been able to retain a good deal of its own political, social and cultural identity. Nevertheless, Scottish nationalism, represented by the Scottish National Party, has become more radical than its Welsh equivalent. Indeed, one wing of the party now supports full independence from Britain. Those nationalists who stop short of demanding full Scottish sovereignty wish to see a large degree of 'devolution' of power. Among their demands are:

- A Scottish legislative assembly which would make laws and oversee government
- A Scottish executive drawn from the Assembly and responsible to it
- Power to raise taxes in Scotland for the direct finance of public expenditure
- Control over existing services maintained and some extension into other services
- More control over industrial and economic policy in relation to Scotland itself
- A large share in the revenues from North Sea Oil
- A more independent Scottish voice in the European Union.

A summary of nationalist aspirations other than full independence

1. A greater degree of self-government, with regional elected assemblies
2. Protection for the national culture
3. An extension in the number of services being locally controlled
4. More influence within the European Union
5. Greater control over the local economy

For exam questions relevant to this unit, see page 493.

4 Democracy

Introduction There are two commonly held beliefs about the term 'democracy', both of which are misleading. These are:

- That democracy is one specific form of government and society which can be readily identified.
- That democracy has been, and still is, considered a universally 'good thing', to be supported by all right-thinking people and pursued by all good governments.

We can illustrate the first fallacy by considering two political systems, both of which have described themselves as 'democracies'. First, the former East Germany, acknowledged widely as as one of the most autocratic and intolerant regimes of this century, nevertheless described itself as the 'German Democratic Republic'. Secondly, we have the USA, with its extensive guarantees of rights and liberties. In the West we would probably hold up the USA as an ideal model of democracy. How can two such contrasting systems both claim the title 'democracy'? The answer is that the term can be used to mean whatever we want it to mean. Above all, its meaning is determined by one's own general political philosophy, be it Conservative, liberal, communist or fascist.

As to the second common error – that democracy has been a universally popular system – we shall see below how, during much of the history of human society, democracy has either not existed in any form, or has been viewed with deep suspicion. It has only been since World War One that democracy has become the accepted form of government for most advanced societies.

Professor Bernard Crick's colourful comment on the concept of democracy may serve to illustrate these problems. 'Democracy', he argues, 'is perhaps the most promiscuous word in the world of public affairs. She is everybody's mistress and yet somehow retains her magic even when a lover sees that her favours are being, in his light, shared by many another.'

In this unit the origins of the idea of democracy will be explored first, taking us to around 1800, by which time France, the USA and Britain had established the basis of modern Western political systems. Following from these early developments, we will see how differing interpretations and forms of the idea arose, just as traditional kinds of regime were declining. Finally, we look at the continuing problems which exist in a modern democratic society.

In an investigation into the theory and practice of democracy the best place to begin is at the beginning, with its origins in Greece.

The origins of democracy

Athens

Classical Greece was not one single state, but a series of city states each of which developed its own political system ranging from despotic monarchy to extremely open forms of direct popular rule. Thus there was more than one form of so-called 'democracy' flourishing in this region. Undoubtedly the best known, however, was the system operating in Athens in the sixth and fifth centuries BC.

The basis of Athenian democracy was that all citizens were granted the right to attend a regular assembly where laws were enacted, executive decisions made and general policy formulated. There was also the opportunity to scrutinise and criticise those city officials who had also been elected by the popular assembly. In order for this to take place the citizens had to be granted political equality, which included the rich and the relatively poor together. In many ways it was this political equality which was the most radical feature of the system. The participation of sections of the wider population was not unusual at that time in Greece, but the concept of granting nearly universally equal status was certainly controversial. Women and slaves were still excluded from such equality, but it was really the equal treatment of different classes which conservatives could not accept.

As Athens, like its Greek neighbours, was a relatively small state, it was quite feasible for the citizenry to gather in one single location for their deliberations, so that the process is often described as 'market place democracy'. Great orators and ambitious politicians addressed the assembly, but any member of the crowd had the right to take part in debates if he could gain a hearing. Thus we can see that Athenian democracy contained several elements to which we can still relate today:

- popular participation in politics
- political equality (at least for free male adults)
- the notion that government should be responsible to the people.

These three principles are all ones which we in so-called liberal democracies find both familiar and desirable, but at the time not all Athens' citizens were seduced by the apparent attractions of the system, among them, its greatest philosopher, Plato.

In fact Plato was democracy's most scathing critic at the time of its heyday. He began his criticism by making clear that he did not believe that the mass of the people were wise or knowledgeable enough to make important decisions. On a more fundamental level he objected to the fact that, as a system, it gave everybody an equal voice even though they were not equal in other ways, especially in education and judgement; he feared it could lead to dictatorship. To him the common people were too ready to follow great orators with a broad emotional appeal. Such leaders, able to exert charismatic control over the people, would become too powerful. Thus he tells us, 'So, from an extreme form of liberty one is likely to get, in the individual and in society, a reaction to an extreme form of subjection, and if that is so, we should expect tyranny to result from democracy, the most savage subjection from an excess of liberty.'

On balance, therefore, he preferred rule by a small group or 'oligarchy' of wise, responsible (by implication also wealthy) rulers.

His pupil, Aristotle, took a similar view, but he was more particularly concerned that the people might not respect the laws which they, themselves, had made. The fear was that, feeling free and self-responsible, the people could make and unmake laws to suit themselves. Why obey a law which no longer conforms to one's wishes if one can simply set the law aside?

We can now summarise the criticisms which Plato and Aristotle laid on democracy:

- The mass of the people are not fit to make laws for themselves.
- An open system gives the opportunity for dictators to arise, raised up by the masses who have been too easily swayed by emotional rhetoric.
- Democracy imposes an unnatural equality upon people. In fact some are more fit to govern than others.
- People will not respect laws they have made for themselves.

In modern terms these would be seen as conservative views on democracy, but much time was to pass before the serious political battles over democracy were to be waged.

Locke and Rousseau　Following the decline of Greek classical civilisation, democracy, in a limited form, made a brief reappearance in Ancient Rome, but then largely disappeared, to be replaced in most parts of the civilised world by absolute monarchies, until the seventeenth century. The English Civil War in the 1640s raised questions about what form of political authority could replace the traditional or divine rule of the Stuart Monarchy. In Cromwell's army and among the Levellers, an embryonic form of socialism, there was much talk of popular forms of government.

The Levellers produced a document in 1647 entitled the 'Agreement of the People' which contained a radical programme for a representative democracy with most, though not all adults having voting rights. At the great debate in Putney, which took place in Cromwell's army as a result of its publication, General Ireton, a close colleague of Cromwell, argued that if the propertyless were to be granted the vote they would surely vote for the abolition of property itself. In other words, he saw democracy as a precursor of communism. The Levellers were quickly defeated, in the event. The propertied middle classes were the true driving force of the Parliamentary rebellion and, since they had much to lose from Leveller demands, ensured that the more radical elements were excluded from power. England, though perhaps the most politically advanced nation of the day, was not ready for modern democracy.

Following the Glorious Revolution of 1688 and the advent of truly parliamentary government in England, the ground was more fertile for the seeds of democracy to be sown again. The Whig philosopher John Locke expounded his theories of representative rule in his 'Two Treatises on Government' in 1689. The first principle for Locke was that government must be based on the consent of the people. Nobody is entitled to judge on our behalf, as individuals, what is best for us. We are the best judges of what is in our interests. Therefore, government must be set up by the people, by a free agreement among them. (This is his so-called 'Social Contract' which gives rise to the term 'Contract Theory' for much of Locke's work). Secondly, Locke insisted that, once set up, government should be continuously responsible to the people. Indeed, he gave the people the right to remove a government, by force if necessary, if it were to break the trust placed in it by the people. Thirdly, Locke envisaged a representative assembly whose role would be to maintain control, on behalf of the people, over government.

Here we can see a much more recognisable conception of a democratic form of government, closer to contemporary forms. However, there needs to be a word of caution here. Locke was very much a representative of the property-owning middle classes, so his representatives would be safeguarding and advancing the interests of property. He did not believe that the uneducated, unpropertied mass of the people should be included in such government. (In this respect he was still close to the outlook of Plato and Aristotle.) This is not to say they were to be ignored. Rather, their interests could best be understood by the more responsible middle classes. The ownership of property was seen as crucial by Whigs such as Locke, for it gave the individual a greater stake in the maintenance of good order. Thus they could be trusted to behave and think in a responsible manner.

Nearly a century later, the French philosopher Jean-Jacques Rousseau was to introduce serious reservations over the growing enthusiasm for Locke's style of democracy, much as Plato had done in Greece. Rousseau's reflections, however, were considerably more sophisticated than those of Plato. He wrote against a background of French political philosophy which much admired the English system of parliamentary government. For him, though, the English were only free at election time. Between elections there was no guarantee that government would act in the interests of the people.

Rousseau's starting point is that man has a right to freedom, but as soon as government is set up over him he loses his freedom, hence his famous maxim, 'Man is born free but is everywhere in chains'. To solve the problem government must be set up by the people and come broadly under their control. However, for the first time in the history of democratic thought, Rousseau recognised the dangers of majority rule if decisions were to be based on a popular vote. He asked, 'On what basis will people make their decisions?' giving the answer that we are driven largely by self-interest, what is best for ourselves. It follows that the will of the majority is bound to conflict with the interests of the minority. Thus simple, popular democracy, based on majority rule, is unjust and dangerous. Of course, he pointed out, if all men were truly enlightened and understood the interests of the whole community as well as their own, the problem would not exist. Thus he tells us, 'Were there a people of gods, their government would be democratic. So perfect a government is not for men.'

Instead, Rousseau discusses the concept of a 'general will', a difficult idea over which scholars have argued ever since. Broadly, it seems to refer to the interests of the people collectively, rather than simply the will of the majority based on a collection of self-interests. So, for example, the majority might vote against a general rise in taxation to improve the public finances, or for relief of the poor, but the true interests of the whole community might lie with such a rise. How then can the 'general will' be arrived at? Rousseau's solution – that only a single, enlightened, perfectly moral individual could perform such a task – has been seen by many commentators as a recipe for a kind of totalitarian rule. Thus, paradoxically, Rousseau has been seen as both a democrat and a supporter of so-called benevolent despotism (sometimes referred to as enlightened dictatorship).

We can sum up the contributions of Locke and Rousseau into the following principles:

- Government must rest on the consent of the people.
- There must be safeguards to ensure that government acts in the interests of the people.
- Government must represent the interests of the people. In Locke's case, this means the interests of the majority of voters; in Rousseau's case, it refers to the collective will of the people.

Paine and Madison If Rousseau proved to be the guiding light of the French Revolution, it was Thomas Paine and James Madison who inspired the American rebels on the other side of the Atlantic. Their conceptions of democratic principles were to be discovered in the American Declaration of Independence of 1776 and the Constitution which was written in 1787. The US Constitution still forms the basis of American government and remains, for many, the clearest example of democracy ever codified.

Tom Paine, celebrated for his authorship of *The Rights of Man*, held almost socialist views, similar to those of the English Levellers. For him, democratic equality meant more than political and legal justice, it also included a fairer distribution of property. Yet it was not his socialist leanings which endeared him to the American revolutionaries. Rather, it was his insistence that any government must be based on the principle that all men are free and have rights which are inalienable, that is incapable of being removed by government, however fairly elected it may be. Such ideas were added to the American Constitution almost immediately after it was first drafted, and form the first ten amendments known as the Bill of Rights.

Madison, a contemporary of Paine, was less radical but made an equally important contribution to the development of democratic theory. His best known writing is contained in the 'Federalist Papers', a series of articles written at the time of the American Revolution to air the various issues the newly independent country would have to face. Madison's concerns centred on two main problems. First, how to stop an elected government becoming too dictatorial. He recognised that, enjoying the increased authority of having been elected by a popular majority, a government might feel it has a mandate to take too much power. Secondly, like Plato, he did not trust the judgement of the mass of the people. They might elect leaders for the wrong reasons and, having elected them, might support them in oppressing minority interests. His greatest fear was the establishment of a political party which would represent a permanent majority and which would dominate the system indefinitely.

In answer to these problems, Madison proposed that government should contain, within itself, checks and balances or internal limitations to its own powers. In other words, for every branch of government there should be another branch able to control it. This would reduce the likelihood of an over-powerful government arising. The problem of the excessive power of the majority was a more difficult one. He hoped to see a democracy work without political parties at all, but this very soon proved to be impractical. More realistically, Madison introduced the notion of indirect democracy. Having rejected outright the idea of a direct democracy of the Athenian kind, he developed a system where the people would elect intermediate bodies between themselves and government. These bodies would serve the purpose of filtering public opinion and reducing the effects of more extreme proposals. Thus, for example, the President would not be elected directly, but by an electoral college of representatives of the people. The college would be guided by the people but would not be its slaves.

Although Madison's ideas were eventually overtaken by the rapid development of democracy during the nineteenth century, his principles still have influence, particularly the notion of self-limiting government.

So, from the American experience, we can see further progress towards modern democracy, notably:

- Individual rights could not be sacrificed to the power of government.
- Government should be limited.
- The influence of popular opinion should be moderated by representative institutions.

As the nineteenth century dawned, the idea of democracy was established as a serious threat to more traditional forms of government. Yet it still had more enemies than friends. The experiences of the French Revolution, the infamous 'Reign of Terror' in particular, and the radical ideas of America's Founding Fathers sent shock waves through Europe. But rapid industrialisation, and the large capitalist middle class which came with it, ensured that popular forms of government would inevitably emerge. It was only a question of how long traditional forms could endure and, when they were replaced, what would be the precise form of democracy to replace them.

Although the democratic spirit began to spread through Europe in the nineteenth century, its implementation had, at first, to be tempered with a need for order and stability. In particular, the role of monarchy and the institutions connected with monarchy, such as the British House of Lords, became a matter of controversy. Could non-elected institutions have any place in a modern democracy? In France the answer was a resounding 'no' and by 1871 she had gone the way of the USA and established a pure Republic following several past flirtations with the idea.

The forms of democracy

Unfortunately for students of the concept of democracy, no sooner had it begun to gain popularity than its theory and practice split into a variety of forms. We can now see how, over the ensuing two centuries, it gained a number of contrasting types.

The first modern democracies were essentially mixed systems. Popularly elected parliaments (invariably elected only by a limited proportion of the population through various limiting voting qualifications) found their authority set against the power of hereditary monarchy. England had set out on the road as long ago as 1688 when the principle was established that, while the King may rule, the elected Parliament should enact laws. Variations on this theme flourished in Europe through the nineteenth century. In Britain, indeed, the concept of combining elected with traditional institutions was turned into a philosophy and became one of the founding principles of the Conservative Party. This was known as 'Tory democracy'.

Tory democracy   This philosophy, largely associated with Disraeli and Randolph Churchill, was principally concerned with balancing the interests of the different social classes which had grown up as a result of the Industrial Revolution. Full-scale popular democracy, while desirable in principle, would lead to social conflict, argued the Tories. One fear was that the working class, now the huge majority, would be able to command large numbers of votes and parliamentary seats. The danger here was that such a huge numerical superiority would sweep away the traditional ruling classes. A second concern for Tories was that the newly wealthy capitalist middle classes, who now held economic power, might convert their wealth into political power. There was a danger that such power in the hands of capitalists could be used to damage working-class interests and provoke revolution, as was common on the continent of Europe. The traditional rulers, drawn from the numerically weak landed gentry and aristocracy, would be powerless to mediate in the great clash of interests which would result. Since the maintenance of order and security was the dominant goal of Conservatism, a solution was imperative.

The answer was to balance the power of elected institutions, notably the House of Commons and its representatives in government, with that of traditional institutions such as the monarchy, aristocracy (represented in the House of Lords) and the Church of England. Furthermore, if the working class could be persuaded to vote Conservative in large enough numbers, the possibility of a 'tyranny' of a working-class majority could be avoided. In this way the clear need to accept the democratic spirit of the age could be reconciled with the desire for stability.

In the event, this model of limited democracy was short-lived. As the nineteenth gave way to the twentieth century, it was the elected institutions, and the parties which dominated them, which came to be seen as the true bearers of democracy. When the principle of full adult suffrage had been established, and when the experiences of World War One made the satisfaction of working-class demands essential, only elected institutions could claim real authority to govern.

Democratic elitism   After World War One the idea of popular democracy ceased to instil fear into those who had a vested interest in maintaining the status quo. At worst it was accepted as an inevitable development, at best it was welcomed as the final maturity of liberal political thought. Few now feared that the capitalist West would be swamped by working-class parties, elected on the back of universal suffrage and dedicated to the introduction of Marxist-inspired socialism. President Woodrow Wilson's so-called 'Fourteen Points', introduced as part of the post-war settlement which set out the future of international relations, gave official approval finally to popular sovereignty and self-determination constituing the only acceptable basis for a modern state.

Yet democracy was still in its infancy as a political system. The modern notion of a society where the citizenry are intensively and constantly active in politics, where information is widespread and sophisticated, and where active participation is common, had not arrived. The political system, and the number of people actively involved in it, remained limited in scope. In effect it was, during the first part of the century, operated by a small political leadership. The clearest description of such a narrow form of democracy is provided by the economist J.A. Schumpeter (1883–1950). Schumpeter understood that the role of the people in political decision making was inevitably limited. It was simply not realistic for people with relatively little knowledge or understanding to become continuously involved in complex political argument. Rather, he observed, their role is reduced to being able to choose freely between different groups of politicians each presenting competing sets of policies. These groups, or political 'elites', would submit themselves regularly to free and fair elections and would usually be open to entry by anyone with sufficient ability and ambition. Between elections, however, the role of the people was only slight. They could not expect to exercise continuous influence or to be regularly involved. He characterised such a democracy as, 'public competition between open elites'. As a further illustration it can be compared to the economic process. The people are the 'consumers' of politics while the elites are the 'producers'. The consumers may choose between competing products in the store, but have little influence over their design and production.

Several other theorists since Schumpeter, largely from American schools of political science, have followed this elitist analysis of democracy. C. Wright Mills referred to a 'power elite' in political society incorporating leaders of business and commerce, the military and politics itself, who continuously hold real power. The democratic competition between parties is, therefore, a mere façade behind which the true decisions are made.

By the 1950s and 1960s such elitist theories had been superseded by new theories, but there are still many who see democracy in terms of such a model. Its main conclusions can be identified as:

- Political issues are, on the whole, too complex for most people to be intimately involved in policy making.
- For most, political participation must be confined to choosing between competing elites at free elections.
- The system can still be described as democratic if these elites are open for most members of the public to join if they have the necessary political skills and will.
- It can further be described as democratic if the competition between these elites is based on a desire to act in the public good.

Pluralist democracy   The term 'pluralism' is one which can be applied to political processes in general. It refers to any scenario where a variety of beliefs, demands and interests are permitted to flourish together. Thus, for example, the former Soviet Union could not have been described as pluralist since competing political ideologies and religious creeds were forbidden. On the other hand, the USA is often held up as the perfect model of pluralism since many political, religious and moral beliefs are tolerated. In the context of democratic politics, we may also look to the USA to provide us with an example of how these two concepts – pluralism and democracy – can be synthesised.

As long ago as 1835, the French democratic theorist, Alexis de Tocqueville, commented on American society that its potential for true democracy lay in its tolerance of many interest groups standing between the mass of the people and their government. At the same time he noted the tendency of the American people to involve themselves enthusiastically in the activities of such groups. The danger of democracy lay predominantly in the fact that majority government might feel itself unfettered by public opinion and so at liberty to adopt dictatorial methods. The best protection against such a danger, observed Tocqueville, was this continuous participation of the people in intermediate political groups.

Over a century later, in the 1960s, Tocqueville's ideas on democracy were echoed in the sociological studies of American political scientists such as Robert Dahl and David Trueman. They rejected the elitist theories of Schumpeter and Mills, replacing them with observations that much of American society was pluralist in nature and that the true character of the political system was extremely complex. It was simplistic, they claimed, to see power as lying exclusively in the hands of a few political elites. Whatever the outcome of elections and the size of the voting turnout, in reality the political process consisted of the interplay of many pressure and interest groups. The role of government was to mediate between the demands of such groups in such a way as to discover a consensus. There were, thus, no majority groups in control, but rather a large number of minorities competing for the attention and favours of the elected government. This process took place from Washington in the centre, to city and county government at the periphery. Such an analysis seems particularly compelling when we consider that in the Britain of the 1990s considerably more people are members of environmental pressure groups such as Friends of the Earth and the Woodland Trust than of the major political parties.

Indeed, the pluralist analysis of modern democracies suggests that many see representation as lying through specialised pressure groups which have direct links with government, rather than through the traditional media of parties and legislatures. In the USA, where parties are diffuse, relatively loose-structured organisations, much political influence now centres around various kinds of interest groups, or through policy communities, notably so-called 'political action committees' which seek to build temporary coalitions for the purpose of securing the passage of legislation. Thus, the pluralist model suggests that there exists an active, politically aware public who see democracy in terms of a series of issues rather than the broader clash of competing parties and philosophies.

Liberal democracy   All contemporary political systems which can be described as 'popular government' are, to a greater or lesser extent, pluralist or elitist as described above. Yet these definitions are not precise enough for the purpose of categorising regimes into more specific types. Perhaps a better description is 'liberal democracy', the common title given to those states which broadly follow a liberal tradition which can be traced back to the eighteenth century. Before establishing detailed criteria, there are two essential prerequisites for maintaining that a system is liberal in nature. These are that:

- government is based on the free consent of the people; and
- government is responsible to the people.

Such requirements correspond essentially to Abraham Lincoln's renowned description of democracy as 'government of the people, by the people, for the people'. But the details are more instructive:

- Government is chosen as a result of regular, free and fair elections in which the whole adult population (with a few justified exceptions) is entitled to take part. It is implied by this description that ballots are secret and that there are adequate safeguards to ensure results are accurate. The question of what kinds of electoral system are compatible with the description 'fair' can be left open in this context and is discussed elsewhere.
- Such elections should be freely competitive. Within reason any political party should be entitled to field candidates (exceptions are likely to be those parties which have illegal aims).
- Government must be continuously responsible to the people, either directly or through representative institutions such as parliaments. It is not sufficient for government only to make itself responsible at elections.
- The rights and liberties of individuals must be protected, preferably in a constitution. These rights should be enjoyed equally by all citizens.
- A wide variety of beliefs should be tolerated, provided they do not threaten the peace of the community and the existence of the state.
- There should be peaceful transition of power from one government to the next. It is a vital principle of democracy that, should a government be removed from power by a popular vote, it should accept the popular decision, step down peacefully from power and agree to obey those laws which may be established by the victors; so too should the supporters of the defeated government.
- The rule of law should prevail. In essence this implies that government must be subject to its own laws, i.e. should not attempt to place itself above the law and should not act in an arbitrary fashion. In addition all citizens should be equal under the law and entitled to a fair trial by a judiciary which is independent of government.
- Government must be limited, that is its powers should be exercised within parameters laid down in a constitution.

Of course no single political regime could hope to meet such stringent conditions in all respects and without some failings. Nevertheless, they do serve as a useful yardstick against which we can assess the democratic credentials of any state.

Representative and direct democracy

Before moving away from what may be termed 'orthodox' conceptions of democracy, it will be useful to cast a glance back to ancient Athens and to compare the merits of direct democracy and the representative forms which now flourish in most economically developed countries. The case against direct democracy has not been proved, nor has representative democracy established itself without serious criticism.

For the past two centuries the practice of expressing the demands and interests of the people through chosen representatives, normally elected, has been known as 'representative democracy'. Virtually all the celebrated democratic theorists, including Locke, Rousseau, Madison and J.S. Mill, have insisted that such a device is vital to the just and effective operation of a state for the following three principal reasons:

- For many, the activity of government is seen as one which can only be undertaken by those who are considered to possess superior knowledge and personal qualities. In short, they would prefer to be governed by their betters. This may seem unconvincing in an age when politicians are frequently brought into disrepute, yet it is still true that most of the electorate do seek to support individuals whom they can respect.
- The electorate may well demonstrate an emotional response to issues which, in reality, demand a more measured, rational consideration. Representatives, removed from the ebb and flow of public debate, may be in a position to judge matters dispassionately. The classic example is the debate over capital punishment. Elected representatives, through the medium of rational and calm discussion, are likely to consider all the practical and moral issues while the voters are more inclined to display a narrower and more emotional reaction. Such a conclusion is not watertight, of course, since in this particular case there are strong moral considerations. Certainly elected representatives cannot be said to enjoy a monopoly of the proverbial 'moral high ground' even if they can claim to carry out their deliberations in the peaceful environment of a Washington or a Westminster. The matter of taxation is a clearer example of how rational thinking may be more desirable than the emotional response. Most of us will feel we would like to pay less tax, but politicians have to weigh up our demands against the broader needs of the country.
- On the assumption (possibly not as over-optimistic as one might believe) that representatives embody a well-developed degree of integrity, there is a good possibility that those whom we elect can reach decisions which are genuinely in the national interest. The alternative is the politics of self-interest where decisions are made to the benefit of narrow sections of the community. Understandably, individuals may wish to support measures which will be to their advantage. The representative may be in a better position to balance the interests of one section of the population against another. The wealthy, for example, may not wish to pay more tax than those of more modest means, but it may be in the interests of the whole community for them to do so. Such a solution is a modern example of what Rousseau meant by his term, the 'general will'. More will be said on this issue when we consider the relative merits and demerits of direct democracy below.

> *The theory of parliamentary sovereignty might suggest that if Parliament enacts legislation all must obey, but the reality is that people are far more likely to conform if a strong case has been made to them and if they themselves have approved the measure.*
>
> Anthony Batchelor. 'Referendums and Initiatives' in *Politics Review*, Vol. 1, No. 3 (February 1992)

A sceptic may view the arguments presented above as hopelessly utopian. Are our representatives really wiser than the collective judgement of the people? Do they pursue the national interest or merely that of the section of the community from which they themselves have emerged? Perhaps they pander to the irrational excesses of public opinion in the hope of ensuring their future re-election. Perhaps by considering the main alternative to representative government – direct democracy – it may be possible to assess the relative virtues of the two forms.

In today's large-scale societies the 'market place' democracy of Greek antiquity is clearly impractical. There are examples of 'town meetings' in some New England communities of the USA and similar devices in the small parishes of rural Britain, but these are rare modern-day exceptions. Indeed, the issues they consider are of only the most local and narrow interest. In general, therefore, direct democracy can only exist today in the form of the referendum.

Two criticisms often levied against the use of referenda can be dispensed with at the outset of this discussion. The first is purely logistical. It is often argued that it would simply be impractical and too slow a process to decide issues by direct popular vote. But technology has now overtaken such an objection. Many hundreds of thousands of viewers now vote in TV talent shows or take part in multiple-choice quizzes through telephone lines or even with the use of interactive TV sets. It seems most likely, therefore, that by the end of the century it will be reasonable to connect all members of the public to a system capable of recording votes instantaneously.

Secondly, there exists a common argument that referenda undermine the authority of elected institutions by removing their decision-making discretion. 'Why purchase a dog and then bark yourself?', runs the logic. However, this argument is not particularly clear. The referendum, by its nature, has invariably been used to fill gaps in decision-making processes left by representative institutions. In other words, if referenda are needed, our representatives have accepted their own inability to come to a decision. The Labour Government's recourse to a referendum over Britain's membership of the European Community (now Union) in 1975 was such a case. The party, and indeed the Cabinet itself, was hopelessly split on the issue. Any decision, either way, might have resulted in a defeat for the Government. Asking the people to decide removed the problem as supporters of both sides of the argument would be forced to accept the ultimate political sovereignty of the people.

We must, therefore, search for criticisms of the referendum elsewhere. The following may be offered:

- Many issues are extremely complex and may be beyond the understanding of a high proportion of the electorate. It is certainly doubtful whether the voters of France, the Irish Republic and Denmark understood all the implications of the Maastricht Treaty when asked to approve it in 1992 and 1993.
- There is a danger that voters, much as they do in British local elections, may use the referendum as a vote of confidence, or disapproval in the government of the day. The true judgement of the people is thus lost.
- Just as Plato and Madison feared, the electorate may be easily swayed by emotional arguments when issues require a more rational response. One only has to consider the excesses of the tabloid press in Britain over recent years to appreciate such a danger.

- It is possible that voters may behave in an illogical and contradictory manner. In the USA, for example, where state level referenda or initiatives are used, the people of California voted for reductions in taxation in 1978 – the notorious Proposition 13. What the voters had failed to appreciate was that such a measure would lead to drastic reductions in the provision of public services, notably the police and emergency services. Shortly afterwards the reduction had to be reversed. The danger which Rousseau identified – that people will vote out of self-interest unless properly informed – is fully illustrated by California's experience.
- Although we now have the technology to hold frequent referenda, there is a strong possibility that 'voter fatigue' may set in. Apathy could become so serious that results, based on very low turnouts, would become meaningless and lack sufficient authority to be implemented.
- Where questions excite the interest of powerful pressure groups there is a danger that the huge financial resources which such groups may possess could distort the referendum campaign. It is, for example, suspected that, in Britain's 1975 referendum on European Community membership, the fact that business interests were broadly in favour of a 'Yes' vote gave rise to a more effective public campaign than that of the opposition.

Despite these objections many states do use the referendum as a means of confirming key constitutional changes where a consensus of support is required. The French voters in 1969 were thus instrumental in the removal of President de Gaulle, while in 1993 the Italians voted to ditch proportional representation just when New Zealanders opted to introduce it. There is also a strong case for suggesting that strictly moral issues, not the subject of party politics, should be resolved by direct democracy. Thus it was the Italians again who voted for the legalisation of divorce against the expressed policy of the Roman Catholic Church.

There are, in addition, a number of strong reasons why referenda could be acceptable as a **complement** to existing decision-making institutions, rather than as an **alternative**. On some occasions party politicians may recognise the need for decisions, but are unable to agree on action. In such cases the clear verdict of the people may help to overcome the log-jam. This has been perfectly illustrated by Britain's inability to reach consensus over its involvement in the European Union. Certainly, if a democracy needs to ensure that key decisions enjoy popular consent, the device of the referendum may prove to be an ideal way of preserving such democratic principles. Direct democracy may be 2,500 years old but there is still no conclusion as to its desirability.

A common objection to the use of referenda is that they are merely tools employed by politicians to deal with their own insoluble problems. Where the **initiative** system is used, decision making is placed more firmly in the hands of the people. Used in parts of the USA and Switzerland, for example, the initiative is a referendum which is demanded by the people rather than the Government. Where they operate, a minimum number of petition signatures is required in order to trigger a referendum.

Referenda and initiatives – the arguments summarised	
For	**Against**
1. They are the most direct form of democracy. 2. They may help to relieve a political deadlock. 3. Decisions resulting from a referendum or initiative may enjoy greater popular consent. 4. Long-term decisions, such as constitutional change, are better made by the people rather than a temporary majority government.	1. Issues may be too complex for many to be able to make a rational decision. 2. The people may use a referendum as a vote of confidence in the Government rather than on the issue itself. 3. People may be easily swayed by emotional rather than rational argument. 4. There is a possibility of contradictory decisions being reached at different times. 5. Too many referenda or initiatives may result in loss of interest and apathy. 6. Rich, powerful pressure groups may be able to exert undue influence during campaigns.

Other forms What we have been dealing with so far has been a more conventional Western–liberal type of democracy. But there are democratic theories which stray a good deal from these typical ideals. It may seem paradoxical to Western ears, for example, when the term 'totalitarian democracy' is used, yet it can have some meaning if one is viewing the concept from a particular perspective. It was Rousseau in the eighteenth century who suggested that a single enlightened ruler, the 'legislator', could express the 'general will' on behalf of the people. The nature of such rule could be considered democratic in a broad sense since the interests of the people were being served. It must also be considered totalitarian, however, since the regime would need wide powers in order to prevent minority interests operating against the collective good. The operation of such powers would thus entail the loss of many other liberties. Indeed, history is scattered with dictators who laid claim to such democratic authority although the conventional institutions of democracy were absent. Napoleon was perhaps the first who drew inspiration from Rousseau's analysis, while others such as Bismarck and Stalin have made similar claims.

The communist argument, that social equality and democracy are synonymous, was not as modern as it may have appeared. As long ago as the 1830s the French democratic theorist, Tocqueville, had expressed the belief that the true democratic spirit of the French and American revolutions had been to create more equality between the classes. This, he argued, was part of a long historical process during which democracy would ultimately prevail over aristocracy and the system of class privilege. Almost prophetically, however, Tocqueville warned that such democracy could result in the kind of tyranny experienced under Stalin. The class system had created stability at least. Social equality introduced the danger of a disordered society and so opened the door for such totalitarianism. As we saw before in the description of pluralist democracy, only an active, enlightened, participatory society could prevent this development.

Equally, as C.B. MacPherson has pointed out in his influential work, *The Real World of Democracy*, we should not be mesmerised by the existence of so-called democratic institutions such as parliaments and elections. Rather, the true test of a democracy is whether it serves the broad interests of its people. In this regard MacPherson suggests we should not reject out of hand the claims of many one-party states to be democratic. They are one-party states often because they have a necessity for singleness of purpose. They may require rapid economic development as is often the case in Asia, or may be searching for a national identity, frequently the problem for former African colonies. Whichever, the existence of a plurality of parties and ideologies would endanger such processes. As long as these regimes do not abuse civil liberties on a wide scale, and as long as the single legal party displays a reasonable degree of internal democracy, they are indeed democratic themselves. He does not extend his blessing of such 'one-party democracies' to the communist type, however, since their widespread abuse of human rights disqualifies them.

The democratic case for communist regimes is made most persuasively by V.I. Lenin who developed a theory known as 'democratic centralism'. As the name suggests, this contains two elements. The term 'democratic' refers to the ultimate goals of the system – equality and justice – which are clearly in the interests of the people according to classical Marxist theory. It also paid at least lip-service to the idea that all were entitled to participate within the process (though they must accept the parameters of socialist doctrine) and to the acceptance of a certain amount of free dialogue within the ruling party. The 'centralist' element referred to the fact that, once firm decisions had been reached, discussion and opposition would end. The higher echelons of the system would impose the decisions upon those below them. In other words influence was to spread down through the system from the centre, rather than up as is the case in the liberal form of democracy. Ultimately, Lenin's successor, Stalin, was to bring the principles of democratic centralism into disrepute by establishing autocratic government which engaged in the systematic abuse of human rights. Nevertheless, Lenin's argument that equality itself could constitute democracy, and that so-called liberal democracy was merely a charade to disguise the institutionalisation of class rule, have enjoyed widespread popularity, at least until recent years.

Before finally moving on to consider some of the problems of democracy we may perhaps return to where we began, with Professor Bernard Crick. He suggests that we should not seek to classify regimes either as democratic or undemocratic. Democracy, he suggests, is more a 'spirit' than a set of institutions. We should judge political systems according to the extent to which they embody such spirit and contain democratic elements. He sums this idea up thus: 'Democracy, then, if we give the word the fairest meaning we may want to give it – if we value liberty, free choice, discussion, opposition, popular government, all of these things together – is still but one form of politics, not something to be hoped for at every stage of a country's development or in every circumstance.'

Problems and issues of democracy

The paradox of democracy

All those theorists who have seen democracy as essentially majority rule have been aware that this constitutes a dilemma of popular government. The problem arises from the enormous degree of authority which is carried by the majority vote of the people. Those of us who live in societies governed by the principle of majority rule must accept that, if we find ourselves in a minority, we must obey the will of the majority unless we are to undermine the whole idea of democracy. We may indeed find ourselves oppressed by this majority will. So a system which is often said to embody freedom may ultimately result in a total loss of freedom for a section of the community. If a society, for example, consistently opposes the introduction of a public health care programme because the majority of its citizens can afford private medical provision, the few who are poor may suffer a permanent disadvantage.

All societies contain minorities of one kind or another. These may be religious, ethnic, cultural or economic, but they all have in common a vulnerability to the rule of the majority. We have said above that tolerance is one of the tests of a claim to liberal democracy, but the majority will may not embody such tolerance. 'If there is free opposition', the argument runs, 'who can complain if the popular vote does not suit the wishes of all?' The problem of Northern Ireland is a typical model of the paradox. The permanent Catholic, largely republican minority there constantly finds itself outvoted in elections. The principle of 'winner takes all' operated up to the 1970s and so there was systematic discrimination against the minority in employment, housing, political representation and welfare benefits. It took direct rule from Westminster to put an end to the worst abuses of majority rule. While this represents a somewhat extreme example, it serves, nevertheless, as a paradigm of a tendency throughout Western democratic society. Those who seek to fight for the rights of minorities whose voice is not sufficiently loud in the democratic arena are often accused of being anti-democratic, even if their campaigns are peaceful.

If we ask, 'can the paradox be solved?' a number of suggestions can be offered. The most compelling concerns the very nature of majority rule. Political systems, such as those operating in Britain or France, frequently award virtually total, uncontrolled power to the winning party. Indeed, Britain's electoral system invariably grants power to a party which does not secure a majority of the popular vote. The relative lack of balancing controls on the power of the ruling party tends to result in unfettered majority rule. This does not have to be the case, however. In the 1950s and 1960s in Britain, for example, an era of so-called 'consensus politics' prevailed. Here the combined deliberations of Parliament, the government and the civil service, together with regular consultations with representative groups outside politics – unions and employers, for example – were aimed at achieving widespread support for policy objectives. It was not considered sufficient for government merely to secure a majority in the House of Commons in order to claim a mandate for its actions. Thus economic, social and industrial policy tried to take account of the interests of a broad cross-section of the community. Of course small minorities could not always be catered for, but, within reason, consensus politics solved many of the problems described above. In this way much social conflict was avoided.

The consensus model of democracy, abandoned in Britain by the late 1970s, has virtually been institutionalised in the USA. There, even if the same party claims control of both Congress and the White House (often the case with the Democrats in modern times), it cannot force through policies which offend substantial minority opinion. The 'checks and balances' built into the system, together with the weakness of the party structure itself, allow minority groups to influence legislators to an extent well beyond their numerical strength. As we shall see below, this in itself causes problems, but there is no doubting the system's ability to safeguard minorities.

The USA's political system contains a further safeguard, perhaps more powerful than checks and balances. This is the constitutional protection afforded to individuals and minorities against the power of a government claiming the authority of electoral victory. Any laws discriminating unreasonably against religious or ethnic minorities are unconstitutional and may be challenged. Although such safeguards do depend, to some extent, on the political leanings of the Supreme Court judges involved, such a device has served to protect the interests of such groups as farmers, fundamentalist Christians and gays in recent political history.

Finally, we may return to the pluralist model, described above. It can be argued that, if the minorities which are endangered by majority rule have open access to decision makers, if there is an active free media and if candidates for election are susceptible to pressure from such groups, there is a good chance that persecution can be avoided. Once again the USA appears to provide us with the ideal model. There, Congress is open to a large, active and effective lobby system and candidates rely on support and funding from a wide variety of groups to secure election.

We can summarise the safeguards against what John Stuart Mill called the 'tyranny of the majority', thus:

- A tradition of consensus, rather than majoritarian politics
- The existence of checks and balances within the system which limit the power of elected government
- The provision of constitutional controls against the abuse of minority rights and interests
- A highly pluralist system which provides minorities with opportunities to protect their own interests.

Lack of direction The nineteenth-century German philosopher, Friedrich Nietzsche, was particularly disparaging about democracy. He described its adherents as 'sheep-like', merely following the will of the majority, and characterised it as 'rule by shopkeepers'. The latter jibe referred to democracy as a political system designed to serve self-interest and small mindedness rather than the broader national interest. Though Nietzsche's general political philosophy, with its fascist undertones, is rather distasteful, he does present a compelling criticism of democracy. It can be said to lack direction. The need to consult, avoid conflict and build consensus may well divert attention away from the pressing need for social progress. There may be times when such progress requires dynamic leadership which is often inhibited by democratic requirements. As

C.B. MacPherson has also pointed out, such overwhelming needs as economic progress, national unification or the restoration of public order may be more pressing than the niceties of democratic ideals.

There is, however, much evidence to refute such charges. The 'New Deal' reforms of President Roosevelt in the USA in the Depression years of the 1930s, the rebuilding of Germany and the creation of the British Welfare State after World War Two and the Thatcherite reforms of the 1980s were all dramatic changes in course for the societies concerned. Yet they were all carried through within the context of democratic politics. A determined enough leadership, it seems, can harness democracy to radical social reform.

Inefficiency A similar criticism to the aimlessness described above, inefficiency refers to democracy's insistence that the people must be regularly consulted if key decisions are to be made. The people are notoriously fickle and often reluctant to allow their rulers to subject them to long-term commitments. The seemingly interminably long progress towards closer European union in the 1980s and 1990s represents a clear example. The supporters of European integration longed for visionary leadership to bring the European peoples together, while their opponents were content to place one obstacle after another in the way of progress.

Of course, in emergencies, all democracies reserve the ability to suspend popular government for the sake of speedy and decisive decision making. War time is the clearest example of the use of such emergency powers, but periods of internal disorder, as in Northern Ireland, provide an additional opportunity. The British system, indeed, has an inbuilt device for such purposes, in the form of the royal prerogative. Here matters of national security remain in the hands of the government acting in the name of the Head of State – the monarch. Such powers are unfettered by parliamentary or public opinion. Unpopular decisions may be made in the broad national interest and, above all, such decisions can be made quickly, freed as they are from the need for extensive consultation. Britain's ability to act so decisively following the Argentine invasion of the Falkland Isles in 1982 demonstrates the effectiveness of prerogative powers. Thus, the charge of inefficiency may have some substance, but democracies can find ways of taking decisive action when an overwhelming need arises.

Whatever our views, democracy, and the liberal form in particular, has become the dominant political form as the twentieth century draws to a close. The ancient Roman maxim, *vox populi, vox dei* (the voice of the people is the voice of God) still holds true today. Its main 'enemies' of the century – totalitarianism and state communism – have been defeated by military or philosophical means, at least for the present. Democracy also appears to have produced greater economic success than these alternative systems.

We can now summarise this study of democracy:

1. Historically there have been a number of usages of the term 'democracy', in particular:

   - Plato's description of a direct, popular decision-making process with equal political rights
   - The idea of a representative system of government, favoured by English liberals such as John Locke or John Stuart Mill and the American, James Madison. Decisions should be made on behalf of the people by elected representatives
   - Rousseau's difficult concept of a powerful leader able to discern and carry out the 'general will' of the people
   - The meaning used by Tocqueville of a society where there is social equality and an absence of class hierarchy and privilege
   - Lenin's communist doctrine of democracy as economic equality with the interests of the people (essentially the working classes) served by a single party
   - Modern 'liberal' ideas of a highly tolerant, pluralistic society with widespread popular participation and influence over government. This is normally characterised by the presence of free elections, competing parties, representative and responsible government and a free media

2. The type of democracy described in the paragraph immediately above, variously described as 'liberal democracy', 'pluralist democracy' or 'democratic elitism' and often containing features of all three, has steadily gained ascendancy during the past two centuries. Of all the political systems which exist today, it appears to be the most popular and the most sought after. This development has become even more marked during the 1980s and 1990s.

3. Despite their apparent success, there remain problems with such democratic systems. They may lack the ability to take decisive action when it is clearly necessary. There are dangers that minorities may be ignored or persecuted in the face of majority rule. Furthermore, if the modern form of direct democracy is used – the referendum – there is a fear that irrational, over-emotional decisions will be taken.

4. A number of solutions have been adopted to reduce the problems described above. Both consensus and pluralist politics go some way to providing safeguards. Individual and minority rights may be protected in various ways, while a well-informed and sophisticated people could prove capable of handling the responsibility placed upon them in a democracy.

For exam questions relevant to this unit, see page 487.

Political parties

Introduction

In this unit the functions of political parties **in general** will be described. Although political parties exist in a number of different types of regime, we will concentrate here on those which flourish within essentially democratic systems. British parties are very much like others in western Europe, but important differences will be identified.

It is usually suggested that Britain's is a 'two-party system' and that the whole of the political system can only be understood in terms of two-party dominance. Thus the meaning and significance of the phenomena of 'party government' and 'two-party government' must be explored. Despite the apparent control exercised by the Labour and Conservative Parties in modern times, there are contrasting analyses of the party system which deserve consideration. 'Do we have a one-party system?' is a question we may pose, so complete has been the supremacy of the Conservatives in recent times. Perhaps, on the other hand, we have a multi-party polity in reality, but one which has been stifled by the characteristics of the electoral system and the nature of parliamentary politics.

The basic philosophies which have inspired members of British parties have been described in Unit 3. However, those descriptions do not tell the full story of the actual **policies** which have been proposed and implemented during the modern era. Therefore, the **practical** aspects of party politics will be discussed, with special reference to the period since World War Two.

The internal structures and procedures of the main parties must also be described. The workings of the party system cannot be understood without reference to the contrasting ways in which British parties go about the business of making policy, selecting candidates for election and raising finance. The various factions and internal groups which make up the parties will also be described.

The functions of political parties

The articulation of demands

Individuals and groups in a community have a wide variety of demands which they place upon the political system. These demands may be the result of **values**, **beliefs** and **ideologies** which prevail in any society. They may also represent the **interests** of specific sections of the community. Examples of such demands might include:

Values, beliefs, ideologies	Interests
Greater freedom	Demands by the poor for better welfare
More social equality	The well off demanding lower taxation
A Welfare State	Women seeking equal rights
Greater law and order	Industry asking for more government aid
Environmental protection	Unions demanding employment protection
Better health care	Consumers requiring better protection
Constitutional reform	Isolated communities needing transport provision

We can see that the left-hand column refers to concerns which may benefit the whole community, while on the right are demands which would benefit only a particular section of the population. In both cases, there is only a prospect that the demands will be met by government if they are properly expressed or articulated, and if it can be demonstrated that there is reasonably widespread support for them.

Two principal methods of furthering one's demands are available. One is to form special pressure or interest groups which will campaign for a particular issue on behalf of a section of the community. The activities of such groups are described in Unit 9. The other is to persuade a political party to adopt its demands as part of its own policy programme. Since parties form governments, control parliamentary voting and have constant channels of communication with both government and Parliament, they are often preferred to pressure groups.

The recruitment of political leaders

Parties perform a key role in training and identifying effective leaders. The skills of persuasion, organisation of support, public speaking, committee work and public campaigning are all required if ambitious individuals are to rise through party ranks and assume public office. Thus, parties are a training ground and also act as a filter, separating the able from the less competent.

Ultimately, it is the parties which select candidates for election to local government and to Parliament. In addition, the parties also nominate individuals to important positions in the public service such as school governing bodies, hospital trusts and a variety of committees charged with the task of protecting the public interest.

Sustaining the system

Any democratic political system requires widespread support among the people whom it governs. Without this continuous 'consent' major problems arise in the implementation and enforcement of laws. It is, therefore, a basic principle of democratic politics that the parties, which inevitably flourish in pluralist systems, should sustain broad public support for the system. Of course they will concentrate on mobilising support for their own particular policies, but underlying this political activity there will normally be an understanding that the institutions and processes of politics must be defended. Some examples from Britain's political system will illustrate this principle:

- Following a general election, losing parties will confirm the **authority** of the winning party to exercise power. Though they may keep up implacable opposition to that party's policies, they will not normally deny its right to govern.
- As it is agreed that Parliament is at the centre of the system and that all politicians should be responsible to it, the parties respect its importance and are generally scrupulous in upholding its traditions and procedures, and in confirming its importance.
- Though the monarch has no political power, his or her status as Head of State is acknowledged and respected.
- In times of crisis, war or other threat to national security, competing parties often suspend political hostilities in the interests of national unity. This has occurred in the two world wars and in matters of policy on many other lesser crises, including the disorders in Northern Ireland.

There are, of course, some parties which are committed to radical changes in the political system, even to its total destruction. Far left 'communists' and the neo-Nazi right wing are examples. However, they are both small and insignificant and largely exclude themselves from the mainstream of democratic politics through their beliefs and methods.

Operating the system

As part of their involvement in system support (described above), parties play a key part in the 'mechanics' of organising political activities within the various institutions which are involved. In many cases these institutions could not effectively operate in their existing form without the involvement of the parties and their leaders. Once again, examples will illustrate:

- Possibly the most vital role parties play in a modern system is the formulation of coherent policy programmes. In this way, when a new government is formed, it will indeed be ready to govern. Its election manifesto will be broadly known not only to many electors, but also to the administrators who will have to implement policy. This gives direction and organisation to the decision-making process. That does not mean, of course, that such policies will prove effective or popular, but at least they are likely to be understood by those who need to understand them. Without the policy-making functions of parties, there is likely to be incoherence, delay and contradiction in the political process.
- As we have seen above, parties recruit candidates for election and then act as a filter to try to ensure that the more able become available for positions of power and influence.
- They also help to run the elections themselves. They 'get the vote out' by ensuring that as many people as possible turn up at the polls, both by giving information and often also by organising transport for the frail and the reluctant. A healthy democracy relies upon good voting turnouts to ensure continuous support among the people. On an administrative level, party representatives also play a vital role in ensuring that elections are conducted honestly and fairly.
- The timetable of Parliament is controlled by the party 'business managers'. Naturally, it is the governing party which dominates, but all play some part in organising the legislative and scrutinising functions of Parliament. Important parliamentary committees constantly need informed, able and committed members. It is the parties who provide the personnel for these committees.

Summary of how parties sustain and maintain the political system

1. Ensuring the peaceful transition of power from one government to the next
2. Maintaining public support for the institutions of the system
3. Ensuring national unity in times of danger and crisis
4. Developing legislative programmes, so maintaining some coherence in policy making
5. Recruiting candidates for election and identifying leaders
6. Helping with the administration and controlling of elections
7. Organising of the business of Parliament

Informing the public

Although we may perceive the parties to be only interested in promoting their own policies, they are also playing a wider role. Without the collective activities of the parties, the public would be deprived of a large amount of information concerning the great issues of the day. The state of the economy, the country's role in world affairs, the major social and legal problems within the community and the transport needs of the country are all examples of issues which have been the subjects of political controversy. As long as the parties seek to mobilise support for their own stance on these issues, they are, in so doing, also informing the public about the problems and the various options available for their solution.

The nature of party government

> 'The conventional view of Westminster democracy has taken for granted that party government was both necessary and desirable. Only by placing the powers of government in the hands of a single party could a country be effectively governed by politicians strong enough to take unpopular but necessary decisions. Only by offering the electorate a choice between the record of the party in office and the criticism of the opposition could the electorate effectively hold politicians accountable.'
> Richard Rose, *Do Parties make a Difference?*
> (Macmillan, 1984)

Professor Rose's view of how party government is generally seen tells us much about its perceived nature in the context of British politics. However much Rose may find it an unfortunate and undesirable feature of the system, there can be no doubting that it has dominated the political scene for much of the twentieth century. British government cannot be understood, nor could it have survived in its present form, without the existence of strong, effective political parties. In practice, what does the term 'party government' mean? The following features can be identified:

- It is normally the case that one **single party** is able to dominate Parliament and to take complete control of the government including the whole machinery of administration. In only one election since World War Two, that of February 1974, has no party succeeded in gaining an overall majority in the House of Commons, thus laying claim to undisputed entitlement to form the Government. Even on that occasion, when Labour was the largest party in the Commons, no coalition was formed and a single party formed a minority government. By 1976 Labour had lost its majority through by-election defeats, but continued to try to govern alone, with a loose agreement with the Liberals for support in return for a few minor concessions. Thus we have come to expect a single party to take control, even in difficult circumstances.
- The doctrine of 'mandate and manifesto' plays a key role in British politics. Each party enters an election campaign with a manifesto, a statement of its intended programme, should it gain office. If it should

win the election, the manifesto is expected to form the basis of its actions. It has, we can say, a 'mandate' to carry out its policies, granted by the electorate at the polls. So we expect a single party's programme to be implemented following election success. In a broader sense too, the doctrine suggests that the winning party enjoys a 'doctor's mandate'. This refers to the idea that the government must have the authority to act in whatever way it feels necessary to deal with a particular problem, even if this was not specifically mentioned in its manifesto. Normally it is unforeseen circumstances which lead to such a situation.

- Parliament is effectively controlled by the parties and dominated by the governing party. Its **legislative agenda** and general business is controlled by party managers; its committees are staffed by party appointees and their agendas are, in turn, arranged by party bosses. There is some room for independent activity by MPs, free of party control, in the departmental select committees which scrutinise the conduct of government. A few pieces of private members' legislation may find sufficient time and support within a crowded parliamentary agenda to come into effect. Yet on the whole the parliamentary scene is dominated by the parties.

- The appointment of all grades of ministers, as well as the senior staff of important committees and other public bodies, is in the hands of the party leaderships. This power of **patronage** ensures a great degree of loyalty to such leaders and again helps the parties to dominate the scene.

- Effective **opposition** is largely confined to the main parties in Parliament which have been unable to form a Government. Though pressure groups and the public may demonstrate their disagreement with government action, it is still the other parties which are able to make their voices most clearly heard in the majority of cases.

So we can see that the whole of the British political scene is dominated by the parties and their leaders. There are, of course, many other actors on this stage, but they are rarely as effective as parties in influencing the decision-making process.

Summary of features of party government

1. It is almost always the case that one party wins a parliamentary majority and so forms a government alone.
2. Parties create policy programmes in the form of election manifestos and have a mandate to carry them out if they secure government office.
3. Parties control the parliamentary agenda.
4. All government posts and many other official positions are under party patronage.
5. The main opposition to government is in the hands of other parties.

Criticisms of party government

Regret is often expressed that the processes of legislation and government cannot be carried out without the influence of parties. As long ago as the 1780s the American constitutionalist and later President, James Madison, was warning against the dangers of party power.

'Complaints are everywhere heard from our most considerate and virtuous citizens, equally the friends of public and private faith, and of public and personal liberty, that our governments are too unstable; that the public good is disregarded in the conflicts of rival parties; and that measures are too often decided, not according to the rules of justice, and the rights of the minor party, but by the superior force of an interested and overbearing majority.'

James Madison, Federalist Paper 10, 1787

Since then the criticisms have continued, both along the lines of Madison's concerns and including some new objections.

The problems of the doctrine of the mandate

Madison referred to the dangers of majority rule and it is still true today that many argue that the 'winner takes all' nature of party government is unhealthy. The doctrine of 'manifesto and mandate' dictates that a winning party has clear authority to carry out **all** its policies. The defeated opposition parties in Britain are given no part in the policy-making process.

Yet the concept of an electoral mandate is flawed. There is no guarantee that a particular policy in the manifesto does indeed enjoy the support of the electors. The party as a whole may enjoy greater support than any other, but this says little about **all** their policies. Despite this clear truth, the winning party claims the right to implement every policy, popular or not. It was clear to many, for example, that the introduction of a Poll Tax, which was in the Conservative 1987 manifesto, was highly unpopular, yet it was indeed implemented after the Tory victory. Subsequent events, including violent riots, a campaign of non-payment of tax and the fall from power of Margaret Thatcher, proved the fallacy of claiming a mandate for such a policy.

What is a majority?

While majority rule may indeed be a dangerous phenomenon, the British electoral system virtually ensures that the winning party in a general election **does not** gain a majority of the popular vote. Since 1945 no party has gained such a majority. Thus there is no real majority rule, yet party government gives the impression that it does exist. The Conservative vote between 1983 and 1992 has held steady at about 43 per cent of the popular vote, yet they have enjoyed 100 per cent of governmental power. The Labour Government which took office in October 1974 was even less favoured with only 39 per cent of the vote and a very narrow Commons majority. Madison would indeed have been dismayed!

Conflict and consensus

British politics are essentially **adversarial** in nature. It is expected that the governing party shall defend all its policies while the other, opposition parties will oppose all that the Government proposes. At first sight this may appear inevitable and healthy. On the other hand, it can be seen as counter-productive. The alternative model is one of **consensus** where policies are only adopted if there is widespread agreement as to their desirability. This may weaken the influence of individual parties, but does ensure more acceptance of policies than can be guaranteed if only those of the governing party are implemented.

Do parties make a difference?

The view of Professor Richard Rose is that party government is merely an illusion. In practice, the government of Britain is largely out of the hands of the party in power. Instead, government is a process of acting in response to events whose course is determined elsewhere. International organisations including the European Union and NATO, together with such international economic phenomena as currency speculation and fluctuating world trade, do more to influence the economy than do party politicians. Even domestically, economic and social problems may not be capable of radical solution by the Government. Small, incremental changes can be made, but certainly not the dramatic solutions which party leaders often claim to be able to offer.

Rose's **ungovernability** thesis is not merely a description of the political system. It is also a criticism, since it suggests that the public are being effectively duped by the parties into believing that they are responsible for successful policies while their opponents are responsible for failures.

The benefits of party government

It would be wrong to suggest that party government is universally criticised. It does have a number of discernible advantages:

- The fact that a single party invariably wins the general election outright and is able to form a government alone does give considerable direction and stability to British government. Major splits in the Government are rare, since party solidarity is usually maintained, both within the Cabinet and in Parliament.
- The doctrine of manifesto and mandate, which has been examined above, does mean that the electorate can be reasonably certain of what policies they are voting for at a general election. They may indeed not support all their favoured party's policies, but they do at least know what to expect.
- Adversary politics provide the public with a clear examination of the Government's policies and of the alternatives presented by the opposition parties. Parliamentary business may appear at times to be excessively hostile in nature, but democracy is being served by the certainty that the Government will be forced to justify itself and its policies.

Summary of advantages and disadvantages of party government

Disadvantages

1. Winning parties are granted too much power to implement policies without effective opposition.
2. The British electoral system means a party can win power without a majority of popular support.
3. Adversary politics leads to unpopular policies succeeding at the expense of consensus policies which can produce more widely supported programmes.
4. The claim that parties control policy may be a dangerous illusion since external factors outside of government control are more powerful.

Advantages

1. It creates clear, united, decisive government.
2. The policies of the Government can be readily understood as they are based on a party manifesto.
3. The adversarial model forces government to be accountable and presents clear alternatives to the electorate.

The two-party system

The conventional view of British politics suggests that it is dominated by a two-party system. In many ways this is undeniably true and these are described below. Nevertheless, there are competing theories of British party politics. The first, and most prominent, is that we now experience single-party dominance and will do so for the foreseeable future. The other is that Britain is a multi-party state in reality, but that various aspects of the political system disguise and inhibit this reality. To begin, we will examine the main aspects of the two-party state:

Dominance of voting support

The table below shows how voting support for the two main parties has developed since 1945:

Election Year	% votes won by Labour and Conservative Parties together
1945	87.6
1950	89.6
1951	96.8
1955	96.1
1959	93.2
1964	87.5
1966	89.8
1970	89.4
1974 (Feb.)	75.0*
1974 (Oct.)	75.0*
1979	80.8*
1983	70.0*
1987	73.2*
1992	76.3*

* From 1974 Ulster Unionist votes were counted as separate from the Conservatives. This accounts for a small drop in voting for the main parties (about 2%)

There are two main conclusions to be drawn from this data. The first is that two parties do indeed dominate voting in British general elections. They have always succeeded in gaining over 70 per cent of the total vote and, if we ignore the special circumstances of 1983 and 1987 when a strong alliance between the Liberals and the short-lived Social Democrat Party achieved unusual popularity, the figure has never been below 75 per cent.

Secondly, it is possible to suggest that there is a long-term decline in support for the main parties. There may have been 'blips' along the way, but there is a clear trend downwards. Thus, generalisations about this aspect of the two-party system must be treated with great suspicion.

A virtual monopoly over seats in the House of Commons

If we examine the same general elections in terms of the **seats** won by the two main parties, rather than the percentage of votes cast, the picture is considerably clearer:

Election Year	% of seats won by Labour and Conservative Parties together
1945	94.6
1950	98.1
1951	98.6
1955	98.6
1959	98.9
1964	98.6
1966	97.6
1970	98.0
1974 (Feb.)	94.2*
1974 (Oct.)	93.9*
1979	95.7*
1983	93.2*
1987	93.1*
1992	93.2*

* From 1974 the Ulster Unionists were counted as separate from the Conservatives. This accounts for some decline in the percentage of seats won by the two parties

The dominance of the two parties is now very evident. The discrepancy between the percentage of votes cast and seats won, which becomes marked after 1970, is due to the unusual electoral system which Britain operates. Whatever the causes, there is no doubt that seats in the House of Commons are almost totally monopolised by the Conservative and Labour parties.

Control over the agenda and procedures of Parliament

Approximately 67 per cent of the time of the House of Commons is directly in the control of the Government or the main opposition party.

This is made up as follows:

Debates on Government Bills	34%
Government Motions	6%
Opposition Motions	6%
Money Resolutions and Estimates	9%
Addresses and Queen's Speech	2%
Others	10%

Taken from *Parliament Today* 1990, Andrew Adonis, MUP, relating to 1987–8

If we were to include Question Times, which are also dominated by the leaderships of the two big parties, the true figure approaches 80 per cent. The minor parties are limited to a few days a year for discussion of their interests in addition to the very limited opportunities their backbenchers might have to raise particular issues.

The same is true of committee work and personnel. The Liberal Democrats, Nationalists and Northern Ireland MPs are awarded individual places here and there on select and standing committees. Otherwise their influence is minimal. The agendas of committees is totally determined by the big party business managers.

The only important exceptions concern the select committees on Wales, Scotland and Northern Ireland, whose work may be influenced to some small degree by these smaller parties. Similarly with the 'Scottish Grand Committee', which is made up of MPs representing Scottish seats and discusses less controversial pieces of legislation relating only to Scotland. Here again, there is slightly enhanced minor party participation.

The story is similar in the House of Lords, even though the two main parties do not enjoy the same dominance in the holding of seats. Indeed, the control is perhaps even more marked with 61 per cent of its business accounted for by Government-sponsored Bills compared to only 34 per cent in the Commons (figures from Adonis, see above table).

Dominance of the political agenda

Much of the conduct of British political processes concerns the presentation to the electorate of a clear choice between just two competing sets of policies. Manifestations of this limited choice are to be seen in a number of circumstances.

- Elections are fought largely on the basis that there are two manifestos, presented by the only two parties which have a realistic chance of being elected. Once a party is elected, it is expected that it will seek to implement most of its programme. The Opposition, by contrast, will have no access to the decision-making process and must therefore wait its turn.
- In parliamentary debates there is a clear struggle waged between the proposals of the Government and the criticisms of the opposition, together with their alternative policies. There is rarely any question of more subtle negotiations with a larger number of options being considered. The choice between just two alternatives is maintained by the

two dominant parties. There have been a few occasions when a more pluralistic approach to problems has been adopted. The Northern Ireland question and Britain's involvement in the Bosnian civil war are two examples. Yet these are unusual. The norm is bilateral conflict.

- While Parliament itself is geared to two-party dominance, with particular stress on 'set piece' occasions such as Prime Minister's Question Time when adversarial politics reaches its height, the media also play their part. It has become their practice to present to the public the impression that there are only two choices in most of the great issues of the day. The tabloid press is particularly prone to treat politics in this simplistic way. Politicians are usually branded as 'left wing' or 'right wing', Government proposals are deemed to be wholly acceptable or wholly unacceptable, parties are to be totally supported or totally opposed. All these perspectives reinforce the 'dualist' view of the party system.

Has Britain become a one-party state?

The evidence, presented above, that Britain is a two-party state, is compelling. Yet there have emerged new theories suggesting that there is, in fact, a single-party monopoly in place. The party in question is, of course, the Conservatives.

> 'Britain's Japanese Question arose out of the Conservatives' fourth successive general election victory in April 1992. It suggested to many that competitive party politics, the hallmark of vibrant liberal democracy, had given way to a dominant party system, the post-war badge of Japanese Democracy.'
> Brendan O'Leary, *Turning Japanese* (Laurence and Wishart, 1994)

This thesis can be expanded as follows: that although there have been Labour Governments in modern times, the Conservative Party is utterly dominant and 'normally' governs. Furthermore, the political agenda is basically determined by the Conservatives, a process which is only briefly interrupted by Labour administrations. The details include:

- Since 1951, at the end of a short but dramatic period of socialist reform, the Conservative Party has governed Britain for 33 out of 44 years. Furthermore, the 11 years of Labour rule included seven years (1964–6 and 1974–9) during which times the party struggled with a tiny Commons majority, a factor which inhibited its ability to govern effectively.
- The Conservative Party won four consecutive elections between 1979 and 1992. All of them were won with comfortable majorities, including two majorities of over 100 (1983 and 1987). Furthermore, the victories of 1983 and 1992 were achieved against the background of recent economic recessions. This last observation suggests that Britain has either become fundamentally conservative in sentiment, or deeply suspicious of the Labour Party, or perhaps both.

- Possibly a cause of Conservative dominance, possibly as a result of it, the financial backing available to political parties has become increasingly biased towards the Conservatives. While Labour's traditional source of finance, the political levy on trade union members, has been drying up, largely due to a decline in union membership, the Conservatives continue to receive large donations from a wide variety of individual and corporate sources. In addition, the Conservative Party has long proved to be the more efficient routine accumulator of funds from its ordinary membership. The Liberal Democrats have a small membership and few corporate backers, thus presenting little challenge to Conservative income. A look at the income of the three main parties in 1990 illustrates this feature:

Annual income of the parties in 1990	
Conservative	£14.900 million
Labour	£6.274 million
Liberal Democrat	£1.600 million

This uneven picture (notwithstanding a decline in Conservative fortunes by 1995) has led to calls by both Labour and the Liberal Democrats for state funding of parties, as occurs in the USA, for example. The **Nolan Committee**, set up in 1995 to investigate the financial conduct of MPs and the general issue of the funding of political movements, is also expected to recommend a more ordered system.

- Since 1951 political policy making has been dominated by the Conservative Party. It was they who introduced Keynesian methods of economic management in the 1950s and then changed to monetarist techniques in the 1980s. Current laissez-faire, non-interventionist politics are a Conservative development. Industrial relations, law and order, the tax system, the operation of the Welfare State, the National Health Service and the education system have all undergone major reform presided over by Conservative administrations. There have, of course, been a few occasions when Labour has led the way such as the expansion of higher education in the 1960s and 1970s, a wide range of employment developments such as protection from unfair dismissal, health and safety measures and equal pay for women. But these have been the exceptions, not the rule. While the Britain of the 1950s may have been shaped by Labour policies, that of the 1990s is almost wholly the result of Conservative reforms.

Is Britain a multi-party state?

The arguments which point to Britain being either a two-party duality or a single-party monopoly are very strong. Yet there are two senses in which a case could be made for it being a multi-party system which do not appear immediately obvious.

First, it can be argued that political allegiance in Britain is more evenly divided among three parties in England and four parties in Scotland. (Northern Ireland, having its own party system, must be treated as a special case from which generalisations about the rest of Britain cannot be drawn.) This reality is disguised by the nature of the Constitution and the political system. Most obviously, the electoral system undervalues the electoral support for those parties with dispersed support, especially the Liberal Democrats. This is translated into the domination of Parliament by the two parties and the illusion, underpinned by the media, that the only policy issues in which the electorate are interested are presented by the two largest parties. Thus, in terms of **true** popular opinion and allegiance, more than two parties are significant.

Secondly, there are regions in Britain where the two-party hegemony has been broken by smaller parties, while at local government level there is no question that multi-party politics is now firmly established. Further details are as follows:

Smaller parties' general election successes

Since 1974 smaller parties have been consistently successful in attracting significant numbers of votes. The data below clearly illustrate this:

Election Year	Liberal % of vote**	% Scottish Nationalist*	% Welsh Nationalist
1974 (Feb.)	19.3	21.9	10.7
1974 (Oct.)	18.3	30.4	11.1
1979	13.8	17.3	8.1
1983	25.4	11.8	7.8
1987	22.6	14.0	7.3
1992	17.8	21.5	8.8

* Percentages of vote only in Scotland and Wales respectively
** Liberal/Social Democrat Alliance in 1983 and 1987. Liberal Democrats in 1992

We can see from the table above that Liberals and their associates have done consistently well and Scottish nationalists even better. The Welsh nationalist vote remains relatively small, but is at least a significant factor in Welsh politics, especially in pockets of nationalist sentiment (four seats were won there!) In addition, there are growing signs in the 1990s that Liberal Democrat support is becoming concentrated and established in the south-west of England.

Thus we are presented with a picture of consistently solid support for smaller parties at parliamentary elections and in three regions – Scotland, Wales and south-west England – where three or four parties are in a genuine competition for poll success. An additional analysis is provided by Professor **Ivor Crewe**, who suggests that England now exhibits two separate two-party systems. In the north and Midlands the contest is between Labour and the Conservatives, while in the south and south-west it is Tories and Liberal Democrats.

Local elections

It has always been true that the two-party domination of politics has been weaker at local level than it has been at Westminster. In recent years, however, this trend has become more marked. The data below show how evenly spread support for at least three parties has been in recent **county council elections**.

Election Year	% Vote Cons.	% Vote Labour	% Vote Lib. Dem.	% Vote Others
1985	38.4	30.0	27.9	3.7
1989	42.2	31.1	20.2	6.5
1993	34.0	32.0	27.0	7.0

The distribution of council seats is remarkably similar to that of votes shown above. Furthermore, of the thirty-nine county councils in England and Wales, twenty-six were without an overall majority for a single party. In other words, a significant majority of these councils have three or more party systems. This is indeed a very different situation from that found in the House of Commons. More remarkably, in the 1995 local polling, the Liberal Democrats secured the election of more councillors than the Conservatives, thus replacing them in second place behind Labour in the control of town halls.

Conclusion

The evidence pointing to the existence of a multi-party system is certainly less convincing than that which underpins the 'two-party' or 'single-party' theses. In particular, it must be remembered that it is seats in the House of Commons which carry most political power in Britain and it is here that the two parties, perhaps just one party, dominate. However 'unfair' we may consider the electoral system to be, there is no immediate prospect of reform so the only important question is: who wins the seats?

We must also be cautious in drawing too many conclusions from recent successes by smaller parties. This success is, in part, due to the collapse of support for the Labour Party in the 1980s. Should Labour recover – and there are signs that it might well enjoy a revival in its fortunes – the smaller parties may well find themselves 'squeezed out' again. Two-party hegemony could certainly return in the future.

Arguments concerning the party system		
Two-party system	One-party dominance	Multi-party system
Labour and Conservative Parties have dominated general election voting since 1945	Conservatives have won the vast majority of elections since 1945	Smaller parties have won significant votes since 1970 but these have not been translated into many Commons seats
The two parties win the majority of seats in the House of Commons	They have won four successive elections between 1979–92	There is significant regional support for smaller parties
The agenda and procedures of Parliament are controlled by two parties	Conservatives have significantly more finance than other parties	Small parties are doing increasingly well in local government elections
The policy agenda is dominated by the two bigger parties	Since 1951 Conservatives have dominated policy making	A large number of local authorities now have multi-party systems

The Labour Party

Origins and brief history

Early days

In 1900 the **Labour Representation Committee (LRC)** was formed in order to campaign for the election of Members of Parliament who could represent the interests of the trade unions in particular and the working classes in general. It was not, strictly speaking, a political party, but rather an action committee. It was the result of a major initiative by a number of different sections of the working-class political movement. The unions were the major element, but there were other groups involved. Radical socialists from the **Independent Labour Party (ILP)**, which had already been in existence for several years, and the **Social Democratic Federation** had come to the conclusion that parliamentary representation was necessary to further working-class aims. The more moderate **Fabian Society** and the **Co-operative movement** lent weight to the Committee which was led by the legendary socialist figure, **Keir Hardie**.

By **1906** it had become clear that, in order to achieve long-term success, the Committee should transform itself into a full-blown political party with a mass membership to add to its union representatives. Thus the **Labour Party** was founded in that year. Three aspects of these early years are instructive and relevant. First, it was clear from the outset that the party was a federation of groupings from a variety of socialist traditions, and that it encompassed a wide range of philosophies from both radical and moderate wings of the whole movement. Secondly, it was formed **outside** Parliament. Thus its most important institutions are not parliamentary, but are external party organs. This has created constant tension between those parts of the party which are inside and those which are outside Westminster. Thirdly, the influence of trade unions existed from the very beginning, when they were the dominant force. Their central position remained crucial throughout the twentieth century.

Growth and consolidation

Support for Labour grew slowly and steadily, with forty candidates elected in 1910. The Constitution of the party was drawn up in 1918. This asserted its aims and objectives, including the notorious Clause IV which committed the party to common ownership of industry and commerce. It also set up the organisation and procedures of the party, a system which endured largely unaltered until 1981.

Some Labour members chose to join the Lloyd George coalition in 1918–22 and thereafter the party spent most of its time in coalition with other parties, apart from the period 1922–31. In 1929 the party achieved a landmark when, in the election of that year, it won more seats than any other party (288 out of 615). However, Labour could still not form a majority government on its own.

Compromise and controversy

In the 1930s, during the dual crises of the Great Depression and the rise of fascism, the party became severely split. Broadly, the controversies included: whether to co-operate with the National Coalition Governments of 1931–45 which were Conservative-dominated (ultimately Labour lost its first Prime Minister, **Ramsay MacDonald**, as their leader over this issue); whether to accept a policy of appeasement with Hitler (**George Lansbury**, leader from 1932–5, was an avowed pacifist); and what was to be the future form of common ownership of industry if and when a future Labour Government was elected. The onset of World War Two brought these issues to an end and real planning for the future could begin.

The socialist reforms, 1940–51

Senior members of the party played a leading role on the domestic front during the war years. Party leader **Clement Attlee** (effectively Deputy Prime Minister), **Herbert Morrison** (Home Secretary) and, above all, **Ernest Bevin** (Labour and National Supply) largely governed the country while Churchill and the leading Conservatives ran the war. At the same time as these Labour members were acting as key ministers, they were also planning for the future. Thus the **Beveridge Report**, setting out the nature of the future Welfare State, was produced in 1942 with much input from the Labour Party. A system of free secondary education for all was introduced through the **1944 Education Act** (introduced by R.A. Butler, a leading Conservative, but inspired by Labour). Above all, the success of national control and planning of production and distribution which had to be introduced for war purposes, convinced the party and much of the electorate that a limited form of socialist planning was desirable after the war.

The landslide Labour election victory of 1945 led to six years of dramatic socialist reforms. A number of large industries were nationalised and local government social and personal services, including housing, were extended. The Welfare State and the National Health Service were introduced among a host of lesser measures.

Consensus politics

After the rush of reforms of 1945–51, Labour spent most of the years from 1951 until 1974 in opposition. Apart from the Wilson Governments of 1964–70 – when technological advances, improvements in the legal and economic status of women and racial minorities, employment protection for workers and the growth of higher education were Labour's main achievements – Labour could only watch while Conservative Governments avoided major political controversies by governing Britain on the basis of consensus. Consensus politics ensured the adoption of broadly agreed and moderate policies which consolidated and built on the reforms of the 1940s. Radical changes were avoided while sound management of the mixed economy and the Welfare State were claimed, with invariable electoral success for the Conservatives.

Lurch to the Left Successive election defeats in 1979 and 1983, together with the clear shift to the 'New Right' neo-liberal policies by the Thatcher-led Conservatives, led to a distinct movement to the left within the Labour Party. A radical leader, **Michael Foot**, was elected in 1980, an internal reorganisation of the party took place in 1981 giving more influence to the traditionally left-wing grass roots membership, and a number of 'extremist' policies were adopted. These were dark days for Labour. Its proportion of the popular vote fell to 27.6 per cent in 1983 and was still at only 30.9 per cent in 1987. A splinter group broke from the party in 1981, naming itself the **Social Democrat Party** and claiming to espouse the true, traditional philosophies of the modern Labour movement. For a few years it threatened, in combination with the Liberal Party, to replace Labour as the main opposition party.

The 1984 election of **Neil Kinnock** to replace Foot was the beginning of the party's long climb back to moderation and hope of future electoral success.

Labour in the 1990s Three successive leaders of the party – Kinnock, **John Smith** (1992–4) and **Tony Blair** (1994–) have brought Labour back to a less radical position and, many believe, have made it electable again. In particular, the **Policy Review** of 1989–9, which Kinnock ordered, set the agenda for Labour's new philosophy. It has been Blair's successful battle to revise Clause IV of the party Constitution which ultimately symbolises Labour's transformation. Formerly, Clause IV committed the party to state owner-ship and control of industry, distribution and finance. By replacing it in 1995 with a more general commitment to equality of opportunity, social justice and the search for maximum employment opportunities, Blair brought to a climax the changes proposed by his two predecessors. The party's stance on policy issues is shown below.

Labour policies

The basic beliefs and philosophies behind the current Labour Party's poli-cies should be viewed in terms of the sections on social democracy and democratic socialism, described in Unit 3. It should also be noted that true policy, whichever the party in question, can only be fully established when election manifestos have been produced and when programmes have been unfurled before Parliament. Nevertheless, general intentions can be established. The schedule shown below is not exhaustive and must, by the very nature of political change, be subject to constant alter-ation. Yet it does indicate the main thrusts of Labour policy in the 1990s.

Policy area	Labour Party policy (early 1995)
Economic Control	Largely pragmatic
Welfare	Committed to a major overhaul of the welfare system based on the Borrie Report of 1994 (Commission on Social Justice). Proposals include a guaranteed minimum state pension, encouragement to all to take out a second, private pension, increased child benefit but this to be taxable for the better off, increased help for lone parents, restoration of reasonable levels of family support. Reform of family welfare to ensure a fairer system.
Employment	Restoration of full employment, or at least greater employment opportunities are a major goal. Subsidies to employers to take on the long-term unemployed. The imposition of a National Minimum Wage. Attempts to establish norms of wage increases each year through regular tripartite discussions between government, unions and employers.
Taxation	An increased top income tax rate for the well off. More taxation on gifts and inheritance. A new lower tax band for the less well off. Possibly more taxation on property and corporate incomes.
Education	Nursery education available for all. More spending on schools. Abolition of the 'Assisted Places Scheme'. Possibly increased tax on private education. More higher education places available, but possibly greater use made of student loan system. Reform of the exam system to broaden the scope of A levels.
Health	Reversal of NHS reforms with a return to the original system. More spending on health. Some charges for health care, but only for those able to pay.
Housing	Vast increases of spending on house building. Greater funds and incentives to local authorities and housing associations to create homes.
Industry	Most privatised industries will remain in the private sector, but government will maintain statutory controls over large industries and possibly purchase large shareholdings to maintain influence. Possibly re-nationalisation of water and railways. Wide range of grants and subsidies available for firms to set up in deprived areas.
Europe	Broad support for all the long-term objectives of the EU. Britain to sign the Social Chapter to improve employment protection, working conditions, health and safety at work, wages, etc. Open-minded on a single European currency and economic integration.
The Constitution	Reform of the House of Lords (abolition of hereditary peers' voting rights). Increased powers and responsibilities and freedom for local government. Probable devolution of power to Scotland and Wales.
Foreign Affairs/Defence	Largely pragmatic.
Law and Order	Few very specific proposals but concentration on the social causes of crime. Reliance on less unemployment and better education to reduce youth crime. Return of the prison system totally to public ownership.
Others	Schemes for employment of the young in Community Work Schemes. Reform of the Child Support Agency. Transport policy to favour rail over private motoring. Further progress towards equal pay for women. A referendum to be held on the possibility of Proportional Representation.

Labour Party factions

The Labour Party, from its very inception, has always been a party of factions and tendencies. This has largely been the result of the number of different varieties of socialism which have always flourished. However, since the mid-1980s there has been a steady drift towards unification within the party. The groups described below are, therefore, very much minorities in the 1990s.

Militant Tendency

This clandestine group appeared in the 1970s, largely within the Young Socialists (Labour's youth wing). It is, or was (since it is not clear whether it has significant membership today) a communist group operating within the Labour Party. Confined chiefly to local government circles, it emerged as a key element in the radical administrations of Liverpool and some London boroughs in the 1980s. Named after the left-wing newspaper *Militant*, its membership remained largely secret until most of its supporters were flushed out by Neil Kinnock. The leader of Liverpool Council, **Derek Hatton**, and MPs **Dave Nellist** and **Terry Fields**, were all ousted. The decline of Militant marked the effective end of communist influence which had dogged the party throughout the century.

Tribune Group

Another, more open and established Labour newspaper is *Tribune*. This paper has campaigned for the retention of genuine socialist traditions within the party. It supported principles such as that of common ownership of production, trade union power, nationalisation of land and banks, extensions of the welfare system and a more pacifist approach to foreign policy and defence. Those who considered themselves on the radical socialist wing of the party thus became known as 'Tribunites' and MPs formed the Tribune Group. During the 1980s, the Group became disenchanted by the failure of the Left to capture popular support and it has moved steadily towards the centre of the party. It is now small and no longer has much significance.

Campaign Group

This faction took over from the Tribunites, seizing the mantle of true socialism which had been dropped by Tribune. Its main concerns still include a return to socialist values, but it is also radical in its support for increased influence in the party for ordinary grass roots members. Indeed, the Campaign Group is generally committed to extensions of democratic principles, both within the party and in the wider political system. By 1995 membership among MPs had fallen to about thirty. Its leading member is **Tony Benn**.

Manifesto Group

Frustrated by the drift to the Left of the party in the 1970s and 1980s, a large group of moderate MPs formed the Manifesto Group, committed to moderate policies which could attract the support of the majority of the general public. They believed that the party's manifesto should make it electable, rather than reflecting purely socialist ideas as had occurred in the 1980s. By 1990 this group had become dominant in the party, guiding its movement towards the centre of the political spectrum.

In early 1996 a small rump of the militant left wing of the party, led by miners' President Arthur Scargill, felt that they could no longer operate within the 'New Labour' party. They founded a new party, the Socialist Labour Party, a development which has threatened to remove, once and for all, the coherent left-wing element in Labour.

Labour Party organisation

The main structure of the party is shown below:

- **The Annual Conference** is made up of delegates from trade unions and constituency parties, MPs, MEPS, representatives from co-operative societies and other socialist societies. Voting is dominated by trade union delegates, who account for 70 per cent of total representation (only reduced from 90 per cent in 1995).

  It is the 'sovereign body' of the party which has ultimate power over decisions. However, its resolutions, while being party policy, do not bind the leadership either to placing those policies in the election manifesto or adopting them as government policy if the party should win power.

  The Conference elects the National Executive Committee of the Party.

1994 Labour Party Conference

- **The National Executive Committee (NEC)**, elected annually at Conference, contains twelve members elected by unions, five by constituency parties and one by socialist associations. In addition, the NEC must include at least five women. Four officers are automatically members – the party Treasurer, Chair of the Young Socialists, party leader and Deputy leader. It therefore represents the broad range of the party membership.

  Its role is to determine party policy on the advice of the Conference and under the strong influence of the party leader. Before elections it writes the party manifesto, although it is accepted that the leader has a veto over individual items.

  The NEC also handles party discipline and approves candidates to be chosen by constituency parties.

- **The Constituency Labour Parties (CLPs)** contain the grass roots members of the party. The CLPs discuss their attitude to policy and may propose resolutions at the Conference. They also send delegates to that Conference and often instruct those delegates on how to vote on each issue. In each constituency the General Management Committee chooses candidates for election to Parliament. Smaller committees in each ward (sub-division of the constituency) choose candidates for local government office.

- **Leader and deputy leader.** Both are elected by a ballot of union members, constituency members and MPs. The weighting given to each of these groups is one-third.

  The roles of the leader and deputy leader are ill-defined but in practice they are the leading figures in policy making, with special control over the election manifesto. Clearly, too, if the party wins power they become the two leading members of the government itself and so gain considerable authority. In particular, a Labour Prime Minister chooses his Cabinet and other ministers, whereas as mere Leader of the Opposition he does not choose the Shadow Cabinet (see below).

- **Parliamentary Labour Party (PLP).** Made up of all Labour MPs, the PLP attempts to exert much influence over policy, especially when Labour is in power. It is divided into a number of policy committees and meets regularly to make its general views known to the leadership.

- **Shadow Cabinet.** Of course this only exists when Labour is in opposition. Its membership of twelve (plus the leader and his deputy) is elected by the MPs annually, but the leader may add members and decides for which policy area each shall be spokesperson. It is a guide as to who is likely to be in a future Labour Government, but no guarantee since, once in office, the leader alone appoints the Cabinet. The Shadow Cabinet meets regularly to discuss and arrange parliamentary business for the Opposition, determining tactics, main speakers in debates and general policy lines. However, its role in long-term policy making is less significant.

Power in the Labour Party

As we can see above, Labour has a wide and complex structure. Traditionally power and influence have been dispersed throughout the party, avoiding the possibility of too much concentration of power in one place. The different sections of the party balance each other out in terms of influence, with particular emphasis on serving the interests of union and constituency members. Since 1981, however, distinct changes in the distribution of power have taken place. These, together with other key features, are described below:

- It must be stressed that, when Labour gains government office, its leader becomes Prime Minister so that there is a marked shift in power towards the leader. He then has enormous powers of patronage, carries the fate of the Government very much in his own hands, and becomes chief policy maker (see Unit 8).
- Before 1981 the leader was elected by MPs alone. At that time, however, a new procedure was introduced. Election was to be by the whole party, with 40 per cent of the votes being carried by trade union leaders. It was assumed and feared in some quarters that this would lead to the election of more radical leaders, but this has not occurred as union leaders have proved to be increasingly moderate.

- In 1994 the party adopted further reforms proposed by John Smith, who died before they could be implemented. In particular, the trade union 'block vote' was abolished. The block vote meant that union leaders could vote, at Conference and in leadership elections, on behalf of **all** their members. Under a system of 'One Member One Vote' (OMOV) each member of the party votes separately both for the leader and for parliamentary candidates. At Conference, meanwhile, each union delegate is free to vote as he wishes. Block delegate voting is now outlawed. This has been seen as a major step forward in internal democratisation of the party. The following year the 'weighting' of union votes at Conference was also reduced from 90 per cent to 70 per cent.
- It used to be the case that the Annual Conference could force policies onto the parliamentary leadership. In the 1980s, for example, the party had to accept nuclear disarmament as a policy when it was clear that this would be unpopular in electoral terms. By the 1990s, however, it has become accepted that, while Conference may embarrass the leadership, it cannot really force it to accept policies which it cannot present to Parliament or the electorate. This was demonstrated in 1994 when a resolution to retain Clause IV was passed after leader Tony Blair had made it clear he wished to reform it. What would, in the past, have been a major internal crisis for the party, proved to be a minor difficulty soon to be resolved. In 1995 Blair was able to force the revision of Clause IV through a special conference.
- It is certainly true that Labour is more internally democratic than the Conservative Party. The Labour leader is not as powerful as his Tory counterpart and he is constrained by a number of other influential bodies in the party. Yet there has been a shift in the distribution of power towards the leader and his parliamentary colleagues. The desperate need to 'stop the rot' and win a general election has gone a considerable way to force such changes upon the party's membership. Following the Clause IV revision in the spring of 1995, further internal reforms are promised by Tony Blair to modernise and democratise the party further.

Summary of Labour Party internal reforms in the 1990s

1. The union block vote was abolished inside constituency parties when selecting candidates for parliamentary and council elections, also at Annual Conference, special conferences and in NEC or leadership elections. Each individual union member's vote is counted separately, instead of being cast on his behalf by a union delegate.
2. All constituency party members now have a say in the selection of parliamentary and council election candidates.
3. The proportion of weighting given to union votes in leadership elections was reduced from 40 per cent to one third.
4. The weighting of total union voting at Annual Conference was reduced from 90 per cent to 70 per cent.
5. Clause IV was revised from a commitment to public ownership of industry to a broader statement of aims concerning social justice, equality of opportunity and reduced unemployment.

The Conservative Party

Brief history

Origins

Unlike Labour there is no specific starting point for the Conservative Party. Its appearance as a coherent group in Parliament was possibly first evident in the 1830s when Robert Peel gathered around him a group of MPs and peers who had opposed the economic, social and political reforms of the time, but who were prepared to accept them in the interests of the stability and unity of the nation.

However, it was Disraeli in the 1870s and 1880s who actually created a political party in the modern sense of the word. Although it was still a party rooted in the House of Commons, there now began the development of Conservative Associations up and down the country comprising leading local citizens who wished to ensure the election of Conservative MPs and to sustain them in Parliament. The philosophies of this group were to unite the nation by accepting social and political reforms, to support the Empire and the nation, to oppose Irish independence and to uphold traditions.

Wilderness years

After Disraeli the reformers among the Conservatives largely deserted the party in favour of Gladstone's new Liberal Party. The rest of the party soon lapsed into a reactionary stance, opposing the rush of reforms which were led by Gladstone. As a consequence, the Conservatives enjoyed only brief periods of government office. Between 1902 and 1922 there was no Conservative Government, with only a progressive section of the party joining Liberal coalitions. Conservatives could only attract about one-third of the working-class vote and a minority of middle-class support, so electoral success was difficult to achieve.

Recovery and protectionism

After the period of extensive reform and progress over which the Liberal Party had presided in the first twenty years of the twentieth century, the Conservatives were able to present themselves as the party of consolidation and stability. With the decline of the Liberal Party and before Labour was able to mobilise enough support to form its own government, the party dominated the political scene through to the 1940s.

The Conservatives governed on the basis of sound public finance, protectionist economics and reliance upon the Empire for economic prosperity. Led by the non-interventionist **Stanley Baldwin** (Prime Minister 1923–4, 1924–9, 1935–7), the party commanded widespread support even during the dark days of the Great Depression. Above all, Conservatism was seen as representing stability while the other parties suggested upheaval and uncertainty. Baldwin himself represented this sense of security under the Tories.

Consensus and corporatism

After the shock of election defeat in 1945, the Conservatives had to take stock of the socialist reforms which were then in full swing. It was the moderates and reformers, led by **Anthony Eden** (Prime Minister 1955–7), **R.A. Butler** and **Harold Macmillan** (Prime Minister 1957–63), who led the party into the consensus era of politics. They accepted the new reforms and campaigned on the grounds that Conservatives were the best party to build on and to manage the new age of the mixed economy and the

Welfare State. Macmillan in particular recognised that there was general agreement about the nature of the reforms so there was no future for the Conservatives if they were to oppose them.

In addition, Butler and Macmillan recognised that the country should be governed in consultation with the representatives of both employers and trade unions. Thus, steady growth and progress, sound economic management and constant consultation with the major interests in society – a form of politics known as 'corporatism' – were adopted with great success.

Selsdon Man and Thatcherism

In the late 1960s a group of prominent Conservatives met at Selsdon Park in Surrey to map out a new form of Conservatism. This group, known as 'Selsdon Man', was concerned that the enormous power of the state, excessively high taxation and the destructive power of trade unions were hindering Britain's economic progress. The first signs of economic stagnation were becoming apparent. They recommended a great reduction of state interference in industry and the economy, large-scale tax reductions, restoration of free markets and curbs on union power.

They persuaded party leader **Edward Heath** (Prime Minister 1970–4) to adopt their position and reforms were commenced in 1970. A succession of economic crises brought these changes to a sudden halt, but this new kind of neo-liberalism had taken hold in the party. When **Margaret Thatcher** was elected in 1979, she revealed herself as a convert to this 'New Right' form of Conservatism as it was becoming known. The next decade saw a transformation in British economic and social life as dramatic as that of 1945–51. It was a decade of privatisation, reductions in personal and corporate taxes, union reform, deregulation of industry and reductions in local government functions. At the same time opposition to European integration became an important feature of the party. By the 1990s, after Thatcher, the question for the party was whether to continue with the process begun by the New Right, or to institute a period of consolidation.

Conservative policies

The divisions within the Conservative Party which have re-emerged in the 1990s make it difficult to establish the future direction of policy. The schedule below describes the 'central' and most generally accepted aspects of party policy. However, there are important variations of many of them which attract significant support within the party. As with the Labour Party, the following descriptions of Conservative policy should be read in conjunction with the analyses of the three types of Conservatism in Unit 3.

Policy area	Conservative Party policy (early 1995)
Economic Control	Largely monetarist, that is, concentrating on minimal interference, confined largely to sound money (i.e. money supply control), inflation and public expenditure control.
Welfare	Scaling down of welfare benefits where possible. Unemployed to prove they are seeking work in return for benefit. No benefits for school-leavers if training is available. Welfare to be only a 'safety net'.
Employment	Unemployment to find its own natural level. Little active policy to create jobs. Instead, sound money and economic policy to increase confidence and keep wages down, so that employment picks up naturally.
Taxation	Continuing shift of tax burden away from income and corporate taxation towards forms of indirect taxes on expenditure. Commitment to further income tax cuts when possible.
Education	Extension of nursery education. Encouragement for schools to opt out of local authority control. Commitment to raising teaching standards through National Curriculum and better teaching methods. Higher education students to contribute more to their own education through loans.
Health	Commitment to further extension of the internal market in the Health Service. Drive for more efficiency in the NHS.
Housing	Further incentives for the private housing and private rented sector.
Industry	Incentives for foreign firms to set up in areas of high unemployment. Deregulation of industry wherever possible. Little direct aid to industry. Further privatisations planned including coal, railways, possibly the Post Office.
Europe	General lack of enthusiasm. Opposition to a future single European currency or to greater integration. Opposition to European Social Chapter. Support for widening of the EU to include more members. Opposition to European Defence Force and ambivalent about common European foreign policy.
The Constitution	Committed to preserve current arrangements. No devolution of power to Scotland and Wales.
Defence	Reduced defence commitment, but only very cautious rundown of forces.
Foreign affairs	Still committed to alliance with the USA, but cautiously willing to accept European policy on some issues. However, still attempting to pursue independent policy lines where possible.
Law and order	Firm line on crime. Stiffer penalties for criminals, especially young offenders. Further privatisation of prisons. Encouragement of community anti-crime schemes. Firmer laws against public disorders, trespassing, squatting, demonstrations.
Others	Heavily committed to a peaceful settlement in Northern Ireland. No specific transport policy, but largely committed to support for private motoring.

Variations The principle challenge to the policies described above comes from the so-called neo-liberal 'right wing', the enthusiastic supporters of the more extreme aspects of the ideology of Margaret Thatcher and her followers. This group, led by powerful Cabinet ministers such as **Peter Lilley**,

Michael Portillo and **John Redwood**, wish to see severe cuts in public expenditure, tax cuts as soon and as deep as possible, drastic scaling down of welfare benefits, as much privatisation as can be achieved and further deregulation of industry. Broadly, they support the maximum degree of 'disengagement' of the state from economic and social affairs as possible.

Overlapping these right-wingers are the 'Euro-sceptics', who wish to see Britain completely out of the European Union, or at least taking a minimum role in its affairs. This group also have representatives in the Cabinet, including **Michael Portillo.**

Those from a purer liberal tradition believe that the Thatcher reforms went too far or at least have gone far enough. They now wish to see consolidation of the 'achievements' of the 1980s and 1990s. They oppose further privatisation or scaling down of the Welfare State. They wish to see more expenditure on health and education, more concern with unemployment and poverty and are worried by the continuing decline of British manufacturing. For them, the state must continue to intervene where social and industrial problems are proving stubborn. Prominent exponents of this moderate form of Conservatism are **Michael Heseltine** and **Kenneth Clarke**.

John Major's role has been to attempt to unite these disparate forces within the party, a task he carried out until 1995 with some success since there were no violent splits within the Cabinet, though the Conservative back-benches are far from united. However, this was at the cost of much unpopularity in the country.

Conservative factions

The Tory Reform Group

The Tory Reform Group is a small group of MPs who are committed to liberal, 'one-nation Tory' policies which would involve the state in a more caring role in the social, economic and industrial fields. They oppose the attacks on the welfare system and support more direct intervention to reduce unemployment and poverty. During the Thatcher years such Conservatives were known as 'wets' and were forced into a minority position which they still hold. It remains an unfashionable position to be in within the party, especially after its founder, **Peter Walker**, retired from active policies.

The Bruges Group

This faction takes its name from a speech made by Margaret Thatcher in Bruges, Belgium, in 1988. In it she made clear her violent opposition to extensions in the power of the European Union, in particular the excessive bureaucracy and regulation coming out of Brussels. The group is, thus, the home for those who are totally or partially opposed to Britain's active membership in the EU.

Monday Club

This group of ultra right-wing, British nationalist Conservatives has attracted much opposition for its suspected links with neo-Nazism. The group takes an extremely hard line on law and order, is opposed to most forms of social reform and takes a traditional line on family values and morality. It is also intensely nationalistic, opposing the European Union and promoting a wider role for Britain in world affairs. It opposes immigration and supports the voluntary repatriation of ethnic minority members. Although its membership in Parliament is small, it is an increasingly influential tendency in the party.

Salisbury Group This, together with a number of other similar factions, is a vehicle for the extreme neo-liberal views described above as the 'extreme right-wing tendency'. The *Salisbury Review* is a periodical which promotes such a philosophy. Its contributors include many leading members of the party.

Conservative Way Forward Overlapping the Salisbury Group, this faction was formed around former close associates of Margaret Thatcher after her downfall. It includes **Cecil Parkinson** and **Norman Tebbit** and wished to see the party continue the Thatcherite reforms and not be tempted to give way to more cautious sentiments. Although it contains a number of influential former ministers and has the backing of Baroness Thatcher herself, it is not particularly well supported among younger, ambitious MPs.

Macleod Group This group was named after Iain Macleod, a Conservative minister in the 1960s and 1970s, who was considered to be one of the most important moderate 'one-nation' Tories of his day. In 1995–6 this group became a significant element in the left–right split which emerged in the party. The Macleod Group were anxious to halt the rightward drift which they believed was the cause of the party's unpopularity at that time. Though small, its influence became significant as the Conservative majority in the Commons dwindled.

Conservative Party organisation

- **The leader** is elected by MPs only. As such he is very much a parliamentary leader. However, it is normally the case that the rest of the party rallies round the choice of their parliamentary colleagues. He is very much chief policy maker and, if he possesses sufficient authority and ambition, can lead the party in the direction he desires. He has complete power of appointment of the parliamentary front-bench, whether or not the party is in power. He will normally write the whole election manifesto, though in practice senior colleagues are usually consulted. In many ways the position of Conservative leader varies greatly from that of a Labour leader. In the latter case, he has more power when the party is in government. A Conservative leader, by contrast, loses some power in office since the Cabinet can prove a greater check to his power than can parliamentary colleagues who do not hold ministerial office.
- **The 1922 Committee** is the collective title of all Conservative back-bench MPs. This semi-formal organisation has an influential chairman and meets on a regular basis, often questioning Conservative Prime Ministers or lesser ministers over policy and tactics. Margaret Thatcher, in particular, learned that it pays a leader to inform and consult with the 1922 Committee as they have the power to remove him or her. Thatcher (1990), Heath (1975) and Home (1965) were all ousted by discontented MPs. MPs are also divided into a number of policy committees which seek to influence the leadership, though ultimately it is only influence which they possess and not power itself.
- **Party Headquarters** comprises both the administrative organisation of the party, or **Central Office**, and its **Research Department**. It is headed by the influential **Party Chairman**. The role of the Chairman and his staff is to organise the selection of a short list of possible parliamentary candidates, to maintain discipline and to handle party publicity and image. As the Conservative Party relies heavily upon its public face, the activities of Central Office become especially important. The Research Department used to have a good deal of influence over the

**Conservative Party
Conference 1991**

leadership, but Margaret Thatcher's preference for external advice
moved it into the background.

- **Conservative Associations** comprise the grass roots members of the
  party. There is an Association in each parliamentary constituency.
  Strictly speaking they are not part of the main organisation of the party
  itself, but are local organisations which exist to support the real party
  in Parliament. Although they send delegates to the annual conference,
  they do not expect to influence policy a great deal. In the main their
  role is to raise finance, select candidates for office from a list presented
  by Headquarters and organise electoral support.

- **Annual Conference** is really the regular meeting of the **Union of Conservative Associations**. Ministers (mere front-bench MPs if the party
  is in opposition), including the Prime Minister, are invited to speak but
  do not have an automatic right to do so. Since this is not really a
  gathering of the party itself, but only its local support groups, Conference has no decision making power. Instead it has a number of lesser
  functions. It is a public relations exercise to demonstrate unity and
  purpose, designed to transmit the general 'mood' of supporters to the
  leadership, and it is a rally of the faithful, an exercise in morale-
  boosting and a time to inspire. There have been occasions when it has
  sought to shift party policy in a particular direction. In the 1990s, for
  example, strong anti-European and pro-authoritarian sentiments have
  been expressed at Conference.

> *'It is a Conservative article of faith that splits spell electoral
> suicide, which is why the party traditionally conducts its
> quarrels in private or in code. Voters expect Labour, not the
> Conservatives, to brawl in public.'*
> Ivor Crewe in *The Major Effect* (Macmillan, 1995)

Power in the Conservative Party

The Conservative Party is very much a 'top-down' party, with power concentrated in its central leadership. It is also predominantly a parliamentary party, a reflection of its origins as well as its belief that its natural position is in government. The ordinary grass-roots members have relatively little influence while the members of Parliament do not expect to exert very much control unless a particularly controversial issue rises. While in the Labour Party the financial backing of trade unions is matched by an important status in the party organisation, the Conservatives' corporate backers – a number of large private companies – do not enjoy such a privileged position. Having said this, the influence of these companies on the party is difficult to assess.

As we have seen, the position of the leader himself can be somewhat ambiguous. On the one hand, he has great powers of patronage and of policy formulation. On the other, MPs have shown themselves not averse to removing a leader who they feel is damaging the fortunes of the party. The halcyon days of Margaret Thatcher's leadership, from 1982 to 1989, indicate the enormous potential power of the leader. By contrast, the less secure leadership of John Major demonstrates the potential power of the parliamentary party and determined groups within it.

The Liberal Democrat Party

Brief history

The modern Liberal Party formed itself into a formal organisation under **Gladstone** in the 1870s. It was a coalition of former Whigs, reformist Tories, Radicals and even some quasi-socialists. Under Gladstone's dynamic leadership they soon came to dominate the political scene. Backed by a network of local party organisations and effective discipline in Parliament, they held power for most of the years between 1880 and 1922, either alone or in coalition with others.

These forty or so years saw the liberals lead the way in reforming the machinery of government, including the civil service, extending the franchise to women, granting freedom to Ireland, establishing education for all, pensions, municipal housing and a wide variety of other local authority services. Both they and the Conservatives were pledged to improving the condition of the people, but it was the Liberals who held most of the power to achieve these goals.

This success came to a rather abrupt end in the early 1920s. The growing Labour movement and a revived Conservative Party began to squeeze the Liberal vote. The reforming stance of the party was taken over by Labour, while the Conservatives stood for stability at a time of great economic uncertainty. There now began a steady decline in support for the Liberals.

The darkest days for the party occurred after World War Two. By 1951 they had won only 2.5 per cent of the popular vote and six seats in the House of Commons. It was even feared that the party might go out of existence.

In the 1970s, however, support for the major parties began to wane. General dissatisfaction with the performance of both major parties set in. The Liberals, together with Scottish and Welsh Nationalists, cashed in. Votes and seats won began to grow slowly but surely.

When the Social Democrat Party broke from Labour in 1981, advocating moderate, centrist policies, it was clear that the new party bore a considerable resemblance to the Liberals. The two leaders, **David Steel** for the Liberals and **Roy Jenkins** for the SDP, reached an agreement known as the **Alliance** which was to fight the forthcoming election along a broadly common front. In 1983 the Alliance won 25 per cent of the votes and 23 seats in the Commons. Despite a number of crises in the relationship, the Alliance staggered on to the 1987 election where it did almost as well as it had four years earlier. However, the hoped-for breakthrough to challenge the hegemony of the two main parties had not occurred. Faced with internal dissension, the two parties merged to form the Social and Liberal Democratic Party. The smaller Liberal and Social Democrat Parties staggered on, supported by a small number of enthusiasts, but these 'rumps' soon passed into political oblivion.

The SLD Party soon dropped its 'Social' tag in order to distance itself from any links with former socialists. It became the Liberal Democrat Party, which it still is today. Despite the name change it can be said that the Liberal Democrats are the genuine heirs to the former Liberal Party. In the 1990s support appeared to have stabilised at between 15 and 20 per cent of the electorate, with occasional dramatic victories at by-elections where sometimes huge Conservative majorities have been overturned.

Liberal Democrat policies

It should be stressed at the outset that **Paddy Ashdown**, the Liberal Democrat leader since 1988, has accepted that the party should not be driven solely by rigid ideology, but should be willing to be pragmatic in its approach. Nevertheless, there are some firm policies to which the party is committed. These include:

- Maintenance of the Welfare State in order to guarantee a decent standard of living for all, protection of the vulnerable in society and ensuring a measure of social justice. However, for those who wish to make provision for themselves in terms of health care, pensions or social insurance, every encouragement should be given by the state.
- There should be strengthening of the state education system with nursery education for all, considerable increases in resources at all levels of education and improvement of teaching standards.
- Continued steps should be taken to grant equality to those who have been traditionally treated 'unjustly'. This includes such groups as women, single parents, the disabled, ethnic minorities and the homeless.
- The National Health Service should be returned to a fully state-controlled system, with additional funds available to improve both national and community health care.
- The tax and welfare systems should be reformed so that more low income groups are taken out of the tax system and the 'poverty trap' eliminated where those on low incomes, but still having to pay tax, are made worse off if they try to earn more. They will lose state benefits because of their higher earnings.
- The introduction of a Bill of Rights to guarantee the rights of all individuals and groups in society against the power of the state. This

would probably mean the incorporation of the European Convention on Human Rights into British law.

- The devolution of considerable legislative and governmental powers to Scotland and Wales. Also greater autonomy should be granted to the English regions.
- Several reforms of the political system. These to include the introduction of a proportional representation system of voting; fixed-term Parliaments where there would be a general election at regular intervals, not at the Prime Minister's discretion; a reformed, elected second chamber to replace the House of Lords. In such ways it is assumed the excessive power of government, controlled by the two largest parties, would be curbed.
- Strengthened government powers to reduce pollution, to stem the destruction of the countryside through development and to protect wildlife and nature generally.
- There is broad support for greater integration with the European Union, including the acceptance of a common European defence and foreign policy strategy.

Summary of current Liberal Democratic policies

1. Strengthening of welfare provisions to protect all vulnerable sections of society
2. Improved state nursery, primary and secondary education provision
3. Legal steps to be introduced to eliminate discrimination against all sections of the community
4. Strengthening of National Health Service provision
5. A fairer welfare and tax system to help reduce poverty and dependence on the state
6. A Bill of Rights to protect individuals and minorities
7. Devolution of power to Scotland, Wales and the English regions
8. Reform of the political system to make it more democratic and reduce centralised power
9. Strengthening of government powers to protect the environment
10. Support for further European integration

In broad terms, Liberal Democrats are seeking greater equality of opportunity, greater social justice and the strengthening of the ability individuals have to influence the political system. At the same time the scope for individual choice should be protected. However, these general goals, it is now accepted, can only be achieved in the context of a secure society and a healthy economic climate. These two latter constraints also require the pragmatic approach which is now advocated by liberal thinkers.

Liberal Democrat Party organisation

It has to be borne in mind when considering the distribution of power and influence in the Liberal Democrat Party that it operates without a realistic prospect of achieving governmental power on its own. The best it can hope for in the foreseeable future is a share of power with a bigger party. It can, therefore, afford the luxury of indulging in extremes of internal democracy, controversy and radicalism without being too concerned with the reaction of the electorate. Its two most recent leaders, **Paddy Ashdown** and **David Steel**, have attempted to curb the independence of local and regional bodies in the party in the interests of unity and clarity of purpose. They have had some success, but the party remains more decentralised and internally democratic than its larger rivals.

**Liberal Democrat Party
Conference 1994**

- **The leader** of the party is elected by the most 'democratic' process of the three principal parties, that is, by all the members of the party, by postal ballot. The small size of the Liberal Democrat Party inevitably means that he appears to dominate. Certainly in parliamentary affairs he is pre-eminent and is very much the spokesman of the party as a whole. The only two other significant figures in a national context are the **Party President** and the **Deputy leader**. In practical terms, this triumvirate has a dominant role to play in policy making.
- **Party Headquarters** has some input on policy, but is mainly concerned with the business of raising money and of drumming up sufficient publicity to challenge the attention paid to the two bigger parties.
- **The Federal Policy Committee** rivals the leader and his two main colleagues in deciding on Liberal Democrat policy. As its name suggests, it comprises representatives from different parts of Britain, that is England, Scotland and Wales. In addition, it is staffed by four MPs, representatives from Liberal local councils and from the House of Lords. Thus, it reflects all aspects of party activity.
- **The Federal Conference** meets annually. It is served by regional conferences which take place earlier in the year. These conferences feed in policy proposals to the main conference. At the latter, representatives from all constituencies act as delegates and pass resolutions which are strongly advisory, but not binding on the leadership. As a body it is known for its independence and often for its radicalism. In the 1990s, for example, there have been calls for the abolition of the monarchy, the legalisation of cannabis and for an electoral pact with the Labour Party from significant sections of the party, but against the wishes of the leadership.
- **Constituency parties** are, in keeping with the democratic and individualistic philosophy of the party, extremely autonomous. As we have said above, they may take an extreme line on policy, are relatively free in the choice of parliamentary and local government candidates, and tend to adopt their own independent procedures.

Small parties

Before reviewing the nature and role of Britain's very small parties, we must consider the reasons why political support is so concentrated on just three parties, at least in England; in other words, why smaller 'fringe' parties are so unsuccessful. The following reasons may be considered:

- Britain is an unusually homogeneous culture. There are few major conflicts of interests within the country. Compared to many other, less prosperous states, there are relatively small differentials in wealth and income among the majority of the population. There is an uncomplicated class structure, with no significant peasant class and a largely unified working class which does not include a significant radical element as do several of its European counterparts. There is also only a weak tradition of extreme right-wing nationalism. Most members of the population are moderate in their political outlook so that their views and interests can be articulated by a small number of parties.
- The electoral system discriminates against small parties. Only those parties with concentrated support – the two main parties and the nationalists in restricted parts of Scotland and Wales – can hope to win significant numbers of parliamentary seats. The electorate, perceiving that a vote for a very small party is likely to be a wasted one, are therefore reluctant to support such a party even if they feel politically inclined to do so.
- Finance has become increasingly important in the process of winning votes and parliamentary seats. Without a significant financial base, small parties are at a serious disadvantage.
- Possibly as a result of the factors described above, Britain's large parties are broad coalitions of belief and interest. Internal discipline enables them to remain relatively unified while, at the same time, being able to attract a wide range of support. This takes the ground away from minority parties.
- An active and influential system of pressure groups flourishes in the British political system. It is therefore unnecessary for parties which represent minority interests and philosophies to exist, as many such demands may be successfully articulated in other ways.

Despite the features of the British political culture described above, some small parties do still function. Among them are the following:

The Green Party A former environmental pressure group, it turned itself into a quasi-political party known as the **Ecology Party**, fought a few election campaigns but was not seriously pursuing significant representation. Following the success of their counterparts in Germany, its name was changed to the **Green Party** in 1985 to signal its serious intention to win seats in Parliament.

Its high point came in 1989 when the party won 15 per cent of a low turnout in the elections to the European Parliament. No seats were won, but the other parties were severely shaken. They reacted by taking the environmental lobby more seriously. Green policies appeared higher on their political agenda. The Liberal Democrats in particular adopted many of the party's policies.

Partly as a result of its political 'clothes' being stolen by the main parties, and partly as a result of a destructive internal schism over tactics and organisation, the tide of Green Party fortunes soon ebbed away. In the 1992 general election their vote fell below 1 per cent. Other than victory in a few rural local government seats, the Greens have ceased to be a significant electoral force.

Nationalists

The aspirations of the Scottish (SNP) and Welsh (Plaid Cymru) nationalist parties are described in Unit 3. In parts of the two countries they have become a significant political force.

It was in the 1970s, when disillusionment with London-based politics set in, and when the Scots realised the potential of North Sea Oil revenues if they could obtain a share of them, that support for the nationalist parties began to grow. In 1974 they both reached the height of their electoral success, with the SNP winning over 30 per cent of the Scottish vote and Plaid Cymru winning over 11 per cent of theirs. Since then support has fluctuated but remained an important factor. Neither has managed to break the stranglehold which the Labour Party has in Scotland and Wales, but nationalist sentiment is again growing in the 1990s. With both Labour and the Liberal Democrats proposing some devolution of power to these national regions, at least some of their hopes seem certain to be realised.

Others

No other party outside Northern Ireland (which is dealt with elsewhere), wins a significant number of votes at any British general elections. Extremists such as the right-wing British National Party (BNP) or the Marxist Socialist Workers Party (SWP) do put a few candidates into the field but with very little success. The BNP did win a shock local by-election victory in Tower Hamlets (East London) in 1993, but this was largely due to peculiar local circumstances and serious errors made by the local Liberal Democrats who should have won the seat. The result was reversed at the next full-scale local elections.

The failure of these and other similar extremist parties is largely due, as we have suggested above, to the general moderate political outlook of most of the British people. Similarly, apparently 'eccentric' groups, such as the Natural Law Party which emerged in the 1990s, are shunned by an electorate which is usually conservative (small 'c') in its voting habits.

For exam questions relevant to this unit, see pages 490–3.

Electoral systems

The current British system

Britain's electoral system, although having much in common with the US Congressional arrangements, is now relatively rare among democratic states. It is known officially as 'simple majority in single member constituencies' but the more common description is 'first-past-the-post'.

It is, perhaps, the simplest system which can be adopted. Each parliamentary constituency returns a single MP who is elected by a **plurality**; that is, whoever gains the most votes, wins. This can also be described as a 'simple majority'. A few salient points should be noted at this stage:

- Each constituent has only one vote.
- There is no need for a winning candidate to win an absolute majority (i.e. over 50 per cent of the vote).
- Voters have no say in which candidate shall be proposed by any party.

The effects of the British system

We must review the results of recent general elections if we are to draw conclusions from them. These are shown below:

General election results October 1974–92 (not including Northern Ireland)		
October 10 1974		
Party	**Seats Won**	**% of Votes Won***
Conservative	277	35.8
Labour	319	39.2
Liberal	11	18.3
Scots Nats	11	30.4
Plaid Cymru (Welsh Nats)	3	11.1
Others	0	0.7
May 3 1979		
Conservative	339	43.9
Labour	269	36.9
Liberal	11	13.8
Scots Nats	2	17.3
Plaid Cymru	2	8.1
Others	0	1.1

General election results October 1974–92 (not including Northern Ireland)		
June 9 1983		
Party	**Seats Won**	**% of Votes Won***
Conservative	397	42.4
Labour	209	27.6
Liberal/SDP Alliance	23	25.4
Scots Nats	2	11.8
Plaid Cymru	2	7.8
Others	0	0.7
June 11 1987		
Conservative	376	43.4
Labour	229	31.7
Liberal/SDP Alliance	22	23.2
Scots Nats	3	14.0
Plaid Cymru	3	7.3
Others	0	0.5
April 9 1992		
Conservative	336	42.3
Labour	271	35.2
Liberal Democrat	20	18.3
Scots Nats	3	21.5
Plaid Cymru	4	8.8
Others	0	1.0

* In the cases of the Scottish Nationalists and Plaid Cymru the percentages relate only to Scotland and Wales respectively.
Source: *British Political Facts 1900–94*, Butler and Butler (Macmillan)

Some immediate observations can be made:

- 'Others', which now include mainly Green Party candidates and the neo-Nazis, have made no significant inroads into gaining voters and are, therefore, scarcely a factor in the results.
- The Liberals, including when they were part of the Alliance with the Social Democrat Party and since they have become Liberal Democrats, are consistently **under-represented** by the system. The starkest result occurred in 1983 when the Alliance (25.4 per cent) was only just

Paddy Ashdown and his wife cast their votes – Yeovil 1992

beaten by Labour (27.6 per cent) in terms of share of the vote. In seats, however, Labour (209) won nearly ten times as many as the Alliance (23). Put another way, in 1992 the Liberal Democrats won over 18 per cent of the total votes, but were awarded only 3 per cent of the seats (20 out of 651).

- Both main parties are **over-represented**. If we study the 1983 result again we can see that if Labour had been awarded the same percentage of the **seats** as the percentage of **votes** which they won, they would have received **179** seats. In fact they received **209**. The Conservatives did even better out of the system. They would have won **276** seats on a strict percentage basis, but actually won **397**. Interestingly, in 1992 the Conservatives won many fewer seats – down to 336 – although the proportion of the votes they won hardly changed from 1983. Thus, the **disproportionality** of the system is uneven from one election to the next.

- The effect on the nationalist parties is mixed. Taking 1992, it becomes plain that the Scottish Nationalists lost out because of the nature of the system. They gained 21.5 per cent of the Scottish vote, but only 4 per cent of the seats (3 out of 72). The Welsh Nationalists (Plaid Cymru), however, did well. Their 8.8 per cent of the Welsh vote was converted into 10 per cent of the seats available (4 out of 38). The reasons for this apparent anomaly will become apparent below.
- It is even possible for there to be a so-called 'wrong-way-round' result, where a party wins less total votes than its nearest rival, but still wins the election in terms of seats. This occurred in 1929, 1951 and February 1974.

Having established some immediate conclusions we must look beyond the figures to make some deeper observations.

Safe seats We may define a 'safe seat' as one where it is extremely unlikely that party control will change hands at a general election. That is, the sitting MP, or a replacement from the same party, is assured of re-election. In the absence of a stricter definition of the term 'safe', no exact number of safe seats can be calculated. However, the figure is probably as high as 60 per cent. The reasons for the existence of so many safe seats are twofold. Either one party is always dominant because of the social make-up of the area (i.e. heavily industrial and much poverty = Labour; middle class, wealthy = Conservative), or the opposition to one party is consistently split between the two other main parties.

It should be noted, however, that in by-elections caused by the death, resignation or retirement of an MP between general elections, there is no such thing as a safe seat. Normal voting patterns do not apply and, in theory, any large party may win. Indeed, it is often the governing party which suffers most. After the 1992 election the Conservatives found themselves incapable of winning **any** by-elections, they were so unpopular. Huge Conservative majorities were overturned on several occasions. This occurred in formerly rock-solid Tory seats such as Eastleigh in 1994 and Christchurch in 1993.

The implications of this high proportion of inevitable constituency results in general elections are possibly the most worrying aspect of the electoral system. It means that the majority of voters who live in such constituencies cannot influence the result of the election at all. Their votes are, in short, worthless. Whichever party they choose to support, the overwhelming level of voting for the dominant party in the locality will swamp their own decision. Only in more 'marginal' seats, where there is a realistic chance of a change of party hands, does the voter feel genuinely empowered. His vote then does count. But marginal seats are a minority.

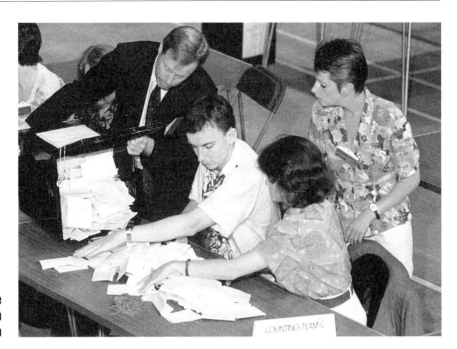

Counting votes at the 1993 Christchurch by-election

Differential voting values   We have already seen above that a vote in a marginal seat is effectively worth much more than one in a safe seat. We can go further, however, by examining all the votes for the parties. The table below illustrates the point:

1992 general election			
Party	Votes won	Seats won	Votes per seat
Conservative	14,092,891	336	41,943
Labour	11,559,735	271	42,655
Liberal Democrat	5,999,384	20	299,969

* Source: *British Political Facts 1900–94*, Butler and Butler (Macmillan)

The figures demonstrate that it takes, on average, many more Liberal Democrat votes to elect an MP than for the other two large parties. This may be interpreted to indicate that each Liberal Democrat vote is worth considerably less than its counterpart for Labour or the Conservatives. Thus, say critics of the system, the principle of 'one-person-one-vote' is distorted in reality by the unequal value of votes.

Liberal Democrat
David Chidgley after
overturning a massive
Conservative majority
in the 1994 Eastleigh
by-election

<u>Concentration of party support</u>   The reason why the two main parties profit from Britain's 'first-past-the-post' system is that they enjoy concentrated pockets of support in certain areas. The Liberal Democrats, by contrast, find their voters scattered much more evenly across the country.

The point may be illustrated by an absurd, but nevertheless instructive illustration. If every party found that its level of support, as demonstrated in the 1992 general election, was **exactly** matched in **every** constituency, the Conservatives would win **every** seat! The result in each constituency in 1992 would have been:

Candidate A (Conservative)	42.3%
Candidate B (Labour)	35.2%
Candidate C (Lib. Dem.)	18.3%
Others	4.2%

* Source: *British Political Facts 1900–94*, Butler and Butler
(Macmillan)

Thus the Conservatives scoop the pool!

Of course, the reality is different. In some places Labour has concentrated support and so wins most of the seats on offer. Yet the figures can illustrate well what happens to the Liberal Democrats and Scottish Nationalists who **do** tend to find the kind of result shown above replicated up and down the country. The areas where they have concentrated support (the West Country for the Liberal Democrats, a variety of localities for the SNP) are few and far between. It is an anomaly that Plaid Cymru, though a small party, benefits because it is a characteristic of Welsh nationalism that it is largely confined to small areas in both the North and South of the principality. There are strange occurrences in Scotland in particular: in 1992 the Liberal Democrats' 13 per cent of the popular vote won them 9 seats, while the Scottish Nationalists' impressive 21 per cent converted to only 3 seats! So beware. The effects of regional voting do not always favour the big parties.

The table below, extracting regional results from the 1992 election, indicates how support for various parties tends to be concentrated in some areas:

1992 general election results by region					
Region	**Cons.**	**Labour**	**Lib. Dem.**	**Scots Nats.**	**Plaid Cymru**
London	48	35	1		
South England	161	10	6		
Midlands	57	43	0		
North England	53	107	3		
Wales	6	27	1		4
Scotland	11	49	9	3	

* Source: *British Political Facts 1900–94*, Butler and Butler (Macmillan)

Clear conclusions can be drawn from the results shown above for the South of England, the North, Scotland and Wales. The figures also give some room for speculation, were regional devolution to be introduced, with elected assemblies!

Tactical voting   A tactical vote is one which is cast by a voter, not for his preferred party, but for another which he feels has a better chance of winning a seat. The voter normally does this to keep out the candidate of a party which he particularly opposes. Typically, this might be a Liberal Democrat voter supporting a Conservative candidate because he knows his preferred choice has absolutely no chance of winning, but he wants Labour to lose at all costs. So he switches his vote. A number of other combinations can be identified.

As we have seen, the poor showing of smaller parties may lead to large numbers of their supporters defecting because they do not wish to waste their vote. There are no second choices in the British system so the tactical voter is simply trying to make his vote count.

In case one might assume that tactical voting always loses votes for smaller parties, it has become noticeable in by-elections in recent years that Labour voters are becoming more willing to support Liberal Democrats or Nationalists to ensure a defeat for the governing Conservative Party. A number of huge Liberal Democrat victories in such former safe Conservative seats as Christchurch demonstrate this development. Whether tactical voting will become more prevalent in general elections as well remains to be seen.

A further kind of tactical vote is the **negative vote**. This occurs when a voter chooses to support one party simply as a way of indicating opposition to another. He or she may not support the party for which the vote is cast, but is simply determined to keep another candidate out. The tendency to cast a negative vote may be temporary. A lifetime Conservative supporter, for example, may be dissatisfied with the Government's performance and so wish to punish them by supporting Labour or the Liberal Democrats. This phenomenon is most commonly seen in by-elections.

> 'Tactical voting matters because its existence carries a message about the voting system . . . it is a symptom of the flaws in the electoral system rather than the root of the problem.'
> Helena Catt, 'Tactical Voting in Britain' in
> *Parliamentary Affairs* (October 1989)

Government formation   The most important feature of the British system lies in its ability to produce decisive outcomes in general elections. This is, of course, at the expense of any sense of fairness towards smaller parties or of giving voters a reasonable degree of choice. Nevertheless, for many this is an acceptable trade-off – clear results in return for equity. A view of all the results since 1945 illustrates how the system works:

Election	Winning party	Size of majority
1945	Labour	+146
1950	Labour	+5
1951	Conservative	+17
1955	Conservative	+58
1959	Conservative	+100
1964	Labour	+4
1966	Labour	+96
1970	Conservative	+30
1974 (February)	Labour	−33
1974 (October)	Labour	+3
1979	Conservative	+43
1983	Conservative	+144
1987	Conservative	+102
1992	Conservative	+21

* Source: *British Political Facts 1900–94*, Butler and Butler (Macmillan)

It can be seen that in every election one of the main parties won an overall majority, with the exception of the election of February 1974. That election resulted in a government which was largely powerless so that a fresh election had to be called within a few months. There have, too, been some close calls, notably in 1950, 1951, 1964 and October 1974, but at least a single-party government could be formed.

The advantages of first-past-the-post

Before examining the advantages of the British system a word of warning is required. This is an electoral system operating in **Britain** and it cannot be separated from the broader political structure. Any conclusions. therefore, can only be applied in Britain. It is important to bear in mind that there is a dominant two-party system, that we expect Governments to be drawn from a single party and that we expect to be represented by an MP who clearly represents the community in which we live. The advantages are, therefore, identified in relation to such political principles:

- It is an extremely easy system to understand. Voters have one choice and, on the whole, understand that they are voting for an MP of a particular party and, by implication, a party which they may wish to see in government.
- It produces clear, usually decisive results, as we have seen above. There is rarely uncertainty after an election; one party is normally able to form a government without any hiatus. This is often contrasted with such countries as Italy or Israel where government formation is frequently difficult as a result of indecisive results with no party being large enough to govern alone.
- The fact that a single party usually wins outright means that the doctrine of mandate and manifesto can operate. This means that parties campaign in elections with a clear manifesto and, if they win, there is no doubt that they have the authority to implement the manifesto. This cannot be said of multi-party government (i.e. coalitions). Voters can never be certain of which policies, proclaimed by their favourite party, will be retained and which will be dropped during coalition-forming negotiations. It has been strongly argued that in Britain at least about 40–45 per cent of the electorate support a specific set of policies adopted by the winning party. With the uncertainties of coalition government and a set of hybrid policies being adopted, **nobody** has voted for the final package.
- There is a strong traditional link between British communities and their MPs. It is expected that the MP will represent their interests, irrespective of party allegiance, both in Parliament and directly to the Government. The single-member constituency system safeguards this link.

The disadvantages of the British system

Many of the problems have been described above, or are implied by the figures. Nevertheless, some key points may be emphasised:

- The system is clearly unfair. It discriminates against small parties and does not give equal value to all votes.
- It encourages tactical voting where voters feel forced into voting for a party they do not support, simply to have a say in the outcome.
- Electors do not have the opportunity to discriminate between candidates from the same party. They must put up with the choice made by a relatively small group of party activists.
- Though the system does produce a single MP to represent constituents, it could be argued that people would prefer to have a representative of their own party.

In addition to these issues, there is a good deal of controversy concerning the relative merits of single-party government, which is almost guaranteed by the current system, and coalitions which would almost certainly result if some form of proportional representation were to be introduced in Britain. Such arguments will be analysed after some alternative systems have been considered below.

Some alternatives

There is a very large variety of electoral systems to be found in the world of democratic politics. Indeed, nearly every European state has a system which is either unique to it, or is an amended version of one of the more popular systems. Most of the systems are proportional and a few are not. We will begin with two similar systems, neither of which is strictly proportional.

The second ballot   Here a first ballot is held very much along British lines. However, in order to be elected a candidate must win at least 50 per cent of the votes. Should no candidate achieve this – and this is common – a second ballot is held some time later. Who qualifies for the second ballot may vary, but commonly it is the top two candidates from the first ballot. Voters are free to choose again. With only two candidates left, one must win an overall majority. Clearly those who support one of the original losing candidates have a second choice. The system operates in **France**.

Alternative vote   This is a variation on the second ballot, and is used in Australia. Each voter makes a first and second choice on the ballot paper. First choices are added together and any candidate achieving over 50 per cent is elected outright. If not the second choices are added to the scores of the top two candidates so that an overall majority must be achieved. The only difference between this and the second ballot system is that voters make both choices at the same time.

We now move on to systems which are described as 'proportional representation'.

The national list or D'Hondt method   This is a simple system which operates in Israel, Holland, Belgium, Spain and Portugal. There are no constituencies and voters choose a party, not a candidate. The proportion of votes cast for each party is then calculated. The parties are awarded the same proportion of seats as votes won. For example, if a party wins 40 per cent of the national vote, it will be awarded 40 per cent of the seats in the legislature. It is up to the parties which individuals will fill the allocated of seats. Normally, a priority list is drawn up before the election and seats are allocated thus. So, if a party has 40 per cent of the seats, those who fill the top 40 per cent of the party's list will enter the legislature.

There are variations where the lists are not national, but regional, but the system is the same in essence. As an additional variation a **threshold** may be stipulated. This is a minimum percentage of the total vote which a party **must** win to gain **any** seats at all. Normally 5 per cent (but lower in Israel, which is notorious for awarding seats to tiny extremist parties), it is designed to eliminate minority parties.

Mixed member proportional systems (Additional member system) This is a hybrid system, operated in Germany and Italy. Electors have two votes each. One is for a constituency MP as in Britain, the other is for a party. The party votes are used as in the d'Hondt method described above. Thus some of the legislature is composed of constituency MPs, while some is drawn from party lists in proportion to votes cast. In Germany the Bundestag (Parliament) is divided half and half between the two. In Italy 75 per cent of MPs represent constituencies.

This system awards seats reasonably, though not precisely proportionally. The table below illustrates this effect.

Results of the German general election under the additional member system 1990			
Party	% of total votes	% of total seats	Number of seats
Christian Democrats	36.7	40.5	268
Christian Socialists	7.1	7.7	51
Social Democrats	33.5	36.1	239
Free Democrats	11.0	11.9	79
Greens	5.1	1.2	8
Democratic Socialists	2.4	2.6	17

Single Transferable Vote (STV) This is possibly the most popular system among those in Britain who wish to convert to proportional representation. It is used in the Republic of Ireland and also in Northern Ireland for European elections only. It is also perhaps the most complicated system.

Constituencies are multi-member (usually four or five). Each party may put up candidates up to the number of seats available in the constituency. Thus the voter is confronted by a number of party lists. There are variations as to how the system operates, but the principles are the same. The next steps are as follows:

- The voter ranks the candidates – all or only some – in his order of preference.
- A so-called 'droop quota' is established which is total votes cast plus one, divided by the number of seats available plus one.
- The first preference votes are counted and those candidates who achieve the quota are elected.
- The candidate with the fewest votes is eliminated but second preference votes are added to first preferences. After this, any new candidates to achieve the quota are elected.
- The process continues with eventually third and subsequent preferences being added until the required number of candidates has achieved the quota.

This complex system is, fortunately, not the concern of the voter who simply places candidates in order of preference. The calculations can be left to someone else. Its popularity is, nevertheless, not due to its simplicity! Rather, it allows voters to discriminate between candidates of the **same** party, while in most systems it is even possible to choose a mixed bag of candidates from different parties. Thus, it offers the most choice for the voter out of all the systems.

An Irish constituency ballot under Single Transferable Vote

Number of seats available: 5   **Electoral quota calculated:** 9301

Candidates, parties and first preference votes received:

Aylward (Fianna Fail)	9219
Gibbons (Fianna Fail)	7032
Langan (Fianna Fail)	1558
Nolan (Fianna Fail)	6998
Crotty (Fine Gael)	8377
Dowling (Fine Gael)	5661
Manning (Fine Gael)	3436
Slattery (Fine Gael)	2665
Meaney (Labour)	1869
Pattison (Labour)	5642
Brophy (Independent)	1021
Jones (Independent)	65
Walsh (Workers)	2189

Candidates elected after second and subsequent preferences were added:

Aylward, Crotty, Gibbons, Pattison, Nolan

Seats awarded to the parties:

Fianna Fail: 3
Fine Gael: 1
Labour: 1

Source: 1982 election in Carlow-Kilkenny. Adapted from *Elections and Voting Behaviour* (Politics Association)

As we have said, this is by no means an exhaustive list, but it serves to demonstrate the principle electoral systems in operation in Europe and elsewhere. It is now possible to draw up a 'shopping list' of electoral systems, with some of the main features of each:

System	Country	Main features
Single member plurality	Britain USA	Simple to understand Clear result usually obtained Favours large parties with concentrated support Very unfair to small parties Good constituency–MP relationship
National list	Israel The Netherlands	Simple to understand The most exactly proportional system Helps small parties as long as the threshold is not too large Voters have no choice concerning party candidates Parties can ensure that certain individuals are elected There is no constituency representation
Mixed member proportional	Germany Italy	Combines the features of the list system and simple pluralities Is both proportional and retains constituencies Helps small parties but not the very smallest
STV	Ireland	Is very complex Is very proportional Maximises voter choice Helps small parties Enables most voters to be represented by an MP of their own party
Second ballot of alternative vote	France	Gives voters a second choice Simple to understand and operate Is fairly but not extremely proportional Favours small, but not very small parties Takes time for results to be finalised

The British system and proportional systems compared

It must be understood that 'proportional representation' (PR) is not a system in itself, but a description of any electoral system which awards seats to a legislature in reasonable proportion to the votes cast for each party. In that sense, all the systems described above are proportional. Even the French second ballot, which is not strictly PR, awards seats more proportionally than does the British/American system. So we can make generalised comparisons between the first-past-the-post system and PR in general, whichever system is concerned.

We must also dispense quickly with the argument about 'fairness', or 'equity'. It is perfectly clear that, taken as a whole, the British system is unfair, both to voters and small parties. This is not in dispute. The result in **each constituency** may be acceptable – the biggest vote-winner is elected – but **overall**, the results distort the real choices of the voters.

What we are concerned with are the **political effects** of the system. How would a new, proportional system affect British political life and would those effects be desirable? In other words, the electoral system we may prefer must have more to do with our perspective on the political system than with our sense of fair play. It would be unrealistic and utopian to think in any other way. So we will consider only these political effects and evaluate them.

<u>Coalition government</u> It is not absolutely certain that the introduction of PR to Britain would result in 'hung' parliaments and a multi-party system. However, we can assume that it would be unlikely that any party would win an overall majority. In the long run this would imply the introduction of coalition government where two or more parties would share ministerial places in the Cabinet. There would also need to be an agreed set of policies between the member parties.

Supporters of coalition government suggest that it would herald the return of consensus politics whereby only policies with widespread support could be implemented. It might also result in a moderating of policies, assuming that the smaller parties in the coalition were themselves moderates and not extremists. The 'adversary' politics of recent times have, it is claimed, resulted in wild swings in policy and a lack of any form of compromise.

Opponents, on the other hand, suggest that coalitions are intrinsically unstable, pointing to Italy, Israel and The Netherlands as examples of systems which have become deadlocked as a result of PR and the multi-party system which it has created. Furthermore, the policies finally agreed within a coalition are unknown at the time of the election. The certainties of Britain's principles of manifesto and mandate would be lost, the argument continues.

<u>Hung parliaments</u> The prospect of a House of Commons with no overall majority for any party opens up new possibilities for parliamentary life. The monopoly power of the governing party's whips would be removed. Without a guaranteed majority, the Government would be forced to secure a coalition of support among MPs. Small parties and factions within parties might enjoy enhanced influence in inverse proportion to the control exercised by the Government.

Some commentators look back to the so-called 'halcyon' days of the House of Commons in the mid-nineteenth century, when there was a fragmented jigsaw of political groupings jostling for advantage. At that time Parliament could make or break Governments with a shift of relatively few votes; ministers were forced to woo smaller political groupings in order to pass their legislation; individual MPs felt empowered. For some this would enhance democracy and limit the over-mighty power of government, balancing it against parliamentary influence. Of course there are many others who fear such a scenario. For them a weak Government, but powerful Parliament, would seriously damage the cause of efficient administration.

Realignment of the party system   Britain already has a multi-party system in terms of voting strengths. This is not, however, translated into parliamentary seats. The introduction of an alternative electoral system would almost certainly break the duopoly of the Conservative and Labour Parties. In Scotland and Wales the likely boost to nationalist representation would lend considerable weight to the movement towards devolved government or even independence. In England, increased representation for Liberal Democrats could begin to drive a wedge between the two larger parties. These are the predictable results of a change. Less clear, however, is the possibility of further fragmentation of the party structure.

Currently, extreme Conservative and Labour factions are forced to stay within the existing party structure. Were they to break away and form their own splinter parties, they would face electoral oblivion. The first-past-the-post system does not allow small minority parties to gain a significant hold at Westminster. Under PR, however, the possibility of some success in parliamentary elections opens up new possibilities for such groups. A new socialist party of the Left or a breakaway nationalist, anti-European grouping on the right might certainly emerge under these circumstances. The two-party system and the existing electoral system reinforce each other. If the rules are changed, the whole party structure might well fragment.

Representation   The British system requires that voters choose a single candidate from a group selected by local parties. It is, therefore, understandable that candidate selection committees which operate in the Labour and Conservative Parties (Liberal Democrat candidates are chosen by all party members) wish to select individuals whom they consider to be most electable. It is regrettable, but not surprising, that they are reluctant to choose members of ethnic minorities and women on the grounds that some voters will find them less acceptable. Liberal values and tolerance are often set aside in favour of pragmatic understanding of how the average voter behaves. It is largely for this reason that women and ethnic minorities are so under-represented at Westminster.

Many proportional systems, especially STV, do not require such a simple choice. Party lists, indeed, are likely to have a reasonable share of members of these groups simply to maximise voter attraction. In multi-member constituencies a mixed group of candidates can be useful. Similarly, List systems do not allow voters to choose individual candidates so that parties may be less fearful about what kind of individuals they select. So it can be confidently predicted that a change in Britain's electoral system would result in the representation of a wider range of characteristics among the candidates.

We are now in a position to summarise the arguments which can be presented in favour or opposed to electoral change to a more proportional system:

British and proportional systems compared

First-past-the-post	Proportional representation

Fairness

First-past-the-post	Proportional representation
• Small parties suffer discrimination. • The value of all votes is not equal. • Many votes are wasted. • Parties with concentrated support have a great advantage. • The relative strengths of the parties are distorted.	• All parties have equal chances. • Voters have greater choice. • Representation in Parliament reflects voting strengths of the parties more accurately.

Representation

First-past-the-post	Proportional representation
• Voters have a simple choice. • There is clear representation of each constituency by an MP. • Women and minorities are less often chosen as candidates.	• Some complicated systems may confuse some voters. • In some systems voters may discriminate between candidates of the same party. • Women and ethnic minority members are more likely to be chosen as candidates.

The political system

First-past-the-post	Proportional representation
• Usually a single party wins outright resulting in strong, united government. • The executive branch is able to control the legislature at most times. • Single-party government enables the doctrine of manifesto and mandate to work. • Small parties, whether extremist or moderate, do not have great influence. • There may be dramatic policy swings as the two dominant parties alternate in power.	• A multi-party system is likely to result, reflecting political opinion more accurately. • Coalition Governments would probably become common, giving rise to consensus politics, but also cause more uncertainty among voters. • Small parties would be able to exert more influence. • There is likely to be a shift in the balance of power between executive and legislature, with the latter having more influence. The lack of a clear Government majority would reduce the power of the whips. • There might be a realignment within the party system.

The balance sheet is, thus, particularly weighted towards one side of the argument or the other. The decision rests between the adoption of a fairer system, with greater voter choice and fairer representation, and retention of the existing system with its current political arrangements. If we are willing to risk the development of a multi-party system and the likelihood of permanent coalition government, proportional representation seems attractive. Those who fear such changes, however, will resist PR.

The waters are further clouded by the conflicting evidence from other countries which use alternative systems. Germany and France are politically stable for the most part, in spite of the persistence of coalition government. Similar systems in Italy and The Netherlands, on the other hand, have resulted in great political disruption.

Electoral reform and the parties

Not surprisingly, all the smaller parties support electoral reform. It is to their advantage and they have long resented the discrimination which the existing systems inflict on them. The Liberal Democrats have a further objection. For them first-past-the-post is undemocratic, whoever may gain or lose by it. Voters are not given a fair choice, their votes are unequally weighted and, above all, Parliament does not reflect political opinion within the country.

As much as Liberal Democrats support reform – most commonly in favour of STV – Conservatives are opposed to it. Being largely traditionalists, they are suspicious of the unpredictable results of proportional systems. Furthermore, they support strong authority and are, therefore, opposed to any constitutional change which is likely to weaken central government.

Less clear is the Labour Party's attitude. Members are split on the issue. Some take a pragmatic view – that the current system serves them well. They believe that change, however desirable in democratic terms, cannot be justified in view of the damage it might do to the party's fortunes. There are others who share the Conservative liking of strong central authority which the system underpins. During the 1980s and 1990s, however, fuelled by four successive election defeats, there has been a ground swell of support for reform. John Smith set up the **Plant Commission** to consider prospects for change. Their 1994 report was just – but only just – in favour of PR, probably the German system. However, there is much uncertainty, with some even calling for a referendum on the issue. In the end one essential question must be answered: Will any government be willing to abandon a system which has brought them to power?

Pressure groups and reform

There are two principal groups which campaign for reform. These are the **Electoral Reform Society** and **Charter 88**. Both draw their support largely from intellectual and academic circles, many members of which are also Liberal Democrats. They are hindered by an inability to mobilise enthusiastic mass support for the issue.

Opinion polls consistently show about two-thirds support for reform, which seems decisive. However, the problem is that few feel particularly strongly about the issue. There are not considered to be many votes likely to be won or lost over electoral reform so the parties are not willing to take a strong line. It seems, therefore, more likely that reform will arise out of political circumstances – probably a hung Parliament in which Liberal Democrats hold the balance of power – than from pressure group activity.

Parliamentary by-elections

Characteristics

A by-election occurs when a sitting Member of Parliament is, for some reason, unable to retain his seat. Most commonly this is due to the death of the member, but may also result from serious long-term illness, or resignation. Resignation can occur through some form of scandal, but is more commonly for business or family reasons. Bankruptcy and the imprisonment of a member will also result in loss of the seat, but such occurrences are extremely rare. The vacancy must be filled within about three months.

The normal characteristics of a general election simply do not apply in by-elections. There are several reasons for this:

- Constituents are aware that they are not electing a government, which is the case at a general election. They may, therefore, relax their normal party allegiance, safe in the knowledge that their vote will not create any dramatic political change. It follows from this that there is no such thing as a 'safe seat' in a by-election. Certainly not, at least, for the party in government.

● Since they are in 'mid-term' of a Government, voters may take the opportunity to pass their verdict on the performance of that Government. Often this is critical. Thus, there is a tendency for the governing party to fare badly in by-elections. Some dramatic results are given below.

● For the reasons described above, smaller parties, especially the Liberal Democrats, tend to do well. There is normally a great deal of media attention paid to by-elections so that smaller party candidates often receive more coverage than would be the case at a general election.

● Turnouts can be much lower than at a general election – often as low as 50 per cent, compared to 70–75 per cent at a general election. This often distorts the picture of party support. Typically, supporters of the incumbent party (the party of the former MP) stay at home in large numbers, feeling no especial urge to vote for a change. In close contests, however, where a major surprise is expected, there may sometimes be a good showing (as much as 80 per cent), as in the Liberal triumph in a formerly Conservative safe seat at Brecon and Radnor in 1985.

● There has been an increasing tendency for 'tactical voting' to take place. This occurs when voters switch their normal allegiance in order to support a party whose candidate has a better chance of winning than their own. The reason is to defeat a candidate whom they particularly oppose, often from the governing party. Certainly three Liberal Democrat victories over the Conservatives after the 1992 general election at Newbury, Christchurch and Eastleigh were partly the result of Labour supporters voting tactically for the Liberal Democrat candidate.

Do by-elections matter? Under most circumstances the answer is 'not very much'. Of course they act as a valuable 'barometer' of support for the parties, especially the government, but, for reasons described above, their results may not be reliable in the long run. Indeed, it is usually the case that, when an incumbent party candidate loses the seat at a by-election, it is regained by his party at the next general election when voting patterns return to 'normal'.

When the government is faced with a small majority in the House of Commons, however, by-election losses can become crucial. This was never more so than when Labour was elected in October 1974 with a majority of only three. By-election defeats, with seats changing from Labour to Conservative at Woolwich and Walsall North, wiped out the Government majority, thus reducing it to a weak and largely ineffective administration.

Similar, though less dramatic events overtook the Conservative Government which was elected in 1992 with a twenty-one majority. By 1995 the Government was so unpopular it was incapable of holding any of its own seats at a by-election, no matter how large the majority. By-election defeats reduced the Government's majority to eleven and, when a further nine MPs temporarily left the party over its European policies, there was again a minority administration for a short time. Important legislation, including the proposed privatisation of the Post Office, was lost in this difficult period. So, the answer to the question concerning the significance of by-elections is that it largely depends upon political circumstances. A Government with a comfortable Commons majority need worry little if it suffers mid-term reverses. Most of them can be reclaimed later.

Local elections in Britain

As with by-elections, the normal 'rules' of electoral behaviour do not apply in local council contests. Again, the most convenient way to understand them is to examine the characteristics which differentiate them from general election patterns:

- Turnouts are always much lower, rarely reaching 40 per cent and sometimes as low as 20 per cent. This means that results can often turn on the switching of a few hundred votes or even less.
- The results owe more to the popularity of the **national** parties, than to the performance of local councillors or to their manifestos. As with by-elections, they are often used by voters as a rod with which to beat the government which has lost their confidence. This was particularly true in the 1995 elections in Scotland and the English and Welsh counties. The enormously unpopular Conservative Party under John Major lost most of its remaining council seats in these elections, even driving some Conservative candidates to describe themselves as independent on the ballot papers to try to disguise their true affiliation and so save their seats.
- Voters are largely ignorant of local issues, not even understanding which services are the responsibility of the local authority and which are centrally administered. Thus, unless there are well-publicised local controversies, the patterns of voting are replicated up and down the country; local variations are relatively minor.

Efforts to make local elections truly local have consistently failed. The most serious attempt revolved around the Poll Tax, introduced in 1988–9. It was hoped by the Government that the tax would accurately reflect the spending practices of local councils. Voters would then be sensitive to local issues, supporting those councillors who kept the tax low, and removing the high spenders. The 1991 local elections indicated some success, with the councils charging a higher Poll Tax doing noticeably worse at the polls than the more frugal authorities. However, before the electoral effects of the tax could be further gauged, it had to be abolished because of its other, well-documented, disadvantages.

European Parliamentary elections

There have only been four direct elections to the European Parliament since Britain became a member of the European Union in 1973. It might, therefore, be premature to draw too many conclusions from them. It must also be remembered that the European Parliament is, with some justification, perceived as a powerless body, whose political make-up has little relevance to the British voter. For this reason it is hardly surprising to note that voters at European and local elections demonstrate similar voting behaviour.

Turnouts are low – 36.8 per cent in both 1989 and 1994 – and they appear to become a referendum on the performance of the Westminster Government rather than a verdict on the effectiveness of Members of the

European Parliament. In all the election campaigns it has been difficult to discern very significant differences in the parties' attitudes to European affairs, apart from the radical stance of the Green Party. Small wonder, then, that an unpopular Conservative Party did badly in both of the last two elections, but did well when its fortunes were at a high point in 1984.

The most dramatic occurrence in these elections occurred in 1989 when the Green Party obtained 15 per cent of the popular vote; not enough to win them any seats, but sufficient to demonstrate to the established parties that environmental issues were at the forefront of many voters' minds. The resultant 'greening' of the policies of all three larger parties owed much to that election result. It also went some way to ensuring that the Green vote diminished considerably in 1994.

Results of elections to the European Parliament			
	Party	**% Vote gained**	**Seats won**
1989	Labour	40.1	45
	Conservative	34.7	32
	Liberal Democrat	6.4	0
	Other	19.0	1*
1994	Labour	44.2	51
	Conservative	27.9	18
	Liberal Democrat	18.4	2
	Other	11.2	0

* Scottish Nationalist

Voting behaviour

The reasons why people choose to vote the way they do has occupied the minds of academics – psephologists, as experts on voting trends are known – since the 1960s. Clearly, political parties are interested in voting behaviour, but it is also important to the student of politics. This is because it can tell us a great deal about the nature of the political culture and the type and scale of the changes which are taking place within that culture. Needless to say, the nature of voting patterns is complex and is constantly changing. We can, nevertheless, identify some of the principal trends of recent years.

Social class

When voting behaviour first came under scrutiny in the 1960s, it was clear that the main determinant of party allegiance was social class. Most members of the working class, defined as manual workers, whether skilled, semi-skilled or unskilled, closely identified with the Labour Party and voted for it without fail. About one-third of this class did have a tendency to vote Conservative out of **deference** – a belief that Conservatives were members of a superior ruling class who could be trusted to govern in the interests of all – but the rest were staunch Labour.

Similarly, most members of the middle class – that is, those broadly in 'white-collar' occupations, from clerks and secretaries to senior business managers – were confirmed Conservative supporters. The Liberals at this time were relatively insignificant, picking up a small percentage of votes from the intellectual middle classes and some independent-minded workers.

The incidence of so-called **deviant** voting – voters supporting a party not normally associated with their class – was relatively rare. There were certainly observable instances of people placing themselves in a different social class to the one in which they objectively belonged (typically, members of the working class considering themselves as middle class for reasons of status). This **self-assigned** class placement, as it is known, can certainly lead to 'deviant' voting, as can individuals moving from one class to another and from one generation to the next. An educated son or daughter of working-class parents might become middle class, but retain working-class attitudes including Labour Party allegiance. Yet it could still be said in the 1960s that social class was the deciding factor in party identification.

> 'Class is the basis of British party politics; all else is embellishment and detail.'
> Peter Pulzer, *Political Representation and Elections in Britain* (Allen and Unwin, 1967)

No sooner had Pulzer (see quotation above) written his key work on voting than the relationship between social class and voting patterns began to break down. This was for a number of reasons:

- **Class de-alignment** began to occur, that is, the connection between social classes and parties began to weaken. A number of explanations have been offered, mainly concerning the increasing **affluence** of some sections of the working class, prompting them to disassociate themselves with Labour. Hand in hand with greater affluence has gone **embourgoisement**. This term refers to a tendency for better-off workers to consider themselves as middle class. They may identify a middle-class lifestyle with voting Conservative and so abandon allegiance to Labour.

> 'It might even be argued that the whole process of dealignment represents an attempt by a more pluralist, heterogenous and less deferential society to break out of the two-party straitjacket.'
> Robert Pinkney, 'Dealignment, Realignment or just Alignment?' in *Parliamentary Affairs* (January 1986)

- **Class fragmentation.** This process is also described above, in Unit 2. As traditional industries such as coal, steel, engineering and ship-building have declined while increased automation has reduced the number of manual jobs available, the traditional working class has become scattered. Increasing employment in service industries has led to a growth in the lower and central middle classes. As a result, there are simply less members of traditional classes who might have been closely allied to one political party.

- **Partisan de-alignment** describes a process whereby the traditionally strong connections between certain sections of the population and a particular party have become weaker. This has been described as a lower level of identification with a party, a phenomenon which might also be described as an emotional attachment. The reasons, identified by researchers such as David Denver and Ivor Crewe, vary from dissatisfaction with the performance of the two main parties to increased awareness of political issues, resulting in voters making an informed choice rather than merely voting out of habit for the same party. William Wale's research indicates a marked decline since the 1960s of voters who 'strongly identify' with any party at all. This implies that they have become volatile, non-class-based voters.

Having said all this, it is still true that class remains an important factor in voting behaviour. Some figures from the 1992 election indicate this:

Class and voting in the 1992 General Election			
Class*	% supporting Cons.	% supporting Labour	% supporting Lib Dems.
A/B	56	20	22
C1	52	25	19
C2	38	50	15
D/E	30	50	15

Source: MORI

* Key: A/B = Professional and managerial classes
C1 = Clerical and secretarial workers
C2 = Skilled and semi-skilled manual workers
D/E = Unskilled manual workers and unemployed

Secular cleavage Ivor Crewe's influential contribution to the debate on modern voting tendencies revolves principally around the concept of secular cleavage. Instead of the old class analysis of party allegiance, Crewe suggests, we must look in more detail at individuals' place in the economic structure and in their lifestyle. Thus, he identifies strong Labour support among those who live in council-provided accommodation, work in the public, rather than private sector, and are members of a trade union. On the other hand, people who own their own homes, work for private companies and are not union members are more likely to vote Conservative or even Liberal Democrat. Thus, the cleavage, or division, of support between the parties is based less on class than on 'section' of the population that people belong to.

Of course, if Crewe's analysis is valid, the traditional Labour Party was certainly doomed to permanent electoral decline, since the kind of voters he identifies as typical Labour supporters are in sharp decline. It is not surprising, therefore, that the modernisation of the Labour Party became inevitable if it was to survive.

Instrumental voting As society experiences social fragmentation and voters become better informed about political issues, there is a tendency for more voters to choose the party which is likely to bring them most personal benefits. This is known as **instrumental** voting. Property owners, therefore, are likely to support a party which is committed to helping them financially and to maintaining a strong position on law and order. Similarly, high-income groups look for tax-cutting parties. The poor, on the other hand, are more interested in welfare and employment policies. The elderly are concerned about health and pensions, young families about education, and so on.

The concept of voters developing a 'shopping list' of demands which will suit them and comparing this list with party manifestos poses a new challenge for politicians who must then attempt to find policies which will maximise their appeal. It is also likely to contribute to more volatile voting behaviour.

Other factors As we have seen, little about voting behaviour is simple any more. There are now many factors which seem to have some effect on voting trends. To begin with, we can identify those factors which seem to have a negligible effect. These include age, sex and religion. There are some trends – a slight tendency for the young to support Labour, for women and members of the Church of England to be Conservative, while Catholics tend to support Labour more often. However, it is likely that other factors discussed above are the real causes of these slight biases.

The question of region is becoming more important. Irrespective of social class, there are important differences in the strength of party support in different parts of the country. The statistics bear this out:

Seats won in the 1992 General Election				
Region	**Conservative**	**Labour**	**Lib. Dem.**	**Other**
London	48	35	1	0
Southern England	161	10	6	0
Midlands	57	43	0	0
Northern England	53	107	3	0
Wales	6	27	1	4
Scotland	11	49	9	3

We can see from the statistics a marked bias towards the Conservatives in the south of England, almost matched by a similar leaning to Labour in the north. Labour dominates Scotland and Wales as much as the Conservatives control the South. These regional variations cannot be totally explained by concentrations of social class in those regions. There are, unquestionably, some regionally based party allegiances. These are almost certainly the result of certain perceptions about how much the parties pay attention to the special needs of different parts of the country.

The Scots, Welsh and northerners commonly believe that Conservative Governments have consistently ignored their demands. The Conservatives are very much seen as the party of 'the south'. The reverse is true in the south of England, where Labour is not seen as the appropriate vehicle for voters' demands.

Summary

If we draw these threads together we can now make some generalisations about the nature of voting behaviour:

- Social class is still an important factor, but a declining one.
- A decreasing number of voters have a strong permanent allegiance to one party or another.
- Voters tend, in increasing numbers, to 'shop around' for the best party to meet their particular needs.
- There is a greater tendency today for voters to understand the issues and to allow them to determine voting rather than relying on traditional allegiances.
- A person's lifestyle and economic status remain key factors in voting behaviour.
- Such factors as religion, age and sex have a relatively minor influence.
- There are marked regional variations in voting patterns.

What determines election results?

Although, as we have seen above, voting is more volatile and unpredictable than it used to be, a substantial proportion of the population know which way they will vote even before an election campaign begins and will, therefore, be unaffected by any short-term factors. This proportion may still be as high as 50 per cent. What of the rest? What makes their mind up? A number of factors may be at work together.

The media

As we saw in Unit 2, the British media have traditionally been biased towards the Conservative Party, certainly the campaigns waged by the *Sun, Daily Mail, Daily Express* and the *Daily Telegraph* helped to underpin support for the Tories throughout the 1980s and in 1992. With the decline in traditional party support, as described above, voters are more open-minded and susceptible to persuasion. The newspapers have filled some of the vacuum left by the reduction in the importance of social class in voting behaviour.

Party image

Commentators such as Dennis Kavanagh have noted that the general image of a party can be as important as the detailed issues which it raises. For example, a disunited party presents a negative impression; if it cannot act concertedly in a campaign, how will it handle government?

Certainly Labour in the 1980s suffered from the image of a working-class party, committed to trade unionism, high taxes and wasteful expenditure. The 'antics' of the so-called 'loony Left' of extreme socialists, much publicised in the popular press, had a disproportionately powerful effect on voters, well beyond its true significance in the party. By contrast, the Conservatives presented themselves as responsible and united, solid attributes with which voters could easily identify. In the closely fought 1992 election, it was the spectre of high taxes which went a long way to ensuring a Labour defeat. The facts did not point to the actual likelihood of significantly higher taxes under Labour, but the image was what mattered more than the reality.

John Major outside No. 10 Downing Street after the 1992 general election

Party leaders

During the 1983 election campaign the contrast between the dynamic, determined and practical Margaret Thatcher, and the uncertain, intellectual, but slightly eccentric Michael Foot could hardly have been more marked. By 1987 Neil Kinnock was in charge of Labour, but he still could not compete with the charismatic image presented by Prime Minister Thatcher.

Neil Kinnock put up a better fight in 1992 against John Major, but still failed to pull off a victory. Kinnock presented a slick, self-assured image by this time, but could still not quite match the trustworthy image which Major conjured up. The election experts agree that it was largely the image of the two party leaders which tipped the balance in favour of the Conservatives in an otherwise close contest.

Party performance

It is often said that the incumbent Government cannot win an election, but it can certainly lose one. This implies a negative side to electioneering which has come to the fore in recent times. Increasingly, elections are fought on the basis of the record of the Government rather than the plans of opposition parties. If there are sufficient negative images, the opposition will win. If not, there is a likelihood that the Government will survive.

The Labour Government, which lost in 1979, for example, had enjoyed a moderately successful period of economic management in the second half of the 1970s, notably bringing inflation down from peak levels of 22 per cent to single figures. In the autumn of 1978 it was expected to win the forthcoming election comfortably. The notorious 'Winter of Discontent' in 1978–9, when a series of public sector strikes over pay led to severe disruption in British life, put an end to this. The voters were left with a strongly negative image of Labour. The second Conservative Government of John Major appears vulnerable for similar reasons.

The campaign

With voters more willing to switch allegiance, the election campaign itself has taken on a new significance. All the parties now hire consultants (the so-called 'spin doctors') and advertising agencies to manage the public campaign. In the 1980s, Margaret Thatcher's association with the advertising agency of Saatchi and Saatchi was seen as a key factor in three successful campaigns. News conferences, speeches by front-bench spokespersons, walkabouts, rallies and conferences are carefully orchestrated to achieve maximum impact. Despite all these carefully laid plans, however, events can be unpredictable.

In the 1992 campaign, for example, Labour believed it had stolen a march on the Tories by finding a child who was suffering because of the failure of the National Health Service to treat her (the state of the Health Service was an important issue that year). This backfired when it appeared that the whole incident appeared to be an elaborate set-up, with little basis in reality. Labour suffered badly from the publicity. Similarly, an ineptly managed rally for Labour a few days before polling day received much negative publicity. Finally, John Major's idea to give speeches in the street from a soapbox was warmly received. Thus, unpredictable incidents can have an important influence on party fortunes. In the end, the 1992 election was probably won, as we have seen, because of the success which the Conservative campaign organisers achieved in persuading the voters that they could expect sharp tax increases if Labour won.

Public opinion polls

Two questions may be asked of opinion polls. First, are they accurate enough to be of any use? Secondly, do they affect the way in which people view politics and the way in which they vote, in particular?

The accuracy of opinion polls

The unexpected result of the 1992 general election, when a narrow Conservative victory shocked the experts who were expecting a comfortable Labour win up to a few days before polling day, brought into question the accuracy of such polls. Some statistics may be helpful here:

Error levels of two leading opinion polls		
1979	**Gallup**	**NOP**
Conservative	− 1.9%	+ 1.1%
Labour	+ 3.2%	+ 1.2%
1983		
Conservative	+ 2.0%	+ 3.5%
Labour	− 1.8%	− 3.3%
1987		
Conservative	− 2.3%	− 1.3%
Labour	+ 2.5%	+ 3.5%
1992		
Conservative	− 4.3%	− 3.8%
Labour	+ 2.8%	+ 6.8%

Source: *British Political Facts 1900–94*, Butler and Butler (Macmillan)

Where the figure shows a plus, it indicates that the polling organisation over-estimated the strength of voting support for a party. A minus indicates an under-estimate. The sample used varies normally between 1,000 and 2,500 respondents and there is usually a possible 4 per cent error in sampling accepted. If we take this 4 per cent margin, we can see that the polls were **always** within their accepted error band, with the exception of NOP's 1992 prediction for Labour.

This suggests a remarkable degree of accuracy, bearing in mind the relatively small size of the samples used and the fact that the actual voting took place a few days after the final poll was taken, time enough for many to change their minds. Indeed, it was understood that the relative inaccuracy of the 1992 polls was not due to poor techniques in opinion research, but rather to a very late swing in voting attention away from Labour towards the Conservatives. Evidently many voters were still making up their minds as they entered the polling stations.

Do opinion polls affect voting?

The French clearly believe so, along with a number of other democracies, as they ban the publication of opinion poll findings a week before an actual election. They fear two effects. One is a 'bandwagon' effect, often observed in the USA, where some undecided voters may throw their support behind the candidate they feel is most likely to win. This is an irrational form of behaviour, but some fear that it happens. Secondly, there is the possibility of tactical voting, which has been described and discussed above. This is a more realistic threat. Opinion polls give voters the information which is necessary for them to plan their voting tactics. Without it they might simply vote for their genuine preference.

There is, however, little evidence to suggest that opinion polls have any significant effect on British elections. They can help the politicians, of course, by telling them whether their current campaigning is gaining or losing ground. It must also be noted that the parties commission their own private opinion polls. But if they do have an influence, it seems to be too small to be discernible.

For exam questions relevant to this unit, see page 492.

7 Parliament

Introduction

The term 'Parliament' actually refers to three institutions grouped into one. These are:

1. The Queen-in-Parliament
2. The House of Commons
3. The House of Lords.

We may dispense quickly with references to the Queen. This is largely an historical hangover from times when Parliament's role was to sustain and legitimise the activities, mostly financial, of the Crown. This role effectively ceased at the end of the seventeenth century. The monarch has not been allowed in the House of Commons since Charles I attempted to arrest a group of rebellious MPs in 1641. Indeed, to this day, the reigning monarch is only permitted to enter the House of Lords once a year to deliver the 'Queen's Speech', a statement of the Government's legislative programme for the year.

Today the monarch's only legislative role is to grant the Royal Assent (i.e. to sign) Bills after they have passed through all the parliamentary stages required. Royal Assent turns a Bill into a statute or law and indicates that the courts should now enforce its measures. Since Royal Assent has not been withheld since 1707, we may assume that it is now merely a formal procedure. The Queen, in reality, has no choice in the matter.

The House of Commons

Structure

The composition and structure of the Commons (also known as the 'Lower House') is as follows:

MPs are elected from constituencies throughout England, Scotland, Wales and Northern Ireland. Those who are not ministers, or senior members of the Opposition parties, are commonly known as back-benchers.

The Speaker The Speaker is chosen from the elected members. This is the result of a ballot of all the MPs. Upon election the Speaker ceases to be a constituency MP or a party politician. Instead (s)he becomes Chairperson of the House, a role in which (s)he must remain politically neutral. Much of this function is simply to organise debates, choose speakers and generally keep order, disciplining MPs if necessary. However, there are rare occasions when the role of the Speaker can be crucial.

There are occasions, for example, when MPs may demand an emergency debate of a current issue. The Government may wish to speed up the passage of a Bill through the House by introducing a 'Guillotine Motion'. Such a device cuts short opportunities for debate in the interests of speed. There may also be a variety of procedural disputes which could affect the fortunes of legislation. In these, and in a variety of other cases, the Speaker may become involved in controversial political issues, but must still remain neutral.

A typical back-bench MP's week

Monday Morning	*Answer correspondence. Attend party policy committee meeting*
Monday Lunch	*Entertain members of lobby group*
Monday Afternoon	*Attend debate on important Bill followed by administrative work.*
Monday Evening	*Attend further debate. Stay for a series of divisions. Dinner with party colleagues. Return to London flat after 10 pm*
Tuesday Morning	*Answer correspondence. Meet delegation from constituency concerning road-building scheme*
Tuesday Lunch	*Entertain delegation from a foreign Parliament*
Tuesday Afternoon	*Attend Prime Minister's questions. Unsuccessful attempt to ask question. Administrative work*
Tuesday Evening	*Attend dinner given by large business company. Attend debate in the House. Stay for series of divisions until 2 am*
Wednesday Morning	*Answer correspondence. Attend Standing Committee*
Wednesday Lunch	*Entertain chairman of constituency party visiting the House*
Wednesday Afternoon	*Attend Transport Minister's questions. Ask question about road plans in constituency. Administrative work*
Wednesday Evening	*Free*
Thursday Morning	*Answer correspondence. Attend back-benchers' meeting*
Thursday Lunch	*Outside speaking engagement at school in London*
Thursday Afternoon	*Attend Prime Minister's questions. Unsuccessful attempt to ask question. Interview with radio station*
Thursday Evening	*Attend outside transport committee meeting. Dinner alone. Return to House for divisions until midnight*
Friday Morning	*Answer correspondence. Party policy committee meeting. Meeting with senior officials at Department of Transport about road plans in constituency*
Friday Afternoon	*Return to constituency. Attend surgery to hear constituents' problems*
Friday Evening	*Attend dinner with local businessmen*
Saturday Morning	*Interview with local newspaper journalist*
Saturday Lunch	*Entertained by senior members of constituency party*
Saturday Afternoon	*Open fête at school in constituency*
Saturday Evening	*Home with family*
Sunday	*Home with family*
Sunday Evening	*Return to London*

The front-benches   The front-benches comprise senior members of the two major parties. In the case of the governing party, these are ministers, while in the Opposition party they are described as 'shadow ministers, or 'spokespersons'. The reason for the name 'front-benches' speaks for itself.

Leader of the House   The Leader of the House is a Cabinet minister whose main role is to organise the business of the House on behalf of the government. Virtually all of the Commons' programme is controlled by the Cabinet. Time allotted to Opposition parties or to individual MPs' concerns is a minority of the total. The Leader of the House, after consultation with the full Cabinet at its weekly meetings, arranges business with the Speaker, including which front-bench members will speak. He then informs the Government whips, who pass information on to the MPs. The Official Opposition party has a 'shadow leader' who organises the small amount of time allotted to his party.

Whips   The whips derive their name from fox-hunting circles where the hounds need to be organised and kept in order. This is an appropriate analogy in the context of the Commons. The Chief Whip (a senior member of his party) with several assistants has the responsibility of ensuring that MPs are informed about parliamentary business, turn up at important debates and, most importantly, remain loyal to the party line. In practice, this means ensuring that MPs vote in line with the Government's wishes. MPs who may be prepared to defy the official party line can expect a visit from a whip who will give them a hard time if they remain obstinate. The role of the whips is central to the operation of government in Britain and will be discussed in some depth below. Whips of the non-governing parties play a similar role, but since the Government's policy is not at stake among the other parties, their function is less critical.

Whips are also described as the 'eyes and ears of the Prime Minister'. It is expected of them to report on the mood of MPs, and to provide answers to such questions as: 'Will they support the party leadership?', 'Can a potential rebellion be headed off?', 'Can a deal be done to head off trouble?' The whips shuttle back and forth between ministers and back-benchers to ensure that Government control over the House is maintained. In the critical days of the minority Labour Government from 1977–9, and during the period of debates over the introduction of the Poll Tax in the late 1980s, the whips were fully employed, with variable success.

Departmental select committees   These were set up in 1979. There are twelve which investigate work of the major government departments, plus committees dealing with Welsh, Northern Ireland and Scottish affairs (though the latter has rarely met owing to a lack of Conservative MPs representing Scottish seats). Each has eleven members, all back-benchers, with a chairperson who may be from the Government or main Opposition party. They may call any witness, including ministers, civil servants, pressure group representatives or any other person who may have relevant views and information. Together with a small research staff, they investigate the efficiency, procedures, effectiveness and related matters concerning departments. In addition, they investigate serious issues and problems which may arise from time to time. These select committees have become a key development in the working and status of the House of Commons. Examples of their work are shown opposite:

Significant select committee work in the 1980s and 1990s

- Successful recommendation to repeal the notorious 'sus' laws whereby police could arrest a person merely on suspicion of planning to commit a crime.
- Measures to protect private pension funds introduced as a result of the Social Services Committee's recommendations following the Maxwell scandal.
- The Treasury Committee's report on the collapse of the BCCI Bank resulted in better control of banks by the Bank of England.
- The Foreign Affairs Committee's condemnation of the exchange of aid (in the form of the Pergau Dam project) for arms sales to Malaysia 1994.

Other select committees   Most other select committees are merely concerned with the domestic arrangements of the House. However, the **Public Accounts Committee** (PAC) is influential in its role of investigating government expenditure, ensuring that it has been used for the purpose for which Parliament has given its approval and that it has been used efficiently. Its independence from government influence is aided by the tradition of ensuring that it is chaired by a member of the Opposition. In 1994 a damning report by the PAC suggested that over £300 million had been wasted by government departments over ten years, thus putting in train a series of investigations into public spending.

Standing committees   These are larger than select committees, with up to forty members. Their role is to consider possible amendments to legislation during its passage through the House. On the face of it this appears to be a key role, but in practice these committees are very much controlled by the Government whips. The Government has a majority of loyal MPs on each committee so that only those amendments of which the Government approves are likely to be adopted. Proposed legislation does have to be tidied up, clarified and modified to take into account various demands for change by interested groups, so it is an important role. However, the standing committees lack independence and, in any case, all their proposals must be approved by the whole House at the 'report stage' of a Bill. A new committee is formed for each separate Bill and, on the whole, MPs treat membership as a chore, however necessary it may be.

Functions   Although Parliament is described as the 'legislature', suggesting its main role is to make laws, in fact the legislative process is a relatively small part of its functions. The House of Commons in particular plays a much wider role in the British political system than the term 'legislature' suggests. We can identify the range of functions as follows:

An electoral college   Since Britain has no formal constitution to determine how a government should be formed following a general election, we must rely on the House of Commons to ensure stable government. Effectively, a Government consists of a Prime Minister and Cabinet which can enjoy the regular support of the majority of the House of Commons. In this sense, the House 'elects' the Government. Since general elections nearly always produce one party which has a majority of the seats in the House of Commons, an actual vote is not required. We simply assume that the leader of the majority party in the House will form a Government and it will be supported by the majority of MPs. Of course, should no party have an overall majority, the House **would** be required to approve a new Government by a vote (this would be in the form of a vote of confidence in the proposed Government).

Thus, the function of being an electoral college is only **implied**. In those states where clear majorities are rare and coalition governments are common, Parliaments play a key role in deciding who shall form a Government. The Commons reserves that function for a time when it might be needed.

It should also not be forgotten that the House of Commons can 'un-elect' a Government and occasionally does so. Thus, in 1979, the Callaghan Labour Government was ousted by the Commons after its failure to secure a measure of autonomous government for Scotland and Wales. In that year a vote of 'no confidence' was passed and, shortly afterwards, Callaghan resigned.

Sustaining government This role is not generally understood or appreciated. It was the nineteenth-century journalist, Walter Bagehot, who discovered a fundamental truth about the British political system. He argued that the system has 'efficient secrets' – aspects which ensure that it runs smoothly and effectively. The power of the Cabinet was the main secret, but the role of the House of Commons was almost as important, he argued. The Commons usually supports the Government (even more so now than in Bagehot's day!) and, in so doing, gives it **authority** and **legitimacy**. The House of Commons has been elected by the people. If it grants approval to what the Government is doing, it is granting authority from the people, albeit indirectly. This strengthens and sustains the Government since it can claim that all its actions have the authority of the people as long as Parliament, in particular the Commons, will support it. It may appear from televised debates in the Commons that there is a constant battle raging between Parliament and Government, but this is largely generated by the minority Opposition. Most of the time the Commons majority supports its own Government.

Legislation This refers to the formal process of passing laws. In order for a law to be enforced in the courts it must have passed through the formal procedures of both Houses of Parliament. Much of this is a ritual since the governing majority in the House of Commons nearly always has its way. Indeed, if the Government suspects it may not be able to carry the support of its own party on a Bill, it will normally drop the measure rather than face a defeat on the floor of the House of Commons. Thus, the Labour Government abandoned proposals to reform trade unions in 1969, fearing defeat in the Commons, while the Conservative administration miscalculated in 1986 and was defeated on its Bill proposing to allow all shops to open on Sundays (since passed). The fact that the only serious defeat of a Government Bill since World War Two was in 1986, is an indication of how much the legislative process is a formality.

Debates on legislation may be interesting, informed and often hotly contested, but the result of a vote in the Commons is rarely in doubt. Nevertheless, the passage of legislation is required to give legitimacy to the laws. Just as Parliament gives authority to government in general, it also grants authority to individual statutes.

The actual legislative procedures are shown in the box opposite.

Legislative process	
First Reading:	Purely formal. No vote is taken.
Second Reading:	A full debate on the principles of the Bill. A vote (called a Division) follows the debate.
Committee Stage:	A standing committee considers possible amendments.
Report Stage:	The proposed amendments are presented to the whole House. A Division is taken on each.
Third Reading:	A further debate on the Bill including amendments. Another Division follows.
Further Stages:	The Bill is passed to the Lords and thence for Royal assent.

Making government accountable   It is a basic principle of the British system of parliamentary government that ministers answer to Parliament, the Commons in particular, for what they do. Accountability effectively means that actions and policies must be explained, justified and open to debate. It also implies that errors may be exposed and, in extreme circumstances, ministers or the Government as a whole may be forced to resign by the Commons. Governments are accountable to the people at general elections, but it is Parliament which makes them answerable on a day-to-day basis.

This function is most apparent during Question Times in the House, either to the Prime Minister every week, or to individual ministers from time to time. Many questions and answers are written and thus never see the public light of day. Nevertheless, the process is taking place continually. General and legislative debates are further opportunities to force government to justify its actions.

The select committees have begun to take over much of this function from the whole House. Here ministers and their officials are subject to questioning, often of an inquisitorial nature. An appearance before such a committee can be a searching test for members of the Government.

Law making   This can be distinguished from legislation in that the latter refers only to the formal process of making Government legislation legitimate. Law making, on the other hand, concerns mostly the infrequent occasions when back-bench MPs themselves introduce and pass laws. These are called **Private Members' Bills**. Only a handful are considered each year and the chances of a successful passage are small. The Government can block such legislation unless it has overwhelming support in the House and, on the whole, it will do so. The reasons for the practice hindering private members' legislation are twofold. First, Governments do not wish to be forced to implement laws they have not produced themselves. Secondly, they will not allow measures which involve them in increased expenditure of taxpayers' money unless they have approved them. In general, therefore, the Commons only initiates legislation if Government approves, or at least does not object. Thus, abortion law reform, various anti-pornography measures and homosexual law reforms have been instigated in this way.

**House of Commons
in session**

There are also unusual occasions when the Government may introduce
a Bill, but allow a **free vote**. Here the whips do not operate and MPs
are free to make up their own minds. Given its independence, therefore,
the House of Commons is actually making law for itself. After its unfortunate 1986 experience, for example, the Government allowed a free vote
on the Sunday Trading issue when it was re-introduced in 1994. However, like Private Members' Bills, free votes are relatively rare.

<u>Representation</u> In a broad sense, the House of Commons represents the
nation and, as such, when it debates an issue, the people as a whole are
indirectly involved. Of course this function is considerably flawed by two
features. First, it is far from being a social microcosm of our society. Less
than 10 per cent of its members are women, there is only a handful of
members of ethnic minorities and the rest are predominantly of middle-
class, professional backgrounds. However much MPs may consult with
their constituents, they cannot be expected to be truly representative,
given such distortions in membership. Secondly, party loyalties are so
strong that MPs are often reluctant to express independent views which
might contradict the philosophy of their political superiors. Nevertheless,
during the great debates of recent years on the issues surrounding wars
in the Falklands, Iraq and Bosnia, the death penalty, Northern Ireland
and law and order issues, the House of Commons can be seen at its best.
Measured arguments mingle with impassioned debate and the public are
informed and educated by the experience.

<u>Redress of grievances</u> This function has been described by Professor
Philip Norton as 'tension release'. Norton points out that individuals
need to feel that, if they are dissatisfied by the way they have been treated
by a governing body, there is some means by which their grievance can
be voiced. Whether or not anything is actually done, it is important that

there is an outlet for complaints. MPs frequently take up issues raised by constituents with relevant ministers or officials, occasionally achieving some success. Matters concerning planning applications, health care, social security and immigration are common examples. Not only must individuals be given help, constituencies as a whole may need representation. MPs have had some success in protecting their constituencies from such problems as intrusive road and rail developments, nuclear-waste dumping and environmental damage.

Influence   Government is subject to a variety of influences in its policy-making procedures. Pressure groups, the media, public opinion in general and committees of experts all have access to ministers. The influence of Parliament is more difficult to assess. However, the fact that many MPs are sponsored by pressure and interest groups, by trade unions, by industrial and commercial concerns and the like suggests they must have some influence. In the 1990s, indeed, there has been a proliferation of professional lobby groups who employ MPs to help them to gain the ear of the Government. At the same time, the departmental select committees have grown in status and are beginning to take a more active role in policy initiation. Despite this, influence is not power, so where key policies are concerned, decision making remains firmly in the hands of the governing party's leadership.

The House of Lords

Structure

The character of the Lords is largely determined by its membership. In many ways it is the most unusual Second Chamber of any political system in the world which claims to be democratic. The membership and structure are as follows:

Hereditary peers   There are about 800 hereditary peers entitled to sit and vote in the House of Lords. In practice, however, most are relatively inactive politically, rarely attending or voting. Of those who express a political allegiance, the vast majority are Conservatives. Their entitlement is based on their being the eldest son of the former holder of the title. It was assumed that, when Prime Minister Wilson declared that he would no longer create any new hereditary peerages, they would begin to die out, literally but Mrs Thatcher began the practice again, creating four new titles after 1983.

Life peers   Since 1958 the Prime Minister (acting in the name of the monarch) has been able to create life peers, whose titles are not passed on to their children. There are about 350 of these at any one time, the number being topped up as life peers die.

Some life peerages are simply granted to prominent citizens as a reward for a deserving career. These are not political appointments and most such peers remain politically independent, declaring themselves 'cross-benchers'. Notable examples have been Lord Olivier, the celebrated actor, and Lord Jacobovits, the former Chief Rabbi.

Most, however, are political appointments, made within the convention that each party may nominate peers in accordance with their relative strengths in the House of Commons. Politicians who wish to move into semi-retirement without completely losing touch with politics are included, such as former Prime Ministers Lord Callaghan and Baroness Thatcher. Lifelong supporters of the party, though not necessarily former

MPs, may wish to serve, such as former trade union leader Lord Feather, or Conservative industrialist Lord Weinstock. In some cases life peerage can be a useful device to bring a colleague into the government who is not an MP. Since ministers must be a members of one of the two Houses (under the doctrine of ministerial responsibility), such a device is occasionally necessary. Mrs Thatcher's close supporter, Lord David Young, was brought into Cabinet in this way in the 1980s.

Lords Spiritual The Church of England is still the 'established' church of the state and, as such, is entitled to send its two archbishops and twenty-four other bishops to sit in the Lords. No other religions have an automatic right to have representatives there. This may seem strange in a multi-cultural society, but it is the result of the historic links between church and state. Normally the bishops sit as cross-benchers.

Law Lords Eleven senior judges are entitled to sit in the Lords. These judges also make up (in groups of five at a time) the highest Appeal Court in Britain, considering cases of great legal or political significance which have been passed up from lower courts of appeal. It is important to stress that when we refer to the House of Lords as a 'court' it is only the Law Lords who are concerned, and the House is here performing a completely different function. At this stage we are considering the House only as part of the legislature where all its members are potentially involved.

Lord Chancellor The Lord Chancellor is unique in British politics, and possibly in the world, in the sense that he is a member of all three branches of government. He is the most senior judge and is thus a member of the judiciary; he is the Speaker, or Chairman, of the House of Lords and so takes part in the legislature; and finally, he is a Cabinet Minister and so is part of the executive.

In the Cabinet he is the Government's senior law officer, advising on legal matters. He is also head of his own department which administers much of the legal system and profession. As a judge he sometimes presides over major appeals. In the Lords he mostly acts as a neutral Speaker, organising debates and general business. (Discipline rarely applies since the House of Lords is nothing if not well behaved, unlike the Commons!) However, from time to time, he may descend from his seat (known as the 'Woolsack') and represent the government in debates. Thus he is expected to play a multi-faceted role and to switch readily from a neutral to a partisan role. He certainly needs rare qualities.

Business managers As in the Commons, there are whips in the Lords and a Leader of the House who organise its business and attempt to maintain party discipline. With many independent cross-benchers and much less party unity (peers are essentially amateur politicians so the power of patronage is very weak) the job for the party bosses is much harder in the Lords than in the Commons. Fortunately for the government, as we shall see, debates and votes in the Upper House are much less critical than in the Commons.

House of Lords in session

<u>Committees</u>   As in the Commons, each Bill requires a stage at which amendments are considered in the Upper House. However, unlike the Commons, the Lords does not form committees as such, but instead the whole House (in practice a relatively small number of interested members) sits as one large committee to consider changes. The fact that all the peers may sit in committee does make it difficult for the Government whips to maintain unity so that small defeats for the Government (all later overturned in the Commons) are not uncommon.

There is a much less developed system of **select committees** in the Lords – this is not considered the proper place for close scrutiny of government – so that just two committees of the House have political significance. These are the committees on Science and Technology and on the European Union. Here the most committed and experienced peers undertake significant work on scrutiny. They have no exact equivalent in the Commons, which gives them greater authority.

Functions   Before we study the functions of the Lords it is important to understand its limitations. There are essentially three realities which control the operation of the Upper House:

- The Parliament Acts of 1911 and 1949. These two Acts declare that the Lords has no control over Money Bills (those involving the raising or spending of public money), that it can only delay any other Bill for up to a year (in practice this means that any Bill passed in two consecutive sessions of Parliament cannot be blocked by the Lords), and that any proposed Lords amendments require the aproval of the Commons.
- Salisbury Doctrine. This was declared in the 1940s when the Labour Government of the day enjoyed an overwhelming Commons majority. The then Conservative Leader of the House of Lords, Lord Salisbury, declared that the Conservative majority in the Upper House did not have the authority to block any measures which had been contained in the ruling party's election manifesto. Salisbury understood that such action would inevitably lead to reform or abolition of the Lords.

- The threat of reform or swampage. Here the elected Government may threaten to reform the Lords so as to make it compliant to the wishes of the Commons, or to swamp it with newly created peers sympathetic to the policies of the Government. (In the 1960s Tony Benn referred to them as his 'thousand peers' taken almost literally off the streets to support the Labour Government.) This threat was to be used to great effect in forcing through the Great Reform Act in 1832, the Liberal Budget of 1909, and sanctions against the rebel regime in the then British colony of Rhodesia (now Zimbabwe) in 1967.

Thus the opportunities for significant action by the Lords are strictly limited. What is left?

Delaying   As we have seen above, the Parliament Acts effectively prevent the Lords from blocking legislation from the Commons. Thus, all it can do is to delay the passage of laws, in practice making the Government think again. The same principle applies to amendments which require Commons approval. In this way the House of Lords may enhance the discussion on policy, but has no real power.

Amending   While it is clearly the case that the Lords is rarely in a position to defy the legislative powers of the Commons, peers may often feel free to make amendments to legislation. In many cases this arises from the fact that the Upper House contains a large number of experts who recognise faults in legislation. This is particularly the case where technical legal matters are concerned. Many former or current lawyers have much to offer and can recognise potential disputes over unclear laws. Thus a number of changes were made to the Community Charge (Poll Tax) regulations in 1988 and to the Police and Magistrates' Courts Act of 1994 concerning the membership of committees controlling these key law enforcement agencies. Pressure groups recognise the potential influence of the Lords and still direct a good deal of their lobbying efforts there to ensure the most favourable legislation.

Debating   Many of the great issues of the day have been the subject of impressive debates in the Lords. These have included questions such as the abolition of the Greater London Council in the 1980s, regular deliberation over the causes of crime and the conduct of economic policy which came to prominence in the early and darker economic days of the Thatcher administration.

We may ask whether such discussions have any real influence over our decision makers and it is true that, in the case of all the examples described above, the government had its way because of its control over the Commons majority.

Safeguarding human rights   There is an assumption that, should a dominant government seek to use its power to threaten individual liberties, the more independent House of Lords stands as a bulwark against what Lord Hailsham called, in 1986, the 'elective dictatorship' of government. Yet once again the Lords' record here is unimpressive. While it is true that an attempt to cancel Greater London Council elections in 1985 was successfully blocked by the Lords, it has failed to hold back steady increases in the powers of the police, despite expressing serious misgivings. Its most notorious defeat concerned the implementation of the Poll Tax legislation in 1988. It was quite clear that the peers considered the tax to be unjust and contrary to the basic principle of taxation that it should be related to the ability to pay. It was clear that they wished to make fundamental changes to the proposals. Faced with the prospect of a disastrous defeat, the Government called up hundreds of normally absent hereditary peers to force the Bill through. Some of the members were so unfamiliar with the Palace of Westminster that they had to be directed to the correct lobby by the whips. Similarly, the Lords' tried to refuse to accept the War Crimes Bill in 1992 on the grounds that no suspected person could be sure of a fair trial when evidence was over fifty years old. Yet, having voted against it, the Bill was simply returned in the same form the following year. Under the Parliament Act rules, the Lords was thwarted once again, being unable to vote against it a second consecutive time.

Thus the evidence suggests that a determined government with a solid Commons majority can defy the Lords whatever it may try to do.

An assessment of Parliament

We cannot attempt any discussion of the importance of Parliament without appreciating the nature of executive control, particularly over the House of Commons. There are a number of factors involved and these can be described as follows:

- It is normally the case that the Government enjoys an overall majority in the Commons. For forty-seven of the fifty years since 1945, the governing party has enjoyed such an overall majority of MPs. Thus normal party loyalties invariably means that unity is preserved. Naturally the **size** of the Government's majority is significant, but nevertheless, simple arithmetic indicates that even a small advantage is crucial.
- Patronage is a key factor in government control. The Prime Minister has about a hundred government posts at his personal disposal, together with a large number of other appointments and honours, notably peerages. Since one of the principal qualifications for political advancement is loyalty, this ensures that a majority of MPs would not think of jeopardising their promotion prospects by defying the instructions of the whips. If we add this group of ambitious members to the ministers and junior ministers themselves who are bound to support the Government under the doctrine of collective responsibility (the so-called 'payroll vote'), few are left as potential rebels. Only when there is a powerful point of principle at stake, such as European integration, are members likely to oppose their political superiors.
- In extreme circumstances a Prime Minister may threaten to resign along with the whole Government and so provoke a general election. MPs with marginal seats are certainly likely to be sobered by threat of defeat, but even those in a secure position would prefer not to fight an election. Furthermore, members generally prefer their own party to be in government. A members' revolt leading to a resignation of the government is more than likely to result in electoral defeat.
- A relatively new phenomenon within the Conservative Party is the pressure placed upon members by their own Constituency Associations. In the great uncertainty over the Maastricht Treaty in 1993, grass-roots members played their part in bringing a number of dissidents into line. Indeed, in the 1990s new alliances were forged between the whips

and some constituency parties to persuade members that compliance would be a wise course of action. This is not a particular feature of the Labour Party, it should be noted however, since constituency parties are often supportive if their member takes a radical, anti-Government line.

- The doctrine of manifesto and mandate generally denies MPs the authority to defy their own Government. It is accepted that most of the electorate vote for a party and its manifesto, rather than for the individual candidates. The MP who then chooses to oppose the manifesto of his own party will be reminded by the whips that (s)he may be betraying the Government's mandate.
- As we have seen above, there are a number of constitutional and political reasons for the weakness of the House of Lords. Apart from embarrassing defeats on amendments, therefore, the Upper House is not a real threat to Government power.

For thirty years after World War Two relatively little attention was paid to Parliament by political commentators. Apart from occasional disputes between a Conservative-dominated Lords and Labour Governments, and short periods during which Governments were vulnerable because of their small majority, Parliament was considered largely irrelevant.

The attitude of MPs themselves tended to confirm such a view. Many continued to pursue other careers almost full time – often in business or the law. They rarely used research assistants and often shared secretarial staff. The practice of holding regular 'surgeries' to hear comments and complaints from constituents did not become common until the 1970s. Select committees, apart from the PAC, held little status and Government defeats were rarely even threatened.

More recently, however, attention has returned to Westminster and there is considerable controversy over its current importance. Attitudes fall generally into two camps, typified by the work of two prominent contemporary experts on parliamentary affairs – Professor Philip Norton and Dr Andrew Adonis.

The Norton view Professor Norton identifies the approximate date of 1970 as a watershed in the behaviour of the House of Commons. He suggests that there have been attitudinal, behavioural and institutional changes in the activities of MPs since that time. He also suggests that the House of Lords has become more professional and independent in its outlook. The result of these changes is that Parliament has been transformed from a supine, unimportant institution into a policy-influencing body. It cannot yet rival the United States' Congress in importance, but has certainly grown immensely in political significance. Thus he suggests:

- MPs expect Governments to listen to them. The experience of Edward Heath's premiership, when they were rarely consulted, led MPs to insist that they should play a more active role in policy formulation, both as a whole and through various policy committees.
- MPs accept to a greater extent that they must represent the interests of their constituents actively and thoroughly. They hold regular consultations with constituents are commonly active in campaigns to protect their constituencies from potentially damaging policies, such as the creation of new motorways or rail routes, or the dumping of nuclear waste. They ask more questions of ministers and are willing to raise local issues in debates on the floor of the House.

- Members consider participation in the work of a departmental select committee to be highly prestigious and useful. In such committees they have a rare glimpse of real influence, normally reserved only for ministers. Seats, and chairmanships in particular, are much coveted. Here they can interrogate ministers and officials without the normal constraints of parliamentary ritual and the reports of such committees have become highly influential on policy.

- The frequency of Government defeats, particularly over amendments, has increased. The 1986 defeat of the Sunday Trading Bill on the second reading was a major event in Commons history, but there have been many occasions when the Government has had a difficult time in passing legislation, often being forced to make important concessions. Thus the Bill to ratify the Maastricht Treaty was only passed on the understanding that Britain would try to hold back the process of European integration. Similarly, the Poll Tax legislation was only passed when thirty or so MPs were 'bought off' with agreement to give certain vulnerable groups of citizens large rebates. MPs no longer consider themselves 'lobby fodder', as they used to be known.

- The House of Lords, with an increasingly representative mix of life peers, has developed what has become known as a 'new professionalism'. As we have seen, it is extremely active in the scrutiny of proposed European legislation. It is also more willing to challenge Government policy, largely through the device of proposed amendments. While such obstructions can be overcome, the Lords has become an important factor in the consideration of future policy making.

Thus, the days when the Government's business managers could disregard Parliament when planning policy implementation have gone. MPs must be consulted fully and often concessions are needed if potential revolts are to be avoided.

The Adonis view   Adonis accepts the Norton analysis in so far as it suggests that Parliament is more important than it was before 1970. However, he insists that it is still only a very small player in the game of policy formulation and implementation. Thus he argues:

- The House of Lords is indeed more active than it used to be and Governments can no longer rely on the smooth passage of legislation through the Upper House. Nevertheless, a Conservative administration can still create a comfortable majority if it so wishes. At the same time, most of its obstruction is little more than a nuisance. Amendments, when successful, are limited in scope and do not alter the fundamental nature of policy.

- The select committees in the Commons are indeed a useful development, but their powers are limited and their influence on policy is yet to be proved.

- There is still no prospect of any major item of public policy being thwarted by the House of Commons. The whips will still have their way. The fact that two key pieces of legislation – the Maastricht Treaty terms and the Poll Tax – were passed despite widespread parliamentary and public opposition, proves that the Commons is still largely politically impotent.

- MPs are still inhibited by the inefficient and archaic procedures of Parliament. There is very limited time for them to raise and pursue issues and the parliamentary agenda is very much controlled by the Cabinet. Private Members' Bills may have wide support, but the Government may block them if it wishes merely by manipulating the procedures. Thus a popular Bill to grant important rights to the disabled was cynically 'killed' by the Conservative Government in 1994, simply by ensuring that it ran out of time.

The 'Adonis view' has many allies in the political arena, notably in the Liberal Democrat Party, but also among politicians of both the Left and the Right, including Tony Benn and Nicholas Winterton respectively. Before we consider the possibilities for reform, we can summarise the apparent strengths and weaknesses of the modern Parliament.

Function:	Legitimation
Strengths:	Parliament is respected by the Government and all policies require the approval of the Commons. Proof of this respect is demonstrated by the need to recall Parliament in times of major crises such as the Iraq War. Even foreign treaties are eventually put before the Commons for its approval. There is the reserve power to defeat legislation, as indicated by the defeat of the Sunday Trading Bill.
Weaknesses:	The process of approval is possibly only a ritual meaning little since the Government is so dominant. Although there is an 'appearance' of conflict, the result of nearly every vote is inevitable.

Function:	Ensuring Government accountability
Strengths:	Select committees have become influential and even feared by ministers and officials. They undertake investigations on such issues as the basis upon which overseas aid is given or the sinking of the troopship *Belgrano* in the Falklands War. They have wide powers, research facilities and are fairly free of the influence of the whips.
Weaknesses:	Ministers' Question Time is largely ritualised and little information is extracted. The limitations of collective responsibility and the traditional secrecy of Government makes ministers wary of being too forthcoming. Select committees find it difficult to obtain information from civil servants, who hide behind their constitutional anonymity. In many cases only official Government policy is revealed. Committees have no way of finding out what information may have been withheld by witnesses.

Function:	Representation
Strengths:	The House of Commons is geographically representative. MPs spend a good deal of time and effort caring for the interests of their constituencies. Many of the major interests in the country are represented by both MPs and active peers in the Lords.
Weaknesses:	The Commons does not accurately represent the strength of support for some parties because of the 'unproportionality' of the electoral system. Liberal Democrats and other small parties are under-represented. Socially, neither the Lords nor the Commons are representative. There are relatively few women or members of ethnic minorities. The Commons is dominated by middle-class, professional groups and the Lords is dominated by older and wealthier members. The hereditary peerage is a denial of democratic principles.

Function:	Law-making
Strengths:	The Commons has the power to amend legislation and the reserve power to block Bills. There are some Private Members' Bills passed which have proved to be popular. Prominent examples have been abortion and homosexual law reform.
Weaknesses:	The Government dominates the parliamentary agenda and so is able to block any legislation to which it is opposed. The House of Lords finds it virtually impossible to introduce legislation with any success.

Function:	Safeguarding rights
Strengths:	Although Parliament rarely exercises a veto on legislation which may threaten rights and liberties, the very fact that it does have the power to do so may affect the Government's deliberations.
Weaknesses:	The whips have great powers to ensure loyalty among the governing party's MPs. Where there is a large Government majority in the Commons, rebellions are easily thwarted, while in situations where the Government is vulnerable the strength of party loyalty and executive patronage usually wins the day. The Lords suffers from the knowledge that it can always be forced into compliance by the Commons majority.

Whichever view we may take on the relative strengths and weaknesses of Parliament, proposals for the reform of either or both chambers are numerous. Below are some of the principal suggestions.

Reform of the House of Commons

We can consider House of Commons reform on two levels. First, relatively minor changes could be introduced which would help to improve its performance, but **without fundamentally changing its role or status**. This might be described as 'tinkering' with the system. Secondly, there could be far-reaching reforms which would **revolutionise the powers and activities of the Lower House**.

Minor reforms

- The working hours of the House could be modified. MPs suffer from long working hours – estimated at fourteen hours per day during the week with much of it largely unproductive, often simply waiting for divisions to be called at all hours of the night or in the early hours of the morning. Morning sittings, together with general streamlining of procedures and the elimination of unnecessary rituals, could lighten the load. It should be noted at this stage that it is partly these burdensome hours which prevent more women who have families from seeking to enter Parliament.

- MPs could be supplied with more research and administrative facilities. Much progress has been made in this regard over the last decade, but members still have poor back-up support to reduce their workload or, more importantly, to enable them to be more effective in their scrutinising and representative functions. Even the physical working environment is considered to be an inhibition to efficiency, so sparse is office space.

- The legislative process could be altered and, to a large extent, reduced. The more radical suggestions have included moving the committee stage – when amendments are considered – to the start of the procedure, thus reducing many time-consuming disputes later in the legislative process. This is the basis of the system in the USA and is considered to be a potentially crucial increase in the influence of the House. However, in the USA members of Congress may 'kill' a Bill in this way and it is unlikely that such a power would be accorded to MPs. A second common suggestion is the removal of a whole stage from the process of the passage of a Bill. This would probably be the third reading which largely duplicates the second stage.

- The problem of the socially unrepresentative nature of the membership centres largely on the lack of women. One solution is suggested above, but a 'quota' system has also been proposed. Thus, devices might be put in place to ensure that a minimum number of women are elected. Similar systems for members of ethnic minorities, or indeed any kind of minority, might also be desirable, but are likely to be less practical than a women's quota.

Major reforms
- The greatest change in the status and powers of the House of Commons would be achieved by changing the electoral system. Proportional representation, of whatever type, would increase the representation of smaller parties. Above all, however, PR might very well result in permanently 'hung' Parliaments, coalition or minority Governments in addition to all the political changes which would accompany such developments. The full implications of the introduction of PR are considered under the section on electoral reform, but it can clearly be seen that the possible inability of future Governments to control the House of Commons majority would result in a fundamental change in the nature of executive–legislature relationships. Similarly, greater numerical strength among smaller parties, notably nationalists, would also produce profound political consequences.

- The select committees have been an acknowledged success in terms of the effective scrutiny of government. Further 'beefing up' of the committee system is, therefore, also a popular proposal. More committees with greater powers, extra payments for members or at least chairmen, and the passage of a 'Freedom of Information Act' to improve their ability to obtain official papers, are some of the suggestions which have been considered.

- The introduction of 'fixed-term' parliaments could have implications which are more far-reaching than may at first appear to be the case. However, the notion of fixed periods between general elections – the Liberal Democrat Party suggests four years – could have great significance. One of the realities which prevents MPs of the governing party from risking defeat for their own Government is the fear that the Prime Minister might call an election and so put all their seats in jeopardy. Indeed, John Major made just such a threat in 1993 in order to bring dissident anti-European MPs in his own party into line over ratification of the Maastricht Treaty. The comfortable knowledge that even an important Government defeat would not result in an election might encourage MPs to be more independent in their actions.

'If it [Parliament] is not proving truly effective at passing legislation that works and if it is only a second-rate scrutineer of the executive, then it is failing at its central tasks.'
Andrew Marr, *Ruling Britannia* (Michael Joseph, 1995)

Reform of the House of Lords

Proposals for reform of the Upper House fall into two main categories: changes in its composition, i.e. its membership, and increases in its powers. (There are no realistic suggestions to reduce its powers since these are so limited already.) It would be a mistake, however, to separate these two types of reform. The powers and composition of the Lords cannot be treated separately. It would, for example, be unthinkable to increase the powers of the Lords while still allowing the hereditary peers their voting rights. Thus, any reform would necessarily combine changes in both areas. Of course the most radical proposal is complete abolition. This, together with lesser changes, are considered below:

- Abolition would make Britain a unicameral system and thus a rarity among liberal democracies. It is suggested that, since the Lords is relatively impotent, its absence would make no significant difference. This view is now largely confined to more radical socialists. Most reformers accept that there is a need for some form of second chamber to protect us against any excesses on the part of the House of Commons majority.
- The removal of the voting rights of hereditary peers would have significant results. In particular, it would radically alter the political balance in the House. The so-called 'in-built' Conservative majority would disappear so that Governments of that persuasion might find themselves confronted by regular opposition which could not be overturned. Similarly, the authority and status of the House would be enhanced. Its better political balance and the knowledge that all its members were there on some kind of 'merit' might indeed result in a more independent attitude among the life peers. Thus, without actually increasing its constitutional powers, the second chamber would naturally become more influential.
- There are a large number of combinations of power and composition changes which have been proposed, notably in the Liberal Democrat and Labour Parties, together with the principal pressure group in the field, **Charter 88**. We may summarise the proposals, bearing in mind that any number of combinations of the following proposals have been suggested:

Composition changes

1. Life peers only, chosen with political balance or independent peers only.
2. An elected second chamber, probably by some form of PR which would have a different political balance to that of the Commons.
3. Some form of combination of elected and appointed members.
4. Representatives nominated by local authorities.
5. Representatives nominated by interest and pressure groups.

> **Power changes**
>
> 1. No great change but more authority resulting from changes in composition as shown above.
> 2. Greater amending powers, but no ability to block legislation completely.
> 3. Power to amend and block legislation coming from the Commons but only with an enhanced majority, such as two-thirds or three-quarters.
> 4. Power to discuss and vote on legislation with **constitutional** significance, such as Europe, local government powers, individual rights or the powers of ministers.
> 5. Power to discuss and vote on issues of **regional**, but not national significance.

The changes suggested above are not exhaustive, but they represent some of the main possibilities.

The possibilities of Lords reform

The last serious attempt to reform the House of Lords occurred in 1968–9, led by the most prominent parliamentary reformer, the Labour Minister Richard Crossman (who had also been the original author of the idea of powerful select committees in the House of Commons). In the event, the proposals were defeated by an unusual alliance of right-wing politicians, led by Enoch Powell, who did not want reform, and left-wingers, led by Michael Foot, who believed the reforms did not go far enough.

Since then political events have never been favourable enough for reform. The Liberal peer **Lord Scarman** has consistently campaigned from inside the Lords itself and it is almost certainly true that the vast majority of the British political community accept that Lords reform is long overdue. To say that reform depends upon the election of a Labour Government or a share of power for the Liberal Democrats is rather too simplistic. What may be an attractive proposition to a party in opposition is less endearing to a ruling Government. It requires great political will for any government to make reforms which will lead to greater limitations upon their own power. Reform of both the House of Lords and the electoral system fall into this category of political action. Labour administrations since 1964 have confined themselves to minor changes such as restoring political balance through the creation of life peerages and refusing to create any new hereditary peerages.

Reform will, therefore, require considerable political will. There is a danger that an unenthusiastic Government may be committed to make changes and may have an electoral mandate to do so, but may put reform to the bottom of its political agenda. Ironically, the very fact that the House of Commons is often overloaded with business may prevent it from tackling the inevitably onerous task of reaching agreement on the necessary legislation.

Conclusion

There is no doubt that Parliament is more important than it was twenty years ago, both the Commons and the Lords. Yet the fundamental truths about its position in the political system remain in place. Both Houses are still utterly dominated by the Government except in exceptional circumstances; there is still no real separation of powers between the executive and legislative branches of government; opportunities for the proper scrutiny of government are still limited.

Norman St. John Stevas – the originator of the departmental select committee system

The televising of both Houses, including departmental select committees, has had a dual effect. On the one hand, public awareness of the work of Parliament has increased, while the political profile of backbenchers such as Dennis Skinner, Edwina Currie and David Alton has been raised. On the other, the poor behaviour of MPs and the apparent lassitude of peers has reduced public respect for the institutions. Once the novelty had worn off, the rather ritualised conflict of the Commons became the subject of some ridicule, as did the often sleepy atmosphere in the Lords.

The question of reform is still confined to the problem of what we want in terms of executive–legislature relations. If we wish to continue to experience strong, dominant Governments which are able to take decisive action without undue obstruction, we should leave Parliament largely alone. If, however, we believe the Government is too powerful, too secretive and needs to be the subject of greater control, then Parliament does need more authority and power.

> 'The modern House of Lords has become a kind of lubricant that helps keep an ancient and rusty machine from finally breaking down . . . Those who want to keep our present dilapidated law-making process as it is . . . are the people who want to keep the House of Lords just as it is.'
> Donald Shell, 'The House of Lords' in *Politics Review*, Vol. 5, No. 1 (September 1995)

For exam questions relevant to this unit, see page 489.

8 Prime Minister and Cabinet

Introduction

Over 100 years ago, the English commentator Walter Bagehot wrote in his great work, *The English Constitution*, that the Cabinet was the **efficient secret** of the British political system. What he meant was that while much of our system, such as the monarchy and the House of Lords, was purely ritualised and ceremonial, it had at its centre something which made everything work. This was the Cabinet. He did not mean it was **literally** a secret (although the deliberations of Cabinet remain confidential for at least thirty years by law). What he did mean was that it is not immediately apparent **why** Cabinet should hold such a strategic position.

Britain has no codified constitution, which makes it difficult to identify the precise role of any of our political institutions. In the case of the Cabinet there is an extra difficulty which is that it is never mentioned in our laws, nor does it appear in any of our great Constitutional Documents. When the British political system was being shaped in the seventeenth and eighteenth centuries, the Cabinet certainly did not exist in its present form. Nevertheless, it has become a central element in the system. Thus, it is no secret, but there is an air of mystery about its development.

'Efficient', as Bagehot called it, was a clearer description. The whole system of policy formulation, law making and policy implementation depends upon the existence of Cabinet and its particular characteristics. Were it absent, or at least relatively weak, Britain might find itself in a similar situation to that of the USA. There, the political system may be extremely open and pluralist, but Bagehot would certainly not have called it 'efficient'! The Americans have great difficulty creating political coherence in policy making and implementation. This is because political power in the USA is so dispersed. The British Cabinet concentrates huge power in one place and this is its 'efficient secret'.

The office of Prime Minister is almost as old as Cabinet itself, dating back to 1721. The Prime Minister was then simply the most senior member of the Cabinet and this is still true today. We must, therefore, consider the two together. However, the Prime Minister's office has also become a separate institution in itself in modern times, so we must also consider it separately, which we will do in the second part of this unit.

In case the student of politics is concerned by the long history of the Prime Minister and Cabinet, he can rest assured that the two have only existed in their **present form** since Bagehot's day – 1867 or thereabouts. What took place before then is more the concern of historians than political scientists. It was the development of the modern party system which created the modern Cabinet. In that regard Disraeli and Gladstone, great Conservative and Liberal Prime Ministers respectively, were key figures. Their Cabinets in the latter part of the eighteenth century resembled more the modern Cabinet than those which had gone before.

John Major's Cabinet in session 1994

The Cabinet

The principles of collective decision making

The theories of individual ministerial and collective responsibility are described in Unit 1, pages 33–4. The discussion below refers to the practical application of these doctrines. Cabinet government relies totally on the notion of collective decision making, also known as **collegiality**. Superficially, it is simply a matter of a group of people who come together in order to reach a series of decisions. It may be a case of several heads being better than one, or it may be that the members of the group represent a variety of views so that a balance is struck. A single voice may be too extreme. Cabinet implies both of these things, but it is much more. It also represents the collective leadership of the ruling party. By constantly repeating demonstrations of unity, the Cabinet is able to translate collegiality into parliamentary control. The MPs and peers of the ruling party can rest assured that all the relevant arguments, including their own, have been aired in Downing Street. Thus they can support the resulting decisions. Ministers and whips will constantly remind them of this principle.

> 'For all that passes in Cabinet, every member of it who does not resign is absolutely and irretrievably responsible, and has no right afterwards to say that he agreed in one case to a compromise, while in another he was persuaded by his colleagues.'
> Lord Salisbury, 1878, quoted in 'The Changing Character of Collective Responsibility' by Peter Dorey in *Talking Politics*, Vol. 7, No. 2, (Winter 1994/5)

The practicalities of collegiality in the Cabinet Room are also not simple. It is not sufficient for the Cabinet to obtain a majority and then ask all its members to concur. Nor is it necessary to continue discussions until all members have been persuaded of the rightness of one view, as might occur with a jury. Dissenting ministers who find themselves in a minority are not obliged to **agree** with the opposing view. All they are required to do is to keep their opposition to themselves and, in public, to **defend the decision that had been taken as if they agreed with it**. This may seem dishonest, and indeed radical politicians such as Tony Benn have said so. On the other hand, it could be argued that this kind of 'false' unanimity is understood by other members of the political community. The feeling is that, if the Government cannot present a united front to Parliament, it cannot survive. Splits in the Government would be easily exploited by the Opposition and would also ultimately result in the splitting of the governing party itself. Thus, whether we call it a necessary evil or part of the 'efficient secret' of the system, without the Cabinet British political life would be very different.

We can gain some clues as to the nature and importance of collective decision making by reviewing two occasions when the system broke down.

British membership of the European Community 1975 Britain had joined the Community in 1973 under the leadership of Ted Heath. In the 1974 elections, the Labour Party manifesto committed a future Government to renegotiate the terms of British membership and to put the issue before the people in a referendum. Accordingly, when Labour came to power, negotiations were completed and our membership was confirmed on better terms. However, the Labour Party and the Cabinet itself were hopelessly split on the issue of our membership. The principles of collegiality and collective responsibility could not survive this split. It had been hoped that the Government would be able, **collectively**, to recommend acceptance of the new terms and continued membership. However, there were seven dissidents in the Cabinet who refused to be bound by the rules of collective responsibility. They included several of the party's most powerful and popular leaders: Michael Foot, Barbara Castle, Peter Shore and Tony Benn. A novel response had to be found to this crisis of government. The answer was to suspend the rules of collective responsibility for the duration of the referendum campaign. In this way the 'rebels' could take part in the campaign without inhibitions.

The referendum approved Britain's membership with a two-thirds majority. The split in Labour was not healed by the referendum, although there was only one ministerial casualty – Eric Heffer, who refused to accept the decision, and the strictures of collective responsibility was dismissed. Two main lessons can be learned from the episode. First, that collective responsibility is vulnerable to a Government split on fundamental issues. Secondly, its survival suggests that there was an acceptance that government cannot operate effectively without it.

The Westland dispute 1986 In 1985 it was clear that the British-owned Westland helicopter company was in financial difficulties and about to collapse. As the main suppliers of helicopters to the British armed forces, this was a major crisis. In Cabinet Michael Heseltine, the Defence Secretary, argued for the amalgamation of Westland with a European company. His colleague, Leon Brittan, Secretary for Trade and Industry, favoured links with the American Sikorsky company. The issue concerned both British jobs and the question of whether we should be promoting closer defence links with Europe or the USA.

Margaret Thatcher and Leon Brittan January 1986

Under normal circumstances Cabinet should have settled the dispute – one of its prime functions. However, the crisis exploded into the public sphere when Heseltine revealed openly that the principles of collective decision making were being undermined by the Prime Minister, who clearly supported Brittan. In the aftermath, Brittan ordered the leaking of critical information about Heseltine which should have been confidential. Meanwhile, Heseltine chose to resign on the grounds that 'proper' collective government had broken down. Brittan followed suit when the dubious nature of his activities was revealed.

Westland has unearthed a number of weaknesses in the traditional view of Cabinet government. It indicated how the Prime Minister could subvert the rules in her own interests. It also confirmed the suspicion that ministers can avoid the rules of collective responsibility simply by leaking their views to the Press and then denying any knowledge of it. As a postscript, the resignation speeches of two of Heseltine's colleagues, Nigel Lawson in 1989 and Sir Geoffrey Howe in 1990, also contained complaints that collective decision making had been undermined by Margaret Thatcher.

The membership of the Cabinet

It is the sole responsibility of the Prime Minister to appoint and dismiss members of Cabinet. In constructing his Cabinet he is engaged in two tasks:

- He is selecting the senior ministers, such as Chancellor of the Exchequer or Foreign Secretary, who will automatically sit in the Cabinet simply **because** they hold high office.

- He is constructing a team which will lead the Government. The formation of the team is one of the most crucial roles for any Prime Minister. He or she has a number of considerations to take into account. These include:

- There may be senior members of the party who are so experienced and popular that to exclude them would be unthinkable. This was true of **Denis Healey** in a number of Labour Cabinets. For Margaret Thatcher and John Major, Douglas Hurd always had to be included.
- There are ministers who have enjoyed an excellent record as managers of their departments. It may be, then, that such a 'safe pair of hands' is an automatic choice. Sir Geoffrey Howe had such a record in the 1980s until he came into conflict with Margaret Thatcher.
- A leading politician may have an important following within the party. His inclusion in the Cabinet, therefore, recognises the group of supporters and may secure their co-operation. Thus Margaret Thatcher kept Peter Walker in her teams, even though they were often political adversaries, he being one of the so-called 'wets'. More dramatically, Michael Heseltine was promoted to Deputy Prime Minister and First Secretary of State in 1995 as a reward for his commitment to support John Major in the Conservative leadership election of July 1995. Not only did Heseltine support Major, he also deliverd the votes of his own followers.
- It is always a temptation for a Prime Minister to promote one or two leading rebels in order to 'buy their silence'. The rules of collective responsibility mean that potential rebels are forced to toe the official line and prevented from stirring up trouble on the back benches. This is very much more a Labour Party problem than a Conservative one. Prominent left-wingers such as Michael Foot and Tony Benn have fallen into this category. It is probably also true that John Major was more comfortable with right-wingers Michael Portillo and Peter Lilley inside his Cabinet than outside it. On the other hand, John Redwood was excluded from Cabinet as a result of his unsuccessful bid for the leadership in 1995. There are limits to how much opposition a Prime Minister will tolerate!
- A confident Prime Minister may feel happier if the Cabinet is packed with his or her own close allies. Margaret Thatcher was able to achieve this objective after her second election victory in 1983. After several years of struggle against the 'wets' – those who opposed her right-wing laissez-faire policies – she was able to dismiss their leading representatives, such as Francis Pym, Ian Gilmour and James Prior. In their place she promoted her own allies, such as Norman Tebbit and Cecil Parkinson.
- The alternative is a 'balanced' Cabinet, designed to unify the party and ensure moderate policies. After John Major formed his second Cabinet in 1994, it was clear that such a balance was his preference. Moderate 'liberals' such as Kenneth Clarke and Stephen Dorrell were set against the right–wing 'Thatcherites' such as Lilley and Portillo. At the same time as a 'left-right' balance was required, a pro- and anti-European balance had to be struck so that both sides in the schism within the wider party could be satisfied.

John and Norma Major with campaign staff, after the leadership challenge in 1995

There are a number of government posts which automatically carry Cabinet membership with them. On the other hand, some ministers are not senior enough to warrant a place in the Cabinet. Effectively, therefore, there are three kinds of ministerial office – those which automatically carry Cabinet status, those which **may** include a place in Cabinet, and those which are too junior for the holder to expect to be included in the Cabinet. Some examples of each are shown below:

Posts always in Cabinet	Posts which *may* be in Cabinet	Posts *never* in Cabinet
Prime Minister	Chief Whip	All 'junior ministers'
Chancellor of the Exchequer	National Heritage Secretary	Sports Minister
Foreign Secretary	Transport Secretary	Local Government
Defence Secretary	Housing	Minister
Energy Secretary	Party Chairman	
Lord Chancellor		
Leader of the House		
Health Secretary		

The actual number of Cabinet members varies according to current circumstances, but it will normally be between twenty and twenty-five. There are some who argue that this is too big to be effective, but others suggest that there is, in reality, an informal 'inner Cabinet' of close associates of the Prime Minister which is able to manipulate the official Cabinet. If we include those MPs who are 'Parliamentary Private Secretaries' – unpaid assistants to ministers – there are about 110 members of the Government in all. Thus, the Cabinet represents about one-fifth of the whole Government.

We should note certain further characteristics of Cabinet membership:

- All must be members of Parliament, either the Commons or the Lords.
- Most come from the Commons, but there must be some members from the Lords who can represent Cabinet there. Since the Lord Chancellor and Leader of the House of Lords are automatic members, there can be no fewer than two representatives from the Lords.
- Although the Cabinet Secretary, Britain's most senior civil servant, attends all Cabinet meetings, prepares the papers and writes the minutes (i.e. the official account) of the meetings, he is not a member and should play no direct part in decision making. (Though informally, as a close adviser of the Prime Minister, he is an influential figure.)

From time to time, junior ministers or civil servants may be invited to address a Cabinet meeting; they too are not members and will be asked to leave once their business has been dealt with. Thus, it is a very exclusive 'club'.

Functions of the Cabinet   Although minutes of Cabinet meetings are subject to the 'Thirty-Year Rule', which means that they remain a secret for at least thirty years, a number of former Cabinet ministers, notably Richard Crossman and Barbara Castle, both Labour ministers in the 1960s and 1970s, have written extensive diaries which inform us about the operation of the Cabinet. It is also common today for ministers to 'leak' information which updates our knowledge of goings-on there.

We can identify six main functions of the modern Cabinet:

Controlling Parliament's agenda   The Cabinet meets, normally, once a week. When Parliament is also in session the weekly agenda must be organised. This will include which ministers are to speak in debates and dealing with any possible problems with the back-benchers. In the medium term, decisions must be made as to when Bills or White Papers (pre-legislative consultation papers) are to be introduced. The standing committees of the House of Commons, which discuss amendments, may also need some discussion.

Dealing with crises and emergencies   All governments must deal with events as they arise. It may be a growing economic crisis, such as excessive inflation or a sudden drop in the value of sterling. Possibly the most serious example of such an emergency was the crisis over speculative selling of the pound on the foreign exchanges in September 1992, known as 'Black Wednesday'. Then Britain's membership of the European Exchange Rate Mechanism – a central element in our economic policy – was threatened and a decision had to be made as to whether to abandon membership and risk a total loss of public confidence. It had to be a collective Cabinet decision for without it the Government could have been hopelessly split. In the event Britain did leave the system, but the Cabinet stood firm in its support for the action. Of course, foreign affairs is another common example of the need for rapid decision making. Wars in the Falklands and Iraq became the subjects of many crisis meetings.

Settling inter-departmental disputes   From time to time problems may arise between government departments and, if the ministers concerned cannot settle their differences privately, the dispute must be brought to

Cabinet for the judgement of colleagues. By far the most common type of problem concerns finance. The Treasury, which holds the purse strings, is engaged in a constant battle with departments to hold down public expenditure. Thus, decisions as to whether a minister's cherished programme can be properly funded despite Treasury opposition may have to be made by Cabinet. However, since one department's spending plans may deprive another of much needed funds, the Chancellor of the Exchequer can usually find plenty of Cabinet allies.

Allocating government expenditure Late summer and autumn are the main season for financial disputes in Cabinet. It is then that the Treasury must finalise plans for overall government expenditure in the following financial year. The Chief Secretary to the Treasury (i.e. assistant to the Chancellor of the Exchequer) will attempt to finalise the plans after negotiations with ministers outside Cabinet. Normally, however, there will be a few remaining problems to be resolved inside Cabinet. Usually this will concern a minister who is holding out for his share of the budget 'cake' despite pressure from colleagues. It is on these occasions that strong ministers earn their spurs and the weak ones fall by the wayside. Senior ministers are often judged by MPs, the press, civil servants and their colleagues on the basis of their ability to secure funds against the opposition of Cabinet colleagues. Indeed, Barbara Castle described Cabinet as little more than a 'battleground'. The public view of a happy, united body was usually false, she suggested.

Policy formulation A number of ministers who served in Margaret Thatcher's Cabinet have reported that there was an almost total absence of discussion of general policy. The Prime Minister considered that a matter for her as party leader and Prime Minister. Cabinet's role was to run the government on a day-to-day basis. So many ex-ministers and journalists have reported this phenomenon that it seems likely to be the case. There is evidence that, under John Major, there is more discussion of policy. The Cabinet is undoubtedly less dominated by the Prime Minister in the 1990s and is therefore more likely to be able to formulate policy itself. In any event, the long-term legislative programme – which matters are to be dealt with now and which can be postponed – must be the subject of Cabinet approval. The establishment of priorities is, therefore, a key function.

Ratifying decisions formulated elsewhere As we shall see below, much of the work of Cabinet is carried out in smaller committees of ministers. Their recommendations must be approved by the full Cabinet before they become official Government policy. In most cases this is a formality; only rarely will committee business cause controversy. It would be an error to believe that Cabinet spends much of its time arguing and agonising over decisions. In fact it is largely a 'clearing house' for business which has been transacted elsewhere.

Cabinet committees Until 1992 the existence and importance of Cabinet committees had been one of the worst kept secrets in Whitehall. It had never been acknowledged that most of Cabinet's work was carried out in committee, nor was it announced which committees existed and who sat on them.

Nevertheless, every MP and political journalist knew perfectly well how the system worked and could, if he were determined enough, find out what the committees were doing. In view of this, and as part of his commitment to more open government, John Major decided to publish details. He kept his promise in May 1992 and revealed that there are two types of committee – **standing** and **ad hoc**. The former are permanent or at least will exist for the foreseeable future. Ad hoc committees, on the other hand, are temporary. The ad hoc committees carry the name **MISC** or **GEN**, followed by a number which identifies them.

In fact, in 1992, only the identity and membership of the standing committees was published. Nevertheless, it gives us a clear insight into the business of government. The list which was first announced ran as follows:

Standing Cabinet Committees (1992)	
Committees chaired by the PM	**Committees chaired by ministers**
Economic and Domestic Policy	Industrial, Commercial, Consumer Affairs
Defence and Overseas Policy	Environment
The Gulf (since disbanded)	Home and Social Affairs
Nuclear Defence Policy	Local Government
European Security	Future Legislation
Hong Kong and other Dependencies	Current Legislation
Northern Ireland	Civil Service Pay
Science and Technology	Health Strategy
Intelligence Services	Public Sector Pay
	European Questions
	Eastern Europe
	Terrorism
	London
	Drug Misuse
	Urban Policy
	Alcohol Misuse
	Women's Issues

We can see above virtually the full range of the Government's responsibilities. In addition, the ad hoc committees are constantly forming and disbanding as new issues come and go. Thus, in the recent past there have been temporary committees on AIDS, on the Falklands crisis and on the European Exchange Rate Mechanism (ERM). More importantly, however, it is increasingly the practice for the Prime Minister to form small committees of his senior colleagues to deal with an issue of great current importance. These ad hoc committees are 'inner Cabinets' of the kind reported by Crossman in the 1960s, but of a less permanent nature.

The use of committees, which first came into existence under Lloyd George's premiership after 1916, has grown considerably since the 1960s. They have since become an integral part of the government machinery. The increased importance of the committees has given rise to several conclusions as to their significance:

- They have dispersed power away from the full Cabinet to a wider group of ministers since non-Cabinet ministers do staff most of the committees alongside Cabinet colleagues. This is illustrated by the fact that regular Cabinet meetings have been reduced from twice to once weekly.
- Smaller groups of ministers are concerned with many specialised decisions. In a sense this is merely an admission of what has always been true – that most ministers do not have either the knowledge or the interest to become involved in decisions which do not affect their own department's work. In other words, they are the inevitable result of the increasing volume and complexity of government business. The Cabinet alone simply cannot cope any more.
- A criticism, certainly before the details of committees were published, was that they formed a kind of 'secret government' from which many ministers were excluded. Although every committee decision must be ratified by the full Cabinet, as we have said there is insufficient time for most ministers to investigate fully what the committees are doing.
- The key committees, standing and ad hoc, are chaired by the Prime Minister. Commentators have suggested that this is one of the modern ways in which the Prime Minister is able to dominate Cabinet government. In addition to holding the chair and therefore controlling the agenda, it is an additional source of patronage for him. Ambitious ministers will seek places on the key committees and rely on the Prime Minister to place them there. In return, he can expect their loyalty.

A note of caution about the committees needs to be struck here. It could be argued that the growth of committees is not an indication of the decline of Cabinet government; rather, it is part of the development of a 'Cabinet system' – still Cabinet government, but with power being more dispersed.

We can summarise the following points on Cabinet committees as follows:

Cabinet committees

1. They have existed for over 70 years, but the main growth in their use has been since the 1960s.
2. They mirror all the main current responsibilities of government.
3. They are either permanent – standing committees, or temporary – ad hoc committees.
4. The structure and membership of standing committees has been public knowledge since 1992. The details of ad hoc committees are still not published.
5. The Prime Minister appoints ministers to committees, determines their agendas and forms new committees when required. He, himself, chairs many of the more important committees.
6. They reflect the increased scope and complexity of government business.
7. They have been criticised on the grounds that they have taken power away from the formal Cabinet and/or that they represent extensions in prime ministerial power.

The rules and political status of the Cabinet

Unlike the complex set of political relationships surrounding the Cabinet, the actual rules of conduct are relatively straightforward. They are governed by a document known as 'Questions of Procedure for Ministers' which is updated from time to time. Some key extracts from Sir Robert Armstrong's 1985 version are shown on page 200.

Cabinet committees

The Cabinet is supported by a system of ministerial committees which has a twofold purpose. First, it relieves the pressure on the Cabinet itself by settling as much business as possible at a lower level. Second, it buttresses the principle of collective responsibility of the government by ensuring that, even though an important question may not reach Cabinet itself, the decision will be fully considered and the final judgement will be sufficiently authoritative to ensure that the government as a whole can be properly expected to accept responsibility for it.

Finance

Proposals which involve expenditure or affect general financial policy should be discussed with the Treasury before they are submitted to the Cabinet or to a ministerial committee; and the results of those discussions, together with the best possible estimate of the cost to the Exchequer, should be indicated in the memorandum.

Oral proposals

When a minister wishes to raise a matter orally at Cabinet, the Prime Minister's consent should be sought through the Secretary of the Cabinet.

Collective responsibility

Decisions reached by the Cabinet or Cabinet committees are binding on all members of the government. They are, however, normally announced and defended by the minister concerned as his own decisions.

It is, therefore, the case that the following apply:

- What takes place Cabinet and at Cabinet committee meetings is secret. The decisions reached, but not the details of discussions or disagreements, are circulated to those ministers and civil servants who need to know for their work. This is covered by the Official Secrets Act so an offence is committed if the rule is broken.
- All members of the government (not just Cabinet ministers) are bound by the doctrine of collective responsibility. This means that ministers must defend in public any Cabinet decisions, or decisions made by a Cabinet committee, and must not show any dissent from them. The alternative is to resign or face dismissal.
- Cabinet committees may make minor decisions themselves without referral to full Cabinet. Otherwise their recommendations must be approved by Cabinet.
- The Treasury has special control over any proposals which involve large amounts of public expenditure.
- The Prime Minister has complete control over the agenda and over which matters are discussed in Cabinet. However, firm decisions are reached collectively in such a way that all ministers feel they can defend them even if they disagree.

Having established the basic rules, it is more difficult to define the precise political status of the Cabinet. Since all proposals, with the exception of actions involving the security forces, secret negotiations with foreign governments and the conclusion of treaties, must be approved by Parliament, we must ask why Cabinet has so much authority.

The answer lies in the unity of the parties in Parliament. The governing party can rely on the fact that, except in exceptional circumstances, the party will support the Cabinet in Parliament. Indeed, if there is a danger that this will not occur, it is the job of the Chief Whip to warn Cabinet. If the problem cannot be overcome, Cabinet will simply drop the policy. This was certainly the case, reported by Crossman in 1969, when the Labour Government was forced to abandon its plans for trade union reform.

Given, then, that Cabinet can count on parliamentary support, its decision becomes both official party and Government policy. It is granted authority by the unity of the party which supports its own leadership. The student may ask himself at this point how and whether the Cabinet system could work if the support of a majority in the House of Commons could not be ensured.

The Cabinet Secretary and Cabinet Office

The Cabinet Office and its Chief, the Cabinet Secretary, are housed at 10 Downing Street, where the Cabinet itself meets. The office operates on two levels – administrative and political.

<u>Administrative duties</u>   The Cabinet and its many committees and sub-committees require a huge amount of administrative back-up. Meetings must be organised, agendas drawn up, official papers prepared and distributed to committee members and minutes of the meetings written and sent to those who 'need to know'. Not only does the Office service ministerial meetings but every Cabinet committee is shadowed by an **official committee** of civil servants who prepare the way for their political masters to reach final decisions later. These official committees have a good deal of influence, especially in specialised areas such as complex European legislation, where ministers do not have sufficient time to investigate fully for themselves. The Cabinet Office organises the official committees too. Most of the work is undertaken by **Assistant Secretaries**, who are fairly senior officials temporarily seconded to the Cabinet Office from other departments. They normally stay for two to three years at Downing Street.

These duties may, at first sight, appear to be neutral and unimportant. This is not always the case. Agendas are important in that their organ-isation can often influence the amount of discussion given to each topic. The minutes, too, may be written in such a way as to influence final decisions to be reached at a higher level. Indeed, the minutes of Cabinet meetings which are drawn up by the Cabinet Secretary in consultation with the Prime Minister may become crucial. The Cabinet minutes form the official policy decisions of the Government. They are circulated to the relevant ministers and civil servants who will have to implement the decisions. The manner in which they are expressed, therefore, can be influential. Richard Crossman reports in his ministerial diaries of the 1960s that Prime Minister Harold Wilson and his Cabinet Secretary, Sir Burke Trend, spent much time on the minutes to ensure they con-formed to Wilson's own view of what had been decided in Cabinet. It should be remembered here that there are not normally formal votes in Cabinet. Agreement is reached informally and it is the Prime Minister's role to sum up discussions in such a way that all members can support

**Harold Wilson with
Richard Crossman**

a resolution. There are no strictly worded proposals to be reported. Not surprisingly, Wilson denied that he influenced Cabinet minutes, but Crossman was convinced he had and even claimed that some committee minutes were – 'doctored'.

It should also be noted at this point that the Cabinet Secretary himself is Head of the Civil Service. He is in charge of the general conduct and conditions of work of the Service. As such, both Sir Robert Armstrong and Sir Robin Butler have had to preside over radical reforms of the civil service in the 1980s and 1990s. Armstrong also found himself in the unusual position of enjoying a high degree of public exposure during his term of office. It is normal for such officials to maintain a low profile, but Armstrong became involved in the Government's attempt to stop publication of *Spycatcher*, an exposure of the British security forces. In this regard he appeared in an Australian court. He also intervened to restore Cabinet unity and confidentiality following extensive leaking of information over the 'Westland dispute'. There was a major Cabinet split over the proposed purchase of foreign helicopters in preference to British-made Westlands. The result was the 1986 publication of the so-called 'Armstrong Memorandum', which set out the principles of secrecy and collective responsibility in Cabinet.

Political role   This is more difficult to establish. Essentially, the extent to which the Office, and particularly the Cabinet Secretary himself, becomes involved in the political arena depends on the Prime Minister. The first Secretary, Sir Maurice Hankey (1916–38), became notorious as a political 'fixer', as did Sir John Hunt (1973–9), who served under four different Prime Ministers. They saw their role as recognising the desired policy, essentially that of the Prime Minister, and then trying to ensure the compliance of the rest of the Cabinet. Less forceful was

Margaret Thatcher's first Cabinet Secretary, Sir Robert Armstrong (1979–88). He saw his role as smoothing the way for the Prime Minister and ensuring that all were aware of her view.

Between 1970 and 1983 the Cabinet Office's position was enhanced by the addition of its Central Policy Review Staff (CPRS), also known as the 'Think Tank'. This group of civil servants and other outside experts, brought in on short-term contracts, was charged with the role of creating entirely new policy initiatives. Hitherto, virtually all policies had originated within government departments. Ted Heath, who set it up, wanted an independent source of policy for himself and the Cabinet as a whole. After a brief period of influence under Heath, the CPRS steadily faded into obscurity until Margaret Thatcher abolished it. She preferred as her independent source of advice the Prime Minister's Policy Unit and external policy agencies such as the Adam Smith Institute. Certainly, it is generally true that the Cabinet Office and the Cabinet Secretary have been considerably less influential since the mid 1980s.

Different views on Cabinet government

This is the orthodox, traditional and, indeed, optimistic idea about Cabinet government. It suggests that, although many routine decisions are reached outside Cabinet, the key policies and strategy of the Government are still discussed and determined in a collegial manner. It was the view suggested in one of the standard works on Cabinet by John P. Mackintosh in 1962, but it is still claimed to be true, even after the onslaught on Cabinet government mounted by Margaret Thatcher in the 1980s.

Cabinet as a central collective decision-making body

'The major task of the Cabinet is not to lead the party, to manage Parliament or to think out policy; it is to take or review the major decisions, to consider any proposals which might affect the future of the Government and to ensure that no departmental interests are overlooked, thus giving the work of Government a measure of unity.'
John P. Mackintosh, *The British Cabinet* (Stevens, 1962)

'Cabinet Government undoubtedly still exists despite rumours sometimes heard to the contrary.'
Hugo Young, Article, 1986

Cabinet as a system

Professor **George Jones** has suggested that it is mistaken to think of the Cabinet in its narrow sense alone. If we do, it will indeed seem to be a remarkably limited body. Instead, he believes, we should think of it as a complete system, with the twenty or so senior ministers merely as the centre around which other elements revolve. The 'satellite' bodies include Cabinet committees, the Cabinet Secretary and his Office, the Prime Minister, the Prime Minister's Policy Unit, senior members of each government department and the Treasury.

It may be true that the **real** decisions are reached among those people and bodies which surround the Cabinet. Nevertheless, they require Cabinet approval to make them legitimate and, where a decision cannot be finalised, there is still one last forum where the matter can be settled.

Cabinet as a battleground

This view suggests that politics is essentially a struggle for power in which the politically strong prevail and the weak fall. At the centre lies the Cabinet, where the final struggles are played out. This was very much the opinion of Barbara Castle in her accounts of government in the 1970s, and of Sir Douglas Wass, Permanent Secretary at the Treasury, at the same time. Thus, Cabinet ceases to be a collective decision-making body and becomes, instead, a struggle for power.

Departmentalism

A common criticism of the modern Cabinet is that ministers are only really interested in their own departments, a characteristic known as 'departmentalism'. According to this view Cabinet simply becomes the place where ministers must fight for their own interests. Thus, it is suggested that collective decision making, where ministers are concerned with the general picture, suffers at the expense of self-interest.

> *'If collective decisions are to be of the right quality then collective decision making has to be the principal, and not the last call on the time and energy of ministers.'*
> Douglas Hurd, Lecture, 1986

> *'Ministers in cabinet rarely look at the totality of their responsibilities, at the balance of policy, at the progress of government towards its objectives as a whole.'*
> Sir Douglas Wass, Reith Lecture, 1983

Cabinet overload

Professor Peter Hennessy has written extensively on the subject of the Cabinet. He believes it has become overloaded with important business, in common with the rest of the central government machinery. It is expected to process so many decisions, that it cannot engage in its real purpose – strategic, long-term thinking and planning. The former Conservative minister, Lord Hailsham, has said much the same, arguing especially that the overload has led to the increasing use of Cabinet committees. Of this development he disapproves.

> *'The volume of work that has to be carried through means that the Prime Minister has tended to govern through smaller sub-groups of Ministers.'*
> Lord Hailsham, Granada Lecture, 1987

> *'If the Downing Street 22 are locked into an energy-sapping, relentlessly deepening downward spiral of overload (as I believe a lot of them are for much of the time), it does affect the rest of us in a direct and important fashion. Our economy and society are not in any condition to carry the luxury of Whitehall and Westminster knocking along at a low level of performance while the rest of us get along running our increasingly prosperous and fulfilled lives.'*
> Peter Hennessy, Article, 1986

Prime ministerial domination

The question of how much British government is now effectively 'prime ministerial government' is discussed fully at pages 214–7. However, we can establish here that it is a common view that the Cabinet is merely an instrument of prime ministerial control. Hennessy has argued that Cabinet is simply what the Prime Minister wishes it to be, so that while Thatcher may have chosen to use it to further her own policies, her successor, John Major, prefers to allow Cabinet to make key domestic decisions. On the other hand, many outgoing Cabinet ministers have claimed that collective decision making no longer exists. Tony Benn and John Biffen, a former Cabinet minister in the 1980s, have been prominent examples.

> *'Cabinet Government remains a putty-like concept. A Prime Minister can make of it very largely what he or she will.'*
> Peter Hennesy, *Cabinet* (Blackwell, 1986)

> *'Thatcher Cabinets, however, have already become political folklore, and rightly so. She is in the corporate mould of the political chairman and chief executive. The days are long gone when, as with Baldwin, the Prime Minister was titular head but gave his great departmental chiefs a free hand.'*
> John Biffen, Article, 1990

As we have said, no study of the British Cabinet can be complete without a full exploration of the position of the Prime Minister. The two institutions are closely tied together.

The Prime Minister

As with the Cabinet, it is difficult to establish the constitutional and political basis of the office of Prime Minister. British constitutional statutes make virtually no mention of the position. At the same time it is clear that the importance of the Prime Minister in today's politics is considerably greater than one could guess from a straightforward description of his powers. In our search for answers we may start by establishing the sources of authority of the office.

Prime ministerial authority

Four sources can be identified:

The Crown The Prime Minister is, technically, appointed by the monarch and thus carries his or her authority. After a general election the Prime Minister-to-be is summoned to Buckingham Palace and asked to form a Government, which will enjoy the support of Parliament. Under normal circumstances, where there is clearly a majority party in the House of Commons and that party has an undisputed leader, this process is a formality. Nevertheless, it is still a necessity, for in the absence of strict constitutional rules the new (or reappointed) Prime Minister needs the legitimacy which the ceremony provides.

The party It is assumed that the Prime Minister is either the leader of the party which commands a clear majority in the House of Commons, or leads a minority party which is being allowed to govern by the Commons, or is the leader of the senior party in a coalition (a situation which has not existed since 1945). Of course, it is virtually always the first of the three circumstances which prevails – a majority party with a clear leader.

It follows from this that, to become and remain Prime Minister, an individual must seek authority from his or her party. If we were in any doubt about this principle we need only remind ourselves of the events of November 1990 when John Major was elected Conservative Party leader in place of Margaret Thatcher. The Conservatives had a new leader and, whether the Queen or the electorate liked it or not, Britain had a new Prime Minister. There had been no election except among Conservative MPs.

<u>Parliament</u> More specifically we mean here the **majority** in the House of Commons. The House of Lords is not consulted and we would expect the Opposition parties not to approve of the Prime Minister. But being a minority, the Opposition view is irrelevant. In principle, it is the whole government, or at least the Cabinet, which requires the support of the Commons majority. However, it is clear that, should the governing party's MPs object to an individual, he or she could not survive for long. Of course, when the Conservatives are in power, the Commons majority **is** the party as far as leadership selection is concerned. For Labour the situation is different. The party leader is elected by **all** party members. Their choice may not have the support of Labour MPs, who only represent one-third of the votes for the Labour leadership. Thus, a future Labour leader could, in theory, be accepted by the party but still rejected by Parliament.

We have to go back to 1940 to witness the potential power of Parliament over the office. Neville Chamberlain was effectively removed by Parliament over his foreign policy conduct. Largely because the country was at war, the new Prime Minister, Winston Churchill, needed widespread, cross-party support in the Commons.

<u>The people</u> Possibly more accurately, we should say 'electorate' here. Research suggests that there has been an increasing tendency in modern times for voters to be influenced by their opinions of the respective party leaders. It follows that the winning party leader can, to some extent, claim to enjoy the authority of the people. This is less clear and less formal than the other three sources of authority described above. Nevertheless, it is widely acknowledged. Similarly, a Prime Minister who can no longer command the respect of the people at large runs the risk of losing office. Certainly, popular opposition played a part in Margaret Thatcher's downfall in 1990, as it did in Ted Heath's election defeat in 1974. And certainly the Conservatives were quick to remove him from their leadership in the following year.

These descriptions show what impressive underpinning there is to prime ministerial power. Those powers can be divided into two types – formal and informal.

Prime Minister profile

Harold Wilson
1964–70, 1974–6

Wilson was the first Prime Minister of the 'Television age', when ownership of TVs became commonplace. He understood how to use the new medium, explaining policies to viewers in an intimate way. He came over as straightforward and down-to-earth and was known as an accomplished communicator.

According to some of his senior ministers, including Tony Benn, Richard Crossman and Barbara Castle, he dominated his Cabinets, frequently using inner Cabinets and personal advisers. Crossman suggested he was an expert manipulator of the Cabinet. He was also admired for his control of Parliament, his skill in debate and cutting wit.

His more radical economic policies failed, especially attempts to introduce centralised planning. Indeed, his greatest failure was probably the poor handling of the devaluation of sterling in 1967. However, he expanded and revitalised higher education, founded the Open University personally and did much to encourage technological advance, including the development of Concorde.

His second term, from 1974–6, was fraught with difficulty as his party only enjoyed a tiny majority in the House of Commons. In that time, however, he reached a vital agreement with the trade unions to limit pay increases (the so-called 'Social Contract') and so began the process of bringing down inflation. He retired in 1976 at the age of sixty, as he had promised, making way to Jim Callaghan.

James Callaghan waving from No. 10 Downing Street after becoming Prime Minister in 1976

Formal powers

The principal group of powers which the modern Prime Minister possesses are derived from what are known as **prerogative powers**. These relate to functions historically performed by the monarch on a discretionary basis. In a modern democracy it is clearly not acceptable that such a state of affairs should continue. First, the monarch is not elected. Secondly, the monarch cannot be made accountable for his or her actions. It is, therefore, part of the Prime Minister's role to perform these functions on behalf of the monarch. They may be carried out in the Queen's name, but she plays no active part in them. There are no statutes or legal rulings to confirm this state of affairs – it is a so-called **convention**, or widely accepted principle, that this is so.

To further complicate the matter, prerogative powers fall into two categories. There are those which are performed on behalf of the monarch as **Head of State**, and those performed as **Head of Government**. The former are duties which would be carried out normally by a **President** in an elective system and are those which are performed on behalf of the whole nation. That is to say, they are outside the party political arena. The latter, which are duties of the Head of Government, are normally carried out by a Prime Minister or the equivalent, but **do** concern party politics. The distinction between the terms 'government' and 'state' in Britain is extremely blurred and this creates confusion over the two roles, especially as our real Head of State – the monarch – is forbidden from becoming involved in the political arena. The USA is the only other leading democracy where such a dual role is accepted. However, while the American President usually makes it clear in which capacity he is acting, the British Prime Minister often does not and need not. A description of the two types of power will help:

1. Powers as Head of State

Head of the armed forces   We could say 'Commander-in-Chief'. This does not mean leadership in the heat of battle, of course, but it does mean direction of the overall conduct of the armed forces. This also includes exclusive control of the Intelligence Services, both at home and abroad.

Negotiation of foreign treaties   This means literally what it says, but also includes general relations with foreign powers and international organisations such as the EU, NATO or the UN.

Granting of honours   This means having the final say as to who should receive peerages, knighthoods and lesser honours. In a minority of cases the Prime Minister nominates individuals himself, but generally he has a power of veto.

Head of the civil service   Although most of the administrative control of the service is left to the Cabinet Secretary, the Prime Minister is in overall control of the organisation and conduct of the civil service. He will also be a major influence over the appointment of Permanent Secretaries – the senior officials in each government department.

Appointment of senior judges and archbishops or bishops of the Church of England   Although this duty is carried out on the advice of the Lord Chancellor and Archbishop of Canterbury respectively, the Prime Minister has power of final approval.

2. Powers as Head of Government

The appointment and dismissal of ministers   This is solely the respon sibility of the Prime Minister, giving him patronage over more than a hundred senior positions.

The appointment of heads of public bodies   This may include having a significant influence over the choice of Chairmen of public corporations such as the BBC or of leading quangos such as the Arts Council or Equal Opportunities Commission.

Dissolution of Parliament   It is the sole responsibility of the Prime Minister to decide when to dissolve Parliament and call a general election. Only under the most unusual circumstance of a Parliament running a full five years from the previous election would there be no choice.

Chairman of the Cabinet   The importance of this role has been discussed on page 189.

Prime Minister profile

**Edward Heath
1970–4**

Heath was, surprisingly, elected in 1970, despite being less personally popular than his rival Wilson. He did not possess Wilson's skills in communication and was seen as a rather aloof figure. He governed on a very individualistic basis with the advice and support of a small clique of Cabinet colleagues. Most importantly, he ignored the opinions of the Conservative back-bench MPs, rarely explaining policy to them and refusing to listen to objections.

Despite his refusal to adopt a collective style of government, he recognised that policy making in the Conservative Party was too haphazard. He therefore set up a number of policy committees in the party and developed the Central Policy Review Staff to feed policy initiatives into Cabinet.

On coming to power he set about implementing laissez-faire policies, restoring market forces in the control of wages, prices and employment, and disengaging government from industrial policy. In fact, his initial policies were close to those adopted by Thatcher Governments of the 1980s. In 1971–2, faced by an alarming increase in inflation and a number of industrial crises, he dramatically reversed policies (the so-called Heath 'U-Turn'). Government adopted a strict wage and price control policy and two firms – Rolls Royce and Upper Clyde Shipbuilders – were even nationalised. His attempts to control trade unions through the Industrial Relations Act was a failure. Possibly his greatest success was to negotiate Britain's entry into the European Community in 1973.

Faced by a damaging miners' strike over pay restraint in 1973–4, he called an early general election in February 1974 as a kind of referendum on his industrial policies. His own unpopularity and public sympathy for the miners combined to defeat him.

Informal powers   Most of the informal powers of the Prime Minister arise from his position as leader of the governing party. Of course this position relies upon the historical reality that there is a **single** governing party, and that it is accepted that the monarch will ask **only** the leader of that party to form a Government. Should there be a coalition, or should there be some dispute as to which individual could command the support of the governing party in Parliament, these existing certainties would be missing. There is no doubt that a future Prime Minister not enjoying the luxury of leading a single, united parliamentary party could not claim such wide powers. However, we can assume for the time being that the status quo will be maintained for the foreseeable future.

Edward Heath signing the Treaty of Accession to the European Community, 22 January 1973

Informal powers include the following:

<u>Chief policy maker</u> The actual extent to which a Prime Minister controls Government policy depends upon which party he leads, and upon his own political command of that party. As we can see in Unit 5, a Conservative leader has a great deal more discretionary power over policy than does his Labour counterpart. Of course, any leader has significant constraints on policy development – from the wider party, from MPs and from the Cabinet – but a Labour Prime Minister has less personal discretion.

We should also take into account the position of the individual concerned. Dominant individuals such as Harold Wilson or Margaret Thatcher both chose, and were able, to play a central role in policy formulation. The less secure, or those who have preferred a collective approach, such as John Major, have played a lesser role.

Chief government spokesman The twice-weekly sessions of 'Prime Minister's Question Time' in the House of Commons have become the principal occasion at which the public and the media can see the Government's current attitudes to the prevailing issues of the day, and how the Opposition challenges those attitudes. Here the Prime Minister **as an individual** is placed under constant scrutiny. But it is not only the individual who is under challenge. The whole range of Government policies is being questioned. The Prime Minister must, therefore, stand alone on these occasions as mouthpiece for the whole Government.

Add to this the constant media attention which is concentrated on him, and we are left in no doubt that ministers must rely on their leader to present the Government case on many occasions. Of course, individual ministers do appear in front of the Commons, the cameras and the microphones, but it is the Prime Minister who has become the key figure.

Leader of the parliamentary party Whatever his position in the wider party, the Prime Minister must lead his MPs in the House of Commons. They look to him for unity and direction. He in turn expects loyalty from them. This sense of loyalty enables the Prime Minister to implement policies even if they may be unpopular in the party and the country at large. Many MPs rely on him for their position as members of the governing party and, for those with marginal seats, they depend on him for their very places in the Commons. Naturally, this is a double-edged sword. If the Prime Minister loses the support of his MPs, the basis of his power is removed, as Margaret Thatcher was to discover.

Summary of the Prime Minister's power

Formal basis of power

1. Acting on behalf of the Crown as Head of State:

(a) Foreign policy maker and treaty negotiator
(b) Control over granting of honours
(c) Head of the civil service
(d) Senior appointments in the judiciary and the Church of England

2. Head of Government:

(a) Power of appointment and dismissal of ministers
(b) Appointment of heads of public bodies
(c) Choose the date of the dissolution of Parliament
(d) Chairman of the Cabinet

Informal basis of power

1. Leading policy maker
2. Chief spokesman of the Government
3. Leader of the governing party in Parliament

Sources of advice to the Prime Minister Unlike other ministers, the Prime Minister has no department of his own. This places him at a potentially great disadvantage against strong-minded colleagues who can call on an army of officials for advice. **Lloyd George (1916–22)** recognised the problem and therefore created the Cabinet Office. Since then there has been a steady growth in the scope of advice available to a Prime Minister.

The Cabinet Office and Secretary Despite its name, the Cabinet Office predominantly serves the Prime Minister. Other ministers can rely on their own officials for policy advice and initiatives. The importance of the Office is discussed on page 201.

The Prime Minister's Policy Unit This was set up in 1974 as a result of an overhaul of the services at 10 Downing Street ordered by Edward Heath. It comprises a number of special advisers, across a broad range of policy issues, brought into government to advise the Prime Minister. Its members are acknowledged experts in their fields who would not normally have access to the policy-making process. The Policy Unit reached its height under Margaret Thatcher, with twelve members, most of whom were politically committed to her radical policy agenda.

Four successive Heads of the Unit exemplified the shift towards neo-liberal policies in the Conservative Party under Thatcher. Sir John Hoskyns (1979–82) was a successful businessman who believed strongly that government should disengage itself from control over industry and commerce. He was succeeded by a right-wing journalist, Ferdinand Mount (1982–4), and then by John Redwood (1984–5). Redwood was later to become an MP and by 1993 was in John Major's Cabinet. In 1995 his unsuccessful challenge for the party leadership was based on radical neo-liberal, right-wing policies, the same ideas which had characterised his leadership of the Policy Unit. He and his team did much to generate the 'Thatcher revolution' in the mid-1980s. Professor Brian Griffiths (1985–90) followed Redwood. Griffiths was a convinced monetarist and formed a powerful alliance with Mrs Thatcher's private economic adviser, Sir Alan Walters.

Since 1990 and the demise of Margaret Thatcher, the Unit has lost much of its reforming zeal. It remains an independent source of advice for the Prime Minister, but has taken more moderate positions than its predecessors.

Individual advisers   All Prime Ministers have been able to choose a number of personal advisers from outside the machinery of government. The most 'notorious' of modern times was Sir Alan Walters, who was the personal economic adviser to Margaret Thatcher in the 1980s. It was the influence of Walters which led to the bitter resignation of Nigel Lawson as Chancellor of the Exchequer in 1989. Lawson claimed that Walters was virtually running economic policy, a role which should have been properly his in consultation with the Prime Minister. Sir Anthony Parsons was a lower-profile adviser on foreign affairs than Walters in the same period.

There has been some disquiet over the growth in the use of such advisers as it may result in a loss of 'balance' of views. While civil servants are trained to provide such balance, to be sceptical and to see different sides of political arguments, private advisers may well be politically extreme and so prevent proper discussion of alternatives.

Policy agencies ('think tanks')   As with individual, special advisers, there has been an increase in the use of such bodies as an extra input to the policy-making process. Prominent in the 1980s were the **Adam Smith Institute**, the **Institute of Economic Affairs (IEA)** and the **Centre for Policy Studies (CPS)**. Much of the privatisation programme at that time was encouraged by the Adam Smith Institute, while the IEA was an important influence on Margaret Thatcher's economic policies. Future Labour Prime Ministers will not find such a ready-made group of think tanks to help, but it is possible that such groups as the **Fabian Society** and the **Commission for Social Justice** may come to the fore.

Inner Cabinets   It was Richard Crossman in the 1960s who first identified the existence of what he called 'inner' Cabinets in Government. He suggested that the Prime Minister used the practice of forming small groups of senior ministers to advise and support him. Indeed, Crossman himself claimed to be a member of such a group under Wilson. This is no surprise, for all powerful figures need close advisers who are also 'insiders'. All Prime Ministers since Wilson have certainly used such advisers from time to time.

'Kitchen Cabinet'   The term 'Kitchen Cabinet' was coined to describe the small group of individuals who were intimate political advisers to Harold Wilson. The most prominent members were his political secretary, Marcia Williams (afterwards ennobled as Lady Falkender), and his press officer, Joe Haines. On the face of it, the positions they held were of relatively minor importance, but they undoubtedly wielded considerable influence. It was the rather closed and domestic nature of their role which gave rise to the title 'Kitchen'. Margaret Thatcher also had an important private team. Again the press officer, Sir Bernard Ingham, was involved, as was Charles Powell, a civil servant transferred to her private office. It was Powell who was the driving force behind Thatcher's attempts to distance Britain from the European Community.

Thus, we have a modern picture of the Prime Minister surrounded by a disparate group of advisers, with no formal organisation. There have, indeed, been a number of proposals to set up a formal 'Prime Minister's Department' along the lines of the top levels of each government department. This would bring advisers under the stricter disciplines of the civil service and ensure greater responsibility. However, there have been no significant moves to bring this about since Edward Heath developed the ideas for the Policy Unit and the CPRS in the 1970s.

It should also be noted that every Prime Minister may choose his own sources of advice. Apart from the sources described above, the party's research department, individual MPs and civil servants may also be used.

Prime Minister profile

Margaret Thatcher
1979–90

Margaret Thatcher dominated political life in Britain more than probably any other Prime Minister in the twentieth century. During her term of office she suffered periods of intense unpopularity (1981–2), but also enjoyed extreme popularity and admiration (1983–7). Yet she was elected Conservative leader as a compromise candidate, expected to be a 'caretaker' until some other dominant figure emerged. On taking office she was forced to accept a Cabinet which was largely made up of senior politicians who were philosophically opposed to her radical, right-wing policies. These were the so-called 'wets' and they were a majority until after the 1983 election. Her dominance was the result of three main factors – the dramatic shift to the left of the Labour Party which resulted in great public suspicion, the British victory in the Falklands War of 1982 and her second election victory, with a huge 144 majority, in 1983. She could now complete the task, started in 1981, of ridding the Cabinet of her political opponents. She surrounded herself with close allies and, thus armed, was able to dominate completely. From then on she was continually accused of converting the government machine into an instrument for her own personal rule. She was also accused of 'politicising' the civil service by ensuring that officials sympathetic to her philosophy were promoted to senior positions. Despite her dominance, she had learned from Heath's mistakes. In particular, she was careful to inform and consult with her back-benchers. She knew that, if she could carry them with her, Cabinet opposition could be defeated.

Her policies are well documented elsewhere, but it should also be noted that she placed Britain in the forefront of world affairs, forming a close relationship with the USA and distancing Britain from Europe.

The terms 'populist', 'presidential' and 'overbearing' were all applied to her and there is little doubt that there is some truth in all of these descriptions. Whether she changed the nature of the office of Prime Minister in the long term is, however, open to question.

Harold Macmillan

Prime ministerial government?

Two events in 1962 opened up the question of whether the British system of government had actually become prime ministerial government. The first occurred in July when Prime Minister **Harold Macmillan** dismissed one third of his Cabinet following a period of great unpopularity for the Government. The second was Richard Crossman's controversial introduction to a new edition of Bagehot's *English Constitution*. In it Crossman, sure to be a minister in a future Labour Government, suggested that the term 'cabinet government' was no longer appropriate. Instead, the term 'prime ministerial government' had become more suitable. Since then there has been discussion as to whether we now see government as totally dominated by the Prime Minister. The evidence to suggest Crossman's view was, and still is, true includes a number of aspects.

Patronage

The Macmillan incident, known as the 'Night of the Long Knives' (after an occasion in 1934 when Hitler had his main political opponents assassinated), illustrated how a strong Prime Minister could use his powers of appointment and dismissal to control his colleagues. The practice of manipulating Cabinet membership to improve prime ministerial dominance was successfully used by Margaret Thatcher in the 1980s. Between 1981 and 1984 she steadily removed opponents, replacing them with close allies such as Norman Tebbit and Cecil Parkinson. Since the growth of Cabinet committees, an additional source of patronage exists. Membership of the key committees is much sought after and lies in the Prime Minister's hands. Thatcher again, for example, was able to secure the compliance of James Prior, a leading 'wet', in return for his place on the key Economic Committee. Callaghan, too, was able to keep the left-wing of the party under control by granting posts to its leading members, Tony Benn and Michael Foot.

When we add the thousands of other honours and appointments at the Prime Minister's disposal, we have a picture of the enormous potential influence which exists.

> *'The present centralisation of power into the hands of one person has gone too far and amounts to a system of personal rule in the very heart of our parliamentary democracy.'*
> Tony Benn, 1979

Cabinet control   Crossman described how it was possible for a Prime Minister to manage Cabinet affairs in the interest of his own position. This included control over the agenda, the minutes and discussions in general. Heath was also accused of making decisions among his own 'inner Cabinet' and then ensuring that the full Cabinet complied by presenting them with policies as though they were already agreed. Thatcher's principal device was simply to ensure that Cabinet never discussed key policy issues. On the rare occasions when they did, she made it clear what her own views were and made it clear that opposition to those ideas would result in sanctions against the offender.

> *'Collective responsibility is based on collective decision-making. Margaret Thatcher is not the first Prime Minister to circumvent her colleagues, nor will she be the last, but this habit is not the sign of a healthy or a happy Government.'*
> Francis Pym, *The Politics of Consent*
> (Hamish Hamilton, 1984)

Prime Minister's advice   As we have seen above, there is considerably more advice available to the modern Prime Minister than there has been hitherto. The Policy Unit, Cabinet Office and special advisers have provided him with enough policy ammunition to be able to challenge even the power of the heads of major ministries. Thus, Wilson, Heath and Thatcher could all **lead** the policy debate rather than merely **preside** over the deliberations of others.

Media   Politics play a greater part in the concerns of the media – broadcast and published – than ever before. The televising of Parliament and the increase in TV programmes dealing with current affairs, together with the press' obsession with political affairs, have thrust politicians increasingly into the limelight. It is, therefore, inevitable that the Prime Minister should have the main attention focused on him. In the case of Margaret Thatcher this was, to some extent, the result of a conscious effort on her part. The media wish to concentrate their attention on someone who represents the government (and indeed the Opposition). The Prime Minister is the obvious target.

> *'The very forcefulness with which Mrs Thatcher has projected her views and style, separate from those of her Cabinet, has also established a model of premiership.'*
> Dennis Kavanagh, *Thatcherism and British Politics*
> (OUP, 1990)

Foreign affairs Britain's entry into the European Community (EU) and the end of the Cold War have resulted in the increased importance of foreign policy-making. A series of complex and dangerous issues have arisen in recent times, including the Falklands War, the Gulf War, Bosnia and the former Yugoslavia, Hong Kong, the Anglo-Irish Agreement, Rwanda and the Maastricht Treaty. The Prime Minister is chief foreign-policy-maker, notwithstanding the role of the Foreign Secretary. It is, therefore, inevitable that the Prime Minister should be thrust increasingly into the public consciousness as Britain's national representative. This has been especially noticeable under John Major in view of his relative weakness in domestic affairs. To compensate, he appears regularly on the world stage with other national leaders, 'batting for Britain', as he is prone to remark.

> *'There is more to Thatcherism than a set of beliefs. It encompasses also a particular style of politics. That style is an aggressive one.'*
> Philip Norton, 'Margaret Thatcher and the Conservative Party' in *Parliamentary Affairs* (January 1990)

Cabinet government?

Despite the weight of evidence, as described above, there are a number of important political commentators who do not subscribe to the view that we now have 'prime ministerial government'.

Peter Hennessy The view of Professor Peter Hennessy is that, under Thatcher, we did indeed experience prime ministerial domination, but this need not be a permanent feature. It was her dominance and style which created the phenomenon, but there is no reason why any other Prime Minister should behave in the same way. The evidence from John Major's premiership certainly bears out the Hennessy view. Indeed, Major came to office promising to restore 'collective government'. Cynics will suggest that Major simply does not have the charisma to dominate as Thatcher did, but in his defence he did set out to adopt a lower profile. Lord (Sir Geoffrey) Howe has also remarked that *any* Prime Minister enjoying as long a term of office as Margaret Thatcher did (over eleven years) is bound to become dominant, simply because she has outlasted nearly all her colleagues.

Hugo Young In his book *One of Us* (published by Macmillan, 1989) the journalist Hugo Young has suggested that Cabinet government was very much alive under Thatcher. Why it **appeared** that she was personally in control was that she had promoted to senior positions in government and civil service individuals who were politically close to her (hence the term 'one of us'). The Cabinet did rule collectively, but they spoke with one voice and it was the same as **her** voice. Thus, it was a different political era, but as Hennessy also points out, it depended upon the dominance of Margaret Thatcher herself. There is no reason why it should be permanent.

> *'The Cabinet may have declined, but the Prime Minister is not the sole beneficiary.'*
> Martin Burch, 'The British Cabinet: A Residual Executive' in *Parliamentary Affairs* (January 1988)

George Jones Professor Jones's main contention is twofold. First, that there was an **appearance** of presidential or prime ministerial government, but that this was largely a question of **style**. Media attention, the prominence of foreign policy issues and the increased tendency for the Prime Minister to act as government spokesman gave the premier a president-like status. Yet there was no real substance to the change. Secondly, that the traditional constraints on a Prime Minister's power are still very much in place. He can, and often still is, outvoted by his Cabinet colleagues. Similarly, a Prime Minister who does not carry his back-bench MPs with him cannot hope to succeed, as Heath was to discover. The removal of Thatcher in 1990 was all the proof we should need to confirm Jones's view.

> 'Cabinet Government and collective responsibility are not defunct notions. Shared responsibility is still meaningful, for a Prime Minister has to gain the support of the bulk of his Cabinet to carry out his policies. He has to persuade it and convince it that he is right. Its meetings do not merely follow his direction. Debate and conflict are frequent. It cannot be by-passed and he cannot be an autocrat. To attempt to become one presages his political suicide.'
> George Jones, *Parliamentary Affairs* (Spring 1965)

Though written twenty-five years before her downfall, Professor Jones's comments, shown above, could be an epitaph to Margaret Thatcher's premiership. He still holds the same view.

> 'Cabinet is a democracy, not an autocracy . . . it is the Cabinet, not the Prime Minister, who decides.'
> Harold Wilson, *The Governance of Britain*
> (Weidenfeld & Nicolson, 1976)

John Major As we have seen above, John Major came to office promising to restore collective government. The use of the word 'restore' is significant since it suggests that his predecessor had indeed undermined collegiality. Certainly, it would be hard to accuse Major of establishing his own personal rule. However, whether collective government has been restored is doubtful. It appears more likely that he has restored power to his ministers as individuals, rather than to the Cabinet as a collective body.

> 'The central policy-making machine was much changed by Mrs Thatcher .... the system has been changed radically again under John Major, with his own hand being felt in the revived collegiality in Cabinet and Number 10, in greater openness, wider consultation and more volatility.'
> Anthony Seldon, *The Major Effect* (Macmillan, 1995)

> 'Mid-term electoral storms, however severe, are not earthquakes; they rarely change the political landscape.'
> Ivor Crewe, *The Major Effect* (Macmillan, 1995)

For exam questions relevant to this unit, see pages 487–8.

9 The civil service and the machinery of central government

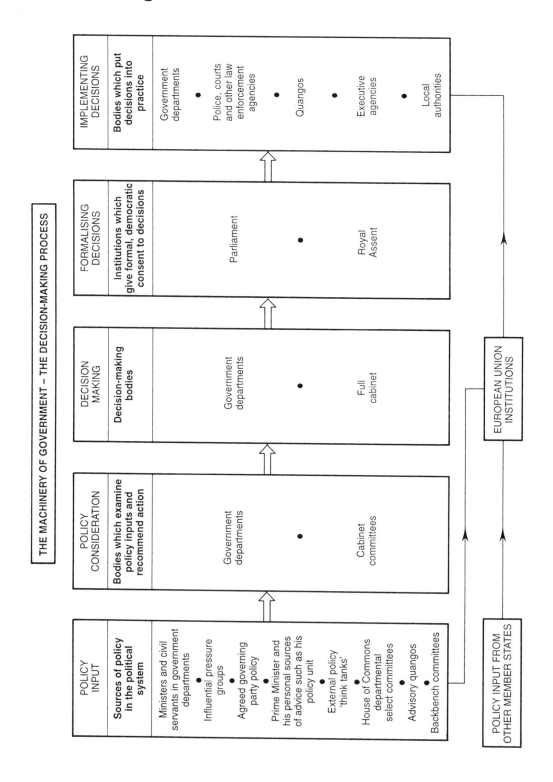

THE MACHINERY OF GOVERNMENT – THE DECISION-MAKING PROCESS

POLICY INPUT — Sources of policy in the political system

- Ministers and civil servants in government departments
- Influential pressure groups
- Agreed governing party policy
- Prime Minister and his personal sources of advice such as his policy unit
- External policy 'think tanks'
- House of Commons departmental select committees
- Advisory quangos
- Backbench committees

POLICY CONSIDERATION — Bodies which examine policy inputs and recommend action

- Government departments
- Cabinet committees

DECISION MAKING — Decision-making bodies

- Government departments
- Full cabinet

FORMALISING DECISIONS — Institutions which give formal, democratic consent to decisions

- Parliament
- Royal Assent

IMPLEMENTING DECISIONS — Bodies which put decisions into practice

- Government departments
- Police, courts and other law enforcement agencies
- Quangos
- Executive agencies
- Local authorities

EUROPEAN UNION INSTITUTIONS

POLICY INPUT FROM OTHER MEMBER STATES

Who are the civil servants?

Civil servants can be described as all those who are directly employed by central government departments. In its fullest sense, therefore, we might include individuals with no political role whatsoever, such as cleaners, drivers, security guards or maintenance staff. Clearly, we need not concern ourselves with them here, although technically they may be within our definition. If we include only those who are directly concerned with the development, organisation, drafting and implementation of central government policy and decisions, we have a more realistic definition of the term. The various roles of this narrower definition can be described thus:

- **Clerical** staff dealing with the creation and organisation of all the paperwork, computer files and other administrative data which central government generates.
- **Information** gatherers who deal with the routine collection of statistics and facts which are needed for both policy and decision making.
- **Researchers** who are at the forefront of progress. They may be engaged in physical and social sciences, medical research, psychological investigation, criminology, economic theory development and a host of other fields of innovation and progress on behalf of government departments.
- **Executive** staff, who form the largest section of the civil service. They carry out the decisions made by departments on an ongoing basis. Some engage in routine operations while others are managers, sometimes employing hundreds or thousands of other staff. The largest section comprises those who operate the social security system through many local offices. They assess and process claims or manage those who operate the system. The Inland Revenue (direct taxation) and Customs and Excise (VAT and other duties) are two of the other large civil service organisations. Since these offices are located all over the country, most civil servants work outside the capital.
- Central **decision makers** are civil servants who are close to their ministers as they are making decisions **directly** on his behalf. No minister, however conscientious, could hope to give proper considerations to all the matters which come before him. He must trust senior officials to pass to him those matters which need his personal attention, and deal themselves with those which do not. Nevertheless, the minister may sign many documents which contain decisions with which he was not concerned. It becomes clear, therefore, how much he is forced to trust his senior advisers. These same officials are also required to draft parliamentary answers, both written and oral.

    Typical examples of such work might be sanctioning local authority plans for educational or transport provision, which require ministerial approval; granting export or import licences; or making senior appointments to agencies which come under the jurisdiction of the department.

Top four levels of the civil service	
1. Permanent Secretary	3. Under Secretary
2. Deputy Secretary	4. Assistant Secretary

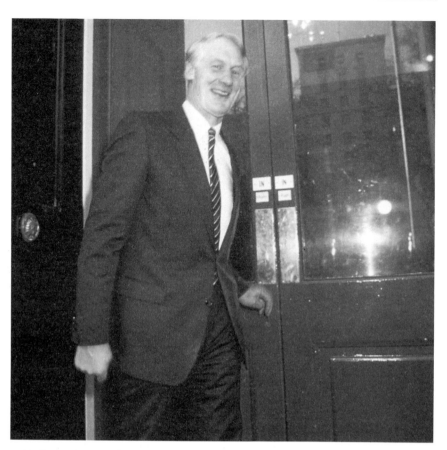

Sir Robin Butler

- **Policy** advisers form the very top levels of the service. It is they who directly advise ministers and the whole Cabinet on Government policy. They have weekly contact with their minister and he relies on them heavily. They operate through a complex system of committees, written memoranda and face-to-face meetings. The information they need is gathered and refined at lower levels so that they are able to distil the decision-making process down to a few manageable options for the minister to consider.

It is with these last two types of civil servant with which this unit is concerned. It is they who are of most political significance. While the whole machinery of central government employs over 500,000 people, these senior policy- and decision-making officials number approximately 2,000, comprising the top four ranks of the service. If we were to further narrow our definition of policy makers, this number might be reduced to only about 400 senior officials who deal regularly with the ministers.

Background to the modern civil service

Northcote–Trevelyan

The structure and operation of the modern civil service has been shaped by three major periods of reform. The first of these took place over a century ago, but the next two occurred during the 1980s and radical reform is still taking place.

In 1854 the Northcote–Trevelyan Report proved to be a damning indictment of the state of the British civil service. It highlighted corruption, inefficiency and, above all, recruitment and promotion on the basis of nepotism. That is, posts were granted on the basis of family and social connections rather than ability. It was, therefore, recommended that a complete reform should take place and by 1870 the necessary changes were effected. The basic principles of the service which were to hold good until the late 1980s were:

- There were to be three main sections of the service – clerical, executive and administrative. There would be little or no transfer between these levels. The elite group – the administrative class – was to represent the very best brains which could be attracted from the universities (in the event, these came mainly from Oxford and Cambridge).
- Admission was to be by competitive examination and interview. In other words, it was to be based purely on merit.
- Promotion was to be based on a combination of seniority – longer-serving officials were to be given preferment – and merit.
- Posts were permanent. That is, the holder could not be dismissed by a minister on political grounds, but only for misconduct. Thus, it was hoped that political pressure could not be placed on officials who would fear dismissal should they disagree on policy with their political masters. In this way it was envisaged that neutral advice would be given.
- Neutrality was also safeguarded by the fact that, when a new minister or government, or even political party, came to office, all officials would retain their position. In other words, civil servants were expected to serve any Government with equal care. Officials were also not allowed to participate in party politics.
- Officials were to be anonymous in that they would make no public statements on policy, nor reveal their personal role in any decision- or policy-making process.
- The principle was established that all senior posts should only be granted to those who had already enjoyed a lengthy career in the service. Outsiders would not, thus, be allowed into the civil service except at the bottom level. The outlawing of such so-called 'lateral' entry created what was known as the 'career civil service'. Put another way, 'civil service' became a 'closed' profession, much as is the case in the law or medicine.

Civil service principles until 1980

1. Recruitment and promotion based on seniority and merit
2. Posts to be held permanently with no political dismissals or appointments
3. Civil servants to be anonymous
4. Civil servants to be neutral and serve any Government or minister equally
5. Only career civil servants to be considered for senior posts

---

For many years the system created by Northcote–Trevelyan appeared to serve British government well. Much admired abroad, the civil service was known for its professionalism, integrity and lack of corruption. By the 1960s, however, concerns began to grow that the service was no longer appropriate in its traditional form to meet the demands of modern government.

The **Fulton Report** of 1968, which was ordered by Prime Minister Harold Wilson as part of his plans to modernise many British institutions, proposed reforms almost as radical as those of Northcote–Trevelyan. However, a stubborn and conservative civil service closed ranks to head off most of Fulton's proposals. There was some tinkering with the system, but overall the existing principles were retained. It was the reforming zeal of Margaret Thatcher which finally brought about dramatic change.

Rayner and FMI

After Fulton, some relatively mild attempts were made to improve the efficiency and management techniques of the civil service, but there was still concern that it was wasteful of public money, inefficient in its operation and certainly larger than it need be.

On taking power in 1979 Margaret Thatcher set up an **Efficiency Unit**, headed by Sir Derek Rayner, Chairman of Marks and Spencer, her favourite successful British company. By 1982 Rayner had produced a major document known as the **Financial Management Initiative** (**FMI**).

FMI was designed to ensure that civil servants would adopt an approach more similar to that followed by typical business managers. Policies were to be considered on the basis of good value for money, efficiency and the achievement of specific goals. The effect was to remove much of the 'political' consideration that went into the making of decisions and the giving of advice, and concentrating more on making government more efficient and effective.

The role of the Treasury had, of course, always been to reduce wastage and keep public expenditure to a minimum. Now, however, all senior officials were forced to adopt the new management style.

At the same time, the reductions in the sheer size of the civil service which resulted from FMI meant that senior officials suffered reductions in their power and status.

Ibbs and the 'Next Steps'

Sir Robin Ibbs, another former businessman, succeeded Rayner at the Efficiency Unit. His proposals, published in 1988 under the title 'The Next Steps', were more radical than Rayner's. The principal measures affected the provision of services rather than policy making and are discussed in more detail below. Nevertheless, senior officials were affected.

Ibbs suggested that many of the routine administrative tasks undertaken by the service did not need to be under the control of senior civil servants. He therefore proposed that a large number of civil service functions be 'hived off' to semi-independent agencies. These would be funded by their sponsoring department and would come under the general direction of a minister, but would, thereafter, be largely autonomous.

The structure of management was to be similar to that found in business and commerce. Specific performance and financial targets would be set and effectiveness would be judged against these targets. The effect on the civil service was to remove operational responsibility from senior officials and to reduce their authority over a large number of key government functions.

Yet although the power and status of senior civil servants was reduced by the Rayner and Ibbs reforms, they did serve to make a clearer distinction between policy making and operational roles. The latter were largely removed. The 2,000 or so senior officials were clearly now advisers rather than managers.

Criticisms of the senior civil service

Since concern over the role of senior officials began to grow in the 1960s, a number of specific criticisms have been levelled at the civil service:

Excessive power

The traditional version of the role of civil servants states that ministers are the masters and officials are servants. Ministers are expected to make policy and officials to carry it out without demur. Of course advice must be given, but this should be confined only to advice and not influence.

A number of former ministers, however, have argued that civil servants seek to wield real power. They are able to do so, it is claimed, because they are permanent and can therefore become experts in their field while ministers are temporary (on average a minister remains for less than three years in one post) and, essentially, amateurs. It is also true that ministers simply do not have the time to check the nature of all the advice they receive. It has long been accepted that ministers are overloaded with work. Officials are, therefore, able to manipulate information and advice. The view of Richard Crossman, a Labour minister in the 1960s and 1970s, was typical:

> *'If civil servants are doing their job properly, there is bound, at the very least, to be a creative and probably co-operative tension between the ministers and their official advisers.'*
> Lord Crowther-Hunt, 'Mandarins and Ministers'
> in *Parliamentary Affairs* (Autumn 1980)

> *'And this is where one's [a minister's] relationships with the Prime Minister are so all-important. If one doesn't have his backing, or at least the Chancellor's or First Secretary's to the Treasury, the chance of winning against the official view is absolutely nil.'*
> *The Crossman Diaries,* April 1965 (Magnum Books, 1979)

More recently, Tony Benn and Barbara Castle, also Labour Cabinet ministers, have expressed similar views. Indeed, more radical critics have suggested that a 'conspiracy' has existed against any government of the Left which proposes serious reforms. In other words, there is an anti-socialist 'establishment' in Britain which is heavily represented within the civil service.

Nevertheless, it should also be emphasised that no such charge has been levelled against the senior civil service by former Prime Ministers Harold Wilson or Edward Heath. They have argued that only weak ministers can be manipulated by officials.

It must also be remarked that, during the 1980s, a large number of radical reforms were carried through despite considerable civil service opposition, not least of which are the deep reforms of the machinery of government itself which are described below and which have considerably weakened the influence of civil servants.

Excessive conservatism

Radical ministers such as Crossman and Benn have also suggested that the British civil service is excessively cautious and anti-reformist. As a prime example, they point to attempts to introduce economic planning in the 1960s and 1970s which were thwarted by the stubborn refusal of officials to co-operate. In case we suspect that this is solely a left-wing accusation, it should be emphasised that Margaret Thatcher, on taking prime ministerial office in 1979, brought with her much the same prejudice. Indeed, Thatcher was determined to challenge the deeply rooted 'conservatism' and opposition to reform which she believed to flourish in Whitehall.

It should be noted that, while socialists such as Crossman and Benn viewed the civil service as the natural friend of traditional Toryism, Thatcher believed them to be more left wing and sympathetic to the retention of state power. Hugo Young's observation below illustrates this:

> 'No Government has been elected whose leader [Thatcher] was as deeply seized as this one of the need to overturn the power and presumption of the continuing government of the civil service; to challenge its orthodoxies, cut down its size, reject its assumptions, which were seen as corrosively infected by social democracy, and teach it a lesson in political control.'
> Hugo Young, One of Us (Macmillan, 1989)

In the event, Thatcher succeeded in forcing through most of her radical programme. However, this was achieved by either by-passing civil service advice, turning instead to independent advisers and policy agencies, and by appointing senior officials who were openly sympathetic to her views.

Exclusivity The Northcote–Trevelyan reforms established a system by which only career civil servants may reach senior positions of responsibility. Furthermore, the recruitment practices of the service have ensured that officials are drawn from a relatively narrow range of social and educational backgrounds. It is, therefore, frequently argued that this exclusive and sheltered group is ill-suited to policy making in a complex and technological modern world.

Professor Peter Hennessy's extensive review of the civil service emphasises this particular criticism as one of its most serious shortcomings:

> 'Whitehall failed to attract the rich mixture of human skills it needed, relying overmuch on a single, if refined, stream of generalist graduates, and . . . it failed to make full use – and still does – of the human capital already in its possession.'
> Peter Hennessy, Whitehall (Fontana, 1989)

The solution suggested by Hennessy (and earlier, in 1968, in the Fulton Committee Report) is to make senior positions open to outside entry, with posts advertised generally. In other words, to eliminate the 'career service' principle. In this way, some of Britain's more able individuals may become available to give advice to Government later in their careers. As occurred in the two world wars, when many experts and academics were drafted into government for the sake of the war effort, ministers might be better served by talented people with wider and deeper experience than career bureaucrats. By 1993 the Conservative Government seemed to have accepted this view and began to implement Hennessy's proposals.

Excessive secrecy

The civil service is not immune from the tendency of British government generally to keep its activities out of the public eye. Of course, civil servants are, according to the rules governing their conduct, expected to remain anonymous in terms of their own individual role. It is also true that they must sign the **Official Secrets Act**, which places a universal requirement for secrecy in all government work unless a minister expressly sanctions publication. Nevertheless, there is, it is often argued, a 'cult of secrecy' within Whitehall.

Again, Hennessy is one of the severest critics:

> *'Secrecy is built into the calcium of the British policy-maker's bones.'*
>
> Peter Hennessy, *Whitehall* (Fontana, 1989)

In practice, this tendency leads officials to attempt to keep policy-making processes from the eyes of both Parliament and the media. Where necessary, reports may be suppressed, information used selectively, and meetings held in private. Letting light into the corridors and committee rooms of Whitehall is certainly discouraged.

Genuine attempts have been made by John Major in the 1990s to alter this ethos. Civil servants increasingly appear before select committees of Parliament, although they are rarely able to be completely frank; a minister for open government now exists to find ways of ensuring publication of information which need not be kept secret; some of the workings of the machinery which supports the Cabinet have also been revealed.

Progress, however, is slow. Many, especially Liberal Democrats, believe that only the passage of a **Freedom of Information Act** will solve the problem.

The conduct and loyalty of civil servants

Whom do civil servants serve?

This may seem a simple question at first sight. It is not. Technically, civil servants are servants of the 'Crown'. Does this mean that they serve the monarch and not the Government of the day? Clearly, if the 'Crown' were a truly independent authority, with an active political role, as was the case before the middle of the nineteenth century, the difference between 'Government' and 'Crown' would be crucial. Civil servants would be subject to a higher authority than that of ministers. But 'Government' and 'Crown' are not really separate in a political sense today. Thus, it may seem, civil servants represent the Crown and the Government simultaneously.

What is already a difficult concept becomes more confusing when we consider further alternatives. Officials (and we must remind ourselves here that this concerns the relatively small community of policy advisers and implementers) might act in a manner which serves the interests of any one of the following:

- The whole Government
- The Prime Minister
- Their own minister
- Their own department, whoever the minister may be
- The ruling party
- Some conception of the 'national' or 'public' good.

These possibilities may be examined briefly in turn:

The Government of the day   In 1985, Clive Ponting, a senior official at the Department of Defence, leaked information to an MP that his boss, Secretary of State for Defence Michael Heseltine, had misled Parliament over Britain's conduct of the Falklands War in 1982. Ponting claimed that he was justified in making the revelation by his higher duty to serve the 'public interest'.

Ponting was prosecuted under the Official Secrets Act. The judge, in his remarks to the jury, clearly rejected Ponting's defence. Officials **do** serve the 'national interest', but this can only be interpreted by the Government. It was not for civil servants to decide what is in the national interest.

In the event, Ponting was acquitted. It seems the jury decided that he was *morally* justified even if he might have been technically guilty. Nevertheless, the case established the principal that there is no abstract or independent conception of the national interest. In other words, civil servants serve the Government alone.

The Prime Minister   Part of Margaret Thatcher's domination of the political system in the 1980s was said to be her control of the civil service. Indeed, it has been argued that she eventually controlled all senior appointments in the service personally. Her aim, it was argued, was to ensure that senior officials shared her own political philosophy. In other words, their highest duty was to serve her purposes.

Hugo Young's description of the Thatcher years in government sums this up in the opening lines of his work:

> '*Is he one of us?' The question became one of the emblematic themes of the Thatcher years. Posed by Mrs Thatcher herself, it defined the test which all politicians and other public officials aspiring to her favour were required to pass.*'
> Hugo Young, *One of Us* (Macmillan, 1989)

There have, certainly, been many fears expressed that the senior civil service was 'politicised' by Thatcher. That is, instead of being appointed on the basis of merit, civil servants were chosen on the basis of their political outlook. The doctrine of a neutral service was, thus, challenged.

Certainly, examples such as Sir Robert Armstrong (Cabinet Secretary), Sir Bernard Ingham (Press Secretary) and Sir Charles Powell (Prime Minister's Private Secretary and Foreign Policy Adviser), were seen as her personal political servants; their first loyalty was to the Prime Minister.

We need to be cautious in this area, however, since Margaret Thatcher's premiership was unusual. It seems unlikely that a less dominant Prime Minister could use the civil service in the same way. Even so, it has been of concern that, if the civil service does become politicised in this way, it becomes unable to serve any future Government with a different political philosophy. The continuation of 'Thatcherite' policies after her fall in 1990 suggests that there may be some truth in this assumption.

Their own minister   The orthodox view on this question is that a civil servant's first duty is to his minister – his political boss. In case there was any doubt, the rules governing conduct were codified by Sir Robert

Sir Robert Armstrong

Armstrong, the then Cabinet Secretary and most senior civil servant, in 1985. The so-called 'Armstrong Memorandum' stated clearly that a civil servant's first duty was to his minister. Should he have any concerns about his role, about integrity or about policy, he was to consult with his minister for guidance.

This appears straightforward but can cause problems. During the open Cabinet warfare surrounding the dispute over the purchase of Westland helicopters – the so-called 'Westland Affair' – it was discovered that some civil servants had been serving their ministers somewhat over-zealously. In particular, officials in Sir Leon Brittan's department (Trade) had illegally leaked information to support their minister's case. So it is unclear whether officials are expected to become involved in internal government disputes on behalf of their political masters. However, before Westland, it had appeared that the position *was* clear:

> *'The constitutional position is both crystal clear and entirely sufficient. Officials propose, Ministers dispose. Officials execute.'*
>
> The Times, 15 February 1977

Their department   One of Richard Crossman's principal criticisms of the civil service was that officials developed a 'departmental view' of various policies. Thus, whoever the minister may be, and whichever party he represents, they will attempt to impose this view on him. In other words, their first loyalty is to their department.

For example, the Treasury is always concerned with maintaining low public expenditure and a balanced budget; the Foreign Office is more interested in relations with the USA than with Europe.

These criticisms, however, have been somewhat overtaken by history. The Thatcher reforms have transformed the civil service and all its former certainties have been challenged. There is now little evidence that the Crossman view is still valid.

The ruling party   It is certainly true that official rules forbid civil servants from becoming involved in party, as opposed to governmental, politics. The advice they give and the decisions they make are to be in the national interest as interpreted by ministers, not in the interests of the ruling party alone. The distinction may, sometimes, be blurred, but it should be made.

The main examples of the problem occur when decisions have to be made which might be to the benefit of the community, but which may damage the popularity of the governing party. Taxation, interest rate policy and public expenditure issues are typical. What may be good for the country, such as tax and interest rate rises, may not be good for the party. Civil servants should make the distinction. The popular comedy TV programmes of the 1980s, entitled *Yes Minister* and *Yes Prime Minister*, stressed these confusions and even Margaret Thatcher was forced to accept that the shows represented something close to reality at times.

The national interest   Finally we come to the Ponting claim – that officials serve the national interest as defined by their own judgement. This has been firmly rejected by constitutional experts and politicians, but remains an issue, especially for radical politicians such as **Tony Benn**. He and others suggest that an official with the problem of such a conflict of interests should be able to appeal to a parliamentary committee, possibly in confidence.

However, it seems unlikely that any Government will be willing to accept such proposals. It remains in the interests of ministers of any party to be able to rely upon officials to serve them loyally. Any weakening of that position is also seen to undermine government itself and so is unlikely to occur.

Increased public profile   The traditional anonymity of the civil service was frequently called into question during the 1980s. The arrival of departmental select committees in the House of Commons in 1979 gave the opportunity for MPs to question civil servants directly. Though officials were under strict instructions to stick firmly to the standard departmental line on policy and avoid voicing their personal opinion, some chinks of light did appear in the dark corners of civil service work.

More importantly, however, senior officials working for Margaret Thatcher's administrations did become increasingly involved in public issues. Her Press Secretary, Sir Bernard Ingham, became a public mouthpiece not just for official Government policy – his legitimate role – but also for the Prime Minister's personal position. Meanwhile, Sir Robert Armstrong, the Cabinet Secretary, appeared both before parliamentary committees and in a court in Australia attempting to block publication there of *Spycatcher*, a highly sensitive book by Peter Wright on the British intelligence community.

A political civil service?

The many problems which have been identified surrounding the relationship between ministers and civil servants have given rise to calls for important changes to the status of officials. Among these is the proposal that ministers should be able to personally appoint a body of advisers in addition to the officials permanently based in their department. These 'political' civil servants would be chosen partly on the basis of their political philosophy. They might be drawn both from within and outside the existing service.

The inspiration for this idea comes from France where each minister has his own 'Cabinet', numbering about a dozen advisers. These both complement and counterbalance the advice offered by the neutral officials. They also answer those criticisms which suggest that the civil service has its own agenda which it seeks to impose on new ministers.

Largely supported by politicians of the Left, such as Tony Benn, the implementation of this plan would break down the traditional barriers in the civil service. Opponents suggest that it is the very neutrality of the existing service which is its great strength. Since the 1970s, however, considerable strains have been placed on that tradition of neutrality.

Four models of the civil service

Dr Kevin Theakston has drawn together a number of views and descriptions of the nature of the civil service and its relationship with ministers. From them he has deduced four 'models' which serve well as a summary:

The four Theakston models

1. **Formal–constitutional** The orthodox view. The service is neutral, loyal, anonymous and professional. It does not serve itself or any other authority, but only the Government and its ministers.
2. **Adversarial** This suggests that the civil service has its own goals and agenda which often involves it in attempting to thwart the plans of new ministers. Included in this model are the radical 'conspiracy theory' and the less extreme notion that officials simply dislike any radical changes in policy. Ministers therefore face a struggle to overcome civil service entrenched power.
3. **Village life** A view that suggests Whitehall is like a community. Everyone in the community – ministers and officials – attempts to find a consensus and to work together to retain his power and maintain the status quo. In other words, they all have a vested interest in helping each other. Clearly this is in direct contrast to the adversarial model.
4. **Public choice** This is another critical view, suggesting that the civil service acts in its own interests which are, typically, to retain its own influence, safeguard the career and financial position of its members and attempt to expand its size. It represents the idea of the great bureaucratic machine of which Margaret Thatcher and her allies were so critical.

Theakston's models may conflict with one another, but they do throw light upon many of the different characteristics of the British civil service. In practice, it embodies all of these characteristics in some measure.

The new civil service

The years between 1980 and 1995 saw radical changes in the nature of the British civil service.

The emergence of rivals

Governments and individual ministers have always used advisers from outside the civil service. The practice was exposed in the years of the Wilson premierships, 1964–70 and 1974–6, when he was known to operate through a so-called 'Kitchen Cabinet' of personal political assistants. In the 1970s and 1980s, however, the process of transferring policy making to private advisers accelerated.

Edward Heath had set up the **Central Policy Review Staff** (**CPRS**, also known as the 'Think Tank') in 1970 to advise the Cabinet as a whole on key policies. The CPRS drew membership from inside and outside politics and was fully independent of the civil service. Although it was abolished in 1983, the 'Think Tank' established the principle of accepting external advice in an organised way.

The Prime Minister's **Policy Unit** is a similar body comprising a dozen specially selected experts who serve the Head of Government and supplement a number of other individual advisers who are increasingly used by different ministers. Margaret Thatcher's dependence on Professor **Alan Walters** for economic and financial policy became notorious when it appeared to challenge the authority of the Treasury.

At the same time, the Conservative administrations of the 1980s and 1990s made much use of external policy agencies such as the **Adam Smith Institute**, the **Institute of Economic Affairs** and the **Centre for Policy Studies**. The introduction of the Poll Tax, much of the privatisation programme and the basis of economic policy have all been the result of proposals from these bodies.

Reduced responsibilities

The three developments described below – that is, the growth of quangos, executive agencies, and increased privatisation and contracting out of services – have all reduced the jurisdiction of the established civil service. This has tended to reduce the status of many officials simply because they have smaller bureaucracies to manage.

The policy-making functions of senior civil servants have been retained in large measure, but the reduction in executive functions has certainly reduced their power base.

Management style

The civil service has had to accept that its traditional administrative methods are no longer acceptable, especially since the Rayner reforms. Decisions on policy and its implementation must now consider the precise goals to be pursued, the methods by which these will be achieved and reviews of performance once action has been taken.

Officials are subject to the discipline of proving that measures provide value for money and will give rise to specific benefits. Should officials fall short of expectations, they can expect that their shortcomings will be exposed. Promotion will, therefore, be based very much on the quality of management shown rather than more traditional administrative skills.

Accountability

The management style described above is expected to make officials more accountable to their superiors for their performance. At the same time, government departments are now expected to be more responsive to public expectations. The **Citizens' Charter**, created by John Major, has given rise to a new ethos for government officials. It has made it clear that they serve the public as well as their political masters. Performance targets are not, therefore, restricted to purely financial considerations, but also to quality of service.

Career structure   The old rigid career structure of the civil service has begun to be broken down despite much resistance. There are proposals to bring in outsiders for senior positions; the new agencies, with their own pay and career structures, have disturbed the traditional expectations of officials; promotion is based much more upon performance than on mere length of service.

With lateral entry and new flexible contracts it is likely that the old career service will decline. If officials can no longer enjoy the job security which comes with permanence, their practices and attitudes may also change. Whether these reforms will be for the good must remain to be seen.

Executive agencies   The Ibbs Report known as 'The Next Steps' resulted an increasing number of governmental functions, formerly carried out by civil service departments, being transferred to executive agencies. The agencies were not quite as independent as quangos but were separated to a significant extent from the civil service itself.

Each agency has its own management structure, with its own pay scales and terms of employment. The civil service, by contrast, has a rigid structure in terms of both pay and careers. The increased flexibility, it is assumed, enables agencies to adjust management performance more effectively. They could also recruit personnel from outside the old civil service, thus enabling them to cast their net wider for appropriate talent.

Although they are funded by their sponsoring department, they have their own targets for both finance and general performance. The outcome of their activities can be measured against these targets so that pay and promotion will depend upon success or failure. This provides incentives which are largely absent from the traditional civil service. In particular, the chief executive, who heads each agency, will have his salary determined by the performance of that agency.

Since 1988, when the Ibbs Report was published, there has been a steady transfer of responsibility to these agencies. Examples include:

Agency	Main functions
Benefits Agency	To assess claimants to a variety of welfare benefits
Child Support Agency	To assess the financial liability of absent fathers for their children and to ensure payment
Drivers and Vehicles Licensing Agency	To administer the issuing and renewing of vehicle and drivers' licences
Central Office of Information	To collect and publish statistical information for educational and research purposes

By the end of the century, Ibbs envisages that the vast majority of government functions will be in the hands of these agencies. This would leave perhaps as few as 20,000 civil servants directly employed by a government department. As we have seen above, only about 10 per cent of this number would be directly involved in policy making.

The effect of the growth of executive agencies would include:

- Opportunities to assess effectively the efficiency of government activities.
- To enjoy reductions in the overall costs of bureaucracy in government.
- To bring in a wider variety of people, with different skills, into the government service.
- To weaken the line of accountability to Parliament since ministers are not directly in charge of their operation.
- To make a clear separation between the policy making and the purely executive functions of government.
- They have considerably more financial flexibility than the civil service, having options to borrow funds from the private sector and even to make profits where possible.
- Should a future decision to privatise their operation be made, they are already prepared for full independence from government.

Quangos

The term 'quango' was coined by journalists in the 1970s. It stands for 'quasi-autonomous national government organisation'.

What is a quango?

A quango is a committee or agency which has the following characteristics:

- It is set up by central government.
- It comes under the general oversight of a government department.
- Its members are appointed by a minister or one of his senior officials.
- Members may be full or part time, paid a salary or expenses only.
- Members may be a mixture of local or central government politicians, local or central government officials, experts and academics, community leaders, pressure group representatives, representatives of unions, business, industry or commerce, or even just interested members of the public, i.e. laypersons.
- It is funded by its sponsoring department.
- It is expected to be independent from departmental or other political influence, i.e. it is expected to act in a politically neutral way.

Types of quango

Quangos have a number of different kinds of function. These include the following:

- **Spending agencies** These are given government funds which they must allocate among competing demands.
- **Advisory committees** Bodies which give informed and non-political advice to ministers concerning policy, legislation and administration.
- **Regulatory bodies** For a variety of reasons it may be seen as preferable that legal regulation is carried out by a body which is independent of government. In some cases, these quangos may even be a prose-

cuting authority with powers to bring possible offenders to court. These bodies may also have powers to grant licences for various types of activity.

- **Administrative bodies** These are given funds to organise and administer activities set up originally by government departments.

Some quangos perform more than one of the functions described above. Examples of quangos and their functions are shown below:

Type of quango	Title	Main functions
Spending agencies	Arts Council	Distributing funds to artistic enterprises and individuals
	Medical Research Council	Granting funds for medical research projects
	District Health Authorities	Distributing NHS funds to hospital and doctors' trusts
	Regional Development Agencies	Granting funds to attract industry to depressed areas
Advisory committees	Law Commission	Advising the Lord Chancellor on issues concerning the law and the legal profession
	Countryside Commission	Advising on measures to protect the rural environment
	Equal Opportunities Commission	Advising the Government on measures to give equal opportunities to men and women
Regulatory bodies	Monopolies and Mergers Commission	Determining whether takeovers or mergers are in the public interest
	Commission for Racial Equality	Implementing laws on racial equality, including prosecutions
	English Heritage	Protecting historic buildings and regulating proposed alterations to them
Administrative bodies	Training and Enterprise Councils	Organising training schemes for the young and for those who need new skills
	Hospital Trusts	Running local groups of hospitals

The growth in the importance of quangos
There have always been bodies similar to the modern conception of the quango involved in the governing process. Between 1970 and 1980, however, there was a vast increase in their number and scope. A peak of 2,167 quangos was reached in 1979 when the new Thatcher administration promised to limit their numbers. This was done and by 1993 there were only 1,389. Despite the fall in numbers, however, quangos control more governmental functions than they have ever done.

'When Margaret Thatcher came to power in 1979 she vowed to prune the political garden of quangos ... a weed, she argued, which grew essentially in socialist soil. Since then we have witnessed an extraordinary burgeoning of this curious plant all over the garden.'

Bill Jones 'The Unknown Government' in *Talking Politics*,
Vol. 6, No. 2 (1994)

Jones also points out that, by 1992, quangos accounted for 20 per cent of total government expenditure. What is more, Jones adds, plans exist for further increases, especially in the Health Service and the police authorities. Figures from 1993, for example, show the following leading expenditure figures of major quangos*:

Legal Aid Board	£1.28 billion
Medical Research Council	£288.35 million
English Arts Council	£225.60 million
Criminal Injuries Authority	£182.50 million
Welsh Development Agency	£151.70 million

* Quoted in *The Independent* by Blackhurst and MacKinnon 2 February 1995

There are a number of reasons for these developments. The scope of government has continually grown since World War Two. This has placed increasing pressure on both ministers and their departments. The temptation to hive off responsibilities to these semi-independent bodies, therefore, has become overwhelming. At the same time, an increasing amount of specialised expertise is required in governing processes. As we have seen in the section above concerning the civil service, British administration at senior levels has tended to be generalist rather than specialist. Quangos draw experts into administration without the need to employ them full time in large numbers.

Some critics have argued that the use of quangos is 'government by stealth'. Here it is suggested that successive Governments have sought to extend their influence into new areas of life, but have disguised the process by operating through quangos which *appear* to be independent. In practice, imply these critics, they merely serve to extend the influence of ministers without increasing their political responsibility. This view – it must however be stressed – is not shared by all political commentators.

The problems of government by quango

Apart from the criticisms described above, considerable concern has been expressed over the increased use of quangos. Among them are the following:

- The line of accountability to Parliament is weak. Their operations are supervised by the **National Audit Office** and ministers are technically responsible for the performance and decisions of quangos, but in practice there is relatively little Parliament can do to oversee their activities.

- Much of their work is carried out in secret. Their proceedings do not take place in public, nor are the media allowed to investigate them too closely.
- They provide ministers with wide powers of patronage since appointment to quangos is in their hands. Thus, although they are designed to be non-political, ministers are able to exercise excessive degrees of influence.
- They are not elected bodies and, in many cases, they have replaced functions carried out by elected councils or ministers. Thus, it may be argued, democracy is diminished by the growth of government by quango.

The advantages of quangos

The picture is not all negative. Quangos can improve the quality of government and administration in a number of ways:

- To some extent key decisions are taken out of the hands of party politicians. Thus, policy may be made in the interests of the community rather than for reasons of party advantage. This is especially true of spending agencies.
- Quangos bring into the governing process a number of people with special expertise who would not otherwise be involved. As we have seen, civil servants often do not possess the necessary outside experience to be able to make technically sound decisions.
- They have gone some way to decentralise government. Although they are not elected, there are some opportunities for local members of the community to become involved in decision making.

Contracting out and privatisation

The effects of the Rayner and Ibbs reforms have been to establish a kind of 'business management ethos' into the operations of government. Those functions which are purely administrative and non-political, it has been argued, should be subject to the same kinds of discipline as private enterprise: they should be cost-effective, target-driven and monitored for performance. The logical next step is, therefore, to travel the full journey and privatise certain functions completely. This involves either 'contracting out', where existing private firms bid to carry out former government functions in return for a stated income – the more efficient their performance, the greater the profit they can achieve – or full privatisation, which implies giving long term contracts to private firms who will simply replace existing executive agencies.

The role of ministers and officials would then be to limited to awarding contracts, ensuring quality, monitoring performance and setting general guidelines.

The process has already begun in the mid 1990s. There are private prisons and contracts have been awarded for the transport of prisoners to and from courts. Similar developments have occurred in the Health Service and are proposed for the less sensitive aspects of the police service and schools inspection.

Whether privatisation and contracting out extends further is likely to depend upon the political fortunes of the main parties. Continuing Conservative Party Government is likely to result in further development. The Labour Party, on the other hand, is most unlikely to allow any more functions to leave the control of Government. It may even be that some of the devolved services will be returned to the direct control of Government ministers.

The new machinery of government

The traditional view of British government was relatively straightforward. Ministers, advised by officials, made policy and the civil service implemented that policy through the Departments of State. The minister was responsible to Parliament for every action of his department. The position is now considerably more complex, with a multi-layered system of committees, agencies, quangos, authorities and private companies on contract to government.

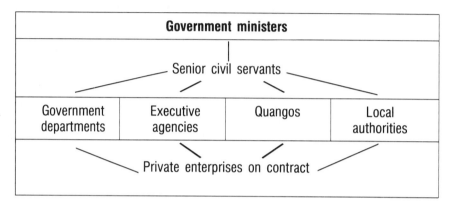

Not only is the system more complex; there have also been marked changes to the way public administration is carried out. The methods and conduct of officials at all levels are now more strictly monitored and based on more specific goals.

Summary of changes to the machinery of central government

1. The civil service as a whole has been reduced in size, from over 700,000 in 1980 to about 500,000 in 1995.
2. Many functions, formerly under the direct control of Government ministers and their senior officials, are now run by semi-independent quangos or executive agencies, or have even been privatised.
3. Civil servants have increasingly become subject to performance targets and budgetary constraints.
4. The rigid career structure of the traditional civil service is becoming more flexible and is now open to outsiders.
5. The political status of the most senior officials has become increasingly ambiguous, with several conflicting demands upon their loyalty.

These changes may seem somewhat confusing, but a clear general picture is emerging of the way in which the responsibilities of the modern machinery of central government are evolving.

The central state used to be a provider of services. Especially when many great industries were nationalised, the goods, services and welfare provisions enjoyed by the community were directly supplied in great measure by ministers and the huge civil service bureaucracy which they commanded. These twin establishments made policies, organised the implementation of those policies and managed the many people who operated the system. The civil service itself was left to control its own internal workings, but, in return, was expected to serve all ministers with equal loyalty and integrity.

> *'Unlike the civil servants of the Northcote–Trevelyan reforms, this reformed civil service did not aim to also deliver those services itself. Instead it bought them in from competing organisations in the public, private and voluntary sectors – government by contract, in other words.'*
> John Williamson in *The Major Effect* (Macmillan, 1995)

All these certainties are now gone. The bureaucracy is subject to greater objective, external scrutiny and is no longer master and mistress in its own house. Its loyalty, still officially owed to ministers, also lies with considerations of commercial and financial effectiveness.

Above all, however, it no longer directly provides all the public services which it used to, as a form of state monopoly. Instead, many services are now supplied by other bodies – the quangos, agencies or private sub-contracting firms which now proliferate in public administration. As with local authorities, central government increasingly 'regulates' and 'enables', but actually produces less and less.

> *'At the broadest level it will be an **Enabling State**. One that encourages beneficial action, but leaves the task of achieving this action increasingly to other quasi-state and non-state agencies.'*
> Martin Burch 'The Next Step for Britain's Civil Service' in *Talking Politics*, Vol. 5, No. 3 (Spring 1995)

For exam questions relevant to this unit, see page 489.

10 Pressure groups

The nature of pressure

In politics pressure is the means by which **influence** is exercised. As is the case with influence, there is no certainty that pressure will actually achieve its ends. Only pure **coercive power** can guarantee success in virtually all circumstances.

While power operates through the ultimate use of **force**, pressure does not enjoy such luxuries. Those who wish to exercise it must, therefore, use more subtle means. Among these are:

Reasoned argument

In an ideal world we might expect that political decisions are all based upon rationality, but it is only on rare occasions that reason alone prevails. Groups which have campaigned for constitutional reforms, such as **Charter 88**, or those which are concerned with rights – of both humans and animals – such as **Liberty** or the **League Against Cruel Sports**, hope that politicians will be persuaded by the force of argument. However, sterner measures are normally required.

Threats of sanctions

Since reason often does not prevail, decision-makers usually need clearer messages in order to stir them into action. Thus, negative pressure may be used. Here the threat of action which will damage, embarrass or hinder the purposes of Government can be effective. In extreme circumstances law breaking may be involved, such as the 'tax strike' organised by the anti-Poll Tax movement in the 1980s. The withholding of local taxes created havoc for local authorities, expense for the Treasury and chaos in the courts, which were attempting to prosecute the non-payers. Trade Unions may organise strikes or lesser industrial action and producer groups may threaten to thwart Government economic policies, should they not receive favourable treatment.

Rewards

Few politicians can resist the lure of the promise of large numbers of voters granting their support at the next election. The achievement and retention of governmental power are meat and drink to these politicians. Pressure which promises to satisfy these appetites is, therefore, likely to be the most successful. It is the large interest groups such as trade unions, home owners and taxpayers which offer these rewards in the greatest numbers. **Finance** is another powerful carrot to attract the attention of the political parties. Groups from both sides of industry – unions and employers – have supported parties in the expectation that they will have some influence over policy. The threat that financial support may be removed can exert as much pressure as voting strength.

There have also been occasions when co-operation, and the promise of it in the future, has been used as a means of persuasion. In the latter half of the 1970s, for example, trade unions were able to stave off the threat of significant reductions in their power by agreeing to co-operate in the Government's battle against high inflation. The agreement, known as the 'Social Contract', was a clear case of political rewards being used as a successful bargaining counter.

Pressure group classification

Definition

Before attempting to place pressure groups into different categories, a **general** explanation is needed. Perhaps the two leading authorities on British pressure groups are Robert Baggott and Wyn Grant. Their descriptions should, therefore, serve us best as precise definitions:

> *'an organisation which seeks to influence the details of a comparatively small range of public policies and which is not a faction of a recognised political party'*
>
> Robert Baggott

> *'an organisation which seeks as one of its functions to influence the formulation and implementation of public policy, public policy representing a set of authoritative decisions taken by the executive, the legislature and the judiciary, and by local government and the European Community [now Union]'*
>
> Wyn Grant

Both quoted in R. Baggott, *Pressure Groups: A Question of Interest* (PAVIC Publications, 1994)

From this pair of definitions we can extract a number of key facts about pressure groups:

- They are **organisations**, which suggests that they have a formal structure of some kind.
- They seek to **influence**, indicating that they have fairly precise goals.
- Their goals are relatively **narrow**, which means that they do not concern themselves with the full range of public policy.
- They are **not political parties** or parts of parties.
- They operate on **any public decision-making body**, whichever is appropriate.

Having established a general description, we can divide pressure groups into two broad types: interest or sectional groups on the one hand, and promotional or issue groups on the other.

Interest or sectional groups

Here a specific part of the population is being represented by a group. Hence we may call it a **sectional** group. It is also known as an **interest** group in that its role is to further the interests of that section of the population. 'Interests' may involve economic well-being, quality of life, rights, or any other desirable goals.

In some cases, membership of these groups may be restricted **only** to those whose interests are being pursued, as is the case with trade unions or the motoring organisations. These may be described as 'restricted membership' groups. In others, membership may be open to all who are concerned, whether or not they stand to benefit. These have been called 'cause' groups as members often feel they have a duty to campaign for those less fortunate than themselves. **Child Poverty Action Group** and **Age Concern** fall into this sub-category.

A slight complication may occur when groups are concerned with foreign countries, as is the case with **Amnesty International**, which campaigns for political prisoners around the world. However, this should not interfere with the basic distinction.

Additionally, there are pressure groups concerned with animals and their 'rights'. It is beyond the scope of this book to discuss the philosophical question of whether animals have rights, but for our purposes here we can add such animal rights groups as the **Animal Liberation Front** or the **Anti-Vivisection League** (which both oppose experimentation on animals) to the 'promotional' classification.

Some of Britain's principal interest or sectional groups are shown below, together with their main goals:

Interest group	Goals
Trade Unions	Furthering the interests of specific groups of workers, including better pay, working conditions and pensions, and health and safety, employment prospects, job security and training opportunities.
Confederation of British industry (CBI)	Securing economic, industrial and financial policies favourable to British industry. Supporting the interests of British Industry in European and world trade bodies.
Automobile Association (AA)	Pursuing policies favourable to the private motorist, including road building, road safety measures, lower fuel prices, etc.
Child Poverty Action Group (CPAG)	Securing policies favourable to poor families, especially welfare benefits, lower taxation and better housing.
MIND	Pursuing the interests of the mentally ill, mainly the provision of research and care facilities.
National Farmers' Union (NFU)	Securing treatment beneficial to British farmers, including provision of subsidies, favourable trade agreements and environmental policies. Largely now concerned with the European Union's agricultural policies.

Promotional or issue groups

These organisations may appeal to **all** sections of the community, but are concerned with a particular issue or group of related issues. We can further divide them into those groups which are likely to remain **permanent**, since the issue is likely to persist, and those which may be **temporary** because they will disappear when their goals have been achieved. Of course some organisations may **hope** to be temporary, but lack of success may turn them into permanent campaigns.

Some prominent examples are shown opposite.

Pressure groups and parties

What distinguishes a pressure group from a party? At first sight the similarities may appear to be overwhelming. Both are formal organisations which have specific goals, engage in campaigns to achieve them, often use similar methods and seek to influence the political system. Yet there are crucial differences:

Permanent issue groups	Goal(s)
Friends of the Earth	Achievement of policies to improve and protect the natural environment, including the protection of endangered animal and plant species
Transport 2000	To promote the cause of public transport, securing more public funds and support for such transport
Viewers and Listeners Association	To prevent the presentation of explicit sex and violence in public performances, mainly the broadcasting media

Temporary issue groups	Goal(s)
Campaign for Nuclear Disarmament (CND)	Securing the worldwide abolition of all nuclear weapons
Campaign for Lead-Free Air (CLEAR)	Achieving the abolition of lead additives in motor fuel
Electoral Reform Society	Securing a change in the British electoral system to some form of proportional representation

- Political parties seek governmental office, either alone or in partnership with others. Pressure groups do not. Any pressure group which adopts the aim of achieving government office automatically turns itself into a political party and must, in such circumstances, change its approach, as we shall see below. There may be some confusion where pressure groups put up candidates for election at local or general elections. Anti-European groups have adopted such tactics in the 1990s and local campaign groups have often put up candidates for councils, sometimes with some success. However, this is not the same as running for office. The purpose of such an action is to seek greater publicity, but little more.

There has been some confusion caused by electoral tactics. The **Ecology Party**, which has since become the **Green Party**, has itself been split on the very issue of whether it is a pressure group or a political party. **Sinn Fein**, too, can scarcely hope to gain office with its very restricted aim of the re-unification of Ireland, but it fights elections and has regularly won seats in both Dublin and London. In the case of Sinn Fein President, Gerry Adams, he refused to take up the seat he had won at Westminster in 1987, indicating that he had no desire to be involved with British government. Adams lost his seat in the 1992 general election, but after the IRA ceasefire which began in the autumn of 1994, Adams began negotiations with the Government on behalf of both Sinn Fein and the IRA. Thus he resumed full-scale political activity.

- Parties must be willing to accept the responsibilities of government, should they be successful at elections. Thus, they must adopt policies across the **whole range** of national concerns. Pressure groups do not have such a problem. They will never seek office and so their aims can be narrower. More importantly still, they do not have to concern themselves with the full potential consequences of their proposals.

In this respect problems arise in distinguishing between pressure groups and factions **within** parties. Such factions also have relatively narrow aims and may neglect the wider implications of their goals. For example, the Conservative **Bruges Group** campaigns against Britain's closer integration in Europe. Similarly, **trade unions** have institutional links within the Labour Party and so form an internal interest group. However, since these groupings exist within the parties, their members are ultimately hoping to enter government in some respect.

- Finally, it must be emphasised that political parties are subject to legal constraints which do not apply to pressure groups. Parties must account for the sources of their funds in order to reduce the likelihood of undue influence. The way in which they choose their leaders, select candidates and operate within political institutions are all carefully scrutinised and controlled by Parliament and its committees. Pressure groups must, of course, abide by the laws, but are much more free in the way in which they conduct their internal affairs.

Methods

As we have seen above, pressure groups are more flexible than parties in the methods they can adopt. This means that there is a wide variety of devices used to influence the governing process. These are described below.

Mobilising public support

If a group is to 'catch the eye' of the government or of Parliament its most effective method is to demonstrate that there is widespread popular support for its aims. High profile campaigning, the organisation of public demonstrations and the dissemination of information are all means by which such support may be attracted and then demonstrated to those in power.

The late 1980s anti-Poll Tax movement was a typical example, as was organised opposition to the imposition of VAT on domestic fuel in 1994. A few years before, a huge campaign to stop the closure of coal pits was almost enough to create a reversal of Government policy and certainly wrung a number of important concessions from the Department of Trade and Industry.

Incorporation or 'insider status'

In the long term, any pressure group is almost guaranteed greater success if it can achieve **incorporation** or what Professor **Wyn Grant** has called 'insider status'.

Much government work is carried out through a variety of official committees, staffed by ministers, officials and other invited members. These committees and quangos make key decisions concerning the allocation of expenditure, licensing of various activities and proposed future legislation. If representatives of pressure groups can be **incorporated** into these bodies, or be regularly consulted by them, they have penetrated the heart of the decision-making process. They have become **insiders**.

Of course, such a status carries responsibilities, but in return pressure groups can expect to be able to exert considerable influence. Not only does this apply to central government in Whitehall, but also in local government and in the European Commission in Brussels.

Examples of groups which have achieved such a status are:

- National Farmers Union
- Friends of the Earth
- National Trust

- Confederation of British Industry
- Institute of Directors
- Royal Society for the Protection of Birds
- Royal National Institute for the Blind.

Yet more crucially, some groups have achieved the ultimate level of incorporation by becoming government-sponsored bodies themselves. Here, certain interest groups are considered so important that their cause must be represented directly. Such quangos undertake research, propose legislation, organise campaigns and may even enforce laws on behalf of key sections of the community or popular interests.

Examples include:

- Equal Opportunities Commission (women)
- Commission for Racial Equality (ethnic minorities)
- Office of Fair Trading (consumers)
- National Heritage (traditional architecture)
- Countryside Commission (environment)

Grant's analysis also identifies groups which are 'outsiders'. These do not have the formal links with political institutions which insiders enjoy. They may be outsiders through choice, as was the case with the Campaign for Nuclear Disarmament (CND), or simply because they have been unable to find acceptance in the political establishment. Greenpeace falls into this latter category.

Outsiders tend to concentrate on mobilising public support in order to put pressure on politicians by the sheer force of numbers and opinion. They often take **direct action**, as was the case with the movements against the Poll Tax in the 1980s and against the export of live animals in the 1990s. Demonstrations, civil disobedience, major campaigns in the media and even intimidatory tactics are typical.

WPC and animal rights protester outside London's High Court, 12 April 1995

Insider and outsider pressure groups – typical methods	
Insiders	**Outsiders**
• Sponsorship of friendly MPs • Direct links with ministers • Participation on official committees • Representation on quangos • Influencing parliamentary standing committees to amend legislation • Testifying before departmental select committees	• Public demonstrations • Petitions • Campaigns of civil disobedience • Media campaigns • Illegal activities to achieve publicity

Parliamentary action

Since the last century, various groups have sought to exercise influence through Parliament. Even as parliamentary influence waned during the twentieth century it remained as a channel for pressure.

The clearest example of the use of this route occurred in 1900, when the trade union movement formed a Parliamentary Representation Committee with the expressed purpose of opening up a new channel of communication to government. Since then many Labour MPs have continued to be 'sponsored' (in terms of expense payments rather than an extra salary) by trade unions in return for which it is expected that they will defend and fight for the interests of their union.

In a similar way, other MPs often receive retainers in return for representation of a whole variety of interests and causes. These include large business companies, employer groups, professional associations, promotional pressure groups, foreign governments and sports associations.

In recent years there has been a growth in the number and activities of professional political lobbying organisations. These lobbyists organise parliamentary exposure by MPs on behalf of smaller groups and companies which could not make such arrangements themselves. In 1994 the extent of their activities was highlighted by revelations of payments to MPs in return for asking questions in the House in order to draw attention to particular issues on behalf of external groups. Although this practice infringes the rules of the House of Commons, it was clear that similar, more acceptable practices were common.

The main purpose of parliamentary pressure is to provide publicity. There is little evidence to suggest that parliamentary activity alone can provide sufficient pressure to produce specific government action, but it can be a useful addition to a broader campaign.

MPs have a variety of means by which an issue can be raised or an interest group promoted. Asking questions of ministers is the commonest method, but speeches during debates, special motions proposed during gaps in parliamentary procedures and direct meetings with officials and ministers are also used. The only truly effective form of parliamentary action is the passage of a Private Member's Bill. Time for such bills is scarce and the government have a number of ways to thwart them. Nevertheless, successful reform of laws relating to homosexuality (led by Edwina Currie MP) and to abortion (David Alton MP) in the 1990s demonstrates that pressure groups can succeed through the parliamentary route.

Very occasionally pressure groups have also succeeded in thwarting a Government itself by organising a sufficiently large back-bench revolt to defeat proposed legislation. Unions were successful in preventing legislative reform in 1969 by mobilising enough Labour MPs to oppose their leadership before the measures known as 'In Place of Strife' were presented to the House of Commons. More dramatically, a combination of church and union groups organised the defeat of a Bill to allow Sunday trading in 1986, the only defeat of the second reading of a Government Bill since World War Two.

Media campaigns

As part of the mobilisation process, the media provide a useful tool in that both the public and the decision makers themselves may be influenced. Most significantly, the impact of TV and radio programmes can be decisive. Certainly various environmental pressure groups have been able to attract support in this way.

An essential ingredient in such campaigns is the gathering of inform- ation and data to support a group's aims. Such research material is often presented in TV, radio and press features. Issues relating to the environment, smoking, cruelty to animals and transport have all been successfully treated in this way. Celebrities are also an effective addition to these campaigns. Cliff Richard (Viewers and Listeners Association, abortion law), Sir Ian McKellen (Homosexual law reform and AIDS issues) and the actor Lord Rix (the mentally handicapped) have all fronted high profile issues.

Direct lobbying

Not only MPs but also leaders of pressure groups and, in some cases, members *en masse* may seek to present their case directly to relevant ministers. Rallies and petitions may be organised, as well as private meetings with the minister concerned or with his senior officials. In practice, however, such methods can only be significant if they achieve sufficient exposure to swing public opinion behind the cause.

Why do pressure groups succeed or fail?

How large are they?

This may seem obvious at first sight. Clearly, a Government is more likely to respond to pressure by large groups simply because there are more potential votes to be won or lost. Thus, such sectional interests as those of motorists or home owners can expect favourable treatment.

Yet the evidence is confusing. During the 1980s, for example, trade unions (total membership about 8 million) and pensioners (about 25 per cent of the population) did not appear to enjoy any political advantage at all. Indeed, in both cases, these large groups suffered considerable discomfort at the hands of ministers.

The answer to this paradox lies in the question of which party is in government at any particular time. The government is more likely to be influenced by large numbers of its **own potential supporters** who make up a pressure group's membership. It was, for example, hardly surprising that Conservative administrations of the 1980s and 1990s were unsympathetic to unions as not many of their members were likely to be Conservatives! Home owners, on the other hand, are predomi- nantly Tory supporters and so had to be nurtured.

Who is in government? Some pressure groups will, therefore, expect better treatment from one party than from another. And success or failure will depend largely upon the philosophy of the government in power.

The table below demonstrates this:

Groups likely to be favoured by a particular party	
Conservative	**Labour**
National Farmers Union	Trade unions
CBI	Caring professions
Institute of Directors	Poorer families
Large companies	Single parent groups
Financial institutions	Education groups
Small businesses	Health Service workers
Higher income groups	Pensioner groups

It can be noted here that some groups which would be best served by the Liberal Party – those favouring constitutional reform, greater protection for individual rights, open government and environmental protection – are, thus, disadvantaged.

Are they well financed? It is a further truism that finance is a crucial factor. It is also possibly the most controversial issue in this area. The availability of funds does not necessarily indicate numerical strength, nor does it say anything about the justice of a particular argument.

There has been considerable disquiet concerning the financial muscle of large companies such as those producing tobacco, public utilities like gas and electricity, the large brewers and motor manufacturers, retail groups and oil companies. The same can be said of trade unions which have use of huge quantities of finance raised in subscriptions from their members.

On the one hand, funds can be used to finance political parties and so receive sympathetic treatment. On the other, they are able to mount expensive campaigns in support of their aims. It is often claimed, for example, that the consistent refusal by governments to ban all advertising on cigarettes is the result of lobbying on a large scale by the big tobacco companies. The same claims are made concerning the lack of action to break the brewers' virtual monopoly over public houses.

Are they well organised? Inevitably, when pressure groups first come into existence they suffer from a variety of disadvantages. They have no public profile, may lack financial resources and have not established formal links with government bodies.

What they need, therefore, is a strong organisation to achieve all these aims before their cases can be properly presented. Those groups which are able to build up such a strong organisation are at a great advantage over less formal, less organised movements. Some of the important features of the well-organised pressure group are:

- A network for the recruitment of members
- An organised system for raising funds
- Research facilities and staff

- Decision-making procedures established and widely accepted
- A strong management structure to give policy direction
- Established methods for creating publicity
- Formal links established with government bodies and . or Parliament.

Do they hold a strategic position? Some sectional groups enjoy special status on the grounds that the community is especially reliant upon them. Those who run emergency services are a clear example, but so too are those who supply households and industry with energy and those who produce our food.

In a similar way, there are those on whom Government itself relies in order to implement key policies. Trade unions used to hold such a position before their status was seriously undermined by the dramatic reforms of the 1980s. Large businesses and commercial enterprises still do. The banks, financial institutions and the City of London are important factors in the success or failure of financial policy. The co-operation of the farming community, too, is vital to the success of policies related to food production and prices, and the preservation of the countryside.

Key strategic groups which may use their position to exert influence include:

- Industries employing large numbers of workers
- Firms and unions involved in energy production
- Businesses which account for large export volumes
- Police, medical and emergency service personnel
- Organisations supplying important information to government.

Are they supported by public opinion? For a variety of reasons, including successful campaigns by pressure groups themselves, public opinion may swing towards a particular issue. As we have seen above, politicians are inevitably sensitive to such movements. Thus, a combination of an effective campaign together with a sympathetic public is a potent combination.

In recent years a number of important policy changes and developments have been the result of such circumstances. For example:

- Equal pay for women
- Controls over experimentation on animals
- Reducing the age of consent for homosexuals to eighteen
- Various incentives to reduce harmful vehicle exhaust emissions
- Relaxation of the alcohol licensing laws.

Do they face powerful opposition? Pressure groups have been portrayed as simply confronting Government with their demands and goals. However, it is often the case that two or more groups are ranged against *each other*. In these circumstances the role of the Government may simply be to act as arbiter between competing claims.

Some recent examples of such contests may illustrate this feature:

- Animal Rights Campaigners   v.   the fur trade
- The Anti-Smoking Lobby   v.   the tobacco industry
- The Campaign for Real Ale   v.   the large breweries
- The Anti-Blood Sports League   v.   the hunting establishment
- Transport 2000   v.   the motorcar industry

The result of these struggles, in which the weapons used are a selection of those campaign methods described above, will depend upon both the effectiveness of action and the attitude of the Government of the day. However, it is clear that in some cases like those shown above, the dice are seriously loaded in favour of one of the combatants.

Factors determining the effectiveness of pressure groups

1. Size of membership
2. Which party is in power
3. How much finance is at their disposal
4. How well they are organised
5. How strategic their position is in society or government
6. Whether public opinion is sympathetic
7. Whether there are powerful groups in opposition to their aims

---

Pluralism, corporatism and democracy

Pluralism

The dominance of political parties in Parliament and government in Britain during the twentieth century has served to disguise the growing importance of pressure groups in our society.

The duopoly of party control had meant that most demands and aspirations within the community were channelled through the parties. Issues came to be seen in adversarial terms – Government versus Opposition, Conservative versus Labour, middle-class demands versus working-class demands. Politicians largely claimed to represent the interests of either one of the great social classes or, alternatively, of the whole nation.

The combination of such dualism and party government left little room for the many competing interests and demands which characterise modern politics. That is not to say that there were no attempts to persuade politicians of either main party to take up a particular cause or interest, but such activities were relatively insignificant in comparison to the great issues which divided the parties.

After World War Two the picture began to change. The influence of social class on politics began to wane, the political system became more open and the dominance of party doctrine was reduced. Between 1940 and 1980, in the era of so-called 'consensus politics' when there were relatively few differences between the policies of the main parties, party leaders concentrated on seeking general, or 'consensus', support for their policies. This search for consensus inevitably led to wide consultation with groups representing different interests and views. The dualism of the party system was being replaced by a 'pluralist' environment wherein group, rather than class interests were generally considered.

Growing prosperity was a further factor in the growth of pluralism. The activities of individuals widened, there was greater access to information, especially with the advent of TV, and an increased awareness that it was possible to exert influence on political leaders.

Even when ideological politics returned under Margaret Thatcher in the 1980s, the greater individualism proliferating in modern society ensured that group membership and activity would continue to grow. Group membership empowered individuals who had previously felt alienated by the party system. Governments have had to respond to these developments and have done so by accepting the pluralistic nature of modern society.

> 'Government, then, has to contend with a society which, in terms of organised interests, is more rather than less pluralist. Furthermore, it has to operate in a political environment in which power is more dispersed than before.'
>
> Philip Norton, *New Directions in British Politics* (Edward Elgar, 1991)

Corporatism A number of factors after 1940 led to a period during which the important pressure groups in society were steadily integrated or **incorporated** into the governing process. This process came to be known as 'corporatism'. The factors included:

- The growth of pluralism described above
- The increasing complexity of the governing process, thus requiring increased information and co-operation from external groups
- The leadership of a group of politicians including Macmillan, Butler and Gaitskell who accepted the need for such incorporation
- An understanding that parties alone could not secure widespread acceptance of policy initiatives.

As a result, a number of institutions were set up to accommodate the new corporatist spirit. Most prominent was the **National Economic Development Council (NEDC)**, set up in 1961 by Harold Macmillan to discuss economic and industrial policy. Its members included union leaders, businessmen, civil servants and ministers. In addition, a wide range of **official committees** came into being, with similar membership structures. Group interests were, thus, officially recognised.

The corporatist era largely ended in the 1980s. Successive Conservative Governments disbanded hundreds of committees and quangos through which group interests had been represented. The abolition of the NEDC was the most symbolic gesture, but it could not alter an important truth. Although pressure groups had lost many of their seats on official bodies, their influence could not be denied.

Pressure groups and democracy As long ago as the 1830s the French writer Alexis de Tocqueville (1805–59) expressed the view that intermediate groups in a society were an essential feature of an effective democracy. Should a people fail to organise themselves into an active **civil society** – his collective term for such groups – they become vulnerable to the power of the centralised government. In a modern context this would imply that the community needs pressure groups to counterbalance the enormously enhanced power of a modern state.

Since Tocqueville, it has become an accepted feature of modern democratic theory that the pluralism represented by pressure group activity must flourish. Indeed, American political scientists in the 1950s and 1960s, such as David Trueman, analysed democracy almost exclusively in terms of the peaceful interplay between such groups.

> *'The total pattern of government over a period of time thus presents a protean complex of crisscrossing relationships that change in strength and direction with alternations in the power and standing of interests, organised and unorganised.'*
> David Trueman, *The Governmental Process* (University of Michigan, 1952)

However, although pressure group activity appears to serve democracy in a positive way, there are some suggestions that they can operate in opposition to democratic principles. Both sides of the argument are summarised below:

Pressure groups as positive elements in democracy

- They act as an effective channel of communication between the governed and the government. They articulate demands and mobilise support for them.
- They provide wide opportunities for people to participate actively in the political process without having to devote excessive amounts of time to such activity.
- They ensure that minority groups and interests are represented within the political system.
- They can act as important checks on the power of the state by mobilising opposition to measures acting against the interests of sections of the community.
- They help to ensure stability by institutionalising peaceful political conflict, so preventing possible disorder and violence.

Pressure groups as threats to democracy

- They can be seen as vehicles for 'vested interests', only concerned with their own welfare and ignoring the broader good of the whole community.
- Some groups may wield disproportionate amounts of influence as a result of financial resources and links with political parties. This influence may be out of proportion to their true importance in society. Both trade unions and big business have been accused of posing such a threat to the democratic process.
- Pressure groups themselves may not be internally democratic. The views expressed by their leaders may not reflect those of their members. Unlike the political system itself, which contains democratic guarantees – especially methods of ensuring responsibility – pressure groups may adopt their own internal systems. Thus, they might become merely reflections of **elitism** rather than true pluralism. Until the reforms of the 1980s trade unions were again suspected of such undemocratic practices, but the same could be argued of the **Automobile Association** (private motorists), the **British Medical Association** (doctors) or the **Football Association**, none of which have well-developed systems for consulting their supporters.

Thus, the case is fairly balanced. Whichever argument holds more truth, there is no doubt that pressure groups have become a central and permanent feature of modern pluralist, liberal democracies.

Future challenges for pressure groups

Europe

Important decision-making processes are steadily being transferred from London to Brussels. This implies two things for pressure groups. One is, clearly, that they must shift some of their operations to the European Commission and the European Parliament. The other is that they must ally themselves with their counterparts in other member countries. This is already occurring.

All large industrial trade unions are affiliated to European federations. The Social Chapter of the Maastricht agreement of 1993 is testament to the influence of these huge organisations. It has improved working conditions, employment protection and other fringe benefits for many millions of workers. A similar development has occurred within the environmental lobby. The European **Green Movement** even boasts representatives in the European Parliament. The movement has made considerable progress in such areas as sea pollution, harmful industrial emissions (including 'greenhouse' gases) and river quality. Some, though less advances have been achieved in the treatment of live farm animals.

Possibly the most powerful of the 'European lobbies' is also the longest established, that is agriculture. This influential group has succeeded in retaining the **Common Agricultural Policy**, which is designed largely to protect farming groups, despite widespread opposition. It has also succeeded in holding back the agreement on a freer world trade system in primary foods through the GATT (General Agreement on Tariffs and Trade, now known as the World Trade Organisation) negotiations. Such an agreement would damage some sections of European agriculture which relies upon tariff protection.

Add to these groups the great industrial complexes, such as steel, motors, oil and gas, shipbuilding and engineering, and we see a picture of increasingly Europeanised pressure group activity. If and when European integration increases, many other lobby groups will have to respond in similar ways.

Ideology

The 1980s saw the return of ideological politics throughout Europe. This style of politics conflicts in some ways with the kind of pluralistic political environment within which group influence may flourish. Governments which take an inflexible, dogmatic approach to policy making are less likely to be influenced by group pressure.

The privatisation of large industries is a case in point. The many vested interests which sought to retain state ownership – particularly trade unions and consumers – were unable to resist the ideological push for such developments. The same has been true of attacks made on aspects of the Welfare State. Large interests representing welfare recipients could not compete with the determination of governments to reduce public expenditure and so find scope for tax cutting.

Even some monopoly businesses, traditionally some of the most influential groups, were forced to accept a more competitive trading environment. Public utilities such as electricity, gas, broadcasting and energy production have had to accept compulsory liberalisation measures.

There are signs in the 1990s that ideological rule is weakening and that new consensus, pluralist-style politics will return. In 1994, for example, attempts to privatise the British Post Office were defeated following persistent lobbying. There are also indications that attacks on the welfare system are being stemmed by a combination of intense lobbying and the influence of public opinion.

It is clear that pressure groups must meet the challenges posed by ideologically based governments and there are also signs that they are succeeding after many years of difficulty.

Communications

The explosion in communications technology which is occurring at the end of the twentieth century is less of a threat, more of an opportunity for pressure groups. There is now considerably more access available to the public through the new information technology.

Those groups which succeed in harnessing these opportunities to be better able to mobilise public support and disseminate information will be the most successful. Not only has there been an expansion in media communications, but there will also be more direct access into people's homes. Pressure groups will learn from the commercial world that the future must lie with these channels of greater communication.

The decline in party identification

Since the 1970s researchers have noted a marked decline in what is known as 'party alignment', that is, the extent to which people identify with the image and goals of a particular party. Herein lies a further opportunity for pressure groups to fill this vacuum of political identification.

To a large extent this has already occurred. As party membership has been steadily declining, membership of pressure groups has increased dramatically. By 1994 membership of the Conservative Party had fallen below one million for the first time since World War Two, while Labour constituency membership had fallen to an estimated 500,000 from a high point of about one million in the 1960s. Meanwhile, pressure group membership has steadily grown, especially in the environmental field. The 65,000 strength of the Ramblers' Association nearly matches that of the Liberal Democrat Party, while the 540,000 membership of the Royal Society for the Protection of Birds compares well with the two main parties' strength.

It is clear that people's aspirations, goals, concerns and interests are now often served by pressure group activity, rather than through identification with one of the main political parties.

For exam questions relevant to this unit, see page 489.

11 Local government and devolution

Local and regional government defined

Those levels of government which apply to areas of territory which are only a **part** of the whole state may be described as **sub-central government**. This implies that there are decision-making institutions which have some degree of independence from central government.

We must be careful not to confuse sub-central **self-government** with **devolved administration**. Administration only concerns the executing of decisions made elsewhere. There are many examples in the UK of bodies which *appear* to be local or regional government, but these are actually only carrying out policies determined at the centre. The Scottish, Welsh and Northern Ireland Offices are the most prominent examples.

Policy for the national regions is made ultimately by Cabinet, with powers sanctioned by Parliament in Westminster. The three Offices shown above exercise these powers. Of course they do so with some degree of sensitivity to local opinion, but there is no organised democratic means of consultation and none of the ministers or civil servants involved are locally elected. Similar comments can be made of such devolved administrative bodies as **Area Health Authorities** (which distribute funds for health care) and **Regional Development Agencies** (distributing funds aimed at industrial development).

Sub-central **self-government**, on the other hand, describes the level at which **policy decisions** are **made**; it is not merely a description of where services are **administered**.

There is no strict distinction between the terms **local** and **regional** government. How do we differentiate between a locality and a region? Clearly the latter is larger than the former, but by how much? A useful pair of definitions might be:

- Local government concerns an area which is small enough that the inhabitants consider themselves a **community**. This might be a group of villages, a town, a city or part of a city, or a county.
- Regional government would involve an area which is too big to be considered a community, but does have some distinctive characteristics with which people can identify. These differences might consist of the economic structure (e.g. industrial, commercial, touristic or agricultural), geographical features (an area dominated by a river or mountain range), culture (often concerned with nationality differences) or the pattern of settlement (e.g. rural or urban).

Summary of definitions		
Term	**Definition**	**Example**
Sub-central government	Decision-making levels below central government	All local authorities
Devolved administration	The execution, but not the making of policy decisions at sub-central level	Scottish Office
Regional government	Decision-making bodies below the centre but above local community level	Isle of Man
Local government	Decision-making at local community level	London boroughs

The constitutional position of local government

The UK is a **unitary state**. This means that legislative sovereignty lies only at the centre. Although Parliament is sovereign, it is clearly true that, under normal circumstances, political decision making lies with central government. We can, therefore, make two assertions. One is that **policy** is ultimately made by the **Cabinet**. The other is that all powers can only be granted under **legislation** passed by **Parliament**.

Local government, therefore, has **no sovereign powers**. Local authorities can make by-laws, that is, laws which relate only to the area under their jurisdiction, such as regulations relating to car parking, dogs and parks. However, these by-laws are subject to parliamentary approval and can be overruled at Westminster. They can also make **local policy**, but this is only within powers granted by Parliament and these powers can be altered or removed at any time.

Local government structure in England and Wales

The way in which local government is organised varies only slightly between England and Wales (which can be taken together as their systems are the same), Scotland and Northern Ireland. Since the vast majority of the population live in England and Wales, the description here is confined to them. The general **principles**, however, apply to Scotland too. Northern Ireland remains a special case and cannot be included here.

The structure of English and Welsh local government is no longer the result of any rational organisation. It is, instead, the consequence of a number of piecemeal changes which have taken place since the 1960s. These changes have largely been the result of short-term political considerations and not long-term strategy. The second half of the 1990s does, however, promise a more permanent restructuring.

It is necessary to distinguish between three types of area: London, metropolitan urban connurbations outside London, and non-metropolitan or rural areas.

London

Most services in the greater London area are delivered by the **London boroughs**, of which there are thirty-two. There is still a sense in which London is considered a region, so that some of the services have to be supplied centrally. Thus, the London Ambulance Service, the Metropolitan Police (controlled directly by the Home Office), Refuse Disposal (though not collection) and a variety of other central services (left over from the days when the Greater London Council existed before 1986) are controlled by **boards**, which are staffed by a combination of appointed officials and representatives from the boroughs.

However, London can be treated as, fundamentally, a **single-tier** system, that is, local government is at one level only.

Metropolitan areas

There are six of these areas which, like London, used to have a central authority until abolition in 1986. Since then they have also become essentially single tier. Again, most services are handled by **metropolitan districts** (sometimes called boroughs), with some joint services still controlled by an upper tier of **joint boards**. The six areas in question are: Merseyside, Greater Manchester, West Midlands, West Yorkshire, Tyne and Wear and South Yorkshire.

Non-metropolitan areas   Often known as **shire counties**, these are areas dominated by small towns and rural areas. These are essentially **two tier**, with a minor **third tier** in the most rural areas. The three tiers are as follows:

- First tier **County Councils** handling larger-scale services.
- Second tier **County Districts** dealing with more personal and household services.
- Third tier **Parish Councils** in villages. These control a very few minor village and countryside matters.

Services

It is a general principle that the more strategic, broad-scale services are handled by larger authorities. The more personal services, which do not necessarily need large-scale organisation and require a great deal of local sensitivity, are handled at the lower level. Some of the main services and levels at which they are controlled are shown below:

Type	First tier	Second tier	Third tier
London	**London boards** Some broad planning Emergency services Refuse disposal Miscellaneous services	**Boroughs** Education Planning Social Services Refuse collection Parks and Gardens Libraries Youth Service Housing Care of the elderly	**None**
Metropolitan areas	**Joint boards** Building planning Some transport Refuse disposal Police Emergency Services	**Met. districts** Education Social Services Child Care Housing Environment	**None**
Non-met. areas	**Counties** Education Housing Social Services Emergency Services Police Broad planning	**County districts** Local planning Leisure services Environment	**Parish Councils** Small-scale planning Village parking Street lights Local traffic

Dilemmas for local government

Before examining the detailed issues concerning British local government, some more general difficulties should be reviewed. The broad, conceptual problems include the following four dilemmas for policy makers:

Uniformity versus local choice

Individuals may expect that, wherever they live, the same type and quality of local services, such as education, environmental control, child care, traffic management and road maintenance should be available. In other words, some may argue that there should be **uniformity** of local provision in all parts of the country. If this is to be guaranteed, however, there must be strict **central control** of services.

On the other hand, many would also argue that, for democracy to be properly served, there must be genuine local choice in these services. Members of the community may wish to choose how funds are allocated between services and how the services should be run. Thus, one community, for example, may prefer a selective form of education provision, others may insist on a strict comprehensive system. There may also be significant differences in views on development planning. Should rural areas be preserved or should development be allowed to stimulate employment? Clearly, if **local choice** is to be satisfied, there must be much looser central control and genuinely **independent local government**.

Efficiency versus democracy

This is also a question of scale. It is generally – though not always – true that larger-scale operations are more efficient than smaller ones. Funds can be used more effectively and a wider variety of services can be offered. Economists know this phenomenon as 'economies of scale'.

Thus, large scale would seem desirable in the field of local government. However, it is also believed by many that larger organisations are less democratic than smaller ones. It is assumed that there is better public access to small organisations – they are more easily understood and generally closer to the community than large bureaucracies.

So there is a dilemma between the attractions of large scale and the fear that this would reduce the democratic nature of local government.

Politics versus administration

We may define **politics** as the making of choices by different groups between conflicting courses of action. Administration, by contrast, is the imposition of decisions based on set rules and guidelines determined elsewhere.

We may then pose the question as to whether such highly sensitive responsibilities as education, care of the elderly, family support services or mental health provision be left to the uncertainties of party politics, or should they be left to bureaucrats who have no political 'axe to grind'? The **Widdicombe Committee** on the operation of local government, which reported in 1986, alluded to this dilemma and recommended that many of these services should be removed from the control of party politicians and instead be administered on a neutral basis.

The national versus the local mandate

Both MPs and local councillors fight elections on the basis of a party manifesto, possibly with a few personal variations. Once elected, these politicians claim they have a mandate to carry out the policies in those manifestos. Unfortunately, it often occurs that local mandates conflict with the national government's mandate. Which has precedence?

In the 1970s, for example, the Labour Government claimed a mandate to introduce comprehensive, non-selective secondary education throughout the country. Many Conservative councils claimed a conflicting mandate to retain selective grammar schools. Similarly, in the 1980s the

Conservative Government passed legislation enabling council tenants to buy their own homes from local councils. This time it was Labour councils which argued that their electors wished them to retain the housing stock in public ownership.

Despite the difficulty in judging between the competing claims of local and national mandates, in practice the national claim is likely to prevail. The outcome of the two issues described above illustrates this. In both cases the central government was able to rely on parliamentary legislation to force its measures through. It should also be observed that local election turnouts are roughly half those at general elections, so the national mandate can claim greater popular authority. Nevertheless, problems are presented when local communities choose to make a clear assertion of their wish to defy central policy.

The Thatcher reforms

When a new Conservative Government came to power in 1979 there were a number of problems with local government which it felt an urgent need to address. The principal perceived difficulties included the following:

The problems

- The Greater London Council (GLC) and six other metropolitan counties had become so large and powerful that they had the potential ability to defy central government policy. Furthermore, they were all controlled by the Labour Party and especially by left-wing local cliques within the party (the so-called 'urban left' or 'loony left', as the tabloid press dubbed them).
- The government was determined to reduce public expenditure but local government accounted for a large proportion of such expenditure and had shown no sign during the 1970s of being willing or able to curb its own spending.
- It was felt that local councils were insufficiently accountable to their electorates. This was particularly true in the area of finance, where there was widespread ignorance of such matters and apparent indifference to high levels of local expenditure and taxation. (This is described in more detail below in the section on local taxation.)
- There was a commonly held belief that local government was inefficient.
- It was suspected that there was widespread 'political corruption' in local politics. That is, decisions were being taken on purely political grounds, to further the interests of a local party group rather than in the interests of the community itself.

In the light of these problems, reform of local government was undertaken on a broad front.

Structural change

In 1986 the GLC and the six metropolitan counties were abolished. Most of their functions were devolved downwards to second-tier authorities, with some strategic services remaining in the hands of special joint boards.

This was followed in 1990 by the disbanding of the **Inner London Education Authority**, a joint organisation run by the twelve inner London boroughs to administer schooling and some higher education. Education was returned to the jurisdiction of the boroughs.

Thus, a powerful tier of local government was removed, administrative costs were reduced and, above all, a powerful challenge to the authority of central government had been eliminated.

Functional changes In the 1980s and 1990s a large variety of services were transferred **out** of local authority control while a smaller number of additional functions were transferred **into** their control. The shift in functions represents the greatest change in the nature of government provision of services since the reforms of the second half of the 1940s, when there was widespread nationalisation and many new responsibilities were given to local government. While the changes described below do not form an exhaustive list, they do represent the principal changes.

1. Functions lost:

Education

- The introduction of the **National Curriculum** for children aged five to sixteen took away local responsibility for the majority of schools' curricula. Instead the school curriculum was to be established by a central Curriculum Council.
- **Local management of schools** removed control over school budgets from councils. Instead, each school was to manage its own financial arrangements through the head teacher and governors.
- Schools were allowed to 'opt out' of local authority control and instead to take up **grant maintained status**. These schools receive finance and are subject to general oversight by the Department for Education.
- The number of places on school governing bodies available for local authority nominees was reduced, giving greater parental control.

Housing

- Local authorities were forced to offer homes for sale to their council tenants at preferential terms. Thus, there was a large increase in private ownership and a reduction in local authority housing provision.
- An increasing proportion of central funding for housing was diverted away from local authorities, being channelled instead through the Housing Corporation and Housing Action Trusts, which finance voluntary housing associations providing low-cost homes for renting.
- Ministers were given discretionary powers to control the level of rents charged to council tenants.

Compulsory competitive tendering

- A variety of services such as refuse collection, road repairs, council home maintenance and parks and gardens were no longer automatically undertaken by local authorities. Instead the work would be offered, by tender, to private firms. Councils were forced to accept the best tender. Thus, many functions were 'privatised'.

Public transport

- Outside London bus and other transport services under local authority control were **deregulated**, that is, private companies were free to provide the services. In most cases, local authorities became a minority provider of public transport.

2. Functions gained:

Children

- Although councils already had broad responsibility for the welfare and care of children in deprived circumstances, these responsibilities were considerably widened under the **Children Act**. Local authorities were now to accept wide responsibility for identifying and caring for children considered to be at some kind of risk.

The mentally ill

- The scheme known as 'Care in the Community' resulted in large-scale closure of centrally funded mental care institutions catering for individuals with low levels of mental illness. Instead, local authoritites were to place such people into homes in the community and to supervise their future care.

The elderly

- Funding was also withdrawn for institutions caring for the elderly, and local authorities were given increased responsibility for dealing with this through private provision or sheltered housing.

Financial controls During the 1980s there occurred a dramatic increase in the level of control exercised over local authority finance by central government ministers. Limitation powers by ministers over both borrowing and large-scale capital spending projects already existed in 1980 and were fully applied as part of the campaign to create more local financial responsibility. However, four further devices were introduced in an attempt to tighten financial discipline. These are described below:

- **Grant Related Expenditure Assessments (GREA)** were introduced by the 1979 **Local Government Planning and Land Act**. Before this an agreed level of annual expenditure for each authority was negotiated and central government grants supplied in order to finance this agreed level. The GREA system (now known as the **Standard Spending Assessment**) changed the situation drastically. Now central government officials alone would assess the spending needs of each authority. This was a fundamental reform. It centralised evaluation of local needs and removed a significant amount of local autonomy.
  Local authorities were given greater flexibility than before as to how the central government grant (known as the **Rate Support Grant**) was to be allocated between different services. However, in the event, the assessments were so financially 'tight' that there was relatively little freedom of action in practice.
  It was immediately apparent that some local authorities were prepared to escape from these strictures by simply raising local taxation (then known as the 'rates') or by borrowing from the banks. Additional controls were, thus, needed:
- **Grant penalties** were introduced for those councils which succeeded in spending above the centrally assessed limit. The central government grant was simply reduced by the amount of the overspend. However, even this measure sometimes failed. The most militant of councils would simply raise local taxes even more to make up the penalty. Eventually, the Greater London Council found itself with no central grant at all! Needless to say, it had to demand extremely high taxes.

**Liverpool City Council
in session 1985**

A third measure was, therefore, introduced:

- Ministers were given the power to place a limit on proposed rises in local tax. At the time it was known as **ratecapping**. Applying a set formula, an authority which was deemed to be raising local rates unnecessarily would be forced to reduce its tax demands. One final attempt to escape from the straitjacket was made by some hard-left councillors. They were prepared to continue to overspend and simply allow the council to become bankrupt.
- Councillors who set a budget which would result in bankruptcy were considered to be committing a criminal offence. The penalties included fining or 'surcharging' them, and/or disqualification from holding office. A number of councillors in Liverpool and Lambeth fell foul of these rules.

> *'For many it seemed that local government had, during the 1980s, been subjected to a death of a thousand cuts.'*
> John Kingdom, *Local Government and Politics in Britain*
> (Philip Allan, 1991)

Professor George Jones of the LSE has described this process as the 'Tom and Jerry syndrome'. Each time central government found a new way of financially trapping local authorities, they, in turn, found a new way of escaping. Margaret Thatcher and one of her favourite policy agencies, the Adam Smith Institute, adopted one final measure to try to end the cat and mouse game. This was to force local authorities to control their spending and taxation levels by making them more accountable to the public. Where ministers had failed, the electorate might succeed.

Earlier in the 1980s Michael Heseltine, as Secretary of State for the Environment, had attempted to introduce a system whereby large rises in local taxation would be made subject to approval by a local referendum.

A trial vote was held in Coventry, but a very low turnout persuaded him that the system would not work. Margaret Thatcher's plan involved the introduction of the **Community Charge** or **Poll Tax**, as it became known. The principles behind this are described below.

Local taxation

<u>Problems with the rates</u> Problems over local taxation emerged in the 1960s as it became increasingly apparent that it was neither easy to administer nor was it levied on a fair basis. Up to 1990 local taxation was known as 'rates'. The rates were based roughly upon the size and value of properties. However, only one person in each household was liable to pay the rates and they were largely levied upon home owners. Furthermore, it was pointed out that the size of one's property does not necessarily reflect one's ability to pay. The ultimate problem could be illustrated by the fact that a single poor person living in a large property would pay the same tax as a large, wealthy family living in a modest property.

A rapid increase in the number of families owning their own homes, together with increased pressures on local finance in the 1970s and 1980s, led to the development of the political will to reform local taxation.

<u>Possible solutions</u> For many years a number of alternatives were suggested and rejected. These included:

- Complete replacement by central **government grants**. This was rejected on the grounds that it would remove local autonomy. Central government would use its financial power to exercise complete control.
- **Local income tax** was attractive as it would be based on ability to pay. However, it was thought too difficult to administer and collect.
- **Local sales tax** is commonly used in the USA, but again it is difficult and expensive to collect. There would also be no room for local variation as people could simply travel to purchase goods where taxes were lower.
- A reformed **property tax** which would reduce some of the anomalies presented by the rates. This was attractive but was, at first, rejected on the old grounds that one's home was not necessarily a reflection of one's ability to pay – one of the fundamental principles of fair taxation.

<u>The Poll Tax</u> The 'Poll Tax' or **Community Charge** was the new form of taxation chosen by the Conservative Government for its 1987 election manifesto. It was an attempt to solve two problems at the same time. First, it was thought to be a fairer form of taxation and secondly, it might go some way to creating greater public accountability in local government expenditure.

The Poll Tax was to be levied as a single, fixed charge on all adults living within a community. A few groups, such as the very poor, would receive substantial rebates, but, essentially, all were to pay the same amount. Thus, it was thought to be fairer and would spread the tax burden more evenly.

Under the rates system only a minority of individual householders actually paid tax. In some poorer districts, where there were very few home owners, as few as 25 per cent of the adult population were paying local rates at all. Yet, it was pointed out, all adults were consuming local authority services. Why should everyone not contribute?

It was also felt that this simple form of tax, paid by nearly everyone, would make electors realise what was being spent by their local council. High-spending councils would therefore have to face an electorate most of whom were meeting the burden of the expenditure through their tax. This had not been the case with the rates. It was hoped that these 'extravagant' councils would, therefore, be pitched out of office by an angry electorate. There would, in short, be greater local financial accountability.

In the event, the Poll Tax met with widespread, militant opposition. Being totally unrelated to one's ability to pay, it was considered unacceptable, even by many whose tax burden was actually reduced as a result. A campaign of non-payment and serious unrest on the Conservative Party back-benches meant the new tax was doomed. Most dramatically, Margaret Thatcher was removed from office by her own party largely as a result of her refusal to accept abolition of the tax.

John Major became Prime Minister and promptly replaced the Community Charge with a modified property tax known as the 'Council Tax'.

Council Tax   By 1992, the Poll Tax had been replaced by the new Council Tax, based on property value, but with a large number of payment 'bands' and exemptions to make it more sensitive to people's ability to pay. This has received widespread support and promises to survive for some time into the future.

Conclusions on local tax   These problems are not merely arguments about the best form of local taxation. They also represent a number of other issues concerning the relationship between central and local government. It is generally true that the power to raise taxes gives any level of government a degree of independence. It is also a key element in the nature of political responsibility. Tax is, furthermore, one of the oldest features of the process of government. It becomes yet more significant when considering national and regional devolution. Some of these broader issues are discussed below.

The changing nature of local government

Central–local relations

All modern commentators on local government in Britain are agreed that, since 1979, the control exercised by both central government, together with a variety of other bodies set up by the government, has increased markedly. Local authorities have considerably less freedom of action and are subject to greater parliamentary and ministerial control than ever before. The nature of these controls falls into three main categories:

Legislative control   The responsibilities which local government must undertake, the services they must provide and the minimum level quality of those services are set out in a large number of Acts of Parliament. Local councils must, therefore, operate within the parameters set by Parliament. Some examples of key legislation include:

- **Local Government Acts** which set out financial provisions and controls as well as general directives as to the way local administration and decision making should operate. Such Acts are passed at regular intervals in order to update procedures and central–local relations.

- **Town and Country Planning Acts** guide local authorities in their role as controllers of building and transport development. Both requirements and limitations are described in these Acts.
- **Education Acts** are, again, passed at regular intervals. The 1988 Education Reform Act was probably the most significant since 1944, when free secondary education for all was first established. The National Curriculum, together with a host of administrative changes in education provision, was established by such legislation.
- **Local Government Finance Acts** set out the arrangements for central financing, local taxation and ministerial control of central government funding.
- **The Children Act** of 1990 laid a number of extra responsibilities for the welfare of children upon local authorities.

These are only a few examples of a regular stream of new legislation coming out of Westminster with the purpose of controlling local government.

<u>Ministerial control</u> Various central government ministers have been granted discretionary powers by Parliament to exercise oversight and control. This particularly applies to such ministers as those responsible for the environment, transport, education and housing.

As we have seen above, the level of local taxation may be 'capped' by the Department of the Environment. Additional examples include the ability to overrule planning decisions, to refuse large-scale borrowing or capital spending projects, or to change educational provision.

<u>Financial and administrative control</u> The principal changes made in the financial arrangements for local government are described in the section on the Thatcher reforms above. In addition, however, the **Audit Commission**, set up in 1982, has powers to investigate the manner in which local authorities conduct their administrative affairs. The Commission is charged with the task of inspecting the efficiency and integrity of local authorities' finances.

The principal office concerned with local authority conduct is that of the **District Auditor**, who is particularly concerned with local financial policy and expenditure. During 1994–5 his office became involved in one of the most serious investigations of local authority conduct when it accused Conservative-controlled Westminster Council of manipulating council housing provision in order to ensure that more potential Tory voters were attracted into the borough and so ensure the survival of existing political control.

In 1992 the **Local Government Commission** was established in order to recommend and establish changes to both the internal workings and the general structure of local government, as well as its financial arrangements. Though still in its early infancy, the Commission promises to become a further important instrument of central government control.

Local authority services Just as observers are agreed that there is now much greater central control over local government, so too do they all point to a fundamental change in the way in which local authorities operate.

It is now clear that in the 1990s local authorities have changed from being **providers** of services to **enabling** bodies. This means that, instead of actually organising and producing themselves, authorities are acting more as **agents** at the centre of a variety of **other** bodies which are now involved in the provision of community services. Instead of being providers, they licence, employ and supervise others who actually fulfil the necessary functions.

This is expressed in the government's own Citizen's Charter:

> *'Local authorities have historically seen the direct provision of services to the community as one of their major tasks. However, we believe that now is the time for a new approach. The real task for local authorities lies in setting priorities, determining the standards of services which citizens should enjoy, and finding the best way to meet them.'*
> Citizen's Charter 1991, quoted in David Wilson, 'The Changing Context of Central–Local Government Relationships', *Talking Politics*, Vol. 5, No. 3 (Spring 1995)

This change can best be illustrated by references to specific services:

- In **housing**, local authorities used to build council homes, maintain them with their own labour force, regulate and collect rents and be directly responsible for the homeless. In these senses, they were **providers** of housing.

  After 1980 the picture changed. Tenants were increasingly encouraged to buy their own homes, thus removing them from the public sector. Building and maintenance of housing was offered out to private contractors under **compulsory competitive tendering**. Increasing amounts of funds, central and local, were channelled through voluntary (i.e. private sector) **housing associations**. The homeless and one-parent families were often housed in private bed-and-breakfast accommodation or hostels. Planning powers retained some control in the hands of the local authorities, but with housing becoming an increasing problem, they had little choice but to accept private sector provision.

- Various **public amenities** such as refuse collection, parks maintenance, road repairs and other environmental services were increasingly put out to private tender. The role of the local authorities changed from carrying out these functions to granting tenders, ensuring quality, dismissing contractors and appointing new ones where necessary, and listening to public comments or complaints.

- Economic development had traditionally been only a marginal local government function, with relatively sparse funds available. However, with a marked increase in the number of agencies set up to distribute both public and private funds, local authorities found themselves at the centre of what has been called a **network** of providers. These have included Development Corporations (such as London Docklands), Enterprise Partnerships (between local government and private enterprise) and Regional Development Agencies (central government-funded). In addition, increasing quantities of development funds for regions and localities are available through the agencies of the **European Union**. Here again, others are responsible for funding, but local authorities must organise the distribution of finance.

> 'Various writers have suggested that in the future local authorities can have a key role in building a network among local organisations and interests to achieve a purpose beyond the ambit of their immediate statutory responsibilities.'
>
> Gerry Stoker, *The Politics of Local Government*
> (Macmillan, 1991)

Structure As described above, the structure of local government in England and Wales (less so in Scotland) has been the product of piecemeal change. It is, therefore, widely acknowledged that reform is needed to create a more coherent, efficient and understandable system.

The **Local Government Commission** is charged with the task of effecting a re-organisation of local government in England, Wales and Scotland by 1998. It recommended the widespread introduction of single-tier authorities, thus eliminating a whole level of government in many parts of England, Wales and Scotland. The threat to a number of historical counties has, however, resulted in much opposition to the proposals. It is, therefore, likely that the simplification of local government structure may be delayed further.

However, these proposals disguise a further development. Although there may be some rationalisation of **elected** local government, there are likely to be a whole series of new bodies, non-elected committees and agencies which will provide services on a broader scale, very much along the lines of the National Health Service. These may include such provisions as higher education, industrial training, transport and development planning. Thus, there would still be two tiers of local service provision, but only one tier of elected government.

Of course, many of these structural proposals may well be eliminated by a change of government and particularly if plans for the devolution of wide powers to Scotland and Wales within the Labour, Liberal Democrat and Nationalist Parties are adopted.

Internal organisation As with the external structure of local government, the internal organisation has also become a subject for reform. Before considering these, however, the traditional model of local democracy and administration must be described.

<u>Councillors</u> The elected representatives form the **full council** whose role is twofold:

- Discussing and agreeing broad issues. In particular the setting of financial priorities between services and the establishment of general policy.
- Ratifying decisions made in the various committees through which all councils operate.

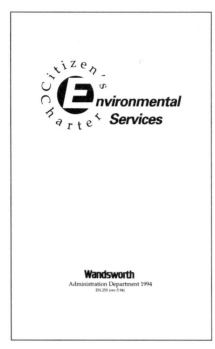

Charter leaflet from Wandsworth Council

All the detailed work of a council is carried out through committees and sub-committees. On these committees councillors may specialise and receive expert advice from the permanent officials who are employed by the council. An indication of council work can be gained by reference to some of the main committees which all councils possess:

- Planning
- Housing
- Education
- Environmental Services
- Police
- Transport
- Social Services.

This is by no means an exhaustive list, but the most important are certainly included. In addition, there are two central bodies which play key roles. These are the **Policy and Resources Committee** and its main sub-committee, **Finance**. As their names suggests, they deal with the main priorities of the council, in particular the uses of finance.

Officials These are the equivalent of civil servants at local level. Their role is to undertake research, identify problems, suggest alternative courses of action and finally to implement the decisions made by elected councillors. They are expected to be neutral and to avoid becoming involved in party politics.

The structure of local administration largely mirrors the organisation of the councillors. A **Chief Executive** serves the full council and the central policy and resources committee. Below him, each committee is served by a **Chief Officer** and his staff. Thus, the essentially 'amateur' councillors are guided and serviced by 'professional' officers.

Local parties In all but the most rural of county districts, most councillors are members of one of the principal political parties. Within the council each party organises itself into groups or 'caucuses', which seek to establish a united party front on every important issue. Thus, before every full council or committee meeting, the party groups discuss the agenda and attempt to enforce collective agreement. Of course, since councillors are not professional politicians, and since there are no highly paid ministerial posts on offer to them, party discipline is more difficult to enforce than is the case at Westminster. Parties on larger councils do have a whip system, but there are few sanctions which can be used to give it real teeth.

Party representation on each committee reflects the relative party strength in the whole council. Thus, if there is a majority party, that same party will enjoy majority membership on every committee and sub-committee. It follows from this that many decisions are actually made within the ruling party caucus and, within this, senior members play a key role.

However, a large number of councils have 'no overall control', that is, they are 'hung'. In such cases parties must reach agreement among themselves whenever important decisions are to be made. Sometimes a permanent 'coalition' is formed between two parties, sometimes each issue must be resolved on an ad hoc basis.

This picture of local authority organisation remained largely unaltered between 1950 and 1980. Since then, however, a number of significant changes have taken place and still remain in force:

- Councils and their officials have simply less to do since the responsibilities of local government have, on balance, been reduced.
- Many local services and responsibilities are now shared with other bodies, both in the public and private sector; this applies at both national and regional level. It has removed much of the independent power of elected councillors. To an increasing extent it must be left to the permanent officials to co-ordinate the work of a wide variety of agencies in the local community context.
- Following the recommendations of the **Widdicombe Report**, political control over officials has been reduced. The general effect has been to increase their authority and to reduce that of local party leaders.
- The **Audit Commission**, as a result of its 1995 report, is now empowered to take steps to force local authorities to introduce greater efficiency and management disciplines within their administration. It is, thus, expected that the size of local bureaucracies will be significantly reduced.

Summary of local government changes since 1979

1. Many services have been removed from local government control.
2. Local authorities have been given some new responsibilities but fewer than they have lost.
3. There is considerably more financial control exercised by central government.
4. Ministers have greater discretionary powers.
5. Many local services have been transferred to the private sector.
6. There is now a wide variety of different kinds of agencies involved in local and regional services.
7. Local authorities have increasingly become enablers rather than providers of services.
8. Within local authorities there has been a shift in the balance of power towards permanent officials and away from elected councillors.

Conclusions on local government

The reduction in the degree of independence of local government has been possibly the most dramatic change in the structure of the political system since the extensions in the role of the state between 1944 and 1950. Self-government at local level scarcely exists, having been replaced by what commentators now describe as 'devolved administration'.

Furthermore, British party politics have polarized on the issue of local government. The Conservatives remain convinced centralisers, while all the other significant parties now wish to restore considerable powers to local and/or regional government.

Devolution

The term defined

Devolution refers to a process whereby significant decision-making functions are transferred downwards, from central government to regional institutions. This does not mean that any sovereignty is transferred since Parliament at Westminster would retain the power to reclaim these functions at any time. Despite this, it is assumed that considerable legislative and administrative functions would be permanently transferred.

Thus, we can summarise by saying that 'devolution is the transfer of significant powers, not including sovereignty, to regional institutions'.

Most commonly, in a British context, devolution has been considered most appropriate in the case of Scotland, Wales and Northern Ireland. This is because these are recognisable **national** communities with stronger claims for autonomy. In recent years, however, there have also been calls for devolution to English regions such as London, the South-West and the North-East.

A note on federalism

Devolution should not be confused with federalism. A federal system, such as prevails in the USA, Germany and India, divides full **sovereignty** between central institutions and regional governments. This implies a much greater degree of independence than mere devolution. A federal Britain could exist under the Crown and so remain the **United Kingdom**, but there is unlikely to be sufficient popular support for such a system in the foreseeable future.

Should European integration become more acceptable, however, the picture may alter. The EU could become a community of **regions**, rather than **nations**. If so, the possibility of divided sovereignty within the regions of the British Isles could become a reality.

The background to national devolution Until about 1970 the question of greater autonomy for national regions was very much a minority issue. In Northern Ireland attention centred on the demands for reunification of Ireland after 1968, opposed by a loyalist community committed to retaining close links with mainland Britain. In Wales and Scotland, however, interest in devolution began to grow during the 1970s.

Three principal causes for this new movement were identified:

- The consistent failure of the Government to deliver promises of economic growth led to dissatisfaction with London-based politics.
- The long-term decline in traditional industries was felt particularly harshly in Wales and Scotland, where such industries were concentrated. Shipbuilding, iron and steel, heavy engineering and coal were notable examples. Again, English government was blamed for this.
- In the case of Scotland, the increasing exploitation of North Sea Oil off the Scottish coast gave rise to a belief that the Scottish economy had the potential to grow at a faster rate than that of the rest of Britain.

In the 1974 general elections those parties which were committed to devolution – The Scottish National Party (SNP), the Welsh nationalists (Plaid Cymru) and the Liberals – enjoyed considerable success. The extent of these advances in nationalist fortunes is indicated by the October 1974 results shown below:

October 1974 election	Seats won	Percentage vote
Liberal	27	18.3
Scottish Nationalist	11	30.4*
Plaid Cymru	3	11.1*

* Percentage of votes in Scotland and Wales only

These results had a galvanising effect on the new Labour Government. They had won a tiny majority in the second 1974 election with a lukewarm commitment to devolution in their manifesto. The party was split on the issue, but two other considerations became paramount. First, they wished to maintain their heavy support in Scotland and Wales and secondly, the leadership recognised that the support of the nationalist parties' MPs might be needed in Parliament if their precarious majority was to be preserved. Now, therefore, they had to take devolution seriously.

Proposals were contained in two Bills – not surprisingly entitled the Scotland and Wales Bills – presented in 1978. Scotland was to have its own elected assembly in Edinburgh with an Executive drawn from this Parliament. The new Scottish government was to have powers over such key functions as education, health, transport, local government, law, industry, welfare and housing. In Wales there was to be no assembly, but a Welsh Executive would have similar powers to those of its Scottish counterpart. Taxation powers, however, were not to be devolved. Instead, both governments would operate through a grant supplied by the British government.

As 1979 dawned, devolution appeared to be a reality. Referenda were to be held in both countries, but there seemed little doubt that the proposals would be approved, especially in Scotland. However, by this time Labour had lost its overall parliamentary majority. The Conservatives who were largely opposed to devolution, recognised an opportunity to embarrass the Government. An amendment was proposed that, instead of a simple referendum majority being required, it would be necessary for at least 40 per cent of the Scottish or Welsh **electorate** to approve devolution. Since the turnout was unlikely to be very high, this 40 per cent threshold promised to be difficult to attain. In the face of government opposition, the amendment was passed with the help of a small revolt among Labour back-benchers.

The 1979 referenda confirmed the Government's worse fears thus:

Devolution referenda	% of total voting in support	% of total electorate in support
Scotland	51.6	32.9
Wales	20.3	11.9

As the figures show, support for devolution in Wales proved to be sparse while in Scotland, although the majority of those who voted were in support, this was not a large enough proportion of the total electorate to satisfy the conditions of the Conservative amendment.

Thus the campaign for devolution failed. The nationalists withdrew support for the Labour Government and, shortly afterwards, a vote of no confidence in the House of Commons led to Labour's resignation.

The revival of support for devolution in the 1990s

During the 1980s interest in devolution waned. Economic growth during the mid 1980s reduced nationalist dissatisfaction with rule from London. However, Scottish and Welsh nationalism refused to die away. The recession of the late 1980s and early 1990s saw a renewal of interest and support. In the 1992 election, the SNP won 21.5 per cent of the Scottish vote while Plaid Cymru secured 8.8 per cent of the vote in Wales.

The increasing unpopularity of John Major's administration was reflected in a growing consensus of support for devolution. Now, indeed, there was also considerable interest in devolution to the English regions. The abolition of the Greater London Council and six metropolitan counties in 1986 had seen the end of a short-lived experiment with regional government.

In 1995 the Conservative Government launched a major offensive against proposals for devolution. Thus, the battle lines were drawn up for the coming general election campaign. The attitudes of the parties involved were as follows:

The Labour Party Scotland, Wales and the English regions would all have elected assemblies and executives drawn from the assemblies and responsible to them. They would have power to raise their own income from taxation. Their most important responsibilities would include:

- the lower tier of local government
- health
- transport
- industrial and commercial development
- housing
- education
- Scotland only to control civil and criminal law
- social services.

The main responsibilities remaining in the hands of the central British government would include:

- foreign policy
- defence
- trade and relations with the European Union
- economic policy
- financial control
- all functions requiring co-ordination between regions.

Nevertheless, it should be emphasised that Labour's proposals do not include **federalism**. As we have seen above, this would involve a transfer of some **sovereignty** to national assemblies. This is not supported by Labour. Parliament in Westminster would reserve the right to reclaim its political powers.

Scottish National Party   The party in 1995 was split into two wings. One view, popular within the leadership itself, was that there should be **Home Rule**. This implied full independence, possibly even removing Scotland from the jurisdiction of the British Crown, i.e. a Republic of Scotland. Naturally, such an independent state would have its own voice in the European Union. The other view was to accept radical devolution, largely along the lines of the Labour Party's proposals shown above. In addition, however, those who support limited devolution still demand a separate Scottish voice in the European Union.

Plaid Cymru   As in the SNP, there is a militant wing which demands full independence, but there is evidence to suggest that this enjoys little popular support in Wales. However, an elected assembly with wide powers is a minimum demand. Broadly, the Welsh nationalists are likely to be content with regional government status, but with special attention paid to the distinctive Welsh culture – especially the arts – and language.

The Liberal Democrats   The philosophy of the Liberal Democrats is to implement **subsidiarity**, that is, the devolution of all government functions to the lowest level possible. In this way, they argue, popular democracy can be best protected. Thus, they envisage four levels of government, each with appropriate functions:

- European
- national
- regional
- local.

The possibility of a federal system – dividing sovereignty between Wales, Scotland and Northern Ireland – is being considered, but remains unlikely to become official policy.

The Conservatives   Until the 1970s it was normal to refer to the Conservative Party by its full title – the Conservative and **Unionist** Party. Indeed, since the great debates over Home Rule for Ireland during the late nineteenth century and early twentieth, the Conservatives have consistently sought to retain a unitary British Isles under the Crown and Parliament. The Republic of Ireland, of course, has long been independent, but in 1994 the Conservative Government accepted that the future of Northern Ireland should be determined by the people of the province. For mainland Great Britain, however, its opposition to further weakening of the union remains implacable. The Conservatives' objection is fourfold:

● They argue that the preservation of the British **Union** is essential to maintain prosperity, unity and stability. They point to the culture and traditions of Britain which would come under threat with devolution. They say that they are worth preserving for their own sake and for the sake of good order.
● They point out that a considerable amount of **administrative devolution** already exists. There are Scottish and Welsh Offices led by their own Secretaries of State and with important powers. In addition, there is a wide variety of other bodies administering policy and public expenditure on a regional basis. These include Health Service authorities, Regional Development Agencies, Regional Arts and Sports Councils and, new in the 1990s, twelve regional Civil Service Offices to allocate central government grants.
● Democratic control is, they suggest, adequately maintained at Westminster so that there is no need for more elected assemblies.
● They maintain that a further level of government would breed more bureaucracy, while regional taxation would increase the financial burden on households.

The future   As was the case in the 1970s, the devolution issue appears to rest upon the electoral fortunes of the various parties. However, should one of the reforming parties win power in London, it may be that devolution has to be put to the electorate in a series of referenda. In that case, the fate of devolution proposals would lie in the hands of the people. There is no guarantee that they will agree with the those politicians who wish to see greater decentralisation.

For exam questions relevant to this unit, see pages 488–9.

12 Constitutional issues

What is a constitution?

Until the late eighteenth century there was no conception of the modern form of 'constitution'. There had been regulated forms of political system in classical Greece and the Roman Republic, but these were elementary and lacked both the sophistication and democratic elements of modern forms.

Through the Dark and Middle Ages, the predominance of monarchy, based on power, order and duty, replaced any need for a constitutional system of government. The development of natural and equal rights, government by consent, limited rule and representative institutions in the eighteenth century introduced the need for a completely new basis for government. Inspired by the ideas of the English philosopher, **John Locke**, the notion of a 'social contract' gained support as the political principle upon which future government should be founded.

The contract of which Locke wrote was to be made between the people and their government. For their part, the people agreed upon the manner in which they were to be ruled. The government, in its turn, was to accept limitations to its role and to submit itself to constant examination by the people. Thus, a modern constitution, whatever its form, can be seen as such a contract. This constitution may be considerably more detailed and refined than Locke's original conception, but it is based on the principle that it is an agreement between the government and the governed.

Under what circumstances do such agreements come about? Almost without exception (Britain is an important one) constitutions come about after a major political upheaval such as a revolution, civil war or the achievement of independence from a foreign power. When a people has been forced to dismantle its former government, reform the political system, and rethink and reorganise the way it is governed, a new constitution invariably comes into existence.

We can find a flavour of this idea in the preamble to the American Constitution of 1787, written and established after British colonial rule had been thrown off. This is shown below:

> 'We the people of the United States, in order to form a more perfect Union, establish Justice, insure*domestic Tranquillity, provide for the common Defence, promote the general Welfare, and secure the blessings of Liberty to ourselves and our posterity, do ordain and establish this Constitution for the United States of America.'
>
> *original spelling

Although we have some clues as to the contractual nature of the American Constitution, it does not explain the several purposes of **any** political constitution. In general, the functions of a constitution can be identified as follows:

- Establishing the distribution of power among the various institutions of government. This also implies a statement of the limits to those powers and the relationships between political institutions

- Defining the limits to the powers of the state as a whole
- Guaranteeing the rights of citizens, both against the state and in their relationships with each other
- Establishing the territory to be governed by the constitution
- Defining the nature and rules of citizenship of the state
- Setting out the method by which the constitution can be amended.

Constitution maintenance

Codification

At its simplest, codification means 'in written form'. However, it implies more. In particular, we can add that it may be written in a single, organised form. This is more than an administrative distinction. Codification also suggests that constitutional rules are **different** to other rules or laws of conduct.

Entrenchment

More crucial than codification, the principle of entrenchment refers to the need to safeguard constitutional laws against the whims of temporary governments and the vagaries of short-term political developments. Parties and governments may come and go, public opinion may change direction with great regularity, but constitutional principles need more stability. They are fundamental and are expected to protect future as well as current generations of citizens.

The practical meaning of entrenchment is that constitutional laws are more difficult to change than other laws. The purposes of such obstacles to change are twofold: first, entrenchment is usually designed to ensure that there is a full and lengthy debate about the desirability of such change. Secondly, it is important that there is widespread, general agreement about constitutional change. We may describe this as **consensus** – having more than just any majority, but a substantial majority.

Consider, for example, the following issues. Some may be the proper concern of a **temporary** government in its task of maintaining the common good (i.e. **political** matters); others are more fundamental and should, therefore, be subject to entrenchment (i.e. **constitutional** matters):

Political matters	Constitutional matters
The level of taxation	Reducing local government powers
Funding health care	Establishing equal rights for women
Student grant levels	Establishing regional government in Scotland
Re-organising the armed forces	Increasing police powers
Subsidising agriculture	Altering trade union rights
	Reforming the House of Lords

A variety of methods exist by which entrenchment may be achieved. In the USA, for example, constitutional amendments require two-thirds majority approval of both Houses of the Senate, plus ratification by three-quarters of the fifty states. The French use referenda to ensure popular support while other states use various forms of enhanced majority voting.

Superiority Part of the distinctive nature of constitutional law is that it must be superior to other law. In other words, if some aspect of 'ordinary' law conflicts with constitutional law, the latter is treated as superior and must prevail in that conflict. If this is not the case, constitutional law could not be properly safeguarded from attacks by temporary political opinion. Thus, superiority and entrenchment go hand in hand.

To illustrate, we might envisage a circumstance where a parliament passes a law granting discretionary powers to a government minister to alter prison sentences handed down by the courts. This might conflict with a **constitutional** principle that the law courts must be completely independent of government. If constitutional superiority is respected, the new law would be set aside. The Parliament in question would have to force through a constitutional change, perhaps against entrenched provisions, in order to introduce its new law.

Once again, we may turn to the USA for illustration of this principle. **Chief Justice John Marshall** declared the following in 1805:

> *'That the people have an original right to establish, for their future government, such principles as, in their opinion, shall most conduce to their own happiness, is the basis on which the whole American fabric has been erected ... The principles, therefore, so established, are deemed fundamental. And as the authority from which they proceed is supreme, and can seldom act, they are designed to be permanent.'*
> John Marshall, *Marbury v. Madison*, 1805

The British Constitution

Although reference is commonly made to the term 'British Constitution', examination syllabuses have been so-named and a key textbook, written in 1867 by Walter Bagehot, was entitled *English Constitution*, it is open to question whether there is indeed such a thing. In reality, there are persuasive arguments suggesting **both** that the British Constitution exists *and* that it does **not** exist. This may appear to be a confusing paradox, but it is understandable if we examine the evidence for both views.

Senses in which the British Constitution DOES NOT exist

1. There is no single **codified document** entitled the 'British Constitution'. Not only that, but where constitutional statutes do exist, they appear to be no different from any other statute.
2. It is not possible to **entrench** constitutional laws and principles in Britain. This is simply on account of the doctrine of **parliamentary sovereignty**. In this context, the doctrine means that Parliament cannot be limited in its actions by any past statute or agreement. Thus, even where constitutional statutes exist, Parliament is free to repeal or amend them by a simple majority vote.

   A clear example of this occurred in 1994 with the passage of the Criminal Justice Act. Before this Act, it was an accepted principle that accused persons had the right to remain silent under questioning and in court, without any assumptions being made that this might indicate guilt. Such a 'right to silence' is certainly a common element in written constitutions elsewhere. After the passage of the Act, however, such silence can be used as prosecuting evidence. However much lawyers and campaigners argued that this abused basic individual rights, Parliament had its way.

By the same principle, of course, lack of entrenchment allows Parliament to **add** to individual rights without excessive difficulty. Thus, race relations and sexual equality have been established through simple, speedy procedures.

3. As we have indicated, there are constitutional statutes in Britain, but these are **not superior** to any other laws. Where there is a conflict between two statutes, Parliament is completely free to determine which shall prevail.

Senses in which the British Constitution DOES exist

1. There is a general sense in which we understand that there are principles by which the political system operates. When such principles are being threatened, there may be stronger opposition from inside and outside Parliament than would normally be the case.

2. Tradition is a powerful influence in Britain. Those constitutional rules which are traditional, such as the maintenance of freedom of expression, the primacy of the Cabinet, the weakness of the House of Lords and the independence of the judiciary, are challenged rarely and with great reluctance by governments.

3. Governments must face the judgement of the electorate at regular intervals. Those which have challenged such traditional principles must consider whether they can maintain popular approval. Thus, the people themselves act as the guardians of some sort of conception of the 'constitution'.

4. Finally, and perhaps most importantly, many constitutional scholars argue that there is such a thing as the British Constitution even though there is no codified document as such. Instead, it exists in a **variety of forms** which may be flexible and constantly developing, but which, nevertheless, have enough substance to replace the more formal constitutions which other states possess. These forms are described in the section below.

Does the British Constitution exist?

NO

1. There is no single, codified document
2. There is no method of entrenchment
3. Constitutional laws are not superior to others

YES

1. There is a general sense of a Constitution
2. Traditional constitutional principles are strong
3. The people may protect it at election time
4. There are accepted forms of constitutional rules

Form of the British Constitution

As we have seen, constitutional statutes do not look different from any others. They are also passed in the same way, by simple majority of both Houses of Parliament. They are, therefore, only recognisable by the function they are performing.

Some examples will illustrate their range:

Statutes

- The **Parliament Acts** of 1911 and 1949 establish the limitations to the powers of the House of Lords.
- **Criminal Justice Acts** concern the functions of the legal system, rights of accused persons and police powers.
- **Local Government Acts** establish and control the powers of local authorities.
- The **Habeas Corpus Act** protects our rights to a trial when accused of a crime.
- The **Race Relations Acts** establish equal rights for members of all races.
- The **Northern Ireland Act 1972** established direct rule by London in Northern Ireland.

Common law

The term 'common law' refers to those laws which have not been passed by Parliament, but which are, nevertheless, recognised as binding. They exist because judges have decided, in past cases, that certain rules of conduct are so firmly rooted in the 'commonly held' traditions of the political system that they have the force of law. But statutes are superior to common law so that, if there is a conflict between statute law and common law, the former must always prevail. However, when statutes are not clear, or when it is not apparent whether a minister or public body is acting lawfully, judges may refer to such common law principles, based on similar disputes in the past.

Common law cases concerning constitutional rules are rare today. They tend to concern the operation of the law courts and the actions of government departments when applying administrative rules. Essentially, common law insists that courts and public bodies deal with citizens even-handedly, with a natural sense of justice and without prejudice.

Conventions

These are unwritten rules which are, nevertheless, considered binding by those who operate them. They have been described as the lubricating oil which makes the machinery of government work, or as a gentleman's agreement by which to operate the political system in traditional ways. They can only be understood in relation to the **royal prerogative**. The nature of the prerogative and prerogative powers are shown on page 278.

The royal prerogative

Before the powers of Parliament were firmly established in the seventeenth century, the discretionary, personal powers of the monarchy were scarcely controlled. Only in the field of taxation were the powers of the Crown limited. The uncontrolled functions of the monarch were known as the **royal prerogative.** Over the past 300 years these powers have been eroded, being largely replaced by parliamentary sovereignty.

However, some roles still remain. These mainly concern two activities. First, the preservation of the security and integrity of the land, involving control of the armed forces, intelligence operations and maintenance of public order, including the judicial system. Secondly, they concern the operation of government, such as the appointment of ministers and the calling of elections.

It would, of course, be wrong to assume from this that the reigning monarch actually performs these functions. We do not accept that the monarch has sufficient authority to carry out such vital roles. Instead, therefore, it is up to Parliament or the Prime Minister to exercise prerogative powers on behalf of the Crown. There may still be emergency or unforeseen circumstances when the monarch might have to step in and take action, but, on the whole, the royal prerogative has passed into other hands.

Most conventions of the constitution derive from this operation of prerogative powers. They are so rooted in the development of the political system that they appear almost to have the force of law. It is difficult to appreciate how conventions can be enforced if they are not laws. In short, we really do not know. This difficulty is compounded by the fact that there are no modern examples of serious breaches of a convention. Writing in 1885, however, the constitutional theorist A.V. Dicey suggested that such a transgression would **eventually** lead to a conflict either with Parliament or the law courts.

Thus, for example, it is a **convention** that a Government must resign if it loses a vote of confidence in the House of Commons. What if a government refused to resign after such a defeat? The answer which Dicey suggests is that Parliament would refuse to approve any of its future proposals and the courts would not uphold the actions of its ministers.

> 'But the sanction which constrains the boldest political adventurer to obey the fundamental principles of the constitution and the conventions in which these principles are expressed, is the fact that the breach of these principles and of these conventions will almost immediately bring the offender into conflict with the courts and the law of the land.'
> A.V. Dicey, *An Introduction to the Study of the Law of the Constitution* (1885)

The main conventions which operate within the British Constitution are:

- The Prime Minister shall be the leader of the majority party in the House of Commons.
- The Prime Minister has the power to appoint all Government ministers.
- The Prime Minister shall have sole power to choose the dates of general elections (although there is a limit of five years between elections established by Statute).
- A Government must resign if it loses a confidence vote in the House of Commons.

- The Prime Minister acts as commander-in-chief of the armed forces and all other security services.
- The Prime Minister negotiates and signs foreign treaties.
- The Prime Minister creates peers, Church of England Archbishops and Bishops, senior judges, knighthoods and grants other honours.
- The monarch always gives the Royal Assent to legislation properly passed in Parliament.
- Cabinet ministers must defend Government policy or resign from the government.

These examples illustrate the extent to which the British political system is governed by conventions. It also possibly over-exaggerates the powers of the Prime Minister. It should be remembered that, although many prerogative powers are exercised by the Prime Minister, he is still subject to the influence of his Cabinet colleagues, his back-bench MPs and his party.

Books and documents of authority
Despite the many statutes and conventions which map out the operation of the British Constitution, there are some areas which have remained the subject of some doubt and confusion. There may be an **awareness** of the existence of such principles as the sovereignty of Parliament or the collective responsibility of the Cabinet, but the **authority** behind such features may be less clear. Here, important documents and theoretical works can help.

- The *Bill of Rights* of 1689 (not to be confused with more recent Bills of Rights which concern the rights of citizens against the state) was an agreement between Parliament and the new King, William III. Its effect was to confirm parliamentary sovereignty, which has been strengthened considerably since then.
- **Walter Bagehot's** the *English Constitution*, published in 1867, went some way to clarifying the status of the Cabinet and the role of party government.
- **Dicey's** *Introduction to the Study of the Law of the Constitution* of 1885 established the importance of the **Rule of Law** and the legal status of **conventions**.

Parliamentary procedures
Many of the rules and regulations of Parliament, largely contained in the reference work, **Erskine May's Parliamentary Practice**, are purely administrative, but it does contain a number of important constitutional principles. Among them are the rights and privileges of MPs, rules concerning their conduct, and the manner in which the government may control the operations of both Houses. At the same time, parliamentary rules guarantee the independence of the Legislature from government.

Rules concerning emergency debates, legislative procedures and the operation of committees affect the political process and must not, therefore, be ignored.

External constitutional agreements
In 1965 Britain agreed to allow her citizens to appeal to the European Court of Human Rights which administers the European Convention on Human Rights. In 1973 we joined the European Community (now the European Union). These two events subjected Britain to constraints

which may be described as constitutional as they affect both the rights of citizens and the jurisdiction of government. They are 'external' in that they affect Britain's constitutional arrangements with other states, individually and collectively.

The **European Convention on Human Rights** is not legally binding on the UK, but the judgments of the Court carry so much **moral** authority that the British Government normally abides by such rulings. It is, therefore, **quasi-constitutional** in the sense that it has virtually the same force as entrenched principles.

The various treaties governing the jurisdiction of the European Union affect the sovereignty of Parliament and the powers of national governments. Thus, they are an integral part of the British Constitution. The agreements include the **Treaty of Rome** which Britain signed in 1972 and the **Treaty of Maastricht** of 1993. In addition, the **European Communities Act**, passed by Parliament in 1972, affirmed that all European law automatically became British law and the **Single European Act** of 1986 established Britain's participation in a unified market.

Should European integration deepen in the future, it may be that further constitutional inroads will be made into the British political system.

Sources of the British Constitution

1. Parliamentary statutes
2. Common law
3. Unwritten conventions
4. Books and documents of authority
5. Parliamentary procedures
6. External constitutional constraints

British constitutional features

Flexibility

The fact that the British Constitution is uncodified and unentrenched renders it extremely flexible. The institutions and practices which characterise the political system have, thus, been able to adjust to changing circumstances without any major upheavals.

Over the past 200 years Britain has seen a number of important changes. These have included the following:

- The development of the party system
- The decline in the authority of the monarchy
- The increasing power of the Cabinet
- A reduction in the power of Parliament, especially the House of Lords
- A considerable increase in the functions of the state
- The development of the European Union.

The response to these changes has been the addition of new conventions and the elimination of old ones. Contrast this history with the experience of France, where five constitutions have been created since the 1789 revolution, often accompanied by violence and disruption. The Americans, meanwhile, suffered a cruel civil war and many bitter battles over constitutional amendments. During the same period, Britain remained relatively stable.

Unitary government

The term 'unitary' refers to the fact that legal sovereignty lies in one place – Parliament. It is not divided as is the case in **federal** systems such as those of the USA or Germany. Although Britain has enjoyed a powerful and vigorous local government system in the past, this has not constituted divided sovereignty. The powers of local government have always been merely delegated by Parliament.

The Parliamentary system

Parliament is the central feature of the political system. Above all, it is the sovereign body, which means that there can be no higher laws than those made by Parliament, and no higher political authority. In addition, government must be drawn from Parliament and is responsible to it.

Constitutional monarchy

Although, in theory, the Crown has unlimited **prerogative** powers in certain fields, including the maintenance of the security of the realm and the operation of the political system, there are important limitations.

Although there is no written constitution, it is understood that it can only operate within strict legal constraints. Most importantly, the sovereignty of Parliament means that the legislature may pass any statute it wishes, including laws which limit prerogative powers. Thus, for example, the monarch (or government acting on her behalf) may not imprison one of her subjects without trial without infringing the Habeas Corpus Act. At the same time, the powers of the Crown are limited by common law rights. In particular, the monarch may not take over private property without statutory authority.

The weakness of the separation of powers

The eighteenth-century French philosopher **Montesquieu** argued that good government must be self-limiting. The most effective way of achieving this, he added, was to ensure that the three branches of government – **legislature** (the bodies which develop and pass laws), **executive** (the bodies which propose and execute the laws) and **judiciary** (the courts which administer and interpret the laws) – should be strictly separated. Not only that, but they should enjoy powers which limit each other.

Although Montesquieu was, at the time, describing his perception of the British system of the day, it was the Americans who enshrined his principles in their new Constitution. To them it became known as the system of 'checks and balances' and it has shaped American politics ever since.

Montesquieu's description of Britain was partially correct at the end of the eighteenth century, but since then the separation has been steadily eroded. It can now be said that the principle of the separation of powers no longer holds true in Britain, with the possible exception of the existence of a semi-independent judiciary. The following features can be identified as the causes of this development:

- Members of the government are all also members of one of the Houses of Parliament.
- The Cabinet invariably dominates the majority in the House of Commons through the party whip system.
- Parliament has surrendered nearly all its genuine law-making functions to the Cabinet.
- Senior judges are appointed by the Prime Minister on the advice of the Lord Chancellor, his Cabinet and party colleagues.

- The Lord Chancellor, the most senior law officer and judge, is a member of the Cabinet and of the House of Lords, thus being unique as a member of all three branches of government.
- The House of Lords, or at least its senior judicial members, acts as the highest appeal court, often considering cases with political significance. Thus, it is part of both the legislature and the judiciary.

It must be stressed that the political independence of judges is protected by the principle that they cannot be dismissed by the government, nor can their salaries be reduced. In this way, it is not possible for any financial or occupational pressure to be placed on them.

The rule of law The principles of the rule of law, confirmed by **A.V. Dicey** in 1885, say much about legal equality and the rights of citizens to a fair trial according to the principles of justice. Their constitutional significance lies in the fact that the government itself must operate within the laws. It is true, of course, that the laws may be designed by the government to suit its purposes, so great is executive control over Parliament, but the rule of law ensures that existing statutory limitations will be respected.

Summary of British Constitutional features

1. It is **unwritten, unentrenched** and therefore **flexible**.
2. It is **unitary** – sovereignty lies in one place.
3. It is **parliamentary** – Parliament lies at the centre of the system.
4. There is a **constitutional**, or limited, **monarchy.**
5. The **separation of powers** is largely absent.
6. The **rule of law** operates in the main.

Does Britain need a written constitution?

The principal pressure group currently campaigning for a codified and entrenched constitution is **Charter 88**, a group of politicians, academics and journalists, mostly of a liberal frame of mind, but including a sprinkling of socialists and even Conservatives. To them can be added the campaign group **Liberty** (formerly the National Council for Civil Liberties), eminent constitutional theorist Professor Fred Ridley and the prominent left-wing MP, Tony Benn. These campaigners wish to see major reform of the constitution, but also wish to safeguard those reforms.

The arguments in favour   The arguments in favour of a written constitution are as follows:

1. There is too much power vested in the executive. A new constitutional settlement is, therefore, needed to disperse power more widely. Most of this redistribution would restore to Parliament much of its former independence.

As we have seen above, the separation of powers between the executive and the legislature has been gradually eroded. No less a Conservative than **Lord Hailsham**, not normally an enthusiast for dramatic reforms, accepted that this was a problem in 1976. His words have become something of a rallying cry for those who have lamented the excessive concentration of power in the Government:

> *'I have reached the conclusion that our Constitution is wearing out. Its central defects are gradually coming to outweigh its merits. I envisage nothing less than a written Constitution for the United Kingdom.'*
> Lord Hailsham, *Dimbleby Lecture* 1976, in *The Spectator*

In the same lecture, Hailsham described Britain as an 'elective dictatorship', referring to the fact that, once elected, a Government can operate without any real controls, so great is its ability to dictate to its own House of Commons majority.

The solution for reformers lies in the adoption of methods to reduce the powers of the executive, including weakening prime ministerial patronage and removing his power to dissolve Parliament and call an election if his government cannot get its way. John Major used this threat twice, in 1993 and 1994, to force through controversial European legislation against the opposition of a group of his own back-benchers.

2. There is too much power at the centre, in London. Particularly during the 1980s, Margaret Thatcher's administrations eroded the powers and independence of local government. More dramatically, a whole tier of local government was removed with the abolition of the Greater London Council, the Inner London Education Authority and six large metropolitan counties.

The rise of Scottish and Welsh nationalism has also heightened interest in regional government. There is a perceived failure by central government to understand or to sympathise with problems in the British regions. The principal of **subsidiarity** which is gaining adherents proposes that, in a modern democracy, decisions should be taken as close to the people as is feasible.

A new entrenched dispersal of powers to the regions and smaller localities would reverse this process and ensure that such centralisation could not occur again.

3. The prerogative powers exercised by government on behalf of the Crown are ill-defined and uncontrolled. Unlike statutory powers, which fall under parliamentary control, prerogative-based actions can only be limited if the courts judge them to be excessive. Such judicial action is rare. The case of **GCHQ** (General Communications Headquarters) in 1984 is considered informative in this respect. The Government's decision to ban trade union membership among civil servants at GCHQ was taken under prerogative powers and thus did not require parliamentary approval. Despite widespread public disquiet, the courts upheld the Government's right to take this action.

Such dramatic decisions as declarations of war, the committal of British troops to battle, the signing of foreign treaties and general foreign policy initiatives are all taken under discretionary prerogative powers.

It is time, say campaigners, that these powers be defined and limited in a constitution. Their extent should not be left in the hands of judges who too often tend to favour state power against individuals. Nor should Parliament be denied the right to exercise some control over such key government functions.

> *'Britain's constitution presents a paradox. We live in a modern world but inhabit a pre-modern, indeed ancient, constitution.'*
> Stephen Haseler, 'Britain's Ancien Régime' in *Parliamentary Affairs* (October, 1990)

4. The rights of citizens are under threat and require greater protection. Although Britain is often considered to be one of the longest-standing guardians of individual liberty, with her Anglo-Saxon rights enshrined in the Magna Carta of 1215 and subsequently exported all over the world through the auspices of the Empire, such traditions are unable to withstand the modern challenges of the powerful expanding state and the current challenges to order which are represented by burgeoning crime levels.

Supporters of the inclusion of an entrenched Bill of Rights, either with or without a broader constitutional settlement, point to a number of developments which threaten individual rights. These include:

- Increased police powers as a result of rising crime rates. Citizens may now be held for lengthy periods without trial. The right to remain silent, under questioning or in court, may now be cited as an indication of guilt under the much-opposed Criminal Justice Act of 1994. Under the same act the police also have greater powers to prevent public demonstrations, while the courts may issue severer penalties for trespass. There has also been a steady increase in police powers to stop and search pedestrians or to detain and question motorists.
- Citizens increasingly come into contact with state institutions and face arbitrary decisions by bureaucracies which are insufficiently controlled. In this way, citizens are exposed to the possibilities of unjust treatment. Social security offices, tax offices, health authorities, local planning authorities, education authorities and housing bodies are all examples of such bureaucratic activity. The individual, it is argued, needs a code of well-protected rights to ensure fair treatment by these bodies.
- An increasing amount of information is held by state institutions about individuals. It is argued that there are dangers that such information may be misused, threatening particularly the privacy of the individual.
- In an increasingly multi-racial, multi-faith, pluralist society, the rights of the many minorities which now flourish are vulnerable to abuse and discrimination. Legal protection is, therefore, vital to allow our pluralist society to flourish.
- The media have become extremely powerful institutions. On the one hand, it can be argued that newspapers and broadcasters must be guaranteed access to official information where it is in the public interest to know; similarly, they need protection from the censorship which government may attempt to impose upon them in order to protect such information. On the other hand, citizens may need protection from the intrusiveness of the tabloid press in particular. Thus, both privacy and freedom of information laws are proposed as part of a Bill of Rights.
- The weakening influence of trade unions during the 1980s, coupled with the growing power of multi-national corporations, has resulted in workers becoming vulnerable to unfair treatment. Rights in the workplace may, therefore, need firmer guarantees.

- Although the courts offer some protection for individuals from unfair treatment by the state, enforcing, as they do, common law rights, it is often argued that our senior judges are conservative (small 'c') in outlook and generally tend to favour the state against challenges by individuals. Furthermore, even if judges do take the side of the individual, they cannot prevent ministers simply passing laws through the sovereign Parliament to give them powers which may have been denied them by the courts.
- The loss of confidence in the institution of the monarchy experienced during the 1990s has led to demands that its 'political' functions be reduced or even abolished. At its extreme, this belief extends to outright abolition of the monarchy and its replacement by a republic. Full abolition seems unlikely, but even **Jack Straw**, a relatively moderate member of the Labour Party front-bench, proposed a 'slimmed down' monarchy in 1994. Should this be implemented, new constitutional rules would need to be codified to replace the old discretionary powers of the Crown.

> *'It is wrong that any government can change laws affecting civil liberties by ordinary and misrepresentative parliamentary majorities – we do need a Bill of Rights.'*
> Professor Bernard Crick in the *Independent*, 19 May 1990

The arguments against Opponents of a written constitution, and indeed an entrenched Bill of Rights, include virtually all Conservatives and many members of the more radical Left. In both cases their main fear is excessive weakening of government as a result of increased constitutional obstacles. In the academic world, Professor Philip Norton leads the 'anti' lobby. Their arguments include:

1. The vital quality of British government, much admired in America and the European continent, is its ability to control the legislature, to carry out its electoral mandate without undue delay or opposition and to deal with unforeseen circumstances without encountering the hindrance of too many constitutional restraints.

Control over financial matters has been the particular characteristic to which opponents of constitutionally limited government point when illustrating the strength of the current system. With the exception of the budgetary opposition encountered by Chancellor Kenneth Clarke in the 1990s, British governments normally enjoy a relatively free hand in financial and economic policy implementation. This is how it should be, runs the argument.

2. The very flexibility which is often criticised can be seen as a strength of the status quo. For traditional Conservatives the political system and the features which characterise it must be allowed to evolve naturally with society. Written constitutions and Bills of Rights are based on fixed principles which such Conservatives oppose.

Certainly, it is true that the British Constitution has been able to adapt to major changes in the setting of our politics as described on pages 52–4. Contrast this with the American experience where responses to the Depression of the 1930s, to economic decline in the 1980s and 1990s, and to a dramatically rising crime rate over the same period have all been hindered by constitutional rigidity. When Presidents and their administrations have attempted to extend their powers to deal with pressing problems, the Supreme Court has been forced to thwart them by enforcing the many constitutional controls over such developments which were put in place in 1787.

3. Philip Norton has maintained that, despite the clamour in the 1990s for additional constitutional safeguards, there is no real need for them. He points out that a number of political features can be identified as sufficient controls over the power of central government. Among them have been the following:

- The existence of many influential pressure groups with sufficient leverage to be able to force government to consult and obtain widespread support for its proposals. The big groups, such as trade unions, major companies and professional bodies have always been there, but in addition the 1980s saw a dramatic rise in the number of small pressure groups which have been able to exert influence. Issues concerning the environment, minority group interests and welfare recipients are all examples of how such groups have been able to control or influence government and Parliament.
- Despite the absence of a codified Bill of Rights, a large number of individual Statutes have been passed since the 1960s which have advanced the cause of individual and group rights. Thus, ethnic minorities (the Race Relations Acts), homosexuals (Homosexual Law Reform), women (Equal Opportunities Legislation, Equal Pay Acts and Abortion Law reform), consumers (Fair Trading legislation) and tenants (Rent Acts) have all benefited from such statutory developments. Norton's contention that rights in Britain have been better protected than in the USA, with its powerful Bill of Rights, is certainly a compelling one.
- Where individual rights are not adequately protected by legislation, the European Convention on Human Rights has proved an effective, if rather slow and expensive, resort for those who are determined to safeguard basic freedoms. On issues such as press freedom, corporal punishment and equal pension rights for women, the European Court of Human Rights has shown its teeth.
- There is yet another remedy for those who feel injustice has been inflicted on them by an official body or a minister. The process of **judicial review** by the courts allows appeals by citizens against unfair treatment at the hands of the state. During the 1990s, for example, the Home Secretaries lost a series of such reviews over their treatment of offenders.
- Although there has been a good deal of centralisation of governmental powers, there remains an important layer of sub-central government which continues to diffuse power. Apart from the obvious local government system, there is a wide range of quangos and local or regional bodies, containing both appointed and elected members, making decisions away from the influence of central government ministers.

- Some power has also passed upwards to the institutions of the European Union. This has removed many central government powers in such matters as trade, agriculture, industry and consumer protection. Thus, power has moved both downwards and upwards away from Whitehall.

> 'A written constitution and a Bill of Rights may sound attractive. The practical reality is that they do not offer what proponents believe they offer. The most effective route for dealing with special problems is the legislative process.'
> Philip Norton, *New Directions in British Politics* (Edward Elgar, 1991)

4. The experience of the many democracies which have written constitutions is that the courts must frequently become involved in resolving constitutional disputes. Since many of these conflicts concern the powers of government, they are political in nature. We could certainly envisage cases involving the exercise of powers by ministers, or local authorities becoming the subject of hotly contested political dispute. The question then arises as to whether judges are fit to pronounce on issues with clear political implications. They are unelected and not responsible. Opponents of written constitutions therefore argue that such conflicts must be left to elected politicians at Westminster.

> 'A Bill of Rights would be a cuckoo in the judicial nest.'
> John Biffen (Leader of the House of Commons 1982–7) in the *Independent*, 19 May 1990

5. An entrenched constitution or Bill of Rights would remove the most basic feature of the British political system – the sovereignty of Parliament. Laws and principles which have a higher authority than other legislation would take away part of what Walter Bagehot, in 1867, called the 'efficient secret' of the system. Remove that sovereignty and there is a danger that British government would lose its most powerful tool.

There are, indeed, some who argue that the creation of entrenched legislation would be futile since Parliament could simply overturn it when it felt necessary and there exists no authority able to stop Parliament doing so.

Thus, there can be no doubt that the introduction of a 'real' British Constitution would challenge the most basic and historic of our institutions including Parliament and the monarchy.

Summary of arguments concerning a written constitution for Britain	
For	**Against**
1. Government is too powerful. Greater controls are needed.	1. Government would lose its power to be able to act decisively.
2. Government is too centralised. Power should be devolved downwards.	2. There would be a loss of flexibility in the political system.
3. The prerogative powers of government are uncontrolled and often abused.	3. The need for governmental control and diffusion of power has been exaggerated.
4. The rights of citizens and groups have been eroded and continue to be threatened by government.	4. The unelected judiciary would be thrust into the political arena.
	5. The sovereignty of Parliament would be lost.

The judiciary and the Constitution

It is often argued that the true guardians of the constitution and, in particular, the rights of citizens are the judges who preside in the higher courts of appeal – the High Court, the Civil Court of Appeal and the judicial section of the House of Lords. In addition, there are now opportunities for citizens and organisations to take grievances to either the **European Court of Human Rights**, which seeks to enforce the European Convention (this court, it should be noted, is **not** part of the European Union), or the **European Court of Justice,** which enforces EU laws.

The principle of judicial review in Britain is described above and has certainly become an important feature of relations between citizens and the state. The strength of this safeguard is, however, reduced by a number of factors:

- Unless European Union law holds precedence, Parliament is sovereign. No courts, judges or legal principles can alter this fact. Thus, if a judgment in favour of an individual citizen runs contrary to Government policy, ministers may simply go back to Parliament and ask members to pass legislation to avoid the problem in future. Executive control over Parliament almost guarantees that new law will replace the judges' verdict. The Criminal Justice Act of 1995, for example, removed a whole raft of traditional rights in such areas as freedom of movement and association and the right to silence for accused people in police custody.
- Even where the courts do have jurisdiction, there is a strong belief that most judges tend to favour the established order, that is, the government and the state, rather than individul rights. It is thought that this is due to their upper middle-class backgrounds and their legal training (encouraging support for the **status quo**). A series of judgments against the miners in their long bitter strike of 1984, for example, gave rise to such suspicions. Judges, on the whole, prefer not to become involved in political issues and so tend to take the safe option by opposing challenges to state power.
- The judgments of the European Court of Human Rights are not binding in Britain. There is no guarantee that a favourable judgment there will lead to a positive response in Britain.

'Judicial review is not a perfect jurisdiction, but in the absence of effective political checks . . . it forms a useful part of the system of mixed checks and balances.'
Dawn Oliver, 'The Judge over your Shoulder' in
Parliamentary Affairs (July 1989)

Nevertheless, there have been occasions when citizens have secured their rights through the courts and, increasingly, the European Union's Court of Justice is establishing employment and welfare rights. The 1994 case which established equal pension rights for women was a landmark in judicial power. Ministers must beware that any suspicion that they may be acting *ultra vires* (beyond their legal powers) is likely to be exposed in the courts.

Add to this the powers of a wide variety of **administrative tribunals** to redress unfair treatment of individuals by public bodies in such areas as taxation, welfare, planning applications and mental health care, and there appears to be an impressive range of judicial controls.

For exam questions relevant to this unit, see pages 490–2.

13 The European context

Background to European integration

Ever since Napoleon dreamed of a single European political and legal 'system' at the beginning of the nineteenth century, there have been grand ideas of solving continental problems by permanent, institutional integration. Until the end of World War Two, however, no such plans ever approached the degree of success which Napoleon nearly achieved.

Two disastrous European wars in the same century finally persuaded politicians that a serious attempt had to be made to eliminate all possibility of a repetition of such events. The key figures were two Frenchmen, **Jean Monnet** and **Robert Schuman**.

Initially, thoughts rested upon an alliance between France and Germany, to avoid future aggression, but Monnet in particular hoped for a broader union to include Britain, Italy and the 'Benelux' countries – Belgium, the Netherlands and Luxembourg. The objectives of European integration were:

- To destroy finally the conditions for future wars between European powers
- To provide stable conditions for increased trade within Europe
- Ultimately to create a single, powerful European economy
- To create a single power able to resist military pressure from the Soviet Union.

Such aspirations were clearly long-term aims, requiring radical changes in the political outlook of the peoples and leaders of Europe. Progress has, therefore, been gradual and piecemeal.

The road to union

European Coal and Steel Community

In 1952 six countries signed the **Treaty of Paris**, establishing the European Coal and Steel Community (ECSC). These were France, Germany, Italy, Belgium, the Netherlands and Luxembourg. Presaging later events, Britain decided not to participate, but to wait and see how matters developed. Ever since 1952, British governments have proved to be reluctant partners in Europe.

The ECSC established a system for the control and integration of the coal, iron and steel industries in the member states. It was an important economic step forward, but its greater significance concerns the political institutions which were set up to administer the Community. These became a blueprint for the future closer union. The constituent bodies of the ECSC were:

- A **High Authority** to administer the industries. This was a 'supranational' body whose jurisdiction stood above that of the member states – a unique innovation in international politics. For the first time, domestic governments showed themselves willing to accept transfer of sovereignty to such an institution. There were safeguards, as shown below, but an important principle had been established.
- The **Ministerial Council** comprising representatives from member governments. Its role was to ensure the High Authority did not act beyond its powers, reserving a veto if necessary.

- A **Parliamentary Assembly**, drawn from the Council of Europe – a consultative body which had existed since 1950 to discuss general progress towards European integration. The Assembly was given no specific powers and was thus a weak body, set up to discuss and propose policy, but little more.
- A **Court**, employing judges from members states, to adjudicate on legal disputes concerning the operation of the rules of the Community.

With the exception of the Ministerial Council, which was later to be given full sovereign status in the Community, these political arrangements were to survive at least until 1996.

The Treaty of Rome Buoyed up by the success of the ECSC, but determined to widen the scope of economic integration, European leaders now moved towards a broader agreement. In **1957** the **Treaty of Rome** was signed by the six member countries. At the same time, an agreement on co-operation in atomic energy production, known as **Euratom**, was completed.

The Treaty of Rome set up the **European Economic Community (EEC)**, often referred to as the **Common Market**. The broad nature of what was agreed in Rome is shown below:

Economic objectives	**Political institutions**
1. Eliminating all import tariffs and other barriers between member states.	1. The **Commission** comprising European civil servants, to develop and implement policy.
2. Establishing common product descriptions and standards in the Community.	2. The **Council of Ministers** drawn from each member state. This comprises Heads of Government (i.e. Prime Ministers) for key decisions, functional ministers for such issues as agriculture, trade and finance. The Council is the **sovereign** body and must agree all laws and regulations.
3. Introducing a common external tariff on goods entering from outside the Community.	3. The **European Parliament** (originally this was known as the Assembly). Its role was limited to general debate and consultation.
	4. The **European Court of Justice** to settle legal disputes over European law arising in member states.

Further functions were added to the EEC after the Treaty of Rome, most notably the **Common Agricultural Policy** in 1967. This was designed to protect European agriculture, stabilise food prices and generally regulate production. The fishing industry was added to the general scheme. Measures to provide help for particular industries which, it is felt, are vital to European prosperity, to give aid to poorer regions and to improve transport facilities are all designed to facilitate trade and greater economic equality between member countries.

The treaty did not deal with the thorny problem of finance. International currency exchanges and movements, together with interest rate policy, are vital in the creation of stable trading conditions. These issues were to come to a head in the 1990s.

British membership As we have seen above, Britain was reluctant to participate in European integration in its early days. Three principal reasons can be identified:

- Britain's tradition of isolation from continental affairs. Historically Britain has seen itself as a world imperial power rather than a continental European one.
- The close association (the so-called 'special relationship') with the USA implied that Britain need not rely on a European alliance.
- The Commonwealth provided Britain with a network of special trade agreements which gave it sources of cheap raw materials and imports, together with ready markets for her exports. This, together with extensive trade links with the USA, rendered economic integration with Europe less attractive than maintenance of the status quo.

From a European perspective British membership was also not wholly supported. The French, in particular, feared that Britain would attempt to dominate the Community, using it for its own purposes. More worrying was a suspicion that a German–British axis might be formed to the detriment of the less wealthy members.

Britain had formed its own European trade community, the **European Free Trade Association (EFTA)**, in 1959 which eventually comprised seven members, but as this was made up of much smaller countries (such as Portugal, Austria and Switzerland), it was limited in scope and was of relatively little economic importance. Essentially, by 1960, Britain was isolated in Europe.

It was Harold Macmillan (Prime Minister, 1957–63) who made the first attempt to bring Britain into the Community. He was thwarted by the French President, Charles de Gaulle, who vetoed British admission in 1962 following major disagreements over entry conditions. At the time, France was moving closer to Germany in economic and political terms. British membership would possibly have threatened this new accord.

Further tentative overtures were also rejected, but two events renewed British interest. De Gaulle was overthrown in 1969, and this removed the major obstacle to British membership. The following year Edward Heath was elected Prime Minister. Heath was a convinced European, determined to negotiate British entry. Talks reached a successful conclusion in 1972 and on 1 January 1973 Britain joined the EEC.

The Labour Government which took office in 1974 renegotiated the terms of British membership, a largely cosmetic exercise, and then held a referendum on the question of whether membership should be retained. This was politically necessary for the party as it was hopelessly split on the issue. Only an expression of the popular will could heal the wound. The result was emphatic support for membership, by two to one.

The single market During 1986 negotiations took place in Luxembourg to complete the task of creating the single market, a process which had started in Rome in 1957. The legislation which was passed – the Single European Act – made a number of political changes within the Community, but its most important provision was to come into effect at the beginning of 1993.

Political changes

- The rules concerning voting in the Council of Ministers were changed. Before the Act, many decisions required *unanimous* approval of the Council to become law. This safeguarded the sovereignty of each state, since there was an effective veto. After the Act most decisions only required a **qualified majority**, that is, more than 50 per cent, but less than unanimity. Thus, member states gave up a considerable amount of control. This marked a significant shift in power from member states to this supranational body.
- The European Parliament's influence was enhanced, but only marginally. It was required to approve proposals from the Commission (civil service) and the Council (ministers). It could now force the decision makers to renegotiate proposals, but not stop them altogether. It was also granted the power to decide on the admission of new members and the appointment of senior officials in the Commission.
- The jurisdiction of the Community was widened to include environmental issues, research and development and more extensive regional policy.

<u>Economic changes</u> One economic principle dominated the Single European Act. This was the establishment of a single market. In practice, this meant that there would be no remaining taxes, regulations or restrictions on the movement of goods, services, people or capital (finance) between member countries. In effect, such movements were to be as free as if they were taking place **within** a single country. This came into effect on 1 January 1993.

The ramifications of this development include the advent of a single currency to apply throughout the community and a single unified economy. Once these two economic changes have taken place the opportunities for closer political integration will increase.

Expansion 1973–95 There were six original members of the Community. In 1973 Ireland and Denmark joined along with the UK to make nine (Norway was due to join at the same time but a referendum there rejected entry). The nine became twelve when Greece joined in 1981, and Spain and Portugal in 1986. On 1 January 1995 Sweden, Finland and Austria made the total fifteen. Most of western Europe was now included.

Apart from the question of a few other Western powers entering, such as Switzerland and Turkey, the main questions over membership at the end of the century concern the 'new' liberal democracies of East and Central Europe such as Hungary, the former Yugoslav states, Poland and Russia itself. However, it seems unlikely that there can be early entry for these former socialist states. Their economies remain in a transitional state while, at the same time, the question of military alliances has not been resolved. The roles of NATO, a possible future European Defence Establishment and the remaining American forces must be decided before there can be further expansion.

Finance Hand in hand with economic integration must go closer financial co-operation. As long as national currencies are allowed to fluctuate in value against each other, there will be trade uncertainty and instability. But this is not merely an economic question. Control over currency values and interest rates, which are closely related issues, requires supranational regulatory bodies which further threaten the sovereignty of member states. Thus, it has vital political significance.

Following earlier modest attempts at monetary regulation, the European **Exchange Rate Mechanism (ERM)** was established in 1980. By 1987 the ERM had developed into a system where each member currency was virtually fixed in value against the value of all the others. The political importance of the ERM was that it required all member states to co-operate in maintaining their currency's exchange rate. This implied that they might have to accept financial constraints for the benefit of maintaining the system, even when this might be damaging to their own economic health. In other words, they might have to accept **short-term national** disadvantages for the sake of **long-term** European currency stability.

This was a price which Britain's Conservative Government was not prepared to pay. Sterling was proving particularly unstable so radical measures would be required to maintain its exchange rate. Thus, the UK stayed out of the ERM. In 1990, however, Margaret Thatcher reluctantly agreed to take Britain in, following intense pressure from other members.

Ironically, it was this event which precipitated the demise of the ERM. Sterling was too weak a currency to maintain its exchange rate without unacceptable measures being taken to protect it. When panic selling of sterling, followed by similar problems for Ireland and Italy, occurred, Britain was forced to leave the system in 1992. A discredited Chancellor of the Exchequer, Norman Lamont, resigned while in Europe the ERM eventually collapsed.

The Treaty of Maastricht   Formally called the **Treaty on European Union**, this agreement was signed in Maastricht, Holland, in 1992. The treaty was a mixture of specific changes and broader, less precise aims. The varied nature of the agreements is indicated in the table below:

The Treaty of Maastricht	
Institutional changes	• Parliament was to have greater influence over legislation, appointment of Commissioners and other future agreements • Advisory Committees on the Regions and on Economic and Social Affairs, plus the European Investment Bank, were given increased status • The name 'the European Community' was changed to 'the European Union'
Broadening the scope of the Union	• Greater powers on environmental issues • More control on social and industrial relations policy (the 'Social Chapter' from which Britain initially opted out) • Increased powers on consumer protection • More control over transport and regional policy
Long-term aims	• Possible future common foreign and defence policy • Increased democratisation, especially increased parliamentary powers • A single European currency by 1999 • Common legal, political and economic rights for all European citizens

On balance, Maastricht was more a promise for the future than an immediate radical reform of the Community. It did little to increase democracy in the Union, did not significantly change the role and powers of the Commission or the Council of Ministers, fudged the issue of citizens' rights and left a number of key decisions to the inter-governmental conference scheduled for 1996.

Possibly the most significant measure was the so-called 'Social Chapter'. This section of the treaty gave the Union powers to regulate the rights and conditions of workers, the powers of trade unions, minimum pay and other benefits, with related implications for welfare, pensions, provision for the disabled and a number of other social policies. This represented a major extension of the Union's jurisdiction. So radical was this development that Britain refused to agree and the other members were forced to allow her to be exempt in order to conclude the Treaty. As we shall see below, Britain was also permitted to reserve the right to refuse to accept a common currency in the future.

The institutions of the European Union

The Commission

The Commission is, effectively, the civil service of the Union. It is made up of nearly 20,000 permanent officials drawn from member states, the number from each state being in proportion to its size. Whichever country an official represents, he is expected to serve the interests of Europe as a whole.

The Commission is divided into seventeen sections, each headed by a **Commissioner** who is an influential policy developer. The Commissioners are selected by the Council of Ministers but their appointment must be ratified by the European Parliament. They come from a variety of backgrounds, but are typically civil servants from member states or former politicians. Among the seventeen sections are Finance, Transport, relations with other states, Agriculture and Industry.

The role of the Commission divides into two. First, it proposes measures designed to further the long-term general goals of the Union,

European Commission meeting

which have already been set by meetings of ministers. It cannot make law and there is no guarantee that its proposals will be accepted. Secondly, it is charged with the task of implementing Union policy. In practice, it could not hope to do this itself because it is a relatively small body. In most cases, the Commission relies upon the institutions of the member states themselves to execute decisions. In this sense its function is largely supervisory.

The Council of Ministers   Though normally referred to in the singular, the Council is not one single body. Instead, it is the collective name for a series of meetings which take place in the EU between representatives from the Governments of member states. The key meetings, where the most significant decisions have to be made, are attended by the Heads of Government. In such cases the title **European Council** is adopted. States take turns to chair the meetings of this Council for a six-month period each. The most significant effect of chairmanship is that the list of items for discussion – the agenda – is determined by the chairing country. Mostly, however, only functional ministers are required where more specialised discussions are taking place. Among them are meetings of finance, agriculture, industry or environment ministers.

The role of the Council, in all its forms, is to ratify decisions which have been proposed by the Commission and discussed by the European Parliament. In short, the Council is the **sovereign** body of the Union. This fact represents the central political feature of Europe. However, it is the system of voting in the Council which is of greatest interest. The basis of the system includes the following arrangements:

- For the most important decisions, such as the admission of new members, currency arrangements, budgetary contributions and changes in the scope of Union jurisdiction, a **unanimous** vote among ministers is essential. In other words, each individual state has a veto on such issues. In this way there can be no total loss of sovereignty for members.
- Member states are awarded votes in the Council roughly in proportion to their size – obviously larger states have more votes than smaller ones. With the arrival of Sweden, Finland and Austria in 1995, the voting strengths were as follows:

      10 votes – Germany, United Kingdom, France, Italy
       8 votes – Spain
       5 votes – Belgium, Holland, Greece, Portugal
       4 votes – Sweden, Austria
       3 votes – Denmark, Ireland, Finland
       2 votes – Luxembourg

  It can be seen immediately that Germany, by some way the largest state, is under-represented and that tiny Luxembourg receives more votes than its size warrants. This is to prevent excessive domination by larger states.
- Some decisions require a **qualified** majority, that is, more than a simple majority of 50 per cent plus, but less than unanimity. In practice, this is approximately a 70 per cent proportion of the total votes in the Council. Thus, a consensus of support is needed for most agreements.

- For minor matters a simple majority of 50 per cent plus is acceptable, but only if the vital interests of member states are not involved.

The qualified majority rule results in a great deal of political 'wheeling and dealing' in the Council. Large states can block proposals by gaining the support of just one other big country, or even two of the smaller members. Alliances constantly shift, often with deals being struck between ministers who are in a position to help each other. The key principles are normally, therefore, **consensus** and **compromise**. Confrontational or adversarial politics of the kind practised at Westminster would be a dangerous course of action for any member as it would run the risk of becoming isolated.

Thus, British support for regional aid to poorer states such as Portugal or Greece could result in their support over issues which affect the UK, such as agricultural quotas and subsidies. Germany may champion protection for the French wine industry against Spanish and Italian competition on the promise of a future French–German alliance in important discussions over budget contributions. Nothing is simple or clear-cut in the Council.

The European Parliament

The intricacies of negotiation within the Council are considerable, but cannot compare with the complexities of the Parliament. Small wonder, since it is a large body, divided both by nationality and by party. The structure of the Parliament following the 1994 elections is shown in the table below:

Structure of the European Parliament after 1994															
Political Grouping	**A**	**B**	**G**	**D**	**Sp**	**F**	**Gr**	**Ir**	**It**	**L**	**N**	**P**	**S**	**Sf**	**UK**
European Socialists	8	6	40	3	22	15	10	1	18	2	8	10	11	4	63
European People's (Cons)	6	7	47	3	30	13	9	4	12	2	10	1	6	4	19
Liberal/Democrat/Reformist	1	6	–	5	2	1	–	1	6	1	10	8	3	6	2
United Left	–	–	–	1	9	7	4	–	5	–	–	3	1	1	–
Forza Europa (Italy only)	–	–	–	–	–	–	–	–	29	–	–	–	–	–	–
Democratic Alliance	–	–	–	–	–	14	2	7	–	–	–	3	–	–	–
Greens	1	2	12	–	–	–	–	2	4	1	1	–	1	1	–
Radical Alliance	–	1	–	–	1	13	–	–	2	–	–	–	–	–	2
Europe of Nations Group	–	–	–	4	–	13	–	–	–	–	2	–	–	–	–
Independents	5	3	–	–	–	11	–	–	11	–	–	–	–	–	1
Total	21	25	99	16	64	87	25	15	87	6	31	25	22	16	87

Source: *The European Parliament* ed. R. Corbett, F. Jacobs and M. Shackleton (Cartermill, 1995)

Key: A = Austria   B = Belgium   G = Germany   D = Denmark   Sp = Spain
     F = France   Gr = Greece   Ir = Ireland   It = Italy   L = Luxembourg
     N = Netherlands   P = Portugal   S = Sweden   Sf = Finland   UK = United Kingdom

The European Union Members 1995			
Country	**Population (millions)**	**Income per head (US$ – 1992)***	**No of MEPs**
Germany	81.2	20,435	99
United Kingdom	58.3	16,340	87
France	57.8	18,590	87
Italy	57.0	17,482	87
Spain	39.1	12,853	64
Netherlands	15.4	17,023	31
Greece	10.4	8,303	25
Belgium	10.1	18,195	25
Portugal	9.9	9,786	25
Sweden	8.6	16,590	21
Austria	7.9	18,096	20
Denmark	5.2	17,813	16
Finland	5.0	14,545	16
Ireland	3.5	12,391	15
Luxembourg	0.4	21,929	6

*Figures from OECD (Organisation for Economic Co-operation and Development)

It can be seen that no political grouping has an overall majority and that each national grouping of MEPs (Members of the European Parliament) is too small to be influential on its own. Thus, there can be little coherence when issues concern one particular state or when they are particularly controversial on a party level. Significant majorities are difficult to achieve and any temporary 'coalition' is likely to be extremely fragile. Though the socialist group of MEPs dominates the post-1994 Parliament, it is not large or stable enough to be able to maintain pressure on the Council or the Commission.

The powers of the Parliament after Maastricht remain uncertain, but they are relatively limited. The description opposite shows the basic elements of the Parliament's powers and functions:

European Parliament powers	
New members	The application for membership of prospective new members must be approved by MEPs.
The Union Budget	Parliament may veto the proposed Union Budget, i.e. the level of expenditure and members' contributions. This gives it a lever to exert influence on other issues.
Appointments	Before senior Commission members, including its President, are appointed, Parliament must give its approval.
Commission proposals	Each legislative proposal by the Commission is passed first to the Parliament which gives an 'opinion'. It is hoped this will influence the Council of Ministers in its deliberations.
Amendments	Parliament may propose amendments to legislation. These may be accepted, but, if rejected by the Commission, force a unanimous vote in the Council to overturn Parliament's view.
Legislative passage*	If a legislative proposal is accepted by Parliament, it passes to the Council of Ministers for normal approval. However, if Parliament rejects a proposed law, it can only be passed by a unanimous vote in the Council. Occasionally, the Parliament may propose its own legislation.

*These procedures apply to most, but not all legislation.

The most significant step after the Maastricht Treaty was to give Parliament the power to force the Council of Ministers into unanimous votes on issues with which Parliament disagrees or wishes to amend. Thus, the Parliament cannot block legislation which the Council of Ministers is determined to approve, but it can place significant obstacles in the way. These new opportunities for parliamentary influence are, briefly, shown below:

- **Consultation** which simply ensures that all proposed legislation is discussed by Parliament, and its opinion recorded, before final consideration.
- **Co-operation** gives Parliament the chance to interrupt legislation and force reconsideration by the Commission and the Council.
- **Co-decision** is required for the most important decisions. Here, Parliament may insist on negotiations between its representatives and those of the Council and Commission before a measure can be approved.

It should also be noted that, in the 1990s, Parliament has increasingly proposed its own legislation, especially on issues concerning social and environmental measures. In order to have any hope of implementation, the Commission must approve such proposals, but this is a possible pointer to a future expanded role for MEPs.

The European Court of Justice

This body should not be confused with the European Court of Human Rights. The latter hears cases brought under the European Convention on Human Rights, which is not binding on all members of the EU, notably the UK. In fact, the Court of Human Rights is not a European Union institution at all.

European Parliament in session

The **Court of Justice**, which sits in Luxembourg, is staffed by judges drawn from all member states. Its functions are as follows:

- Adjudicating on claims brought by the Commission that a member state has infringed Union law. Should such a claim be upheld, the Court will order appropriate action.
- Settling disputes between states arising out of the application of Union law. Typically, this might concern taxes, subsidies or quotas being imposed by one state to the detriment of another.
- If a court within a member state requires clarification of European law, the judges in Luxembourg will give an opinion which is binding on that lower court.

It is important to note that it is normally the responsibility of the courts of member states themselves to enforce European law. The Court of Justice only steps in to settle disputes or deal with problems which cannot be handled in those national courts.

Democracy in Europe

The evolving political system

The political system of Europe is still evolving and is unlikely to become permanently established before the end of the century. It is also a unique structure in the political world. Fifteen, soon to be more, sovereign nation-states bonded into an economic and political union has never been attempted before. It is, therefore, inevitable that many serious problems will arise.

Every step towards closer union must be painstakingly negotiated in the European Council and then ratified by each member state. By way of comparison, the Founding Fathers of the USA established their Constitution in just three months in Philadelphia, while it took only three further years for agreement by the thirteen member states. This same Constitution is still fundamentally in force in spite of its being created in such a short time.

The main difficulty in establishing political institutions and processes in Europe is that all the member states remain sovereign and so retain the right to veto any developments which they feel may not be in their national interests. This problem was illustrated graphically by the process of ratification of the Treaty on European Union (the Maastricht Treaty). Only unanimous approval by the twelve states which negotiated the Treaty was acceptable. In most states this was not a problem, especially since nine of the states required only parliamentary majorities for ratification. Only in the UK did this prove a difficulty as a result of the Government's small majority and a revolt among a sizeable section of its own back-benchers. It was the referenda which three states were forced to hold which caused the stumbling block.

In Ireland the people voted decisively in favour of the Treaty. In France there was a nail-biting contest; 51 per cent voted in favour of France's signing, but the country was clearly split leading to fears that future progress towards union might prove difficult. It was the Danes who nearly destroyed the Treaty. By a tiny 40,000-vote majority they rejected the agreement. Thus, one of the smallest states in the EU threatened to bring progress to a halt. In the event, the Treaty was amended to ease Danish fears, allowing the Danes to opt out of several important elements. Nearly a year later a second Danish vote reversed the decision and the Treaty was saved. But the lesson of Maastricht is that future developments may prove difficult. The UK, France and Denmark are again likely to prove the main obstacles as there are serious popular misgivings in these countries about European integration.

A parliamentary system?

Approaching the 1996 inter-governmental conference, the European Union is **not** a parliamentary system. Rather, it is a system with a Parliament. To be truly parliamentary three features would need to be present:

- The Parliament would have to be the legislature, i.e. the law-making body. This is not the case in 1996. The Council of Ministers makes law and the Parliament only has an advisory role.
- The government of the Union would be drawn from the Parliament and would thus draw its authority from that Assembly. Again, this is not the case. The governing Council is made up instead of representatives from member states.
- The executive branch of the Union – the Council and the Commission – would have to be fully accountable to the Parliament and, in theory at least, removable should they lose the confidence of a majority of MEPs. Even though Maastricht provided increased opportunities for the Parliament to scrutinise the Commission's work, this does not add up to real accountability.

There is little immediate possibility of a truly parliamentary system evolving in Europe. Member states are reluctant to hand over too much sovereignty to a directly elected assembly. In addition, the fact that the Parliament will always be split on both national and party lines suggests that it would be unlikely to be stable enough to sustain a united government.

Subsidiarity and federalism

The Maastricht Treaty declares that the European Union shall operate on the basis of **subsidiarity**. This implies three principles:

- The institutions of the Union shall only be given the powers which they need to carry out the policies of the Union.
- Any powers not granted to Union institutions automatically belong to the member states individually.
- Decisions should be taken as close to the citizen as possible.

It is hoped that this will both limit the powers of central European government and ensure the greatest degree of democracy possible. It is also designed to replace the principle of **federalism**.

Federalism implies a system where the sovereignty of the central government, of the member states and of any further sub-regions which might be established is strictly defined by a constitutional settlement. The difference between subsidiarity and federalism is not readily apparent and may, in practice, turn out to be merely semantic. However, the opponents of such a settlement suggest that federalism would result in a once-and-for-all loss of sovereignty for member states. Subsidiarity, on the other hand, is seen as a more flexible arrangement which ensures that the central Union establishment will never be able to claim powers without the full consent of the members.

There is a widespread fear in Europe that there will be a creeping shift in the distribution of power towards Brussels. The principle of subsidiarity, it is hoped, if properly enforced, would prevent such a process. In addition, Liberals especially suggest that subsidiarity would actually result in an **increase** in the powers of regional and local government, powers which are being denied to them by national governments at present.

The 'democratic deficit'

Despite the advances made in the influence of the European Parliament under the Single European Act, which are described above, there continues to be concern that the political system of Europe is not democratic enough. This problem has become known as the 'democratic deficit'.

It can be claimed that democracy is served by the fact that all decisions must be ratified by elected ministers from member governments. Since these ministers are accountable to their own peoples, the argument continues, the requirements of democracy are satisfied.

These claims can be challenged on the grounds that the line of accountability is too indirect. Member parliaments and electorates simply cannot maintain vigilance over what their ministers are doing in the Council. It is also pointed out that the unelected Commission, which plays a major role in policy formation and implementation, is not accountable at all.

A more pressing concern than the issue of accountability is the problem of **consent**. In domestic general elections each party produces a manifesto. When a party wins and takes control of government, it has a **mandate** to implement the policies in its manifesto, together with an understanding that it must deal with unforeseen circumstances in accordance with its broad political philosophy. It is the mandate which makes laws **legitimate**. In the European Union the principles of mandate and manifesto are blurred. The directly elected Parliament has no such mandate and, in any case, does not make law. The ministers in the

Council, who **do** make laws, only have a mandate from their own peoples, not from the electorates of other states. Thus, the status of European laws may be uncertain. The former Conservative Cabinet minister Lord Tebbit expressed these concerns at a Young Conservative Conference in 1995:

> *'But we are now drifting – perhaps being driven – into a situation in which more and more people will regard the decrees emanating from Brussels as unjust laws, laws which do not have the consent of the British people and therefore laws without legitimacy which would not be obeyed.'*
> Lord Tebbit, Speech to Young Conservatives, 2 February 1995

Proposals for strengthening European democracy centre largely upon the Parliament, so as to provide the accountability and legitimacy described above. This has two inherent problems, however. First, there is a danger that procedures would become so slow and cumbersome that decision making in the EU would grind to a halt. Secondly, as we already see, the Parliament itself is an unwieldy body, representing a huge electorate of over 350 million and still growing. The widely differing economic interests, political philosophies and cultures represented in the Parliament are difficult to reconcile. Agreement on important issues will always be difficult to achieve. The Council and Commission may be less democratic institutions, but they are, at least, more efficient.

Issues for 1996

What are the questions which will be addressed at the 1996 intergovernmental conference? Some of them were established at the Maastricht Conference in 1992, but others have longer-running histories. The most important questions include the following:

- Is Europe ready to move to a single currency, a process known as **European Monetary Union (EMU)**? The key criterion, identified in 1992, is whether there has been sufficient **convergence** in members' economies. Convergence involves subjective judgements, but implies that inflation rates, wage levels, interest rates and economic growth levels are similar in all states. Once these economic indicators have levelled off, it is argued, there can be a single currency to allow trade on exactly equal terms within the Union.

  In itself, this may not be particularly contentious. More significant, however, is the belief that EMU will result in the necessity for centralised economic and financial policy-making institutions. In particular, it is assumed that a European **central bank** would have to be established to regulate the common currency. Such a bank would inevitably control Union finances and so remove important policy-making powers from member states.

- A **common defence and foreign policy**, with the institutions necessary to develop such a position, has been considered for some time. Piecemeal attempts have already been made to adopt concerted EU military action in a number of crises, notably the Gulf War of 1991 and the Bosnian civil war. These have been largely futile, with patchy or non-existent co-operation by member states. The concept of a permanent apparatus which the Maastricht Treaty envisaged, therefore, appears somewhat utopian at present.

Member states have traditional alliances and views which might be threatened by a common foreign-policy establishment. Austria and Sweden, for example, have retained a position of strict neutrality since World War Two. Britain has strong links with the USA and its Commonwealth allies while Spain, France and Italy all have historically close relations with Mediterranean states. Any of these, or others, might cut across attempts to adopt common European attitudes towards the outside world. If troops have to be committed to action, national interests will become all the more sensitive.

- Maastricht tentatively moved towards the creation of the concept of **European citizenship**. The free movement of citizens of member states within the Union, EU passports and the existence of many common **economic rights** have gone some way to establishing such a reality. However, it is the prospect of an entrenched, enforceable collection of rights and freedoms, common to all European citizens, which now beckons. Currently, individual rights are safeguarded by domestic constitutions, all of which differ, the European Convention on Human Rights, which is not legally binding on all, and a number of Union laws which are limited in scope.

  A European **Bill of Rights**, binding on all member states and enforceable in all courts, European or national, would represent a significant shift in sovereignty away from member states. Nevertheless, there are many Liberals, Social Democrats and other radicals in Europe who wish to see it come about.

- Since 1957 the European Community has grown from just six to fifteen members, with others waiting in the wings. The question of future **widening** of membership will be on the 1996 agenda. Turkish membership depends largely upon improvements in the human rights record of that country. The admission of other countries of western Europe such as Norway is less contentious. It is the central and eastern European states, formerly communist systems, which present a greater problem.

  Part of the difficulty arises from the military and foreign policy issues described above. Many are also concerned, however, that the poor condition of the economies of these countries would represent a severe burden on the more prosperous members. There are some in Britain who would like to see extensions in membership, hoping that this will dilute the power of the Union.

- It is envisaged that further progress will be made towards greater **political union**. In the main, this will be effected by increasing the number of decisions which can be made by a majority of ministers in the Council. Unanimous voting prevents the transfer of power from individual member states to the Union. Majority voting, on the other hand, transfers sovereignty in the opposite direction. Those who wish to see greater political integration will be hoping to extend the scope of qualified majorities. The less enthusiastic countries, such as Britain, may resist such developments.

- The operation of the **Common Agricultural Policy** has come under increasing criticism. Designed to provide protection for farmers, its system of subsidies, quotas and guaranteed prices is seen as a retrogressive device which prevents the operation of a truly free market in food (and indeed fisheries, although there are issues of conservation involved there too). There has been stubborn opposition to reform, especially in France, but countries such as Britain will be determined to persuade enough allies to make significant changes, perhaps even to abolish the CAP.

- **Immigration** to the Union is a sensitive issue. With the free movement of people allowed in Europe, immigrants from anywhere might end up in members' countries, often when they are not wanted. Most states wish to retain the option of closing their borders to unwelcome immigrants. A common immigration policy will, therefore, be difficult to negotiate. Nevertheless, an attempt will be made to settle the issue in 1996.

Britain and Europe

The treaties

Britain's unusual arrangements with regard to foreign treaties creates some confusion over her commitment to them. Normally, treaties are signed by a Head of State which gives **legitimacy** and **permanence** to them. This is not the case in Britain. The prerogative powers of the Crown are exercised by the Government of the day. Thus, treaties are negotiated and ratified only by ministers. Parliament may express a view but is not asked to grant approval.

The problem was illustrated when Britain signed the Maastricht Treaty in 1992. There was a danger that a vote to approve the Treaty in the House of Commons would go against the Government. An alliance of the Labour, nationalist and Ulster Unionist Parties, together with a group of Conservative anti-Europe MPs, threatened defeat for the Government. Foreign Secretary Douglas Hurd made it clear that the Treaty would be ratified even if Parliament did disapprove. It had been agreed under prerogative powers so that parliamentary sovereignty would not apply. In the event, the Government survived the vote, but the incident illustrated the constitutional confusion which exists.

If treaties are negotiated by temporary Governments enjoying temporary majorities, and if they do not need the approval of either Parliament or the people, there is a danger that future Governments will not accept the legitimacy of the treaty in question. Thus, in 1974 the new Labour Government could demand the right to renegotiate Britain's membership terms. In the future a Conservative Government might not approve of agreements on social and industrial policy which Labour has promised to sign if it were to come to power.

It is these concerns which have led to calls, from all parts of the political spectrum, for a **referendum** to approve any major agreements over Europe which affect Britain's sovereignty and vital interests. Popular approval, it is felt, could provide the permanent legitimacy which current arrangements lack.

Europe and Parliament   The **European Communities Act** of 1972 makes it clear that any European law properly agreed in the Council of Ministers **automatically** becomes UK law which must be enforced in British courts. In other words, Parliament does not have the ability to block EU law after it has been passed.

Parliament's role is, therefore, limited to the following functions:

- In general debates, motions, etc, Parliament has an opportunity to express its view on new proposals in Europe. This may exert some influence on ministers in their negotiations with the Council. However, such influence depends upon voting rules in the Council. Those few key decisions which require unanimous approval could be blocked by Parliament if it can persuade the British minister to dig his heels in and exercise a veto. This was, broadly speaking, the case when Britain refused to sign the Social Chapter (providing a number of protective measures for workers) at Maastricht. When a measure requires only a qualified majority, however, Britain's representative cannot veto the proposal alone, so that Parliament's opposition may prove futile.
- A number of committees, but mainly the House of Lords Select Committee on the European Communities with its functional sub-committees, scrutinise proposed European legislation and pass their opinions to ministers. Much of the work is highly specialised and often technical. Ordinary members cannot, therefore, hope to play a significant role.
- Parliament may urge British ministers to campaign for changes to European law. For many years, for example, there has been all-party support for reform of both the Common Agricultural Policy and EU policy on fishing quotas. However, success depends upon the determination of those ministers and their ability to persuade their European colleagues to support them.

Europe and British courts   As we have seen above, European law is British law which must be enforced in domestic courts. Should a citizen or a body wish to appeal against a decision made under European legislation, they must first exhaust all possible remedies in Britain. Thereafter appeals are passed to the **European Court of Justice** for a final ruling. Their judgments are binding on all courts in the UK.

Should there be a conflict between domestic law and European law, as occurred over Britain's discrimination on pension provision between men and women, the latter must always prevail. Courts cannot pick and choose which laws to enforce.

Europe and the British political parties   The Liberal Democrats, Scottish and Welsh nationalists are the only major parties which unequivocally support greater European union. Both the Labour and Conservative Parties are seriously split on the issue.

Labour   The Labour Party has succeeded in keeping its own internal split over Europe under control since the referendum on membership in 1975. Of course, for most of that time it has been in Opposition so that other matters, related to winning back power, have tended to distract the party from European issues. Indeed it is unlikely that internal conflict will break out again before Labour returns to power.

The schism cuts largely along left–moderate lines. It is the socialist wing of the party which is mostly suspicious of further European integration. Their beliefs in the necessity of restoring social justice, as they see it, would be hampered by the need to co-operate with our European partners. For them, the rest of Europe is simply not socialist enough, so Britain must go it alone. Moderates, on the other hand, are prepared to accept the inevitable march towards European union. Many of the measures now being adopted, especially progress towards greater workers' rights, fair wages, better distribution of welfare, consumer protection, industrial competition control and environmental protection, are very much in accord with their own policies. For them Europe is largely social democrat in nature. It is, therefore, an acceptable vehicle for their own aspirations.

The Conservatives   The agenda for internal division was established when Margaret Thatcher made a dramatic speech in **Bruges** (Belgium) in 1988. Alarmed by the intentions of European Commission President, **Jacques Delors**, to speed up progress towards economic and political union, she described the proposals as a prelude to 'a European super-state exercising a new dominance from Brussels'. This Bruges speech (which later spawned an anti-European faction in the party, known as the 'Bruges Group') rallied the Conservative Party's nationalist right wing around the anti-European cause.

As Britain became increasingly isolated in Europe, Margaret Thatcher moved steadily further away from any plans for closer union. In October 1990 she returned from a European Council meeting in Rome and reported her fears to the House of Commons.

> *'The President of the Commission, M. Delors, said at this conference [an EU summit meeting in Rome] the other day that he wanted the European Parliament to be the democratic body of the Community, he wanted the Commission to be the Executive and he wanted the Council of Ministers to be the Senate. No. No. No.'*
> Margaret Thatcher in the House of Commons,
> 30 October 1990

This precipitated the resignation of **Sir Geoffrey Howe**, the Leader of the House of Commons, which in turn led to the leadership contest which Mrs Thatcher subsequently lost.

Since then the Conservative split on Europe steadily widened. An alliance of authoritarian, nationalist right-wingers, who feared loss of sovereignty for Britain, and neo-liberal 'Thatcherites' who saw Brussels as too bureaucratic and socialist, grew up. There are some, such as **Sir Teddy Taylor**, who would have preferred to see Britain leaving the European Union altogether and others, such as **William Cash**, who accepted the benefits of economic union but would not accept political integration.

The pro-Europeans led by **Michael Heseltine** and **Kenneth Clarke**, both Cabinet ministers, were barely able to maintain collective Cabinet responsibility on the issue. They and anti-European Cabinet colleagues, such as **Michael Portillo** and **Jonathan Aitken**, stretched the rules of Cabinet unity to their very limit. So bitter had the issue become, that by 1995 it was threatening the integrity of the Cabinet and the Conservative Party.

Smaller parties   The **Liberal Democrats** are enthusiasts for closer European integration. Though sovereignty would be lost to Brussels, they believe that more effective regional and local government would also result. They strongly support the principle of **subsidiarity** – that decisions should be taken as close to the citizen as possible – and believe Europe can provide this. They also expect that there will be better protection of citizens' rights and environmental control within Europe.

Scottish and Welsh **nationalists** take a similar line to that of the Liberal Democrats. European union, they hope, will free Scotland and Wales from rule by London. While they too would have to grant a good deal of political and legal sovereignty to Brussels, they believe that the power they would gain from London would more than compensate. **Ulster Unionists**, on the other hand, oppose European integration. This, they fear, would loosen Northern Ireland's ties with the British Crown, the retention of which constitutes their main *raison d'être*.

The **Green Party** sees European integration as its main hope for further progress. Green politics are more prominent in Europe than in Britain and there are a number of Green members of the European Parliament, though none from the UK. Indeed many environmental issues, such as toxic emissions, sea pollution, farming methods, conservation and energy production can only be treated at European level.

Europe has never been the major issue at any British general election. In 1996 or 1997 there are some indications that it might well be **the** key issue.

For exam questions relevant to this unit, see page 487.

The meaning of 'ideology'

Before we embark on an investigation of the various world ideologies which have flourished over the past two hundred years, the term 'ideology' itself needs to be clarified.

The original meaning of the expression, coined by the French philosopher **de Maistre** at the end of the eighteenth century, was the 'science of ideas', in essence the study of the dominant ideas and philosophy of the age. People assumed at that time that there was a single discoverable set of ideas which characterised and moulded the society within which they lived. It was, therefore, a relatively uncontroversial term, though it was a revolutionary notion that such a concept as 'ideology' should exist at all.

At the same time, the German philosopher **Hegel** was also stressing the crucial role of great ideas in the study of history, religion and society. Although he preferred the term 'spirit' or 'zeitgeist' (literally 'spirit of the age'), he was certainly referring to a similar concept.

Karl Marx was a follower of Hegel but took a more critical view of ideology. For him, and for all subsequent Marxist thinkers, the ideology which dominated each age was a product of the ruling class's efforts to ensure that it retained its dominant position and was able to oppress 'inferior' classes. Thus, the ideology of **capitalism** and of **liberalism**, which was associated with it, were views of the world promoted by that ruling class. Unlike de Maistre or Hegel, Marx considered an ideology to be a false picture of society, a version which underpinned class rule.

Nowadays the term is used quite differently. Rather than a single dominant view, whether an objective one as Hegel suggested, or a false one as Marx had claimed, we more often use ideology to refer to **any** established, coherent political philosophy. Thus, there can be more than one ideology in common currency at any time. If a set of political ideas includes the following:

- firm beliefs about the nature of man and society
- a clear set of values which may guide political action
- a coherent vision of how society should be organised,

it may then be described as an 'ideology'. Beliefs held by individuals or political parties which are less precise than this should not be described as ideologies. Rather, they are merely philosophies or perhaps doctrines.

Thus, we may describe socialism, feminism, Marxism itself or even 'Thatcherism' as modern ideologies which compete with each other and which attract large numbers of followers. All may claim to be an accurate view of the world, but, as objective observers, we may take a more detached attitude and see them as competing sets of beliefs which contain both clear truths and mere theories.

Communism

Introduction

Though most people associate the term 'communism' with Marxism, **Karl Marx** (1818–83) himself did not 'invent' it. He drew his inspiration for the name from some of the more radical elements during the French Revolution of fifty years or so earlier. Indeed, the basic **principles** of communism can be traced still further back in history. The English 'diggers' of the mid seventeenth century, for example, organised land sharing and social equality very much along Marxist lines. During the nineteenth century, too, the 'Narodnik' movement stirred up the Russian peasantry, encouraging them to seize and redistribute land among themselves.

It should further be stressed that, in the middle of the nineteenth century when Marx was writing, anarchism was growing in popularity, especially in Germany, France and Russia. The anarchists themselves, as we shall see below, were often described as 'communists'. It was not until the 1870s, when Marx split with the great anarchist revolutionary, **Mikhail Bakunin** (1814–76), that Marxism and anarchism could be fully distinguished. At that time communism referred to the practice of setting up small-scale, self-governing communes, with common ownership of property, internal democracy and economic equality. If we adhere strictly to this definition, as Bakunin himself argued, Marx was not really a communist at all! Nevertheless, when the workers of Paris set up their own government in 1871 just as the city was about to fall to the invading Prussian army, and called it the **Paris Commune**, their main inspiration was Marx. Thus, Marxism and communism have become almost synonymous.

Since regimes calling themselves 'communist', 'socialist' or 'people's republic' have all claimed to be based upon the ideology developed by Marx, any study of communism must begin with an analysis of his philosophy.

The historical analysis

<u>Economic determinism</u> All societies, argued Marx, have their own distinctive economic structure. By this he meant the manner in which the production and distribution of goods was organised. This might involve such questions as who owned land and who did not. How was the land held – was it owned or rented? How were goods sold? Who controlled other forms of production? How was trade organised? It was this economic structure which determined the whole character of society. Its political system, its ideology and dominant beliefs, its social structure and even its religion were all determined by economics. Thus, he was an 'economic determinist'. Once one understood the nature of a society's economic 'infrastructure', one could understand the whole of that society.

> 'The history of humanity must therefore always be studied and treated in relation to the history of industry and exchange.'
> Karl Marx, *The German Ideology*

<u>Dialectic materialism</u> Marx made a detailed empirical (that is, with reference to observable events and processes) study of the processes of historical change. He argued that history moves in discernible cycles. These cycles or 'epochs' may last for hundreds of years. At the beginning of a cycle there is a state of **harmony**. The organisation of production and distribution, and the economic relationships which arise from

production do not contain conflicts in such a state of harmony. When great civilisations in the past reached their height, such stability could be recognised, as in the classical Greek and Roman periods.

However, as such societies mature, they develop internal conflicts, or **contradictions**. Put simply, this results in the interests of one or more **social class** coming into conflict with the interests of other classes. In general, Marx suggested that there is always one small dominant **ruling class** and another large **exploited class**. There may be other smaller social classes but they are of less significance. At first, the exploited class does not appreciate its position and, indeed, believes it is benefiting from the economic system. But it is inevitable that exploitation increases and intensifies. As this occurs, the exploited class becomes aware of its true situation. The result is growing social conflict.

The class conflict, or 'contradictions', which arise sooner or later in all societies is known as a 'dialectic' process. That is, one sector in a society is confronted by its own opposite, or 'negation'. In this case, the ruling class is confronted by the exploited class whose interests are totally opposed to its own. The ever-increasing clash of class interests is, thus, a 'dialectic process'. Eventually, the conflict becomes so intense and violent that the whole system collapses. A new order is ultimately established, with a new harmony. But the whole process then begins again. Since these changes are taking place within the **material** economic world (as opposed to the world of ideas, philosophy and religion), it is known as **dialectic materialism**.

> 'The history of all hitherto existing society is the history of class struggles.'
> Karl Marx and Friedrich Engels, *The Communist Manifesto* (1848)

All the other phenomena which we can observe in a society – its religious conflicts, political events, wars, civil wars, revolutions and rebellions – are merely **reflections** of the economic, material conflict taking place all the time. Thus, Marx claimed to be a truly **scientific** historian, claiming that he understood the true processes of history. He maintained that others merely observed the superficial changes taking place and analysed them in unscientific ways. Indeed, he went on to charge historians with explaining history in such a way as to justify the position of the ruling class. Marx viewed history very much from the point of view of 'exploited' classes.

The feudal age – a Marxist model

Productive system	Class structure	Politics and religion	Contradictions
A hierarchy of land tenure, with land granted in return for a proportion of its output or duties such as military service Trade carried on for the sale of surplus production in towns, including imports and exports	A ruling class made up of the monarch, aristocracy and feudal nobility An exploited class of peasants or serfs A small class of yeomen or independent small farmers An additional small class of merchants and craftsmen	Absolute monarchy ruling with the support of the aristocracy Mostly Catholic or related churches, teaching the importance of obedience and the worthiness of poverty and meekness Dominant philosophy is 'conservative' stressing the need for order and a natural hierarchy	Exploitation of serfs becomes intolerable resulting in increasing revolts and unrest. Food production becomes inadequate under feudal conditions Traders and merchants become more economically significant, challenging aristocratic power Emerging primitive capitalism cannot operate in a feudal environment. Result is outbreak of 'bourgeois' revolutions

The analysis of capitalism

Marx applied the same principles of analysis to the capitalist age (at the height of which he lived and worked), just as he had done for all other historical epochs. Productive forces and economic relations were its basis. The class structure was typical, and progress towards its demise was predictable.

Before describing Marx's analysis, it should be stressed that he was observing capitalism in the middle of the nineteenth century, largely as it operated in Britain, the most advanced industrial country of the day. The nature of capitalism has changed markedly since then. Some would say that the changes have been so radical that Marx's analysis is no longer valid. Nevertheless, it forms the basis of the philosophy of subsequent Marxism and is therefore essential to an understanding of the ideology.

Class under capitalism   There are two great classes. The **bourgeoisie** own and control all the means of production, that is, the factories, mines, workshops, banks, etc. These 'capitalists' are the ruling class who also control the dominant ideology, religion and political system of capitalism. The **proletariat**, or working class, own none of the means of production. They must sell their labour to the bourgeoisie in return for money wages. For Marx, this is the exploited class.

Marx identified a smaller class – that of the **petit bourgeois** – consisting of those who earn their living independently, such as individual craftsmen, professionals, tradesmen and merchants. These, he suggested, were relatively insignificant, but, more importantly, would be absorbed into the other great classes. This process was known as **class polarisation**. As more and more people are drawn into the two great economic classes, the antagonism between them would intensify.

The class system on the land, the remnants of the dying feudal age, was of less concern to Marx. The landlords, or **rentier** class, were losing their economic and political power and would continue to do so. The **peasants**, another exploited class but with less revolutionary potential than the industrial working class, would ultimately attempt to free themselves, but their fortunes were of less concern to him than those of the proletariat.

It was a key element of Marx's criticism of capitalism that the interests of the two main classes would come increasingly into conflict. This would occur as capitalism developed and became more productive.

Surplus value Capitalism extracts from its workers a surplus value, argued Marx. The system is organised so that the worker is paid only a fraction of the true value of his own production. The rest is surplus value, which is expropriated, or stolen, by the capitalists. Furthermore, as the productive capacity of capitalism increases, and the value of workers' output grows, the degree of surplus also increases. The worker does not, however, benefit.

Wages were determined in free labour markets. These markets ensured, claimed Marx, that wages remained at subsistence (minimum) or certainly very low levels. This was guaranteed by the fact that workers would compete with each other for scarce jobs and so employers could pay low wages. A permanent pool of the unemployed, women and even children was maintained to ensure that workers who claimed higher wages could always be replaced. Thus, even though workers' productivity constantly increased, wages did not. The degree of surplus value extracted steadily grew.

It was largely this fact, however, which sounded the death knell of capitalism. As the exploitation of workers increased, and the gap in living standards between the classes widened, the proletariat would become steadily more aware of the nature of that exploitation. The overthrow of the ruling class by the oppressed class would surely follow.

Alienation The term alienation is not exclusive to Marxism. It refers to any state of mind where an individual feels that the world around him is strange and alien to him; he is not at home in it; it confronts him as something hostile and threatening. In Marxist analysis, particularly, it referred to the condition of workers under capitalism.

For Marx, the activity of labour is central to man's existence – it is his 'life force'. Under capitalism he is forced to sell his labour to somebody else. Thus, it is no longer his own, but has been exchanged for money. Furthermore, the workers have no personal interest in the goods they are producing, often being unable to afford to buy them. The **division of labour**, whereby workers become increasingly specialised in the productive process, adds to the alienation, since the worker is further separated from what he is producing. Thus, herded into factories, mines and offices to produce goods and services at the behest of the capitalist, having no control over production or financial rewards, workers are alienated in the workplace. For Marx, this was the principal evil of capitalism. Modern Marxists believe much the same, while suggesting that the precise nature of the alienation has changed under modern conditions.

> *'The worker feels himself at home only during his leisure, whereas at work he feels homeless. His work is not voluntary but imposed, forced labour. It is not the satisfaction of a need, but only a means for satisfying other needs.'*
> Karl Marx, *Economic and Philosophical Manuscripts*

The capitalist state   Every epoch has its own particular form of state, but all have one feature in common, argued Marx. The state is always the agent of the ruling class. Its main purpose is to maintain class rule. This is an easy concept to understand when considering absolute monarchies, or the oligarchies of wealthy citizens which governed the classical world. Less clear, however, is the charge laid against representative democracy – the typical kind of state operating in capitalist societies. Of course, at the time Marx was writing, universal suffrage was extremely rare. Voting normally carried a property or income qualification. Thus, it was understandable that he should claim that this represented merely bourgeois rule under the guise of democracy. Marx's claims, however, have been transferred to political systems where the working classes were granted the vote.

> *'The State is the form in which the individuals of a ruling class assert their common interest.'*
> Karl Marx, *The German Ideology*

For Marx, democracy as a whole was a charade. The real apparatus of the state – its bureaucracy, legal system, armed forces and police – were the truly permanent instruments of class rule. Their role was to maintain the status quo and ensure the continued oppression of the exploited class. Passing governments were of no lasting significance. It followed from this analysis that if capitalism were to be destroyed, so too must the state which supports it be swept away.

The destruction of capitalism   Marx was largely a **determinist**. He asserted that there are social and economic forces which are beyond man's control. He is, therefore, not in control of his own future. But the same uncontrolled forces which sustained capitalism, he insisted, would also destroy it. Capitalism contained the seeds of its own destruction – principally the exploited working class – and these seeds would steadily grow into a lethal force. Thus he identified a clear road to revolution.

Class consciousness   In the early stages of capitalism, the proletariat were not aware of the position in which they found themselves. They saw themselves as individuals, in competition with each other for scarce employment and wages. They did not understand that they might have common interests. As their exploitation intensified, however, **social solidarity** began to grow. The common experience of exploitation would breed class consciousness. This involved both an understanding of the nature of their oppression and the appreciation that there was more to bind them than divide them.

The symptoms of growing class consciousness were the formation of trade unions, frequency of strikes and demonstrations and political agitation. At first, the state was able to contain such unrest, but capitalism, he suggested, could not prevent its own development which brought with it greater exploitation and, therefore, deeper working-class consciousness.

The crises of capitalism Marx foresaw the passage of capitalism through a number of stages leading to its final end. It suffers from an inherent tendency to over-produce, he observed. This led to periods of falling prices and profits, unemployment and declining wages. The working classes, faced with these slumps, would naturally become increasingly discontented. The true nature of capitalism would be increasingly apparent to them.

Intense competition for scarce markets among capitalists would lead to two further developments. First, countries would seek to create or expand empires abroad. Secondly, a series of wars would ensue, both for control of these empires and directly as a result of market rivalry. As an ultimate irony, the working classes would be asked to fight and risk their lives defending a system which exploits them. The Franco-Prussian War of 1870–71 was just such an example. World War One represents the most dramatic example to illustrate Marx's predictions.

Booms and slumps, increasing in intensity, wars and imperial rivalry, growing unrest among the working classes, would all be signs of the impending final crisis of capitalism.

Revolution As class consciousness grew among the proletariat, the development of revolutionary parties, and some bourgeois intellectuals joining the working-class cause, represented the prelude to revolution. Marx was certain that the ultimate revolution would be a violent one since the capitalist state, he believed, would defend itself with all the coercive forces at its command. He suggested that Britain, possessing the most mature democracy in the world, might achieve a transition to socialism by peaceful, democratic means, but in other cases only bloody revolt would destroy capitalism.

> 'The communist revolution . . . abolishes all class rule, along with the classes themselves.'
>
> Karl Marx, *The German Ideology*

There has been controversy surrounding Marx's revolutionary theory. Some argue that he believed it to be inevitable. Others, however, suggest that this was not so. Rather, the **conditions** for revolution would certainly arise, but it would require the organised efforts of leading members of the proletariat to overthrow the state. Should the latter be true, it can go some way to explaining why so few capitalist states were destroyed. If the working class failed to organise, the state could perhaps survive.

The dictatorship of the proletariat

Possibly the most controversial aspect of Marx's theories concerns his vision of the post-revolutionary world. He insisted that society could not move directly to communism. There would, instead, be a transitional phase. This he describes as the **dictatorship of the proletariat** or the **socialist** phase.

The old capitalist state would be replaced by a new state, charged with the task of building first socialism and then creating the conditions for the transition to a communist society. All states are instruments of class rule, Marx asserted. This would be no exception. The formerly oppressed class would become the rulers. They would now oppress the old ruling class – the bourgeoisie. The powers of the new workers' state would be used for this purpose. This form of socialist state, apparently lacking in democratic institutions, individual liberties or any pluralist institutions, was to characterise the practical application of communism for over seventy years after the Russian Revolution.

Marx intended that the dictatorship of the proletariat would persist until the last remnants of capitalism had been abolished and, even more importantly, all forms of 'bourgeois consciousness' had disappeared. In other words, society would have become totally classless, without private property and with no possibility of capitalist tendencies re-emerging. Then, and only then, would the state be able to 'wither away'. Complete economic equality would exist and all the means of production would be in common ownership. Without the need for any government or coercion, each would receive rewards according to need and all would contribute freely to society without the need of compulsion. Communism would then ensue.

The nature of communism

Marx is less clear about the nature of communism. His description of communism is full of generalities and lacking in practicalities. A number of clear features do, however, emerge from his work:

- All property (though not personal possessions) would be in common ownership.
- There would be no classes as every individual would have the same relationship to the means of production.
- There would be no political state. Thus, there would be no coercive power in the form of law enforcement or sovereign government.
- Rewards would be distributed strictly on the basis of equality.
- The division of labour would cease to exist. Every individual would be free to choose his occupation, avoid specialisation and possibly even undertake a number of different occupations at the same time.
- Problems of alienation would have disappeared.
- Communism would contain no internal contradictions. Thus, the dialectic process of history would be at an end. The communist epoch would last for the foreseeable future.

It should be noted that those states which espoused the Marxist creed often referred to themselves as 'communist'. Their systems, however, clearly did not conform to Marx's description of communism. In fact, the term 'communist' was used to express long-term goals. In reality, all these states were in fact in the 'socialist' phase of development.

The Soviet experiment

<u>V.I. Lenin (1870–1924)</u> In 1917 Lenin led the first successful revolution which was openly inspired by Marxist theory. Yet this revolution took place in a largely peasant-based, neo-feudal society. There was a small industrial working class in a population dominated mostly by poor peasants. Capitalism was still in its early stages. It was true that

there was a powerful, autocratic state under tsarist rule and the small proletariat which existed were certainly treated badly by their employers. Russia was also heavily involved in a war which, in terms of Marxist analysis, was a symptom of competition between capitalist powers. Yet these were far from the conditions which Marx had described as the prelude to revolution. Much of Lenin's contribution to Marxist thought was, therefore, to explain how socialism, and ultimately communism, could be established in such an undeveloped economy. Broadly, his justifications for such a revolution were as follows:

- Marx had underestimated the ability of a well-organised, professional revolutionary party to overthrow the state even when the 'classic' conditions for the destruction of capitalism were absent. In other words, Lenin was more of a 'voluntarist' than Marx, insisting that men can take control of their own destiny.
- His theory of **imperialism**, a truly original contribution to Marxism, saw the world increasingly divided into exploiting and exploited nations. Russia was one of the latter countries and so might never develop a fully capitalist system. Only by striking quickly could the Russian workers prevent this development. Simply waiting for economic progress to take its course would prove futile.
- Third World Marxists were particularly influenced by his concept of **uneven development**. This suggested that countries could move towards socialism at any stage of their economic development. As long as there were large exploited classes – mainly peasants and workers – they should take control of events and overthrow their oppressors. Thereafter socialism could be built alongside industrialisation and the new workers' state. The industrial proletariat was always, for Lenin, the principal vehicle for socialist development, but this did not disqualify other classes from revolutionary activity.

The more controversial elements of Lenin's career concern his political beliefs and actions. He created a state in Russia on the principles of **democratic centralism**. Originally, this was designed to be a two-way flow of power and influence. A party hierarchy was formed, with free access for anyone who wished to be politically active. Each level would nominate members to represent them at the higher level. This continued up to the top level – later to be known as the **Politbureau** – at which all key national decisions were to be made. The demands and interests of the people, as long as they conformed to broad socialist principles, were to be passed up through the system. However, once decisions at the higher levels were made, they were imposed on society strictly. Thus, he envisaged a combination of a **workers' democracy** and the **dictatorship of the proletariat**.

As events in Russia unfolded and Lenin was beset by economic and political problems, the system evolved into a mere dictatorship. Influence from below was steadily cut off and, instead, the leading members of the party simply imposed their policies on Russian society. The government – a hierarchy of committees or 'soviets', which were theoretically democratic – was steadily brought under the ruthless control of the Communist Party. The notorious Soviet form of dictatorship was virtually in place by the time Lenin died in 1924.

It remains an open question whether Lenin intended to create the autocratic, oppressive regime which the Soviet Union became, or whether he was a sincere democrat who was forced to adopt temporary authoritarian methods to overcome his country's immediate problems. Whichever is true, his successor, Joseph Stalin, completed the development of a totalitarian regime which had begun to emerge under Lenin.

<u>Joseph Stalin (1879–1953)</u> After Lenin's death, Stalin engaged in a long-drawn-out struggle for power with his rivals in the Communist Party, notably Leon Trotsky. By 1927 he was in control. The very method by which he achieved power established a political feature of the Soviet Union which was to attract a good deal of criticism. There was no open, democratic competition for power in which large sections of the population could take part. Instead, there was a closed, secretive struggle among a few leaders about whom little was known. The Soviet Union was to retain its undemocratic methods of transferring power until the late 1980s.

The system which was ultimately to become known as 'Stalinism' included the following features, all of which were the personal creation of Stalin:

- **Socialism in one country** was Stalin's description of his belief that the Soviet Union must protect itself at all costs from the antagonism of the capitalist world. Its principal role was to build socialism, ensure that it outdid capitalism in terms of production and developed sufficient military strength to protect itself. Rather than actively supporting revolutions in other parts of the world, the Soviet Union was to provide a perfect 'model' for other working-class movements to emulate. So he cut the country off from the outside world, adopting an inward-looking, isolationist approach to world affairs.
- Stalin preferred **bureaucratic rule** to democratic institutions. Unelected officials, or bureaucrats, could be easily controlled by ensuring that they operated to set procedures imposed from above. Politicians, on the other hand, could be influenced from below and so become unreliable. Thus, he created a hugely bureaucratic state, unresponsive to the demands of the people, but strictly under party control.
- He was determined that his own position as party leader and, therefore, his country's **absolute** ruler, should not be challenged. He saw himself as the pure embodiment of orthodox Marxist thought. Thus, the fortunes of the working class and the future road to communism were in his hands. Those who opposed him were branded as **revisionists**, enemies of socialism and the working class. The party was regularly purged to ensure absolute obedience to its leader.
- The population was kept under control through the use of **terror** – the public use of force, propaganda achieved by total control of the media and the use of an extensive secret police to root out any signs of dissidence.
- The position of the **peasantry** was a major problem for Stalin. Like Lenin before him, Stalin mistrusted them, often describing them as basically petit bourgeois in outlook. He suspected that most of them were only interested in acquiring their own land and working it for their own benefit. He did not accept that they might become true

socialists in the way that industrial workers could. His answer was to introduce enforced **collectivisation** of the land. Land was organised into huge collective farms which employed peasants as though they were factory workers. The total product of the collective farms belonged to the state and the workers were paid a wage. No peasant was allowed to own his own land. The disruption and ruthlessness of this process led to millions of deaths in the 1930s, but it solved the problem of how to control the Soviet Union's masses.

The notorious Stalinist regime brooked no internal opposition and no alternative interpretation of the works of Marx and Lenin, but it did have one implacable enemy – Leon Trotsky.

<u>Leon Trotsky (1879–1940)</u> Trotsky was one of Lenin's closest associates and, many say, his chosen political heir. But Stalin defeated him in the struggle for power which followed Lenin's death. He was exiled and ultimately assassinated by a Stalinist agent in Mexico in 1940. While in exile, he maintained a campaign of criticism of the Stalinist system. For those who professed to be Marxists, but could not stomach the excesses of Stalinism, Trotsky became a hero. He was to inspire communists from the 1930s to the 1980s.

Much of his thought was in diametric opposition to Stalinism. His principal ideas included the following:

- The communist revolution should not be a single event, but a longer process wherein various aspects of capitalism and bourgeois thought would be attacked. He termed this proposal 'permanent revolution'. Stalin, by contrast, had created a static political system which had ceased to develop. Indeed, many of the evils of capitalism had re-emerged, such as the oppressive state, alienation of workers, an unfair wage system and the creation of a new ruling class – the party elite.
- Instead of 'socialism in one country', with an inward-looking, isolated Soviet Union, Trotsky urged **world revolution**. Unless the capitalist world were to be converted to socialism, its intense opposition to the Soviet Union would ultimately prevail. The task of the Soviet Communist Party must, therefore, be to sponsor revolution wherever possible. Thus, revolution was to be permanent and universal.
- Trotsky described Stalin's proposed road to socialism as 'socialism from above', that is, it was imposed by the ruling party elite. He preferred 'revolution from below'. Here the spontaneous actions and demands of the masses should be involved in building socialism. He accepted popular democracy as a positive force. Stalin had feared and therefore suppressed it.

    The bureaucratic 'monster' which Stalin created in the Soviet Union was a denial of real proletarian democracy, Trotsky insisted. He added that the workers must govern themselves. The faceless machine of the Soviet state created a form of alienation as damaging as anything capitalism had produced.

Trotsky's popular version of socialist revolution and his rejection of any limits to action were attractive to New Left communists of the 1960s and beyond. The notion that all alienated groups – including workers, the young, ethnic minorities, the poor, oppressed women and Third World peasants – could have a role to play in overthrowing capitalism was preferable to the undynamic Stalinist world of orthodoxy and strict adherence to the political line set by a ruling party elite.

Other modern Marxists Outside the Soviet Union, Marxist-inspired communists were developing alternative applications of the basic philosophy. The persistence of capitalism after the Russian Revolution, and a number of other failed socialist revolts which followed it, required new explanations and there was no shortage of them. Some are described below:

Antonio Gramsci (1891–1937) The founder of the Italian Communist Party, Gramsci sought to explain why capitalism had not collapsed when Marxist theory suggested it should. He identified two particular reasons for its survival.

First, capitalism had learned to **control its own development**; it had not, as Marx suggested, simply intensified its exploitation of the proletariat to the point where it was bound to be overthrown. Instead, capitalists were able to head off revolution by avoiding the worst excesses of industrialisation. Popular democracy, tolerance of trade unions, improved wages and some social reforms were introduced. When democracy failed to prevent the advance of socialism and communism, capitalism developed a distortion of itself in the form of fascism.

Secondly, his theory of cultural **hegemony** analysed the very deep hold bourgeois ideas were able to exert upon working-class consciousness. Through the institutions which transmit cultural values – schools, the arts, the media and the political system itself – capitalist ideas were rooted deeply into society. They exerted a domination, or hegemony, over the industrial workers. To combat this hegemony, Gramsci, along with the contemporary **Council Communist** movement, urged the setting up of workers' councils, educational institutions and other cultural organisations to counter bourgeois culture. After its hold had been loosened, progress could be made towards revolution.

Gramsci's ideas were somewhat discredited after the defeat of fascism and the restoration of liberal democracy through most of the capitalist world. Interest in them revived, however, within the New Left movement of the 1960s and 1970s. Gramsci provided a cogent explanation for capitalism's durability as well as pathways towards its future destruction. The creation of 'counter-cultures' within capitalist societies was inspired in part by his writings.

Mao Tse-tung (1893–1976) Mao led an extensive peasant communist movement in China between 1928 and 1949, at which time his forces overthrew the weak and corrupt nationalist Government. He was partly a land reformer working among discontented peasants, and partly a Marxist. But his modifications of Marx's ideas proved so radical that 'Marxist' was scarcely an accurate description. He was, however, broadly a 'communist', as he supported the self-sufficient commune, with common ownership of land as the ideal form of economic organisation.

His main contributions to communist thought are shown below:

- In any society the most exploited class is the most revolutionary. Thus, in societies such as that of China, the peasants were the true vehicles of the revolution. By the same token, the principal enemies of the people were the landlords who exploited the peasants.

- Although the Communist Party must play a leading role in society, it should maintain close links with the people, be guided by them as well as guiding them, and avoid becoming separated from them and over-bureaucratic.
- Whereas Lenin and Stalin had insisted that only leading members of the Communist Party could interpret and impose Marxist theory, Mao believed that the masses, if broadly guided, could develop true social solidarity spontaneously. Instead of the sullen, obedient population which Stalin commanded, Mao encouraged a highly volatile, enthusiastic and sometimes violent reaction to social problems among the masses. Unfortunately, his mass campaigns frequently ran totally out of control!
- Third World societies are all subject to direct political or indirect economic imperialism, Mao observed. There must, therefore, be a constant struggle by communists against domination by foreign, capitalist powers. In China itself, he saw the external threat of Western powers such as Britain and the USA as more dangerous than internal revisionism.
- Although he had a warm relationship with China's masses, Mao was a ruthless dictator. Despite his anti-bureaucratic, anti-elitist and anti-intellectual ideas, he would brook no opposition to his personal rule. Like Stalin, he claimed to be the ultimate embodiment of true communism.

Mao's faith in the revolutionary potential of the peasantry and his awareness of the dangers of Western imperialism ensured that he became an inspirational figure for Third World communist movements. In addition, his experience and writings on guerrilla warfare tactics became guides for those carrying out communist actions in Asia, Africa and South America.

Frantz Fanon (1925–61) In addition to Mao, Fanon, a French West Indian, proved to be a champion for Third World Marxists. He, too, recognised the international power of capitalist imperialism and believed that freedom fighters should, therefore, concentrate on undermining its hold as well as seeking to overthrow colonial and post-colonial governments which encouraged imperial penetration of their countries.

Fanon also analysed the nature of the developed world's exploitation of poorer countries. He revealed the complex trade and financial systems through which Third World countries were exploited. Indeed, he pointed out, the proletarians of the developed world, far from feeling themselves exploited, threw in their lot with their capitalist masters. They now believed that their best interests lay in co-operating with capitalism's international conspiracy against the exploited masses in Africa and Asia. Thus, the revolutionaries of the future would be not the industrial workers of developed capitalist countries – the classical Marxist model – but what he called the 'wretched of the earth' – the Third World peasantry.

The synthesis of intense nationalism – the struggle against imperialism – and socialism, which Mao and Fanon advocated, was to be the main inspiration for movements led by revolutionaries such as **Fidel Castro** in Cuba and **Ho Chi Minh** in Vietnam. It was also popular among Western Marxists since, like Gramsci, Fanon provided an alternative way forward to replace the traditional models of revolution provided by Marx.

Herbert Marcuse (1906–79) The left-wing-inspired youth protest movements of the late 1960s and early 1970s acknowledged a number of 'gurus', among whom Marcuse was a leading example. He moved further away from traditional Marxist analysis of capitalist society. He de-emphasised the role of class – a central feature of Marxist ideology – developing instead a theory of **mass society**.

According to Marcuse, all parts of society have become exploited, as consumers as well as workers. He described capitalism's control of society as a new type of totalitarianism. The political form of totalitarianism – fascism – had failed, but been replaced by a more subtle, economic and psychological type of control. He argued that we adopt lifestyles and consumption patterns which have been created for us by capitalism's need to produce more and more. Our lifestyles are not, therefore, of our own choosing; we are manipulated and exploited. Thus, there is still alienation under capitalism, but of a different, more sinister form than had existed before.

Marcuse was pessimistic about the prospects of overthrowing capitalism and the society of the masses. He therefore suggested that individuals must seek to liberate themselves by choosing their own, distinctive lifestyles. In the age of sexual liberation and hallucinatory drugs, these ideas were, understandably, popular among young radicals.

The decline of communism

The destruction of the Soviet political system which **Mikhail Gorbachev** set in motion in the mid 1980s, led to a 'domino effect', causing one communist regime after another to collapse, to be replaced by more liberal democratic forms of government. At the same time, the centralised, planned socialist economies in such states have been largely dismantled and transformed, fully or partially, into capitalist states. In short, Marxism appears to be in full retreat.

Some modern socialist writers, such as **Ralph Miliband** and **Nicos Poulantzas**, have always argued that capitalism continues to be an exploitative system, disguised by the façade of liberal institutions. It follows that, although communist regimes are in decline throughout the world, Marxist-inspired socialism is still relevant. However, there can be little doubt that, at the end of the twentieth century, communism is largely an historical phenomenon. It is an open question as to whether it may re-emerge in the future.

Anarchism

Introduction

The term 'anarchy' literally means 'an absence of government'. It does not mean, as many might suppose, 'a state of chaos'. We often use the word to mean disorder, but this is a distortion of the real philosophy known as anarchism. Nor does anarchism automatically imply violence. The image of the bomb-throwing or gun-wielding assassin actually represents very few anarchists.

Rather, as we have observed above, anarchists are, on the whole, essentially communists who have a well-developed sense of order and peace. It is true that many anarchists have been revolutionaries, but for them violence is merely a means to a peaceful end. It is also true that there have been violent anarcho-individualists who have wreaked havoc in civilised society and attracted much hostile attention. But these are a minority, most of whom can be described as 'nihilists'. The analysis shown below will concentrate on mainstream, social forms of anarchism – a **positive** rather than a negative philosophy.

Basic principles <u>The nature of man</u> No understanding of anarchism can be achieved without prior comprehension of how anarchists see the basic nature of mankind.

> *'From his birth not a single human being is either good or bad.'*
> Mikhail Bakunin

There are four different conceptions of natural man to be found among the prominent exponents of anarchism:

- The most common view is that man is basically good, sociable and displays natural empathy towards his fellow human beings. The fact that he does not always do so is because imperfect societies have corrupted him.
- Similar to this is the notion that man is born neither good nor bad. He is, rather, a **tabula rasa**, a blank sheet upon which any characteristics may be inscribed by the social environment. Thus, if he lives in a corrupted society, he will be corrupt, while in a good society he will be good.
- Less optimistic anarchists have suggested that man has two sides to his natural character. On the one hand, he is egotistical and individualistic; on the other, he is sociable and sympathetic to others. Such characteristics give rise to co-operation and mutual aid.
- The most radical anarchist philosophers suggest man is a pure egotist. For these 'nihilists' any form of social organisation is unnatural to mankind and cannot, therefore, be justified.

The first three conceptions all have in common the hope that man is perfectible. Either he is naturally good and simply needs to be returned to such a natural state, or he possesses the **capacity** to be good and sociable if a perfect social order can be established. Only the nihilists and extreme anarcho-individualists take a pessimistic view of the possibility of the creation of a truly 'communist' society.

<u>Freedom</u> As with liberalism, anarchists see individual liberty as a key value, so much so that some have claimed that anarchism is simply an extreme form of liberalism. This is to misunderstand the anarchist conception of freedom, which is fundamentally different to that of liberalism.

Liberals distinguish carefully between **licence** and **freedom**. 'Licence' refers to a state where there are absolutely no restrictions on human action. In these circumstances, they argue, there is no true freedom since the exercise of licence by one person will inevitably lead to interference with the actions of others. A simple example concerns private property. As soon as one person claims some land for himself, he deprives another person of enjoyment of that same land. The problem becomes particularly acute when land is scarce. To deal with it liberals argue that there must be legal regulation of property distribution and ownership.

Thus, 'freedom' can only exist where people operate within laws which protect them from each other. A person can only be **free** to enjoy his property if it is protected from encroachment by others. This gives rise to an apparent paradox. In order to be truly free, mankind must accept restrictions. Of course, liberals argue that this is an acceptable trade-off. In addition, the laws must be openly agreed by the people, so that there is full **consent** to the restrictions. Anarchists reject this proposition. They argue instead that there need be no distinction between licence and freedom.

Anarchists start from the basic premise that man, in a natural, uncorrupted state, will **not** interfere with the liberty of others. Furthermore, he would deal with such problems as scarcity through natural co-operation and equality, rather than through legally controlled competition. Returning to the problem of private property, for example, anarchists believe that **common** and not **private** ownership is natural. Thus, laws regulating the ownership of property should not be needed at all. Freedom for the anarchist consists of **private judgement**, the individual making his own decisions concerning his conduct. If the social conditions can be created within which such private judgement conforms to **natural law**, there is no need for artificial, man-made laws.

'Social solidarity is the first human law; freedom is the second.'
Mikhail Bakunin

Liberals have a similar conception of natural law – the way in which individuals would behave in a natural state – to that of anarchists. Both philosophies suggest that mutual respect and tolerance, justice, the protection of life and the importance of co-operation to overcome social and economic problems are natural. The difference lies in how such natural laws can be applied. Liberals argue that they must be enshrined in human laws, underpinned by coercion. Anarchists maintain that if mankind is morally perfected, everyone will follow natural laws without compulsion. It is possibly this particular aspect of the anarchist philosophy which has been most often criticised as **utopian** and, therefore, unattainable.

The anarchist critique of modern society

The state Since anarchists insist on the creation of a free society in which all may exercise private judgement, there can be no place for the state in their philosophy. The fundamental purpose of the state is to concentrate coercive power in its institutions in order to enforce laws (even though they may represent the genuine will of the people). Indeed, no man has the right to exercise power in any form over another man. Some anarchists shared the Marxist analysis of the state as the means by which a ruling class is able to maintain its dominant position. Nevertheless, it was the anarchist insistence on the complete removal of any form of state which was the main cause of their split with the Marxists around 1870.

'Anarchy means the government of each by himself.'
Pierre-Joseph Proudhon

Laws Since laws restrict the anarchist conception of freedom, as we have seen above, they clearly could not be justified. Liberals counter this argument by suggesting that, if laws are the result of a freely made agreement among men, nobody can claim to have been coerced. Yet **social contract theory**, as this is usually described, is also not accepted by anarchists. The individual cannot be coerced by the group to which he belongs, even when there is unanimous agreement. There is no guarantee that he will always agree and he may, at the outset, have been unduly influenced by others.

This is not to say that anarchists reject law as a concept. For them, it is a natural phenomenon, not an artificial creation. Either man is born with the sense of natural law which limits his activities, or he will be forced to obey social laws which are necessary to his survival and well-being. In both cases, he should know or learn how to act spontaneously. He should not be coerced.

Private property For many anarchists the existence of private property is both the most corrupting influence upon human society and the root of a number of other evils which have emerged since the first time a man placed a barrier around some land and claimed it as his own. Again, there is a sharp contrast with liberalism here as the latter sees ownership and enjoyment of private property as a basic right.

The anarchist view is that the idea of private property is **not** natural and runs contrary to natural law. Furthermore, its existence gives rise to laws which are needed to protect that property. The need for laws also necessitates the existence of the state to enforce them. Private property also provides opportunities for those who possess it to exploit those who are propertyless.

There is a sense that all the fruits of nature belong to all mankind collectively. Thus, common ownership of all resources is natural, as is equal distribution of the rewards gained from it.

Artificial communities Modern societies, argue the anarchists, have created a number of artificial groupings into which man is forced to gather. The industrial factory system clearly herded workers together into artificial working communities, but it also gave rise to the proliferation of cities, another unnatural phenomenon. On a larger scale, even the concept of 'nation' was criticised by most anarchists. It is understandable that the political manifestation of nations – the state – should be condemned as coercive, but the nation appears at first sight to be natural. Not so, they suggest. Even common culture, language, religion and history are false values; communities, therefore, should not be based upon them. Furthermore, nationalism has given rise to rivalries, aggression and warfare.

It is essential that any community should be voluntary if the anarchist ideal of a society without coercion is to be achieved. Only then can it be guaranteed that all will conform to the norms of the community. Should they not wish to do so, they should be free to leave and join a different group with which they can identify more clearly. Only complete social outcasts would, therefore, be excluded.

<u>Capitalism and industrialisation</u>   The anarchists' objection to capitalism is clear. It is based on private property, exploits workers and underpins the coercive modern state, they complain. There is another criticism of capitalism, however, which not all anarchists share. This concerns the nature of industrialisation which has accompanied the growth of capitalism.

The division of labour, the nature of the modern workplace and the loss of much of the creative element in work are all aspects of modern economic progress which must be reversed. Workers have become brutalised and automated by modern work methods. Long hours, poor conditions and low wages are also to be abhorred, of course, but the alienation experienced by the unskilled, production-line worker can only be removed if the whole system is dismantled. This is a romantic aspect of the anarchist creed since it suggests a return to a simpler form of existence in which the creative instincts of workers are released and production is organised on a smaller scale.

Summary of anarchist beliefs

1. Mostly there is a belief that man is naturally good and sociable, or at least is perfectible.
2. Liberty consists not of freedom within artificial laws, but of the exercise of private judgement which leads, in the uncorrupted individual, to good acts.
3. No man has a right to exercise power over another man.
4. The state and government should not be tolerated, even if they are established by consent.
5. Since the existence of a state cannot be justified, there can be no artificial laws. Man should, however, conform to natural laws.
6. Private property is unnatural and should, therefore, be replaced by common ownership.
7. All communities should be natural and voluntary.
8. Capitalism, and possibly many of the features of industrialisation, should be abolished.

Conceptions of an anarchist order   It is at this point in our analysis of anarchism that a clear distinction must be made between **anarcho-individualism** and **anarcho-communism**, together with its related forms. Both share many common basic beliefs, but their prescriptions for the creation of a new order differ markedly.

<u>Anarcho-individualism</u>   The anarcho-individualists stress the egotistical aspects of man's character. For them, all forms of social organisation are unjustified limitations upon his liberty, even if they are voluntary associations. Instead, they wish to see a world where the individual is a sovereign being, free to exercise his own judgement as to how he behaves. Within this tradition there are two further sub-divisions of belief, each of which is dependent upon the anarchist's conception of human nature.

Social Darwinists, sometimes described as **anarcho-capitalists**, draw their inspiration from the biological theories of Charles Darwin, applying them to life in human society. In this analysis each man is engaged in a personal struggle against his natural and social environment. He must compete in order to survive, or at least succeed at the expense of others. In some ways, this is a logical extension of the intensely individualistic liberalism which flourished in the nineteenth century at the height of the development of capitalism. In the USA it has a longer tradition, arising out of the 'frontier' spirit of the early days of the Union. There, on the edges of civilised society, the influence of government and laws was especially weak. Each individual was, therefore, responsible for himself.

In its modern form, anarcho-individualism is considered to be a right-wing phenomenon, sometimes described as libertarianism. Here there is an intense suspicion of the activities of the state. It is seen as an instrument of repression, seeking to impose artificial values and to inhibit man's natural instincts for survival.

A gentler individualist tradition also flourished in nineteenth-century America. There, genuine anarchists believed it was possible for absolute individual liberty to exists alongside peaceful community life. Each could, therefore, choose to be self-sufficient or to co-operate with his fellow man. This was seen as a world of mutual respect and peace, but without social organisation. Man's natural egotism would not bring him into fierce competition with others, but would simply allow him to withdraw from social life.

Anarcho-communism   The more influential and widespread form of anarchism which proliferated in the nineteenth century was a communist form, which, as we have seen above, was closely associated with more radical forms of revolutionary socialism. This tradition stressed the sociable nature of man's natural character. Instead of individualism, the anarcho-communists stressed social solidarity and mutual aid. In contrast to the Darwinian approach, they stressed man's desire to live in voluntary communities. The emphasis lay, therefore, in communal living and economic co-operation. Although this has formed a philosophy rich in its diversity, certain common characteristics can be discerned, as follows:

• Man can live in communities without need of state organisation or laws.
• Wherever possible these communities should be self-sufficient.
• If communities were forced to co-operate, systems of mutual benefit and fair exchange would be developed.
• Although individual sovereignty would be maintained, each member of the community would naturally conform to its norms of behaviour.
• Decisions would be made by direct democracy with all members participating.
• All property would be in common ownership.
• Goods would be distributed on the basis of absolute equality.

Two principal variants of this theme also flourished. The most popular was known as **anarcho-syndicalism**. This movement based its prospective social and economic organisation upon the existing trade union structure. The nature of men's occupation was seen as the most powerful force which binds them together. It was therefore logical that social organisation should be based upon that criterion. The union structure was also ideal, having in place its own internal democratic structure. The syndicalists enjoyed an additional advantage since, in order to destroy the existing political and social order, trade unions were ideally placed to organise the working classes.

The proposed post-revolutionary social structure was, in essence, to be a highly decentralised form of socialism. Workers were to enjoy common ownership of their own industries. These were to be managed in a highly democratic manner, with economic and social equality respected. The industries would find it necessary to co-operate with each other on a voluntary basis, using a series of trade agreements created for mutual benefit. The more idealistic of the syndicalists – the anarchists themselves – believed that this could be achieved without the need for any form of coercive state.

The most developed form of such a decentralised system was known as 'federalism'. In this conception a multi-layered hierarchy of communities, ranging from the very small locality to a world system, would be formed on the basis of occupational groupings. At each level co-operation would take place freely. At the highest level, a federation of workers would be formed on a worldwide basis. Thus, the nation-state would also be abolished as an entity.

So it can be seen that communist forms of anarchism range from conceptions of very small, autonomous, voluntary communities with relatively little to do with each other, through to a great international workers' co-operative with a complex system of trading and mutual aid in place to support it.

Some prominent anarchists Since there are almost as many anarchist proposals as there are anarchists, and since it is a philosophy with so much diversity, a review of the beliefs of some of the principal anarchists will prove to be the most effective way to illustrate the many ideas which have flourished.

William Godwin (1756–1836) (English) Godwin developed the notion of private judgement, allying it to the principles of utilitarianism. Thus, he argued, each person should make a decision each time he acts. Will the result of the action do more good to others than harm? If so, it should be undertaken. He differed from the mainstream utilitarians such as Bentham, however, in that he believed that it was for each individual to determine for himself whether the results of his actions would be beneficial.

Godwin shared with Rousseau the belief that, in an ideal world, each man should be able to govern himself, so that there should be no need of government, even of the most democratic kind. The difference between these two close contemporaries, however, was that, while Rousseau was pessimistic about men becoming moral and wise enough to govern themselves, Godwin was more idealistic and looked forward to a world without government. For him, man is completely perfectible, given the appropriate social environment. Thus, while his critics described him as intensely utopian, he saw himself as realistic. His most influential work was entitled *An Enquiry Concerning Political Justice* (1793).

Michael Bakunin (1814–76) (Russian) His principal contribution to the anarchist tradition was the notion of federalism as described above. He was a close associate of Marx until they split over the issue of the dictatorship of the proletariat. He broadly shared Marx's analysis of capitalism and his vision of a communist world. He could not, however, accept the need for an interim state – the dictatorship of the proletariat.

Like Marx, he saw labour as man's fundamental activity. Thus, the nature of a man's work – his occupation – should also form the basis of social communities. In common with many other anarchists of his time, Bakunin was a revolutionary who saw the destruction of the existing repressive state as the first priority for his movement.

Peter Kropotkin (1842–1921) (Russian) Kropotkin was Bakunin's fellow revolutionary and possibly the purest example of an anarcho-communist. In his book *Fields, Factories and Workshops* (1901) Kropotkin extolled the virtues of the small, voluntary community based on the village. It was, he argued, the breakdown of such small communities which had led to the development of the modern repressive state.

The post-revolutionary world would, for him, be concerned with the restoration of such voluntary communities. If possible, they were to be self-sufficient, but he accepted the need for some large-scale industrial organisations. Like Bakunin, he was an internationalist, viewing the nation as an artificial community. These two Russian anarchists were also scathing in their condemnation of religion as a means by which men have been repressed by a ruling class.

Georges Sorel (1847–1922) (French) One of the most violent of the anarchists, he developed the political creed of anarcho-syndicalism. For him, man is constrained not only by laws and governments, but also by moral scruples. In order to see society for what it is and to be able to act effectively to destroy it, these moral restraints must be removed. The exercise of one's individual will through extreme violence was the means of achieving this.

The state was the instrument of the will of a ruling elite, he argued, so that only the superior will of the mass of the working class could secure its downfall. Thereafter, a stateless society based on self-governing trade unions could be achieved. His stress on the importance of individual will and decisive action endeared him also to later fascist philosophers as well as modern existentialists.

Pierre Proudhon (1809–65) (French) As well as being one of the more scientific of the anarchist philosophers, Proudhon was responsible for its best-known maxim – 'All property is theft.' Yet, despite his apparent opposition to the concept of private property, he did not, unlike virtually all other anarchists, recommend its abolition. He understood that property ownership was the principal cause of the existence of the oppressive state and its attendant laws. Property, once established, had to be protected by force. But he also accepted that its ownership was so deeply rooted in society that it could not, realistically, be abolished, however desirable this might be.

His practical theories became known as mutualism and were a compromise between capitalism and socialism. Each person would produce goods either as an individual or in voluntary association with other workers. These goods would be sold, not in free markets, but at prices determined by the amount of labour which had been put into their production. Instead of money, therefore, goods would be priced in 'labour value'. In this way, a free semi-capitalist system would be retained, but neither workers nor consumers would be exploited. The fact that there was no exploitation meant there would be no need for a state since a state only exists in order to maintain conventional forms of capitalist exploitation.

Proudhon rejected other forms of socialism or communism on the grounds that they were collectivist doctrines, forcing men into mutual co-operation. His scheme, he claimed, gave rise to voluntary mutual arrangements with individuals retaining their own personal liberty.

Henry Thoreau (1817–62) (American) During the late 1960s and early 1970s interest in certain forms of anarcho-individualism was rekindled within the youth protest movement. Thoreau, and in particular his most celebrated book, *Walden*, became one of the inspirations among radicals of the Left. In his early years as a philosopher he did not propose any detailed form of alternative order to that of the modern state, but rather recommended that each individual should free himself from its restrictions by withdrawing from it and becoming self-sufficient. He practised this philosophy himself in rural America where he was considered an amiable eccentric. Later, he was to become more militant, recommending that protesters should engage in civil disobedience against the oppressive nature of the modern state.

His combination of individualism and self-sufficiency appealed to those radical thinkers who wished to escape both from the restrictions of the all-powerful state, and who were concerned by the destruction of the environment caused by modern production methods.

Max Stirner (1806–56) (German) Stirner's rejection of all forms of social organisation as a denial of the human ego earned him the title 'nihilist', one of those extreme anarchists who became notorious for their radicalism. His view of human nature was that man has two sides to his character, egoism and sociability. In an ideal society, the opportunities for man's social nature to manifest itself would be maximised, but he recognised this aspiration to be utopian. The alternative was to accept man's egoism and to give it full rein.

In *The Ego and His Own* (1845) Stirner rejected all social theories on the grounds that they would result in alienation for the individual. Thus, governments, laws, morality, religion and society itself must be rejected by man who will then take control of his own life. The extreme negativity of Stirner's philosophy was too much even for most other anarchists to stomach, but he remained an important philosophical inspiration for the anarcho-individualists.

Robert Nozick (1938–) (American) Nozick represents contemporary interest in libertarianism which is both a form of anarcho-individualism and an extreme type of conservatism. For him, every individual should be responsible for his own actions and, most importantly, should also be responsible for his own self-protection. The notion that the state and its laws exist to protect free individuals from each other is rejected in favour of self-help of a kind which had been advocated by the nineteenth-century English essayist, **Samuel Smiles**.

In Nozick's world there would be only a minimal state, preferably no state at all. Capitalism would be virtually uncontrolled and a number of voluntary agencies, to which individuals could subscribe for their own protection and welfare, would replace state institutions. Rewards in such a society would be distributed purely on the basis of power in the market place. Popular among many modern libertarians, Nozick's ideas flourish at the confluence of individualist anarchist, New Right Conservative and extreme liberal traditions.

The relevance of anarchism In nineteenth-century Russia, largely among the peasantry, anarchist ideas did enjoy a certain degree of support. There was, during the Spanish Civil War in the 1930s, a substantial anarchist presence, members of which actually controlled Barcelona for a short period. Yet no large-scale community has ever been established for any length of time along anarchist lines. Furthermore, the movement has never attracted mass support. It may, therefore, be asked whether it has any great significance as a world philosophy.

There can be two responses to these observations. First, the role of anarchism must be recognised as having inspired many of the alternative lifestyles which have sprung up since the 1960s. The 'hippy' commune movement and its modern successors, the New Age Travellers, certainly espouse many anarchist principles. So, too, do some environmental groups who have been attempting to establish self-sufficient, sustainable and simple forms of lifestyle in small voluntary groups. Though still on a small scale, interest in such new lifestyles continues to grow steadily as a reaction to modern living.

Secondly, anarchism serves as a challenging and diverse philosophical criticism of modern society. Though most of its proposals may seem impractical today, many of its observations upon such institutions as the state, property and capitalism are still relevant and stimulating. If it is true that the sovereignty of individuals continues to be challenged by these institutions, then reference to anarchist ideals may serve to remind us of what may be lost.

Totalitarianism

Introduction

The term 'totalitarianism' refers to a political and social system rather than to any specific ideology. We could argue in some instances that the mere exercise of absolute power by a regime can become an end in itself and, therefore, an ideology, but few rulers would admit to this. George Orwell's novel *Nineteen Eighty-Four* suggests that the dictatorship portrayed there was only interested in the pursuit of power and had no other reason for its existence, but the book is a political allegory so we must be wary of generalising on the basis of what it says.

Certainly, as we shall see below, all totalitarian regimes claim to be motivated by ideology, and it is this which drives them to exert total control, rather than the enjoyment of power alone. It is therefore useful to include an analysis of totalitarianism in this section rather than elsewhere. Having done so, we may examine three ideologies which have been most closely associated with absolute regimes. These are fascism, Nazism and Soviet socialism.

Totalitarianism and autocracy

Between the two World Wars it became apparent that a new form of political regime had come about. The term 'autocracy' could be used to describe those systems which did not conform to the new ideas of liberal democracy, but it was inadequate in describing the dictatorial governments of the likes of the Soviet Union, fascist Italy and Nazi Germany.

Hannah Arendt, the historian, and herself a refugee from the Third Reich, provided a clear distinction between the two forms of rule, thus:

- Autocracy is merely a form of government which denies democratic and individual rights. Totalitarianism, on the other hand, is a complete social system, not just a style of government.

- With autocracy a clear distinction is made between what is in the public sphere, i.e. the concern of government, and what is private and therefore not to be interfered with by the state. For totalitarian rulers, no such distinction is recognised. Everything is relevant and may be subject to control or transformation.
- The role of ideology may not be paramount in an autocratic system. Totalitarians always espouse an ideology, using it as the guide by which they wish to transform society and bend it to their will.
- The autocratic ruler seeks fear and obedience among the governed, but is not necessarily concerned with any deeper control or even enthusiastic support. Those who have led totalitarian states, by contrast, have attempted to exert psychological control over their subject peoples, sometimes resulting in adulation and absolute faith in the ruling ideology and its embodiment – the leader.

Thus, Arendt stresses the 'totalness' of such regimes. She emphasises total relevance of the ideology, total control and total obedience to a single leader. **Bernard Crick** summed up this idea some time later:

> *'The totalitarian believes that everything is relevant to government and that the task of government is to reconstruct society utterly according to the goals of an ideology.'*
> Bernard Crick, *In Defence of Politics* (Penguin, 1962)

The nature of totalitarianism

A distinctive phenomenon?   Scholars have entered into much dispute as to whether there is a distinct form of state which can be described as 'totalitarian'. Some have suggested that it is merely a distorted form of democracy which arose out of the peculiar historical conditions which existed during the inter-war period in Europe. The conditions necessary for its emergence have been variously identified as:

- an unstable political system
- a series of economic crises
- the imminent threat of socialist revolution feared by the middle classes
- in larger countries, difficulty being experienced in maintaining national unity
- perceived threats to the dominant culture of the society.

Certainly, many of these phenomena can be discerned in Germany, Italy, Russia or Spain in the first part of the twentieth century. In Britain, France and the USA, the main victors in World War One, most of the conditions were, by contrast, absent. Only the Great Depression was experienced by all the European powers.

Thus, there is a strong argument for suggesting this was merely a passing historical phenomenon arising from the failure of democracy to deal with pressing national problems. However, the counter theory – that it was a distinctive form of regime arising largely out of adherence to a dominant ideology – remains the more popular.

Theories of totalitarianism   The belief that totalitarianism is indeed a distinct form of society is asserted by a variety of schools of thought. Some of these are described opposite.

Talmon, an historian, sees much in the work of Rousseau to provide clues as to the origins of the system. The concept of a **general will**, which Rousseau developed, gave the people a collective voice which could cut through the confusions and majoritarianism of democracy. Thus, minorities would not feel persecuted, majorities could not persecute them and each individual could feel part of an organic whole rather than drifting in a competitive sea. The problem of how to determine such a collective will, if indeed one can exist at all, cannot be solved by democratic methods, Rousseau feared, so a single ruler with perfect knowledge and understanding of his people must be found to declare the 'general will'. Thus, when democracy appeared to fail in certain countries, this notion was put forward as an explanation. In each case a dynamic individual emerged as the embodiment of the popular will. This, suggests Talmon, is what characterises totalitarian rule.

Friedrich proposed a more detailed version, but at the same time a less sophisticated one. For him, totalitarianism arose out of a combination of the **desire** for a more concentrated form of rule, arising from various economic and political problems, and technological advances which enabled such a concentration of power to be successfully attained. Thus, it is the result of a coincidence of phenomena. He expressed the results in a six-point scheme:

1. There is a single state ideology. No alternative is tolerated.
2. The state has a monopoly of the communications media.
3. There is a similar monopoly of economic power.
4. The state employs terror – the public use of force – to maintain obedience.
5. All significant weapons are in the hands of the state.
6. There is single-party rule which uses an obedient bureaucracy in order to govern.

It has been suggested that these phenomena are not distinctive enough, that they represent merely exaggerated forms of autocracy, but they certainly conform closely to the characteristics to be seen in Nazi Germany and the Soviet Union.

Arendt, as we have seen above, stresses the psychological nature of totalitarianism, as well as its totalness. She observed how 'civil society' – the intermediate social groups such as families, religions, political parties, interest groups and trade unions – are broken down by the state. They are either absent or are replaced by 'puppets' which are not independent at all but compliant to the will of the government. There is, therefore, no social organisation between the central state and individuals. The minds of the people are, thus, laid open to both psychological and coercive control.

This view also lays great stress upon the role of the governing ideology since its goals must be attained at all costs and no private interests can be allowed to stand in its path.

We can now move on to review the two principal forms of totalitarian regime which have flourished in the twentieth century. Since Marxist ideology, which underpinned the Stalinist system in the Soviet Union, is described elsewhere, it is appropriate to begin with fascism.

Fascism

Philosophical origins

The most important philosopher to have inspired twentieth-century fascists has undoubtedly been **Friedrich Nietzsche (1844–1900)**. This strange, complex and, ultimately, insane thinker was largely concerned with the struggle between rational thought and action. For him, the world was being ill-served by rational thinkers who developed such ideologies as democracy and liberalism. He maintained that individuals should not be fettered by the disciplines of rationality, but be free-spirited and ready to engage in a struggle against their fellow men, a battle of wills in which only the strong can succeed. In this way, society is guided by strength and purpose rather than by weak ideology.

Democracy was the subject of Nietzsche's most scathing criticism. Slavish adherence to the wishes of the majority would render society directionless and without noble purposes. Furthermore, each man, by subjecting himself to the will of the majority, denies his own individual will. This Darwinian world which he envisaged, and in which only the fittest can succeed, must yield up a superior being in each society, a man whose personal will is superior to all others. This being, he describes as the '*übermensch*' or 'superman', an individual who can inspire whole nations into dynamic action. When we add Nietzsche's love of war and conquest to this philosophy, it is easy to understand why such characters as Hitler and Mussolini were so influenced by Nietzschean ideas.

The anarchist **Georges Sorel** (1847–1922) adopted a similar Darwinian approach to that of Nietzsche. He saw politics in terms of the struggle between competing elites. The elite which holds power is able to retain it through the strength of its will. Aspiring elites who wish to take over power must, therefore, demonstrate superior dynamism to succeed. In this way, modern states can guarantee to be ruled by powerful leaders for it becomes inevitable that the weak must fail. Both Sorel and Nietzsche echo the much earlier works of the Italian Renaissance writer, **Niccolo Machiavelli (1469–1527)**, whose most celebrated work, *The Prince*, exhorted rulers to exhibit more ruthlessness, cruelty, cunning and, if necessary, deceitfulness than their rivals. All these 'evils' cannot be justified, he admitted, unless they are used for the purpose of defending the state. But if the state is threatened – and it frequently is, both internally and externally – there are no limits to which the ruler cannot go.

Like Sorel, **Friedrich Hegel** (1770–1831) did not belong strictly to any totalitarian movement, being more in the continental conservative tradition, but he nevertheless provided much inspiration in his philo-sophical works for later fascists. Hegel's historical theories (which also heavily influenced Marx) suggested that the alienation and disharmony which had characterised all past societies could be eliminated, heralding a new age of peace and freedom. This could only occur, however, if the will of every individual could become identical to the will of the whole society. There would then be no contradiction between individual free-dom and the collective purposes of the state. Nobody would feel con-stricted and individual liberty would not interfere with the harmony of the whole community. Though Hegel almost certainly would have opposed modern fascism, his ideas were used by the fascists to justify the practice of submitting individuals to a subservient role in relation to the state. In other words, what Hegel intended to be a perfect form of collective freedom was interpreted by fascists to be the complete abolition of individual liberty.

Features of fascism As we have already seen, the nature of fascist regimes has been totalitarian, demonstrating the characteristics described by Arendt, Friedrich, Talmon and the like. However, these phenomena do not present us with a complete picture. Thus, although all fascist regimes have been totalitarian, they have also displayed a number of other distinguishing features.

Will and action The ruler of a fascist regime does not claim to be its legitimate leader on the grounds that he has been elected or that he represents a political party which has been installed in power by the people. Rather, he claims the right to govern on the grounds of his superior will, his ability to act decisively and to move the nation in a direction which is the result of his own inspiration and not of a democratic process. Mussolini was, thus, prone to remind his people that he may not have observed the rules of democratic politics but he had succeeded in making Italian trains run on time.

The leader principle This term, coined by Hitler, refers to the claim that the leader of a fascist regime is the single embodiment of the will of its people. The granting of all power to one personality ensured that there would be a singularity of purpose which is lacking in more pluralist political systems. If a nation is to move decisively towards its future goals, it must have this single-mindedness, claimed the fascist dictator. Hitler argued that his will was merely a reflection of the clear destiny of the German people – to create a superior civilisation and to conquer inferior races. Mussolini, on the other hand, was prepared to admit that he was creating his own myths concerning the Italian people, heralding a new imperialist age for them. In both cases, however, the principle was the same – clarity of purpose and direction.

The implications of this principle were twofold. First, that those who chose to defy the will of the leader were, automatically, traitors against their own people. Secondly, it denied any possibility of organised opposition or democratic processes. Mass participation in politics was allowed and, indeed, encouraged, but this could only manifest itself in demonstrations of enthusiastic support, not in meaningful dialogue.

> 'Fascism insists that government be entrusted to men capable of rising above their own private interests and of realising the aspirations of the whole collectivity.'
> Alfredo Rocco (adviser to Mussolini) 1937

The state In democratically-based political systems, the state – the permanent apparatus of government – is subject to the will of the majority of the people as expressed through their representatives. This is not so in a fascist system. There, everything is subservient to the purposes of the state; everything, that is, except the leader himself, who is the embodiment of the state.

It was Mussolini's closest associate, Giovanni Gentile (1875–1944), who brought this concept of the state to its highest form. For him, the state can take on a life of its own and become an individual on its own account provided that the people collectively bury their own individuality beneath the will of the state. For those who have been raised within a democratic tradition, this is a difficult concept to understand since individual liberty, pluralism and tolerance are stressed by democrats. The fascists attempted to break out of this mode of thinking. 'Statism' became a kind of religion within which there can be only one form of allegiance. Naturally, since fascist regimes were totalitarian, everything was the concern of the state. There was no private sphere, no independent civil society and no higher authority.

Nationalism   The most powerful synthesis of fascism and nationalism occurred in Hitler's Third Reich and is described in more detail below. However, all the prominent fascist regimes used nationalism as a means by which the solidarity of the state could be maintained.

An important distinction needs to be drawn at this point between German and Italian fascism. For Hitler, there was a higher purpose than the consolidation of state control which was the greater glory of the German people and their culture. Thus, the state was to **serve** German nationalism. In Italy, on the other hand, Mussolini and Gentile used nationalism as a means to maintain allegiance to the state. So the positions of state and nation were reversed.

Nevertheless, in both cases nationalism was a powerful instrument for maintaining state unity. The belief that a people are bound together by common ancestry, culture, language and history sits well with the struggle to create an organic state. Indeed, the term 'fasces' derives from the Latin noun describing a roped bundle of sticks, symbol of the need to bind disparate peoples under one authority in the Roman Empire. The concept of 'nation' and 'national destiny' proved an easier idea with which to inspire people than the more abstract notion of an organised political state.

> 'It is not nationality which creates the state, but the state which creates nationality, by setting the seal of actual existence on it. It is through the conquest of unity and independence that the nation gives proof of its political will, and establishes its existence as a state.'
> Giovanni Gentile, *The Genesis and Structure of Society*
> (1937)

Economics   Though fascism is generally thought of as a right-wing philosophy, it is not sympathetic to the free operation of capitalism. The economic forces exerted by free markets are seen as a denial of the individual will. Each person should be able to engage in an unfettered struggle against the social and economic environment. Capitalism threatens this process. It is also the case that market capitalism conflicts with the fascist obsession with state power. It becomes a contradiction in terms to have absolute state power but a free, individualistic economic system.

Similarly, though fascism is a collectivist doctrine, its adherents oppose socialism and its extreme form, Marxism. This is not to say they reject all the principles of socialism. Many fascists admire the social solidarity and collective principles of socialism. Indeed, the three most 'successful' fascist leaders – Hitler, Mussolini and Franco – displayed socialist tendencies in their earlier years. The principal objections to socialism are twofold. First, its reliance upon a rational ideology threatens the operation of free individual will. Secondly, it is a class-based movement, which divides society into at least two social groupings. Fascists pursue a complete, undivided organic state so that class conflict is not acceptable. Of course, the goals of fascism and Marxism may appear to be similar in that they are seeking a classless society, but this is as far as the similarity goes. The persistence of the all-powerful, coercive state is not acceptable to Marxists.

To replace both free market capitalism and state socialism, the fascists developed a theory of economic management of their own, known as the 'corporate state' or 'corporativism'. Its most developed form was introduced in Italy by Mussolini. Here, economic enterprises remained under private control, but their relations with the workforce were to be overseen by 'syndicates' or 'corporations' who would ensure that all interests were served by each industry, i.e. those of employers, workers, consumers and, above all, the state. Thus, there was neither complete state control, nor absolute laissez-faire capitalism. In the event, only in Italy was the corporate state created in the full sense of the term. Even there it was corrupted by the domination of the fascist party in every corporation, and war soon overtook their operations. In wartime, although private enterprise was maintained, the purposes of the state became ever more pressing so that the semi-independence of the corporations was largely lost.

Irrationality and myth As we saw in the philosophy of Nietzsche, fascists are opposed to the application of rational theories in politics. They have, therefore, been described as 'irrational' thinkers, not in the sense of being socially maladjusted, but in that all appeals to reason are rejected.

Instead of appealing to the people on rational grounds, fascists prefer to play on emotions, fears and prejudices. Thus, for example, xenophobia (fear of foreigners or strangers) was seen as a more powerful force in moving the masses than economic self-interest. Similarly, the fostering of a sense of racial superiority could inspire people more effectively than drives for greater efficiency in production. Neither of these emotions, any more than religious bigotry, historical destiny or conspiracy theories, had any basis in reason, but, for the fascist, this is less important than the effect they have on the people.

It was Hitler who was to use the device of national and racial mythology as the most potent form of irrational appeal. The theories of the superior 'Aryan' race whose culture and will were superior to those of all other peoples were to become the basis of his own version of the fascist creed – National Socialism.

These theories are described more fully below. Both Franco in Spain and Mussolini in Italy persuaded their people that they were leading them to a new 'Golden Age' whose origins lay in dubious historical interpretations. Neither, however, was to develop the extensive mythology which Hitler's advisers were able to achieve.

<u>War and conquest</u> Nietzsche had proclaimed that 'the Nation which gives up war and conquest is ready for the rule of shopkeepers and democracy', a condemnation born out of his belief that a people are at their most dynamic and purposeful when they are at war. He saw the conquest of weaker peoples as the greatest act of will attainable. In war the individual is totally free because he subordinates his ego and his interests completely to those of the state. His will and that of the state become one; there are no contradictions to hold him back.

This was very much the fascist view, especially of Hitler. War and conquest were noble aspirations. There was a natural duty for members of a superior culture to impose themselves on the world. Not to do so would be a denial of their destiny. To the last days of World War Two, Hitler believed that failure was the result of a lack of will. Death was, therefore, preferable to defeat.

Summary of fascist beliefs

1. The state must be totalitarian in form. Everything becomes the concern of the state.
2. The state should be driven forward by the force of men's will and their ability to act decisively.
3. Democracy is an unjustified denial of the human spirit, based on reason and it is therefore too weak to serve the state.
4. If a state is founded on the basis of the competitive struggle of wills, a superior leader is bound to emerge.
5. The state is superior to all other organisations and individuals except the leader. All activity must be directed to the purposes of the state.
6. The most effective means of creating the collective, organic state is to emphasise nationalism as a popular binding force.
7. Both state socialism and free market capitalism are detrimental. Corporativism – state-led co-operation among all sectors of industry – is preferred.
8. Leaders use irrational emotional appeals and the creation of myths to inspire the people to action.
9. Warfare is exalted as the supreme act of service to the state.

National Socialism

National Socialism, or **Nazism**, as it became known, was that particular form of fascism which was developed by Adolf Hitler and his associates, notably **Alfred Rosenberg**. It should be stressed at the outset that the Nazis were fascists in every respect, but added a number of features to that philosophy to give it its distinctive German form.

A description of its principal beliefs need not, therefore, repeat the characteristics described above. The main additional features were as follows:

<u>Racism</u> The German race was superior to all other races. That was, claimed Hitler, its historical legacy. Following the theories of the nineteenth-century French philosopher, **Count Gobineau**, he accepted

that the dynamism of the German people had been weakened over the centuries by the mixing of blood with inferior races. If Germany were to re-establish the superior culture which had existed in the Middle Ages, blood purity would have to be restored. In other words, the classic Aryan 'type' was to be recreated.

In addition to these quasi-scientific theories, Hitler was influenced by the ideas of an English adviser, **Houston Chamberlain** (no close relation to the British politician of the same name). Chamberlain suggested that the Aryan (also known as Teutonic) people had long been engaged in a struggle for supremacy against the Jews. These myths were attractive to the Nazi Party since the theory of a Jewish conspiracy was an ideal explanation for Germany's misfortunes in World War One and the subsequent economic slump.

The results of these two beliefs concerning race and racial superiority led to the horrific persecution of the Jewish and other so-called 'inferior' peoples, as well as the strict race laws which were designed to ensure racial purity. Indeed, those modern fascists who are described as 'neo-Nazis' still proclaim similar beliefs about race.

<u>Volkism</u> As we have seen, fascists have always emphasised the key role of nationalism. The Nazis were to take this a stage further. For them, the basis of nationhood was predominantly race. It was blood, not merely common experiences, which truly binds a people together. Thus, mere traditional nationalism is seen as a largely rational idea. Racial purity, on the other hand, is intensely romantic and therefore irrational. It becomes – naturally for a fascist – a superior aspiration to the liberal-democratic forms of nationalism which were common in the nineteenth and twentieth centuries.

In addition to race, the term *volk* suggested several other qualities which defined a people's superiority. Such attributes as intellect, artistic talent, honour and dynamic will were stressed. Since this *kultur* – a specifically German term for such a collection of qualities – was indeed superior, those who displayed it were entitled to conquer other peoples and so obtain territory (so-called *Lebensraum*) where their culture would have more room to flourish. Indeed, a people who have spilled their blood in a noble struggle to conquer land are entitled to possess it. Thus, a combination of race, culture and territorial claims characterises *volkism* as a special form of nationalism.

<u>Socialism</u> To some extent, as many historians will confirm, Hitler added the term 'socialist' to his party's name purely in the hope that this would attract support from Germany's working class. However, it was not merely an exercise in opportunism. Hitler did admire the social solidarity of the working-class movement and his speeches often referred to the 'heroism' of the workers. Unlike the peasantry and the middle classes, who were largely driven by self-interest, the workers could claim to be a genuinely collective social group.

The Nazis did develop notions of social equality, abhorred the vested interests of capitalism and the bourgeois state, and preferred the enthusiasm of the masses to the intellectualism of the educated middle classes. So, in very general terms, the Nazis were rudimentary socialists. Certainly, Nazism is a philosophy of collectivism and not individualism, so the term is not wholly inappropriate. It should be stressed, however, that Hitler completely rejected the scientific socialism of Marx and his followers. As we have seen above, the romantic and utopian anarchist, Sorel, was to prove a more attractive inspiration.

Soviet socialism

The basic principles of Stalinist thought and practice are described above in the section on communism. However, the Soviet system needs to be examined specifically in terms of the nature of totalitarian rule.

While there is no doubt that the Soviet Union under Stalin and his successors conformed largely to Friedrich's six-point scheme (see above), some additional features need to be emphasised:

- There was great stress laid upon **ideology** – in this case, Marxist–Leninism. The relentless adherence to the orthodox interpretation of the doctrines led to extreme repression of even the slightest variance from the 'official line'. Such revision was ruthlessly put down.
- The power of the party **bureaucracy** was raised to new levels under Stalin. Party membership became an essential prerequisite to opportunities and a good standard of living. Furthermore, since all official action had to be sanctioned by party officials initiative was stifled in favour of procedural correctness.
- As Orwell observed in his allegorical work, *Nineteen Eighty-Four*, the Soviet regime made a practice of manipulating history, current news and statistics to justify its own exaggerated claims. **Propaganda** was used extensively, not merely on an emotional level, as fascists practised it, but also by the publication of false production figures and inflated achievements of the party machine.
- Possibly the most important distinction which can be identified was the total control of the **economy** exercised by the state. The totalitarian economy forbade all forms of private enterprise and would not allow any free markets to operate. Even at its height the Third Reich did not attempt to wield such power.

Nationalism

Before examining the several strands of nationalism which have, and which still do flourish around the world, two terms must be defined. These are 'nation' and 'state'.

The nation

The concept of the nation is a relatively modern one, dating from the latter part of the eighteenth century. Before then peoples were differentiated by territorial boundaries and the jurisdiction of monarchs. Thus, the 'French' were deemed so because they were subjects of the French King and inhabited those territories over which he ruled. Of course, they displayed some elements of national pride and common experience and, of course, mostly spoke the same language, but there was no real sense of 'nation' which could stand above political rule.

The modern idea of what constitutes a nation, however, does suggest that people have forces which bind them other than the fact of a common ruler. Among these forces are the following:

- **Race or ethnicity** is possibly the most popular criterion for identifying a particular nation. The Chinese and the Arabs certainly place this factor above all others in expressing their national heritage.

- Common **ancestry**. In some extreme cases even a single common ancestor can be a criterion, as is the case with the Jewish nation. This is also true among peoples who describe themselves in terms of 'clan' or 'tribe'.
- Common **historical experience** refers to an understanding that a people have been bound together over a long period of time. The English display this sentiment particularly strongly.
- **Language** may be an important factor. The Welsh stress this feature, as do the Basques.
- **Geography** can play a significant part with island nations often created by their isolation.
- More difficult to define, but no less powerful for that, is **culture**. The Irish nationalist movement was especially affected by the cultural traditions of the Irish people, which were very distinct from those of their English masters. This has always been a significant force in Germany even before the Third Reich.
- Finally, we can identify **religion** as an important factor in some cases. Jews and Muslims are clear examples of where religion can be a key factor in national sentiment.

Of course, various combinations of these features can be identified in different forms of nationalism. What is important in all cases, however, is that the idea of 'nation' is a state of mind. It may not derive from objective historical truths and may be based on mythology, but this is not crucial. All that matters is that when a people think of themselves as a nation, then they become a potent political force.

The state While, as we have seen, the idea of **nation** is largely a collective state of mind, the **state** is a political reality. It embodies the existence of a specific territory which is governed by political institutions. Nothing need be said about the legitimacy of this political phenomenon, since all that concerns us here is whether the state has the necessary coercive power to maintain control over its defined territory. If it does, then it is a reality. We can, therefore, say with certainty that France is a state, and so are Italy, Germany and Israel. This could not be said of Bosnia in 1995, however, since no single political entity is able to maintain control.

On the other hand, arguments may rage as to whether some nations are indeed nations as they claim. Does it apply to the Arabs, for example, or to Catalans in Spain or Tamils in Sri Lanka? Nobody can doubt the **claim** of these peoples to be genuine national groupings, but the reality is more difficult to establish. This is not true with states. The acid test is whether some institutions do indeed exert a monopoly of coercive power within a territory.

The nation-state It was Napoleon who first attempted to put together the relatively new ideas of nation and state into practical form. His vision of a Europe with common legal and political systems, but within which each nation should possess its own government, was futuristic but undoubtedly realistic.

It was at the end of World War One that the notion of the nation-state was to come to fruition. The two great multi-national empires of the nineteenth century – the Ottoman and the Austro-Hungarian – had collapsed. America's President **Woodrow Wilson** declared the principle that every nation should also become a state with its own sovereign institutions. Most of the European powers concurred and the concept of the nation-state was realised. However, the principle was to have little credence outside Europe. Colonial possessions still persisted, national groupings were denied statehood in the Middle East and the great Russian (later Soviet) Empire still held sway over subjugated peoples.

After World War Two new life was given to the movement towards nation-states. The United Nations Organisation declared the principle of national self-determination, colonial empires were beginning to break up – a process almost complete by 1990 – and eventually, in the 1990s, the Soviet Empire collapsed freeing many nationalities to struggle for full statehood.

Despite the great progress towards the achievement of independent nation-states on a universal basis, it is still true that there are nations which are not yet states. The Palestinians have nearly achieved territorial sovereignty, but groups as disparate as the Scots, Kurds and Basques are still searching for nation-statehood. It is also true that there are some states which are not nations. The clearest example is the USA. Despite the intense patriotism displayed by most Americans, they are not one nation and are unlikely to be so for many years. The ethnic and cultural backgrounds of the American peoples are so diverse that true nationhood is far off. Yet they are a state in every sense of the word. This was also true of the former states of Yugoslavia and Czechoslovakia, as their subsequent disintegration indicates.

Having established our terms, we may now investigate the different branches of nationalism which have flourished.

Liberal nationalism In its early life nationalism was an exclusively liberal movement. It was concerned with the problems of government by consent and the self-determination of peoples. Having removed the traditional authority of hereditary monarchies in the late eighteenth and nineteenth centuries, liberals faced the difficulty of how to define the political community. Under monarchy the question was answered by establishing the extent of the territory which was rightfully controlled by the ruler. All those living within that territory thus formed the state. The issues of consent or sense of collective identity did not normally arise except as devices used in warfare in order to inspire troops.

In the liberal age the state could only be founded upon consent, but how were boundaries to be set? The concept of nation provided the solution. Here was a force which was able to bind a people together and justify the establishment of such a political community – the nation-state. For those nations who already enjoyed independence and unity, nationalism was not particularly important in establishing popular governments. In Britain and France, for example, the nation was well established so it was only necessary to transform the system of government for the new kind of state to come into existence. Elsewhere, however, there were greater problems to surmount before a nation-state could be formed. These difficulties were of three main types:

- Independence from a foreign power had to be established. This was particularly the case in the crumbling Austro-Hungarian Empire of the nineteenth century. Hungarians, Serbs, Slovaks, Slavs, Czechs and a host of other national groups sought to establish freedom, self-government and, in most cases, popular democracy. It was their nationalist sentiments which bound and inspired them to seek their freedom. A parallel scenario occurred after 1990 when the Soviet Empire collapsed. Then it was the likes of Georgians, Uzbeks, Latvians, Lithuanians and Estonians who were, simultaneously, seeking to express their nationhood as well as their release from domination by a foreign power. Indeed, this liberal form of nationalism was to become one of the dominant ideologies of the 1990s.

- In the nineteenth century there were several peoples who had become divided into a number of separate states, largely through the splitting of inheritances among unstable monarchies. The two prime examples were Germans and Italians. The unification movements in those two regions were not exclusively liberal, but it was a desire for full self-determination which was the driving force behind movements led by Bismarck and Mazzini, the two great unifying nationalists of their age. The desire for a union of Slavic peoples was not successful in the nineteenth century, nor has the desire for the establishment of an Arab nation in the second half of the twentieth century been fulfilled.

- Finally, some liberal nationalist movements have been described as 'republican' in nature. Here, the state already exists as a discrete entity, but is governed by rulers – normally hereditary – who are considered to be alien and an obstacle to the exercise of fully popular democracy. In the British Isles this is an apt description of both Irish and Scottish nationalism. Similar movements flourish in Spain (the Catalans) and in Belgium (the Flemish).

One of the characteristics of this kind of nationalism is that it may not be permanent. After its main goals have been achieved, there is no particular reason for its existence. It may persist in other forms – national pride and patriotism – but not as a specifically liberal movement.

Anti-colonial nationalism   This kind of movement is very specific in its goals and therefore easier to define. Clearly, peoples who have been subjected to colonial rule may develop nationalist sentiments in order to throw off the yoke of foreign rule. The dissolution of most of the great empires after World War Two gave rise to a large number of such movements.

However, the desire to remove colonial rule has been the one common feature of such nationalists. Thereafter, they have taken a variety of forms. These have included:

- socialist, as in Zimbabwe and Vietnam
- liberal-democratic, such as Kenya or India
- religious, for example, Pakistan.

It is also true that the claims to genuine nationhood have varied in strength from one case to another. Since colonial boundaries were often drawn up on an arbitrary basis, with little regard to history or ethnic and tribal divisions, newly independent territories were not natural nations. The problem of fostering national sentiment was, therefore, one which had to be continued long after the anti-colonial struggle had succeeded. Very often this post-colonial form of nationalism has led to the formation of authoritarian, one-party states. The need to create national unity among disparate peoples has eliminated the possibility of tolerating pluralist systems. That would be too much of a threat to the building of the successful nation.

Socialist nationalism

As a response to the economic imperialism experienced by many poorer developing countries, as well as by some long-established societies such as China, there have been revolutionary movements which have created a synthesis between the goals of nationalism and socialism. The ultimate objective has been the establishment of a new order to replace the economic domination of foreign powers.

In order to move such oppressed peoples to rise up against their governments who have been unable or unwilling to free themselves from dependence upon richer countries and multi-national corporations, a sense of national identity has had to be fostered as a rallying force. It may have **appeared** in such states as Cuba, El Salvador, Nicaragua and Algeria that foreign companies were providing employment and export markets while international banks were providing credit, but socialist nationalists argued that only dependence had been created. Independent economic life, sponsored largely by state socialism, was seen as the solution to inferior status and relative poverty. Thus, there was a symbiotic, interdependent relationship between nationalism and socialism. Its most successful exponents – Fidel Castro (Cuba) and Frantz Fanon (Algeria) – were able to overcome the natural suspicion of nationalist sentiment which most socialists harbour.

Conservative, right-wing nationalism

It is tempting to presume that all forms of right-wing nationalism are to be deplored on the grounds that they are associated with totalitarian regimes which have displayed aggressive, expansionist tendencies. Nazism was certainly the example *par excellence* of such a distasteful system, with Italian fascism and, more recently, Serbian nationalism in the Balkans following closely behind. This would, however, be a false picture as there have been conservative nationalist movements which have not demonstrated such extreme forms of behaviour.

Any political system which has an overwhelming desire to unite a people who show an inclination to disintegrate is likely to attempt to foster an organic society by using nationalistic symbols and forces. By stressing the factors which give people a common identity, there is a hope that such unity will prevail. The concept of an organic society led by a powerful state has been a conservative goal throughout the developed world since the early nineteenth century. Disraeli stressed such sentiments at a time when class conflict threatened the fabric of English society in the 1870s. So, too, did Bismarck in Germany. There was certainly little which could be described as sinister about such philosophies. It may be true that right-wing Conservatives have suggested that nationalist sentiments sponsored by a dominant ruling class could replace popular democracy, but this did not amount to totalitarianism. At worst, it could lead to benevolent despotism.

Nevertheless, conservative nationalism of this kind has had a tendency to drift towards totalitarianism. If the demands for national identity and pride are overwhelming, they may become as powerful as any other ideology. As we have seen above, the determined imposition of ideological rule of this kind does tend to lead towards a totalitarian society. China under **Chiang Kai-shek** before the 1949 revolution, Spain under **Franco** after 1939 and Chile under **Pinochet** in the 1970s and 1980s may serve as examples. Such nationalist, semi-totalitarian, almost fascist systems have also become endemic in Africa and South America.

In the latter cases, fear of socialism has been a further motivation in the creation of an authoritarian system. Nationalism has been seen as a valuable replacement for emerging class consciousness.

Apart from the development of authoritarianism, right-wing nationalism has also manifested itself in expansionist tendencies. Yet the apparent desire of such regimes for warfare is not merely born out of dreams of conquest. Paranoia – the fear that the country is suffering a constant external threat – can also be the seedbed of nationalism. **Nasser** in Egypt in the 1950s and Iraq under **Saddam Hussein** more recently have been typical in this regard.

We can, therefore, summarise the bases of right-wing nationalism as follows:

- a pressing need to unite a disparate people
- a conservative desire to create an ordered, organic society
- the need to replace socialist sentiments with an alternative form of social consciousness
- in extreme cases, a need to underpin the development of a totalitarian system
- a desire to reinforce expansionist tendencies
- a need to inspire a people to defend the state against a perceived external threat.

Ideas related to nationalism

Patriotism This should not be confused with nationalism. The term patriotism can be defined as a strong sense of pride and attachment to a **state**, that is, a political **reality**, not a mere dream or future goal. Where a people aspire to statehood, such as Palestinians or Kurds, we should refer to their sentiments as 'nationalism', not 'patriotism'. Conversely, it is possible to feel patriotic towards one's state even if no nation exists.

This is best illustrated by reference to the USA, which is a multi-national society characterised, nevertheless, by a well-developed sense of patriotism. Indeed, to a large extent these sentiments have been deliberately fostered by government in order to unite its disparate peoples. Thus, schoolchildren regularly salute the flag *en masse*, are taught sections of the Constitution and revere the office of the Presidency, even when the incumbent is personally unpopular. Similarly, we may find many Scottish nationalists who are, nevertheless, British **patriots**. In other words, they accept the existence of the British **state** and are loyal to it, but their **national** allegiance is to Scotland. The same analysis could be applied to such states as the former Soviet Union, Yugoslavia and Czechoslovakia, perhaps even South Africa.

<u>Chauvinism</u> Where patriotism becomes extremely exaggerated, the term 'chauvinism' can be applied. There are overtones of superiority attached to chauvinism, especially where patriotism becomes associated with nationalism, or even racism. The manifestations of chauvinism include sporting fanaticism, racial prejudice and exaggerated attachment to symbols such as patriotic songs and flags. Where the symbolism becomes overwhelming, the term 'jingoism' applies. Very often personality cult and heavy satirical criticism of foreigners may occur. Mao Zedong, China's great communist leader, was able to inspire many millions of his people to violent action by use of jingoism, largely directed at the USA and Britain.

<u>Racialism and racism</u> These two terms are often treated as interchangeable and clearly they are closely related, both being concerned with racial issues. However, we can distinguish between the two.

Racialism refers to a number of scientific or quasi-scientific theories about racial or ethnic differences between peoples. The theories presume that racial differences are significant in terms of human behaviour and/or characteristics. If racial origin does indeed influence behaviour in any meaningful way, it follows that it becomes relevant to political theory. Racialism can, therefore, be defined as any political philosophy which bases some or all of its principles upon racial differences.

Racialism existed in possibly its purest form in the white-dominated regime which governed South Africa for over thirty years until it was deposed in 1994. Its policy of 'apartheid' (literally 'separateness') actually proposed that different racial groups could not exist together in the same society. The culture, religion and abilities of different races were seen as eternally different so that peaceful co-existence would prove impossible. It became a by-product of this belief that, if separate states could not be established, the 'superior' white race should deny the other ethnic groups full citizenship and force them to live in separate areas.

While the white South Africans were unable to establish fully separate, racially-segregated states, Hitler in Germany certainly did see such an aspiration as a realistic goal. It was, indeed, a central feature of Nazi philosophy and played a large part in most other fascist regimes. There have been many historical examples of states or civilisations which have considered themselves to be of a superior race. The ancient Greek and traditional Chinese Empires, for example, certainly took the view that all other peoples were 'barbarians'.

There have also been some examples of racialist thinking which have been of a more benign character. Moderate Zionism, for example, bases the existence of the state of Israel upon ethnic/religious origin. Similarly, some Arab regimes have attempted to achieve a degree of racial exclusivity. Saudi Arabia and other Arabian Gulf states demonstrate such a tendency. Of course, all these examples have also their militant wings.

Racism represents a more emotional response to race than a political one. Certainly, racists have a highly developed sense of racial superiority and a disdain for what they perceive to be inferior races. Racism's most important manifestation is, as we have seen above, a desire for racial exclusivity, and it is normally the case that racists wish to rid their native country of foreigners. More commonly, however, racism shows itself in the form of prejudice, sometimes expressed violently, and systematic intimidation. It is also important to stress that, while racism is an utterly irrational mode of thinking (racists, for example, tend to place great store by skin colour alone), racialism does at least claim some scientific basis, however tenuous it may be.

Feminism

Origins

Despite the legendary existence of matriarchal (female-dominated) societies such as the warrior race of women known as 'Amazons', ideas concerning female equality did not emerge until the seventeenth century. The English 'diggers', for example, a quasi-communist movement which reached its height in the 1640s, did include some supporters of improved property and political rights for women. After that, only minor evidence of early feminist ideas can be found until the period of the French Revolution. Some, at that time, did argue that equal rights should be extended to women. In the same period in England, Mary Wollstonecraft (the wife of William Godwin, one of the first anarchist philosophers, and mother of Mary Shelley, the novelist who created the character Frankenstein), was campaigning for women's rights, notably for equal opportunities to obtain a good education and to pursue meaningful careers. The great liberal thinker, John Stuart Mill, together with his wife, led a campaign to achieve property rights for married women. His work *The Subjugation of Women* (1869) was an immediate precursor of the **Married Women's Property Act**, passed in the following year. This Act gave married women the right, for the first time, to own their own property. It was a significant step in freeing women (at least wealthier middle-class women) from financial reliance upon men.

However, it was the campaigns for women's suffrage – voting rights – which brought the question of the status of women to the fore in political circles. The suffrage movement gained momentum during the 1890s and early twentieth century, but it was not until 1918 in Britain, 1920 in the USA, that votes for women were guaranteed. Elsewhere, in the fields of education, career opportunities, family law and finance, progress was slow. Indeed, it has been suggested that the achievement of women's suffrage actually set back the cause of women's rights. It had been assumed that with votes would come representation. More women in Parliament would, the campaigners believed, result in political progress towards further rights and opportunities. As a result of this confidence, the movement was largely disbanded, but the expected advances in the women's cause did not arrive. Few women entered parliamentary politics, and women did not use their votes to further their own interests, but tended to persist with the same class-based allegiances to parties as men.

During and between the two World Wars, although relatively little legislative progress was made, changes were taking place which were to transform attitudes towards women irrevocably. Among them were:

● The experience of women working during the wars, often in responsible jobs formerly monopolised by men.

- The spread of knowledge and increased practice of family planning among women enabled them to take more control over their own lives and to limit the burden of childbearing.
- A great deal of literature was increasing public awareness of the inferior status of women. The liberally inspired 'Bloomsbury Group' of writers and artists and the novelist D.H. Lawrence were prominent examples.
- Some information about the improved status of women in the Soviet Union was filtering into the West. News of high numbers of female undergraduates, managers, workers, party officials and even officers in the armed forces inspired many middle-class intellectuals.

Nevertheless, the women's movement remained both small and almost exclusively middle class until the 1960s. It was at that time that modern, more radical forms of feminism were to emerge.

> 'The primary goal [of feminism] is women gaining power in order to eliminate patriarchy and create a more humane society.'
> Charlotte Bunch, *Class and Feminism* (Diana Press, 1974)

Feminism and the New Left

During the 1960s a new political movement emerged in Europe and the USA which was to become known as the 'New Left'. It was partly Marxist-inspired, but was also a reaction, not only to post-industrial capitalism, but also to the totalitarian, state-controlled socialism which had been established in eastern Europe. This was a more individualistic, anti-state group of philosophies, closer to anarchism than Marxism and with a more pluralist outlook upon modern society. Instead of viewing society from the point of view of economic class distinctions, New Left thinkers were concerned with the position of the many minority groups which appeared to be alienated from the dominant culture.

The ruling culture, argued the New Left, was dominated by white, middle-class, male, heterosexual society. Thus, the poor members of ethnic minorities, gays and women were alienated from such a culture. It was as part of this new political movement that modern radical forms of feminism came into existence. At the same time, interest was aroused in more liberal branches of the women's movement. Thus, as the 1960s came to a close, it was clear that two developments were taking place. First, there was a dramatic increase in interest in issues concerned with women. Secondly, the movement itself was fragmented into a number of different philosophies. We may now examine these various strands of feminism.

Liberal feminism

In common with all other philosophies which are based upon liberal principles, this branch of feminism is limited in its scope. Such feminists recognise that there are aspects of life which are not their concern. In other words, there is a clear distinction between public and private spheres. Thus, for example, individual sexual orientation, the structure of the family, and sexual and romantic relationships between individuals are the private concern of those involved and no one else. However, where there is systematic discrimination against women in the workplace or in education or if women are portrayed as inferior, liberal feminists in any medium claim the right to campaign for reform.

Similarly, we can say that liberal feminism is a reforming but not a revolutionary movement. There is no desire to transform the structure of society in order to realise women's goals. Rather, there are specific aspects of society which are seen to require reform. The kind of reforms which are proposed are suggested by the following liberal goals:

- Women should enjoy absolutely equal legal and political rights. This objective had been virtually completely achieved in Britain by 1990.
- The creation of equal opportunity for girls in education. This implies that girls should have equal access with boys to the whole school curriculum. In addition, there is a need to change attitudes among teachers and parents who may have lower expectations of girls.
- There should also be equal opportunities for women in virtually all forms of occupation. In recruitment and promotion practices women should be given equal treatment.
- The principle of equal pay for equal work should be established. The European Union had developed laws to provide for this by 1992.
- The state should provide pre-school education for children to enable women with young children to take up paid employment should they so desire.
- Financial help for single parents so that they may choose either to take up employment or to concentrate on child rearing.
- Abortion on demand.
- The outlawing of references in the media and the arts which overtly encourage attitudes suggesting male superiority.
- Encouraging and enabling more women to enter active politics.

The list shown above is not exhaustive, but it summarises the broad objectives of liberal feminism. However, one further aspiration must be emphasised. Betty Friedan, whose 1963 book *The Feminine Mystique* was a key early work of authority for feminists, suggested that women themselves must liberate their own minds. Her original contribution to feminist thought was to maintain that the inferior status of women was not solely due to men's desire to dominate society. Rather, she suggested, it has been the attitude of women towards themselves which has caused them to be regarded as inferior. The proposed remedy – that women should demand the right to pursue occupations outside the home – has been a central feature of liberal feminism ever since.

Radical feminism   Although Friedan's work was a crucial element in the early years of the modern women's movement, it was to be overtaken by considerably more radical writings after 1970. It was in that year that two books were published which together were to transform feminism completely. These were *The Dialectic of Sex* by Shulamith Firestone and *Sexual Politics* by Kate Millett.

Firestone, as the title of her book suggests, adapted Marx's dialectic approach to historical development, but substituted sexual conflict for class conflict as the crucial driving force behind social change. Similarly, while Marx had seen economics as the basis of all societies, Firestone identified the nature of male–female relations as the most significant characteristic of any community.

Millett focused upon sexual relations between men and women as the key factor in patriarchal, or male-dominated society. She defined such relations as 'political' in nature and claimed that, for this reason, they were the root cause of the conflict between the sexes. For her, domination began not in school, the workplace or the kitchen, but in the conjugal bed.

These two extraordinarily radical feminist tracts demonstrate the two features of this kind of feminism which distinguish it from the liberal variety:

- Patriarchy is seen as a complete **system** of domination of women by men. It pervades all aspects of life. It is not, as liberals suggested, one undesirable aspect of society, but its whole basis.
- There is nothing in society which is not the concern of feminist politics. Even the most private aspects of sexual relations are relevant and, indeed, may form the very basis of female oppression.

It follows from this that radical feminism is a revolutionary philosophy. This does not necessarily mean that there is likely to be a violent uprising by women against their male masters. Instead, it suggests that such feminists are seeking a complete transformation of existing, patriarchal society.

Just as radical feminism's critiques of patriarchal society are fundamental, so too are the solutions which have been proposed. The principal examples are shown below:

Radical reform   These measures include all the liberal proposals shown above, but go considerably further. For example, all so-called 'sexist' (meaning the display of attitudes demeaning to women or which express male domination) pornography, or sexist portrayals of women in theatre, films, literature and on television are to be outlawed. The militant anti-pornography campaigner, **Andrea Dworkin**, sees sexist portrayals of women as not merely distasteful, but actually violent, opposed to equal rights and exploitative. Similarly, Millett attacks the way in which women have been encouraged by men to appear feminine and 'sexy', thus accepting inferior status. It was this view which led to notorious 'bra burning' episodes and a tendency for feminists to dress in an asexual manner.

These attacks on attitudes which express male superiority have largely given rise to what is now known as 'political correctness'. Here, the use of language is seen as crucial since it is language which conveys so many of our cultural attitudes and transmits them from one generation to the next. Germaine Greer, in *The Female Eunuch*, referred to the importance of cultural transmitters as long ago as 1972. For the radical feminist reformer then, all sexist allusions in the written and spoken word should be eliminated.

Separation   Those who are less optimistic about the chances of destroying patriarchal society have suggested that women must set up their own social groupings from which men are excluded. In this way, female consciousness can be heightened and solutions to women's problems found without having to use institutions which are patriarchal in nature.

Women's communes have been set up, the most celebrated of which in Britain joined the permanent resident protest against the siting of American Cruise missiles at Greenham Common. So too have consciousness-raising groups, refuges for women suffering physical abuse by male partners and a variety of other community initiatives.

<u>Lesbianism</u> For those feminists who stress the exploitative nature of heterosexual relations, believing them to be intrinsically characterised by male domination, the only resort has been to encourage lesbianism as a means of freeing women from the most basic aspects of patriarchy. This has also been associated with the notion of separateness described above.

There is an assumption that lesbian relations are not exploitative in nature and are, therefore, the most natural form of human bonding. It may be difficult to accept that this is a call for heterosexual women to **become** lesbians even when their sexual orientation points elsewhere, but the most radical of feminists are suggesting just that.

<u>Matriarchy</u> In a parallel of Marx's hopes that the oppressed working class would one day rise up and become the masters of the class which formerly oppressed them, some feminists wish to see women replace men in dominant social roles. Underlying this aim is an assumption that women are different to men and are, indeed, superior.

Feminists claim that the nature of this superiority lies to some extent in biological differences and that women's genetic attributes which are designed to aid child-rearing also give rise to natural humanity, goodness and a lack of aggression. Feminists criticise men's aggressiveness and militarism, blaming them for many of the world's social ills. Women do not normally possess such characteristics, they argue. A matriarchal world, therefore, is likely to be peaceful and contain true social justice.

Marxist or socialist feminism This branch of feminism is inspired to some extent by Marxism, but is not necessarily so militant, so can take the milder title 'socialist'. In either case, it is a philosophy which suggests that the inferior position of women is based largely upon economic factors. Marx's close collaborator, Friedrich Engels, had suggested such an idea in the 1880s and continues to provide inspiration for women on the left of politics.

This economic branch of the feminist movement propounds the following ideas:

- The traditional nuclear family is, in itself, a repressive institution. Women are forced to provide a cheap source of labour in child-rearing and care of the home. Men are the beneficiaries in the home as they are freed from this burden at relatively little financial cost. Juliet Mitchell in *Women's Estate* (1971) drew attention to these domestic aspects of women's exploitation at a time when radical feminists were concentrating on what were considered 'big' issues, such as employment opportunities and education. She maintained that exploitation begins in the home.

- A more Marxist-led account of economic exploitation considers that women have been used in capitalist systems to provide a cheap source of labour. Marx had pointed out that a labour surplus was essential under capitalism to ensure that there would never be labour shortages which might cause wages to rise and profits to fall. Thus, an army of unskilled women waiting to step into vacancies would keep wages down.
- It is noted that much of the large accumulation of private property has been monopolised by men. This in turn deprives women of that property and, therefore, reinforces economic inequality for women. The answer is seen as the redistribution of that property without any question of preferences between the genders.

Broadly, therefore, the Marxist and socialist feminists believe that a complete transformation of society along socialist lines is required to liberate women. Like radical feminism, it is a 'revolutionary' movement.

Summary of feminist beliefs

Liberal feminism

- Women must enjoy equal legal and political rights.
- There should be equal opportunities for women.
- Overtly sexist attitudes should be discouraged.
- Women should have wide choice as to how they lead their lives.
- There should be equal economic rights for women.
- There should be a more female-led focus on such issues as rape, abortion, pornography and violence in the home.

Radical feminism

- Patriarchy is a complete system affecting all aspects of society.
- Even private sexual relations are political in nature.
- There must be a complete transformation of society to achieve feminist aims.
- Radical measures are required to rid institutions, the language, the arts and culture generally of sexist attitudes.
- Women should choose to set up a separate culture and/or develop purely lesbian sexual relationships to free themselves from male domination.
- Society should be matriarchal which would result in it being more humane, peaceful and just.

Socialist/Marxist feminism

- The oppression of women is fundamentally economic in nature.
- The traditional family is itself an oppressive and exploitative economic institution.
- Women are used by capitalism as a cheap source of labour to be exploited for greater profit.
- Private property is largely owned and controlled by men, thus depriving women of economic opportunities.
- Only the creation of a socialist society will liberate women.

Environmentalism

Introduction

Just as socialism or feminism can be conveniently divided into broadly liberal and radical wings, so too can two distinct forms of environmentalism be identified. The liberal form is reformist, but not revolutionary. It proposes important changes in the way we treat the natural environment and the living things within it, but stops short of suggesting that we need radical changes to the nature of our society. Radical environmentalists, also known as **ecologists**, on the other hand, insist that a far-reaching transformation in our thinking and way of life is essential if we are to survive as a species.

Both movements, however, have their origins in the New Left movement of the 1960s, to which we alluded in the section on feminism above. As we have seen, the dominant theme of the New Left was **alienation**. In the case of the environmental, or 'Green', movement it was alienation from our natural environment which was of concern. All Greens, radical and liberal, believe that we are in danger of losing sight of the fact that man as a species is intricately connected with the living and physical world. If we lose this perspective – become alienated from the natural earth – serious or irreparable damage will be done to human society.

Liberal environmentalism

It is within this philosophy that most of the groups which form the broad Green movement operate. They are, for example, European Green Parties, Friends of the Earth, Greenpeace and the Council for the Preservation of Rural England. Each tends to concentrate upon a relatively limited range of environmental issues, but all are essentially liberal in nature. The kind of issues concerned are shown below:

- Protection for the atmosphere through controls on air pollution, in particular those gases and chemicals which damage the ozone layer, cause the 'greenhouse effect' of global warming, and are responsible for a variety of human, animal and plant health damage.
- Control over industrial, transport and residential development in order to protect the rural environment.
- The elimination of all forms of water pollution, affecting the sea, lakes and rivers.
- Protection for endangered species of plant and animal life.
- Controls on the depletion of the world's natural resources, including fossil fuels, forests, fish and wild animals, and rare minerals. This is known as the theory of 'sustainable growth', that is, that economic progress should only be pursued if it is not at the expense of our natural resources.
- Decent treatment for wild, farm and domestic animals.
- A halt to the spread of economic development which endangers the traditional culture of primitive communities such as South American, Arctic and African tribal peoples.

All of these objectives, the less radical environmentalists argue, could be achieved within existing economic, social and political structures. Changes in policy and practice are needed, but this does not necessarily involve fundamental changes. The groups involved in seeking to bring about such reform have adopted a variety of tactics to achieve their goals, including lobbying politicians, publicity campaigns, civil disobedience, putting up candidates for election to representative institutions and placing representatives on administrative bodies which are concerned with environmental protection. However, none of these methods can be described as especially radical. It is **ecologism** which engages in such fundamental thought and practice.

Radical environmentalism or ecologism

At the heart of this movement lies the concept of **Gaia**, developed largely by the radical thinker James Lovelock in 1972. This 'hypothesis', as he titled it, suggests that the earth is one single organic whole. In short, it is a complete living thing. Everything, both living and inanimate, is interdependent. This 'biosphere', as it is also called, is in desperate need of protection and it is man's duty to provide that.

Arising out of the Gaia hypothesis is the startling suggestion that man himself is not the centre of this biosphere called earth, but is merely one part of it. We therefore have no special rights to treat the earth as if it exists solely for our own benefit. Jonathon Porritt describes the belief that man is pre-eminent as 'anthropocentrism' and he rejects it outright.

Underpinning the hypothesis stands a new kind of physical science, a prominent adherent of which was **Fritjof Capra**. Instead of treating physical phenomena as separate entities, Capra and his followers saw everything in nature as connected and interdependent. If anything happens to one part, there will be some effect on all the other parts, however disconnected they may appear to be. It follows from this that we cannot predict the effects of any change to any single part of the earth (sometimes this is described as 'chaos theory' according to which phenomena can occur without any possibility of adequate explanation or prediction). Traditional physical science had suggested that all changing phenomena could be explained. The environmental application of Capra's ideas lies in the fear that human activity which affects the natural environment is unpredictable in its results. We are, in short, interfering with nature without any idea of the ultimate effects of our actions.

Whether or not we accept the Gaia hypothesis, the implications are clear. There must be a fundamental change in man's thinking about the way in which we interact with the earth. This, in turn, will involve us in a deep rethinking about the way we organise society. The principal aims and beliefs of radical environmentalism are given below:

- Much of the cause of environmental damage lies with capitalism. Its constant need for economic growth gives rise to a reckless exploitation of the natural environment. Only if capitalism is abolished, probably to be replaced by socialism, can this relentless desire for economic growth be checked. Thus, sustainable growth, proposed by the liberals, does not go far enough. The concept of growth itself must be attacked.
- With regard to the critique of the capitalist obsession with growth, the radicals wish to put an end to the assumption that there will always be a steady increase in prosperity. Indeed, it is noted that much prosperity is achieved at the expense not only of the natural environment, but also of the poorer sectors of the world's population.
- The earth's resources may only be exploited in a sustainable manner, that is, man should not use any natural resources unless he can replace them.
- Industrialisation should be reduced or even abolished. This presupposes a return to a simpler way of life and, in this regard, ecologism can be equated with some forms of anarcho-communism.
- Since man is not considered to have higher status than any other living organism, we must show respect for all other living things.

- The exploitation of poor Third World countries is not only an economic evil, it is also an additional example of the abuse of the planet's natural ecology. Susan George, the celebrated modern campaigner for Third World protection, notes how the compulsion of developing countries to grow cash crops for export instead of natural local products disturbs the natural relationship between man and his environment.

Of course, the radical environmentalists share virtually all the goals of the liberals, but their views are considerably more philosophical and even spiritual. In many ways, ecologism is the most fundamental of all political ideologies.

For exam questions relevant to this unit, see page 493.

15 The social and political context of American government

The United States

The United States of America came effectively into existence with the creation of the Constitution in 1787. At that time, there were thirteen member states. Since then a further thirty-seven states have joined the Union, making a total of fifty. The last two to be added were Alaska and Hawaii in 1959. The states vary greatly in size and population. California, the largest, has a population close to 25 million, while Alaska has about 300,000 inhabitants.

Each state has its own constitution, legislature and government. These must all operate within the boundaries laid down in the federal Constitution. Each state elects two Senators to attend the federal Senate and a number of Representatives, depending on the size of its population, who pursue the interests of their constituencies in the House of Representatives.

The states are divided into **counties** and **cities**, which form the most local form of government. These smaller units enjoy a considerable degree of independence from the state government. The term 'city' must be treated with caution. Geographically, of course, the expression refers to a large urban conurbation and in the USA this is also true, but **politically** a city is a small unit of local government; American 'cities' can be just small towns as well as great metropolises such as New York.

The **District of Columbia** (the 'DC' in Washington DC) is not a state, but the territory immediately surrounding the capital city. It is administered directly by Congress and, thus, does not have its own government.

The USA has never possessed overseas colonies in the way that European powers have. There are, however, a number of territories which fall under American protection and are, broadly speaking, administered by Washington. The Pacific island of Guam, the American Virgin Islands and Puerto Rico in the Caribbean come into this category.

A multi-national country

The USA is not a 'nation' in the true sense of the word. Its people come from too many cultural and ethnic backgrounds for nationhood to be claimed. Americans themselves often refer to themselves as a nation, but this relates more to their aspirations to unity than to any historical reality.

Although the largest 'ethnic' group consists of the white descendants of the original British colonists, there are also substantial communities of other origins. These include:

Black Americans	Mostly descended from slaves
Hispanics	Immigrants from Mexico, Central America, Philippines, Cuba, etc
Asians	Mostly from Japan, China, Korea and Pacific islands
Jews	Largely refugees from oppression in Europe
Irish	The result of several migrations in hard times
Various Europeans	Escaping oppression and poverty at home

These groups are all 'Americans' and remain, on the whole, loyal and patriotic. This is not to say, however, that ethnic differences have no political significance. Their origins and sensitivities must be taken account of. Apart from the clear educational needs of more recent immigrants, politicians must also take heed of national sentiments. Modern examples have included the following:

- Policy in the Middle East is tempered by the need to maintain support from the large, influential Jewish population. America's relations with Israel are extremely delicate for this reason.
- In order to placate the largely Irish Catholic population, American politicians have been tempted to involve themselves in the Northern Ireland troubles. Indeed, it has been a common practice among Presidents, notably Kennedy and Reagan, to stress their Irish origins.
- The strong anti-communist position which the USA has taken in Central America and Asia has partly been driven by the demands of immigrants from those regions who came to the USA to escape such regimes.
- All immigrant groups have a tendency to suffer discrimination from the white majority. There is, therefore, a constant need to develop political measures to combat the abuse of civil rights.

The importance of section

The British term 'region' is described by Americans as 'section'. The USA is extremely large geographically, but more importantly, its sections have experienced different patterns of development, both economically and ethnically. Account must, therefore, be taken of the very different conditions which prevail in different parts of the country. A brief description of the main sections will give an indication of the political significance of 'sectionalism'.

The South

This really refers to the south-east corner. Texas dominates the South economically, but not culturally. It is, untypically, a mixture of conservatism and liberalism. Most of the South comprises old-established states such as Mississippi, Arkansas and Alabama. This is the heart of the former slave-owning part of the country. It has, therefore, a large black population. The white inhabitants are largely descended from English and French origins. It is also the least prosperous part of the USA, the result of the decline of agriculture and decades of economic neglect there following the Civil War and the freeing of the slaves in the 1860s.

The white, often poor, population tends to be deeply conservative in outlook, often racist and anti-federal government. These poor whites (also known as 'rednecks' or 'good ole boys') resisted civil rights legislation in the 1950s and 1960s and consistently discriminated against the equally poor blacks. There has been some economic recovery towards the end of the century and some degree of liberalisation of politics there. However, it remains an isolated, untypical part of the political map.

The East Coast

Dominated by New York, Washington and nearby Philadelphia, this is one of the oldest-established parts of the country, and includes some parts of the original British and Dutch colonies. It is more cosmopolitan than elsewhere, an extremely rich mixture of ethnic groups, especially in the cities. Its prosperity is based upon industry, finance and business, which are, in turn, dependent upon international trade. This is middle-class America, but **liberal** middle class, not conservative.

The people here, therefore, tend to be more progressive and international in their outlook. Until the growth of California in the middle of the twentieth century, it was the centre of American commercial and political life. To some extent it still is, though the West is now an important rival.

New England This is the most 'English' part of America – hence its name – and also one of the wealthiest regions. It comprises the north-eastern states, such as Massachusetts, Maine, New Hampshire, Vermont and Maryland. Boston is the principal city. The old-established families there, including the Kennedys, are the nearest thing the Americans have to an aristocracy and they have certainly played a dominant role in American life in modern times.

The people are, broadly speaking, liberal in their political outlook, but above all tend to be parochial. There is a very old, established tradition of independent local government within the hundreds of small communities. Many decisions are still made at 'town meetings' where the whole population gathers to exercise the most direct form of democracy known. This is a throwback to the way in which the original settlers carried on their politics, demonstrating how much tradition still colours the nature of American politics.

New England town meeting

The Mid-west The term 'Mid-west' describes the great states in the centre of the country, with scattered populations and great empty spaces – the landscapes so often seen in 'Western' films. Illinois dominates the area, which also includes Ohio and Indiana. It is largely agricultural, although much of its former prosperity has moved further west to California as a result of 'over-farming' in the early part of the twentieth century. In the 1930s a large proportion of the rural inhabitants moved west (the subject of John Steinbeck's epic novel, *The Grapes of Wrath*), as a result of which parts of the region have become seriously depopulated.

Outside its larger cities, such as Indianapolis, Cleveland and Chicago, most Mid-westerners live in small isolated communities. Not surprisingly, they tend to be inward-looking, conservative people. They generally oppose American involvement in the outside world and have supported firm policies of protection for agriculture against international competition.

The West Coast This is 'new' America – the later additions to the Union, now becoming the most prosperous. It is dominated by California and its three largest cities: Los Angeles, San Diego and San Francisco. It is here that America's newer and most modern industries – the 'sunrise' economy – are centred, including electronics (the original 'Silicon Valley' is in California), wine and exotic agriculture, and, of course, entertainment. In some ways, California and its neighbouring states are cut off from the rest of the USA. They are becoming increasingly more prosperous than the rest of the country and now look more to the Far East, towards Japan and China, than to Europe for their trading links.

Politically, the West Coast is very much a microcosm of the rest of the country. The liberal, urban middle classes in the north of the region are contrasted by the conservatives of Los Angeles and the agricultural communities.

Religion

Religious observance is more established in the USA than in most of Europe. Furthermore, there is developing an increasing diversity of faiths. The Christian religion is widely followed, but is gradually becoming more fragmented as there develops a steady increase in the number of sects and splinter groups. We have already seen how the Jewish and Irish Catholic communities can affect politics, but the revival of religious interest goes still further.

Many of the new fundamentalist Christian groups are deeply conservative in their moral outlook, taking a reactionary line on such issues as divorce, abortion, crime and even welfare. The New Right movement which grew during the 1980s, under the protection of Ronald Reagan's presidency, was partly religious in its inspiration. It regretted the loosening of morals, blaming rising crime, homosexuality and divorce rates on liberal social and moral attitudes. Many of the new members of Congress who swept into power as part of the Republican triumph in the 1994 elections were motivated by a deep religious sense of morality which was opposed to President Clinton's progressive social outlook.

At the same time, an increasing number of the black population are turning to Islam as the answer to the problem of their persistently low status in American society. Leading members of the black community, such as world boxing champions Mohammed Ali and Mike Tyson, have followed in the footsteps of more radical black leaders of the 1960s and 1970s, so rendering Islamic belief more respectable. The move to Islam threatens to usher in a new radical era in black politics. Adherence to the Muslim faith poses a challenge to traditional American social and political values.

The economy

Although America remains the most prosperous large country on earth, it still suffers a number of chronic economic problems. It has not experienced the same extremes of unemployment and inflation, the twin evils that have dogged Europe since the 1960s, but this does not signify a healthy economy. There are pockets of serious unemployment in the big cities, resulting in crime and other social problems, but these are not considered as pressing as the longer-term imbalances in the American economy.

The main problem in the American economy is debt, both domestic and international. For many years the federal government has run a huge deficit, that is, its spending has far exceeded its revenue from taxation. The accumulated debt – largely raised by borrowing from the public (in the form of bonds) and from the banks – places an enormous burden on the American taxpayer. There is a vast amount of interest to pay on the debt every year, as well as a proportion of the original sum which must regularly be repaid. Repeated attempts by Presidents and Congress have failed to make inroads into the debt. There is heavy pressure not to raise taxes on the one hand, but also resistance to reductions in public spending on the other. So the problem persists from one year to the next.

The USA has also suffered a long-term deficit in its balance of payments account. Put simply, there is a constant tendency to import more goods than it is exporting. This also results in debt, much of it overseas in this case. There is pressure to introduce protective measures against imports of cheap food from the Third World and manufactured goods, especially cars, from Japan and the Far East. But American governments recognise the importance of trade and are reluctant to jeopardise links with its allies. Attempts to make American industry and agriculture more competitive have also failed. The once almighty dollar has become a weak currency, prone to bouts of selling which cause disruption to the financial life of the country.

It would be mistaken to suggest the American economy is in crisis, though it suffers from periodic recessions as the other major world economies do. Rather, it is the case that the political system finds it increasingly difficult to maintain smooth economic growth in the way that the country is used to.

The media

As is the case with the political system in general, the American media is largely decentralised. Newspapers are all localised to cities and states, as are most of the TV and radio stations. There are a few network organisations, such as ABC and CNN, as well as some public service (non-commercial) broadcasting, but most coverage is regional. The effect is to ensure that local political issues are given a prominent place in the media, often rivalling all but the most dramatic national and international issues.

The Press is extremely independent and the great newspapers all have a strong tradition of investigative journalism. The openness of the political system gives extensive access to journalists and they put it to full use. This was never more evident than when two reporters – Woodward and Bernstein – were able to reveal the full extent of the dishonest practices adopted by President Nixon's staff in the Watergate scandal of the 1970s. The USA now has a Freedom of Information Act, which ensures that the Press is able to see official documents, ensuring that the work of journalists, such as the Watergate investigators, can continue to be an effective check on government.

The broadcasting media is similarly independent, though there is less political involvement than that undertaken by the Press. TV and radio are seen predominantly as providers of entertainment rather than information. Documentary or investigative programmes are, therefore, relatively rare. Politicians are able to buy time on TV and radio, and this has become one of the most important forms of political campaigning. Although there are statutory limits to spending by individual candidates, there is, essentially, open access to the broadcasting media for candidates for election of all kinds.

Social problems

Crime

Of all the economically developed democracies in the Western world, America suffers most from high levels of endemic crime. It is widely assumed that liberal gun laws are partly to blame – the right to carry weapons for self-defence is safeguarded by the Constitution – but this is not the only cause.

A popular explanation proposes that the wide gulf between the ostentatious wealth of many sections of the population and the extreme poverty of some groups, often from ethnic minorities, and frequently concentrated in the cities, is the main culprit. There is an assumption that large numbers of the urban poor, especially the young, have become alienated from the rest of America's prosperous society. Some look more critically at the American culture, suggesting that the extreme individualism which it has always promoted (as exemplified by the western 'cowboy' tradition) can lead to self-seeking criminal behaviour.

Whatever the true explanations, there is a considerable split within the political community concerning remedies. The conservative Right suggests draconian punishments to act as a deterrent to crime. Extensive use of the death penalty, long custodial sentences and tougher prison regimes have all been suggested. The liberal response is that there should be a greater focus on the economic and social causes of crime, including measures to relieve inner-city poverty and unemployment, to provide better social education and to curb the sale of guns. Though the problem continues to grow, political deadlock prevents dramatic action in either direction.

Inner-city decay

It would be a mistake to assume that the USA is completely riddled with criminal behaviour. In fact, most crime is concentrated in the centres of the great cities, notably New York, Los Angeles, Miami, Washington, Chicago and New Orleans. It is no mere coincidence that the rise in crime has coincided with the continued decline in both the social fabric and the physical environment of these cities.

Housing is run-down, schools are deprived and disordered, there are few employment opportunities and little hope for the young to improve their living conditions. In addition, there are ghettos where members of

Homelessness and poverty are major problems in many inner cities in the USA

ethnic minorities are heavily concentrated, so that there is constant tension and violence between neighbouring communities. Finally, and perhaps most seriously, drug abuse has become a serious and growing problem, leading to both criminal behaviour and broken lives.

As life in the cities has become less tolerable, there has been a growing exodus to the suburbs, especially by the middle classes, leaving poverty yet more concentrated in the city centres. Presidents Kennedy and Johnson began to tackle the problem of the inner cities in the 1960s, but since then the economic problems, to which reference is made on page 360, have prevented serious attempts to make inroads into the crisis. Bill Clinton declared, on his election in 1992, that he intended to tackle the problem of the cities, but a reluctant Congress is unwilling to release the huge funds needed to relieve the deprivation and decay. The high levels of crime and periodic rioting which have been seen of late seem set to continue.

Drugs Wars on the drug problem are periodically declared by American politicians, but progress has been slow. As with crime, its most severe incidence occurs in the cities and among the poor, but it has become an issue which now affects all levels of American society.

The USA has a huge coastline and land border, making it extremely difficult to prevent the import of drugs. Being so prosperous, it is also seen as an ideal target for the commercial interests associated with drugs. So, the problem appears to be intractable and no political party or leader has been able to propose viable solutions. There has been some entanglement with America's chief suppliers of drugs, such as Colombia and Panama, but these have resulted only in embarrassment and failure.

The political culture

Politically, the USA is extremely complex. This is mainly the result of a political culture which is full of paradoxes and subtle variations. As we have seen above, too, generalisations must be treated with caution as there are wide sectional variations in the political life of the country. Nevertheless, some general observations may be useful to an understanding of American politics.

Suspicion of Governments

On the whole, Americans are extremely suspicious of Governments. This sentiment can be traced right back to the origins of the Union, when British rule became very discredited, and even further back to the origins of the first settlers. Many of them arrived to escape from Governments which had been oppressing them. Ever since then, new waves of immigrant groups have followed, many of whom have also suffered from tyranny. It was, indeed, small wonder that the Founding Fathers ensured that the Constitution placed large obstacles in the way of any future administrations with ambitions to extend federal power.

There are variations in anti-government feeling, from the very conservative 'states'-rights' campaigners, who wish to see more power transferred from Washington to the state capitals, to more moderate politicians who simply wish to protect the constitutional safeguards against centralised power being further eroded. All have in common, however, a determination to prevent government becoming overbearing.

The relatively low turnouts at presidential and congressional elections may be seen as symptoms of the traditional dislike of big government. It is common for only 40–50 per cent of the electorate to vote in such elections, compared to about 75 per cent in Britain. A close parallel may be drawn between the British electorate's relative indifference to campaigns in European parliamentary polls (turnouts close to those of the USA) and that of the electorate in the United States. The reasons are similar. Governments in both Washington and Brussels are viewed as remote, ineffective and wasteful. By contrast, however, Americans are enthusiastic participants in local politics, especially where interest and pressure groups come into conflict with governmental institutions such as school boards, water authorities and police departments. They may be reluctant to vote for party politicians, but not to exercise their right to take direct political action.

Individualism

Few, if any, Western democratic countries give greater rein to the freedom of the individual than the USA. Individual liberties are firmly protected by the Constitution. Economic enterprise is not only protected, but also actively encouraged. Americans tend to like people who take responsibility for their own lives and are unsympathetic to those who rely on others when they could help themselves.

For this reason, collectivism has never been popular as a way of achieving goals among Americans. There is no organised public health service, little publicly provided housing, only a basic welfare system and trade union membership is not widespread. Not surprisingly, then, socialism, even social democracy, has never gained a significant toehold in the political scene.

Parochialism   Despite the existence of many huge cities, America is basically a country of small towns. In these towns the sense of community tends to be very strong. The level of political activity on a national scale is relatively low when compared to European democracies. National election turnouts only reach about 50 per cent and there are few national party activists. At local level, however, the story is very different.

Local politics is extremely vigorous and well supported. Community interest and pressure groups abound. Local issues are often hotly disputed through the media and in the form of direct action. As we shall see below, many local officials are elected, whereas in Europe they would be appointed. This makes for a lively and interesting local political environment.

The story is similar at state level. As we have seen, many Americans see federal government as remote and largely irrelevant. What goes on in their state and their county, on the other hand, affects them more directly. For these reasons American politics is mostly parochial in nature.

Conservatism   One of the paradoxes of American political life is the fact that, in a country which has proved to be one of the most dynamic and innovative societies in the modern world, the people are, on the whole, conservative in outlook. Radical politicians are treated with great suspicion, as are the radical measures which they may propose.

The recent revival in religious observance has underpinned this deep-seated conservatism, since most of the new Christian groups are fundamentalist in character. The media, too, tend to avoid too many radical positions, though this may be the result, rather than a cause of American moderation.

Some caution needs to be expressed at this point, since there are regional variations on this issue. As we have seen above, the states of New England, the Deep South and the Mid-west may be largely conservative, but there have been pockets of political radicalism in the eastern cities and on the West Coast which have emerged from time to time, never more so than in the 1960s, when America appeared to be taking a political turn to the left. By the mid 1970s, however, the apparently stronger conservative tradition had reasserted itself.

Patriotism   Few nations can rival the USA in the love their people show for their country. It is true that patriotic symbolism is heavily stressed in American schools. The flag, the anthem and the Declaration of Independence are well-known images to all American children. Yet patriotism is also a reflection of a natural sentiment which was noted as long ago as 1830 by the visiting French political philosopher, Alexis de Tocqueville. For him, it was one of the country's most endearing qualities and he saw it as essential to the stability of the political system.

Even when government is unpopular, the President receives a loyal welcome wherever he travels. There is an understanding among most Americans that there is a difference between the **office** of the President, which they respect, and the policies of the **individual** who holds that office, which they may oppose. Similarly, they may fight to defend the **Constitution** even when they find government repugnant.

In a country that is the home of citizens with such diverse ethnic origins, cultures and religions, patriotism becomes the key to the unity of the country. As we have said above, America is not really a nation, but it is able to compensate for that through the degree of loyalty to the country shown by most of its people. Apart from its powerful patriotic symbols, the USA has also come to embody the 'American dream'. The dream is that anybody, no matter how humble their origins, has the opportunity to realise their full potential. In a free society, with no social or ethnic barriers to success, Americans believe that every individual has the same life-chances. Though aspects of American life may fall some way short of the dream, it sustains many of the people in their love of the country.

For exam questions relevant to this unit, see pages 493–4.

16 The United States' Constitution

Background

Historical development

In 1765 British America was comprised of thirteen colonies which came under the jurisdiction of Parliament in London, and whose people were subjects of the King (George III at that time). Each of the colonies had its own political institutions, but these were relatively powerless, with no legislative and few executive powers.

In that year Parliament in London passed the notorious **Stamp Act**, effectively a tax on all official documents and contracts. What may seem a relatively unimportant event was to light a spark which became a conflagration. The tax was bitterly resented and gave rise to calls for greater American control over such matters. The maxim 'No taxation without representation' was born at this time. The colonists pointed to the long English history of allowing Parliament, with its representatives from the towns and counties, to oversee the King's use of taxation and public expenditure. Why were they denied such representative rights?

Unrest led to the **Boston Massacre** in 1770, when British troops fired on a crowd protesting over British monopolies in trading rights. Three years later the famous **Boston Tea Party** saw the destruction of tea imports taking place for similar reasons. The stories – largely exaggerated – of the exploits of the Bostonians and the British repression which followed it, gave rise to the calling of the first **Continental Congress** in 1774. Representatives from twelve of the colonies met in what became the first seedbed of independent American government. They called on George III and his Government to grant a number of rights to the colonists. These calls went unheeded, however, and unrest grew in the colonies.

By the time the second Continental Congress met in 1775, the War of Independence had begun. On 19 April the battles of **Concord** and **Lexington** took place. The Congress lasted for five years and was, effectively, the provisional Government of the American revolutionaries. Its most important achievement, other than the raising of an army to fight the British, was the publication of the **Declaration of Independence** on 4 July 1776. The Declaration was largely written by **Thomas Jefferson** of Virginia who was to become the effective leader of the new country. Though **George Washington** was later to become its first President, Jefferson was the dominant political figure.

After the Declaration all the states claimed to be sovereign political units and most of them adopted written constitutions. These events of 1776–81, therefore, were to prove to be key historical moments in the development of the concept of constitutional government. The **Massachusetts State Constitution** of 1780 still exists today (albeit with many amendments) and is the oldest codified constitution still in force anywhere in the world.

By 1781 a constitution for all the thirteen states had been established, known as the **Articles of Confederacy**. This created a loose union between the states, each of which retained its own sovereignty. The Confederacy was to control the armed forces, foreign affairs and treaties on behalf of all the states, exercise broad economic and currency control, and deal with disputes between states. However, it did not deny the claim of the thirteen former colonies to be independent sovereign states. The Confederate Congress was drawn from delegates from the states and there was no true executive Government set up. It was, in short, a compromise between a **unitary**, centralised state, as Britain was, and a **federal** system, which was to evolve in America after 1787.

The **Treaty of Paris** in 1783 formally brought to an end the War of Independence, which had effectively been won two years earlier. Britain accepted the independent status of the thirteen states. It was soon clear, however, that the Confederate system could not work. The states were too weak, militarily and economically, to survive alone. A closer union was needed, with some sort of centralised leadership. If America were to join the international community of states, it needed a new political structure. After an abortive attempt to create a union at **Annapolis** in 1786, representatives from the thirteen states met at Philadelphia in the summer of 1787, charged with the task of creating the United States of America.

The 'Founding Fathers', as the Philadelphia gathering became known, worked quickly (and in secret, which explains much of their efficiency), producing the **United States' Constitution** in the autumn. There then began a long process by which each of the thirteen states' assemblies had to ratify the document. By the time the state of Rhode Island narrowly approved the new Constitution in May 1790, all the other thirteen states had ratified it. Before that, however, the first President, George Washington, had been sworn in on 30 April 1789. And it is this date that marks the creation of the United States.

The road to the Constitution – a chronology of events

1765	Passage of the Stamp Act
1770	Boston Massacre
1773	Boston 'Tea Party'
1774	First Continental Congress
1775	War of Independence begins
	Second Continental Congress
1776	Declaration of Independence
1781	Articles of Confederacy signed
	War of Independence ends
1783	Treaty of Paris formally ends war
1786	Annapolis Convention
1787	Constitution written at Philadelphia
1789	Washington sworn in as President
1890	All thirteen states ratify the Constitution

Philosophical principles

Democracy   It may seem obvious today that the Founding Fathers should choose democracy as the basic form of government to be adopted. However, in 1787 the matter was less clear. The French Revolution had not yet occurred so that no large-scale democratic political system had been established. Many feared the power of the mass of the people and the disorder which might result from the abandonment of absolute government.

But it was the democrats who won the day decisively. Of course, it was to be a democracy of property owners and not the mass of the people. Slaves were certainly excluded, as were women. For free men the issue was less clear. In fact, it was not until later in the nineteenth century that universal male adult suffrage was to be established. Yet this does not alter the fact that the American Constitution was firmly rooted in the concept that citizens of the state should be able to influence and participate in government.

<u>Government by consent</u>   The principle objection which the American colonists had laid against the Government of George III was that it gave no opportunities for those who were governed – the subjects of the Crown – to give their agreement to the power being exercised over them. A hundred years before, the English philosopher, **John Locke**, had insisted that any government could only be legitimate if it enjoyed the consent of the people. Thus, the Constitution was designed to ensure that there would be mechanisms for establishing such consent. The system chosen was for an elected legislative body (Congress) to agree to laws or taxation **on behalf** of the people.

> 'Nor can any edict of anybody else, in whatever form soever conceived, or by what power soever backed, have the force and obligation of the law which has not its sanction from the legislative which the public has chosen and appointed.'
> John Locke, *Second Treatise of Civil Government*, 1691

<u>Individual rights</u>   It was something of an oversight that the original Constitution of 1787 did not contain a clear statement of the rights of individuals. Nor did it include provision for the protection of such rights. During the ratification process, however, there was an insistence that such a provision be included. The revolutionaries had clearly been motivated largely by a desire to grant such rights to the people of America, rights which had been denied by British government. In the event, the first ten Amendments to the Constitution expressed the need for the entrenchment of individual rights. These amendments have become known as the **Bill of Rights**.

They arose from two traditions. One was the historical development of 'common law' rights which were part of Anglo-Saxon culture. In the early days of the USA, most of the citizens were of Anglo-Saxon stock so that they understood the principles. Such rights as trial by jury, private enjoyment of property and freedom from imprisonment without trial were ancient privileges which had been enjoyed by free Englishmen for centuries. They had been enshrined in the Magna Carta of 1215, but the Americans added the device of entrenchment as an added safeguard. Thus, rights were not only stated clearly, they were also protected from encroachment by government.

The second origin of the protection of rights in the Constitution arose out of the conception of natural rights which had been developed by such philosophers as Thomas Hobbes, John Locke, Jean-Jacques Rousseau and, above all, **Tom Paine**, an Englishman who had, despite his nationality, joined the American cause.

The inspiration for the Declaration of Independence had come largely from Paine's revolutionary pamphlet *Common Sense*, published in 1775. The Bill of Rights arose largely out of his later work, *The Rights of Man*.

> *'The end of all political associations is the preservation of the natural and imprescriptible rights of man . . . liberty, property, security and resistance of oppression.'*
> Tom Paine, *The Rights of Man*, 1790

Political principles

Limited government The American colonists had suffered from the experience of the arbitrary government of the British monarchy and the uncontrolled sovereignty of Parliament in London. It was, therefore, hardly surprising that the Founding Fathers wished to establish the principle of limited government. They developed a concept which was, at the time, completely unique. This was the use of a written constitution to establish the limitations upon government.

Philosophers such as Locke had suggested that the way in which government could be controlled was through the ability of the people to remove it. However, this ignored the possibility that a tyrannical Government might simply refuse to be so removed. By making government subject to the limitations of a constitution, underpinned by the principle that its laws would be unenforceable if they did not conform to constitutional rules, the problem was largely solved.

The principle, also known as 'constitutionalism', establishes that part of the Constitution will clearly set out the boundaries within which each branch of government may operate. Its authority will not run beyond these boundaries.

Judicial review Associated with the concept of constitutionalism stands the principle of judicial review. This establishes that any dispute concerning the meaning or application of the Constitution must be resolved by a review carried out in the courts, ultimately the Supreme Court. Such review, however, does not take place **before** a law is passed or a government order made. Rather, it must first be challenged by an individual, an organisation or a state through the courts and later, if necessary, through an appeals procedure.

If a law or government action is deemed to have contravened the Constitution, it is declared **unconstitutional**. The courts will not enforce it and so it must be set aside.

The separation of powers The French philosopher, **Montesquieu**, one of the inspirations behind the French Revolution, had argued that, if tyrannical government was to be avoided, it was necessary for it to be **internally** limited. The principle of constitutionalism, as described above, establishes an **external** control. Montesquieu was more concerned with the nature of government itself.

Montesquieu first identified the three branches of government as **legislative** (law making – the Congress), **executive** (policy making and implementing laws – the President and the agencies he controls), and **judicial** (law interpretation – the courts, especially the Supreme Court).

He then suggested that each branch should possess powers which would limit the other two. As long as they were separate and mutually powerful, there would be an automatic mechanism whereby no single branch of government could become too powerful. The concentration of power in too few hands was to be avoided for the sake of balanced and controlled administration of the laws.

The American version of Montesquieu's principles has become known as 'checks and balances'. The powers granted by the Constitution to each branch of government were carefully matched against those granted to a rival branch. To illustrate, the President has the power to veto laws passed by Congress. This is balanced by the fact that the President can issue no laws without congressional approval. Thus, they control and rely on each other.

Similarly, the President may appoint judges to the Supreme Court, but this is balanced and controlled by the fact that his nominations may be set aside by Congress. In addition, since judges are appointed for life, the President cannot remove them if he is dissatisfied with their decisions.

> '*US government is in reality based not on separated but on shared powers which give each branch of government considerable powers in the legislative, executive and judicial functions of government.*'
> Howard Elcock, 'American Government in the 1990s' in
> *Talking Politics*, Vol. 6, No. 2 (Winter 1994)

Federalism The biggest problem which the Founding Fathers faced in 1787 was how to reconcile the demands of the thirteen states to retain some autonomy while, at the same time, creating a strong union which would not disintegrate at the first sign of political controversy. Allied to this difficulty stood the danger that the new union could be dominated by the larger, richer states. The result, forged out of a number of compromises, was known as the 'federal settlement'. It should be immediately apparent that the kind of controversies which raged in Philadelphia over 200 years ago are still being played out in the struggle to find a structure for the European Union in the 1990s.

The nature of the federal compromise was something of a masterpiece of both legal theory and political reality. The legal device used was to split sovereignty between the central institutions of government and the several states. The division of sovereignty was protected by the extremely entrenched nature of the Constitution itself. It was made so difficult, as we shall see below, to alter the terms of the Constitution that the states were satisfied that their sovereignty would be safeguarded except in highly unusual and unlikely circumstances.

Two particular principles were designed to protect what are called 'states' rights'. One was a limitation upon the powers of the federal Congress and the Presidency so that there could be no significant erosion of state power. The other was to assert that any powers not covered by the Constitution would automatically be granted to individual states. Thus, even if the scope and functions of future government were to increase, it would not automatically lead to greater centralised power.

**Part of the original
Constitutional
document**

The Founding Fathers were, however, also realists and understood that the Constitution should not be too rigid in its division of sovereignty. Thus, some of the wording remains vague and, therefore, capable of future interpretation. Terms such as 'trade' and 'commerce' are prominent examples of the compromise.

Despite some problems during the two hundred years of its life, the federal settlement has proved such a successful constitutional device in reconciling political unity with regional autonomy that many other states have adopted similar devices since. Germany, India and Russia have been important examples of federalism.

The structure of the Constitution

The Articles of the Constitution (effectively sections) reflect the thoughts of the founders on the appropriate nature of constitutional government, together with the philosophical principles established by the likes of John Locke, Tom Paine and Montesquieu. There are seven Articles in all, as listed below.

The Articles

Article 1 The powers and limitations of the Federal Congress
Article 2 The powers and limitations of the President and his Administration
Article 3 The role of the judiciary, especially the Supreme Court
Article 4 The nature of membership of the Union and citizenship defined
Article 5 Procedures for amendment of the Constitution
Article 6 An affirmation of the supreme authority of the Constitution
Article 7 Arrangements for the original ratification of the Constitution

One area was omitted – a clear statement of the rights of citizens. This was put right before the ratification procedure was completed. The ten amendments forming the Bill of Rights are described below.

The Bill of Rights These amendments (confusingly, also known as 'Articles') are a description, varying in clarity, of the rights which American citizens can expect to enjoy. Article 6 of the main Constitution makes it clear that all laws and Acts of government, whether federal or state, must conform to these rights. The rights which are established are as follows:

- freedom of religion
- freedom of speech and expression
- freedom of association and assembly
- freedom to petition government for redress of grievances
- the right to carry arms for self-protection
- freedom from enforced billeting of troops in private houses in peacetime
- protection from searches of private homes, except following legal procedure
- the right of accused persons in serious cases to have a preliminary hearing before a 'grand jury' – effectively a randomly selected group of members of the public
- the right of accused persons to remain silent during interrogation and trial in case they should incriminate themselves (the famous 'fifth amendment', hence the term 'pleading the fifth' when a defendant refuses to answer questions)
- protection from being tried for the same crime twice ('double jeopardy')
- accused persons must be quickly brought to trial and not held in custody without such a trial
- the right to trial by jury in serious cases
- the right to be represented by a lawyer in criminal cases
- protection from excessive bail and 'cruel and unusual punishments'
- any other rights enjoyed by individuals or the states are automatically protected unless expressly removed by consent of the people.

Though this forms an impressive list, the Bill of Rights still leaves a number of important questions unanswered. Examples of these issues include:

- Do these terms grant the right to privacy?
- Should there be limits to the right to carry weapons?
- Does 'cruel and unusual punishment' include all judicial executions, some types or none at all?

Apart from these open issues which have continued to exercise the minds of lawyers, judges and politicians ever since, a number of further rights issues have come to light, with some being resolved and others not. Voting rights were left out and the issue of slavery was fudged. Discrimination against racial minorities and women was to become a key issue in the 1950s and 1960s and the latter remains to be resolved. Freedom of information became an issue with the growth of government functions in recent times. So, too, has the question of censorship and pornography. Yet, apart from questions arising specifically out of modern developments, unforeseeable by the Constitution writers, the Bill of Rights remains a guide against which all legislation must be judged.

Amendments Any amendment to the Constitution requires the approval of two-thirds of both Houses of Congress, together with ratification by the legislative assemblies of three-quarters of the states (38 out of 50). It is a long and difficult procedure, as was fully intended when the Constitution was drawn up. This is an entrenched Constitution. Changes were only to be considered if there was a broad consensus of support for such changes. The principle of 'government by consent' lives on in these amendment procedures.

During its life of just over two hundred years the Constitution has only been amended twenty-seven times. This is testimony both to the complexity of the amendment procedures and the skill of the Founding Fathers in creating such an enduring system. The contents of the first ten amendments are detailed on page 372; some of the most important of those which have been passed since are shown below:

		Constitutional amendments
Number	Year	Detail
13	1865	The abolition of slavery
14	1868	Establishment of equal rights, including their right to vote, for all males over 21
15	1870	Voting rights not to be denied to anyone on the grounds of race, colour or religion
18	1919	Prohibition of manufacture and sale of alcohol
19	1920	Voting rights for women established
21	1933	Repeal of the 18th Amendment (Prohibition)
22	1951	Presidents to have a maximum of two terms of office (8 years)
26	1971	Voting age reduced to 18

The difficulty in amending the Constitution can be illustrated by the problems encountered by two important proposals in recent times. The Equal Rights Amendment (ERA) was designed to force all states to outlaw discrimination against women. Having passed both Houses of Congress successfully, its ratification journey was halted in 1982 after thirty-five states had given their approval. Thus, it fell just three states short of enactment. In 1995 a proposal by Republican Senate leader Robert Dole to force future administrations to achieve a balanced budget (where government expenditure would be matched by revenue from taxation) fell two votes short of success in the Senate, having passed through the House of Representatives with a large majority.

The status of the Constitution

Marbury v. Madison

Chief Justice John Marshall was possibly America's greatest constitutional lawyer and judge. He was Chief Justice of the Supreme Court from 1801–35 at a time when a number of important cases were heard, cases which shaped the meaning and status of the Constitution. The most significant of these cases was *Marbury v. Madison* in 1803.

The case was a dispute over the appointment of judges. In making his judgment, Marshall made a declaration concerning the status of the Court and the Constitution which has been considered binding ever since. Three main principles were established:

- The Supreme Court has the right to undertake **judicial review** of cases brought before it in which constitutional principles are at stake.
- If the Supreme Court declares a law to be unconstitutional, it has no force and must be set aside.
- If there is a conflict between any ordinary law and a constitutional law, the latter must prevail.

The key section of Marshall's judgment is shown below:

> *'It is emphatically the province and duty of the judicial department to say what the law is. Those who apply the rule to particular cases, must of necessity expound and interpret that rule. If two laws conflict with each other, the courts must decide on the operation of each.'*
> Chief Justice John Marshall, *Marbury v. Madison*, 1803

McCulloch v. Maryland

It was Marshall again who enhanced the status of the federal Constitution in 1819 in a case where the state of Maryland was attempting to defy federal law. The state was brought before the Supreme Court where a far-reaching judgment was made.

Marshall ruled that, in any dispute between the laws of the federal Constitution and the laws of a particular state, the federal Constitution must prevail. Thus, although legal sovereignty is divided in the USA, there can be no doubt that the central authority of the Constitution is supreme. Marshall's words are clear in their implication:

> *'This great principle is, that the Constitution and the laws made in pursuance thereof are supreme; that they control the Constitution and laws of the respective states, and cannot be controlled by them.'*
> Chief Justice John Marshall, *McCulloch v. Maryland*, 1819

The living Constitution

The Supreme Court and the Constitution

John Marshall's term of office confirmed the status of the Supreme Court in the maintenance and development of the Constitution. Although, as we have seen, there have only been twenty-seven **formal** amendments to the Constitution, this should not be interpreted to mean that it is a fixed, rigid document. On the contrary, it is constantly evolving and changing its practical applications.

The reasons for the evolving nature of the Constitution are threefold:

- First, circumstances are constantly changing; fresh situations arise which have not been addressed by the terms of the Constitution. For example, the development of the communications media has thrown up new problems concerning censorship, privacy and federal control of broadcasting.
- Secondly, the make-up of the Supreme Court itself is permanently changing. As judges retire or die and new members are appointed by the President, the political balance of the Court alters. Thus, for example, while a 'conservative' Court might allow capital punishment to be imposed, a more liberal bench might outlaw it. Similarly, some of the judges have been sympathetic to federal power and have, therefore, allowed a degree of centralisation; others have been staunch defenders of the rights of the individual states.
- Thirdly, the nature of American public opinion is in a permanent state of flux. Political sentiments and moral views do change over time. Thus, during the 1980s and 1990s a new moral movement has taken hold. This is reflected in a series of cases over such issues as abortion in which individual rights have been reconsidered from a constitutional point of view. When America is in a liberal mood it is also civil liberties which often take the attention of the Supreme Court. Although some 'conservative' legal commentators have argued that the Supreme Court should not be influenced by movements in political and moral opinion among the general public, it has always been true that the judges have reflected changing public feeling.

Thus, the nature of the Supreme Court and its use of judicial review ensures that the Constitution is always evolving. To illustrate, some of the most celebrated constitutional cases are described briefly below:

Gibbons v. Ogden 1824   The Constitution gives power to the federal government to **regulate commerce** but does not explain the precise meaning of the term 'commerce'. The pioneering Chief Justice John Marshall ruled in this case that commerce should be interpreted widely to include trade between the states and therefore, by implication, the general regulation of industrial and commercial activity. His words were clear: *'Commerce undoubtedly is traffic, but it is something more – it is intercourse. It describes the commercial intercourse between nations and parts of nations, in all its branches, and is regulated by prescribing rules for carrying on that intercourse.'* The limited interpretation of federal power was, therefore, rejected by the ruling, and central government power has tended to increase ever since.

Dred Scott v. Sandford 1857   A conservative Court was asked to judge whether black slaves could become citizens if they resided in a state where slavery was outlawed. It was ruled that, as slaves were 'property' they could not claim the same rights as 'free' men. The decision was one of the factors which led to the Civil War when the southern states sought to protect their right to maintain slavery. Though seen as a retrograde decision, the Court had opened the issue to public debate and, ultimately, the Constitution was amended to end slavery.

Pollock v. Farmers' Loan and Trust Company 1895 This test case affirmed that the federal government did *not* have the constitutional right to levy taxes on income. The resultant debate over the issue led to the ultimate passage of the sixteenth amendment in 1913, allowing government to raise such tax.

Schechter Poultry Corporation v. United States 1935 President F.D. Roosevelt's attempts to extend the power of the federal government into the field of industrial relations during the Great Depression (as part of his **New Deal** policies designed to regenerate American industry) was stopped in its tracks by this judgment. The **National Industrial Recovery Act (NIRA)** included measures to restrict working hours and so provide increased employment opportunities. Schechter challenged the Act on the grounds that the Constitution did not allow federal government to take such powers. The Court, which was unsympathetic to the New Deal policies, found in favour of Schechter. The NIRA was now virtually useless and it took Roosevelt a further two years, when a more friendly Court was in place, to restore his programme.

Brown v. Topeka Board of Education 1954 In a number of the ultra-conservative southern states schools were usually segregated until the 1950s, to avoid the mixing of black and white pupils. In this case the practice was challenged and the Court held that blacks had the right to attend any school. The civil rights movement was, thus, given a boost which was to culminate in President Lyndon Johnson's Civil Rights Act of 1964, securing equal rights for all races.

Baker v. Carr 1962 This case illustrated the ability of the Court to interpret constitutional principles broadly. The fifteenth amendment states that there must be equal voting rights for all. *Baker v. Carr*, however, concerned a claim that electoral boundaries were being manipulated to favour one political party, a practice known as **gerrymandering**. It was considered that such gerrymandering denied certain voters equal rights, since they were disadvantaged by the artificial creation of the electoral boundaries. This was indeed a liberal interpretation of the wording in the Constitution, but was still effective in establishing a new political principle – that the creation of such electoral boundaries must be seen to be neutral and fair to all parties.

Furman v. Georgia 1972 The Court specifically abolished the use of the death penalty in this case on the grounds that its use varied so much from state to state and from court to court that it had become a matter of pure good or bad fortune whether a convicted murderer was put to death or not. Thus, it constituted an 'unusual' punishment, forbidden by the Constitution.

Gregg v. Georgia 1976 A protracted debate followed the *Furman* case as a result of which the Court reconsidered its earlier decision. Public opinion was also slowly returning to supporting the use of capital punishment. The Court finally declared that, under most circumstances, execution for capital crimes could be constitutional after all.

Roe v. Wade 1973 This case, concerning abortion, reflected the rising power of feminism in the USA. By forbidding anti-abortion laws it affirmed the right of women to seek an abortion during the first three months of pregnancy.

Casey v. Planned Parenthood of Pennsylvania 1992 As opinions on abortion began to change in the 1980s away from the liberal stance of the previous two decades, the Supreme Court was asked to reconsider the earlier *Roe v. Wade* judgment. The *Casey* case was a compromise whereby states were given powers to limit the circumstances under which abortions could be performed, without allowing them to introduce outright prohibition.

Adarand Constructors v. Pena 1995 This case concerned a challenge to the principle of 'affirmative action', or positive discrimination, which is commonly implemented in American states. Normally, there is a legal requirement that larger employers take on a certain 'quota' of members of ethnic minorities in order to counteract the apparent negative discrimination which such groups suffer. Despite President Clinton's appointment of two liberal justices who might have supported this kind of device, a 5–4 majority outlawed many forms of affirmative action as an unconstitutional interference in commercial practice. Indeed, even the Court's one black judge voted with the conservative majority. The decision further confirmed the 1990s conservative reaction to civil rights progress.

This brief selection of Supreme Court cases illustrates the breadth of judicial action on developing the meaning and applications of the Constitution. Among them we can find examples of interpretation, responses to shifting public opinion and adaption to changing circumstances. Thus, the Constitution is, indeed, alive and growing.

Legislation The twin processes of constitutional amendment and judicial review ensure that the Constitution is constantly evolving, but these procedures are not enough to ensure that the business of government and politics can develop quickly enough to meet shorter-term contingencies. More flexible devices are necessary to deal with rapidly changing circumstances. Here, ordinary legislation can be used to flesh out the skeleton of the Constitution. Though Acts of Congress do not carry special labels if they are of constitutional significance, we can recognise them as such from the nature of their content. They form a part of the 'living' Constitution in the same way as the other devices which have been described above. Some of the most important constitutional Acts are shown below:

Federal Regulation of Lobbying Act 1946 Responding to the growth in the activities of pressure and interest groups in Congress, this Act requires all such groups to register with Congress in order to have access to legislators. It also forces them to declare the nature of their activities, the sources of their funds and the use to which they have been put.

This was a clear case of legislation being needed to meet a fresh circumstance not covered by the Constitution. Being a technical and detailed regulation, it was not practical to use the method of constitutional amendment. In addition, the Act can be easily adjusted by Congress in the future without recourse to the long and complex constitutional amendment procedures.

Civil Rights Act 1964   President John F. Kennedy was the architect of this legislation, but was assassinated before he was able to enact it. His successor, Lyndon Johnson, guided it through a sympathetic Congress a year after Kennedy's death.

In essence, the Act prevented federal funds being given to any enterprise where racial discrimination was practised. Although its main effect was on educational provision, which relies heavily on such funds, by outlawing racial discrimination it had the broader effect of bringing southern states into line with the rest of the country. The constitutional provisions had not proved clear or detailed enough to prevent discriminatory practices, so additional legislation had been required.

War Powers Resolution 1973   The Constitution asserts that war may only be **officially** declared by Congress, a requirement which delayed the USA's entry into both World Wars. However, the Constitution also clearly states that the President is Commander-in-Chief of the armed forces. The question therefore arises: who has constitutional authority when war is **undeclared**?

This question was brought into focus when President Nixon engaged in increasingly secret armed operations in Vietnam and Cambodia against communist insurgents during the 1970s. Congress demanded the right to be informed and consulted, while Nixon quoted his own constitutional powers to justify his actions. Congress passed the War Powers Resolution in 1973, despite the President's attempts to veto it. This Act requires that the President informs congressional leaders immediately after he has committed American troops to combat. Thereafter Congress may order withdrawal after sixty days, giving the President a further sixty days to comply. Effectively, this means that the President may commit troops to combat for a period of four to five months without declaring war and without being forced by Congress to withdraw.

The constitutionality of the Resolution is still in doubt, but there has not been an opportunity for the Supreme Court to test its validity. Operations by American forces since the end of the Vietnam War have been short and limited. Invasions of Grenada (1983), Lebanon (1983–4) and Haiti (1994) in attempts to restore ordered government, the bombing of specific targets in Libya (1986) in retaliation for acts of terrorism, and the Gulf War (1991) were all too restricted to present a threat to the Resolution. Nevertheless, it is a clear example of how legislation can redefine constitutional statements.

Gramm–Rudman–Hollings (GRH) Act 1985   Named after its congressional sponsors, the GRH Act was a response to the growing fiscal deficit being experienced by the federal government. The deficit – an excess of public spending over receipts from taxation – had grown to alarming proportions when President **Reagan** came to office in 1983. He was, therefore, happy to support such legislation.

It required that the President and Congress should adopt a medium-term strategy for bringing down the deficit and, eventually, eliminating it altogether. It was a 'constitutional' measure in that it sought to place important restrictions on the activities of central government in the interests of taxpayers and inflation control.

In the event, the Act proved to be virtually unworkable and the deficit has since continued to grow. Senator Bob Dole's attempts to convert the basis of the GRH Act into a constitutional amendment narrowly failed in 1995, but the issue remains a priority for the Republican Party.

Foreign policy declarations The Constitution makes no mention of specific foreign-policy issues, other than to describe the powers of President and Congress in the conduct of war and the negotiation of treaties. The actual **objectives** of American foreign policy have never been declared in constitutional form. There have, however, been two key doctrines established which shape such policy:

The Monroe Doctrine 1823 Alarmed by political disorders in Central and South American countries, resulting in interference by European powers, President **Monroe** resolved to establish America's place in its own hemisphere, or 'backyard' as it has come to be known.

In the interests of the security and self-defence of the USA, Monroe declared that western hemisphere affairs were the rightful concern of the USA and that it would, henceforth, claim the right to intervene to maintain order in that part of the world. The blockade of Cuba in 1963 by John Kennedy in order to force the removal of Soviet missiles, and the invasions of Grenada and Haiti described above, are clear recent examples of the operation of the doctrine.

> *'The United States looks on any attempt on their [foreign powers'] part to extend their system to any portion of this hemisphere as dangerous to our peace and safety.'*
>   President James Monroe, 1823

The Truman Doctrine 1947 After the end of World War Two, it became apparent that the Soviet Union was engaged in a programme of expansionism. President Truman met this threat by committing the USA to the defence of the so-called 'free world'.

Since then there have been several examples of American forces being used in response to the need to defend vulnerable peoples from external invasion. Clear examples are the defence of West Berlin in 1949, Korea 1950–3, Vietnam in the 1960s and 1970s, and Kuwait in 1991. (Technically Kuwait and Korea were United Nations operations, but there was no doubting that the USA was the driving force.)

> *'It is the policy of the United States to support free peoples who are resisting subjugation by armed minorities or outside pressures.'*
>   President Harry Truman, Address to Congress, 1947

These doctrines are neither constitutional requirements nor Acts of Congress. Nevertheless, they have been considered so powerful that Presidents since have considered them binding in foreign-policy considerations.

Informal amendment As in Britain, written principles do not give the full picture of how the United States' Constitution works. There are also 'conventions' or informal practices which determine the real operation of government.

Executive agreements are a typical example. These are pacts or contracts made by the President with foreign powers. Not being classed as 'treaties', they do not require the formal approval of Congress. It is understood that, in the conduct of foreign policy, the President must have some flexibility and this device provides him with such freedom. Yet we will not find regulations governing such agreements written down formally in the archives of Congress.

There are similar 'conventions' affecting the operation of Congress. Though both Houses have similar powers with regard to the development of the federal budget, it is understood that the House of Representatives plays a leading role and the Senate will be led by the House. In foreign affairs the position is reversed. The House may debate such foreign issues, but is not expected to attempt to usurp the Senate's pre-eminence in the field.

The doctrine of the separation of powers, enshrined in the Constitution, also disguises the existence of an important political practice. Although, unlike Britain, the executive branch is not strictly **responsible** to Congress and its members, including the President, and cannot be removed by Congress for purely political reasons, it is clear that there is a constant requirement for officers of the administration to report to Congress and respond to its criticisms. Powerful congressional committees regularly submit Department Heads to close scrutiny and it is understood that, should criticism become severe enough, the President must remove the individual in question even though he is neither constitutionally nor legally obliged to do so. This particular development in the practical operation of government has simply arisen over the years and is, therefore, an informal, gradual amendment to constitutional doctrine.

Summary of constitutional development and change

1. Formal amendment, such as women's voting rights, 1920
2. Interpretations by the Supreme Court, such as *Roe v. Wade*, 1973
3. Legislation, such as Gramm–Rudman–Hollings, 1985
4. Presidential doctrines, such as the Truman Doctrine, 1947
5. Informal amendment, such as the growth of executive agreements

The British and American Constitutions compared

Philosophical principles

The American Constitution is predominantly a **liberal** document, while Britain's counterpart is essentially **conservative** in nature. The implications of this difference are deep and far-reaching.

Such liberal ideas as limited government, government by consent, the separation of powers, the desire to safeguard individual rights and the need to establish legal and political equality are all fixed for the foreseeable future in the American Constitution. It was never expected that these principles would be threatened, and so it has proved.

In Britain, by contrast, the conservative traditions of the political establishment have demanded that the system should not be subject to such unchanging, abstract principles. For a Conservative, the Constitution is a part of the living, changing society and culture. It is rooted within them. It should, therefore, be allowed to grow and develop in sympathy with social change. Thus, it cannot be a fixed set of principles, but should, instead, be allowed to reflect constantly shifting public sentiment. So when it is felt that some individual rights should be sacrificed in the interests of public order – when there is a marked rise in crime, for example – the British Constitution is flexible enough to allow this to occur. Similarly, when it is widely accepted that government should be granted more powers – such as at the time of the creation of the Welfare State – this can be achieved without major constitutional upheaval. American leaders and legislators are hampered by the rigid liberal principles of their Constitution, and while this reassures the people, it makes fundamental political change difficult. Though liberals and socialists in Britain may disagree with this philosophy, the pre-eminence of conservatism over the past two centuries has ensured the retention of the traditional character of the Constitution.

Status

The different philosophical foundations of the two constitutions, as described above, give rise to important contrasts in their status. In the USA it is clear that the Constitution is absolutely supreme. All laws and acts of Government are subordinate to it. Where there is a conflict the Constitution must always prevail. So declared Chief Justice John Marshall nearly two hundred years ago.

In Britain it is accepted that, while constitutional principles are important, they can be subordinated to the needs of government and the wishes of Parliament. Provided the correct procedures are adopted, ordinary law and decisions taken under properly delegated powers cannot be constrained by the Constitution. This principle will always be upheld by the courts.

Codification

The clearest difference which can be discerned lies in the very clear way in which the American document is laid out, with all the major aspects of the political system included. The British Constitution is not codified at all, there being no single document entitled 'The Constitution'.

This is not the same as not being 'written', however. Parts of the British Constitution are written in the form of statutes and important documents. It is also not the case that the whole of the American Constitution is written. As we have seen above, there are elements which are purely 'convention', in particular the relationships between the executive and legislative branches of government.

It may be, however, that the closer links with the European Union which Britain must contemplate bring closer the implementation of codified constitutional constraints. The original Treaty of Rome and the Maastricht Treaty of 1992 are both examples of quasi-constitutional codification.

Entrenchment

Here again a wide difference can be seen. The American Constitution is exceptionally deeply entrenched, possibly the most stubbornly safe-guarded of all the major constitutions in the democratic world. This is far from the case in Britain.

The sovereignty of the British Parliament, its inability to bind its successors to constitutional principles, renders the Constitution extremely flexible. It can mean changes being made merely through the passage of a statute, an event which can take less than two days and requires only a simple majority of both Houses of Parliament. Some entrenchment does exist in the unwritten conventions which make up so much of the British Constitution. Since conventions only develop over long periods of time, and certainly need a consensus of support in order to become established, they are, in practice, entrenched through tradition. However, it still remains true that, in most cases, a statute could overturn a convention if there were enough support.

The extensive increase in the scope of government in the 1940s, and the dramatic changes which have taken place in the balance of power between central and local government in the 1980s, bear testimony to the flexibility of the British Constitution. In the USA such reforms would have required a considerably longer period of time to effect and, indeed, could probably not have been contemplated. The rigidity of rules governing the distribution of political power in the USA is difficult to overcome. President Clinton's vain attempts to increase federal responsibility for health care in the 1990s demonstrates the difficulties involved.

We must also refer again to Europe here. Though Britain's Constitution remains flexible, those European regulations which now apply in Britain are deeply entrenched, often requiring the unanimous approval of all the member states of the EU for change to be effected. The advent of a European Constitution, similar in its status to that of the USA, may not be far off.

Judicial review

Despite the key differences in the nature of the entrenchment of the two constitutions, there are a number of similarities in the processes of change. Of course, formal amendment is far more difficult in the USA than in Britain, but the less formal processes are similar.

Judicial review is carried out in the British courts – usually the Court of Appeal or the House of Lords – in much the same way as the Supreme Court operates. Challenges may be made to the constitutional validity of executive actions and the judges are required to test those actions against established constitutional principles. In both countries the courts have the power to set aside governmental decisions. Even in Britain, where such judgments may in turn be set aside by resultant legislation, the Government is always loathe to risk incurring unfavourable judgments by the courts.

What is more important about judicial review, however, is that it provides opportunities in both systems for the Constitution to be interpreted and re-interpreted according to circumstances. Parliament plays a bigger role in the process than does Congress, but it remains true that both constitutions rely heavily on judges to ensure their systems remain up to date.

For exam questions relevant to this unit, see pages 494–5.

17 The United States' Congress

Introduction

The US Congress is unlike any other legislature. In particular, it possibly deserves the term 'law-making body' more than any of its rivals. While Congress initiates, debates, amends and creates laws, other assemblies are either mere charades, as is the case in many one-party systems, or are so dominated by the executive branch that they cannot claim to be truly independent, as is the case in Britain. Such assemblies may have adopted formal procedures for the passage and legitimisation of legislation, but none of them can claim to be genuine law makers. Not so Congress. In respect of its other functions – scrutiny and control of government and representation of interests and political philosophies – it may not appear to be extraordinary. It is its ability to develop law which singles it out from the rest.

We can find few clues to this special quality in the Constitution. While it is true that all Congress's current functions are to be found, explicitly or implicitly, in the provisions of the Constitution, it is not immediately clear why Congress has not developed in the way that legislatures in other liberal democracies have done. It may help us to consider first why other legislative assemblies have failed to become true law makers. Having developed some theories, we may discover what it is about Congress which makes it so different. Three features are apparent:

The committee system
Most elected assemblies are too large to be able to develop coherent legislative programmes. Of course, Congress is also very large, but it has developed a committee system which ensures that legislation which has widespread support **can** be created and passed without the organisation and discipline normally provided by government. Each committee becomes a relatively small policy community in itself.

Checks and balances
It is normally the case that the executive branch dominates the legislature. Not unexpectedly, Governments will use their control to demand a virtual monopoly over law making. Indeed, most democratic Governments claim an electoral mandate for their legislative programmes. They argue that their authority is derived from the electorate. Representative assemblies are also elected, of course, but they cannot assert the same authority as the governing party or coalition which owes its position to public support for specific policies. Such domination of the legislature by the executive is not possible in the USA. The system of 'checks and balances' which was included so carefully in the Constitution gives Congress its independence. While the President can claim his own separate electoral mandate, he is aware that members of the Congress have a continuous direct line of communication to the electorate through the open access which it allows to the many interest and pressure groups which form the lobby. The balance of power is, thus, both a constitutional and a political reality.

The party system
American parties are considerably less coherent and unified than most other democratic parties. They may be efficient in such functions as candidate selection, electioneering and finance raising, but as policy-making machines they make little impact. Where parties are concentrated, disciplined centres of policy development, legislative power can be retained by them when they achieve governmental office. In the USA there are few effective party institutions in the field of law making. The vacuum is filled not only by the President and his administration, but equally by Congress.

The Constitution clearly intended that Congress should exercise a great deal of control over public finance, both the raising of taxes and government expenditure. So it has proved. Taxation had been a particularly sensitive issue in the Americans' dissatisfaction with British rule, so it was hardly surprising that special provisions regarding this were included when the Union Constitution was written. What was perhaps not envisaged was the effect that financial control would have over general policy. Most government programmes require large amounts of money to make them work. Congress's control over such funds has the effect of giving it power over the policies themselves. Such programmes as health care, welfare, defence or transport initiatives may be proposed by the President and he may obtain congressional approval for them **in principle**. Yet if the necessary funds are not approved, the exercise may prove futile.

Newt Gingrich's Contract with America

Shortly before the congressional elections in November 1994, over 300 Republican Party candidates for the House signed a document known as the Contract with America. Newt Gingrich, the inspiration behind the Contract, insisted that it be read before every session of the House to remind members of their promise.

The Contract detailed ten key measures which were to be enacted within four months of the new Congress and, with the Republicans having won a majority, there was a good possibility that a number of the proposed Acts would reach the statute book. The ten terms of the Contract were:

1. The Fiscal Responsibility Act to ensure a balanced government budget by 2002.
2. Congressmen's terms of office to be restricted to six years in total, Senators' to twelve.
3. Tougher anti-crime measures, including more use of the death penalty.
4. Tightening up of the rules entitling various groups to welfare benefits.
5. Reduced taxes for middle-income groups.
6. Increased defence expenditure but reduced contributions to the United Nations.
7. Reductions in the amounts of damages paid in civil disputes.
8. Reduced taxes on capital gains to encourage investment.
9. Reduced taxes on pensioners.
10. Banning of homosexuals in the armed forces.

The significance of the Contract can be seen in terms of a first attempt by an American party to create a detailed election manifesto along the lines of those produced by British parties. Presidential vetoes and the likelihood of a Democratic recovery in the 1996 elections make it unlikely that all the measures will be enacted. Nevertheless, the swing to the right in American politics in 1994 is illustrated by the radical nature of the Contract.

As we have suggested above, all legislatures assert the right to exercise some degree of control over government. The Congress is no exception. There can be little doubt that most of the Founding Fathers would have been delighted by the way in which Congress has developed its scrutiny role. The traditional American fear of central government power is expressed in modern times through the way in which members of Congress insist on regular questioning, even interrogation, of representatives of the federal government.

It is normal for the representation of interests to operate largely within government agencies. In democratic systems it is recognised that policy is largely in the hands of senior officials and ministers so that pressure must be concentrated there. Legislatures are subject to lobbying everywhere, of course, but this is invariably a secondary activity. The greater

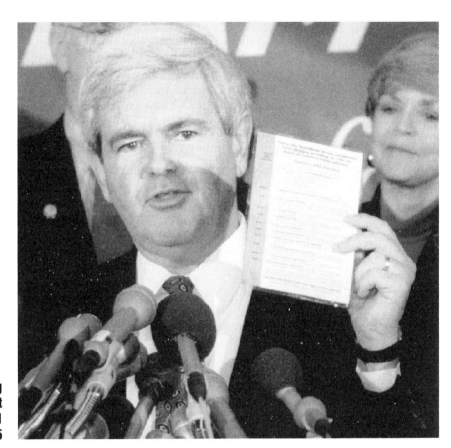

Newt Gingrich, holding a copy of the 'Contract with America', 11 January 1995

influence which the American Congress enjoys forces lobbyists to split their efforts between the administration at the White House and Congress on Capitol Hill. The American system is remarkable for the open access it allows to all those who legitimately seek to influence. Indeed, the institutions of Congress, principally its committees, operate as the forum within which the three main elements of policy development can meet. Here, representatives of interest groups, members of Congress and senior office-holders in the administration can communicate and negotiate. The term 'pluralism' is possibly most aptly used in this context. Congress is not simply a legislative assembly, it is very much a market place in which demands, influence and political decisions are traded.

We can now summarise the principal features of Congress. These are shown below:

Main features of Congress

1. It is very much involved with the process of making law.
2. It is a forum of negotiation between the administration, interest groups and elected members over legislation and finance.
3. There is open access to interest and pressure groups.
4. It exercises close scrutiny and control over the executive branch.
5. Its power is balanced delicately against that of the President.
6. The party system is relatively weak and diffused.

The composition of the Senate

Senators

There are a hundred Senators, two from each state. Since each state has the same representation, some small states, such as Alaska and Wyoming, are 'over-represented', while larger states, such as Texas and California, are relatively 'under-represented'. Senators are elected on a six-year term of office, but Senate seats are not all contested in the same year. Every two years one-third of the seats are contested. Thus, the composition of the Senate changes gradually. For each state the Senator who has served for the longer period is called 'Senior Senator', while his colleague is called 'Junior Senator'.

The reason for the uneven representation of states is largely historical. The smaller members of the original Union in 1787, such as Rhode Island, feared the power of their larger neighbours, notably Virginia. Had there been representation on the basis of population, two or three states of the original thirteen would have been able to dominate proceedings by holding a permanent majority in the legislature. As we shall see, the House of Representatives is based on equal geographical representation, but the Senate, with virtually equal powers, acts as a balance against the power of the big states. Although this is less critical today, with fifty states in the Union, the system offers some protection against the powerful majority. It is interesting to note at this stage that the same kind of problem faces the European Union as it seeks to develop democratic institutions. For Virginia read Germany, and for Rhode Island read Portugal, and the difficulty becomes clear.

President of the Senate

The President of the Senate is the Vice President of the United States. Effectively, this makes him the 'Speaker', as he would be called in the House of Representatives or in the British House of Commons. In this role he is expected to be neutral. His function is to maintain good order, organise debates and deal with procedural disputes. He is, of course, in an ideal position to act as the President's representative in the Senate. However, since his neutrality is required, this must be handled with some degree of subtlety and sensitivity. He cannot vote, not being an elected Senator himself, but will resolve a tied vote. Since the Vice President must inevitably be absent for much of the time on duties of State, he is often replaced by the **President Pro Tempore**. This is a senior Senator of the majority party who, although neutral in maintaining discipline and organisation, is allowed to vote.

Senate majority leader

The Senate majority leader is the key party leader in the Senate. As the name suggests, he is chosen by the Senators of whichever party holds the majority of the seats in the Senate. In modern times this has usually been the Democrats, although there was a significant period from 1981–8 when the Republicans were in the ascendancy during the Reagan years (at that time the House was still Democrat dominated). The majority leader has a number of roles, as described below:

- Attempting to ensure that legislation to which his party is sympathetic receives sufficient debating time to stand a chance of success.
- Mobilising support, particularly within his own party, for such legislation. It should be noted here that achieving 75 per cent party unity behind a measure is deemed to be a success in congressional politics.

**Senate Republican
leader Robert Dole**

Republican **Howard Baker** (majority leader 1981–5) achieved an average of 80 per cent unity for President Reagan's proposals in the Senate and was thus a key figure in the reforms of that period.

- Mobilising support for the President's proposals, provided, of course, that the President is of the same party. There may be a few occasions when the majority leader and a President of the same party may disagree, but this is unusual.
- Playing a leading role in the appointment of his own party's members on committees.

Thus, while the President may have a higher profile on the international scene, the Senate majority leader, and his equivalent in the House, is a key personality in American domestic politics, carrying as he does great authority and influence. Republican **Bob Dole** took over in 1995, forming a powerful alliance with the Speaker of the House of Representatives, **Newt Gingrich**. This extremely conservative alliance acts as a strong barrier to presidential influence.

Possibly the most successful majority leader of modern times was Lyndon Johnson (1953–61), who was to become Vice President and later President. He was a Democrat confronted by a Republican President (Eisenhower). Nevertheless, he was able to lay the groundwork for the civil rights and welfare programmes which he and President Kennedy were to complete in the following decade. Indeed, Johnson himself formed a vital alliance with majority leader Mike Mansfield (1961–77) to steer through many liberal reforms.

Senate minority leader

The Senate minority leader, as the name suggests, does not enjoy the luxury of a party majority behind him. Even so, several of his functions are similar to those of the Senate majority leader. Of particular importance are those occasions when the minority leader is of the same party as the President, a situation which occurred during the Republican presidencies of Richard Nixon and Gerald Ford (1968–76). With a Democrat majority in both Houses of Congress, the role became particularly difficult, especially during the complex foreign policy issues caused by the Vietnam conflict and the continuing Cold War.

He has relatively little influence over the legislative programme, but is still expected to attempt to mobilise his party, either in opposition to, or support for, particular measures. Being in the minority, his party will also enjoy fewer committee seats than the opposing party. It is largely up to him to allocate such places.

Whips   Both parties have whips who have the unenviable task of attempting to maintain party discipline in a system where members are notoriously independent. The whips of both parties have little hope of persuading a Senator to change his mind over an issue when he is being placed under great pressure from constituents, lobbyists or Policy Action Committees, upon whom he relies for re-election sooner or later. In practice, the whips become the principal assistants to both the majority and minority leaders. They may help to persuade, cajole or forge deals with wavering Senators, but they cannot bully them into compliance.

Party committees   Party committees should not be confused with the standing and select committees of the Senate. As we have seen, party organisation in Congress is notoriously weak and this is reflected in the relative lack of importance of party committees. Nevertheless, both parties attempt to influence the course and fortunes of legislation through such committees. The **Democrats** have a **Policy Committee** which seeks to determine which legislation may have a chance of success, and a **Steering Committee** to ease the passage of such Bills. The **Republicans** limit themselves to a **Policy Committee** with both functions. Unlike the Democrats, Republicans have a **Committee on Committees** which largely determines which Senators sit on which congressional committees. Its chairman wields considerable influence in the party, since patronage over committee seats is an important element in political authority.

Party caucuses   From time to time, all Senators from the respective parties will meet to discuss matters of common concern. Such sessions are known as party **caucuses**, or **conferences**. Once again, we must take into account the relative lack of party unity and discipline in the USA. The caucuses may be the scene of heated debates from time to time, but the real horse trading and persuasion goes on in private committee rooms and offices.

Before we move on to describe the congressional committee system, the most important feature of the politics of the legislature, we must examine the House of Representatives.

The composition of the House of Representatives

Congressional Districts

Unlike Senators, members of the House represent roughly equal constituencies, known as Congressional Districts. The size of each district is between 550,000 and 600,000. Although they are inevitably smaller in very small states, there must be at least two members from each state. In 1994 there were 435 members. They must seek re-election every two years when the whole House goes to the polls. This is perhaps the shortest term of office of any representative assembly in the West. We shall see its effects later, but it is immediately apparent that membership may change more rapidly than that of the Senate.

Speaker

The affairs of the House are presided over by a Speaker who is, by tradition though not by law, a leading member of the majority party. He has a dual role. When acting as Chairman of the House he is expected to be even-handed and will not take part in debate, although he is allowed to vote. As a senior member of his party, however, he has considerable patronage over committee posts and is influential in determining what legislation is likely to survive to reach the statute book. He is also expected to play a leading part in keeping the party together and is, thus, an auxiliary whip. The best-known modern Speaker was **Tip O'Neill**, a Democrat who did much to thwart the plans of his own party's President (Carter), and then did little to stop President Reagan, in theory an opponent, gaining control over the federal budget. However, in 1995, following the success of his party in the 1994 congressional elections, Republican **Newt Gingrich** took over the post. Gingrich, a right-winger with a strong antipathy to federal government power, holds something of a stranglehold over presidential proposals in the House.

Floor leader and whip

As in the Senate, the majority party elects a 'floor leader' and a whip. Their role, jointly, is to try to maintain some degree of party unity and to engineer support for Bills which the party as a whole can support. Assisted by a small army of assistant whips, they engage in much the same negotiating and persuasion which characterises the Senate. Representatives are perhaps even more independent-minded than Senators. Their short term of office means they are virtually fighting a permanent election campaign. They are under pressure from constituents and financial sponsors alike. Their voting records are well publicised and may determine their ability to raise funds and win votes for the next election campaign. Thus, the floor leader and whips have their work cut out in creating party cohesion. The minority party has a similar team with the same role, although, being in a minority, they are often fighting a rearguard action.

Both floor leaders have a special relationship with the President, whether or not he is of the same party. If the President can gain the support of either or both floor leaders for his policies, his chances of success are considerably increased.

Party caucuses

The two parties have similar structures to those of the Senate, with a caucus of all members, together with **Policy** and **Steering Committees**. Both parties, but especially the Democrats who invariably hold a majority in the House, have attempted to make these institutions into a more formalised and centralised structure for the sake of greater party unity.

Little success has been achieved, however, so that the formal structure is of much less importance than their equivalents in many European legislatures.

We can now summarise the structure of the two Houses, excluding the standing and select committee systems.

Senate	House
Senate President (US Vice President)	Speaker
Majority leader	Majority floor leader
Minority leader	Minority floor leader
Majority whip	Majority whip
Minority whip	Minority whip
Party conferences (caucuses)	Party conferences
Party Policy Committees	Party Policy Committees
Democratic Steering Committee	Democratic Steering Committee
Republican Committee on Committees	Republican Committee on Committees
100 Senators (six-year term)	435 Representatives (two-year term)

The committee system in Congress

The committees in setting

The Constitution of the USA makes no mention of congressional committees. This was hardly surprising since, with only thirteen states in the Union and a relatively limited population, Congress was very small to begin with. Add to this the fact that the volume of business was relatively limited at that time, and we can see that committees were scarcely necessary. Today, by contrast, several thousand measures are proposed in each session of Congress. Many of these are extremely complex and often contentious. They must all be studied, sifted and filtered. The small number which do receive a hearing require careful

Russian President Boris Yeltsin addressing a joint session of Congress

US House of Representatives

consideration and often radical amendment. Congress as a whole cannot, and often radical amendment. Congress as a whole cannot, therefore, hope to perform such an enormous task without resorting to a form of streamlining. Thus we have the committees, in particular, the standing committees.

We may begin with a list of the standing committees in both Houses:

Senate	House of Representatives
Appropriations	Appropriations
Finance	Ways and Means
Foreign Relations	Foreign Affairs
Armed Services	Armed Services
Budget	Rules
Agriculture etc.	Agriculture
Banking, Housing and Urban Affairs	Banking, Finance and Urban Affairs
Commerce, Science and Transport	Education and Labor
Energy and Natural Resources	Government Operations
Environment and Public Works	House Administration
Government Affairs	Judiciary
Judiciary	Merchant, Marine and Fisheries
Labor and Human Resources	Natural Resources
Rules and Administration	Post Office and Civil Service
Science and Space	Public Works and Transport
Small Business	
Standards of Official Conduct	
Veterans' Affairs	
Ways and Means	

This impressive list of committees goes some way to illustrating the complexity of Congress. Indeed, the legislative process is often described as a labyrinth, with many avenues and dead ends. As we shall see, few proposals are able to make a successful passage through it.

If we are to enter the maze, we will need a map.

The following procedure refers to a Bill originating in the House. Bills beginning in the Senate have the same procedure, with the Senate stages taken first.

Bill is instituted by the President or a representative or group of representatives on behalf of an outside group.

↓

The Speaker sends the Bill to the appropriate standing committee.

↓

Standing committee examines the Bill. It may simply 'kill' it by doing nothing, amend it slightly or radically, or pass it on unamended. If passed on, it is said to be 'Reported out'.

↓

Rules Committee places the Bill on the House agenda. If it is placed low on the agenda, it is unlikely to be passed. All Presidential Bills are given priority by Rules Committee.

↓

The Bill is considered by the whole House. There is a debate and a vote. Amendments may be proposed and voted on unless the Bill has been protected from amendment by the Rules Committee.

↓

If passed in the vote, it will go to the Senate.

↓

Senate procedures are similar except that the Rules Committee is replaced by a Majority Party Committee which determines its place on the agenda.

↓

If there are differences in the form of the Bill passed by the House and the Senate, it goes to a Conference Committee of both Houses which will resolve the differences if possible and pass an agreed Bill to the President.

↓

The Bill is passed to the President. If he signs, it becomes law. He may veto the Bill, in which case it is passed back to both Houses together with his objections. If passed by a two-thirds majority, the veto is defeated and the Bill becomes law. If not, the Bill fails.

Subject standing committees

Every aspect of governmental and legislative activity is covered by a congressional committee. Since these committees are permanent, with some members spending most or all of their careers on the same committees, they become considerable experts in their field. They have access to a large research staff which may be augmented from time to time for special consideration of legislation, and extensive finance is available. Members may travel around the country, or even abroad when appropriate, in pursuit of information and opinion. They may also commission major private investigations.

Although their principal role is to consider and amend legislation, committees are engaged in a permanent scrutiny of those government agencies which deal with their work. They get to know officials well and have the right to demand what is going on in policy formulation. The USA has a tradition and, indeed, laws of freedom of information. The chronic secrecy which characterises British government is largely absent. Questioning of officials may be inquisitorial or friendly, depending on the situation, but whichever obtains, there is a relatively free flow of information between executive and legislature.

When a committee is considering a Bill, it will call witnesses from a variety of sources to assist in its work. Thus, other members of Congress not already on the committee may appear, together with government officials and representatives of interest and pressure groups who have a vested interest in the legislation. Add to this impressive list any number of outside experts or academics who may be required, and we have a picture of a full-scale inquiry every time a new law is proposed. Where a matter of great public concern and interest is at stake, hearings may be broadcast, sometimes on live TV. Where necessary, votes are taken among the members and again these are matters of public record.

The committee chairman is a key figure. He has a major influence over the agenda, determining which Bills will be considered and which will be 'shelved'. Committees are presented with far more business than they can possibly transact within the allotted time. If a Bill is put aside for later consideration, it is being effectively killed. The committee chairman will also have a significant influence over proposed amendments. Again, those considered first will receive a proper hearing, those which are postponed will never see the light of day. The only rule which must be followed is that Bills presented by the President are given priority. This does not mean they have a better chance of success, although the President does have political advantages over other groups. It does mean, however, that everything he proposes will be given a fair hearing. Were a committee to ignore this courtesy to the President, it would risk the heavy hand of retribution in the form of a storm of vetoes against cherished congressional programmes.

Thus, in some senses committees are part of the governmental as well as the legislative process. They are not passive bodies, waiting for policy proposals to be presented to them. Indeed, in some cases, committees actually draft Bills themselves. Certainly, they are a permanent element in the policy-making community. In Britain and most other Western democratic systems, many of the functions of these committees are carried out by government departments. Consultation, research, drafting, refining and support recruitment, with all the other aspects of creating the necessary legislation to implement policy, are as much the concern of congressional committees as they are of government agencies in the USA.

As we can see above, if the committee majority approves, and when all amendments have been considered, the Bill is 'reported out'. It may be almost unrecognisable from the original proposal if it has been extensively amended, or it may emerge largely untouched. Whichever, it has several hurdles still to encounter. In particular, it must find a prominent place on the congressional agenda. For this it must go to another committee.

House Rules and Senate Majority Policy Committee

If a Bill successfully negotiates its standing committee, it must find a place on the agenda of the relevant House. Its chances of success depend upon how early in the session it will be heard. If it is placed too low down on the agenda, it will suffer one of two fates. Either it will never be debated because time has run out or, if it is only debated in the last ten days of the session (Congress tends to save up a large number of Bills until the end and then rushes them through in a short time), it may fall foul of a Presidential **pocket veto**. The pocket veto occurs when a President receives a Bill for his approval in the last ten days of a congressional session. Normally, the President is required to give reasons for a veto and this may make him reluctant to use it, usually if the measure is a popular one. A pocket veto is somewhat different. It is operated by the President simply sitting on the Bill (i.e. 'pocketing it') without signing it. Once the congressional session is over, within these last ten days, the Bill simply fails. Here, the President does not need to give reasons for his veto. Thus, it is an attractive course of action for a President who objects to a Bill and an early 'rule' is much sought-after by supporters of a Bill.

In the House of Representatives it is the function of the **Rules Committee** to place a Bill on the agenda. The House has a more crowded agenda than the Senate so this is a more critical stage than its counterpart in the Upper House. The chairmanship and membership of the Rules Committee is largely in the hands of the House Speaker and majority leader and so is very much controlled by the majority party. The Chairman is one of the most influential politicians in the system. The committee enjoyed its 'heyday' in the 1960s when a congressional majority of liberal legislators found themselves confronted by a conservative House Rules Committee (a coalition of Republicans and conservative southern Democrats). It was not until President Johnson gained control over the Democrat majority that reform could be effected. The Committee may also boost a Bill by granting it a 'closed' rule, which effectively forbids any further amendment by the whole House. Excessive amendment can delay a Bill fatally, or change its character fundamentally, often rendering it worthless. The closed rule is, therefore, a valuable asset.

In the Senate it is the **Policy Committee** which performs the function of the House Rules Committee. Unlike Rules, it is exclusively a party committee, staffed only by members of the majority party. However, it is slightly less influential than its House equivalent. The Senate's agenda is less critical and Senators are less inclined to allow their agenda to be controlled by a small group.

If a Bill has a favourable rule granted, it will be debated and voted on by the whole House. It may seem strange to an outsider that this is a relatively insignificant part of the legislative process, at least in terms of time. Debates are usually formal and brief. Most of the real political action has already taken place long before the full floor debate on a Bill. The arguments have been rehearsed and mostly resolved in the committees. It is true that, if amendments are still being proposed, there may be much to do, but generally there is less contentious material to be considered at this stage. Bills which do not have widespread support will have been filtered out by a committee at an earlier stage of the process. This is not to say there are not close votes after full sessions of Congress, but it is recognised that this is not the place for detailed debate. Speeches are made largely for public consumption, with congressmen simply wishing to place on record their attitude to a Bill. Before long they will all have to face re-election and their speaking and voting records will be studied by many of the voters.

Having been passed by both Houses, most Bills will have two different forms, since each House may have made its own amendments. These differences must be resolved and yet another committee is needed.

Conference committee Such committees are formed when a Bill emerges from Congress in two different forms. Members are drawn from both Houses. If such a conference is needed the agreed form of the Bill must return to each House where it cannot be amended again. Thus, there is still a stage when a Bill may fail, owing to lack of agreement, even if both Houses approve. However, the days when powerful conference committees were able to change the form of a Bill completely are largely gone. It is usually accepted that the will of Congress must be accepted, so genuine efforts are made to achieve an acceptable compromise.

Sub-committees As the business of Congress has grown it has been increasingly necessary to resort to the use of sub-committees to deal with specialised legislation. This has had two effects. On the one hand, it has reduced the power of committee chairmen and diffused it among the heads of the sub-committees. On the other, it has broadened the opportunities for more members of Congress to become closely involved in the business of law making. The diffusion of power in Congress is not only the result of the development of sub-committees, it is also due to the decline of the seniority system in the selection of committee chairmen. This is examined below.

Committee chairmen In many ways congressional committee chairmen are as powerful, perhaps even more so, than the Department Directors and Secretaries who are appointed by the President to run the administration. This is especially true of key committees such as House Rules, Appropriations, Foreign Relations and several others which stand as watchtowers over vital legislative programmes. It used to be the case that chairmen held the key to the success or failure of government action or congressional legislation. Their position was strengthened by the **Seniority Rule** which was in force until the 1970s. This simply meant that, when a chairmanship became vacant, the post would automatically fall to whichever member of the majority party had served on the committee for the longest period, i.e. the senior member. This prevented much political manoeuvring, but gave such security of tenure to chairmen that they tended to become politically invincible. The situation today has changed considerably. Chairmen may lose their position and be replaced by younger, ambitious congressmen. Vacancies are filled by those who enjoy the support of their party or a faction of that party, rather than by those who have been waiting for the longest period. As we have seen, the development of sub-committees has altered the position of chairmen, but perhaps the most important change is the advent of public hearings. When committees met in private, manipulation by the chairman was allowed to continue unchecked. Since the media and public have been allowed to observe proceedings, however, such blatant tactics have become unacceptable. Thus, chairmen are still key political figures, but lack the influence they used to enjoy.

Col. Oliver North taking the oath before the House Foreign Affairs Committee, 9 December 1986

Select committees

From time to time, one of the Houses of Congress may wish to conduct a special investigation, usually into some aspect of the conduct of the administration, or into a feature of American life which is causing concern. Although such committees are normally temporary, the most notorious example lasted for nearly forty years before its abolition in 1975. This was the House of Representatives Un-American Activities Committee, set up to investigate groups and individuals who might have been operating against the interests of the USA at best, or who were suspected traitors at worst. Led in the early 1950s by Joe McCarthy, the committee conducted a witch-hunt against suspected communists, especially targeting public figures from the world of entertainment and the arts.

More recently the so-called 'Watergate' Committee of the Senate attracted much attention. This committee was set up to investigate the alleged spying on Democratic Party Headquarters at the Watergate Building by aides of President Nixon, who was seeking re-election in 1972. The subsequent 'cover-up' and discovery that election funds had been improperly used became the subject of a series of dramatic hearings which were carried live on national TV. The committee chairman, Sam Ervin, and other prominent members such as Howard Baker and Daniel Inouye became household names and, in the last two cases, found their political careers were given a great boost by the episode.

In 1988 the **Iran–Contra** affair received similar media coverage when the Senate investigated it. Here, Colonel Oliver North gave a series of dramatic accounts to his inquisitors about the use of funds from arms sales in Nicaragua to the 'Contra' rebels to secure the release of American hostages in Iran. The concern was that the President, through his representative North, was conducting foreign policy without informing

Congress. This has been a particularly sensitive issue in Congress, especially the Senate, since a succession of Presidents – Kennedy, Johnson and Nixon – conducted extensive military and intelligence operations in Vietnam and Cambodia without securing the approval of Congress. In the event, North became something of a folk hero and was adopted as a Republican Senate candidate in 1994.

These are three examples of prominent select committees, but there have been many, less-publicised examples, investigating such matters as penal reform, abortion, the operations of the CIA and the intelligence community, and overseas aid.

We can now summarise features of committees, which we have established so far.

Features of congressional committees

1. They are both legislative and investigatory committees.
2. They may develop, draft and pass their own legislation.
3. Legislation developed elsewhere may be rejected, amended or accepted in full.
4. Committees have large permanent staffs and extensive research facilities, often augmented by special investigators.
5. They may call witnesses from Congress, the administration or outside bodies.
6. Most hearings are in public and the voting record of members is known.
7. The procedural committees – Policy in the Senate, Rules in the House – have the ability to kill or severely hinder legislation.
8. Committee chairmen are powerful political figures, although less so than twenty years ago. Chairmanships are much sought after.
9. Select or special committees may be formed by either House.

Congress and public finance

In most parliamentary systems, public finances – the raising of revenue, mostly in the form of taxation, together with the allocation of funds to spending programmes – remain largely in the hands of the Government. There will always be public scrutiny of finances, but this is normally **post facto**. In other words, it is a check that money has been spent on the purposes for which expenditure was approved, that it has been spent wisely and that there has been no corrupt use of money. Congress, however, reserves the right to play a more creative role in finance, involving itself **before** money is allocated and spent. There is an understanding here that policy cannot be separated from finance as nearly all legislation will involve the federal government in expenditure. The control of expenditure exercised by Congress is, thus, another aspect of its influence over public policy. Where taxation is concerned, as we have said above, there are strong historical reasons why Congress should be sensitive to tax proposals, as President Bush (1988–92) was to discover when he wished to break election pledges not to raise taxes. Members of Congress are highly susceptible to pressure from their constituents, and Americans dislike being taxed more than do most people in the West.

An overview The federal system of budgetary control has a number of inherent problems:

- Although Congress reserves the right to have a major say in the level of taxation and expenditure, it does not have the ability to exercise overall control. Both Houses have Budget Committees which propose a general budget and, in particular, the extent to which expenditure shall be allowed to exceed tax revenue. (The USA has for many years experienced budget deficits where more is spent than is raised in taxation. Prospects for a surplus remain remote in the 1990s.) If these budget proposals were to be accepted, they would form guidelines for total levels of expenditure within which departments of government should work. However, the Budget Committees are weak compared to the specialised standing committees and the Appropriations Committees which control expenditure within particular areas of policy implementation. Thus, expenditure ceilings become a futile objective.

- Most programmes involve ongoing expenditure. Serious cuts can only be made, therefore, if the programme itself is cancelled. Such a course of action is unlikely to be acceptable to a Congress which originally approved them. Thus, much expenditure control is 'incremental' – each year relatively small adjustments can be made.

- As we have seen, Congressmen are under immense pressure from their constituencies to keep taxes as low as possible, but to protect federal spending programmes which will be of benefit to the area. So there is always a tendency for taxes to be held down, but for expenditure to creep up.

- While the President may have the ability to take an overview of the budget and to develop long-term targets, he can only exercise limited control over Congress and its key financial committees. At the same time, if he is in his first term and must, therefore, seek re-election, he is limited by the need to nurture public opinion. The American public care more about low taxes than about budget deficits.

- In practice, expenditure and taxation are generally considered separately by Congress. This makes overall control exceedingly difficult.

Appropriations All legislation or proposed federal programmes require approval for the necessary expenditure from the Appropriations Committees of both Houses. Indeed, if a law has been passed which requires such approval, a further Bill must be presented to approve the necessary funds and the whole process is effectively repeated, albeit more quickly.

Appropriations Committees have huge amounts of business to transact over a wide variety of subjects, from defence to agricultural subsidies, from transport to welfare programmes and inner city reconstruction. Thus, they must divide into a large number of sub-committees, each with a fair degree of independence.

These committees cannot reject legislation and spending programmes, but they may cut, sometimes severely, the funds available for them. The effect may amount to something close to rejection. Certainly, over the past two decades, such programmes as space research, health care, welfare and anti-crime programmes have suffered at the hands of these sub-committees. Indeed, it is normally the case that original requests for funds from the Government are cut, and the vital question is really the extent of these cuts. At the same time, Congress's own measures are more likely to enjoy much fuller funding. There is, thus, a constant tension between the spending plans of the President and those of Congress.

No real target for **overall** expenditure is accepted by Congress, even though the President may propose one. At the same time, the committees and sub-committees are autonomous. The result is that total expenditure for the year is randomly determined, despite all attempts to stay within set limits.

Taxation
Congress does not itself propose tax measures, but those which are presented by the President require congressional approval and may be amended. The **House Ways and Means** and **Senate Finance Committees** deal with taxation, and membership of these committees is much sought after, so crucial is their role. As with appropriations, these committees do not operate with overall budgetary targets. Thus, while appropriations may be allowing expenditure to rise, they may also be determined to keep taxes down. The fact that this may result in a burdensome borrowing problem for the Government is of little concern to them. It is partly traditional and partly practical that the House Ways and Means Committee is the more influential of the two. The shorter term of office of Representatives and the closer scrutiny exercised over them by constituents renders them more sensitive to taxation issues.

The Gramm–Rudman–Hollings Act
The election of **President Reagan** in 1980 heralded new concerns about the level of borrowing by the Government, in particular the effect it was having on inflation and interest rates. With the support of the three Congressmen (Gramm, Rudman and Hollings) after whom the Act is named, Reagan supported legislation to ensure that the budget deficit would be eliminated by the 1990s. The Republican Party's opposition to higher taxation meant that the objectives of the Act could only be met if spending programmes were cut back.

At first, some progress was made with Appropriations sub-committees co-operating by reducing expenditure. Much of the reduction fell on welfare and housing programmes and thus became the subject of considerable controversy. President Bush (1988–92) was committed to pursuing the Act's goals, although it was becoming increasingly apparent that the problem was not going to be solved by spending cutbacks alone. Bush's problems were exacerbated by the influx of many new Democratic Senators and Representatives who were opposed to cuts, which were having a devastating effect on America's poor, especially in the inner cities where poverty, rising crime and drug abuse, poor housing and education, and declining health care facilities had become endemic.

In the event, Bush was forced to abandon the intentions of the Act, and the goal of a balanced budget – with expenditure equalling tax revenue – was postponed further. At the same time, he was forced to raise taxes in order to protect vital spending programmes. The tax increases proved to be a major factor in Bush's defeat by **Bill Clinton** in the 1992 election.

The election of Clinton brought a fresh view of the budget problem. He asked the American people to accept the prospect of higher taxes both to reduce the budget deficit and to finance vital housing, welfare, law and order and, especially, health care programmes. Having achieved a decisive victory at the polls, and with comfortable Democrat majorities in both Houses, he could set about persuading the key financial committees to back his plans.

Summary of Congress and public finance

1. Congress considers both expenditure and taxation plans before they are finalised.
2. Although an overall federal budget is proposed, there is no compulsion for Congress to operate within its limitations.
3. Appropriations Committees in both Houses play a key role in the implementation of legislation as well as federal spending programmes.
4. Taxation must be approved by Senate Finance and House Ways and Means Committees.
5. Congress has found it difficult to engage in budget planning, but in the 1990s there is a new resolve to tackle budget problems.
6. There is a constant tension between President and Congress over budgetary control.

Congress and foreign policy

Background

Although the President is understood to be pre-eminent in the field of foreign policy – after all, he is Head of State as well as Head of Government – Congress now demands a major say in the key foreign policy decisions which arise from time to time. Naturally, Congress cannot hope to be involved in the day-to-day business of foreign policy, but it expects to be concerned at important times. The role of Congress is shaped by three main factors:

- Section 8(11) of the Constitution, which grants to Congress the sole right to declare war.
- Article II, Section 2(2), which deals with presidential powers, states that foreign treaties made by the President require the approval of two-thirds of the Senate.
- The War Powers Act of 1973, which requires the President to inform Congress within sixty days if American troops are committed to action abroad. It also requires that those troops be removed if Congress insists on this.

Until the 1950s relatively little attention was paid to foreign affairs in Congress. Apart from its reluctance to involve the USA in what were seen as European wars – reluctance which was to be overcome by events in 1917 and 1941 – the USA normally stayed aloof from world affairs. Historically, with the exception of involvement in problems with close neighbours such as Mexico or Cuba, America was isolationist in outlook. The wars in Korea (1950–3) and Vietnam (1962–75), together with the onset of the Cold War with the Soviet Union and her allies, signalled a major change in American foreign policy. The House of Representatives has remained reluctant to become involved, but the Senate has remained closely concerned with presidential action.

It is the power the Senate has over treaty ratification which has resulted in the Upper House being more concerned with foreign policy than the House of Representatives. The House is usually too embroiled in domestic affairs to look outwards. The President has a traditionally close relationship with the chairman of the key Senate Foreign Relations Committee. Normally, he will find an ally here. Congress, and the Senate in particular, recognises that it may be seen as unpatriotic if it places obstacles in the way of presidential policy.

Presidential pre-eminence

Despite the apparently impressive powers which Congress has over the conduct of foreign policy, in practice the balance of power lies firmly with the executive branch. Several developments have been important in this respect:

- The extensive use of **executive agreements** has avoided the need for the President to seek treaty ratification in the Senate. These agreements are not full treaties even though they commit the USA to a variety of agreements with foreign powers. Most of them concern trade and aid, but it is such devices which are the currency of modern foreign relations. Executive agreements tend to outnumber treaties by over ten to one.
- All three Presidents who were involved in Vietnam discovered that, while the 'war' was undeclared, Congress lost much of its influence. It was Nixon's totally secret invasion of Cambodia in the 1970s which led to the passage of the War Powers Act. There have been several examples of 'minor' military actions which have never been considered 'wars' so that Congress was unable to prevent them. The invasion of Grenada in 1983 to restore democratic government was such a case.
- Although the War Powers Act theoretically gives Congress the power to order troops home, many actions are so short-lived that the sixty-day rule does not apply. The Grenada incident and the bombing of Libya in 1986 fell into this category.

Thus we can see that congressional powers in this area are relatively weak, existing more in theory than in practice.

Additional functions

Advice and consent

The Senate has the power to reject presidential nominations for posts in the Cabinet or for a position on the Supreme Court. This has only proved a major problem for the President in recent years, with Bush having **John Tower**, and Clinton **Zoe Baird** rejected on the grounds of personal conduct. Even President Reagan found difficulty in gaining acceptance for appointments, in his case largely on political grounds. However, it is not the actual rejections which demonstrate Congress's true power. Long before actual committee hearings take place at which nominees are questioned by Senators, the President must discuss his plans with important members of the relevant committee. Those who are unlikely to gain approval will never be nominated. Thus, the Senate does have some input into the political and personal make-up of the administration and the Supreme Court.

Impeachment

Before 1974 the power to try impeachments was reserved to the House and to carry them out by the Senate would scarcely have warranted a mention in a textbook on American politics. Such a device – the removal of a President from office on the grounds of misconduct – was simply not envisaged. The aftermath of the Watergate Affair, however, reminded the political community of this forgotten function. In the event, the House recommended an impeachment trial and it was widely accepted that the Senate would have voted to remove the President. Nixon resigned rather than face the ignominy of impeachment.

Since then there has been no more talk of such a device, but Nixon's experience remains as a warning to all future Presidents.

Constitutional amendment

The Constitution requires that proposed amendments to the Constitution need the approval of two-thirds of both Houses of Congress before they are taken to the states for their ratification. This device recognises that constitutional change warrants a consensus rather than a majority of support.

There have only been twenty-seven amendments over the two-hundred-year history of the Constitution, so this is a rarely used function. The last amendment – in 1992 – limited Congress's ability to raise their own salaries. Recent attention has centred on the so-called 'Equal Rights Amendment', which would forbid all laws that are discriminatory on the grounds of gender. Congress passed the proposal in 1972, but it failed to achieve sufficient support in the states. In 1982 a further attempt failed in the House where it enjoyed a majority, but not a large enough one. The battle continues in the 1990s.

Additional features

The parties in Congress

As we have seen above, the parties in Congress are relatively unstructured and disunited. There have, however, been signs in the past twenty years that party unity is increasing. Two main developments are responsible for this. First, there has been a degree of concentration on philosophy in the Republican Party following the rise of the 'New Right' ideas, a movement fronted by President Reagan. Secondly, the Democratic Party has become more 'nationalised'. Traditionally, Democrats from the southern states have been extremely conservative in outlook. This has partly been a legacy of Civil War days, but, more practically, was a result of the need to attract the support of the majority of the poor whites in the area. This group's opposition to liberal reforms, especially in the area of racial equality, outweighs the need for social policies to alleviate poverty. The southern Democrats, or 'Dixiecrats' as they are known, have been in decline. The Republicans in the South have captured their old constituencies, while the increased voting among the black and immigrant population in the South has led them to fall into line with their more liberal colleagues in the North.

The effects can be seen in the voting records of the parties since 1975. Taking the percentage of party members who supported the majority line on voting, we find the following:

Democrats	1975–1984	69%
Democrats	1985–1992	80%

Republicans	1975–1984	71%
Republicans	1985–1992	75%

We can see that, in both parties, there has been an increase in party unity. Nevertheless, it is still true that divisions which cut across party lines are often more important than party strength in the Congress. On some issues, especially appropriations, sectional (regional) groups become important. When social legislation is at stake, it is the conservative-liberal split which becomes decisive. Committees which may **appear** to have a Democrat majority may, in fact, still have a **conservative** majority which is more crucial.

Congress and the lobby Provided a group has been registered as an official lobby group, its members have virtually open access to both Houses of Congress. Indeed, they maintain permanent offices on Capitol Hill. Attention centres on the standing committees, with lobbyists seeking to testify in open hearings. They may be promoting legislation, opposing it, or merely seeking to secure important amendments.

Lobbyists are also active in gaining the support of individual members. They have a variety of incentives available, including election funds and the guarantee of electoral support. At the same time, there are sanctions against those who try to resist their overtures. The successful lobbyist is likely to be the one who can persuade a member of Congress that his support for, or opposition to, a measure will win him many votes when he is seeking re-election. In this regard extensive campaigns take place to ensure that there is widespread support for the issue in question.

The President and Congress We have examined the President's role in Congress in Unit 18. However, a few key points may be useful at this stage. The President has six main objectives in his dealings with Congress:

1. securing the passage of legislation he has proposed
2. opposing congressional legislation of which he disapproves
3. ensuring that he secures funding for his spending programmes
4. gaining approval for his taxation plans
5. obtaining support for his foreign policy initiatives
6. gaining approval for his nominations to Government and the Supreme Court.

In order to achieve his objectives, he now has a large congressional office whose job is to lobby the House and the Senate in the interests of the President. He also relies on the support of key congressional figures, usually from his own party, who may be his permanent allies.

The President has a number of factors in his favour, including the natural loyalty and patriotism he should enjoy as Head of State and the fact that he is leader of his party. If that party enjoys a majority in the Congress, this is especially useful. He also carries the threat of the use of the veto to thwart the Congress in its own legislative goals. The veto is his greatest weapon, but Congress, especially a Congress whose majority party is not the same as the President's (most Republican Presidents in modern times have had to deal with a Democrat-dominated Congress), can override his veto and can defeat his own legislation if they wish.

Thus, there is a fine balance in President–Congress relations, as the Founding Fathers intended in 1787.

Pressure on members   Members of Congress, Senators and Representatives alike, face contrasting pressures when deciding which causes to support and how to vote. These include:

- **Party loyalty**. Apart from the normal feeling that he ought to support his party, a member is aware that he owes his election to the army of party workers at home. They usually **expect** him to toe the party line on most occasions. He may also wish to continue to enjoy the political companionship of his fellow members in Congress. As we have seen, such loyalty in voting is on the increase.

- **From lobbyists**. It requires considerable funds today to fight elections so that the financial contributions offered to sitting members are a great (and perfectly legal) temptation. This is also true of the many Political Action Committees, local pressure groups and corporate backers who seek their support. Today most sitting members can almost guarantee re-election and this is because of the huge financial rewards which are available to them if they are compliant.

- **From constituents**. The voting and speaking record of a member is sure to be publicised at election time. The member who defies public opinion in his constituency, therefore, is playing a dangerous game. This factor is more significant for Representatives, who must seek re-election after only two years and whose constituencies are much smaller than those of most Senators. The Senate's longer term of office – six years – releases them from this pressure. Indeed, it used to be the case that Senators were notorious for their defiance of public opinion. Safe in their 'citadel', as the journalist William White called the Senate in the 1950s, Senators formed an exclusive 'club', and were largely immune from external pressure. This is less so today and Senators are more sensitive to public opinion than ever before.

- Many members have strong personal philosophies, whatever their party allegiance. Thus, Senator **Edward Kennedy**, for example, is a convinced liberal and supporter of social reform and a greater degree of economic equality. At the other end of the spectrum, Republican Representative **Newt Gingrich** is a firm conservative who would oppose most economic and social reform. Personal convictions, in such cases, will often be a more powerful influence than any of the other factors.

Differences between the Senate and House of Representatives

In contrast to most bicameral systems, the two Houses of Congress have remarkably balanced powers. The titles 'upper' and 'lower' House are largely meaningless, unless we accept that Senators enjoy higher political status than Representatives, a development which was spurred by the fact that two great Presidents of modern times – Kennedy and Johnson – were former Senators. However, there are important differences.

Possibly the strangest feature of the Senate which differentiates it from the House is the '**filibuster**'. Any Bill which runs out of debating time is automatically lost. It follows from this rule that a determined group of Senators may seek to defeat a Bill simply by 'filibustering', which means speaking indefinitely (about any subject they choose) until time runs out for further consideration of the Bill. Senators have been known to stay on their feet for over twenty-four hours to ensure a successful filibuster!

To stop a filibuster, supporters of a Bill must introduce a motion of 'cloture' (a corruption of the word 'closure'). Unfortunately, a cloture motion needs the support of 60 per cent of the Senate. It therefore follows that a Bill effectively needs a 60 per cent majority; 51 per cent will not do if there is serious opposition. In the House of Representatives a simple majority **will** bring a Bill to the vote so the filibuster would be futile.

The effect of the principle of filibustering is to make the passing of legislation through the Senate slightly more difficult. However, the fact that the Senate is smaller at least means that only sixty Senators need to be persuaded to support a Bill, whereas the simple majority in the House is 218.

All of the distinctions between the Senate and the House can be divided into those of **powers** and **authority** and those of **characteristics**.

Powers and authority

Senate	House of Representatives
To impeach the President	To conduct preliminary impeachment hearings
To approve or reject presidential nominations to the Cabinet or Supreme Court	Special power over tax proposals
Ratification of foreign treaties	More influence over appropriations
More say in national issues	More authority over domestic issues
Filibuster block available	No filibuster possible

Characteristics

Senate	House of Representatives
Senators are less open to pressure from constituents	Representatives are very sensitive to constituency opinion
Senators tend to take a 'national' outlook	Representatives are more concerned with domestic issues
Party and committee leaders are less powerful	Power is more in the hands of key party leaders
There are fewer Senators and so they are better known nationally	In the bigger House, Representatives have less prestige
Bills have more chance of success	Bills are more likely to fall foul of the powerful Rules Committee

Conclusion The picture we have now seen of the US Congress is undoubtedly of one of the most pluralist bodies in Western democratic politics. Power is extremely diffused and access to the key centres of power is remarkably open. The great question over which American commentators argue is whether these characteristics render the Congress too weak to be effective, or whether this absence of concentrated power is the perfect safeguard against the tyranny of a powerful majority.

The US Congress and British Parliament compared

Contrasts

The relative positions of these two legislatures in their political settings are shaped by four particular features.

The separation of powers

The eighteenth-century French political philosopher, **Montesquieu**, was a great admirer of the British political system. He believed, with relatively little justification, that the secret of the British system was the separation of the powers of the three branches of government – judiciary, executive and legislature. This separation, he argued, prevented the concentration of power in too few hands. Each branch of government would balance the power of the others. His romantic vision of British government was one of the major influences on the writers of the American Constitution. It is, therefore, ironic that, while the American Constitution insisted on the separation of executive and legislative power, the British system moved steadily away from Montesquieu's vision. What does this imply in practice?

In the USA:

- There are separate elections for the Presidency and the Congress. Thus, each branch has its own source of authority.
- The President is required to attend Congress once a year for his annual 'State of the Union Address'. Otherwise, he and other members of his administration may only come to Capitol Hill if invited.
- In addition, members of the administration may not sit as members of Congress.
- The Constitution lays down completely separate powers for the Congress and the President. If one of the two were to attempt to encroach upon the power of the other, the Supreme Court would quickly intervene to prevent it.
- The survival of the administration does not depend upon favourable votes in the Congress. Indeed, the President may lose a large proportion of his legislation at the hands of an unfriendly Congress, but he must carry on regardless. US Presidents have no record of resigning on the grounds that they are unable to control the legislature.

In Britain:

- Members of the Government are, and indeed **must**, be drawn from either House of Parliament.
- It follows from the above that ministers are invariably present in Parliament and are expected to lead debates if they concern the minister's area of responsibility.
- It is understood that Parliament and Government do not have separate mandates from the electorate. Thus, the party which wins power can claim authority to carry out its manifesto without obstruction from Parliament.
- There being no entrenched and codified Constitution in Britain, there is no clear separation of the responsibilities of Government and Parliament.
- Government **does** depend upon the continuous support of the majority in Parliament.

The party system
The contrast between the parliamentary behaviour of British and American parties could hardly be more striking. Unity scores on legislation among both Democrats and Republicans, as we have seen above, usually lie between 75 per cent and 80 per cent. In Britain such scores would represent disaster for a government and almost certain resignation. The governing party in Britain invariably marshals over 95 per cent support and often 100 per cent among its MPs. Why is this so? We only have to ask what the respective whips in the two systems have at their disposal to maintain discipline to answer this question.

In Parliament MPs may be threatened with loss of career prospects, temporary suspension, the enmity of their colleagues, deselection by their constituency party and even the ultimate sanction of expulsion from the party. Indeed, in the 1993 battles to keep the Conservative Party in line over ratification of the Maastricht Treaty, the whips were said to have used a variety of 'dirty tricks', including revelations of extra-marital affairs, to bring the most stubborn into line. As a last resort the whips may point out that an issue is a matter of confidence in the Government in general. If sufficient dissidents insist on defying the party line, resignation of the government and the threat of an election will usually prove enough to cool down the hotheads. This is indeed an impressive array of weapons!

Pity, then, the poor American whip. He can appeal to the loyalty of the party. If a presidential proposal is at stake, he may appeal to the member's patriotism. He may have at his disposal potentially damaging knowledge of the member's private or financial affairs to use as a threat. If he is very lucky, he may have something at his disposal with which to strike a bargain – the compliance of a member on one issue may be rewarded with a valuable government contract going to his state or district. When whips are representing the President himself, the member's support may be secured in return for the President's sympathy in a different area of policy dear to the member's heart. Yet these are mere bows and arrows compared to the heavy artillery available to British party whips.

There have been a few occasions when the British Labour Party whips have encountered the same kinds of obstacles as their American colleagues. Prominent left-wingers such as **Tony Benn** have felt secure enough in their beliefs to be independent-minded, while others have come under such extreme pressure from militant constituency members or trade union backers that they have been forced to defy the whip. The Conservative Party, less troubled by such pressures, has had a few of its own rebels – **Nicholas Winterton** being a prominent example – but they are relatively rare. Nevertheless, despite such exceptions, the behaviour of British parties in Parliament is markedly different from that of the parties in Congress.

'Damn your principles, stick to your Party,' declared Conservative leader **Benjamin Disraeli** over a hundred years ago. The appeal of this instruction still holds largely true in Britain and the result is a remarkable degree of predictability about voting in the House of Commons. In Congress, party membership is only one of several forces acting on members so that the outcome of most proposals is uncertain.

In the House of Lords, of course, party loyalties are of less importance than in the Commons. Indeed, for the many cross-benchers parties are not a consideration. However, as we shall discuss below, the weaknesses of the British Upper House render such comparisons largely irrelevant.

The sovereignty of Parliament or checks and balances

At first sight it may appear that Parliament has considerably more power than Congress. After all, it enjoys almost unlimited sovereignty, is omni-competent, having no restraints on its powers over domestic affairs, and is not bound by a supreme Constitution. Congress, by contrast, is strictly limited in its jurisdiction by the terms of the Constitution. But this is only a superficial view.

In effect, the sovereignty of Parliament becomes the sovereignty of Government. Since Government exercises virtually complete control over its majority in the Commons, the legal strength of Parliament translates into barely limited executive power. On the other hand, Congress's powers are actually **guaranteed** by the Constitution. The executive branch simply **cannot** usurp these powers. The checks and balances built into the system both limit and enhance congressional independence.

Of course, should it become the case that British Governments cannot regularly command the support of a majority, which would most probably be the case if 'hung' Parliaments became the norm, the circumstances might be very different. For the foreseeable future, however, parliamentary sovereignty results in parliamentary weakness.

The Upper House

In some ways, the House of Lords may appear similar to the two Houses of Congress. Its members enjoy a great degree of independence, debates are less party-dominated and there is much concern with legislative amendment. Indeed, the intense controversies over two major pieces of Government legislation in 1994 closely resembled the deliberations of American standing committees. The **Police and Magistrates' Courts Bill** and **Criminal Justice and Public Order Bill** were extensively amended in the Lords, both as a result of intensive external lobbying and the concerns of peers with a background in the legal profession.

However, even when the Lords engages in one of its periodic bouts of rebelliousness, it is always in the knowledge that the Government, through its Commons majority, can undo everything it has tried to achieve.

By contrast, the powers of the two Houses of Congress are almost equally balanced. A measure which enjoys success in one place may still encounter obstacles in the other.

Having established these points, we may now make some detailed comparisons:

Legislation

Congress

Congress may initiate, draft, amend or reject legislation.

The executive branch is not guaranteed favourable treatment for its legislation. Carter (1977–80) enjoyed about 75 per cent success rate, Reagan (1981–8) achieved between 43 per cent and 82 per cent, Clinton achieved 89 per cent success in 1993.

There is extensive expert examination of all legislation.

External lobby groups have considerable influence.

Parliament

Very little legislation originates in Parliament. Usually less than five Private Members' Bills are successful per session. Most are rejected.

Virtually all government legislation is guaranteed success. Only one Bill – the Sunday Trading Bill of 1986 – has been defeated on the floor of the Commons since World War Two.

The amending function in the Commons is largely meaningless, with only government-approved changes being accepted.

Government domination means the parliamentary lobby is relatively weak.

Finance

Congress

All taxation proposals require congressional approval. There is liable to be significant amendment to tax measures.

All expenditure for every purpose must be separately approved

Legislation may be favourably or unfavourably affected by appropriations votes.

Congress does not consider any overall levels of expenditure, taxation or long-term budgetary constraints.

Parliament

Parliament is remarkably powerless in its consideration of public finance even though it spends considerable time debating the annual Finance Bill.

Even controversial tax proposals can be forced through Parliament. Thus, Poll Tax (1988) and VAT on domestic fuel bills (1993) were accepted by Parliament despite fierce public opposition.

Expenditure is not seriously questioned before it is made. The Public Accounts Committee does scrutinise expenditure effectively, but **after** it has taken place.

Parliamentary weakness allows Government to exercise budgetary control.

Representation of interests

Congress	Parliament
There is extremely open access for lobbyists.	There is access allowed to lobbyists, but this is relatively limited.
Members rely heavily upon interest groups for finance of election campaigns and political support. The weakness of the party system frees members from party commitment, allowing them to support external groups more openly.	MPs can be sponsored by outside groups, including trade unions, business, and cause groups, but there are many reservations about such influence, as indicated by the disciplining of two Conservative MPs who accepted bribes in return for asking parliamentary questions. Also, individual campaign spending for MPs is very limited by law, so there is little need for financial support from such groups.
The committee system relies heavily upon information and opinion from interest groups.	There is limited access to legislative and investigatory committees. Most lobbying activity is centred on government departments.
Members, especially Representatives, take special care to protect the interests of their constituencies, securing favourable and opposing unfavourable legislation and supporting a fair share of federal spending and government contracts.	MPs take care to represent the interests of constituencies. Whips accept that this may transcend party loyalty. Thus, members of the governing party have defied government policy over such issues as nuclear waste dumping sites and the siting of motorways and railways.

Scrutiny of government

Congress	Parliament
Congressional committees have wide powers to call witnesses and see papers. Freedom of Information Act ensures the right to see official documents.	Select committees have fewer powers to see government witnesses and papers. Official documents may not be forthcoming.
American government does not have a strong tradition of secrecy.	The Official Secrets Act and tradition of secrecy inhibit ministers and officials in their evidence to committees.
Important hearings are well publicised and broadcast.	Committees are generally low profile.
There is no doctrine of collective responsibility so members of Government can be more frank.	The doctrine of collective responsibility prevents ministers from expressing personal views.
Public officials are freer to express views.	Civil servants must only repeat official government policy and cannot discuss policy making, their own role in it or their own views.
Appointment of government members and Supreme Court judges are subject to Senate approval.	Parliament has no influence on public appointments.
Congress has the right to investigate the work of the CIA and intelligence services.	Question Time on the floor of the House has become largely ritualised and Government-controlled.

Some similarities

There can be little doubt that there are considerably more contrasts than similarities between Parliament and Congress. They play fundamentally different roles in their political systems. Nevertheless, we can identify a small number of parallels.

Social composition

Both bodies are notoriously unrepresentative of the broader population. The table below shows some revealing statistics taken in 1992. (The House of Lords, being an unelected body, is not included in this comparison.)

	Congress	House of Commons
% Women	10	9
% Ethnic minorities	12	1
% Former manual workers	9	11

* Figures rounded to the nearest whole number.

There is also disproportionate representation of professions in both – in 1992, 45 per cent of members of Congress were lawyers, while 42 per cent of British MPs were from a professional background; the average age of members of Congress in that year was 53, remarkably similar to the average of 52 in the House of Commons.

Constituency representation

In both the House of Commons and the Congress it is expected that members should pay special attention to the interests of their constituents, both as individuals and as a whole. While it is true that Congress members have more means at their disposal – notably, influence over the allocation of federal funds and contracts around the country – MPs are also expected to lobby Government in the interest of their constituents. Certainly, there has been a trend in Britain for such activity to increase in modern times as voting becomes more volatile, but this feature has always been present in the USA where it is an essential ingredient in re-election campaigns.

Committee work

Although American committees are vastly more influential than their British counterparts, we should still note the similarities which now exist in committee structures. It is true that the House of Commons separates legislative and investigatory committees, but the essential functions exist in both systems. In both countries, the debates on the floor of the House are of considerably less importance than the background work going on in committee rooms (in the case of Britain, often unnoticed).

Legitimation

Both Congress and Parliament have the key role of giving authority to legislation. Neither the people nor the courts will accept laws which have not been legitimised by the elected legislature. It may be largely a meaningless ritual in Britain compared to the hard-fought battle that takes place in the USA, but in both cases it is the central activity.

The future...

There are some indications that Congress and Parliament may be moving towards a greater similarity in their characteristics. This is not dramatic, but is certainly perceptible:

- Congress is developing greater party unity as we have seen above. This has always been notable when a new President first takes office and enjoys a so-called 'honeymoon period' and Congress behaves most like the House of Commons, but there has been a noticeable trend towards greater party discipline.
- The development of departmental select committees in the House of Commons since 1979 has been a significant step in the direction of the congressional system. There are even signs that the committees are beginning to take legislative initiatives, pointing the way to future policy as a result of their investigations.
- Britain's position in Europe being a major policy issue has had the effect in the 1990s of splitting the main parties across the traditional ideological lines. These have become open wounds in the Conservative Party, but are also significant in the Labour Party, which has managed to keep them under the surface while it seeks to gain power. The question of devolution – the granting of greater autonomy to Scotland and Wales – represents a further potentially divisive force for Labour. Should these issues indeed split the parties, Britain will be faced with the same kind of competing schisms which exist in Congress. The traditional north–south split in the Democratic Party, and the centre-right divide among Republicans, have inhibited unity; Europe and devolution may play the same role in the future of British parliamentary parties.
- As Professor Philip Norton has pointed out, since 1970 there has been a new prevailing attitude among British MPs that they are not mere lobby fodder. They are more independent-minded and are willing to defy their party leaderships on such clear issues as taxation, Europe and defence policy. The removal of Margaret Thatcher as Prime Minister by her own MPs was indeed a dramatic development. There has also been a recent increase in the Commons' determination to create some of its own legislation. Important changes to abortion law in 1993 and to laws relating to homosexuality in 1994 were prominent examples.

Over the same period, the House of Lords has become more active in its scrutiny of legislation. While its powers remain limited, it has certainly attempted at times to behave like the USA Senate.

Conclusion

It is somewhat ironic that, while many British parliamentarians look wistfully across the Atlantic, wishing that they too could enjoy the influence of their American colleagues, American government officials remain envious of the British Government's ability to force even unpopular measures through a weak and compliant Parliament. In many ways these emotions illustrate the principal contrasts between Congress and Parliament.

For exam questions relevant to this unit, see page 494.

18 The United States' Presidency and administration

Section 1 The executive power shall be vested in a president of the United States of America. He shall hold his office during the term of four years.

Section 2 The President shall be Commander-in-Chief of the army and navy of the United States, and the militia of the several States, when called into the actual service of the United States; he shall require the opinion, in writing, of the principal officer in each of the executive departments upon any subject relating to the duties of their respective offices, and he shall have power to grant reprieves and pardons for offences against the United States, except in cases of impeachment.

He shall have power, by and with the advice and consent of the Senate, to make treaties, provided two-thirds of the Senators concur; and he shall nominate, and, by and with the advice of the Senate, shall appoint ambassadors, other public ministers, and consuls, judges of the Supreme Court.

He shall, from time to time, give to the Congress information of the state of the Union, and recommend to their consideration such measures as he shall consider necessary.

Section 3 The President, Vice President and all civil officers of the United States shall be removed from office on impeachment for, and conviction of, treason, bribery, or other high crimes and misdemeanours.

Introduction

The Founding Fathers faced, in 1787, a number of problems when shaping the future government of the USA. Among them was the precise relationship between Congress and the executive. They were aware of the danger that government might be dominated by one or two large states, notably Virginia and New York, and that there might be no figure who could represent the Union as a whole. The twin objectives of uniting the states, while also giving government a firm direction, seemed to conflict with each other. At the same time, there was a pressing need to establish the USA in the world community (not least, in order to secure some financial credit to pay for the armed forces!) and to protect it from external threats. The answer was to create the Presidency.

The office of President of the USA is unique in Western democratic politics. It is the only case where the positions of **Head of State** and **Head of Government** are combined in one post. The incumbent is, therefore, expected to perform the two basic functions described below.

Head of State

Here he must undertake a number of responsibilities:

- to represent the whole country in relationships and negotiations with other states
- to unite the country in times of emergency and crisis
- to understand and further the interests of the whole American community, irrespective of party allegiance; he must attempt to take into account the interests of specific groups as well as those of the people collectively

- to undertake the security of the USA from both external and internal threats
- to act as a figurehead, representing the spirit of America, its culture and traditions
- to be able to maintain national unity even in the face of bitter political controversies.

Head of Government   These functions are distinct from those the President performs as Head of State:

- to promote a specific programme which has been sanctioned during his own election, as part of his party's political programme
- to support those sections of the Congress which, he believes, are promoting policies with which he can concur
- to mediate between competing views on policy arising out of congressional debates
- to ensure the implementation of legislation passed by Congress in such a way that it conforms to the interests of the country
- in some cases, to veto legislation which he feels is impractical or not in the interests of the people.

There is little doubt that the framers of the Constitution intended that the President's role as Head of State would be the more significant. They saw policy making as largely the preserve of the Congress; the President was to oversee the process of government, appoint its officers and ensure continuity, but little else. Despite James Madison's hopes to the contrary, it was the emergence of political parties which changed the picture. As it became clear during the nineteenth century that the President was becoming head of the majority party, his **political** role as Head of Government began to dominate. By the time **Abraham Lincoln** (1861–5) took on the southern states over the slavery issue, it had become clear that the direction of government was in the hands of the President.

Since his role as party leader has become a key factor, our understanding of how the Presidency works must begin with the process of his election.

The election of the President

Party nomination

In theory, any citizen of the USA who meets the necessary constitutional conditions may run for election as President. In practice, however, a candidate has no realistic chance of being elected unless he is nominated as the official choice of either the Democrat or Republican Party. There have been occasions when heroic campaigns have been waged by independent candidates or those representing minor parties, but these have always ended in failure. **John Anderson** won 6.1 per cent of the popular vote in 1980 and **Ross Perot** achieved the remarkable figure of 19.0 per cent in 1992, but neither was a realistic contender once the polls opened. It follows that the first major step on the road to the election of a President is the securing of a major party nomination.

The process may begin as long as two years before the actual election, which always takes place in November. Indeed, by March 1995 a total of nine prospective Republican candidates were beginning their campaigns for the 1996 election.

Ross Perot talking to the Press during his 1992 election campaign

Both parties choose their candidate at a **National Convention** in the summer before the election. Party delegates from all the states (the number being proportional to the population of the state) assemble and are balloted to determine whom they wish to see as their party's presidential candidate. There is an exhaustive ballot where losing aspirants drop out until one of the nominees achieves an overall majority of the delegate votes. As we shall see, however, most of the activity takes place before the Convention.

Most of the delegates are committed to support one individual by the time they arrive at the Convention. They are only free to switch their support if their nominee is eliminated in an earlier ballot. The delegates become committed to one nominee by one of two processes, both used by the two parties in much the same way. These are either **primary elections or caucuses**:

<u>Primaries</u> These are basically private elections held among the supporters of each party. Voters must register for one or other of the parties to be eligible to take part in a primary. There are a number of variations in the way in which the primaries are organised and in the degree to which they bind delegates to the Convention. In principle, however, they apportion the delegates to various nominees in two main ways. **Either** the nominee who wins a primary receives the support of **all** the party delegates from that state, **or** delegate support is apportioned according to the proportion of votes won by each nominee in the primary. Primaries for the presidential nomination are currently used in twenty-eight states. New Hampshire is traditionally the first primary, usually in February or March, and the rest follow over the next three or four months.

<u>Caucuses</u>   These are meetings of party activists rather than open elections. Again, delegates are chosen at the caucuses some of whom are committed to a nominee, some of whom are not. The delegates chosen attend a state convention which **does** normally bind the delegates to the National Convention to a particular nominee.

<u>The National Convention</u>   Both major parties hold their Convention in the summer before a presidential election. This is the most important event in the life of an American political party, serving a number of functions:

- It is a mass rally of key party workers, designed to boost morale before the arduous task in the autumn of campaigning for their candidate – not just the presidential candidate, but all the other office-seekers (at national, state and local level) who are also elected in November.
- It is a public relations exercise with much high-profile publicity. The party and its candidate must appear confident and competent before the election.
- The presidential candidate for the party must be chosen.
- Once a candidate is chosen, a political programme must be approved, and it must be one upon which both the chosen presidential candidate and members of Congress can agree. Most of the process is a formality, but some issues remain to be resolved at the Convention.
- Finally, after the battle for party nomination, the Convention seeks to unite the whole party, including the losing aspirants, behind the nominee.

In some cases, one of the candidates has already secured an absolute majority of the committed delegates **before** the Convention, through successful caucuses and primaries. This was the case with **Walter Mondale**, the Democratic nominee in 1984 (though this did not prevent his being heavily defeated by Republican **Ronald Reagan** in the real election). In such a case, the Convention turns into a triumphal rally and a great show of unity.

If there is to be balloting, each party hopes for a decisive result on the first ballot to avoid damaging in-fighting. A bitterly fought Convention presents a poor image of the party to the public. The Democratic Convention of 1968 in Chicago, for example, in which **Hubert Humphrey** beat off the challenge of **Eugene McCarthy** amid much acrimony, was contrasted with the Republican display of unity behind **Richard Nixon** in Miami. Not surprisingly, therefore, Nixon beat Humphrey, the earlier favourite, in the following November's election.

The election   Every four years, early in November, the whole of the United States is entitled to vote in the presidential election. As we have seen, small party and independent candidates are a distraction, but not a serious factor. This is a contest between the nominated candidates from each of the two main parties. It is not, however, a straighforward popular election. The President is actually elected through the **electoral college** system. This device requires careful explanation:

Ronald and Nancy Reagan at Republican National Convention, 23 August 1984

Richard Nixon at Republican National Convention, 8 August 1968

<u>The electoral college</u> Effectively, in a presidential election each state holds its own 'mini-election'. That is, the votes for each candidate are counted **within** the state and a winner is declared. The winner in each state receives **all** the 'electoral college' votes for that state. The number of such electoral college votes gained depends upon the population size of the state. Thus, the very small states have only **three** electoral college votes (the minimum permissible), while the largest – California – has fifty-four. After the election, the electoral college votes of each candidate

are added up and the winner is elected. Should no candidate win an overall majority of the college vote, there are procedures for settling the deadlock but, since this has not occurred in the twentieth century, we need not describe them here.

The results of two modern presidential elections illustrate the effects of the electoral college system:

Year	Candidate	Total votes gained	Electoral College votes
1980	Carter (Dem.)	35,483,820	49
	Reagan (Rep.)	43,901,812	489
	Anderson (Ind.)	5,719,722	0
1992	Clinton (Dem.)	43,728,275	370
	Bush (Rep.)	38,167,416	168
	Perot (Ind.)	19,237,247	0

We can see that the effect of the electoral college is to distort the true popularity of the candidates. Ross Perot's zero score in 1992 disguised a good showing by him in terms of popular support. Similarly, a fairly close contest in 1980 looked like a landslide for Reagan if we only look at the electoral college. However, despite these distortions, in every election since World War Two the candidate with the largest popular vote has also won the election. Thus, the college system does not produce the 'wrong' winner, it merely exaggerates the size of the victory. Even so, hoping for an unusual result, candidates campaign much harder in those states with most electoral college votes. A narrow victory in California or Illinois is worth much more than a thumping majority in a small state such as Iowa or Rhode Island.

We can now summarise the stages on the road to the White House:

A successful campaign for the Presidency

1994	Tentative feelers are put out to test potential strength of support.
March 1995	An announcement of an intention to run for President is made.
Summer 1995	A drive to raise campaign funds is initiated.
Autumn 1995	A firm commitment to run is made. More fundraising activity.
February 1996	Campaigning in the primaries and caucuses begins.
Summer 1996	The National Convention takes place. The candidate becomes the party nominee.
Autumn 1996	Campaigning and fundraising intensify.
November 1996	The presidential election is held.
January 1997	The new President takes the oath of allegiance and takes office.

The powers of the President

As Head of State

These powers concern mostly the conduct of foreign policy, military action and the maintenance of public order within the USA. Although all of the functions performed under the auspices of his role as Head of State are subject to constitutional and congressional controls (part of the general principle of 'checks and balances'), it is in this area that the President has most discretionary freedom. Indeed, they are sometimes described as 'prerogative powers', similar to those enjoyed by a British Prime Minister acting on behalf of the Crown. The most important are detailed below.

<u>Treaties</u> The negotiation and signing of **treaties** is carried out by the President and his advisers, notably the Secretary of State. During the Cold War, several issues arose concerning the control of nuclear weapons which required extremely sensitive treatment during discussions with the Soviet Union and its allies. The **Nuclear Test Ban Treaty** (signed by John F. Kennedy in 1963), **Nuclear Non Proliferation Treaty** (signed by Lyndon Johnson in 1968) and **Strategic Arms Limitation Treaties (SALT 1, 1970 and SALT 2, 1977)**, for example, were negotiated in great secrecy and with relatively little domestic interference.

JFK signing partial Nuclear Test Ban Treaty, 7 October 1963

However, although the President may conduct his discussions in relative freedom, the final treaty requires the approval of a two-thirds majority in the Senate. This is by no means automatic. The 1968 Test Ban Treaty was delayed by a year so that Richard Nixon took the credit for Johnson's work; SALT 2 was never ratified owing to the Senate's suspicions that the Soviet Union could not be trusted to comply with the requirement to reduce its weapon stocks.

<u>Executive agreements</u> Executive agreements replace formal treaties, being arrangements made with other countries concerning trade, military co-operation, mutual friendship or the like. They are binding but, not

being treaties, do not require ratification by the Senate. These comprise, in the true sense of the phrase, prerogative presidential powers. They must, of course, be reported to Congress, but no formal action can be taken to undo them.

Control of the armed forces   As **Commander-in-Chief** of the armed forces, the President also enjoys considerable freedom of action. Congress must approve formal declarations of war but, thereafter, the President is in full control. Indeed, before the **War Powers Resolution** was passed in 1973, the President could do as he wished with American forces in undeclared conflicts. The conduct of the Vietnam War between 1962 and 1975 changed this situation. Successive Presidents – Kennedy, Johnson and Nixon – sheltered under their powers as Commander-in-Chief to wage an undeclared war, often under the cloak of secrecy, and even after the support of public opinion for the action had clearly been lost. Congress now demands overall control of such conflicts.

Nevertheless, as we have seen above, several short-term military adventures have been carried out by Presidents, unhindered by the limited terms of the War Powers Resolution. In Grenada, Somalia, the Arabian Gulf, Lebanon and Haiti, Presidents Reagan, Bush and Clinton have felt at liberty to commit and command American forces without hindrance by Congress.

Control of the National Guard   As well as external forces, the President commands the **National Guard**, a domestic 'army' whose role is to put down major outbreaks of public disorder and to deal with other emergencies, such as natural disasters. During the 'Youth in Protest' movement of the late 1960s and early 1970s, largely directed against the Vietnam War, Presidents Johnson and Nixon were forced to resort to use of the Guard to control student rioting.

More commonly, however, it is the incidence of natural disasters such as major flooding, hurricanes and earthquakes which see the National Guard in action. In the most serious examples, the President himself may be seen taking personal control.

The intelligence services   The intelligence services are the responsibility of the President himself. The principal body is the **Central Intelligence Agency (CIA)**, whose Director is appointed by the President and reports directly to him. This relationship remained relatively uncontroversial until, after the creation of the CIA in 1947, it became clear that its agents were increasingly acting as instruments of clandestine presidential policy abroad. In the 1970s CIA operatives were discovered to be conducting covert operations in Vietnam and Cambodia, in communist-dominated Nicaragua, and in Chile, where the autocratic regime of General Pinochet was said to be supported heavily by the CIA despite its record of human rights violations. As a result, Congress now demands greater information concerning CIA operations and a special committee has powers to demand full information concerning its activities.

Appointment of ambassadors   All USA **ambassadors** are appointed by the President. Of course, a new President does not replace all his ambassadors, but he is certainly expected to replace those holding key positions in such capitals as Moscow, Beijing, London and Paris. In this way he can ensure that they become his personal envoys and important instruments in his foreign policy plans.

<u>Acting as a figurehead</u> The President, as we have observed above, is expected to represent all the American people. He is, therefore, a figurehead, who will attempt to unite the country at important moments in its history. In times when important domestic and foreign events threaten to have a major impact on American lives, it is his role to lead the country. In this regard, he has total access to the **media**. In particular, he is empowered to take broadcasting time on both TV and radio in order to speak to the people. He is not entitled to use this privilege to promote his own or his party's policies, but he may tell the American people why he feels certain courses of action are necessary. The commitment of American troops to battle are clear examples, as are regular requests for people to show patience in times of economic difficulty.

As Head of Government We can divide the President's role as head of the executive branch into four areas. These are legislation, appointments, budgetary control and federal expenditure. We examine each in turn:

<u>Legislation</u> Congress is the principal legislative branch of government. The Constitution states this and it is still, broadly speaking, true. What the Founding Fathers did not anticipate, however, was that the President would come to play a key role in law making. Although the Constitution states that the President should, from time to time, make recommendations for action to the Congress, the concept of a full legislative programme to be developed by the President and his advisers was not expected.

The legislative role of the President falls into two categories. First, he initiates a good deal of legislation, either himself or through the various executive agencies which he influences. In modern times, for example, we have seen programmes of civil rights protection and poverty relief from Presidents Kennedy and Johnson, of reform in the system of distributing federal funds to the regions (revenue sharing) from Richard Nixon, new energy initiatives by Jimmy Carter, deregulation of the economy by Ronald Reagan and new health and crime initiatives by Bill Clinton.

Secondly, the President has the power to **veto** legislation proposed by Congress. This effectively means that he can block new laws unless they are backed by a two-thirds majority of the legislature. He does this either by refusing to sign the Bill and so denying it legitimacy, or through a 'pocket veto'. The pocket veto means that, at the end of a congressional session, he simply delays signing until the session ends; the Bill then runs out of time and is lost simply by default. This device is useful to a President who does not wish to enter into bargaining over a piece of legislation and is possible because there is no opportunity for Congress to overrule the veto with its two-thirds majority.

At first sight the veto may appear to be a purely negative device, but a skilful President can use his power of veto creatively. It may be effective as a bargaining counter with the Congress. In return for withholding a possible veto, the President may secure the compliance of the Congress over a piece of his own legislation. Similarly, although the President is **not** able to propose specific amendments to legislation (what would be called a 'line veto'), he can make it known in advance that he will veto a Bill unless certain changes are made. Thus, there are subtle ways in which the power of veto can be a useful legislative tool for the President.

How well this can work largely depends upon the political complexion of Congress, whether it is broadly in philosophical sympathy with the President, as was the case with Lyndon Johnson, or whether there is strong opposition, as under Bill Clinton.

The different uses of the veto can be illustrated by the contrast between the Presidencies shown below:

President	Office years	Total vetoes	No. overruled	Average per year
F.D. Roosevelt	1933–45	635	9	53
D. Eisenhower	1953–61	181	2	22
R. Nixon	1969–74	43	7	8
G. Bush	1989–93	46	1	12

Roosevelt was faced with a largely sympathetic Congress, supportive of his radical 'New Deal' policies, but there were, nevertheless, frequent stand-offs, illustrated by the high rate of veto. Eisenhower, a traditional Republican, was simply opposed to federal power and interference so he blocked many congressional initiatives.

Richard Nixon, on the other hand, had good relations with his Congress for much of his presidency and was prepared to let them take the leading role in domestic policy. Thus, he interfered relatively infrequently.

<u>Appointments</u>   When a new President takes office, he has the opportunity to make about 4,000 appointments of his own choosing. These comprise ambassadors, as we have seen above, but more importantly, all the senior officials in his own office (the White House Staff) together with the Heads and senior officials in the executive agencies which form the new administration. He may select whomsoever he wishes and often nominations come from such varied quarters as Congress itself, the universities, business, pressure groups and, of course, from among the President's own close political supporters. It is generally expected that those who have done most to help in the President's election campaign will obtain a senior post. Even nepotism is acceptable; John Kennedy appointed his brother, Bobby, as Attorney General, but more controversially, Jimmy Carter chose, amid considerable embarrassment, his hard-drinking brother, Billy, to serve on his personal staff.

The President has less discretion over the appointment of judges to the Supreme Court. Here, he must wait until an incumbent judge dies or retires as there can only be nine judges at any one time. The President may not dismiss any judges so that his freedom of action depends largely on circumstance. The nature of the relationship between the President and the Supreme Court is discussed in more detail on pages 430–1.

Budgetary control In conjunction with the **Bureau of the Budget**, the President plays a leading role in the formulation of the federal budget each year. He proposes tax changes and the new levels of existing taxes, together with appropriate levels of expenditure on the various activities of the federal government. At the same time, the President is setting the agenda for broad economic policy, for which he is also responsible. He may wish to deflate the economy by raising taxes and cutting public expenditure, or to promote expansion by taking the opposite measures.

His freedom of action in this field, however, is heavily limited by congressional action, especially that of the House of Representatives. The annual announcement of the federal budget proposals is the prelude to a prolonged series of negotiations with congressional leaders. Frequently, the Congress will wish to reduce taxes since constituents invariably judge their representatives on their ability to reduce the financial burden that central government imposes upon them. At the same time, however, many Congressmen and Senators will also be campaigning for increased federal expenditure if it means more jobs and prosperity for the region which they represent. So the President inevitably has difficulty in reaching budgetary agreement with the legislature.

Democrat President **Bill Clinton** faced a more unusual problem with Congress in the 1990s. Confronted by a hostile, Republican-dominated House of Representatives, his plans to raise taxes in order to finance a new health care plan and law and order measures were vehemently opposed. Speaker of the House **Newt Gingrich** and Senate majority leader **Bob Dole** led a campaign to force Clinton to reduce expenditure while also keeping taxes down. Their interest lay in achieving a more balanced budget to combat possible inflation and to reduce the enormous burden of accumulated debt on the federal government. The result was a series of setbacks for Clinton. He was unable to implement his policies, simply for lack of the necessary funds.

Thus, what is apparently a key tool of presidential policy is, in fact, substantially limited by congressional powers. While Congress cannot produce its own budget, it does possess significant influence over public finance.

Federal expenditure (appropriations) As well as setting an overall sum to be spent by each federal department, the President must determine the allocation of funds to projects within different states and in particular regions. This might include such items as agricultural subsidies, scientific research funds, transport initiatives, environmental projects, industrial grants or the establishment of federal operations in a particular city. In such cases there are significant implications in terms of job opportunities and the general prosperity of an area.

Appropriations, as such allocations are called, provide the President with a significant weapon in the struggle to win support from members of Congress. The apportionment of large amounts of federal funds to a Senator's state or to a Congressman's district can work wonders when it comes to seeking their support for a cherished presidential policy.

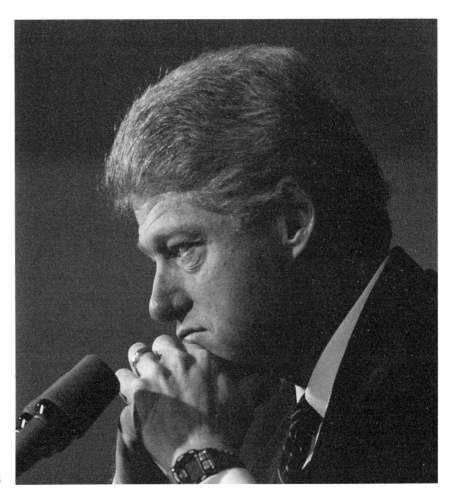

Bill Clinton in 1993

As with the federal budget, however, the House of Representatives, through its powerful **Appropriations Committee**, can make substantial amendments to the President's plans. Indeed, it can be a bargaining counter for use by Congress itself, as well as by the President. Nowhere within the American political system is the system of checks and balances better illustrated than in the horse trading which takes place over federal appropriations.

Conversely, when Congress itself apportions federal funds to projects which it supports, the President has the power to cancel or **impound** them. Impoundment can be thwarted through the use of legislative vetoes, but only if in both Houses, and the process is difficult and time-consuming.

The President and Congress

Party strengths

It is in the relationship between a President and the Congress where the system of checks and balances operates most clearly. The careful balance of power which the original writers of the Constitution created is not constant, however; it is significantly affected by the relative party strengths at the White House and on Capitol Hill, where Congress meets.

We can see the variety of combinations of party majorities which can exist by reference to the political make-up of Congress since 1961, shown against the party of the incumbent President:

Term	President	House of Representatives		Senate	
		Democrats	Republicans	Democrats	Republicans
1961–3	Democrat	262	175	64	36
1963–5	Democrat	258	176	67	33
1965–7	Democrat	295	140	68	32
1967–9	Democrat	248	187	64	36
1969–71	Republican	243	192	58	42
1971–3	Republican	255	180	54	44
1973–5	Republican	242	192	56	42
1975–7	Republican	291	144	61	37
1977–9	Democrat	292	143	61	38
1979–81	Democrat	277	158	58	41
1981–3	Republican	243	192	46	53
1983–5	Republican	268	167	46	54
1985–7	Republican	253	182	47	53
1987–9	Republican	258	177	55	45
1989–91	Republican	260	175	55	45
1991–3	Republican	267	167	56	44
1993–5	Democrat	258	175	57	43
1995–7	Democrat	204	230	47	53

We can also see that it is normal for the Democrats to hold a majority in both Houses of Congress, especially in the House of Representatives where the first Republican majority since 1955 appeared in 1994. This may suggest that only a Democratic President is able to achieve significant success. It is, indeed, certainly true that one of the most 'productive' Presidencies was that of **Lyndon Johnson**, a Democrat (1963–9), who enjoyed very large Senate and House majorities. At their height, between 1933 and 1939, the Democrats dominated the Senate by 76 to 16 and the House by 331 to 89. Not surprisingly, Franklin Roosevelt was able to enact the most extensive legislative programme ever seen in American politics.

Nevertheless, the picture is not always so clear. Among the Democrats there is always a sizeable conservative group, especially among Congressmen from southern states, who can obstruct a progressive President. **Jimmy Carter** (1977–81) was to experience such opposition. Conversely,

Lyndon Johnson reviewing Vietnam War troops, 28 December 1967

Ronald Reagan (1985–93), although a right-wing Republican, was able to enact considerable reforms by creating a coalition of support between a united Republican Party and a group of southern Democrats.

The most striking example, however, of how the party balance in Congress can work against a President occurred in the mid 1990s when Democrat Bill Clinton found himself completely blocked by Republican majorities in both Houses from the beginning of 1995. To add to the problem, Clinton was a relatively liberal President, while the new Republican Congress leaders, notably Bob Dole (Senate) and Newt Gingrich (House) were, on the whole, extremely conservative.

Yet the fact that American parties are rarely as united and disciplined as their British counterparts does mean that a President can make some headway against an apparently hostile Congress, provided he possesses sufficient political skill, the backing of public opinion and a strong team of congressional managers. Of all modern Presidents, Reagan and Johnson possessed all three qualities to the greatest degree.

Reciprocal veto power   As we have seen, the President's use of his veto over congressional initiatives can be used both as a negative and a positive tool. Thus, a conservative President such as Ronald Reagan was able to keep the progressives in Congress at bay through his use of the veto. At the same time, he could bargain with congressional leaders to ensure that his own policies – mainly in the fields of crime control, welfare and economic management – were given a fair hearing.

On the other hand, Congress has, since 1932, been able to exercise a **legislative veto** over executive actions by the President or one of his agencies of government. Apart from lesser executive agreements in foreign policy, it is the appropriation of federal funds for different projects and regions which is most often subjected to such vetoes.

Appropriations and impoundments

Some of the fiercest battles waged between the President and the Congress concern the apportionment of federal funds. The conflict is ensured by the fact that **both** Congress **and** the executive branch, led by the President, have power to spend such monies. Naturally, Congress may wish to spend funds on its favourite projects, such as inner city renovations, anti-crime measures or environmental projects. As representatives they wish to show their constituents that they have been fighting for the wellbeing of their area. Members of the House of Representatives are particularly sensitive to federal spending as they are forced to seek re-election every two years.

At the same time, public expenditure forms a vital part of presidential policy making, especially in the fields of defence and foreign affairs. Apart from the huge expenditure on the armed forces, which the President controls directly, overseas aid must be apportioned to maintain America's world-wide network of allies. Space and weapons research are additional favourite items of presidential spending. Both Reagan and Bush, for example, cherished dreams of seeing through the 'Star Wars' project – a fabulously expensive plan to create a laser-based anti-missile defence umbrella for North America.

Presidential–congressional conflict over public expenditure came to a head under President Nixon in the 1970s. The problem had become exacerbated by two features. First, Nixon was spending vast sums on the wars in Vietnam and Cambodia, of which Congress was increasingly disapproving. Secondly, a liberal and progressive Congress, determined to reduce poverty and urban deprivation, was frequently falling foul of Nixon's conservatism and dislike of excessive domestic spending.

Ultimately, the **Budget and Impoundment Control Act** of 1974 attempted to clarify the issue. Although the financial relationship between the President and Congress remains complex, while the use of impoundments and legislative vetoes is subject to constitutional dispute, some order was restored in 1974. Basically, the President may stop or defer any congressional spending programme through impoundment. However, a legislative veto by **both** Houses of Congress may overturn the impoundment. Similarly, Congress may thwart presidential spending programmes, but the President may simply retaliate by using his veto to make life difficult for the Congress.

It is such a balance of power – some may say 'deadlock' – which has been faced by Bill Clinton in relation to his second Congress, elected in 1994 with a Republican majority in both Houses. His two great spending programmes on health care and crime control have been destroyed by an unfriendly Congress. Sadly for him, however, the conservative nature of the Congress means that even some of his retaliatory vetoes may be overturned by a two-thirds majority.

Advice and consent

As we have seen, the Constitution insists that some presidential actions require the approval of Congress. The Congress describes this stipulation as 'advice and consent'. It applies to foreign treaties and the appointment of Supreme Court judges or senior executive officials.

Until the 1970s most Congresses scarcely used their reserve powers to thwart presidential plans. They had been considered very much as merely 'reserve' powers, for use only if a President appeared to be becoming

George Bush in 1992

dictatorial. In more recent times, however, it has become a reflection of the growing authority of Congress in their relations with the Presidency that the advice and consent power has been increasingly used.

In the 1970s, for example, the Senate consistently refused to ratify SALT 2 (the second strategic arms limitation treaty with the Soviet Union), thus usurping some of the President's authority in foreign policy and defence matters. More recently, President **George Bush** found his nominee for Defense Secretary, **John Tower**, rejected in 1989 on the grounds that the Senate did not trust his financial motives for seeking the post. Similarly, Bill Clinton's nomination for Attorney-General (the senior law officer in the administration), **Zoe Baird**, was refused in 1993 as she had employed illegal immigrants in her house, so it was felt she could not be relied upon in a senior post. The highly publicised Tower and Baird rejections represent a stronger tendency for the Senate to question presidential nominations more searchingly now than in the past.

The President and the Supreme Court

The Supreme Court judges are, in theory, **neutral** guardians of the spirit of the Constitution. It would be naive, however, not to understand that a President would prefer to face a Court which is sympathetic to his own political outlook. The political views of prospective candidates for appointment to the Court are often well known, so that it is certainly the case that there are some opportunities to 'pack' a Court with judges of a particular philosophical persuasion. It may be, of course, that only occasionally do cases come before the Court which have great political significance, but any President would want to be ready for such eventualities.

The most important incidence of the key political role of the Court occurred in the 1930s. Franklin D. Roosevelt had swept to power as President in 1932. His 'New Deal' for America pledged to bring the country out of the Great Depression, then at its height. This would require, however, great extensions in the powers of the federal government. The question was: Would the measures be challenged in the Supreme Court as unconstitutional? Further, would the Court block the President's plans in this way? During Roosevelt's first term these fears were, indeed, realised. A conservative Court, in a series of challenges to extensions in federal authority, thwarted the New Deal policies. Roosevelt threatened to amend the Constitution, possibly even to give himself powers to flood the Court with his own new nominees. In the event, such drastic measures were not needed. By 1937 he had been able to make a number of legitimate appointments, so that he faced a Court generally divided five to four in favour of the new interpretation of federal power.

Though each judge has an equal vote in Court decisions, there is no doubt that the **Chief Justice** is a key figure. He leads the discussion and generally sets the tone for the deliberations. We have already referred to the influence of **John Marshall** in the early days of the Constitution's life; more recently, two further Chief Justices have made a significant impact on the American political climate. These are described below:

- In 1953 **Earl Warren** was appointed Chief Justice by Dwight D. Eisenhower. Warren presided over the Court until 1969. During that time, dramatic changes were effected in America's political culture, especially under Presidents Kennedy (1961–3) and Johnson (1963–8). In particular, a string of measures to establish equal rights for racial minorities and increased welfare provision for the poor were implemented. Successive constitutional challenges were rejected by a fundamentally liberal Court.
- Richard Nixon, who succeeded Johnson as President, appointed an apparently conservative Chief Justice, **Warren Burger**, in 1969, in the hope that he would be able to lead the Court towards reversal of many of the liberal decisions made by his predecessor, Earl Warren. Furthermore, a total of six judges had been appointed by Republican Presidents – Nixon, Ford and Reagan – by 1983. The scene was set, apparently, for reaction against the reforms of Kennedy and Johnson.

  In fact, the very opposite occurred. One after another of the Warren Court's decisions were confirmed, despite determined challenges. The progress towards civil rights and increased welfare for the poor and underprivileged continued unabated.

The experience of the Burger Court illustrates the uncertainty of the relationship between the President and the judges. Without any means of putting pressure on them, he cannot guarantee that they will not simply decide to act independently and without regard to their past political record. The conservatism of Burger disappeared once he took office, but this has not been the case with his successor, **William Rehnquist**, who took over in 1986. Rehnquist is a fierce defender of states' rights and illiberal on social and moral issues. Ronald Reagan found a willing political ally in him in a way which Richard Nixon missed under Burger.

Summary of presidential powers	
Power	**Limits**
Commander-in-Chief of the armed forces	Only Congress may declare war The war powers resolution Congress may withhold appropriations for military purposes
Negotiation and signing of foreign treaties	Treaties require support of two-thirds of the Senate
Making executive agreements with foreign powers	Legislative vetoes
Appointment of Supreme Court judges	May only act when there is a vacancy Senate must approve all appointments
Appointment of administration officials	Senate must approve all appointments
Setting the federal budget	Congress may refuse to enact the budget
Proposing legislation	Congress may refuse to pass presidential legislation New law may be declared unconstitutional by the Supreme Court
Veto of laws passed by Congress	May be overriden by a two-thirds majority
Implementation of federal programmes	May be declared unconstitutional by the Supreme Court May be limited by a legislative veto in Congress
Impoundment of congressional spending programmes	Legislative veto of both Houses of Congress
Speaking on behalf of the whole country	None significant
Using the National Guard in a state of emergency	None significant

The Presidency – an overview

Two descriptions of the American Presidency reflect the condition of the post in modern times. One refers to 'two Presidencies', the other describes the office as the 'separated Presidency'.

Two Presidencies The US President is often described as the 'most powerful man on earth'. This is how he is seen from the perspective of foreigners, however. The view refers to the fact that the President plays the leading role in American foreign policy and military affairs. It also takes note of the fact that the USA is the world's richest and mightiest country, so its leader is bound to cut an impressive figure on the world stage.

From a domestic standpoint the picture is very different. Congress makes an equal claim to authority over domestic affairs. As we have seen, the President faces considerably more constraints in policy making at home than he does when dealing with the rest of the world. At the same time, he must accept that Congress, too, makes policy and if there is a clash of objectives, between Congress and the President, it is often the former which prevails, as Bill Clinton has found to his cost.

Thus, there are indeed two Presidencies. One is the powerful world leader who can command great armies, impose American authority on weaker nations, distribute largesse in the form of foreign aid, negotiate treaties with other great nations and is capable of pressing a single button which would initiate a devastating nuclear attack. The other is a domestic policy maker, often facing an uncooperative Congress, struggling with immense financial constraints, attempting to control volatile public opinion and facing a struggle to be re-elected four years hence if he is in his first term.

The separated Presidency

The separation of powers which was incorporated in the American Constitution works extremely effectively in the field of congressional–presidential relations. This has become increasingly apparent since Richard Nixon alienated his Congress in the early 1970s.

In addition to this widening schism, American public opinion has become less reliable and more independent. The voters treat congressional elections very differently to those occasions when they are choosing the President. There may, therefore, be little in common between the political make-up of the Congress and the philosophy of the President himself. He has, in other words, become increasingly separated from the world of congressional politics. For a powerful, popular communicator such as Ronald Reagan, this presented fewer problems. But the less popular Jimmy Carter, George Bush and Bill Clinton have found that Congress is more of an adversary than a partner.

The Vice President

Powers and functions

It is a cliché, but no less true for that, that the Vice President is a heartbeat away from becoming the most powerful man on earth. Should the President die, resign or become permanently incapacitated, his deputy automatically steps into his place until the next scheduled election. Harry Truman in 1945, when Franklin D. Roosevelt died suddenly, Lyndon Johnson in 1963, when John F. Kennedy was assassinated in Dallas, and Gerald Ford, when Richard Nixon resigned in 1974, have experienced these occurrences. Thus he is a deputy to the President, but only in an emergency situation. He is not expected to make any decisions **on behalf** of his senior, as most deputies do, unless the President is totally unavailable.

The second important function of the Vice President is to preside over, or be Speaker of, the Senate. This is a largely ceremonial position, but it can occasionally carry some responsibility. He is, for example, a key presidential spokesman among the Senators and may perform the task of informing and persuading them of the merits of the President's proposals. In the event of a tie in the Senate, the Vice President has the power to give the casting vote. This last occurred in 1993 when Bill Clinton was experiencing difficulty securing the passage of the budget. **Al Gore**, his loyal and respected deputy, was able to break the deadlock in favour of the President.

The presidential 'ticket'

In many ways the importance of the Vice President is only noticed during the months leading up to a presidential election. In the presidential election the candidate for President is harnessed to a particular deputy. In other words, voters are presented with a team of two and they cannot

Gerald Ford with vice presidential choice, Nelson Rockefeller, 20 August 1974

vote for one without the other. So the pair must appeal to as wide a spectrum of electoral opinion as possible. It is often the case, therefore, that an attempt is made to 'balance the ticket'.

Should a presidential candidate be, for example, a known progressive liberal, with particular appeal among the poor, ethnic minorities and the educated middle class, he may lack appeal in the more conservative southern and mid-western states. It is therefore tempting to choose as a 'running mate' a candidate who is more conservative in his outlook. It is also the case that some candidates appeal to a particular part of the country because of their background. Again, a balance is needed. It was for this reason that Jimmy Carter, a southerner and, therefore, mistrusted by the established northern heartland of the Democratic Party who saw such southerners as conservative, chose Walter Mondale (1977–81) to fight the election with him. Mondale was a more traditional Democrat and may have swung electoral fortunes decisively Carter's way. In 1960 John F. Kennedy selected Lyndon Johnson (1961–3) for the opposite reason. Kennedy was an intellectual northerner (from Massachusetts), while Johnson was a Texan, much respected among the more conservative Democrats in that region.

The fact that presidential running mates can have so much influence on voters is largely illogical. Having few functions and, normally, less influence, the choice of Vice President is of little practical consequence. Yet voters may be swayed. More importantly, so too may the key party workers who help to secure the votes for their own candidate. They need to feel that one of the candidates on the presidential ticket is one of their own and not a stranger.

A flexible role Most Vice Presidents have played no significant role in American politics. **Dan Quayle** (1989–93), for example, George Bush's deputy, was allowed only ceremonial duties. Even less was seen of **Spiro Agnew** (1969–73), Richard Nixon's first Vice President, who was to resign over allegations of tax evasion after three years of undistinguished office.

Jimmy Carter with Walter Mondale, 15 July 1976

There have, nevertheless, been some deputies who have found a positive role to play. Lyndon Johnson had been Senate Democrat majority leader before Kennedy chose him as running mate. Kennedy's intention was to find an experienced, respected congressional leader who understood the nature of the kind of deal-making and coalition-building which a President needs to control Congress. In the event, Johnson was of little help to Kennedy, but his background was to prove a vital factor during his own Presidency. George Bush (1981–9), Reagan's Vice President, had been a Director of the Central Intelligence Agency. His experience of foreign relations was, therefore, of great use to Reagan, who was a complete beginner in this area. Bush acted as a kind of roving ambassador for the USA during his eight years as Vice President.

Thus, we can see that the post of Vice President can vary in its importance, depending on the incumbent's abilities and background. But, however large a role he may be given, he can never rival the authority of the key figures in congressional party politics, such as the floor leaders, senior committee chairmen and the like.

The future President? Either because they have been in office upon the demise of a President, or because they choose later to run for office, a high proportion of Vice Presidents go on to become President. Since World War Two the list reads impressively: Harry Truman, Richard Nixon, Lyndon Johnson, Gerald Ford and George Bush.

Lacking in influence he may be, but the Vice President does have a privileged position in the White House. He sees most of the action from the inside, may be present at high-level discussions and can learn how the office of President works. It has therefore become one of the several typical 'apprenticeships' which an aspiring President may undertake.

The executive office of the President

Introduction

Also known as the White House Office, or Staff, the executive office represents a collection of powerful bodies which serve the President directly, helping to shape his policies and advising on the nature of their implementation. The date of its creation by Congress – 1939 – is significant. It followed a period of unprecedented growth in the scope of presidential power during the first half of Franklin D. Roosevelt's incumbency, the New Deal era. With the expanded role of the Presidency he clearly needed a bureaucracy of his own to be able to sustain all the functions expected of him. At the centre of the White House organisation sits the White House Office itself.

The White House Office

These are the most personal advisers to the President – those who may expect to see him on a day-to-day basis when he is in Washington. The most senior member is the **Chief of Staff**, the President's personal aide, who keeps him informed of what the rest of the Office staff are doing and, in turn, informs them of the President's current thinking. Behind him stand a number of **assistants** and **special assistants** who are assigned specific roles in the White House machine. The **Counsel to the President** advises him on legal matters, while the **Press Secretary** deals with the media on behalf of the White House. Under normal circumstances it is expected that these staff are mere reflections of the President's own thinking. During Richard Nixon's Presidency, however, it became clear that several of the White House staff were actually running the policy-making process themselves, often without consulting the President. Three of Nixon's closest advisers, **Bob Haldeman** (Chief of Staff), **John Erlichman** (special assistant) and **John Dean** (legal counsel) formed, with the aid of a number of other officers, notably Attorney-General **John Mitchell**, an inner circle whose legal, semi-legal and even illegal activities formed a kind of 'hidden executive' from which Congress and the public were excluded. The revelations of such a situation, which resulted from the **Watergate** hearings, were to bring about Nixon's downfall. More recently, Ronald Reagan's Chief of Staff **Donald Regan** (the similarity of names was a mere coincidence) was said to wield considerable influence in White House politics.

The National Security Council (NSC)

This body, chaired by the President and with the Vice President in attendance, deals with White House policy in foreign affairs, national defence and the intelligence services. As such, its members include the Director of the Central Intelligence Agency, the Chairman of the Military Chiefs-of-Staff, the Secretary of State (i.e. Foreign Secretary) and Secretary for Defence. Backed by a team of experts on defence and foreign affairs, the NSC is the hub of the President's policy-making machinery in all matters related to the security of the USA.

Office of Management and Budget

This is a key office for the President. The preparation, presentation and implementation of the annual federal budget is possibly the most complex operation which he must undertake. Furthermore, he expects, in a normal year, to face difficulty in negotiations with Congress over the precise terms of the budget. Bill Clinton in the nineties has faced especially heavy opposition for his plans for higher taxes and federal spending so that he has had to rely heavily on the OMB for support.

The work of the OMB is year-long. It must deal with the various executive secretaries and agency heads who wish to claim a share of the federal expenditure kitty, and also with representations from the fifty states who seek federal help with their spending plans. On the other hand, taxation has to be considered, along with the general economic consequences of budgetary plans. Liaison with the President's economic and financial advisers is, therefore, also needed.

Once a budget proposal has finally been crafted out of this complex set of negotiations and consultations, Congress must be faced, especially the House of Representatives which has the senior role in budget negotiations. As we have said, in the case of Clinton's progressive budgeting, opposition was so fierce that a virtual reconstruction of his budgets had to take place before Congress would accept them.

The Council of Economic Advisers

Normally this Council comprises three economic advisers (whose appointment requires the consent of the Senate) helped by a permanent team of professional economic researchers. Their role is to provide economic information to the President, advise on possible courses of action to deal with economic problems and help prepare the President's annual address to Congress on the state of the national economy.

When it was set up in 1946, the Council had fairly specific tasks, including the maintenance of full employment, monetary stability and a healthy overseas balance of payments. Broadly speaking, these have remained the objectives of the executive branch. During the Presidency of Ronald Reagan, however, it adopted a 'monetarist' stance, concentrating on anti-inflationary policies through control of interest rates and the money supply. It became committed to the reduction of both federal taxation and expenditure. Under President Clinton, attempts have been made by the Council to return to expansionary policy, but congressional opposition has hindered its work.

A considerable amount of liaison takes place between the CEA and the OMB, as well as with the USA Treasury and the Federal Reserve. Although the President himself must mediate between competing policy demands from these bodies, he has come to rely increasingly upon his Chief Economic Adviser for guidance.

Other offices

The **Office of Policy Development** is a catch-all organisation, dealing with all the matters of domestic policy not covered in the other sections of the executive office. It is headed by an assistant to the President who must act as his guide on a host of miscellaneous concerns. The title of the **Council of Environmental Quality** speaks for itself, as does that of the **Office of the United States Trade Representatives**. The **Office of Science and Technology Policy** has played an important role in advising the President on space and weapons research policy, though the end of the Cold War has reduced these matters to a lower priority. Finally, the **Office of Administration** does what its name suggests – providing administrative back-up for all the other departments.

Conclusions

The list of organisations in the executive office of the President makes impressive reading. It comprises a formidable array of expertise and specialist knowledge upon which the President can call. Of all Western democratic leaders, the American President has, perhaps, the most powerful machine backing him. Yet he certainly needs it. In many ways he stands alone as the chief executive. Elected separately by the people, they expect him to achieve great progress in a variety of ways. He cannot devolve responsibility elsewhere, to a Cabinet or to his ministers. He must face the electorate alone when they come to judge his performance.

At the same time, he faces the impressive authority and power of the Congress. He must be able to negotiate and persuade, bully and cajole the legislators into accepting all or part of his plans. These White House advisers must, therefore, be prepared to operate on the floor of Congress, furthering the cause of presidential influence.

The executive departments

The Cabinet

Those who have grown up with preconceptions about Cabinet government as it is practised in Britain must not make the error of assuming its American counterpart is in any way similar. It is different in virtually all respects except its name. When the President's 'Secretaries', who head the departments, meet together from time to time, they may **look** something like the British Cabinet, seated around a large table with the President at its head, but the similarity ends there.

The principal difference is that it is **not** a collective decision-making body. Indeed, it makes no decisions at all. Discussion may centre around key elements of the administration's policy, but these consultations do not result in binding decisions. They are discussions and little more. It is clearly understood in American government that all major decisions are made by the President, but that decisions specifically related to the work of one department are made by its Secretary. Some Presidents, such as Dwight Eisenhower (1953–61) and Ronald Reagan (1981–9), have relied heavily upon the advice of Cabinet colleagues. They both took a limited view of the presidential role, seeing it as more of a public relations role than a policy-making one. Others such as John Kennedy (1961–3) and George Bush (1989–93) have largely ignored the Cabinet, meetings becoming formal and meaningless.

The Cabinet comprises thirteen members, all Secretaries, who are appointed by the President subject to ratification by the Congress. The Constitution specifies that they must not be drawn from the Congress (thus preserving the principle of the separation of powers), so the President must look elsewhere for his nominees. Civil servants, retired politicians, academics, pressure group leaders and senior managers from the worlds of finance, business and commerce are favourites, as are successful officials from state governments.

The thirteen positions are the Secretaries of or for:

- State (foreign affairs)
- Commerce
- Treasury
- Labor
- Defense
- Justice (Attorney-General)
- Health and Human Resources
- Housing and Urban Development
- Transportation
- The Interior
- Agriculture
- Energy
- Education.

Each Secretary is backed by a number of assistants and an army of lesser civil servants. The senior officials are also appointed by the President, though in effect the Department Head has the major voice in lesser appointments.

Department Secretaries are considerably limited in their powers by a number of factors. First, they may be overruled by the President himself in his capacity as head of the executive branch. Secondly, their legislative plans may be thwarted by an unsympathetic Congress. Thirdly, and perhaps most importantly, they must rely upon the Congress for the appropriation of funds required for their programmes of action. Thus, it would be a mistake to compare them directly with 'ministers' who lead European-style democracies. They are very much presidential assistants, rather than political leaders in their own right.

There have, nevertheless, been important exceptions to the norm. Some Department Secretaries have played a leading role in American policies. **Henry Kissinger**, for example, was President Nixon's Secretary of State and, as such, played a leading role in the conduct of the Cold War, the Vietnam conflict and American involvement in the Middle East. **Bobby**, brother of John Kennedy, was an enormously influential Attorney-General, taking the lead in preparing the ground for important civil rights legislation.

It must also be stressed that these senior officials have the vital task of appearing regularly before Congress to explain administration policy. A good showing before a congressional committee will not only enhance a Secretary's prestige, it will also further the cause of presidential power.

Executive agencies It is a matter of great potential confusion in American government that agencies whose heads are below Cabinet rank have been given a variety of titles, such as 'agency', 'commission' or 'administration'. They have in common, however, the fact that they are operational agencies, charged with the task of implementing policy which has been determined at a higher level. The agencies form the bulk of the federal administration (though not all are based in Washington). They vary in the degree of independence they enjoy, but it must be emphasised that their senior members are appointed by the President and may be removed by him. They are, therefore, still subject to presidential jurisdiction.

There are a considerable number of agencies, but a selection of the most significant should include the following:

- Environmental Protection Agency
- Federal Communication Commission
- Federal Reserve System
- Interstate Commerce Commission
- Securities and Exchange Commission
- Tennessee Valley Authority
- Veterans Administration
- National Aeronautics and Space Administration (NASA).

We are now in a position to summarise the structure of the federal administration:

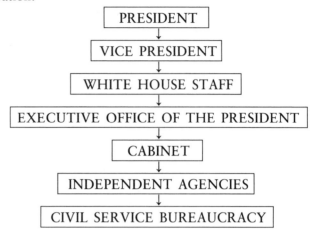

Comparisons – the American President and the British Prime Minister

In some ways such a comparison is spurious since there is a key difference between the constitutional positions of the two posts. The American President is **both** Head of State and Head of Government. The Prime Minister is **only** Head of Government. Nevertheless, there are a number of respects in which similarities can be found as well as distinctions.

Similarities

- Both have extensive powers of patronage, with hundreds, even thousands, of important political posts at their disposal.
- They are the chief policy-makers within the political community.
- Both are heads of the governing party.
- Foreign policy is very much in their hands.
- Both play the role of Commander-in-Chief of the armed forces.
- In times of crisis and emergency they may speak on behalf of the country.

Distinctions

This is the more complex part of the comparative analysis since, although the similarities are clear, the variations in power are more subtle. The easiest way to deal with this problem is first to identify those elements of the President's role which give him **greater** power or influence than the Prime Minister, and then to reverse the position and see where a Prime Minister gains in contrast.

Presidential advantages

- Being Head of State, he has the authority to speak for all American people.
- His authority is not shared with the Cabinet. He dominates it, whereas the Prime Minister is only 'first among equals' in his Cabinet and can be outvoted by them.
- The whole of the administration serves him and is subject to his direct patronage. He does not have to share powers with departmental ministers.
- He cannot be removed from office for political reasons by the legislature. Thus, he may suffer political defeats, but remain in office. The Prime Minister must rely constantly upon parliamentary support.

Prime Ministerial advantages

- He is not limited by an entrenched Constitution. The extensive nature of prerogative powers which he exercises is flexible and not subject to legal or parliamentary constraint. The President's powers are constitutionally circumscribed. Since a Prime Minister can control Parliament his powers are enormously enhanced.
- His powers of patronage are not limited by the need to seek the approval of the legislature. The President must seek the 'advice and consent' of Congress.
- The Prime Minister's party is normally united behind him. Presidents, on the other hand, head weak, decentralised and independent party machines.
- The Prime Minister leads a Government which is normally able to dominate Parliament. By contrast, the President cannot rely on congressional support and often faces stiff opposition.
- Britain's unitary state means the Prime Minister does not face strong regional forces, whereas the President has limited jurisdiction among the states.
- The Prime Minister may choose the date of a general election to his and his party's advantage. The President faces a fixed four-year term and so is less in control of his political fortunes.

The 'balance sheet' is, therefore, difficult to interpret. However, a reference back to the phenomenon of the 'two Presidencies' described above may help us. In the field of **foreign policy** we can certainly say that the American President does, indeed, possess unsurpassed powers. If we consider **domestic affairs**, on the other hand, it is evident that the British Prime Minister enjoys considerably enhanced freedom of action and possesses a more impressive array of unconstrained powers. One proviso must, however, still be added. The pre-eminent domestic position of the Prime Minister depends upon his ability to control both his party and Parliament. A President can still govern despite remarkably severe political opposition; a Prime Minister cannot.

For exam questions relevant to this unit, see page 494.

19 Parties and pressure groups in the United States

Parties

Introduction

Unit 5 of this book describes the functions of political parties in general. It was apparent that British parties have as one of their prime functions, perhaps *the* prime function, the articulation of demands. They spend much of their time developing and refining policy programmes which can be placed before the electorate at elections and, if that election is won, which can be turned into government action. Although American parties are concerned with this same process, it is certainly not the principal feature which characterises them. Indeed, all our European preconceptions must be put aside if we are to understand American party politics at all.

The most striking feature which we will notice is that there is considerable variation in the political philosophy of the parties depending upon which part of the country they are operating in. This geographical divergence can be observed to a limited extent in Germany and Italy, but to nothing like the same extent as in the USA. There is also no real concept of the 'election manifesto' in America. Individual candidates may produce their own manifestos, but the parties as a whole do not have organised political programmes to put before the electorate.

In some ways, the party system in the USA resembles that which prevailed in Britain in the first half of the nineteenth century. A party label such as 'Tory', 'Whig' or 'Radical' gave a clue to the philosophy of the candidate, but it was only a clue. He was not tied to a fixed set of party policies nor was he subject to any central discipline. One might be able to predict how he would vote in the House of Commons on such issues as protectionism versus free trade, the Irish question, or constitutional reform but one could guarantee nothing. So it is today in the American Congress at Washington and in the state legislatures.

What we can say with some certainty, however, is that there is a two-party system of sorts. In all but the most local elections, the endorsement of either the Democratic or Republican Party is essential if a candidate for public office is to have a realistic chance of success at the polls. It is true that the precise nature of the two-party system may vary from place to place, but there is always the same duopoly.

The origins of the parties

There have been a number of defining periods in American political history which have helped to create the modern Democratic and Republican Parties.

The Civil War Broadly speaking, it was the Democratic Party which supported the breakaway of the southern states over the issue of slavery in the 1860s. The Republicans, who were determined to maintain the unity of the country, proposed the abolition of slave-holding. Having won the Civil War in 1865, the Republicans dominated the political scene for the next seventy years. Those Democrats who were based in the northern states were virtually completely excluded from power. In the South, however, a strange, more resilient kind of political animal had been born. This was the 'southern Democrat', or 'Dixiecrat', as he was to become known.

In the South the Democrats completely dominated the political scene and, to some extent, they still do. Nationally they formed a minority, so there was little chance of a Democratic candidate being elected President (**Grover Cleveland** in 1884 and 1892 was the only exception). The Dixiecrats were conservative in outlook, unwilling to grant the freed slaves full civil rights and opposed to the power of federal government which had defeated them militarily. To make matters worse for them, the Republicans were supported by an alliance of business interests, the growing industrial working class and freed slaves. These were all seen as economic threats to the poorer South, which was dominated by estate owners, small tenant farmers and agricultural labourers.

The Industrial Revolution The old North–South divide which followed the Civil War and determined the two-party system of the day, began to break up with the onset of America's late but rapid industrial revolution, which became politically significant in the 1890s.

The challenge of **William Jennings Bryant** to the Republicans was based on support from the small, independent farmers, craftsmen and traders who felt threatened by the rise of big business interests. Although Bryant, a Populist by title, was embraced by the Democrats, his real influence was felt among the Republicans. Effectively, they were split over the issue of whether to support the great new industrial and commercial interests, or whether to champion the 'small, independent' man as Bryant had done. Ultimately, the Republicans tried to secure the support of both groups. The northern Democrats, meanwhile, had their eyes firmly on the new, expanding working class which was centred in the growing cities. The Republicans still drew much support from workers, but their hold over them was beginning to slip. The Democrats forged links with the trade unions and the poor sections of the community, both black and white. Meanwhile the southern Democrats, frozen in time, retained their parochial, conservative outlook.

The New Deal era By the 1930s the Republicans were still hanging on to their dominant political position, especially in presidential elections. The Great Depression, which struck in 1929–30, changed American politics for the rest of the century. The Republicans appeared to have no answer to the economic slump. **Franklin D. Roosevelt** persuaded the Democrats to nominate him as their candidate in 1932 with a radical programme, proposing massive federal intervention in industry and commerce to bring the USA back to full employment and prosperity.

Roosevelt's dramatic victory, added to the domination of the Congress by Democrats which followed it, forged a new coalition of support for the Democrats. This comprised the working classes (particularly in the northern cities), the more educated middle classes and, as before, the poorer elements in urban society. Republican support shrank to include only the Mid-west farming interests, owners of small businesses, and the salaried employees of big businesses, banks, etc. The Democrat voters accepted the expanded role of the federal government which Roosevelt had brought about. As long as central government served their economic interests, they were prepared to put aside the traditional American suspicion of governmental power. Republicans, more conservative and traditional in their outlook, were not prepared to see federal interference with economic enterprise and feared the erosion of the independence of the states in the face of growing federal authority.

Once again, while all these changes on the political map were taking place, little changed in the South. The Dixiecrats continued to hold on. Although the South suffered from the Depression along with the rest of the country, their Democratic members of Congress resisted many of Roosevelt's reforms. Like the northern Republicans, they were still fearful of federal power, a legacy of the Civil War. There was, in other words, a conservative anti-Roosevelt coalition, which cut across party lines. This continues to be a common feature of the American political system in Washington.

The civil rights era   1960 saw the election of **John Kennedy** as President. He was supported by a new kind of Democratic coalition. This contained, as we would expect, the poor blacks and whites in the cities as he promised to bring civil rights to all and to introduce anti-poverty, welfare and housing programmes to combat the growing problems of America's cities. He also attracted the votes of many young Americans, traditionally a politically apathetic group. They saw him as a new kind of politician, a man of vision who promised to break the hold of the old political establishment and so make real changes for the better in American society.

However, as well as attracting new elements of support for the Democrats, Kennedy opened up the process of breaking the hold of conservative Democrats in the South – a process initiated in 1948 by Truman's espousal of civil rights. His civil rights policies, designed to end racial discrimination, angered the poorer whites in the South who opposed such liberal proposals. Indeed, Kennedy's, and his successor Lyndon Johnson's, generally liberal and progressive philosophy was deeply unpopular in the South. The Republicans began, albeit slowly, to pick up support there from defecting Democrats. This change in the political balance of the South was largely responsible for the Republican domination of the White House from 1968 to 1992 (apart from the brief Democratic incumbency of Jimmy Carter from 1977 to 1981).

Modern party alignments   As we have seen, it is an error to think of American parties as single, unified entities. They are highly decentralised organisations whose support varies considerably from one part of the country to another. It used to be the case, therefore, that generalisations about party alignments were dangerous and certainly futile exercises. The regional pattern of party support was at least fairly predictable, but even that has now broken down.

Since the movement to the right of the Republican Party in the 1980s, and the weakening of the conservative Democratic hold over the South, the precise nature of party alignments among the electors has become even less certain. Voters tend to be more volatile, more influenced by the individual candidates than by their party label. As has occurred in Britain, there has been a considerable degree of 'partisan dealignment' in the USA. Traditional attachments to parties are weaker; issues and personalities now rival them in the mind of the typical voter.

Nevertheless, some discernible patterns can still be identified. The principal elements of **national** party support are shown below.

National party allegiances	
Republicans	**Democrats**
Mid-western farming interests	Members of ethnic minorities
Business executives	Liberal eastern middle classes
Small business entrepreneurs	Some poor whites in the South
Some southern whites	Industrial workers
Religious fundamentalists	Young liberal idealists
Commercial interests in the East	Members of caring professions
Wealthier families in the West	

Party philosophies The decentralised nature of American parties is not merely an organisational feature. The great sectional variations which exist in the political culture are also reflected in the philosophies of both Democrats and Republicans. Thus, it is dangerous to make any generalised comments about basic beliefs. The clearest example, as we have seen, is the phenomenon of the southern, conservative Democrat. There are also pockets of progressive, more liberal Republicanism in the cities of the East such as New York and Boston.

We must also be aware that every candidate for election is relatively free to create his own political programme, based on his own philosophy and the nature of the constituency which he is seeking to represent. A Republican who may normally be opposed to federal government power, for example, would need to mollify his views if he were running for the House of Representatives in a district which relied heavily on federal government funds or contracts. Similarly, a normally progressive Democrat, with strong views on civil rights for ethnic minority groups, has to be cautious where there is a high level of racial tension. His liberal views would need to be tempered by a possibly more conservative view on law and order. In addition, virtually every candidate needs financial help from a variety of sponsors and supporters. The interest groups, business enterprises and individuals who are supporting him in this way inevitably expect him to take their views and demands into consideration. Only the candidate who is sure of being elected, or can finance himself independently, can afford to resist such pressures when developing his personal manifesto.

Thus, any general statement about the philosophies of the two parties must be seen against two important variable factors. These are the region or section in which the party is operating and the nature of the individual **candidate**, who is financing him and what pressures are being placed upon him within the community. Nevertheless, the typical, broad beliefs and goals of the two parties can be described as follows overleaf:

Typical party philosophies

Republicans

- Suspicion of federal power; preference for greater independence for the states
- Opposition to high levels of taxation and public expenditure
- Support for policies favourable to business and commerce
- Dislike of government-organised welfare, housing and health schemes
- Belief that individuals should be prepared to support themselves
- Strong defence of those parts of the Constitution which guarantee individual liberty
- Stress on firm policies on law and order
- Support for protectionist measures in defence of agriculture and industry against foreign competition
- Opposition to American involvement in foreign affairs outside the immediate vicinity of North America
- A conservative view on moral issues

Democrats

- Support for full equal civil rights for all
- An acceptance of federal intervention in order to exercise economic control
- General sympathy for measures to improve health, welfare and housing provision through positive action by federal government
- Concern for the environment and an acceptance that government intervention is needed to curb environmental damage
- Opposition to protectionism and an acceptance of the benefits of free trade
- Support for stiffer gun control laws, but a general belief that the crime problem needs social as well as legal remedies
- A stress on education as a key element in social order and prosperity
- A generally tolerant, liberal attitude on moral issues

Party organisation American parties do not have single, unified, national organisations as most European parties do. It must also be borne in mind that there is no real concept of party membership in the USA. There are small numbers of regular workers and a larger group of 'activists', who are willing to support party candidates at elections, but who then cease to participate in politics until the next polling day. Without a permanent mass membership, and without a hard core of active workers, there cannot be an extensive established party organisation.

The organisation of the parties can only be understood as a series of layers, which correspond broadly to the various levels at which American government operates. Not only is party organisation multi-layered, it is also multi-faceted. The character of party activity varies at each of the levels. Descriptions here begin at the most local tier.

<u>Precincts</u> These are the smallest units within American government. Here, there may be political clubs or caucuses which meet irregularly and which have their own, unique organisations. Their role is largely threefold. First, they may be called on to nominate delegates to the state party convention whose role is to select the candidates for state positions and to try to create some sort of political programme for the forthcoming elections. Secondly, they must try to raise funds for the candidates representing their parties at all levels, from local school

board members to the presidency itself. Finally, they will campaign locally to try to persuade the voters to turn out in support of their candidates.

Wards, counties and cities   The small units of local government, wards (occasionally boroughs), make up the counties and the cities. In each case there is likely to be a party committee and a chairman. Their role only becomes significant when they are required to attend meetings of the state party committee or even the state convention, which plays a crucial role, alongside primary elections, in candidate selection. Otherwise, they are expected to help at election time, raising money and canvassing support, but will largely disappear from view between elections. The big cities used to have more formal and powerful committees in the days of 'machine politics', but these have now declined so that even in such large units of local government as Los Angeles, Chicago or New York, party committees make little impact on the political scene.

The states   There is a more formal organisation operating at state level. Each party has a central committee, headed by a chairman. Their tasks are similar to those at the levels below them – fundraising, candidate nomination and election campaigning. In addition, however, they attempt to co-ordinate the work of the party's various elected representatives within the state. These will include those Senators, Governors, Lieutenant-Generals and members of the House of Representatives who may be members of that party.

Within the state legislature itself, the party representatives organise themselves into as tight a group as they can for the purposes of voting as a block, especially when the State Governor is of their party and so needs their support. Majority or minority leaders are, therefore, chosen by the members as are party whips whose role it is to try to maintain some sort of disciplined unity. As in Washington, this may not always be possible, but at state level there is more party cohesion than there is at federal level.

National parties   As in the states, there is a national committee, headed by a chairman. The most important task these committees carry out is the organisation of the National Convention, at which the party's presidential candidate is chosen. Thus, they are only prominent every four years when those conventions take place. It used to be the case, when leadership of a party carried with it considerable influence, that the national committees were able to interfere with the nomination process at the Convention. This is less true today, since most delegates are now tied to supporting a particular candidate through the results of state primary elections. Thus, their role is now largely ceremonial and symbolic.

Congress and the White House   The real party work at national level takes place within Congress. The party whose nominee secures the Presidency is in a special position. The President is automatically head of his party. It becomes his, and his staff's, role to try to secure the support of colleagues in the House and the Senate. Together with his party floor leaders (both the majority leader and the minority leader) and the whips, attempts are made to create unity. Success in this regard

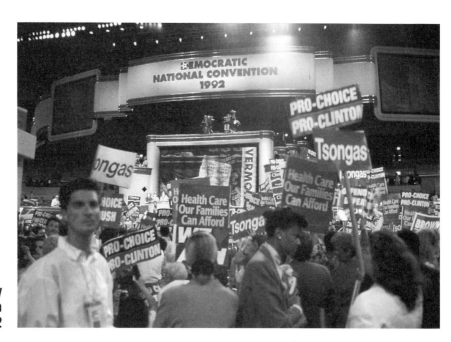

**Democratic Party
National Convention
1992**

is variable. The Democrats, in particular, find difficulty in forging a coalition between the liberal northerners and the conservatives from the South. To a lesser extent, the Republicans may also find themselves split between their right wing and the moderates within the party.

Where the Presidency is held by its rivals, a party has no real leader. If they hold a majority in one or both Houses of Congress, however, their floor leaders become the most powerful members of the party. If they are able to carry the rest of the party with them, they can put themselves in a position of parity with the President. He will depend on them to secure the passage of his legislation and, in return, congressional party leaders may gain his backing for some of their cherished programmes.

The worst scenario for a party in Washington is to lose the Presidency and to be in a minority in both Houses of Congress. In these circumstances, it becomes largely impotent, reduced to sniping at the administration, trying to be as obstructive as possible and, in some circumstances, attempting to link with some disaffected members of the majority party to form a temporary majority on a specific issue. The Republicans faced this situation in the 1930s and again in the 1960s. In both cases the result was a successful programme of radical reforms by the triumphant Democrats, largely untroubled by their opponents, except when some conservative southern Democrats were willing to throw in their lot with the Republicans over a particularly repugnant measure.

Parties and elections

The parties' task

In the USA a large proportion of officials are elected, officials who, in other political systems, would be appointed by some sort of superior body. Thus, in any election (November is election season in America), the following candidates may be placed before the electorate:

- President
- Senator

- Representative (Congressman)
- State Governor
- State Lieutenant-General
- State Attorney-General
- County or city mayor
- County judge
- County sheriff
- School board representative.

In addition to this list, there may be other officials whose titles and roles vary from state to state. Thus, the party organisations, loose and informal though they may be, have an enormous task supporting so many candidates.

The workers must organise meetings and rallies, fundraising events, dinners, opportunities for ordinary people to meet the candidate and exposure in the media. On the day of the election itself, it is their job to go out to persuade people to cast their votes. Americans are notoriously reluctant to vote, so a great deal of cajoling needs to be done. The platforms of the candidates must be explained (often in the simplest terms), their personal qualities emphasised and, if they already hold office, the better aspects of their political record highlighted.

Primary elections As we have seen in Unit 18, the USA enjoys a unique system for determining which individual should represent each party in elections. In European parties candidates are chosen by the party leadership, by small committees of local party activists or by ballots of registered, permanent members. The American primary election is different in character, which has quite marked effects on the nature of the final ballot. It does not yet operate in all states, but the majority – thirty-eight – now use the procedure.

Primaries can be **open**, where all registered voters may vote, or **closed**, where only those who are registered as a party's supporter can vote. In either case they have the effect of bringing into the candidate selection procedure a broad section of the electorate. For some period before an election, at presidential, congressional and state levels, aspiring party candidates compete with each other, through the primaries, to demonstrate that they can attract sufficient support to be able to win office for their party.

The effects of the use of primaries are several, and most are considered by Americans to improve the quality of their democracy:

- They widen political participation, allowing ordinary voters to express a preference between candidates of the same party.
- They open up the political system to a wider variety of aspiring office-holders. In British parties virtually all candidates have to serve a long apprenticeship in a party, otherwise they have little chance of being adopted. In the USA it is possible to enter and win primary contests without such a background. Thus, many more able people may qualify for consideration.
- Since voters are normally more moderate in their political outlook than party activists, their participation in primaries tends to produce more moderate candidates. The 'extremes' are usually filtered out in primary contests.

The results of elections depend upon a wide variety of factors, many of which cannot always be explained by political tradition. The factors which determine results include the following:

The individual campaign   The average American voter does not have a strong allegiance to either party. In other words, 'partisan alignment' is relatively weak. It follows then that the character, image and performance of each individual candidate is most important. How well the campaign is conducted, how much exposure there is in the media and how adept the candidate is at avoiding offending important groups of voters, are all of great significance. A charismatic individual can 'buck the trend' against his party, just as a poor candidate may help the opposing party which would have little chance under normal circumstances.

Section   In some areas there is, effectively, a one-party system. There are still parts of the Deep South which are completely controlled by the local Democrats. Texas and Alabama are notable in this respect. Some cities, such as Chicago, are also Democrat monopolies. The Republicans, too, have their strongholds, such as Pennsylvania and Kansas. Here, one party is virtually guaranteed victory in all elections above those at the most local level.

The legacy of city machines   It used to be the case that one or other of the parties maintained a political 'machine' in one of the great cities. The city machines were rare examples of established organisations, more closely related to the European model than to the normal American style of loose-knit party political organisation. In every precinct or ward of the city the party which dominated the city could boast groups of party supporters on whom they could rely for fundraising and electioneering. In many cases, where Democrats held sway, trade union officials would be recruited in this way. The reward for their work for the party was the promise of a job with one of the city's departments, or some other form of preferential treatment, guaranteed by the party's established control of City Hall. As well as controlling voting patterns in the cites, the machines also determined the way in which delegates to the National Party Convention, where presidential candidates are chosen, voted. Thus, a few powerful party leaders carried much influence within the national party.

The machines are all but gone now. It was at the Democratic National Convention of 1968 in Chicago, when the all-powerful mayor, Dick Daley, openly 'rigged' the result of the nomination process in favour of Senator Hubert Humphrey (standing against the radical candidate George McGovern), that 'machine politics' was finally discredited. Nevertheless, the legacy of that domination of the cities by one party or another still remains. Most cities are still almost dominated by electoral support for one party.

Individual voter circumstances   Although social factors are less important in American voting than is the case in Britain, there are still a number of discernible patterns in the USA. Some of the principal factors are shown on the next page.

Some personal circumstances affecting voting patterns

Circumstance	More probable party allegiance
Protestant	Republican
Catholic	Democrat
Jewish	Democrat
College graduate	Republican
Failed to graduate from High School	Democrat
Trade union member	Democrat
Non-white	Democrat
Male	Republican
Female	Democrat
Young	Democrat
Old	Republican

The social, ethnic and age structure of a particular constituency is, therefore, a significant element in determining how well each party is likely to perform at the polls.

Incumbency   More important than all these factors, however, is that of 'incumbency'. There is a considerably greater chance that the incumbent Senator, Congressman, state assemblyman, governor or the like will be elected than a new challenger. Of course, this is largely due to the fact that some constituencies, because of their social make-up, are bound to return a candidate of the same party. Nevertheless, there is still a tendency for voters to prefer the representative they know to one who is an unknown quantity. A word of caution is needed at this point, however. The 1994 congressional elections saw a rout of many apparently 'safe' Democrat seats. There is also a stronger likelihood that the incumbent President will be beaten than used to be the case. Indeed, fighting against a President who was seeking a second term was usually seen as a futile exercise. In recent years, however, three Presidents – Ford (1976), Carter (1980) and Bush (1992) – have all been denied such a second term. The incumbency factor, still important within the states, seems to have broken down at federal level.

Ticket voting   The sheer mechanics of voting in American elections can be a factor in the behaviour of the electors. At every poll the voter is faced with a ballot paper listing candidates for as many as fifty different posts, for each of which there are at least two, sometimes more, candidates. Faced with a bewildering choice, the voter may prefer to simply cast all his votes for candidates of his preferred party. This is known as 'voting the straight ticket'. To help the voter there is, in many states, a voting machine which allows him to cast a number of votes simultaneously, provided, of course, they are all for the same party. 'Split ticket' voting, where a voter supports different party candidates for different posts, involves more effort and more special knowledge.

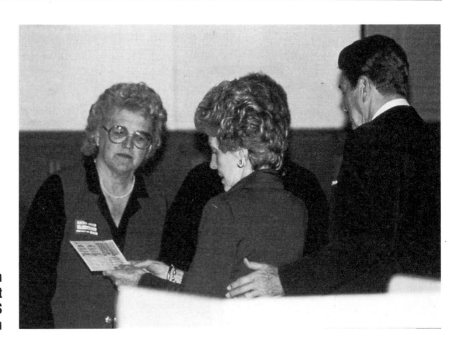

Nancy Reagan inspecting a ballot paper in the 1984 US election

Clearly, some candidates benefit from this factor, picking up votes simply because they stand for the party which is the voter's choice. Voting machines are not universally used so that this only applies in the more populated districts, often the big cities.

<u>Coat-tailing</u>   In a similar way, a phenomenon known as 'coat-tailing' can occur. Here, a popular party candidate for a senior post – say the Presidency itself, or the post of Senator – may carry along other lesser-known candidates from the same party on their 'coat-tails'. In other words, less popular or less well-known individuals may be elected on the reputation of another candidate. The opposite may happen where there is an unpopular candidate leading his party's challenge.

The financial bandwagon   Finance and the 'bandwagon' effect can also go a long way to determining election results. The many pressure groups and businesses which use the financing of candidates' campaigns to help further their cause are extremely sensitive to the chances of success of each of the candidates. They invariably wish to sponsor successful office-seekers since otherwise they would be of no use to them. Supporting losing candidates is seen as a waste of money. It follows, therefore, that when a candidate seems to be gaining ground during the campaign, he will automatically attract more financial support. In the primary elections, which last several months, this effect is especially noticeable. One by one, the less popular candidates drop out through sheer lack of funds. Those who are doing well, on the other hand, gallop ahead with ever-increasing campaign funds swelling their coffers. This is known as a 'bandwagon' effect, as more and more financial supporters climb on the candidate's election train. Of course, the more funds a candidate has, the greater his chances of success.

Some comparisons   At this point it may be instructive to draw some comparisons between the factors which tend to determine the outcome of American elections with some of those which are influential in Britain. A summary is shown below.

Determining factors in British and American elections

Factors common to both the USA and Britain

1. Regional patterns of party support
2. Influential factors – which policies benefit which voters
3. The political record of existing office-holders
4. Voters' occupations
5. Quality of the campaign itself

Factors more influential in the USA

1. The incumbency factor
2. Religion
3. Ethnic origin of the voter
4. Success in raising finance
5. Personality of the candidate himself
6. Coat-tailing and the bandwagon effects
7. Straight ticket voting

Factors more influential in Britain

1. Social class of the voter
2. Party image
3. Sectoral cleavage – personal circumstances of the voter

Other parties   The USA has a two-party system which is more entrenched than possibly any other in the Western democratic world. Small parties are remarkably unsuccessful. Independents may win some very localised elections, but at the wider state and federal levels they never win. Indeed, the permanent, 'established' minor parties such as socialists and liberals are totally insignificant. It is only temporary 'third' parties, centred round the personality of one individual in presidential elections, which gain any substantial numerical support. There are a number of reasons for this lack of success:

- **Finance** is a vital aspect of party success. Candidates cannot make an impact without huge financial backing to fund media advertising, hiring of support staff and travelling expenses. Those who are willing to back candidates – largely businesses and pressure groups – will only commit money to those who they think can win, otherwise the exercise would be pointless. They seek political influence and this can only be achieved through those who hold public office. This is unlikely to be a representative of any party other than the Republicans or Democrats.
- Americans are notoriously reluctant to vote. The candidates therefore need a considerable organisation to help cajole and transport

supporters to the polls. The established parties have extensive **electoral machines** in place in most parts of the country. This is not the case with other candidates.

- In most states small parties are not permitted to hold primary elections to determine who will be their candidates. This may not be a problem where there is only one viable candidate, but it does reduce the opportunities for publicity, which are so vital to electoral success.
- All candidates for election must show that they have a reasonable amount of support in order to be placed on the ballot paper at all. This is in the form of a 'petition' signed by electors. In many states this may not present a problem as the numbers required are quite small, but in some states, such as Illinois and California, up to 100,000 signatures may be stipulated in presidential elections.
- Many voters feel a strong emotional sense of attachment to a 'traditional' party. This often causes them to vote for candidates of that party even when they are largely ignorant of the issues at stake. It is difficult for a new party candidate to break these traditional allegiances.
- As we have seen in Unit 15, Americans are notoriously conservative in their political outlook. They do not take easily to new social and philosophical ideas. Radical candidates are, therefore, at an immediate disadvantage.

Despite all these problems, a number of presidential candidates from parties other than the Republicans and Democrats have done tolerably well. Some examples are shown below.

Presidential election year	Candidate	Party	Votes won	Electoral college votes
1912	Theodore Roosevelt	Progressive	4,119,507	88
1948	Strom Thurmond	States' Rights	1,176,125	40
1968	George Wallace	American Ind.	9,906,473	46
1980	John Anderson	Independent	15,719,722	0
1992	Ross Perot	Independent	19,741,065	0

Comparisons American parties, as we have clearly seen above, are extremely unusual in contrast to their counterparts in the rest of the democratic world. It therefore becomes difficult to make meaningful comparisons. Parties should be judged by reference to their objectives. The very fact that the goals of American parties are somewhat different to those of British parties, for example, hinders analysis.

Nevertheless, if we accept that the organisation and characteristics of American parties are **bound** to be different, given the nature of their objectives, some interesting observations can be made.

Policy formulation Herein lies the principal distinction between American and British parties. Indeed, it is in this area that respective objectives are so divergent. The typical British party is organised at its centre almost entirely with a view to developing a policy programme which can be placed before the electorate. American parties cannot do this. They possess neither the organisation nor the philosophical cohesion to be able to create a unified programme which most of their candidates could support.

Structure   The second key distinction between British and American parties lies in their very different structure. The fact that they operate in extremely different political systems is of vital importance. The American federal system ensures that the parties there must have a decentralised structure. They must fight on two or more fronts at the same time. Small wonder then that there are more like one hundred American parties (two per state). The unitary state in Britain, with weak local government, means that the parties must be highly centralised. National politics is so much more important than regional and local variations.

Candidate selection   As we have seen, British election candidates come from a narrower range of possible nominees. They must satisfy a relatively small number of party activists to be adopted as the official nomination. It follows from this that British candidates, at both national and local level, are often in the image of the party workers who select them – highly committed, usually loyal and often significantly ideological in their political philosophy. In the USA access to the ballot is more open. Prospective candidates must appeal to the ordinary voters rather than to party enthusiasts. They are, therefore, likely to be more moderate and more populist in their appeal.

Party systems   The American party system only boasts two parties. This is the result of a series of factors, some historical, some financial and some political. Since about 1970 Britain has had a three-party system with, in Scotland and Wales, the added complication of a fourth significant contender in the form of the nationalists. This results in slightly more complicated electoral arithmetic. In the USA one party must beat its opponent fair and square. In Britain one party may gain from the fact that two other parties might split the vote against them. Certainly, the Conservatives have enjoyed the effects of this factor in particular.

Parties and pressure groups   Although there has been a marked increase in the importance of pressure groups in British politics in the last quarter of the twentieth century, it is still true that parties remain the principal means by which demands are articulated. This process of a transfer of activity away from parties towards pressure groups has been in train for much longer in the USA than is the case in Britain and has had more profound effects. The reason lies in both the extreme pluralism of the American political culture and in the weakness of parties in being able to promote public policy. Political participation is widespread in America, but it is more usually in the form of activity on behalf of pressure and interest groups than in solid work on behalf of a party.

Membership   British parties have been characterised by large mass memberships. The Conservatives have, in the past, been able to boast over one million members, even though many have only been, in truth, social members. The Labour Party, excluding union subscription payers, has reached 300,000 constituency members and even the Liberal Democrats have over 75,000 adherents. Thus, they are in continuous active session and have permanent access to an army of enthusiastic supporters. In the USA the parties only really mobilise themselves fully at election time. State and National Conventions, where candidates are confirmed, may be impressive occasions, characterised by much publicity and razzmatazz, but they are the only occasions when there appears to be any coherence in their activities.

Pressure groups

Introduction

The United States' political system is generally thought of as perhaps the most pluralist of all democratic systems. This is not to say there is a **broad** spectrum of political opinion which flourishes in the country. That claim can be better made in such countries as France, Italy and Spain. By contrast, America's political culture displays a remarkably **narrow** range of political philosophies. Rather, the description 'pluralist' refers to the fact that large numbers of factions, interests and campaigning organisations co-exist in a crowded political forum, jostling for prominence, determined to be heard above the noise made by all the others and sometimes resorting to grand gestures in order to be noticed.

It is customary to point to the relative weakness and lack of ideological coherence of the two great political parties when explaining the extensive nature of pressure group activity. This is undoubtedly true to a degree. Parties and their candidates, from the President downwards, cannot guarantee to fulfil any commitments which they may have made during election campaigns. Power at federal, state and local level is so diffused and so subject to checks and balances, that decisive political action becomes extremely hazardous. Individually and in groups, Americans are aware of this. As a response, therefore, they need to take more direct political action in order to further their political goals. Reliance on their elected representatives is simply not enough. So active pressure groups come about.

Nevertheless, party weakness is not a sufficient explanation for the abundance of American pressure groups. A number of other reasons – institutional, social and political – must be found.

The causes of pressure group activity

<u>Institutional</u> The decentralised nature of American government means that much political action must be conducted at two or more different levels at the same time. Federal government is limited, both by the Constitution and by the relative political independence of the states, so that it is not sufficient for pressure to be confined to Washington. The lack of a significant focus of power means that there is a great deal of access available for pressure groups to exercise leverage. Decentralisation, then, is both a challenge and an opportunity for pressure groups. The parties certainly do not have the necessary tight-knit organisation to cope with such an open system. Campaigning and interest groups, on the other hand, are often organised enough at all levels to be able to operate on a broad front.

The first amendment to the Constitution guarantees to American citizens the right of free speech and free association. There have, therefore, never been legal limitations on the establishment of political campaign groups. Alexis de Tocqueville noted this in the 1830s when researching for his great work, *Democracy in America*. For him, no democratic system could survive if it did not allow and encourage an active 'civil society' – the collective term for the many different groups to which citizens may belong and which act as a 'buffer' between the individual and the state.

<u>Political</u> We have already referred to the loose nature of American parties and the effect this has had on pressure group activity, but there are other political features which are of relevance. It has always been the case that American representative institutions at federal and state level have been remarkably open. The traditional suspicion of governmental institutions has resulted in an insistence that they carry out their deliberations in public. Publicity has, however, also come to mean access. American laws do place some restrictions upon the activities of pressure groups, but they also guarantee that political institutions open their doors to the many campaigning groups that seek entry.

<u>Social</u> America is a remarkably diverse society. It is divided into many ethnic groups, cultural backgrounds, religions and economic sections. Nevertheless, all of these consider themselves to be American and are, therefore, proud of American democracy. Most of them, therefore, express their differences and their diverse demands **within** the legitimate arena of democratic politics. There have been occasions when some alienated and disaffected groups have sought extra-legal methods to make their demands heard. During the late 1960s, for example, urban black groups, sections of the most poor and many college students resorted to direct, sometimes violent, action to express their opposition to American policy in Vietnam and to what they believed to be a corrupted political system. But it is usually the case that America's diversity is contained within the realms of legal activity. The fact that pressure groups enjoy guaranteed liberties and access to political institutions makes this possible.

Types of pressure groups We can divide American pressure groups in the same way as we can their counterparts in Britain. Essentially, there are **interest** groups, which represent a particular economic, social or ethnic section of the population, and cause groups, which are concerned with a particular issue. Some of the main examples are shown overleaf.

American pressure groups	
Those representing sectional interests	
Group	*Representing*
American Federation of Labor–Congress of Industrial Organizations (AFL–CIO)	Trade unions
American Farm Bureau Federation	Agricultural Interests
National Association of Manufacturers	Industry
American Bar Association	Legal profession
National Association for the Advancement of Colored People	Black and other non-white minorities
National Organization for Women	Women's rights
Cause groups	
National Rifle Association	Defending the right to carry guns
National Wildlife Federation	Environmental issues
National Right to Life Committee	Anti-abortion
Christian Coalition	Conserving traditional moral values
Common Cause	Rights for consumers and citizens against inefficient or unfair government

Interest groups have always played a major part in American politics, but it is largely since the 1960s that cause groups have begun to take over the scene. Indeed, there has been a tendency for these campaigns to amalgamate to form conglomerates with others who have similar demands. These are sometimes called 'externality' groups and have large memberships and extensive political influence. **Public Citizen**, run by veteran consumers' campaigner **Ralph Nader**, is an amalgamation of consumer protection groups, while the **Heritage Foundation** combines a variety of conservative causes in its work.

A further element in the lobby group activity is the development of so-called 'think tanks' – organisations which carry out research in a designated area of public policy and which are financed by many of the kinds of interest groups described above. The **Urban Institute**, for example, is concerned with welfare, racial and housing issues as they affect life in the poor districts of the cities. The **American Enterprise Institute**, by contrast, prefers to discourage government intervention in order to allow free-market capitalism to flourish.

We have, therefore, a remarkable plurality of organisations which operate the American lobby system. This partly reflects the diversity of interest and concerns within the political culture, and partly the fact that there are many different points of access to the political system, which may require different approaches and tactics.

Where pressure groups operate

<u>Local government</u>   At county, school board, large and small city level officials are constantly subject to lobbying, both by smaller community groups and by local branches of larger campaigns. Typically, issues will concern education, the environment, transport, agriculture, controversial planning decisions, law and order and public amenities. The very

well-developed sense of community spirit which flourishes within American society results inevitably in constant pressure being brought to bear on the lowest level of government. The political parties may not be fully organised at this level, but campaign groups often are, and can raise the finance necessary to make their voices heard.

In addition to high levels of local pressure group participation, the fact that so many local officials are elected gives considerable leverage to campaigners. The record of such officials is carefully scrutinised and publicised, especially at election time. This renders local representatives extremely sensitive to public opinion within their community. Local democracy, therefore, consists very much of pressure group politics.

The states As we have seen, state governments are very much microcosms of the national political system. State legislatures are extremely open to lobbying, while they also all possess active committee systems, which requires a good deal of interaction with lobby groups. Witnesses may be called to provide information to state representatives and evidence of public opinion, and to ensure that issues are seen to be given the fullest deliberation possible. Thus, there is a 'symbiotic' relationship between the state legislatures and the many groups which operate around them. They depend on each other. The groups need influence and this can be provided within the state legislature, but representatives also need the groups, for both financial support in their re-election campaigns and political support to help them with their own programmes.

At the same time, the governments of the states, the department heads and the officials who run the various services supplied at this level are constantly subjected to lobbying. In some cases, a single state may become the target for a national pressure group which is particularly concerned by its activities. Where major environmental damage is threatened, for example, the full weight of a group such as **Friends of the Earth** may be brought to bear on the state government. Similarly, anti-abortion **Right to Life** campaigners may target one state where they feel there is a possibility that restrictive legislation may be introduced. It may indeed be difficult for a smaller state political system to resist the pressure of a national campaign group.

Federal Congress It is in this arena that the highest-profile operations of pressure groups, collectively known simply as the 'lobby', operate at their highest level. Approximately 5,000 groups are registered with Congress (that is are given legal access to the members of Congress in general and the committees in particular). A further 10,000 or more may operate without such privileged access, but still consider it useful to be in Washington. The army of lawyers, agents, professional campaigners and public relations executives who operate here were collectively known in the 1980s as 'Gucci Gulch', such was their apparent affluence and fashionability. It can also be described as an industry, so extensive are their activities.

Operations are mainly on two levels. First, individual Senators and Congressmen may be targeted by groups as the most likely to be sympathetic. Members of the House of Representatives are considerably more vulnerable to such pressure. They must face a re-election campaign every two years. Their voting record will be carefully checked during the campaign, as will their congressional speeches. In many congressional districts, certain pressure groups are particularly important. Thus, in industrial areas the support of trade unions must be nurtured; where there are large ethnic minorities, or even majorities, the issues which concern them will come to the fore. The same is true for interest groups concerned with agriculture, business, foreign trade or specific industries. If one of these activities is prominent in a Congressman's district, the groups which represent them gain great influence over him. Secondly, congressional committees become a centre of pressure group interest.

Whenever legislation is being considered, the standing committees become involved at one stage or another. This may be to decide whether to devote any time at all to a proposed Bill, whether to give it a favourable place on the agenda or whether to suggest various amendments. Pressure groups will clamour to be heard by the relevant committee if the outcome of the legislation is important to them. At the same time, the committees are happy to call witnesses from the interest groups in order to gather information and to gauge the strength of support or opposition to a measure.

The federal administration The many departments and agencies which make up the administration, including the executive office of the President and the White House Staff, are almost as open as Congress to pressure group activity. Indeed, in some cases a permanent relationship can be built up between an agency and those groups most affected by its work. Thus, for example, it is vital that the Department of Education is in constant touch with organisations representing teachers, while the same kind of relationship must exist between the Department of Agriculture and the various farm groups which operate in Washington. Sometimes, in fact, the relationship can be too cosy, resulting in a phenomenon known as 'agency capture', where a pressure group seems to have developed so much influence over the agency that it appears to be running it.

Whether or not too much influence can be wielded by the lobby in Washington's bureaucracy, there is no doubt that, as at state level, there is an interdependency between interest groups and government agencies. Information changes hands, deals are done, involving the use of influence and finance, and powerful coalitions may be formed to push through important legislation or, where necessary, to thwart unwanted initiatives from Congress.

Iron triangles This term refers to the observation that there can develop a strong three-way relationship between interest groups, a government agency and a congressional standing committee. If all three are working towards the same objective, it is argued, the coalition is so strong that it cannot be resisted. The triangles thus become policy-making communities in themselves – 'governments within government'.

Typically, this analysis has been applied to the agriculture lobby, where pressure for protection from world competition has become irresistible. The same has also been true of the automobile industry in the 1990s. Energy policy has also been the subject of successful lobby group relationships, with such a triangle being able to thwart even the plans of the President himself.

The iron triangle analysis has been weakened somewhat in recent years, to be replaced by the concept of 'issue networks'. This is a more complex concept, suggesting that pressure groups are being forced to operate on a broader front. The standing committees in Congress, it is suggested, are no longer as influential as they were. At the same time, there is considerably more fragmentation within the parties in Congress so that lobby groups must seek the help of smaller groups of Congress members in order to build a wide coalition or 'network' of support. In short, policy making is not as simple as it once was. The groups must be more sophisticated in their campaigns. Power in Congress is more diffuse today and the groups must respond accordingly.

How pressure groups operate

Public campaigns and initiatives   One of the most effective means of putting pressure upon legislators and government officials is to demonstrate that there is widespread public support for a group's interests or for an issue. Public petitions or write-in campaigns may be organised and demonstrations held – those run by the National Association for the Advancement of Colored People in the 1960s were extremely influential. Write-ins involve large numbers of individuals writing to representatives and officials, all making the same demands, in the hope that the recipient will be persuaded that there is sufficient public support to warrant positive action.

In those states which incorporate an **initiative** system, pressure groups have a more direct form of leverage available to them. They may be able to gather sufficient signatures to trigger an initiative – effectively a referendum – and then have the resources to be able to conduct the resultant campaign for a favourable vote. Anti-tax groups are particularly active in this field.

In some cases, more extreme measures may be adopted. During civil rights campaigns in the Deep South in the 1950s and 1960s, a great deal of civil disobedience was used, especially against segregation in schools, universities and other public places. Later in the 1960s students rioted on their campuses, blacks in the city centres and the poor marched on Washington, squatting in their thousands in front of the White House to publicise their plight. More recently, in the 1990s, anti-abortion groups have attacked abortion clinics and they even assassinated one of the surgeons who had performed terminations. However, public demonstrations remain, on the whole, relatively peaceful and law-abiding.

The media   Access to the media is very open to any lobby group which has the funds to pay for the space or the time. Press advertising is a common feature of pressure group activity, as are slots between radio and TV programmes, provided the group in question has the necessary finance. Indeed, on those shows which are unashamedly religious or morally conservative in nature sympathetic groups may not need to pay for their time. The broadcasting stations might themselves be a prominent feature of the campaign. Such publicity takes three main forms.

First, it may be designed to give information to members of the public. Environmental, moral and legal issues, for example, need to be brought to the attention of viewers and listeners. Statistics, scientific facts and viewpoints may effectively be conveyed through the broadcasting media.

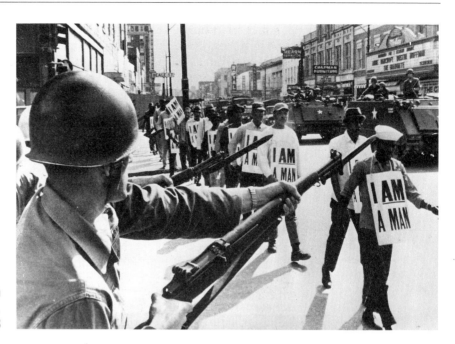

Civil rights march in Memphis, Tennessee, 30 March 1968

Secondly, attempts may be made to persuade the public to support a cause. Here, an appeal may take on the appearance of any other commercial. Finally, the more subtle campaigns may publicise the personal record of elected officials, especially those who show antipathy to the cause. In this way, pressure is placed on them to conform to the wishes of the lobby group, under the threat that they may lose public support as a result of the campaign.

<u>Through the courts</u>   America is an exceptionally **litigious** society. This means that it is relatively easy to have access to the courts and that citizens are not reluctant to use this freedom. At both state and federal level, court orders may be sought to prevent governmental action which may be considered to be contrary to current law or, in extreme circumstances, unconstitutional. If official or legislative actions are thought to offend such principles as individual rights, privacy, freedom of expression or freedom of association and movement, court orders may be used to prevent or merely delay the process.

In these circumstances, where courts, and especially the federal Supreme Court, are judging official actions against fixed legal principles, a lobby group may be considered *amici curiae*, meaning 'friends of the court'. This means that the group may be given the privileged role of adviser to the court, providing facts as well as legal opinion. All large campaign groups employ constitutional lawyers for such purposes. Typically, pro- and anti-abortion groups, law and order campaigners, environmentalists, consumer protectionists and 'Common Cause', the citizen's group described above, use the courts wherever possible. A number of examples of such key cases can be found in Unit 16 on pages 375–7.

<u>Congressional committees</u>   Of considerably more importance than either House of Congress are the congressional committees, which are the main target for pressure group activity at federal level. Those standing

committees which are concerned with such matters as agriculture, transport, environment, industry, defence, finance and the economy are constantly pressed by the relevant lobby groups to consider favourable legislation, to resist measures which are considered unfriendly or to amend Bills in ways they consider desirable.

There is a great deal of informal lobbying of committee members, but groups are also frequently required to give evidence at well publicised formal hearings. Indeed, lobbying may take place well before this stage is reached. When committees are being formed at the beginning of a new Congress, lobbyists will seek to ensure that representatives and Senators who are known to be sympathetic to their cause will find a place on those committees which are relevant to it.

The federal administration Here pressure groups begin by attempting to give themselves a privileged place within the central bureaucracy. First, they may attempt to ensure the appointment of sympathetic officials or to prevent the promotion of less friendly individuals. With favourable officials and congressional committee members, any group places itself at a great advantage. Secondly, the larger groups will seek a privileged, permanent position within the organisation of the agency. They need to ensure that they are regularly consulted and have ready access to important members of the agency. In Britain this process is known as 'incorporation' but in the USA it is often described as 'agency capture'.

The phenomenon of 'iron triangles' has been described above, but this depends upon the co-operation of members of Congress. Without them, lobby groups must rely on the ability of administration officials to operate successfully on the Congress floor and in the committee rooms. In these cases, the relationship may be described as a partnership rather than a triangle.

Initiatives In a number of states citizens may call for a referendum if they can collect a sufficiently large quantity of names on a petition. If a pressure group can force through such an initiative, causing it to appear on the normal ballot paper in November, there is an excellent chance that public opinion will back its demands. Politicians, faced with such a device, have little choice but to accept the verdict of the people. The best-known example of such an initiative was **Proposition 13**, which was passed in California in 1978. This had been promoted by anti-tax groups and the result was a significant cut in state taxation.

Political Action Committees (PACs) These are a relatively recent development on the American political scene. They are partly the result of the fragmentation of pressure groups, and partly of legislation limiting the financing of candidates for public office. PACs are umbrella groups that collect finance from a variety of lobby groups which are all concerned with a similar issue. There were as many as 4,000 PACs in existence by 1990. Although no individual may give more than $5,000 to a particular PAC, there is no limit on how many PACs may receive such funds and no limit on how many PAC contributions any election candidate may receive. This gets round the legal limits on **direct** contributions to candidates, which cannot be made by businesses or any other organisations. PACs can receive such financing provided no single donation is above $5,000.

Typical examples of PAC concerns can be illustrated by their titles:

- Business–Industry PAC
- Committee for Responsible Government
- National Conservative PAC
- AFL–CIO Political Education PAC.

Some PACs are simply representatives of large interest groups such as employers, farmers, professions, trade unions, women, students, banking, business and commerce. Others are more ideological in nature, pursuing conservative, liberal or progressive causes of one kind or another.

Although PACs operate extensively on the floor of Congress, their principal activity on behalf of their clients is the financing of candidates at all levels of government. They seek out those who are likely to be sympathetic to the cause and try to ensure their election through financial aid to their campaigns. To an increasing extent PAC work has become one of the prime political methods used by pressure groups.

Are pressure groups in decline?

Since the rise of 'New Right' politics in the 1980s, there has been much speculation that the influence of the lobby is waning. There is an assumption that the return of more ideological politics has closed many points of access to pressure groups. There is little research evidence that the voting patterns of representatives have been particularly affected by PAC contributions to their election campaigns. There has also been something of a reaction by legislators against the activities of pressure groups. Americans may be proud of their pluralist, open democracy, but they have also become concerned by the increasing influence of lobby groups who do not appear to be politically responsible to anyone.

Two incidents in the 1980s illustrate the new conflict between the lobby and Congress in particular, and politicians in general. In 1983 the welfare system was extensively reformed through the **Social Security Reform Act**. This was done in the face of intense pressure from lobby groups to abandon or amend the proposals. More dramatically, in 1986 the **Tax Reform Act** was discussed and passed almost in secrecy in order to avoid pressure group influence. All the lobby could do was to kick its heels while decisions were taken behind doors which had been closed to them.

The reaction against pressure group activity is the result of concerns that the enormous financial influence which the lobby wields is unhealthy in a modern democracy. There has also been a feeling that it has had the effect of rendering politicians largely impotent in that **any** form of political action is likely to meet with so much opposition from lobby groups that it is immensely difficult to achieve any significant change. Issues such as gun control, abortion, anti-crime measures, health reform, public spending cuts, energy policy and agricultural aid have all been subject to the stifling effect of pressure group activity. There are now renewed demands to curb these groups' activities still further.

For exam questions relevant to this unit, see pages 495–7.

20 Federalism and the states

The origins and nature of federalism

The Constitution

During the political manoeuvring which preceded the development of the federal Constitution in 1787, three main groups emerged. The first favoured a continuation of the very loose **confederation** which already existed. Central government would be meagre and relatively powerless. A second faction was content to see a strong, unified political system, within which the states would have some independent powers, but sovereignty would reside firmly in the Union capital. Between them lay a party, led by **James Madison**, known as 'federalists', who wished to see either a confederation or a unitary system. Its campaign, centering on a series of political pamphlets known as the 'Federalist Papers', was ultimately successful, and a federal system was introduced. This was the first such political system ever to be fully devised and represents America's most important contribution to constitutional theory.

Why a federal system was adopted

We can identify three principal reasons why the Founding Fathers opted for a federal solution and, indeed, why their system has only come under serious challenge twice, the first being in the Civil War era of the 1860s and the second in the modern era of 'New Federalism' which will be discussed below.

- The American people were, and indeed still are, fiercely independent. They dislike strong government, viewing it as a threat to their liberty. In addition, the experience of the autocratic rule of the British monarchy had left them with a natural antipathy to political authority. Federalism, therefore, guaranteed a measure of independence while accepting that some form of centralised state was inevitable.
- The thirteen original states were very varied in character, especially in their economic structure. They ranged from the predominantly agricultural areas such as Virginia, to the trading states of New York and Rhode Island and the 'frontier lands' further west. Federalism reflected this diversity, allowing it to flourish, but within an ordered national framework.
- Madison himself recognised the dangers of concentrating too much power in too few hands. He understood that a method of reducing such a danger was to divide government. Federalism was one way of doing this (separating the powers of the three branches of central government was the other). The guaranteed powers and independence of the states could act as a check on the power of the central state. So an important constitutional principle was born with the creation of the federal union.

'It is a known fact in human nature, that its affections are commonly weak in proportion to the distance of diffusiveness of the object. Upon the same principle that a man is more attached to his family than to his neighbourhood, to his neighbourhood than to his community at large, the people of each state would be apt to feel a stronger bias towards their local governments, than towards the government of the union, unless the force of that principle should be destroyed by a much better administration of the latter.'

Alexander Hamilton, federalist (1787)

Disputes about the exact **balance** of power between the federal government and the states have continued, but there has never been a serious attempt to end the federal system altogether.

How federalism works

The Constitution and its subsequent amendments establish how **sovereign** powers are to be divided. It is important to stress the term 'sovereignty' since it is clear that, once the Constitution has allocated powers to the federal government, to the states or to a combination of the two, they cannot be taken back or overruled, as is the case in a unitary constitution such as Britain's. The only way in which the division of sovereignty can be altered is by constitutional amendment. Since such an amendment would require not only congressional approval but also the agreement of three-quarters of the states themselves, the federal settlement is safety protected. The states can only be required to give up sovereign powers by their own consent.

The allocation of powers works as follows:

- Some powers are reserved **only** for one or more of the branches of federal government.
- Some are reserved **only** for the states.
- Some are left open for the federal Congress to determine who shall exercise them.
- Any powers not allocated by the Constitution or by Congress automatically are reserved for the states.

In practice, we can see how the system works by enumerating the powers which are now exercised either by federal government, by the states or by both:

Powers exercised ONLY by federal government and forbidden to the states

National defence and internal security of the United States
Negotiations and treaty-making with foreign powers
Regulating trade with foreign powers
Regulating the United States' currency
Regulating interstate trade

Powers exercised by BOTH federal and state governments

Development and enforcement of criminal and civil law (MOSTLY controlled by states)
Health care, welfare and housing programmes
Care of the environment
Transport provision
Regulation of broadcasting and the media
Regulating industry and commerce within the state itself
Taxation of individual and corporate incomes
Arrangements and funding of educational provision

Powers exercised ONLY by the states

Taxation on property and goods
Control over local government
Control over city government

The list shown above, though not exhaustive, illustrates how few powers are now reserved completely for the states compared to those which only federal government exercises. But the real dynamics of the federal system concern those powers which are shared. It is here that the ebb and flow of the balance of powers between state and federal government takes place. On the whole, there has been a steady shift of power and function towards the centre since the federal system was first established. More recently, however, as we shall see below, the tide has been stemmed and a reaction is under way. Calls for transfers of powers back to the states have been growing louder and more insistent.

The changing nature of federalism

<u>Dual federalism</u>   In 1791 the tenth amendment to the Constitution was passed. This was an attempt to clarify the relationship between the states and federal government. The wording of the amendment is shown below:

> *'The powers not delegated to the United States* by the Constitution, nor prohibited by it to the States, are reserved to the States respectively, or to the people.'*
> Amendment 10 of the US Constitution. Ratified 1791

*Here the term 'United States' refers to federal (central) government

By granting all 'reserve' powers to the states, it was assumed that the independence of the states would be protected from future encroachments by the federal authorities. This was the establishment of what is known as 'dual federalism'. It confirmed the principle that the federal and state governments should run in parallel, each with their own institutions and powers. Relatively little overlapping of powers was envisaged. However, as time has gone by, the principles of dual federalism have been steadily eroded.

<u>The interstate commerce clause</u>   In the case of *Gibbons v. Ogden*, which came before the Supreme Court in 1824, the precise meaning of the term 'interstate commerce' came into question. The Constitution states in Article 1, Section 8, that the Congress shall have power to 'regulate commerce **among the several states**'. Does this imply that the federal Congress, therefore government, should have the power to regulate all forms of trade which affect more than one state (effectively virtually all trade)? Yes, said the Court led by Chief Justice Marshall. Thus was established federal jurisdiction over commerce, later industry, and this ultimately became full economic control.

Five years earlier, in the case of *McCulloch v. Maryland*, the pre-eminence of federal government in matters concerning taxation had also been established by the Court. Put together, these two judgments made it clear that, whatever the tenth amendment might say, areas of jurisdiction not covered in the Constitution were, in fact, likely to fall into the hands of the federal Congress or the President.

> *'We admit, as all must admit, that the powers of the govern-ment are limited, and that its limits are not to be transcended. But we think the sound construction of the Constitution must allow to the national legislature that discretion, with respect*

> to the means by which the powers it confers are to be carried
> into execution, which will enable that body to perform the high
> duties assigned to it, in the manner most beneficial to the people.'
> Chief Justice John Marshall, *McCulloch v. Maryland*, 1819

The Civil War   The attempt by a number of southern states to secede from the Union over the slavery issue was not merely about the principles of slavery itself. It was also about the authority of the federal government to dictate to the various states. When proposals were made to instruct all states to end the practice of slavery, the slave states revolted. Here was the most direct confrontation yet between those who claimed the rights of the states to run their own affairs and the power of federal government.

The military victory which Abraham Lincoln, the President, and the supporters of federal power (the so-called 'Union' side in the war) achieved, established the ability, if not the authority, of the federal government to exercise wide powers. Since then, there has been a lingering resentment in the South, so that both Democrats and Republicans continue to be suspicious of the power of Washington. When Presidents Nixon and Reagan promised to shift some of the balance of power back to the states in more recent times, they found ready allies in the South.

The sixteenth amendment and taxation   In 1913 the federal government was granted constitutional powers to raise taxation on individual and corporate incomes. This was a significant development since it enabled the federal government to raise considerably larger amounts of its own funds and thus to initiate more expansive policies. Without these taxation powers, the President, or Congress, was forced to persuade the states to spend their own money if new programmes were to be implemented.

Grants-in-aid and co-operative federalism   This device was first used in the 1860s during Lincoln's Presidency, but it was hampered by lack of funds. With the sixteenth amendment came fresh opportunities and grants-in-aid began to form the main basis for federal–state government relations.

The system had a number of features which all led to increased federal control. In essence, the federal administration can propose a policy to be implemented in a particular state. This may be, typically, road building, agricultural subsidies, welfare programmes, hospital building, an energy production scheme or education initiatives. The funding was to be shared between federal and state sources. Essentially, each dollar used by Washington would be matched by the state government. Although voluntary, any state would be reluctant to refuse a grant-in-aid as the money, raised from its own citizens, would only then be used for a project in a different state.

This system gave rise to a new term for this kind of federal action. **Co-operative federalism** supplanted the old mutual variety. However, co-operation was not a strictly accurate description. Though it may appear to operate on the basis of voluntary agreements, the projects are invariably controlled by the federal government which dictates how the money shall be spent and may lay down minimum standards in the provision of services. In addition, the original initiative normally comes from Washington. The states are in a weak position because they cannot themselves propose extensive programmes without the financial co-operation of the federal administration.

As well as grants-in-aid, the new style of federalism also meant that federal government felt freer to use its own funds exclusively, without state involvement, to introduce new schemes. Much of Roosevelt's New Deal measures, described below, were achieved without matching-fund schemes. So, in one way or another, the period between 1913 and World War Two saw a marked extension in the responsibilities of central government and a matching decline in states' independence.

The New Deal President Roosevelt came to power in the 1930s with a clear popular mandate to extend the scope of federal government into new realms. Social security systems were introduced using federal funds to help poorer families. The creation of the **Tennessee Valley Authority** also opened the way for federal initiatives in state investment, infrastructure development, agricultural subsidies and employment creation schemes. Together with a variety of further measures to ensure fair wages, improved working conditions and recognition of trade union powers, the New Deal policies established the principle that federal government had authority to intervene in the economic and industrial structures of the states, provided, of course, there was an electoral mandate to do so.

A number of challenges were made in the Supreme Court to Roosevelt's policies, challenges which were, at first, successful in holding back progress. By 1937, however, Roosevelt had established greater control in the Court and the New Deal policies were finally granted constitutional approval.

The Great Society The commitment of **John F. Kennedy** (1961–3) and his successor, **Lyndon Johnson** (1963–9), to further intervention by the federal administration in the fields of welfare, education, medical care for the poor, urban renewal and housing programmes was known as the 'Great Society'. Aided by a friendly, Democrat-dominated Congress, Johnson in particular was determined to ensure that the traditional ear of central government power would not prevent him from reversing what he saw as many years of neglect by state governments in their own social fabric.

Both grants-in-aid and straightforward federal expenditure were used to establish radical increases in the responsibilities of American government. By the time Richard Nixon took over the Presidency in January 1969, the tide of federal power had reached its high point. Nixon was determined to turn this tide back and claimed a clear mandate to do so.

New federalism Nixon's plan was relatively simple. First, he cancelled a large number of specific grants which could only be spent by the states on programmes specified by federal government. They were replaced by 'block grants' which could be used in whatever ways a state chose. The policy was known as 'general revenue sharing'. This was clearly designed to return a measure of independence to the states. Secondly, he reduced the number and cost of grants-in-aid. The states were presented with a greater expenditure burden through the loss of federal funds, but at least they were freed from a good deal of federal intervention in their affairs.

After Nixon, **Jimmy Carter** (1977–81), whose term of office proved to be a brief Democratic interlude in a period of Republican domination of the White House, began by promising to restore many of the federal aid programmes, which Nixon had abolished, to the states. However, he was thwarted by determined resistance in both Congress and the state governments. The process of federal disengagement which Nixon had started could not be stopped.

Ronald Reagan (1981–9) introduced the most radical phase of the 'New Federalism' era. He transferred responsibility for a large number of welfare, anti-poverty, housing and health programmes to the states. He also made deep cuts in federal expenditure in order to finance substantial tax cuts. Between 1980 and 1991 federal grants to the states fell by almost 20 per cent, mostly as a result of the 1981 **Omnibus Reconciliation Act**, which set the cuts in motion. Some of the states, notably in the South, were happy to pick up the gauntlet thrown down by Reagan. They took over the programmes relinquished by federal government, even though it involved them in higher financial commitments. This was a fair trade-off in return for greater autonomy. In other cases, however, the expenditure cuts resulted only in hardship. Some of the cities, notably New York, were effectively bankrupt. A number of states had to make severe reductions in police, emergency and social services to make up for the loss of federal funding. Even California, the Union's wealthiest state, struggled to maintain educational and social provisions.

Thus, New Federalism has had its price and the states have had to pay it. Either by raising their own taxes or reducing services, shortfalls have been made up. But the pressure is still on. Like Carter before him, President **Bill Clinton** hoped, on his election in 1992, to resurrect federal initiatives with his plans for a comprehensive health care scheme and extensive crime control measures. Tax increases and reductions in other items of federal expenditure, such as defence, were to pay for the plans two years later. However, a conservative, Republican-dominated Congress was elected. Its leaders, Bob Dole and Newt Gingrich were determined to resist any further increases in federal expenditure and power. Clearly, the spirit of New Federalism was still alive.

The future for federalism   The rise of New Right conservatism in the 1980s and 1990s has heralded a new era in federal–state relations. Federal government has been under attack for a number of reasons:

- It is thought to be corrupt, inefficient and wasteful.
- It is associated with high taxation which stifles enterprise.
- Rising federal expenditure increases its power and threatens state independence.
- The faulty policies of federal government are blamed for the poor economic performance of the USA in recent years. The failure to 'balance the federal budget' since 1969 is, it is argued, caused by extravagant federal officials.

Apart from these specific criticisms, however, there is a growing feeling that the power of central government is threatening the liberty of individuals. Herein lies a parallel with the British Conservative right wing's fear of the growth of European Union power. Only by restoring autonomy to a lower level of government, argues the right, can individualism be restored. In some extreme cases in the USA, calls are beginning to be heard for the complete independence of some states. As yet these are very much an extreme minority view, but centrifugal forces have certainly become more powerful.

Thus, the definite shift in the balance of power between the centre and the states seems set to continue as long as conservatives hold sway in Washington. It may, nevertheless, be that economic recovery will end the criticisms of federal power and equilibrium will be restored.

State government

The state constitutions

Every state has its own constitution because it is a **sovereign** power. In most cases, these constitutions were written at around the time when the state became a member of the Union. However, in other cases a completely new document has been written and adopted since. The list below shows when some of the states established their current constitution:

Date of adoption of current state constitutions	
State	**Date of current constitution**
Massachusetts	1780
New Hampshire	1784
Vermont	1793
Indiana	1851
California	1879
New Mexico	1912
New Jersey	1948
Hawaii	1959
Louisiana	1975

Each of the constitutions contains provisions similar to those in the federal document. They set out the distribution of powers between the counties, cities and other units of local government, and establish the legal limits to the jurisdiction of each level of administration. They also all contain a statement of the rights of citizens in the state. These may not go as far as the federal Bill, but sometimes may go further. For example, there are states which legally guarantee equal rights for women, a provision not yet established at federal level. Of course, such rights are only mandatory within the borders of the state.

State constitutions are subject to regular amendment and, in many cases, a full rewriting may be required. Louisiana, for example, established its eleventh constitution in 1975! Georgia is close behind with ten and South Carolina has had seven. However, such drastic measures are not normally needed. A number of states, notably Kansas and Oregon, still operate their original constitutions.

Methods for amendment vary. A common method is the **voter initiative** system. Seventeen states operate a system where citizens may collect a petition which calls for constitutional amendment. These petitions are known as 'initiatives'. Provided sufficient names – normally a fixed percentage of the votes cast for Governor at the last election – are forthcoming, the amendment may be included in a ballot. Thereafter, a majority of voters may approve or reject the amendment. Otherwise, proposals for change are often the result of *legislature initiative*. Here the state legislature brings forward the amendment. However, the approval of the voters is still required.

The most dramatic examples of popular democracy at work occur in fourteen states where there is a mechanism for the regular calling of an elected **Constitutional Convention** to review the existing document. New Hampshire, for example, has held seventeen such conventions since the establishment of the Union. At the most recent convention, 175 amendments were proposed, but only ten were passed.

Although every state constitution must conform to the federal Constitution, their existence and importance illustrate the key role of the principle of **government by consent** in the USA. Whether citizens themselves initiate change, or are simply asked to approve changes proposed by their elected representatives, it is clear that American government remains very much in the hands of its people.

The state administrations

<u>The Governor</u>   Every state elects a Governor who is the chief executive in the state and head of its administration. The Governors normally operate on four-year terms (three Governors must seek re-election every two years) and voting coincides with congressional elections in November. Broadly speaking, the role of the Governor is similar to that of the federal President, except, of course, that he need not concern himself with foreign affairs or the defence of the country. These last two roles are forbidden to him by the Constitution.

In most states the Governor's functions include the following:

- Legislative proposals. The Governor is the state's chief policy maker.
- Exercising a veto over legislation which he opposes.
- Oversight of the state's administration.
- Representing the state in negotiations with other states.
- He is the state's representative in negotiation with the federal administration and Congress, especially over grants-in-aid. He must attempt to secure funding from Washington for many of the state's key services.
- Appointment of **some** of the state's senior officials, though many, as we shall see below, are directly elected.
- Quasi-judicial functions such as the right to approve paroles or pardon convicted criminals.

<u>The administration</u>   Here, there may be some variation from state to state. However, it is normal for there to be a **Lieutenant-Governor** who is a deputy to the Governor. Like the federal Vice President, he must take over if the Governor dies or resigns, but otherwise has few powers or functions. In the main, he deputises for the Governor on ceremonial occasions.

In addition, there may be a **Treasurer**, in charge of the finances and economy of the state, a **Secretary of State**, another largely ceremonial role, and an **Attorney-General**, controller of the legal and criminal enforcement systems in the state. Otherwise, the precise titles and nature of posts in the administration are subject to considerable differences from one state to the next.

It is difficult to generalise about the manner in which administration officials are chosen. Some may be appointed by the Governor, others are elected. In the latter cases, of course, problems may arise if an official is of a different party to that of the Governor. However, since they are normally elected together, at the same time, voters will normally elect them as a 'team'.

State court systems   Most criminal and civil law in America is under the jurisdiction of the states. It is, therefore, inevitable that state courts play a greater role in American life than do their federal counterparts. The basic 'pyramid' of courts is also subject to variation, but in most states courts are organised as follows:

- At the lowest level, where minor criminal cases and civil disputes are heard, there are **Justices of the Peace** or **Magistrates' Courts** in the rural counties and the smaller cities.
- The larger cities have **Municipal Courts** in which more senior judges sit. These courts are further divided into levels depending on the nature of the crime or the financial size of a civil dispute.
- The main state courts are normally called **General Trial Courts**. Here, most criminal and civil cases are heard. The state is divided into a number of **districts** or **circuits**, each presided over by a court. In the criminal district courts, prosecutions are carried out by **district attorneys** who are sometimes elected, sometimes appointed by the state Attorney-General.
- **Appeal Courts** deal with more routine appeals arising from cases in lower courts. Where an appeal concerns important principles of state law, or constitutional matters, it must be carried higher.
- The **State Supreme Court** is the summit of the legal system in the state. It hears the more important appeals which may have wider legal implications. It also considers challenges to state laws and executive actions which may offend the state's own constitution. Despite all this, perhaps its highest-profile role is the consideration of final appeals against the execution of offenders in those states which operate the death penalty.

On rare occasions there may be some conflict between the operation of state laws and those which are federal and therefore apply throughout the USA. This may especially arise in matters concerning government or major commercial civil cases arising out of disputes in more than one state. In these cases, the problem must be resolved in a federal appeal court or, if important enough, in the Supreme Court in Washington itself. It should also be noted that if a crime is committed in more than one state, the case must be heard in a federal court. A fugitive from justice, for example, who crosses a state line, automatically becomes a **federal** criminal and comes under the jurisdiction of the Federal Bureau of Investigation (FBI).

Judges may be appointed in one of three ways, depending on their state. Some are appointed by the Governor or his Attorney-General. Others are appointed by the state legislature and finally, and most controversially, some states elect their judges. However, it is most common for a combination of these methods to be adopted. Only in thirteen states are all judges elected. Appointment by the Governor is the most common method.

It may seem strange that a supposedly neutral official, such as a judge, should be elected. In fact, most candidates do not stand under a party label, and those who do still claim to be politically impartial. The reason for the persistence of such elections arises simply from the American love affair with direct forms of democracy. It is believed that judges 'represent the people' in the administration of justice. To ensure that this continues, they must be elected. The practice is, however, slowly dying out.

State legislatures

<u>Voting</u> Until the 1960s the principle of 'one-person-one-vote' was not finally and irrevocably established in all states. Although the federal Constitution had long since established universal suffrage, some states were able to discriminate against certain classes, mainly blacks, by introducing such barriers to voting as a literacy test. The Supreme Court judgment in *Reynolds v. Sims*, a 1964 dispute in Alabama, finally declared that all discriminatory practices were unconstitutional.

Similarly, the drawing of electoral boundaries had often been subject to discrimination by ruling parties. The practice of 'gerrymandering' – drawing electoral boundaries to favour one party – was ultimately outlawed in the Supreme Court judgment in *Baker v. Carr* in 1962.

<u>Bicameralism</u> All states have two legislative chambers – a smaller Upper House and a large Lower House. The practice of bicameralism is a reflection of the American determination to avoid concentrations of power by dividing government into two branches. Systems vary, but on the whole legislation requires the approval of both Houses, which are elected at different times and on different bases. In this way, no party majority can guarantee to govern unopposed for any significant length of time.

The organisation of state legislatures is similar to that of Congress in Washington (though their actual titles vary). There are standing committees dealing with the agenda, rules and amendments. The chairmen are equally as influential as their counterparts in Washington, as are party leaders on the floor of the legislatures. Bills go through a lengthy, often complex procedure and then must be approved by the Governor who can, and often does, veto them. In a few cases, certain categories of legislation, usually concerning finance and taxation, may have to be put before a referendum of the people for their approval.

State legislatures do not meet as often as the federal Congress so that representatives need not be full time. Indeed, many are paid by the day rather than receiving an annual salary. Most have outside interests, often full-time jobs. However, in some large states such as California being a legislator is a complete career.

Parties are highly organised at state legislature level. Unlike the national parties, which are extremely fragmented and subject to wide regional variations in philosophy, the state organisations are more cohesive. Indeed, in some states where one party completely dominates, there may be an extremely tight-knit hierarchy. Party discipline is stronger and, if the Governor is sympathetic, policy programmes can be coherent and predictable. Such party control is based upon patronage and a network of links with local business and interest groups. It is therefore the case that the political system in many states resembles the European picture much more closely than does federal government.

Local government

The structure of local government varies considerably from state to state. Nevertheless, certain basic institutions and principles can be established which are, more or less, applicable in all cases.

Counties

These are the building blocks of nearly all states. They vary in size a great deal, from a few thousand to over seven million in Los Angeles County, California. Only Connecticut and Rhode Island do not have them. About half the states determine the nature of county government through their constitution, but the other half allow counties to make their own arrangements. It is in the area of county government that state constitutional amendment is often proposed.

Typically, a county board is elected and, in turn, appoints a variety of full-time officials to run the county, such as engineers, planning officers, health inspectors and financial controllers. Some officers may also be directly elected, including prosecuting attorneys, judges, coroners, treasurers and sheriffs.

The functions of counties normally include law enforcement, prisons, road building and maintenance, planning controls, some welfare for the elderly and the poor, public works, refuse collection and disposal, environmental protection and a variety of other public services. Though most education is in the hands of separate school boards, some schooling is within county jurisdiction.

Counties receive their finance in the form of grants from state government. They do collect taxes, but this is not on their own account, it is on behalf of the state authorities.

Towns and townships

These are a throwback to America's early origins. They are common in the New England states, in the states of New York and New Jersey, and in the mid-West. Replacing county government, the town or township is a small community, based on one or more small towns or villages. It is characterised by the phenomenon of the 'town meeting'. Here, all voters meet to make decisions directly. This may include the election of town officials, key decisions on transport or public works and even levy-ing of tax. The towns are given a remarkable degree of independence by the states. This can even extend to some financial independence.

Though not a major factor in American local government, the town-ship system is an interesting example of the most direct form of demo-cracy in the modern world, an echo of the market place democracy of ancient Athens and the 'New Leveller' movement in England in the 1640s.

School boards and special districts

Overlaying the local government system sit special authorities (whose officials are normally elected) which run various specialised services. School boards are everywhere, operating with state funds and under the general auspices of the state administration. In addition, some authorities are responsible for providing water, police, environmental protection, emergency services, libraries, sanitation and public transport.

Special districts do not necessarily conform to other local government boundaries and are not normally subject to jurisdiction at county level. The system can, therefore, be extremely confusing. The average citizen may find himself in a bewildering variety of county, school board, police, transport and water supply jurisdictions. When he goes to vote, he will be presented with a ballot paper listing candidates from several different levels of government.

Cities

As we have observed earlier, caution needs to be exercised when describ-ing American cities. It is more a local government term than a geo-graphical description. Thus, cities vary greatly in size, from huge conurbations such as Chicago to relatively modest towns. Whichever is the case, cities are granted **charters** by state legislatures, allowing them to control their own affairs. It follows that the government of cities varies both between states and within them.

Despite this, a few generalisations can be made. All cities elect a **mayor**. The mayor may be a 'strong' official who is **chief executive**, appoints officials, makes policy and controls the city budget. This applies in New York and Chicago, for example. Such mayors have often become major national figures. Dick Daley of Chicago led a notorious party machine in the 1960s and New York's chief executive is always a high-profile politician. In the states of the South it is now common for mayors to be black, reflecting the concentration of ethnic minority groups in urban ghettos and their new willingness to vote in larger numbers.

The mayor may also be in a much weaker position, being merely a figurehead. In such cases his officials are separately elected and he is not expected to formulate policy. The most celebrated example of such a ceremonial figure was actor Clint Eastwood, who became mayor of Carmel, California, in the 1980s.

Councils are elected to run cities alongside the mayor. Where the mayor is weak, the city council is strong, and vice versa. In particular, the strong councils have powers to appoint officials and take the lead in policy making. More than rural areas, the cities rely heavily upon outside financ-ing. In particular, the large conurbations rely upon federal funding for housing renewal, anti-crime measures, relief of the poor and health programmes.

Clint Eastwood becoming mayor of Carmel

Many of the larger cities have experienced severe social problems in the 1980s and 1990s, including drug abuse, general crime, racial tension, poor housing and schools, and general poverty. Since the decline in federal funding which began during Ronald Reagan's Presidency, many cities have found themselves unable to cope. They have been squeezed between increasing problems and declining revenue. Police and medical services have been particularly disadvantaged. The mayor and council may, therefore, appear to be independent and powerful, but in practice they are hampered by financial stringency.

Conclusions on sub-central government in the United States

The decentralised nature of American government makes generalisation difficult. However, some useful observations can be made.

The elective principle

Hundreds of thousands of representatives and officials are elected in the American political system. There are approximately 82,000 units of local government alone. Add to this the fifty state governments and legislatures, and the federal system, and we see an impressive array of politicians who owe their position, not to the patronage of party leaderships, but to the approval of the people in their own community. Their record in office is a matter of public concern, they face regular re-election campaigns and may be removed every two, four or six years, depending on their role, if the people are not satisfied. No other political system in the world elects so high a proportion of its politicians and officials.

Decentralisation

We know that America is a federal system. This is not unusual. A large number of other states, including Germany, India and Russia, have similar systems. What is remarkable in the USA, however, is the degree of independence enjoyed by levels of government below state level. Counties, towns and cities are broadly self-governing. As we have already observed, the township meeting is the most ancient and direct form of democracy known to mankind. Particularly striking is the extent to which financial independence is allowed. Although taxes are basically only levied at two levels – state and federal – there are three or more tiers of government where expenditure is largely free of controls from superior authorities.

Complexity   The decentralised nature of the political system, and the degree of independence which each level of government enjoys, makes sub-central administration in America extremely complicated. Most citizens have a fairly adequate grasp of those local institutions which govern them. Should a resident move to another part of the country, however, he must begin a whole new learning process to discover what taxes he must pay and to whom, who supplies his water, public transport, schooling for his children and policing, and which representatives or officials he must elect in November's ballot. If he is especially fortunate, he may even find himself voting on local taxation or on proposed changes to his state's constitution. The lack of uniformity in government is certainly striking.

Comparison with Britain

Here we can find a number of dramatic contrasts. Indeed, the nature of government below the centre in the two countries is radically different. Some of the main distinctions are as follows:

Distribution of sovereignty   The position here is clear. The USA is a federal system in which sovereignty is divided between the centre and the regions. Britain is a unitary state, with sovereignty residing in one place – Parliament. Any powers which are passed down to regional or local bodies in Britain are only **delegated**; they may be overruled or withdrawn.

Regionalism   There is no democratic regional government at all in Britain. Since the abolition of the Greater London Council and the six other metropolitan counties in 1986, even the great conurbations have no government of their own. There are regional quangos, such as Regional Development Agencies and Sports and Arts Councils, but these are not under direct democratic control, do not enjoy full financial independence and are certainly not elected. There are also government departments for Scotland, Wales and Northern Ireland, but these are examples of 'devolved administration' rather than regional government. They are not accountable to regional assemblies and are very much under Cabinet jurisdiction.

   The contrast with America could hardly be starker. Regional government is constitutionally guaranteed and, far from being in retreat, has been growing in strength in recent years. Of course, America is a much larger and more diverse society, but this does not completely account for the power of regional forces. Regionalism has political roots in America. It is a reflection of the individualism of her people and their fear of concentrated power.

Local democracy   Although British local government is elected, none of its officials are. Furthermore, turnouts in local elections are notoriously low and the outcome has more to do with national politics than with local issues. People recognise that British local government has little independent power, especially since 1979, so that the outcome of electoral contests is of relatively little importance. Local councils are heavily dictated to by ministers in London. They have little control over finance and their actions are heavily circumscribed by legislation and by ministerial controls.

In America, if anything, citizens are more interested in the politics of their state and their community than in the goings-on in Washington. Their daily lives are clearly affected more by the nature and performance of local government than those of British citizens. American local democracy is, therefore, more lively, more meaningful and more cherished than it is in Britain.

Federalism in Europe

The problems faced by America's Founding Fathers in creating a unified country, while at the same time preserving the aspirations of the thirteen states to maintain their identity, are largely mirrored in the European Union.

Each member is concerned to preserve its own culture, maintain control over its economy and determine its own social policies. Two further complications, not faced by the Americans, are the questions of language and relations with other countries. Yet, at the same time, there are powerful forces working towards greater unity.

A federal system is to be established in Europe. Therefore, these questions must be answered:

- What is the acceptable balance between the transfer of sovereignty to federal institutions and the maintenance of national self-interest?
- How can a federal settlement be made flexible enough to accommodate change, without being so weak that centralising forces cannot be resisted?
- How is it possible to avoid a federation being dominated by one state (say Germany), or a few large states (Germany, France, Italy, Britain)? In other words, how could the interests of small weaker states be protected?
- How can institutions such as the Parliament and the Council of Ministers become genuinely supranational, genuinely **European**, rather than mere battlegrounds where the competing national interests of individual members are fought out?
- Will it be possible to establish a system for creating a real, single Head of State?

The Americans solved some of their similar problems by such devices as:

- the bicameral system where small states were given equal representation in the Senate, but not in the House;
- the separately elected President as Head of State whose primary role is to unite the country;
- strict constitutional safeguards to protect the sovereignty of the states.

European federalists may learn from this experience, both from those devices which have been successful such as the bicameral system, and from the failures such as the inability of central government to overcome powerful regional interests.

For exam questions relevant to this unit, see page 498.

The British political system in a comparative context

Comparative politics

There are a number of key elements which can be used as a means of comparing different political systems. These include:

- the relationship between the legislative and executive branches
- the degree of independent power enjoyed by the Head of Government
- the role of the Head of State
- the operation and functions of the legislature
- the relationship between citizens and the state
- the distribution of power between central government, regions and localities
- the nature of the main political parties within the system.

We can, therefore, place the British system in context by comparing these elements with those which prevail in the USA and in Europe.

Legislative–executive relations

As **Walter Bagehot** commented in 1867 in *The English Constitution*, the fusion between the Government – in the form of the Cabinet – and the legislature – largely the House of Commons – is the 'efficient secret' of the political system. Indeed, since his day, there has been a strengthening of that bond, so much so that by 1976 Lord Hailsham was able to describe British Government as an 'elective dictatorship'.

The reason for the ever-increasing strength of Government and its growing dominance of Parliament lies predominantly in the development of party discipline and unity. In practice, the House of Commons places a Government in power and can remove that same Government by a simple majority vote, as occurred in 1979. But this reserve power is rarely exercised to any great effect. A number of factors have contributed to this reality:

- the power of prime ministerial patronage
- the extremely unified nature of the parties
- the constitutional convention that the Government cannot survive an adverse vote on a key issue in the House of Commons
- the frequency with which winning parties achieve comfortable Commons majorities
- the obsessive fear which MPs have of losing their seats at a general election. They are, therefore, reluctant to precipitate an election by defeating their own Government.

The manifestations of executive power are clear to see. They include the rarity of defeats on major pieces of legislation (the difficult periods for Labour in the late 1970s and the Conservatives in the mid 1990s were notable exceptions), the inability of Parliament to force through legislation proposed by back-bench members and of parliamentary committees to pass amendments against the Government's wishes.

At the same time, and despite the introduction of departmental select committees in 1979, ministers and officials find it relatively easy to evade meaningful investigations into their policy-making procedures. Ministers and civil servants tend to be obsessed with secrecy and attempts by MPs to open up government to public view have all failed.

In almost all respects the circumstances in the USA present a marked contrast to the British experience. The powers of the executive and legislative branches control each other; they are both separated and balanced. The causes of this phenomenon can be identified as follows:

- The Constitution guarantees that each branch has powers to limit the other: the system of 'checks and balances'.
- The parties lack unity and discipline. Members of Congress are independent in their thinking and their actions.
- The system of fixed-term Congresses means that the executive (i.e. President) cannot be removed from office during his four-year term. Legislators, therefore, do not fear to vote against the President, even when he is from the same party as themselves.
- Since members of the Government (administration) are often not drawn from Congress, the President's powers of patronage *vis-à-vis* Congress are weak.

Thus, while the British system may be described as **executive dominance**, that of the USA should be seen as **balanced**. This balance is further illustrated by the fact that, although Congress has important powers of scrutiny without the smokescreen of government secrecy which prevails in Britain, the executive, in the form of the President in his role as Head of State, enjoys relatively independent powers in the formulation of foreign policy.

We can find a further contrast in the political system of the European Union. Here, there is very little relationship of any kind between the executive branch – the Commission, the Council of Ministers and the legislature – and the European Parliament. Their sources of authority are completely separate and there is relatively little interplay between them. The Parliament possesses no real powers at all, only nebulous influence.

The EU system can, therefore, be described as **executive dominance** with only **token legislative control**. Nevertheless, it must be remembered that each individual member of the Council of Ministers is subject to influence from his own domestic legislature. If his national parliament's power is considerable, as is the case in Spain or Italy, a minister in the Council may find his freedom of action considerably restricted. This is not the case in Britain, however, where parliamentary control over relations with Europe remain notoriously weak so that ministers have a free hand in negotiations.

Heads of Government The position of a Head of Government (also known as **chief executive**) depends upon a number of factors. These are:

- leadership of a unified, disciplined party which controls government
- ability to control the legislature
- control over the rest of the government machinery, including the bureaucracy
- powers of patronage unencumbered by other bodies
- access to the media.

The British chief executive – the Prime Minister – enjoys most of these privileges. The principal check to this impressive list of powers lies with the Cabinet which does, from time to time, overrule him. Otherwise, he enjoys what may be described as a **dominant** role in all fields. A similar role is played, for example, by the Chancellor of Germany, although the federal nature of German government means that the latter's power may be rivalled by influential provincial leaders.

The President of the USA cannot boast the same advantages, even though he combines the roles of chief executive and Head of State. He leads a party (whether it be Democrat or Republican) divided into factions. That party is made up of independent-minded (and independently funded) legislators who all have their own political agendas. Patronage is limited by the Senate's constitutional power to veto the President's nominations for important offices. There is no guarantee that his proposed legislation or budgetary proposals will pass successfully through Congress.

The French Prime Minister is in an equally ambiguous position. His power is rivalled by that of the separately elected President and, indeed, he may be removed from office at any time by that same President. He does not fully control the membership of his own Cabinet and is often not even leader of the principal governing party. Any French chief executive, frustrated by his lack of independent power, must look enviously across the Channel at his dominant British counterpart.

In the European Union there is no effective chief executive at all! The post which fits this description most closely is that of **President of the Commission**, but he is an unelected official who can only advise, persuade and cajole the Council of Ministers. He has no decision-making powers of his own and lacks nearly all the advantages enjoyed by the British Prime Minister.

Heads of State   Three models can be identified to distinguish the different roles played by Heads of State:

- the symbolic figurehead
- the power-sharing Head of State
- the dominant leader.

Clearly, the British monarchy conforms to the first model, with most of the functions of 'Head of State' being performed by the Prime Minister on behalf of the monarch. The fact that the Crown's role is almost entirely ceremonial leads to a number of problems. For example, it may be difficult to separate the **national** interest from the interests of the **Government** itself. Similarly, maintaining national unity on key issues may be difficult for a Government which does not enjoy the support of the majority of the populace. However, as we shall see below, the structured party system enables the processes of government to run smoothly under most circumstances. Were it not for party dominance, the system would often need the intervention of an individual who could stand aloof from short-term political controversy. This would be the role of an active Head of State which Britain does not possess. Weak monarchical systems also operate in The Netherlands, Belgium, Australia and Canada.

More powerful Heads of State may have to share their power with elected Governments. This is certainly the case in France where the President has control over foreign policy and defence, but must co-operate in domestic policy-making with the Prime Minister and his Government. France, therefore, conforms to the second model.

The dominant leader is exemplified by the new Russian President. He enjoys extensive control over membership of the Government, is clearly the key figure in both domestic and foreign policy and is able, in a number of policy fields, to govern virtually by decree. He does experience some opposition from within the Parliament, but, in the absence of a coherent party system, he is able to avoid significant control by them. With greater reservations, the US President can be classified as a dominant type. However, his position depends upon shifting political fortunes. When confronted by a Congress dominated by a party other than his own, as has been the case for Bill Clinton, he becomes a power-sharer. Should he enjoy significant congressional support, on the other hand, he can become the dominant political figure in Washington.

Legislative bodies

How can we compare such institutions? They come – literally – in all shapes and sizes. Indeed, the rectangular form of both Houses of Parliament is often quoted as an illustration of the bipolar, adversarial nature of British politics. By contrast, the typically semi-circular shape of legislatures in Washington and most European capitals is seen as a model of more complex, fragmented party systems. But we should search for less superficial comparative features. The following questions must be answered regarding each legislative body:

- Does it have the power to remove the Government from office?
- Is it able to initiate legislation independently of the executive branch?
- How effective are its powers of scrutiny of government institutions?
- Is it subject to extensive constitutional controls?
- How much power does it have over budgetary measures?
- Can it block legislative proposals emerging from Government effectively?
- Does it have effective powers to amend legislation?
- Are individual legislators able to represent the interests of their constituents effectively?

On virtually all counts the British Parliament (principally the House of Commons) scores low marks. Theoretically, it possesses the decisive ability to pitch any Government from office by a simple vote of no confidence, but this power is rarely exercised. Instead, over the past century it has surrendered most of its powers of legislation, amendment and budgeting, handing them over to the Cabinet.

On the plus side, the departmental select committees have beefed up Parliament's powers of scrutiny, but they are still hindered by government secrecy and the reluctance of MPs to challenge executive power. Members of the governing party usually avoid drawing attention to their independence of thought, lest they incur the displeasure of the powerful party whips. There are ample opportunities for MPs to raise constituency business and there is increasing evidence of greater activity in this field. Most significantly, however, it is the existence of parliamentary sovereignty which **appears** to invest Parliament with almost complete freedom of action. But the true position is less clear.

In view of executive dominance, which is described above, the unfettered sovereignty of Parliament becomes largely the sovereignty of government. The legislature's very independence is, thus, turned back on itself and contributes to its own weakness.

If Parliament does badly in this scheme of assessment, the US Congress provides a dramatic contrast. It fulfils virtually all the requirements of what might be described as the 'dominant legislature' model. Indeed, Congress only suffers from one important limitation, which is that created by constitutional restraints. It cannot, unlike Britain's sovereign Parliament, claim powers which are denied to it by the Constitution. Nor can it infringe individual liberties without falling foul of those constitutional requirements which guarantee citizens' rights.

Between these two extremes lie most European legislatures. The fragmented Italian Parliament comes closer to the American model, while the weaker German Bundestag is not dissimilar to Britain's experience. Party control in Germany is strong and usually well founded.

Turning to the Parliament of the European Union, however, we find a completely new model. Every political system which describes itself as a democracy must include an elected, representative body. This is also true of the European Union. But the Parliament represents little more than a token claim to real effectiveness. In other words, it is essential to satisfy the democratic requirement, but performs few other functions. The 'charade' parliaments which were set up by the French *ancien régime* in the eighteenth century and by the Russian Tzar in 1905 (the 'Duma') were designed to head off demands for democratic reforms. They were not expected to achieve any real change. The European Parliament is, therefore, little more than a democratic symbol. Its limited role of advice and consultation renders it perhaps the weakest example among modern parliaments. Supporters of further European integration do, nevertheless, understand that any further political progress will have to be accompanied by extensions in parliamentary power. Otherwise, the 'democratic deficit' in Europe will worsen.

The citizen and the state

Throughout Europe, both within individual countries and in the EU as a whole, guarantees of individual rights against the power of the state abound in the form of codified, entrenched constitutions, Bills of Rights, Basic Laws and legal conventions. In the USA the whole Constitution, the Bill of Rights section in particular, plays a similar role. Redress of individual grievances is made possible through powerful constitutional courts and most citizens feel they do have access to such bodies. However, there remains the difficulty that different judges interpret the Bill in different ways.

Britain's lack of constitutionally guaranteed rights stands in dramatic contrast to other democracies. British government, indeed, enjoys prerogative powers which cannot be controlled even by Parliament. Redress through the European Court of Human Rights is possible but, as we have seen, is not binding. Yet it would be wrong to suggest that the British suffer under tyrannical government. The combined forces of tradition and parliamentary representation have succeeded in preventing serious infringements of basic rights. The contrast between Britain and the USA or most of the European democracies is largely confined to the **potential** power of government and the fragile guarantees of civil rights. In **reality**, rights have been preserved in Britain almost as effectively as they have in other constitutional democracies.

The distribution of power   It is useful here to classify political systems in the following way:

- highly centralised systems with no significant regional institutions and with local government enjoying very little independence
- centralised systems but with strong local and/or regional self-government
- federations where sovereignty is granted to regional government
- loose confederations with strong regional government and limited power at the centre.

The reforms in local government structure and provisions which occurred during the 1980s and 1990s moved Britain from the second category towards the first. The centralisation of power was not complete, with many new regional quangos having been created, but there were marked reductions in the freedom of action of local councils. Much of that local power was transferred to central government ministers and official agencies.

Italy, though not a federal structure, grants considerable independence to city governments and so has a more decentralised system than Britain. Clearly, the USA, Russia and Germany are federations with constitutional guarantees for regional government. When we consider the European Union, however, we see an example of the fourth category – a loose confederation of states with central government institutions having a remarkably narrow range of jurisdiction.

Parties   Britain and the USA present us with sharp contrasts between the respective roles and structures of their parties. This produces significant effects upon the political system in general. While the American Republicans and Democrats are loose, decentralised organisations, with weak discipline and without the ability or inclination to develop coherent national policy programmes, British parties are notable for their unity and discipline.

Furthermore, these differences can be identified as key determinants of several other political phenomena. The British Parliament and Government are both shaped by the nature of the parties. They could not exist in their present form were it not for the persistence of an ordered two-party system. The lack of a formal, codified constitution means that executive–legislative relations and the process of government formation depend upon the near certainty that a single, unified party is able to win government office decisively and then to maintain itself in power.

No such features exist in the American central government system (though in some states and localities party rule can exist in a similar way to that described above as existing in Britain). Political processes depend, instead, on constitutional rules, personal patronage and complex sets of relationships between individual legislators, government officials and agencies, pressure groups and shifting party factions. American parties simply do not have the cohesion to be able to run the system in a meaningful way.

The European Union displays similar characteristics to those found in the USA. No coherent party system has emerged as yet in Europe. There are – to add to the complexities of non-party politics – national interests to take into consideration. The party groupings are, therefore, of minor political significance. Elsewhere in Europe, party political systems vary considerably, from the chaotic Italian system where coalitions are created and destroyed with great regularity, to the stable Swedish system, dominated as it is by the Social Democrat Party.

Conclusions

What makes the British system so uniquely different from those of the USA and Europe? All the features which are described above have played a part, but which are the more crucial factors? What are, to borrow Bagehot's words, the 'efficient secrets' today? A few realities stand out:

- the lack of separation of powers between the executive and the legislature
- the strength and unity of the parties
- the ability of a single party to win governmental power on its own
- the concentration of powers in central government
- the accumulation of powers placed in the hands of the Prime Minister
- the sovereignty of Parliament converted into government dominance.

Selected examination questions

Britain and General
Concepts

1. Can there be equality in a free society?

(Oxford 1993)

2. What, if anything, transforms political power into political authority?

(Oxford 1993)

General British politics

1. Why is it thought desirable that everyone should participate in voting, election campaigns and the activities of political parties and pressure groups? Are those who decline to participate indicating satisfaction with the political system or alienation and rejection?

(AEB 1992)

2. To what extent did the conviction politics of the 1980s bring to an end the post-war political consensus?

(AEB Specimen)

3. 'Dissension and division rather than consensus and homogeneity are now the key feature of British political culture.' Discuss.

(NEAB 1994)

Democracy

1. (a) What are the distinctive features of 'liberal democracy'? (b) How accurate is it to describe the British political system as liberal democracy?

(ULEAC Specimen)

2. How democratic is the British system of government?

(ULEAC 1994)

3. 'A referendum is unsuitable for the resolution of complex issues.' Discuss.

(UCLES 1994)

4. Is there any conflict between the principles of liberalism and democracy?

(ULEAC 1994)

The European context

1. Is national sovereignty still possible within the EC (European Community)?

(UCLES 1994)

2. Discuss the impact of the European Union on British political processes.

(ULEAC Specimen)

3. 'Membership of the European Community seriously threatens the British Constitution.' Discuss.

(NEAB 1993)

PM and Cabinet

1. 'First among equals', how adequately does this describe the role of the Prime Minister in the British Government?

(UCLES 1994)

2. How could the power of the Prime Minister be reduced?

(ULEAC Specimen)

3. Consider the view that the most significant constraint upon British Prime Ministers is the power and influence of Cabinet colleagues.

(NEAB 1994)

4. 'Collective cabinet responsibility is only for public consumption.' Do you agree?

(Oxford and Cambridge 1994)

5. Compare the relationship between the Prime Minister and the Cabinet during the Thatcher and Major administrations.

(Oxford 1994)

DATA RESPONSE QUESTION

Study the following extract and then answer questions (a) to (c).

The Scott Inquiry

'The Inquiry was told that the guidelines limiting defence-related exports to Iran and Iraq were originally drawn up in late 1984 but ministers and civil servants decided not to announce them publicly in a high profile way, opting instead to let them "trickle out". They were finally made public after a parliamentary question in October 1985. Lady Thatcher conceded: "It might have been better it we had published earlier."

Despite asking to be kept informed of "all relevant decisions", Lady Thatcher said she was never told formally that the guidelines were subsequently revised in 1988 .... "It may have been mentioned to me by one of my secretaries. I have no recollection if it was ... I had 19 departments and 83 ministers ... if I had seen every copy of every minute when I was in government I would have been in a snowstorm."... She said that she only got involved if policy matters arose. Administrative details did not concern her. Her ministers only bothered her with the "big issues".

(Adapted from the *Independent*, 9 December 1993)

(a) Use the extract to illustrate the limitations on the power of the Prime Minister.

(b) What does the extract tell us about 'responsible government' in Britain?

(c) How could ministers and civil servants be made more accountable?

(ULEAC 1995)

Local and regional government

1. Discuss the changing nature of the relationship between central and local government.

(ULEAC 1992)

2. 'Local authorities should be free to spend how much they like, on what policies they like, as long as they get the support of local electors.' Discuss.

(UCLES 1993)

3. Why and with what consequences was the Community Charge (Poll Tax) introduced?

(Oxford 1993)

4. Assess the arguments in favour of devolution and regional government. Why did these issues return to the political agenda?

(Oxford 1993)

Parliament

1. In what ways could government be made more accountable to Parliament?

(ULEAC Specimen)

2. How much power and influence do backbenchers have in Parliament?

(UCLES 1994)

3. How well does the House of Commons perform its main functions?

(NEAB 1993)

4. Can the House of Lords be justified in a modern democracy?

(Oxford 1994)

Pressure groups

1. (a) Why is Parliament subject to so much lobbying by pressure groups? (b) Should there be greater control over lobbying?

(ULEAC 1992)

2. Do pressure groups have an undue influence in the political process?

(UCLES 1994)

3. To what extent do pressure groups strengthen or undermine the democratic process in Britain?

(NEAB 1994)

4. What makes a pressure group successful?

(Oxford 1994)

Civil service and machinery of government

1. How has the role of the civil service changed in recent years?

(ULEAC 1994)

2. 'Civil servants may be civil, but do they serve?'. Discuss this comment respecting the political relationship between ministers and civil servants.

(UCLES 1994)

3. 'The reforms of the 1980s have made the Civil Service more efficient but less accountable.' Discuss.

(Oxford 1994)

DATA RESPONSE QUESTION

'It is extraordinary that the first Thatcher government crusaded against the quangos of the corporate state. Indeed the assertion is still being made that quangos have had their wings clipped since 1979. Yet the official picture is a distortion. A recent study reveals that nearly a third of all public expenditure – some £46.6 billion in 1993 – is now being channelled through the appointed and contracted-out state. There are some 5,521 quangos (three times the official figure) and over 70,000 quangocrats put there by ministerial appointment compared to 25,000 elected councillors.'

(Adapted from an article by Tony Wright MP, the *Guardian*, 23 May 1994)

To what extent is the role of quangos an issue in a system of representative and responsible government?

(AEB Specimen for 1995 onwards)

Political parties

1. To what extent does Britain have a two-party system?

(ULEAC 1992)

2. What are the main functions performed by parties in the British political system?

(UCLES 1993)

3. Discuss the distribution of power within either the Conservative Party or the Labour Party.

(NEAB 1993)

DATA RESPONSE QUESTION (1)

Study the following extract and then answer questions (a) to (d).

'Judges have, by their education and training and the pursuit of their profession as barristers, acquired a strikingly homogeneous collection of attitudes, beliefs and principles which to them represents the public interest . . .

The judicial conception of the public interest . . . is threefold. It concerns, first, the interests of the State (including its moral welfare) and the preservation of law and order, broadly interpreted; secondly, the protection of property rights; and, thirdly, the promotion of certain political views normally associated with the Conservative Party . . .

My thesis is that judges in the United Kingdom cannot be politically neutral because they are placed in positions where they are required to make political choices which are sometimes presented to them, and often presented by them, as determinations of where the public interest lies; that their interpretation of what is in the public interest and therefore politically desirable is determined by the kind of people they are and the position they hold in our society; that this position is a part of established society and so is necessarily conservative and illiberal. From all this flows that view of the public interest which is shown in judicial attitudes such as tenderness towards private property and dislike of trade unions, strong adherence to the maintenance of order, distaste for minority opinions, demonstrations and protests, indifference to the promotion of better race relations, support of governmental secrecy, concern for the preservation of the moral and social behaviour to which it is accustomed, and the rest.

Professor Mancini of the University of Bologna has singled out "the susceptibility of English judges to be analysed as a politically cohesive group" – what I have called their homogeneity – as the factor distinguishing them from judges in Italy, France and Spain.'

(Source: J.A.G. Griffith, *The Politics of the Judiciary*, Collins Publishers, 1985)

(a) Explain why some observers of judicial decision-making believe that the judges have acquired 'a strikingly homogeneous collection of attitudes, beliefs and principles'.

(b) Outline a recent case concerned with civil liberties which illustrates a 'judicial conception of the public interest'.

(c) State an argument *against* the view of the role of judges put forward by Griffith.

(d) What is the relevance of Griffith's argument to the question of whether we should have a Bill of Rights?

(ULEAC 1991)

DATA RESPONSE QUESTION (2)
The Labour Leadership Contest 1992

Following the 1992 general election campaign it was demonstrated that opinion polls had been systematically overestimating Labour support for some years. In the event Labour were defeated and Mr Kinnock resigned formally. He also indicated Mr Hattersley's intention to resign. The two issues which surfaced during the first week were the timing of the leadership election and the names of the candidates for the two vacancies.

The nomination process produced two candidates for the leadership: John Smith (162 nominations) and Bryan Gould (63). There were three nominations for the deputy position: Margaret Beckett (89), Bryan Gould (69) and John Prescott (64). The important theme which developed concerned the role of the trade unions and their relationship to the Labour Party. The trade unions provided the Labour Party with most of its money. They also, through the 'block vote' system, wielded enormous influence in the decision-making process.

By early June the weight of support for John Smith was clear, and the final few weeks of the campaign were virtually meaningless. It was abundantly clear that John Smith would win by a thumping majority because he was backed by so many unions, constituencies and MPs. It was equally clear that Mrs Beckett would win the deputy contest although it looked at one stage as if John Prescott might take her to a second ballot. The special conference took place on Saturday July 18th and yielded the following unsurprising results:

Leadership: John Smith 91%; Bryan Gould 9%
Deputy Leadership: Margaret Beckett 57%; John Prescott 30%; Bryan Gould 13%

A political cartoon on Monday 20th July showed John Smith, equipped with climbing gear, on top of a summit marked 'Leadership'. Ahead of him loomed a massive rock-face marked 'Reform' – if Labour is to win the next election then continued reform within the Party would be necessary dealing with such things as relations with the trade unions and in-party democracy.

(Adapted from Bernard M. Jones in *Talking Politics*, Vol. 5, No. 2 [1993] pp. 94–8)

(i)   How does the Labour Party choose its leader and deputy leader?
(ii) Account for the importance of the *timing* of the leadership election.
(iii) Explain the phrase 'it was demonstrated that opinion polls had been systematically overestimating Labour support for some years'.
(iv) To what extent did the trade union 'block vote' represent a cause for concern within the Labour Party?
(v)   Subsequently, internal Labour Party reform has focused on the issue of 'one member, one vote.' Evaluate John Smith's campaign to introduce this principle into Labour Party affairs.

(Oxford and Cambridge 1994)

Constitutional issues

1. Can the British Government act unconstitutionally?
(UCLES 1993)

2. Discuss the problems in drawing up a written Constitution for Britain.
(ULEAC 1994)

3. To what extent do the major political parties have different views on the British Constitution?
(NEAB 1994)

4. What aspects of constitutional reform are needed in Britain and why?
(Oxford and Cambridge 1994)

Elections

1. To what extent and in what ways do opinion polls mould rather than reflect the opinions of the general public? Why do political parties commission private polls, the findings of which they rarely publish?
(AEB 1992)

2. 'Class is no longer a major factor in determining voting behaviour.' Consider the arguments for and against this view.
(UCLES 1993)

3. Did the 1992 general election demonstrate once again that the 'first past the post' system is undemocratic?
(UCLES 1994)

4. Outline and account for the major parties' views on electoral reform.
(Oxford and Cambridge 1994)

5. Why does the turnout of voters vary between local government elections, general elections and elections for the European Parliament? What factors might explain the differing amounts and proportions of support given to the major parties at these elections?
(AEB Specimen)

Results of the 1992 General Election in Britain			
Party	MPs elected	Votes per seat	Pure PR result*
Conservative	336	41,942	275
Labour	271	42,646	237
Liberal Democrat	20	299,922	101
SNP	3	209,850	17
Plaid Cymru	4	38,609	3

* i.e. the number of seats which would have been gained if they had been allocated strictly proportionally to votes cast

It is sometimes claimed that electoral systems are always either unfair in the way they 'convert' votes into seats or so fair that they can create political instability. Thus, a new system of voting is often demanded for quite different reasons.

With reference to the UK and at least one other country, consider how far this view can be justified.

(AEB Specimen for 1995 onwards)

British and alternative ideologies

1. How far may changes in support for nationalism in Scotland, Wales or Northern Ireland be accounted for purely in terms of economic factors? Should the causes and consequences of nationalism in Scotland, Wales and Northern Ireland be seen primarily in political, economic or cultural terms?

(AEB 1993)

2. Do modern liberals have a consistent view of the state?

(ULEAC 1993)

3. How consistent are the political and economic doctrines of the New Right?

(ULEAC 1992)

4. Do conservatives place pragmatism before principle?

(ULEAC 1994)

5. 'Conservatives are more concerned with the preservation of stability and order than with freedom.' Discuss.

(ULEAC 1992)

6. Do you agree that socialism is the culmination of liberalism rather than its antithesis?

(ULEAC 1992)

7. To what extent is nationalism a rational doctrine?

(ULEAC 1993)

8. Critically examine the Marxist view that there is no place for nationalism in the modern world.

(ULEAC 1992)

9. How distinctive is the Marxist concept of revolution?

(ULEAC 1993)

10. What role does Marx ascribe to the state and how adequate is his explanation?

(Oxford 1993)

11. Are anarchists simply uncompromising, extreme liberals?

(ULEAC 1993)

12. 'Fascists value struggle and war.' Discuss.

(ULEAC 1994)

13. Is it reasonable to compare Nazi Germany with Stalinist Russia, given the contrast in their respective ideologies?

(ULEAC 1993)

14. 'The concept of patriarchy cuts right across social class.' What problems does this raise for Marxists and feminists?

(ULEAC 1994)

15. Why have modern feminists criticised so much of past political thought?

(ULEAC 1993)

16. How do the traditions of political thought react to feminism as a twentieth-century issue?

(AEB Specimen)

USA

General

1. 'Far from being a melting pot, racial and ethnic tensions within American society threaten to tear it apart.' Discuss.

(UCLES 1994)

2. Examine the impact of the principles of 'checks and balances' and separation of powers on the relationship between the legislative and

executive branches when facing such controversial issues as the budget deficit or in leading the international rejection of Iraq's seizure of Kuwait. To what extent and in what ways does the relationship change when a crisis arises?

(AEB 1992)

3. Assess the desirability of having a President and Congress of the same party. What effects do party divisions between Presidency and Congress have on the operation of constitutional checks and balances?

(AEB 1994)

4. Which political system, the UK or the USA, more effectively allows for the views of the people to be promoted?

(Oxford 1993)

Presidency and administration

1. President Truman said his only power was the 'power to persuade'. How far is this view of presidential power still valid?

(UCLES 1993)

2. 'Domestic issues are more important than foreign affairs in determining the outcome of presidential elections'. Do you agree?

(UCLES 1993)

3. Do the processes by which presidential and vice-presidential candidates have been selected since 1944 suggest that the US system puts too much emphasis on 'electability' and does not give enough consideration to the skills and experience needed to undertake either job?

(AEB 1992)

4. How important is the President's Cabinet?

(Oxford 1994)

Congress

1. Why does the US Senate have more power and prestige than the House of Representatives?

(UCLES 1993)

2. Assess the relative importance of political parties and interest groups in influencing decisions made by the two Houses of Congress. Consider whether members of Congress pay too much or too little attention to public opinion in their state or district when making decisions.

(AEB 1992)

3. 'Ultimately it is the Senate and not the House of Representatives that wields congressional power.' Discuss.

(ULEAC 1994)

4. How far has Congress been able to exert control over foreign policy and defence in the last twenty-five years?

(Oxford 1993)

5. Examine the claim that it is in the committee rooms that the real work of Congress is done.

(Oxford 1994)

Constitution and Supreme Court

1. 'We are under a Constitution, but the Constitution is what the Supreme Court says it is' (Chief Justice Hughes). Examine the decisions of the Supreme Court since 1969 in the light of this comment.

(UCLES 1993)

2. Is the Supreme Court a political or judicial institution?

(ULEAC Specimen)

3. Why has it proved so difficult to amend the US Constitution?

(UCLES 1994)

Parties and pressure groups

1. Critically examine, giving appropriate examples, the role of pressure groups in the US political system.

(UCLES 1994)

2. To what extent is the United States governed by the lobby system?

(Oxford and Cambridge 1994)

3. Consider why American political parties were often claimed to be 'in decline' in the 1980s and assess their significance at state and federal level in the 1990s.

(AEB 1994)

4. Given the de-centralisation of American politics, why is there basically a two-party system?

(ULEAC 1992)

5. 'It has been claimed that, for all their apparent differences, US party conventions and UK party conferences are in fact identical in their ultimate purpose of legitimating decisions taken elsewhere.'

Assess the accuracy of this statement and consider whether party conventions and party conferences are equally important in the two countries.

(AEB 1993)

6. Consider why, if British voters expect Conservative, Labour, Liberal Democrat, Nationalist or Green candidates in most parliamentary constituencies, US voters seem to be satisfied with just Republican and Democrat candidates in most congressional election contests. Would it be desirable for most UK contests to be limited to two parties or for US elections to involve three or four candidates in each district or state-wide election?

(AEB 1993)

7. Examine the view that although pressure groups are supposed to underpin democracy, they effectively overwhelm the political process in the USA and are virtually ignored in the UK. Consider whether there should be more controls on the spending and activities of pressure groups in either country.

(AEB 1993)

DATA RESPONSE QUESTION

Selection of Party leaders

Political parties in UK and USA

Source A

Writing in 1981 and making direct comparisons with the selection process of British prime ministers, (Professor) Anthony King listed eight apparently serious flaws in the 1980 presidential selection process. It is worth repeating these.

1. The two winners in the United States had entered politics in middle age and neither had much experience of government.
2. Neither winner in the United States had ever served in any capacity in national government. Moreover, at the time of their nomination, neither held any public office whatsoever.

3. The candidates in the United States were assessed and voted on by party activists in some states but mainly by voters in primary elections. No special weight was attached to the views of those who had worked with the candidates or had a chance to view them at first hand.
4. The campaigns for would-be presidential nominees lasted for a very long time.
5. Campaigns for presidential nomination involve an enormous amount of wear and tear on the part of the candidates and their families.
6. The campaigns cost enormous sums of money and the candidates and their staffs have to devote a great deal of time and effort to raising money.
7. The process of selecting presidential candidates is by no means a party process.
8. Electoral consideration may have loomed large in the minds of party regulars who attended party caucuses in 1976 and 1980 but they probably figured scarcely at all in the minds of most voters in the primaries.

(From *American Politics and Society* by David McKay, 1993. Professor McKay is quoting from Anthony King's *How not to select Presidential candidates: a view from Europe*, first published in 1981.)

Source B

Election of Conservative Party leader November 1990

First Ballot November 20	
Margaret Thatcher	204 votes
Michael Heseltine	152 votes
Abstentions	16 votes
Second ballot November 27	
John Major	185 votes
Michael Heseltine	131 votes
Douglas Hurd	56 votes

Source C

Election of Labour Party leader July 1994, first ballot July 21

	Trades Unions %	Party Members %	MPs/MEPs %	Overall Percentage
Tony Blair	52.3	58.2	60.5	57.0
John Prescott	28.4	24.4	19.6	24.1
Margaret Beckett	19.3	17.4	19.9	18.9
Total number of votes cast	779,426	172,356	327	952,109

(a) What are the 'primary elections' referred to in Source A? How significant are they in American presidential elections?

(b) Identify and account for the main differences between the ways in which the British Conservative and Labour parties choose their leader, as shown in Sources B and C.

(c) How far are Professor King's arguments in Source A supported by political developments in the UK and the USA since 1981?

(d) How justified is Professor King's attack upon the American method of choosing its political leaders when compared with the British?

(UCLES Specimen for 1995 onwards)

DATA RESPONSE QUESTION (1)

US parties and pressure groups The intense ideological debate on NAFTA (North American Free Trade Association) was Washington's bitterest and most divisive lobbying battle of modern times.

About $7 million was spent by big business supporters of NAFTA in last minute lobbying and advertising against $6 million by opponents.

The figures are dwarfed, however, by the $17 million donated to Congressmen's campaign chests by anti-NAFTA Trade Union, environmental and consumer associations. Political Action Committees of 35 of the largest corporations distributed around $9.3 million to 'sweeten legislators'.

Ross Perot accused President Clinton of 'buying NAFTA votes with tax-payers' money' through the Federal 'pork barrel'. Ralph Nader, the consumer rights activist, said a 'NAFTA pork patrol' was needed.

The vote in Congress was as follows:

Party breakdown vote in House of Representatives on the establishment of NAFTA			
	Democrats	Republicans	Total
Voting 'yes'	102	132	234
Voting 'no'	156 (+1 Ind.)	43	200

(Adapted from the *Independent*, November 1993)

What does the above tell us about the operation of the American political process?

(AEB Specimen for 1995 onwards)

DATA RESPONSE QUESTION (2)

American Courts can deal with social or political issues only when cases are brought before them. Law suits involve time and expense, which makes it difficult for most private citizens to use the judicial system to protect or assert their rights. To correct this imbalance in the area of civil rights, special interest groups such as the American Civil Liberties Union (ACLU), the National Association for the Advancement of Colored People (NAACP) and the National Organization of Women (NOW) have arisen.

These organisations are not only effective in the legal area, they also conduct very impressive educational and lobbying programmes. By building public support, and thereby influencing the executive and legislative branches, these civil rights organisations bring political pressure on the courts.

(Adapted from P. Woll and S. Zimmerman, *American Government: The Core*, McGraw-Hill)

What main factors influence the degree of success of the interest groups, such as those mentioned above, in the protection and assertion of the rights of American citizens? To what extent is the system of government in the United States more accessible to interest group lobbying in the field of citizens' rights than the system of government in the UK?

(AEB Specimen for 1995 onwards)

Federalism
1. Assess the changing relationship between the federal government and the state.

(UCLES 1994)

2. How significant are the 'reserve powers' that the constitution grants to the states?

(ULEAC 1992)

3. Is a federal system of government still appropriate for the United States?

(ULEAC 1994)

4. To what extent has power shifted away from the federal government towards the states in the last twenty-five years?

(Oxford 1993)

Selected reading list

General UK

A New Introduction to British Politics, Peter Madgwick (Stanley Thornes, 4th edn 1994)

British Political Facts 1900–1994, D. Butler and G. Butler (Macmillan, 1994)

British Politics Today, Bill Jones and Dennis Kavanagh (MUP, 5th edn 1993)

Contemporary British Politics, Bill Coxall and Lynton Robins (Macmillan, 2nd edn 1994)

Developments in British Politics 4, Patrick Dunleavy (ed) (Macmillan, 1993)

Government and Politics in Britain, John Kingdom (Polity, 1991)

Politics UK, Bill Jones (ed) (Philip Allan, 1st edn 1991)

Public Policy in Britain, Stephen Savage (ed) (Macmillan, 1994)

Ruling Britannia, Anthony Marr (Michael Joseph, 1995)

The British System of Government, Anthony H. Birch (Harper Collins, 8th edn 1990)

The Major Effect, Dennis Kavanagh and Anthony Seldon (Macmillan, 1995)

Unit 1 Political concepts

British Politics: Ideas and Concepts, Keith Pye and Richard Yates (Stanley Thornes, 1990)

In Defence of Politics, Bernard Crick (Penguin, 4th edn 1992)

Political Ideas, David Thomson (ed) (Penguin, 1966)

Political Ideas and Concepts, Andrew Heywood (Macmillan, 1994)

Unit 2 The United Kingdom – social and political context

Annual Abstract of Statistics (HMSO) (published annually)

Aspects of Britain (HMSO) (published regularly)

Friends in High Places, Jeremy Paxman (Penguin, 1991)

Key Data (HMSO) (published annually)

Thatcherism and British Politics, Dennis Kavanagh (OUP, 2nd edn 1990)

The Essential Anatomy of Britain, Anthony Sampson (Macmillan 1993)

Unit 3 The ideological context of British politics

British Political Ideologies, R. Leach (Philip Allen, 1991)

Nationalism in Scotland and Wales, Duncan Watts (PAVIC Publications, 1994)

Party Ideologies in Britain, L. Tivey and A. Wright (Routledge, 1989)

Politics in Britain, from Labourism to Thatcherism, C. Leys (Verso, 1989)

Unit 4 Democracy *Democracy*, A. Arblaster (Open University Press, 1987)

Democracy in Britain, J. and A. Lively (Blackwell, 1994)

The Real World of Democracy, C.B. McPherson (OUP, 1972)

Unit 5 Political parties *British Political Parties*, A. Ball (Macmillan, 1989)

Do Parties make a Difference?, Richard Rose (Macmillan, 1984)

The British Party System, S.J. Ingle (Blackwell, 1989)

UK Political Parties since 1945, Anthony Seldon (ed) (Philip Allan, 1991)

Unit 6 Elections *Elections and Voting Behaviour in Britain*, David Denver (Philip Allan, 2nd edn 1994)

The British General Election of 1992, D. Butler and D. Kavanagh (Macmillan, 1992)

Unit 7 Parliament *Does Parliament Matter?*, Philip Norton (Harvester-Wheatsheaf, 1993)

How Parliament Works, P. Silk (Longman, 1989)

Parliament Today, A. Adonis (MUP, 1993)

Unit 8 Prime Minister and Cabinet *British Cabinet Government*, S. James (Routledge, 1992)

British Government: The Central Executive Territory, Peter Madgwick (Philip Allan, 1991)

The British Prime Minister, A. King (ed) (Macmillan, 2nd edn 1985)

The Crossman Diaries (Condensed), Richard Crossman (Magnum, 1979)

Unit 9 The civil service and machinery of central government *Governing the UK in the Nineties*, R. Pyper and L. Robins (eds) (Macmillan, 1994)

The Civil Servants, Peter Kellner and Lord Crowther-Hunt (MacDonald, 1980)

The Evolving Civil Service, R. Pyper (Longman, 1992)

The Private Government of Public Money, Hugh Heclo and Aaron Wildavsky (Macmillan, 2nd edn 1981)

Whitehall, Peter Hennessy (Fontana, 1989)

Unit 10 Pressure groups *Pressure Groups: A Question of Interest*, Robert Baggott (PAVIC Publications, 1st edn 1994)

Pressure Groups, Politics and Democracy in Britain, Wyn Grant (Philip Allan, 1st edn 1989)

Pressure Politics, Martin Smith (Baseline, 1995)

Unit 11 Local government and devolution *Local Government and Politics in Britain*, John Kingdom (Philip Allan, 1991)

Local Government and Thatcherism, Hugh Butcher *et al* (Routledge, 1990)

Local Government in the United Kingdom, David Wilson (Macmillan, 1994)

The Politics of Local Government, Gerry Stoker (Macmillan, 2nd edn 1991)

Unit 12 Constitutional issues

Debating the Constitution, A. Barnett (Polity, 1993)

New Directions in British Politics?, Philip Norton (ed) (Edward Elgar, 1991)

Unit 13 The European context

Britain in the European Community, Andrew Geddes (Baseline, 1993)

Europe, Leon Brittan (Hamish Hamilton, 1994)

European Community, John Pinder (OUP, 1991)

European Union and European Community, C.H. Church and D. Phinnemore (Harvester Wheatsheaf, 1994)

Ever Closer Union?, Desmond Dinan (Macmillan, 1994)

Government and Politics of the European Union, Neill Nugent (Macmillan, 1994)

Understanding the New European Community, W. Nicoll and T.C. Salmon (Harvester Wheatsheaf, 2nd edn 1994)

Unit 14 Alternative ideologies

Ideals and Ideologies of Modern Politics, M. Hagopian (Longman, 1985)

Marxism After Marx, D. McLellan (Macmillan, 1979)

Political Ideologies, Andrew Heywood (Macmillan, 1992)

Political Ideologies, R. Eccleshall *et al* (Routledge, 1984)

General USA

American Government, M. Skidmore (St Martin, 1993)

The American Political Process, Alan Grant (Dartmouth, 5th edn 1994)

The Government and Politics of the United States, Nigel Bowles (Macmillan, 1993)

The New American Political System, A. King (ed) (AEI Press, 1990)

Understanding American Politics, R.V. Denenburg (Fontana, 3rd edn 1992)

Unit 15 The social and political context of American government

American Political Ideas, Michael Foley (Manchester University Press, 1991)

Developments in American Politics, G. Peele *et al* (eds) (Macmillan, 1992)

The American Political Tradition, R. Hofstadter (Cape, 1967)

Unit 16 The United States' Constitution

Constitutional Conflicts Between Congress and the President, Louis Fisher (Princeton University Press, 1985)

Constitutionalism and the Separation of Powers, M.J.C. Vile (OUP, 1967)

The Burger Court, V. Blasi (ed) (Yale University Press, 1983)

The Supreme Court of the United States, T. Walker and L. Epstein (St Martin, 1993)

Unit 17 The United States' Congress

Congress, M. McCubbins and T. Sullivan (Cambridge University Press, 1987)

Congress Today, E. Schneier and B. Cross (St Martin, 1993)

The US Congress, C.J. Bailey (Blackwell, 1989)

Unit 18 The United States' Presidency and administration

Leadership in the Modern Presidency, F. Greenstein (ed) (Harvard University Press, 1988)

Ronald Reagan and the American Presidency, David Mervin (Longman, 1990)

The Presidential Branch, J. Hart (Pergamon, 1987)

Winning the White House, Aram Bakshian (Ross Anderson, 1984)

Unit 19 Parties and pressure groups in the United States

American Parties in Decline, Martin Wattenberg (Harvard University Press, 1990)

American Political Parties, D. McSweeney and J. Zvesper (Routledge, 1991)

The Interest Group Society, J.M. Berry (Little Brown, 1989)

The Power Game, Various (Random House, 1988)

Unit 20 Federalism and the states

American Federalism, T. Dye (Lexington, 1990)

Reagan and the States, R. Nathan and F. Doolittle (Princeton University Press, 1987)

The New Federalism, M. Reagan and J. Sanzone (OUP, 1981)

Glossary

The following terms may be described in the main text but are included here as a ready reference. Other explanations of terms may be found by reference to the index.

Absolutism A system of rule where a leader or small group holds complete power within a political system. There is no serious, effective opposition.

Affirmative action See under 'Positive discrimination'.

Autocracy A system of rule where the leader or leaders are not subject to democratic controls or accountability. Internal opposition is not tolerated and decisions are reached without seeking the consent of the people.

Back-bencher Any British MP who is not a senior spokesperson for his party.

Bill The formal proposal for legislation before it has been passed by the legislative process.

Bill of Rights A constitutional document which sets out the basic rights of the citizens of a state. Such Bills are normally entrenched by special safeguards and are binding upon law makers and government. Also the name of an agreement made in 1689 between the English Parliament and King William III, whereby the King gave up the right to make law without the sanction of Parliament.

By-law In Britain a law which is passed by a public body subordinate to central government, mostly local authorities or public corporations.

Capitalism Description of an economic system where the distribution of finance, raw materials, incomes and goods is determined by free markets where there is free movement of goods, labour and money. It has formed the basis of the economic structure of the developed world since the industrial revolution.

Charisma A quality in an individual which refers to their special ability to inspire a following through the force of their personality, not merely the plausibility of their message.

Citizenship The right granted to an individual to enjoy the privileges associated with belonging to a particular state. Usually, but not always, it includes the right of abode in a country.

Civil service A name for the body of officials who are directly employed by a central government department.

Classical liberalism A term used to describe that form of liberalism which is concerned with the extension of liberty and tolerance, and which flourished in the middle part of the nineteenth century.

Coalition Specifically a Government where ministerial posts are shared among more than one party. Generally it can mean any grouping of politicians with varying beliefs, who come together temporarily to promote some form of action to which they all agree.

Coercion The use of force to achieve a particular end.

Collegiality A state of affairs where a group is able to make decisions on a genuinely collective basis and not just through a majority vote. Normally related to Cabinet government, it suggests that ministers in the cabinet can all support the same decision.

Consensus General agreement which is more than a mere majority, but includes the vast majority of a community. In political life consensus refers to a circumstance where a large proportion of the population and the political community are agreed on certain values. The period 1940–70 is often described in Britain as the 'era of consensus politics'.

conservative (small 'c') A description of a person who places a high value on traditional institutions, values and ideas and who is suspicious of excessive amounts of change.

Conservative (capital 'C') A follower of one of the political movements which have flourished in the eighteenth, nineteenth and twentieth centuries. The movement has supported such ideas as 'order', tradition and social cohesion and has opposed strong ideologies such as liberalism, socialism and fascism.

Constitution A document or set of principles which sets out the distribution of power within a state, establishes the relationship between citizens and the state and specifies the limits of the Government's jurisdiction.

Corporate state In fascist states, notably Italy, this referred to a system where regional bodies, comprising representatives of unions, industry and the ruling party planned public policy. In a modern context, it refers to a tendency, noticeable in Britain in the 1960s and 1970s, for government to incorporate important interests into the governing process.

Deference A tendency among some people to show excessive respect and a sense of inferiority towards those whom they consider to be of superior status or ability.

Democratic deficit Description of a situation where, within a political system, there is a gap in the democratic process. Normally, this relates to a circumstance where a governing body is not sufficiently accountable to an elected institution. Most often applied to the relationship between the European Parliament and the rest of the Union's government.

Doctrine A firmly held belief, normally concerned with politics. It is used as the basis, or partial basis, of political action or a wider ideology.

Drys The opposite of 'wets' – see below. Those Conservatives who, during the 1980s, were most supportive of Margaret Thatcher's radical policies.

Electoral College A term used to describe a body which is elected with the expressed purpose of itself electing a higher political authority. The best-known example is in the USA where the electoral college, now only a formal body, is popularly elected to choose a President. In effect, all the votes of this college are fixed in advance by the original election.

Elite A description of a group of people which is considered, for some reason or another, to be superior to others. In politics it refers to those who have achieved some kind of exclusive access to power.

EMU European Monetary Union. The proposal that the European Union should adopt one single currency to be used by all members.

Executive In politics that part of the state which oversees the implementation of public policy and the laws of that state. Normally, the executive will also be heavily involved in the formulation of policy.

Faction A distinct group within a political party which holds views which differ from the central policies of that party. However, these views are not so incompatible with the norm as to warrant them forming a separate party.

Filibuster A device, commonly used in the US Senate, where a speaker in the legislature continues to talk for so long that a piece of legislation runs out of its apportioned time and so fails.

General will A term associated with the eighteenth-century philosopher Rousseau. It suggests a collective will of the people as opposed merely to the will of the majority.

Gerrymandering The practice – usually illegal – of drawing up electoral boundaries in such a way as to favour one political party.

Government (capital 'G') That group of individuals who control the operation of the state at any particular time. In a democratic system this group will have been elected.

government (small 'g') The act of governing OR a term relating to the broader institutions of government, not just elected ministers. Thus, it includes non-elected civil servants, advisers, public bodies, etc.

Grass roots A description of those supporters of a party who do not hold any office, but do form the basic membership.

Head of State The individual who is able, on appropriate occasions, to represent all the people of a state.

Hung Parliament   In Britain, a situation where no one party is able to command an overall majority in the House of Commons. As with the term 'hung jury', it suggests that it is difficult to reach decisions under such circumstances.

Impeachment   A means of removing an individual from public office for reasons which could not be enforced through the conventional law courts. Can happen in the case of political, rather than financial, corruption.

Initiative   A referendum which has been called on the initiative of a section of a community, rather than by government itself.

Judiciary   The individuals and bodies, normally judges and courts, which administer the laws. This includes the resolution of civil disputes, disputes between citizens and the state, trial of suspected criminals and interpretations of the meaning and applications of the laws.

Laissez-faire   A description of a style of government which prefers not to interfere with the life of its people. It refers mainly to the economic and industrial field. It is associated with liberalism, modern neo-liberalism, monetarism and free trade.

Law   A system of rules which are binding on all and which are enforced by the state.

Legislature   The body which formalises the laws of a state. It may also be involved, though not always, in the policy-making and policy-influencing process.

Liberal   An individual whose outlook and values include tolerance for the ideas of others, respect for the freedom of others, social justice for all, equal rights and powerful democratic controls over governmental power.

Mandate   The authority or consent given by the people of a state to its Government to carry out certain policies. In a democratic system such a mandate is normally granted at elections. In international politics it can refer to a situation where one state is given responsibility for governing a territory temporarily while arrangements for permanent sovereignty can be completed.

Manifesto   A statement published by a political party, normally before an election, containing its stated philosophy, aims and intentions when it gains public office.

Monetarism   An economic philosophy which has as its basis a belief that the only positive interference in the economy which should be undertaken by government is the control of the supply of money and, therefore, of interest rates. Control of taxation and public expenditure for economic reasons should, thus, be avoided. Monetarism is associated with laissez-faire policies and a belief in the operation of free markets.

Neo-liberal A term used to describe one who follows the ideas of so-called right-wing, or 'New Right' thinkers of the late twentieth century. It is an adaptation of classical liberalism, encompassing ideas of laissez-faire economics, monetarism and free trade.

New Left A term for a collection of radical movements which developed in the 1960s and early 1970s. It included feminists, environmentalists, pacifists, black rights activists, anarchists, gay rights campaigners and a broad socialist youth movement.

New Right A conservative movement which arose in the late 1970s, mainly in the USA and Britain. It encompasses neo-liberal ideas (see above), a stress on traditional moral values, a strong position on law and order, and is nationalistic and xenophobic. In the case of the USA, it extols the Christian religion.

One-nation Conservatism A description of a section of the Conservative Party which embraces its traditional values, referring back to Benjamin Disraeli. The term refers to the idea that these values will unite the nation and prevent social conflict.

Paternalism A tendency among some, especially politicians, to claim that they have a deeper understanding of how to improve the condition of individuals and society than the people themselves. They may suggest they know what is best for people who, having inferior knowledge, do not understand what is in their own best interests. The relationship between paternalists and the people can be described as similar to that of father and child. Associated with the idea of a 'superior' ruling class.

Plebiscite A popular vote organised within a community where people vote to decide who shall exercise sovereignty over them; in other words, in which state they shall live.

Political Action Committee An American device to raise funds and to campaign for political action to benefit a section of the community or to further a popular cause. They arose in the 1970s as a way of avoiding tight federal laws on the funding of the campaigns by candidates for public office.

Political culture A term referring to the dominant political values, attitudes, traditions and emotions which exist within a community.

Poll Tax A tax, used in British local government in the late 1980s, based on a flat rate charge levied on all adults.

Pork Barrel An American term for funds which are available to federal government for distribution among projects in different parts of the country. Regional interests compete strongly for these funds.

Positive discrimination A description of measures designed to give a section of a community which is considered to suffer unfair disadvantages special privileges to restore the principle of equal opportunities. It may involve special quotas for jobs or political offices for members of ethnic minorities or women.

Pragmatism   A style of decision-making which is based not on firm principles, but on an understanding of what appears to be the best course of action in the short term, with the fewest potential problems.

President   A name used in politics to describe a Head of State other than a monarch. It is also sometimes used at a lower level to describe a lesser position at the head of an organisation as in 'President of the Board of Trade'.

Primary   An election held within a political party to decide which of a number of competing individuals should be the official candidate of that party in a public election. Most commonly used in the USA.

Proportional Representation   A description of an electoral system which awards seats in a legislature in close proportion to the votes cast for each party and.or candidate.

Public corporations   In Britain this refers to enterprises which are publicly owned and run by the Government. They are separated from the rest of government by having their own management structures, financial arrangements and legal status. There were a large number of such corporations until 1980, but most have now been privatised. The BBC is an example which still remains.

Quango   This stands for 'quasi-autonomous national government organisation'. A body established, appointed, overseen and funded by national government to carry out some function or functions of the state on behalf of the Government.

Reactionary   One who strongly opposes new ideas and innovations. The reactionary prefers what has gone before to new developments.

Referendum   A popular vote organised in a community to decide on an important issue. It may or may not be binding upon the government of that community.

Revolution   An event or series of events which brings about a complete transformation of the political system, not merely a change in the personnel of government. It may or may not be violent.

Social Contract   A philosophical idea associated with such thinkers as John Locke and Jean-Jacques Rousseau. It suggests that the appropriate basis of government should be a free agreement between the people, who will submit themselves to the laws, and a Government which agrees to respect natural laws and rights. Thus a political, or social contract is formed. It is the basis of all constitutional government. It also relates to a voluntary agreement in the late 1970s between trade unions and the British Government to moderate wage demands.

State   The permanent apparatus of government which enjoys a legal monopoly of the means of coercion. It represents the permanent interests of the whole country in the long term. It expresses where sovereignty lies permanently, whoever may form the temporary Government.

Subsidiarity Where government is carried out at the most local level appropriate to efficient administration. Each level of government has its suitable geographical level. It is believed to enhance democracy.

Suffrage The right to vote in public state elections.

Terror The public demonstration of force used by a state to instil fear and obedience in its people. Typical examples include public executions, open troop movements and public 'show trials'.

Ticket An American expression meaning a list of candidates from the same party appearing on the same ballot paper.

Tory A popular nickname for a member of the Conservative Party. Modern Conservatives often use it to describe one who espouses traditional, rather than modern, Conservative values. A more extreme version of the latter is 'High Tory'.

Totalitarianism A system of rule where the leadership maintains complete control over all, or virtually all, aspects of political, social, cultural and economic life, usually on the basis of a ruling ideology.

Trust An American expression for what the British call a 'monopoly'.

Welfare State A term used to describe a national system where all citizens are required to contribute through taxation or other contributions to the provision of social services such as health, education, financial benefits, pensions, etc. These services are available to all according to need on a free or subsidised basis.

Wets A pejorative term used in the 1980s to describe those leading Conservatives who were opposed to the radical policies of Margaret Thatcher. The term 'wet' was used to suggest weakness of resolve.

Index